Arms and the University

Military Presence and the Civic Education of Non-military Students

Alienation between the U.S. military and society has grown in recent decades. Such alienation is unhealthy, as it threatens both sufficient civilian control of the military and the long-standing ideal of the "citizen-soldier." Nowhere is this issue more predominant than at many major universities, which began turning their backs on the military during the chaotic years of the Vietnam War. *Arms and the University* probes various dimensions of this alienation, as well as recent efforts to restore a closer relationship between the military and the university. Through theoretical and empirical analysis, Donald Alexander Downs and Ilia Murtazashvili show how a military presence on campus in the form of the Reserve Officers' Training Corps (ROTC) (including a case study of ROTC's return to Columbia and Harvard universities), military history, and national security studies can enhance the civic and liberal education of non-military students, and in the process help to bridge the civil–military gap.

Donald Alexander Downs is Alexander Meiklejohn Professor of Political Science, Law, and Journalism at the University of Wisconsin, Madison. He is the author of five books: *Nazis in Skokie: Freedom, Community, and the First Amendment*; *The New Politics of Pornography*; *More Than Victims: Battered Women, the Syndrome Society, and the Law*; *Cornell '69: Liberalism and the Crisis of the American University*; and *Restoring Free Speech and Liberty on Campus*. He is the co-founder and director of the Wisconsin Center for the Study of Liberal Democracy at the University of Wisconsin and a frequent contributor to local, state, national, and international media.

Ilia Murtazashvili is Assistant Professor at the Graduate School of Public and International Affairs at the University of Pittsburgh. He earned his Ph.D. in political science from the University of Wisconsin, Madison, and his research interests include institutional design and political economy.

Arms and the University

Military Presence and the Civic Education of Non-military Students

DONALD ALEXANDER DOWNS
University of Wisconsin, Madison

ILIA MURTAZASHVILI
University of Pittsburgh

CAMBRIDGE UNIVERSITY PRESS
Cambridge, New York, Melbourne, Madrid, Cape Town,
Singapore, São Paulo, Delhi, Mexico City

Cambridge University Press
32 Avenue of the Americas, New York, NY 10013-2473, USA

www.cambridge.org
Information on this title: www.cambridge.org/9780521156707

First published 2012

Printed in the United States of America

A catalog record for this publication is available from the British Library.

Library of Congress Cataloging in Publication Data
Downs, Donald Alexander.
Arms and the university : military presence and the civic education of non-military
students / Donald Alexander Downs, Ilia Murtazashvili.
p. cm.
Includes bibliographical references and index.
ISBN 978-0-521-19232-3 (hardback) – ISBN 978-0-521-15670-7 (paperback)
1. United States. Army. Reserve Officers' Training Corps. 2. Education, Humanistic –
United States. 3. Soldiers – Education (Higher) – United States. 4. Civil–military relations –
United States. 5. United States. Army – Recruiting, enlistment, etc.
I. Murtazashvili, Ilia, 1975– II. Title.
U428.5.D68 2012
355.2′232071173–dc23

2011032229

ISBN 978-0-521-19232-3 Hardback
ISBN 978-0-521-15670-7 Paperback

To Jen, Leo, Zoe, Susan, Jacqueline, and Alexander; and to the student cadets and veterans who have striven so ably and honorably to foster the citizen-soldier ideal and to bridge the gap between the military, the university, and society

[Lincoln] expressed the new idea in the Gettysburg Address.... He addressed Tocqueville's worry about the longevity of liberal democratic governments. ... But the Civil War raised the question of whether such a government could survive, "testing whether that nation or any nation so conceived and dedicated can endure"...

But what gave force to this argument was the occasion and setting of his speech. He delivered his remarks at a battlefield cemetery, dedicating the site. His speech was about death. ... He said nothing to suggest that death was good. ... He did not think, as Qutb did, that martyrs go on living in some respect, and that death is a garden of delights. He did not find brotherhood in death – did not see his highest aspirations realized in a field of the dead, as the totalitarians of the twentieth century have done, and are still doing. ...

But neither did he avert his eyes from death. He spoke about death as "the last full measure of devotion," which Union soldiers had given.... Death was not their goal; but death was the measure of their commitment. "From these honored dead we take increased devotion," he said. He was explaining that a liberal society must be, when challenged, a warlike society; or it will not endure.

Paul Berman[1]

[1] Paul Berman, *Terror and Liberalism* (Norton, 2003), pp. 169–70.

Contents

List of Tables		*page* ix
Acknowledgments		xi
PART I. A NORMATIVE AND PEDAGOGICAL FRAMEWORK		
1	Introduction: The Closing of the University Mind: The Military–University Gap and the Problem of Civic and Liberal Education	3
2	Education in the Regime: How a Military Presence Can Enhance Civic and Liberal Education	40
PART II. ROTC AND THE UNIVERSITY		
3	ROTC and the University: An Introduction	77
4	ROTC and the Ivies: Before the Storm	103
5	ROTC and the Ivies: The Divorce	131
6	ROTC, Columbia, and the Ivy League: Sisyphus Renews His Quest to Renew a Troubled Relationship	161
7	Post-DADT: Sisyphus Ascends the Mountain	198
8	Pedagogy and Military Presence: The Educational Influence of Student-Soldiers in Their Own Words	226
9	Winning Hearts and Minds? The Consequences of Military Presence for Non-military Students	256
PART III. MILITARY HISTORY EXAMINED		
10	Military History: An Endangered or Protected Species?	283
11	Half Empty or Half Full: Military Historians' Perspectives on the Status of Military History at the Leading Departments	320

12 Military Presence in Security Studies: Political Realism (Re)Considered 356
13 Security Studies in the Wake of the Cold War University: Paragons of Productive Friction, or Throwing the Baby out with the Bathwater? 381

PART IV. CONCLUDING THOUGHTS
14 Conclusion: Placing the Military in the University 411

Index 425

Tables

8.1 Cadets' Reasons for Joining ROTC *page* 235
8.2 Cadets' Views on the Importance of ROTC to the Military and University 237
8.3 Negative Experiences of Cadets 242
8.4 Positive Experiences of Cadets 246
8.5 Cadets' Perceptions of Benefits of ROTC on Campus 248
8.6 Cadets' Self-Described Impact on Campus 249
8.7 Influence of Non-ROTC Students in the ROTC Classroom 253
9.1 Student Interactions with ROTC 258
10.1 Military History and National Security in History Departments: A First Take 308
10.2 Traditional and New Military History in History Departments 311
10.3 Traditional and New Military History in Political Science Departments 317
11.1 Faculty in Various Military History Orbits 325
11.2 Courses in Various Military History Orbits 328
13.1 Orientation of Security Studies Departments 385

Acknowledgments

Many individuals helped us with the making of *Arms and the University*, including those who granted us interviews in person or in e-mails; those who offered guidance regarding research, information, and points of view; and those who provided encouragement and other forms of support. We are grateful to all who gave us aid and comfort in this complicated project and would like to extend specific thanks to several individuals here. One of the benefits of conducting this type of research is the opportunity to meet exceptional individuals who have much to offer and teach the researcher. The individuals we thank here are exemplars of this benefit.

We begin with those who represent America's future and who were the guiding light in the movement that led to Columbia University's reopening of the Reserve Officers' Training Corps (ROTC) door in April 2011: the students who led the ROTC movement over the course of the last decade and who granted us interviews and gave us important information. The success of the Columbia ROTC movement was due, first and foremost, to these impressive students. Those who gave us the most assistance among this group include Yoni Appelbaum, Austin Bird, Eric Chen, Elizabeth Feldmeier, Learned Foote, John McClelland, Joe Naughton, Jose Robledo, Tao Tan, Robert Wray, and Riaz Zaidi. It was a true pleasure interacting with these exceptional young men and women, who instill needed confidence in our struggling nation's future prospects.

Beyond the students, special thanks go to professors Allan Silver and James Applegate of Columbia University, who have encouraged and contributed to the progress of this book almost from its inception. Allan and Jim represent the best that higher education has to offer on many levels, including a commitment to campus citizenship, which is highly relevant to the subject of our book. Allan helped us with his extensive knowledge of the military and its complex relationship with society, with his distinctive and inimitable insights into the vicissitudes of higher education and Columbia as an institution, and with information about the ROTC movement. Allan's deep and subtle understanding of the civic implications of the ROTC question had a profound impact on our work, and we are indebted to his insights even on those occasions when our views on certain matters and his part ways. Jim granted us very useful interviews and on-the-spot information as the ROTC movement progressed, including his own penetrating insights into the labyrinthine nature of the Columbia University political process and the rationales for ROTC. Our numerous interactions with Allan and Jim have been invaluable and inspiring, and we are honored to list them among our colleagues from "abroad," so to speak.

Professor Stephen Van Evera, an international relations political scientist and key member of MIT's Security Studies Program, gave us two lengthy interviews while also furnishing us with one of the book's most important models of pedagogy: Hans Morgenthau's notion of the "higher practicality." Deeply and enthusiastically committed to scholarship, teaching, and policy, Van Evera strives to unite intellectual understanding and policy relevance, discerning the theoretical and historical significance of important international relations policy questions. Steve's perspective and commitment helped to inspire the pedagogical aspects of *Arms and the University*.

Other individuals with ties to Columbia and the ROTC movement also helped us in noteworthy ways. Ted Graske, captain, U.S. Navy (USN) (Ret.), and the leader of the alumni group Columbia Alliance for ROTC, gave us generous assistance, including interview time, relevant material, and wise insight. Mickey Segal, a Columbia graduate who mans the general Advocates for ROTC website (www.advocatesforrotc.org/), assisted us with a lengthy interview and with the provision of many articles that chronicled the ROTC political movement that has burgeoned over the course of the last decade. Paul Mawn, captain, USN (Ret.), the leader of Harvard alumni's Advocates for ROTC, helped us with two probing interviews and useful material. Tom Mathewson, the secretary of the University Senate at Columbia, generously arranged for coauthor Downs to attend the senate vote on April 1, 2011, that opened the door for ROTC to return to Columbia. We would also like to thank the staff at Columbia's Butler Library Rare Book and Manuscript Library, who provided Downs with excellent assistance while he was researching the 1960s material in the library's collection entitled "University Protest and Activism Collection, 1958–1999."

John T. S. Keeler, dean of the Graduate School of Public and International Affairs at the University of Pittsburgh, and Phil Williams, director of the Matthew B. Ridgway Center for International Security Studies at Pitt, provided us with an opportunity to bring together a diverse group of scholars to discuss the issues presented in this book. The conference, which addressed the themes considered in this book, was tremendously valuable. We were fortunate to gather insight from several exceptional military historians at the conference, including John Lynn, Michael Neiberg, and Peter Karsten. We have also learned much from their scholarly writing. Captain Geoffrey Heiple and Forrest Morgan, U.S. Air Force (USAF) (Ret.), offered practical insight into the relationship between the military and universities that informed our approach. Geoff also deserves special credit for alerting us to important dimensions of leadership studies, ROTC, and American universities that we had not fully considered. The conference also provided a forum that brought us in contact with many other students with military experience at the University of Pittsburgh. One of these student-soldiers in particular, Lieutenant Christopher Zenk, now a newly commissioned officer in flight school, was always willing to take time from his demanding schedule to offer insight into the themes presented in this book. This book would not have been possible without the insight offered by the many experts in military affairs with whom we were fortunate to talk.

Jennifer Murtazashvili has provided constant insight into the themes presented in this book as well as personal encouragement on this project. Her practical insight into the importance of engaging with the military – insight gained in part through years of field work in Afghanistan – affirmed our belief in the importance of the topic of this book while also humbling us. On an academic and personal note, she deserves special acknowledgment for her courage in honestly striving to discern the appropriate balance between the military and the academy.

We would also like to thank the Wisconsin Alumni Research Foundation (WARF) at the University of Wisconsin, Madison, and the Political Science Department for providing funding that greatly assisted the project. The department granted Downs a professorship in 2000 that included ample research funds that were later used in launching the research in 2007–8; and WARF awarded Downs a named professorship in 2010 that included research funding that greatly assisted in the final stages of the work.

PART I

A NORMATIVE AND PEDAGOGICAL FRAMEWORK

1

Introduction

The Closing of the University Mind: The Military–University Gap and the Problem of Civic and Liberal Education

> War is an ugly thing, but not the ugliest of things. The decayed and degraded state of moral and patriotic feeling which thinks that nothing is worth war is much worse. The person who has nothing for which he is willing to fight, nothing which is more important than his own personal safety, is a miserable creature and has no chance of being free unless made and kept so by the exertions of better men than himself.
>
> – John Stuart Mill[1]

> The progress of our arms, upon which all else chiefly depends, is as well known to the public as to myself, and it is, I trust, reasonably satisfactory and encouraging to all.... Both parties deprecated war, but one of them would *make* war rather than let the nation survive, and the other would *accept* war rather than let it perish, and the war came.
>
> – President Abraham Lincoln[2]

The inspiration for this book arose several years before either of us actually sat down to begin the research that led to its publication. It was born when we observed events that took place on American campuses in the immediate aftermath of al Qaeda's terrorist attacks on September 11, 2001. Most of the campus ceremonies and "teach-ins" addressing the attacks that we read about in the press emphasized such things as counseling students to resist the impulse to fight back and to think hard about why America was responsible for bringing this action upon itself. Various versions of pacifism were espoused on many occasions. A ceremony on our own campus in Madison, Wisconsin, that drew an estimated twenty thousand witnesses on September 14 fit this pattern to a "T."[3]

[1] John Stuart Mill, "The Contest in America," *Fraser's Magazine* (February 1862); later published in *Dissertations and Discussions* (1868), vol. 1, p. 26.

[2] Abraham Lincoln, Second Inaugural Address: http://www.ourdocuments.gov/doc.php?flash=true&doc=38.

[3] "Gathering Remembers Victims of Terrorism," *Badger Herald*, September 17, 2001: http://badgerherald.com/news/2001/09/17/gathering_remembers_.php. See also "Student Leaders, Professors Prepare Nationwide Peace Rally," *Badger Herald*, September 20, 2001: http://badgerherald.com/news/2001/09/20/student_leaders_prof.php.

Along with many of our colleagues, we understood and appreciated these remarks, but we also felt that something was missing.

Our consternation should not be taken the wrong way. We duly respect those who question American policy, and we hold pacifists in high regard when their beliefs are genuine and when they accept the implications of their truths. Nor are we among those who deem America blameless for its actions in the world. Among other things, we are students of the political and moral realism espoused by such thinkers as theologian-philosopher Reinhold Niebuhr and international relations theorist Hans Morgenthau, who taught that no nation or individual is free of self-interest and dirty hands (sin, if you will). No nation or individual has a monopoly on virtue. We also realize that the moral calculus of foreign policy and military policy is complex, subtle, and unavoidably full of contradictions. We try to steer clear, to borrow words from Niebuhr, of the children of light as well as the children of darkness.[4]

But what troubled us at the ceremonies at Madison and elsewhere was the lack of recognition that a military response might be appropriate under the circumstances. Some type of military response is hardly presumptively irrational when a nation is attacked as the United States was, and when the enemy who perpetrated the attack continues to operate in a sanctuary or safe harbor that is identifiable. (To be fair, at the time of the ceremonies, it was not yet clearly established that al Qaeda was behind the attack. But many speakers' admonitions were not contingent upon who was responsible.) Most importantly to us, the lack of a military dimension was not simply a *policy* problem, but a *pedagogical* one as well. At a university, we are supposed to take seriously all ideas that are germane to the question at hand. So the failure or refusal to address the military question seemed to be an *intellectual* problem – and that is what should matter at a university.

With this observation, we embarked upon a long conversation regarding the relationship between the military and the university. As we conversed with students, we found that many of them harbored the same misgivings or second thoughts that we shared. They desired to hear the other side of the argument in order to be fully informed. To rephrase Allan Bloom, a kind of "closing of the university mind" seemed to exist regarding the military, at least in certain domains of consequence.[5] Though universities pride themselves on being liberally minded and open to challenging ideas, this pride seemed less merited when it comes to the military, even though the military is one of the most important institutions in American society.

[4] See, e.g., Reinhold Niebuhr, *The Children of Light and the Children of Darkness: A Vindication of Democracy and a Critique of Its Traditional Defense* (Charles Scribner's and Sons, 1945); Hans J. Morgenthau, *Politics Among Nations: The Struggle for Power and Peace*, 3rd Edition (Alfred A. Knopf, 1965). On the ethical realism of both of these thinkers, see A. J. H. Murray, "The Moral Politics of Hans Morgenthau," *Review of Politics* 58 (1996): 81–107.

[5] Allan Bloom, *The Closing of the American Mind: How Education Has Failed Democracy and Impoverished the Souls of Today's Students* (Simon and Schuster, 1987).

Accordingly, in this work we address an important yet vexing question in higher education, a question that has spawned intensifying national attention over the course of the last several years: *What is the appropriate role or presence for the military and military-related studies in American higher education?* Military presence on campus can take several forms, the most important of which are the operation of Reserve Officer Training Corps (ROTC) programs and the provision of courses that deal with the military, such as military history and strategically oriented national security/defense studies. Though they differ in their respective objectives and approaches, ROTC and courses treating military and security issues are similar in one major respect: They provide knowledge about the military and war, to varying degrees. They are also similar for another reason: They are often embattled within American universities.

In the years since 9/11, however, activists have sought to return ROTC and related programs to schools that had turned their back on the military in the aftermath of the Vietnam War; most notably, this movement has challenged the retreat of ROTC from the Ivy League and such schools as Stanford University. A similar movement supported and publicized by documentary filmmaker Rob Roy and his allies has been brewing in Canada, which dropped the Canadian Officer Training Corps (COTC) nationwide in 1968 at the hands of a government initiative. Though these efforts have not met meaningful success in Canada as of this writing, they have elevated the issue to the level of national attention, occasioning a serious consideration of the issues raised by Roy and his allies.[6] There has also been a concerted effort to enhance the status of military history as an academic discipline in the United States, a movement that has encountered some success after years of appearing to be a losing battle. More surprisingly, the pro-ROTC movement in the United States began to enjoy unexpected success as we were preparing to go to press in late summer 2011, as Columbia University, Harvard University, Yale University, and Stanford University had decided to bring ROTC back after having effectively barred the program for over forty years. Fortunately, we were able to capture this historically significant turn of events in Chapter 7 just before sending the book to the production process. These and other developments suggest that many domains of higher education are now striving to repair their relationship with the military. This advance has gathered force during the three and a half years that we have been researching and writing this book. We consider this book to be part of this ongoing process.

Whereas our consideration deals directly with the relationship between the military and the university, it also beckons a broader inquiry into the meaning of higher education itself. What are the ends of liberal and civic education, and how might – or might not – an appropriate military presence on campus contribute to these ends? We will argue that an appropriate military presence – including

[6] On the revival of COTC, see Tim Johnson, "Will Universities Salute a New Campus Corps?" University Affairs/Affaires Universitaires, April 6, 2010: http://www.universityaffairs.ca/will-universities-salute-a-new-campus-corps.aspx. Also interview with Rob Roy, Head of "Seven Year Project," Breakout Educational Network, October 2010.

appropriate physical presence of the military, course offerings, and faculty versed in military history – can indeed contribute to the civic and liberal education of non-military students, especially in the context of higher education today. The traditional justification for ROTC, for example, considers the positive impacts such programs have on the military and, by virtue of this, on society itself – that is, bringing the university to the military. Though we hold this rationale in high regard, our main question points in the opposite direction: *Can an appropriate military presence on campus contribute in itself to the education of non-military students*? In this introduction, we lay out the background from which this inquiry emerged and then discuss the format by which we will proceed.

Above and beyond these concerns are the crucial questions of civic equality and equal duty. One percent of the American population today bears the burden of fighting our wars, and, as we will see throughout this book, military representation and status at many prestigious institutions of higher education is marginal. Whether or not this status is harmful to the conducting of military policy and war, it certainly poses a problem for citizenship more broadly construed. As Columbia University sociologist Allan Silver – a leader in the pro-ROTC movement at that institution – has remarked on more than one occasion, this state of affairs amounts to "a corrosive civic scandal."[7] In addressing this problem, some students of civic life have seriously considered the propriety of reinstituting the peacetime draft.[8] We do not take this bait, accepting the fact that such a revival poses as many problems as it answers; absent genuine democratic consent or a national military emergency that would necessitate a draft, we are consigned to the All-Volunteer Force (AVF). But this position does not mean that a civic problem does not exist. An appropriate military presence on campus could provide one partial, yet meaningful, remedy to this predicament.

The civic scandal is a problem for universities, too, for their missions include commitments to fostering citizenship, equality, and diversity, all of which are deeply implicated in the questions we pose regarding the military. Most importantly, universities strive to expose their students to the problems and issues stirring in the world around them. As Jose Ortega y Gassett declares in his classic book *Mission of the University*:

> Not only does it [the university] need perpetual contact with science, on pain of atrophy, it needs contact, likewise, with public life, with historical reality, with the present, which is essentially a whole to be dealt with only in its totality, not after amputations *ad usum*

[7] Allan Silver, "The Military and Academe," paper and talk presented at National Association of Scholars Conference, February 19, 2009: http://www.nas.org/polArticles.cfm?doctype_code=Article&doc_id=569&Keyword_Desc=NAS%20Conference%20Video.

[8] See, e.g., James Fallows, *National Defense* (Vintage, Random House, 1982), ch. 5; William A. Galston, "A Sketch of Some Arguments for Conscription," in *Community Matters: Challenges to Civic Engagement in the 21st Century* (Rowman and Littlefield, 2005), pp. 61–72. Congressman Charles Rangel has also spoken in favor or reinstituting the draft. "Rangel Eyes Draft Return," *New York Post*, July 8, 2010.

Delphini. The university must be open to the whole reality of its time. It must be in the midst of life, and saturated with it.[9]

We will also deal with another matter that directly implicates civic equality: the effects of the congressionally mandated Don't Ask, Don't Tell (DADT) policy, which prohibited the open expression of homosexuality in the military. DADT has been the most prominent reason that many universities have resisted the military and/or ROTC. The policy violates principles of antidiscrimination and civil rights that Americans – especially those in higher education – hold dear, and we have consistently agreed with the opposition to it. In December 2010, Congress finally managed to repeal the policy, and President Obama's signature drove the final nail into its coffin.[10] Pending the military's implementation of the repeal, the end of DADT has added one bookend to the civic equality shelf; finally opening the mind to the military completes the task. This said, disquiet regarding the military extends beyond the DADT issue in many quarters of higher education, meriting a broader inquiry.

We acknowledge that tension between the university and the military is only natural given the respective institutions' different natures. Universities are, at least as ideal types, the institutional heirs of the Enlightenment, in which the light of reason and progress holds sway over the endorsement or exercise of force, which appear retrograde. The realities of war and force are often either disavowed or relegated to the shadows of consciousness.[11] Universities have often stood in the forefront of antiwar and pacifist movements throughout history. (At the same time, however, they opened their doors to extensive military training, war preparation, and research during World Wars I and II and the Cold War.) As an ideal type, universities also pride themselves on free and creative thought, while the military – according to its ideal type – emphasizes hierarchy and command.[12] In discussing the politics of ROTC later in this book, we will witness many claims that "the military and the university are incompatible"

[9] Jose Ortega y Gassett, *Mission of the University*, edited and translated by Howard Lee Nostrand (Norton Library, 1966), pp. 88–9. By "science," Ortega means theoretical and academic knowledge, which includes the humanities, the social sciences, and the physical sciences.

[10] For a good treatment of DADT, see, e.g., "'Rum, Sodomy, and the Lash': What the Military Thrives on and How It Affects Legal Recruitment and Law Schools," panel remarks at 2006 Lavender Law Conference, September 8, 2006. In 14 *Duke Law Journal of Gender Law and Policy* 1143 (2007); "Colleges Rethink R.O.T.C. After 'Don't Ask' Repeal," *New York Times*, December 21, 2010.

[11] On how social theory has largely ignored questions of war and peace because of its inconsistency with academic sensibility, see, for example, Hans Joas, *War and Modernity* (Polity, 2003), ch. 7, "Between Power Politics and Pacifist Utopia: Peace and War in Social Theory."

[12] For a thoughtful account of the fundamental differences between the military and the university that is duly respectful of each side, see Pat C. Hoy, "Soldiers and Scholars: Between Harvard and West Point, a Deep – and Dangerous – Cultural Chasm," *Harvard Magazine* 98, 5 (1996). We will discuss Hoy's insights more fully in the next chapter. (Note that throughout this book, we do not always consistently provide pages numbers for cited articles. Page numbers are provided if there is a quotation or if the idea or point discussed was from a distinct page or set of pages in the article.

for these and related reasons. We certainly agree that universities should *not* be like the military, lest they risk losing their moral charter – their raison d'être – by becoming that which they are not. To guard against any militarizing impacts of ROTC on campus, universities must uphold their own standards of academic quality, academic integrity and freedom, and equal respect for all members of the campus community. Indeed, we will encounter many examples of such exertion of academic control in our chapters dealing with ROTC. But the key question for our purposes is whether a dialectically constructive relationship can exist that facilitates mutual advantage.

A PROBLEM FOR THE CONSTITUTIONAL ORDER AND EDUCATION, AND THE CITIZEN-SOLDIER RATIONALE

In the normative framework we set forth, the state of affairs to which we have just alluded – quasi-benign neglect at best, outright hostility to the military and military affairs in the academy at the worst – is detrimental to the constitutional order, civic equality, and the civic and liberal education of non-military students. We join a large community of scholars, leaders, and citizens in maintaining that the constitutional order *requires* a civil–military relationship that protects military professionalism and appropriate military autonomy while also honoring the principle and practice of civilian control. Historically, the major worries about an inappropriate relationship between the military and civilian society (including disquiet about a military–society "gap") have centered on three concerns: (1) the dangers of a military takeover – a worry that scholars rightly consider exaggerated (at the least) in the modern American context; (2) undue military interference with civilian strategic judgment that tilts the appropriate constitutional balance; (3) and uncooperative military–civilian interaction in the policy process, which can lead to bad policy decisions. These are obviously important considerations, and they are relevant to our inquiry; but they lie toward the periphery of our concern. Our emphasis is upon higher education, civic equality, and the learning process. In this vein, we believe that ignorance of the military and war can lead to four problems:

- Uncritical support of the military, often accompanied by what historian (and former Army lieutenant colonel) Andrew Bacevich calls the "new American militarism," which entails an undue and unrealistic enthusiasm for military power and adventure.[13] Such support is misbegotten because the military – like any institution or group, however noble and worthy of respect – is rife

Often the point made in the main text applies generally to the basic theme or themes in the entire article, so there is no need in our view to cite specific pages.)

[13] Andrew J. Bacevich, *The New American Militarism: How Americans Are Seduced by War* (Oxford University Press, 2005). While militarism is a threat that arises when civil–military balance breaks down, it is a strong claim to describe American society as militaristic, the latter describing societies that value war in itself. While many may disagree with the ends of American policy, there are few reasons to believe that the recent conflicts in Iraq and Afghanistan reflect the United States fighting war for its own sake. Misadventure is not the same thing as militarism.

with conflicts and imperfections. Military leaders and soldiers make mistakes, sometimes egregiously so, and the politics of defense and defense spending is notoriously messy and laced with institutional and bureaucratic self-interest, as President Dwight D. Eisenhower accentuated when he warned against the shenanigans of the military–congressional–industrial complex in his famous presidential Farewell Address. As an Army lieutenant colonel with twenty-five years of service told us in an interview, "The military can have a significant bullshit problem."[14] A recent example is the military's initial distortion (some claimed it was a cover-up) of the truth behind the killing of Army Ranger Pat Tillman in Afghanistan on April 22, 2004. The Army claimed that the former football star's death was caused by enemy fire, and it was only after Tillman's family publicly pursued the matter that the Army acknowledged the embarrassing fact that Tillman was killed by friendly fire.[15] The university's relationship with the military must be duly respectful, but also critical. As the great military sociologist Morris Janowitz wrote in a letter to a colleague in 1971, warning against what he called "unanticipated militarism," "A new intellectual, critical, and truly academic relation between the universities and the military will have to be created – since such contacts will be essential for effective civilian control and a meaningful military policy."[16]

- Endorsement of an opposite, antimilitary ideology that perceives the military as evil or as the "other." As we will see in our section on the politics of ROTC, some students berate ROTC cadets as "baby killers" and similar embodiments of evil, or uncritically assume that universal peace would prevail if nations only laid down their arms. A healthy relationship between the military and civilians on campus should help to dispel negative stereotypes and myths about the military and the legitimate uses and abuses of the deployment of military force.
- A simple lack of knowledge regarding the military and strategic security matters, a lack that amounts to a failure of civic education and responsibility. National security and the appropriate use of force are vital matters of national interest, so understanding these phenomena constitutes an important aspect of citizenship. As former Democratic senator Russ Feingold and former Democratic congressman (and former vice chair of the 9/11 Commission) Lee Hamilton remarked in a 2009 editorial, "Protecting our national security

[14] Interview with Rob Sayre, Army Lt. Col., October 2010. Dwight D. Eisenhower, Presidential Farewell Address, January 17, 1961: http://www.americanrhetoric.com/speeches/dwightdeisenhowerfarewell.html. For an interesting portrayal of the historical institutional persistence of the military services' conceptions of their self-interest, and how such interest is the primary source of national military policy, see Carl H. Builder, *The Masks of War: American Military Styles in Strategy and Analysis* (Johns Hopkins University Press, 1989).

[15] See Josh White. "Army Withheld Details About Tillman's Death: Investigator Quickly Learned 'Friendly Fire' Killed Athlete," *Washington Post*, May 3, 2005: http://www.washingtonpost.com/wp-dyn/content/article/2005/05/03/AR2005050301502.html.

[16] Morris Janowitz letter, quoted in James Burk, "Morris Janowitz and the Origins of Sociological Research on Armed Forces and Society," *Armed Forces & Society* 19, 2 (1993): 178.

is the most solemn responsibility of members of Congress, one that should transcend both partisan politics and the parochialism of the current appropriations process."[17]

Bacevich detects a common denominator winding through all three of these postures. "Here we confront a central paradox of present-day American militarism. Even as U.S. policy in recent decades has become progressively militarized, so too has the Vietnam-induced gap separating the U.S. military from American society persisted and perhaps even widened. Even as American elites become ever more fascinated with military power and the use of force – Vice President Cheney, for example, is a self-professed war buff with a passion for military history – soldiering itself is something left to the plebs."[18] Bacevich's concern points to the civic duty and equality aspects of the gap problem.

- The fourth problem concerns the military itself: the rise of an undue sense of moral superiority to civilian society. To some extent, this problem is inherent to the military. Competent soldiers engage in rigorous training that turns them into soldier-warriors who possess special skills and forms of courage that lie beyond the ken of the average citizen. (The need for courage, of course, depends upon the role a soldier performs, for not all military roles involve combat.) This disparity can engender a feeling of moral superiority that is detrimental to an appropriate relationship between the military and civil society. As Machiavelli relates at the beginning of *The Art of War*, a trained soldier wearing a uniform often finds it difficult to respect his fellow citizens who lack such accoutrements.[19] A widening gap between the military and civilian society exacerbates this problem.

A productive relationship between the civil order and the military can be fostered in a number of ways, but one important vehicle involves the university. In many respects, the university is a microcosm of the relationship among the military, civil society, and the government. Student soldiers and non-military students can interact in ways that foreshadow their interactions in the political realm in their role as citizens, politicians, and members of the military. The model of the citizen-soldier, which is the primary rationale for ROTC, is predicated on this aspiration.[20] This rationale holds that exposing a host of future officers to the intellectual virtues of civilian universities improves and broadens the military mind, contributing to maintaining appropriate civilian influence and control. Our task is to understand how well the university contributes to broadening the

[17] Russ Feingold and Lee Hamilton, "The Intel Committees Need the Power of the Purse," *Wall Street Journal*, February 8, 2009, p. A19.

[18] Bacevich, *The New American Militarism*, p. 28.

[19] Niccolo Machiavelli, *The Art of War*, translated by Neal Wood (Bobbs-Merrill, Library of Liberal Arts, 1965), p. 4.

[20] The definitive work on the citizen-soldier republican rationale of ROTC is Michael S. Neiberg's *Making Citizen-Soldiers: ROTC and the Ideology of American Military Service* (Harvard University Press, 2001).

horizons of military and non-military students, and to discuss possible avenues for improvement.

THE "GAP": A BROADER PROBLEM IN ACADEMIA?

As our inquiry commenced and widened, we noticed that we were not alone, as other observers had similar misgivings about the status of military-related ideas on campus. The reasons for the broader problem are many, and the posture toward the military portrayed in the preceding transcends the issue of DADT, raising broader questions about the military–university relationship.

To be sure, the picture that emerged as we progressed in our investigation was complex. On the one hand, military-related inquiry is present in many sectors of research and pedagogy, especially those dealing with national security. For example, international relations departments and programs offer courses treating the uses of force, and the field of civil–military studies (comprising primarily political science, history, and sociology) has enjoyed a "renaissance" in the post–Cold War era.[21] Such research is a response to the fraying of the more typical cooperation that had prevailed between civilian and military leaders during the Cold War, when the Soviet Union reigned as a common enemy that compelled relative consensus in the strategic realm.[22] Furthermore, a revival of interest in the attendance of veteran students and in ROTC has arisen on many campuses in just the four-year period during which we have been researching and writing this book – a phenomenon we designate the "return of the soldier" on campus. On the other hand, we came across consternation regarding such matters as the status of military history in leading history departments, a decline in attention given to military matters in the broader social sciences, and the continued exclusion of ROTC from many of the most distinguished institutions in American higher education. A few of these concerns merit attention in this introductory chapter.

ROTC Issues

First, we encountered a growing concern about the geographic distribution of military recruits and ROTC and regarding ROTC's lowly status on elite campuses. As the military has become more separate from American society after the advent of the All-Volunteer Force, fewer young men and women from the middle and upper educational, social, and economic echelons of American society

[21] See Peter D. Feaver and Erika Seeler, "Before and After Huntington: The Methodological Maturing of Civil-Military Studies," in Suzanne C. Nielsen and Don M. Snider, eds., *American Civil-Military Relations: The Soldier and the State in a New Era* (Johns Hopkins University Press, 2009), p. 87.

[22] One theory of civilian–military leadership harmony is that cooperation is encouraged by agreement on external threats, breaking down when such threats go away. See Michael C. Desch, *Civilian Control of the Military: The Changing Security Environment* (Johns Hopkins University Press, 1999).

participate. As Gary Schmidt and Cheryl Miller pointed out in a recent essay in the *Wall Street Journal*, soldiers now hail from an increasingly narrow segment of American society geographically and culturally. Almost half of all Army recruits come from military families and close to half of the soldiers in all the services are Southerners. Meanwhile,

> ... the middle-class suburbs surrounding the nation's largest cities – New York, Los Angeles, Chicago, Boston and Philadelphia – produce relatively few service members despite having a large percentage of the nation's youth population. ... The homogeneity of today's military is partly a product of self-selection, as the services seek out the most eager volunteers. But it is also a product of green-eyeshade budgeting and policy decisions by the armed services and government.

ROTC is complicit in this problem, as its leaders have concentrated the program in less urban areas of the South and the Midwest, marginalizing highly populated urban areas. "In Virginia, for example, there are 7.8 million residents and 11 Army ROTC programs. New York City, home to over eight million people and America's largest university student population, has two Army ROTC programs. The entire Chicago metro area, with its 10 million residents, is covered by a single Army ROTC program, as is Detroit. Alabama, population 4.7 million, has 10."[23]

Though the situation is more complex than many critics and apologists aver, evidence also supports the claim that a substantial gap has yawned between the military and many major institutions of higher education. Such schools as Harvard, Yale, Columbia, Stanford, Brown, and Cal Tech forsook ROTC, and the programs at such schools as Cornell and Princeton have garnered less-than-enthusiastic participation. As Yale professor David Gelernter remarked in Kathy Roth-Douquet and Frank Schaeffer's book, *AWOL: The Unexcused Absence of America's Upper Classes from the Military – and How It Hurts Our Country*, "Here in academia, my colleagues seem determined to turn American soldiers into an out-of-sight, out of mind servant class who are expected to do their duty and keep their mouths shut."[24] Accordingly, we can discern at least three "gaps" that exist regarding ROTC: a gap between academics and student-soldiers, between elite and non-elite institutions, and a regional gap

[23] Gary Schmidt and Cheryl Miller, "The Military Should Mirror the Nation: America's Armed Forces Are Drawn from an Increasingly Narrow Segment of American Society," *Wall Street Journal*, August 26, 2010: http://online.wsj.com/article/SB10001424052748703632304575451531529098478.html. Schmidt and Miller are director and program manager of the American Enterprise Institute's Program on Citizenship. See also Cheryl Miller's widely cited new monograph, "Underserved: A Case Study of ROTC in New YorkCity," American Enterprise Institute Report, May 5, 2011: http://www.citizenship-aei.org/2011/05/new-aei-report-why-nyc-needs-rotc/; Steven Trynosky, "ROTC and New York City," presentation at Columbia University conference "Service and Society," October 2, 2010. See also Lt. Col. Anthony G. Dotson, "Fixing the Reserve Officer Training Corps' Recruiting Problem," M.A. Thesis, U.S. Army Command and General Staff College, 2003; and Greg Jaffe, "Urban Withdrawal: A Retreat from Big Cities Hurts ROTC Recruitment," *Wall Street Journal*, February 22, 2007, p. A1.

[24] Gelernter, quoted in Kathy Roth-Douquet and Frank Schaeffer, *AWOL: The Unexcused Absence of America's Upper Classes from the Military – and How It Hurts Our Country* (Harper Collins, 2006), pp. 48–9.

between the major urban areas and the new redoubts of ROTC in the less urban areas of the South and Midwest. The decisions by Columbia, Harvard, Stanford, and Yale to welcome some form of ROTC back in early 2011 justify some optimism regarding the amelioration of all of these problems, and we will explore these possibilities in Chapter 7.

The Broader "Gap" Question

Second, we considered the growing literature on the "gap" that has opened between the military and civil society more generally. Secretary of Defense William Cohen addressed this concern in a speech he delivered at Yale University in 1997, in which he raised the specter of "a chasm ... developing between the military and the civilian worlds, where the civilian world doesn't fully grasp the mission of the military, and the military doesn't understand why the memories of our citizens and civilian policy-makers are so short, or why the criticism is so quick and so unrelenting."[25] Cohen's apprehensions were widely shared among scholars, journalists, and other observers, many of whom we will encounter in this book. For the most part, the evidence indicates that there is a gap about which we should be duly concerned, especially between officers and the general society in respect to attitudes and social-political values. Concern has also emerged over the rise of undue religious influence – especially evangelical Christian influence – over sectors of the officer and chaplain corps and the service academies, which began in earnest with the traumatic impact of the Vietnam War on the military. (We tend to focus on that war's impact on American society and politics, often neglecting its equally profound effect on the military.) Relevant factors in this development included the military's reaction to its growing isolation from American society during and after the Vietnam War; that war's impact on military morale; and the military's response to the breakdown of military ethics that sometimes took place in the conduct of the Vietnam War, which included such war crimes as the massacre at My Lai.[26] In general, however, research suggests that the differences – though significant on many measures – are not grave enough to constitute a "crisis"; furthermore, the attitudinal and value gap that stretches between enlisted (non-officer) soldiers and civilian culture appears to be appreciably less stark than the gap that looms

[25] Secretary of Defense William Cohen, speech at Yale, quoted in Peter D. Feaver, Richard H. Kohn, and Lindsay P. Cohn, "Introduction: The Gap Between Military and Civilian in the United States in Perspective," in Peter D. Feaver and Richard H. Kohn, eds., *Soldiers and Civilians: The Civil-Military Gap and American National Security* (MIT Press, 2001), p. 1.

[26] See, e.g., Anne C. Loveland, *American Evangelicals and the U.S. Military 1942–1993* (Baton Rouge: Louisiana State University Press, 1996); Laurie Goodstein, "Evangelicals Are a Growing Force in the Military Chaplain Corps," *New York Times* (Late Edition [East Coast]), July 12, 2005. The gap between the military and society has even been implicated in the My Lai massacre. See Ed Berger, Larry Flatley, John Frisch, Mayda Gottlieb, Judy Haisley, Peter Karsten, Larry Pexton, and William Worrest, "ROTC, Mylai, and the Volunteer Army," *Foreign Policy* 2 (1971): 131–60.

between officers and society. A recent comprehensive survey found that the attitudes and values of enlisted men and women in the Army generally reflect those of the general population.[27] The bottom line is that we should be "concerned," but not "alarmed."

Nevertheless, the very content of this research does point to an unsettling divide and alienation between the military and society, of which the university community is a prime, more extreme, example. The "gap" question has two fundamental dimensions: (1) cooperation between civilian and military leaders on policy making and the execution of policy, which is primarily a policy problem; and (2) the relationship between the military and the general society and culture, which is essentially a cultural problem. The two major scholars addressing these questions, respectively, were Samuel Huntington and Morris Janowitz, whose insights continue to shape the debate regarding civil–military relations even among those who disagree with their fundamental conclusions.[28]

Cooperation between military and civilian leadership frayed with the demise of the Soviet Union as a common enemy and the emergence of new military missions in the 1990s in such places as Bosnia, Kosovo, Somalia, and Haiti, where American national security was not directly threatened. Poisoning the waters further, Bill Clinton had not served in the military and was the first president to have been active in antiwar resistance as a youth; his administration's early initiative to end the ban against gays in the military added fuel to the fire. The combination of these and other factors engendered several instances of open military dissent against the administration, unleashing new anxieties about military–civilian relations at the leadership level. The strategy and tactics with which the Bush administration fought the Iraq War, conjoined with Defense Secretary Donald Rumsfeld's strong-armed efforts to reform and streamline the

[27] See the essays in Feaver and Kohn, *Soldiers and Civilians*. This work presents many of the findings of the Project on the Gap Between the Military and Civilian Society and the Triangle Institute for Security Studies (TISS) at Duke University and the University of North Carolina. It is the definitive source on the gap issue. The best source on the attitudes and beliefs of enlisted soldiers is Jason K. Dempsey, *Our Army: Soldiers, Politics, and American Civil–Military Relations* (Princeton University Press, 2010). Dempsey's work is the most exhaustive survey of the attitudes and beliefs of enlisted soldiers; he concludes that the enlisted Army is generally representative of the general population in terms of attitudes and beliefs. This is less the case for the officer corps. Our concern is not with the ideology of soldiers, however, but rather with the expertise of cadets, officers, and veterans regarding the military as an institution and regarding matters of war relative to nonmilitary students – differences that become the core of our argument that military presence is a source of "productive friction" that enhances prospects for civic and liberal education.

[28] See James Burk, "Theories of Democratic Civil-Military Relations," *Armed Forces & Society* 29, 7 (Fall 2002). Burk maintains that the theories of Huntington, Janowitz, and the civil–military distinction have declined in relevance since World War II because of such developments as the blurring of the political and military spheres in policy making; the outsourcing of military work to private organizations; the declining relevance of the citizen-soldier as an ideal; the movement toward transnational military institutions such as NATO; and the growing influence of international organizations, governmental and nongovernmental. That said, Burk acknowledges that the "gap" is a major concern in the era of "our own revolution in civil–military affairs" (p. 24). His point is simply that we need to think of new solutions.

military, further heightened tensions that had been let out the bottle during the Clinton administration.[29] At the same time, the representation of veterans in national politics has declined. The number of veterans serving in the House and Senate, for example, declined from 398 in 1971 to just 113 in the 112th Congress, which convened in January 2011. Meanwhile, given the likely makeup of the Republican presidential contenders for 2012 and President Barack Obama's lack of service, "the odds are that in two years, Americans are likely to cast their votes in the first presidential race in nearly 70 years where neither major party nominee has ever worn the nation's uniform."[30] Of course, these odds likely changed, as Texas governor Rick Perry, a former captain in the Air Force, announced his candidacy shortly before we went to press with this book. Nonetheless, the preceding facts suggest that there have been important changes in representation of veterans in national politics.

Unease also arose over the widening gap between soldiers and American society more generally. Following the Vietnam War, national leaders had concluded that the failure to mobilize the Reserves in that war had "disrupted an historical linkage between the American military and the American people," according to military sociologist David R. Segal.[31] Journalist Thomas Ricks helped to relaunch this concern in a seminal *Atlantic Monthly* essay and a best-selling book, *Making the Corps*, which were published in 1997, the same year that Cohen delivered his speech at Yale. Ricks jumped right to the point in the *Atlantic Monthly* article's first paragraph:

> After following a platoon of Marine recruits through eleven weeks of boot-camp training on Parris Island in the spring of 1995, I was stunned to see, when they went home for post graduation leave, how alienated they felt from their old lives. At various times each of these new Marines seemed to experience a moment of private loathing for public America. They were repulsed by the physical unfitness of civilians, by the uncouth behavior they witnessed, and by what they saw as pervasive selfishness and consumerism. Many found themselves avoiding old friends, and some experienced difficulty even in communicating with their families.[32]

In *Making the Corps*, Ricks pointed to several factors that have intensified the Marine Corps' (and the military's) alleged isolation from American society, including the establishment of the All-Volunteer Force and the concomitant

[29] See, for example, the debate between Michael Desch and his critics in *Foreign Affairs*. Michael C. Desch, "Bush and the Generals," *Foreign Affairs* 86, 3 (2007): 97–108; Desch, "Responses: Salute and Disobey? The Civil–Military Balance, Before Iraq and After," *Foreign Affairs* 86, 5 (2007): 147–56.

[30] This quotation and the statistics of veteran representation in Congress are from Kasie Hunt, "MIA in 2012 Field: Military Service," POLITICO, November 13, 2010: http://www.politico.com/news/stories/1110/45067.html.

[31] David R. Segal, "Current Developments and Trends in Social Research on the Military," in Giuseppe Caforio, ed., *Social Sciences and the Military: An Interdisciplinary Review* (Routledge, 2007), p. 52.

[32] Thomas E. Ricks, "The Widening Gap Between the Military and Society," *Atlantic Monthly*, July 1997.

termination of the draft; the intensification of military professionalization that has further isolated the military from civilian thinking; the closing of military bases in the Northeast and the Far West (a process that parallels trends in the distribution of ROTC); and the "privatizing" or outsourcing of many military functions, which decreases opportunities for many soldiers to work with civilians. Ricks' apprehensions are echoed by ROTC researcher and advocate Steve Trynosky (an Army major), who maintains that the Army has further separated itself from society by restricting the geographic reach of ROTC and by the formal adoption of a new Soldier's Creed in 2003 that included a "Warrior Ethos." The new creed is designed to instill a sense of distinction and valor that distinguishes the warrior from the society he or she serves. The previous Soldier's Creed placed more weight upon soldiers' duty to country and to fellow citizens.[33]

Robert Sayre, a well-connected lieutenant colonel whom we interviewed (he has served in the Balkans and Afghanistan and worked with General David Petraeus and other high-ranking officers) defended the previous Soldier's Creed, which was rooted in the logic of military professionalism espoused by such military theorists as Samuel Huntington and Carl von Clausewitz, who stressed that the military's main duty is to execute policy and strategy formulated by political leaders. "The model of the soldier is being smart and aware of one's position, like Eisenhower or Marshall. A soldier is crafty and disciplined. Being a 'warrior' makes you something other than being an instrument of policy on behalf of the nation. It is war for war's sake." Nevertheless, Sayre agreed that it is perhaps a matter of definition: When we mentioned Annapolis instructor Shannon French's model of "the warrior code," which portrays the ways in which warrior identity throughout history has been intimately bound up with character, moral psychology, and ethical limits – so violating the code exacerbates the mental and emotional trauma that accompanies war – he said that he agreed with the warrior ethic so framed.[34]

In the end, perhaps a propitious balance of warrior and soldier ethics is called for – we do, after all, want our soldiers to possess warrior virtues. More generally, we must remind ourselves that troubling tensions between the military and civilian leadership have erupted periodically throughout American history, and that a proper measure of tension is even desirable, comprising part of the

[33] Ricks, *Making the Corps* (Scribner, Simon and Schuster, 1997), ch. 9. *Making the Corps* is a remarkable work that tells the powerful story of Marine Platoon 3086 while integrating this story into a broader discussion of the military and American society. Interview with Stephen Trynosky, April 2008. See Vernon Loeb, "Army Plans Steps to Heighten 'Warrior Ethos,'" *Washington Post*, September 8, 2003.

[34] Interview with Sayre; Samuel P. Huntington, *The Soldier and the State: The Theory and Politics of Civil–Military Relations* (Harvard University Press, 1957); Carl von Clausewitz, *On War* (Penguin, 1968). Clausewitz pays special attention to the cerebral powers and judgment of officers, especially in combat-related situations – keeping a cool head and reason under pressure and the "fog of war." Shannon E. French, *The Code of the Warrior: Exploring Warrior Values Past and Present* (Rowman and Littlefield, 2003).

checks, balances, and constructive disharmony that our system promotes to effectuate thorough consideration of policy and to protect rights.[35] Furthermore, though the percentage of veterans in Congress is now at an all-time low, one study has concluded that this situation has not measurably influenced lawmaking, at least not yet.[36]

Along these lines, political scientist Richard Betts throws some water on the heat generated by undue consternation over the status of civil–military relations at the policy level. Betts pinpoints the three major reasons why civil-military relations should be of greater concern than other political relationships: (1) "the military has the hypothetical capability to impose its political will by force" in the form of a coup d'état; (2) mistakes in communications between civilian and military policy makers can lead to catastrophic consequences; (3) poor communication and integration can "produce strategic incoherence that wastes blood and treasure." Betts dismisses the first concern as not credible in the United States; the second concern is indeed worthy of consideration, but had greater saliency during the Cold War, when "mistakes could hypothetically trigger World War III." As for the danger of strategic incoherence, "The third risk is constant." It is simply part of the cost of doing business in our federated, pluralistic political system.[37]

We agree with Betts' refusal to be seduced into alarm (he entitles one of the sections in his article "A Problem Without a Crisis"); but we note that his skepticism regarding the negative effects of a gap is addressed to the realm of policy making, which poses a somewhat different set of questions from our pedagogical concerns. Our concern is that the university may not do enough to encourage appropriate military presence on campus – neglect that may not lead to a breakdown of civil–military relations but one that certainly appears to undermine not only prospects for civic and liberal education, but also for more effective public policy. Specifically, our primary concern is with the status of the military and military-related fields of inquiry, the pedagogical effects of military presence on campus, and the implications of the status of the military on campus for civic equality, civic duty, and engagement. Our interest thus overlaps that of noted military sociologist Morris Janowitz, whose work centered on the civic implications of the military–civil relationship and on the problem of preserving democratic and republican values in a militarized state. Janowitz maintained, empirically speaking, that the military was becoming more like the general society in several telling respects, including burgeoning bureaucratization, the

[35] On how such conflict is often productive in the defense policy area, see, e.g., Harvey Sapolsky, Eugene Gholz, and Caitlin Talmadge, *U.S. Defense Politics: The Origins of Security Policy* (Routledge, 2009). On the benefits of conflict in the American system, see Samuel P. Huntington, *American Politics: The Promise of Disharmony* (Harvard University Belknap Press, 1981).

[36] See William T. Bianco and Jamie Markham, "Vanishing Veterans: The Decline of Military Experience in the U.S. Congress," in Feaver and Kohn, *Soldiers and Civilians*, ch. 7.

[37] Richard Betts, "Are Civil-Military Relations Still a Problem?" in Nielsen and Snider, eds., *American Civil–Military Relations*, ch. 2, esp. pp. 26–7.

growing importance of educational and technical expertise, the ascendance of a managerial ethic and careerism at the expense of the traditional heroic military ethic, and the intensification of interaction with civilian society. Normatively, Janowitz believed that this process of fusion or "civilianization" is a good thing because it helps to preserve republican influence and checks on the military as an institution. (In this respect, Janowitz's position stood as the most prominent counterpoint to Huntington's position on military–civilian relations, for Huntington believed that "fusion" threatened military effectiveness and professionalism – although each scholar was fundamentally concerned with ensuring civilian control of the military.)[38] Some trends that have intervened since Janowitz's prime (roughly between the 1950s and the late 1980s) have undercut his empirical conclusions, as they have widened the gap between the military and the society it serves, including such phenomena as the institutionalization of the All-Volunteer Force, the explosion of international terrorism, and the onset of the cultural differences that we have addressed. But these trends make Janowitz's normative position all the more compelling for those who take the civic implications of the military seriously.

Thus, even if Betts is correct about the civilian–military gap in *government*, his assessment does not translate to the situation in *universities*. Indeed, Betts was one of eighteen Columbia University faculty members to sign a public statement in September 2010 supporting the return of ROTC to Columbia in the event of DADT's repeal. Among the statement's eight declarations are the following, which embrace the concerns we have broached thus far:

- It is damaging to democratic ideals of equality that graduates of highly selective, private universities are so underrepresented in the nation's officer corps;
- Our students' prevailing experience is of great personal distance from military service, limiting preparation for citizenship;
- Reciprocally, military leaders are often uncomprehending of the values for which Columbia and its peer institutions stand;
- Diversity in the student body including students preparing for military service would help alleviate this situation.[39]

The Status of Military History

Our third observation after embarking upon our inquiry was that the status of military history has generated much contention since the early and mid-1990s, as the generation of military historians who had come of age during the Cold War

[38] Morris Janowitz, *The Professional Soldier: A Social and Political Portrait*, Second Edition (Free Press, 1971). Brian McAllister Linn also depicts a tension among professional role conceptions in the Army ("guardians," "managers," and "heroes") in *The Echo of Battle: The Army's Way of War* (Harvard University Press, 2007). But Linn traces the existence of such roles back to the nation's inception. Huntington, *The Soldier and the State*.

[39] "Faculty for a Reserve Officers Training Program at Columbia," Public Statement, September 2010. The leading promoter of the petition was Columbia emeritus professor Allan Silver, whose participation will be discussed in Chapters 6 and 7.

has not been replaced by many junior colleagues in the field upon their retirements. As our inquiry proceeded, we came to see military history as the natural complement to physical presence of the military on campus: Intellectual consideration of war complements physical presence of the military, and it is military history that generally produces the most profound and realistic knowledge of war. Yet the status of military history on campus is far from settled. In the introduction to his 2008 book that focuses on Abraham Lincoln's actions as commander in chief during the Civil War, James M. McPherson offers an interesting observation that reflects the status of academic military history: "In the vast literature on our sixteenth president, however, the amount of attention devoted to his role as commander in chief is disproportionately far smaller than the actual percentage of time he spent on that task." In fact, as McPherson shows, Lincoln considered his position as commander in chief to be his most important responsibility as president. McPherson proceeds to provide telling examples of conferences, edited volumes, and books in which this topic does not see the light of day, concluding, "Perhaps it is time to recognize the truth expressed by Lincoln himself in his second inaugural address, when the Civil War had been raging for almost four years: On 'the progress of our arms . . . all else chiefly depends.'"[40]

McPherson is not alone in his perplexity. In 1997, military historian John A. Lynn wrote an essay that amounted to a call to arms in *The Journal of Military History*, entitled "The Embattled Future of Academic Military History." Lynn grieved at the virtual vanishing or marginalization of the field from leading journals of history, a dismay that extended to a 2008 essay in *Academic Questions* in which Lynn surveyed the 150 issues of the bellwether journal, *The American Historical Review (AHR)*, from 1976 to 2006. According to Lynn, "During this time, the *AHR* failed to publish a single research article focused on the conduct of the Hundred Years' War, the Thirty Years' War, the Wars of Louis XIV, the War of American Independence, the Revolutionary and Napoleonic Wars, and World War II." In addition, no article on Vietnam appeared, and only two on the Civil War, one of which was simply an address by the recently enthroned president of the American Historical Association. Lynn also found that of the top ninety-one programs in history, only four offered military history as a field for Ph.D. examinations. (He assumed that departments need at least two faculty members in the area to constitute a "field" – a standard that some critics say biased his findings in a pessimistic direction.) He also reported that when the last military historian at Purdue University retired a few years ago, his department chair informed him that the department would not be replacing him because "there was no *social* purpose to the study of military history."[41] Our eyebrows were raised like Lynn's, especially when we found that the status of military history was marginal at some of the nation's elite history

40 James M. McPherson, *Tried by War: Abraham Lincoln as Commander in Chief* (Penguin, 2008).

41 John A. Lynn, "The Embattled Future of Academic Military History," *Journal of Military History* 61 (1997): 777–89; John A. Lynn, "Breaching the Walls of Academe: The Purposes, Problems, and Prospects of Military History," *Academic Questions*, March 2008: http://www.nas.org/

programs – despite some of these departments having substantially more than fifty members. We will see, however, that even Lynn is now beginning to reassess his pessimism due to factors we will discuss later in this volume, and that our own findings suggest some cause for (guarded) optimism.

The Military and Social Science

Finally, we encountered similar, though less gloomy, concerns about the status of the military and military-oriented strategic studies in political science and international relations. The alleged retreat of military history parallels the broader marginalizing of military-related matters by mainstream social science and social thought. For example, in *War and Modernity*, published shortly before 9/11, sociologist Hans Joas observes that, "The major theories that are the subject of general discussion [in social theory] today – let us take [Jürgen] Habermas, [Niklas] Luhmann, or the post-structuralists as examples – contain hardly any mention of war and peace."[42] And political scientists Kenneth R. Mayer and Anne M. Khademian noted a dearth of political science literature on defense policy making in the early 1990s, surmising that it "is possible that political scientists have shied away from studying military defense issues out of an ideological bias against the military, a legacy of the Vietnam War and the critical view of the military-industrial-academic complex."[43]

On another front, a major study/report on the troubled state of civic engagement in America issued under the aegis of the American Political Science Association (APSA) in 2006 signifies a similar – though hardly stark – unease about the military. The APSA authors, experts in the fields of civic engagement and deliberation, depicted the decline in various national indicators of civic participation and presented ways that citizens (especially young citizens) can get involved in politics and public service. Though the authors enthusiastically and ably made the case for public service, they mentioned the military as an option on only three of the book's roughly two hundred pages, and the authors did not consider the consequences of the decline of ROTC on campus for civic participation. The report exhibited no hostility toward the military, but rather what might be called quasi-benign neglect. To be fair, the authors do remark in their section on national service that, "Most significantly, military service is often regarded as a powerful instrument of civic education." Yet why would a group of political scientists dedicated to the study of civic participation pay so

polArticles.cfm?Doc_Id=10. See also Lynn, "The Embattled Future of Academic Military History," *Journal of Military History* 61, 4 (1997): 777–89. Emphasis added.

42 Hans Joas, *War and Modernity* (Polity, 2003), ch. 7 ("Between Power Politics and Pacifist Utopia: Peace and War in Social Theory"), p. 126. And the postliberal or postmodern domains of higher education, which question such Enlightenment tenets as universal reason, are not known for being comparatively more hospitable to the military.

43 Kenneth R. Mayer and Anne M. Khademian, "Bringing Politics Back In: Defense Policy and the Theoretical Study of Institutions," *Public Administration Review* 56, 2 (1996): 180–90, at p. 181. See also Stephen M. Walt, "The Renaissance of Security Studies," *International Studies Quarterly* 35 (1991): 211–39, p. 216.

little attention to what is, in their words, a *powerful* instrument of civic education? Political theorist Jeffrey Isaac discovered a more severe neglect when he inquired how the major journals in political theory had dealt with the demise of the Soviet Union and the end of the Cold War. In the several years after this momentous historical event, Isaac found a "deafening silence," with only three articles dealing with it – and two of these not very much. Isaac attributed the silence to political theorists' reluctance to address significant events that exist outside the predominant paradigms of the discipline. These paradigms did not include taking the Cold War – including the demise of the Soviet Union and the failure of Communism – seriously.[44]

Of special significance is the status of the military and military studies in security studies programs, which is the branch of the university most likely to participate actively in the national security process. As one would expect given the overall trends identified so far, there has been some conflict over the status of the military in security studies, in particular security studies as practiced during the early period of the Cold War. According to strategic studies expert Richard Betts, scientific studies dealing with war and strategy in the United States comprise a "missing discipline" that has – unlike in Britain – no distinctive departmental status. Accordingly, academic work addressing strategy "is sponsored elsewhere, primarily in the service war colleges and the National Defense University." Security studies acquired a distinctly "realist" feel, in part because of its close association with the military and its ascension during the period of the Cold War University.[45] In its minimal ideal type, political realism gives priority to such matters as national interest and security (which it conceives as universal categories regardless of time or place) over such factors as morality, ideology, and socially constructive contingencies.

Some political scientists have expressed misgivings about the status of national security-strategic studies in political science and international relations. Like the discipline of history, the field of international relations has broadened considerably over the course of the last thirty years to include perspectives that go well beyond a military-strategic focus. Cultural, constructivist, and critical schools of thought now challenge the once dominant school of political realism. For realists, power is the *ultima ratio* in international politics; justice is, to paraphrase Thucydides, what the stronger say it is. Of realism's competitors, constructivism – a variant of postmodernism – is the most serious challenger. Constructivism in international relations is generally less hard-wired with

44 Stephen Macedo et al., *Democracy at Risk: How Political Choices Undermine Citizen Participation, and What to Do About It* (Brookings Institution, 2006), p. 145. The authors also emphasize the "citizen-soldier" model of service on page 152. See also Jeffrey C. Isaac, "The Strange Silence of Political Theory," *Political Theory* 23, 4 (1995): 636–52, and the several responses in the symposium on Isaac's essay in the same volume.

45 The term "Cold War University" is used to depict the profile of many major universities during the Cold War period, which entailed the rise of defense policy–relevant instruction and research accompanied by vast amounts of funding by the government, foundations, and corporations. We discuss the dilemmas, pros, and cons of the Cold War University in Chapter 4.

postmodernism than many fields in the humanities, and many scholars have reasonably advocated using both constructivism and realism when appropriate, with due regard for the strengths and weaknesses of each.[46] And such expansion of international relations has broadened our understanding of human reality in the field. The problem arises when movements such as constructivism crowd out traditional work on security studies characterized by a deeper appreciation for military history and military perspectives, thereby leading to *less*, rather than more, diversity in the field. Our reading of security studies as a field also suggests that what separates political realism from its competitors is that many of the latter have fortified their approaches within the walls of the academy, for it is political realism that is most closely associated with *practical* knowledge. As such, the broadening of academic horizons may have in important ways undermined the practical significance of the discipline – yet as we show, the nation's most prestigious security studies programs remain an important abode for political realism and historically oriented security studies.

Our perspective does not suppose that the military perspective should dominate security studies. Rather, we emphasize the importance of balancing a military perspective with different perspectives. As Betts reflects, "If strategy is to integrate policy and operations, it must be devised not just by politically sensitive soldiers but by militarily sensitive civilians. Either of these types makes third parties in politics or academia uncomfortable."[47] When considering the status of security studies, we seek to understand the extent to which programs strike this type of balance between the military and civilian perspectives.

Finally, we should offer a brief word about other social sciences, especially sociology. Before World War II and the Cold War, psychology dominated social science military work because of its role in developing psychological and personality testing for the services. This interaction established a perception – grounded in reality – that social science's relationship with the military was functional or "applied" in nature, thereby relegating the field to second-class academic citizenship. In the 1960s, however, sociologists and other social scientists became more interested in the military as a subject of analysis, with Janowitz (sociology) and Huntington (political science) leading the way with their classic studies of civil–military relations. Ferment over Vietnam and the social-political revolutions of the 1960s aroused sociological interest in such topics as the nature and legitimacy of compulsory service, race, gender, class, sexuality, and organizational functioning – a trend reflected in all the social sciences and many of the humanities, such as history and literature. Military sociology also incorporated these trends and thrived within its own bailiwick; but it has remained largely ghettoized, unconnected to the broader discipline.

In the early 1960s, Janowitz and others formed the Inter-University Seminar (IUS) on Armed Forces and Society, which created its own journal, *Armed*

[46] In general, see the various essays in Walter Carlsnaes, Thomas Risse, and Beth A. Simmons, eds., *Handbook of International Relations* (Sage, 2002).

[47] Richard K. Betts, "Should Strategic Studies Survive?" *World Politics* 50, 7 (1997): 22–4.

Forces & Society. This journal served the field of military sociology because the profession's mainstream journals were not publishing works on the military. According to sociologist Eric Ouellet, military sociology has remained marginal for both substantive and ideological reasons. Substantively, it was the only subfield dedicated to a particular institution, and it was perceived to be more "applied" than other subfields. And this isolation "is certainly compounded by a simple lack of interest for military matters by sociologists in general. Yet, military sociology also suffers from the problem of guilt by association.... As stated by [James] Burk, historically 'there were concerns that obtaining data from the military required political contacts and that one was a 'friend' of the military.'"[48] (Edward Bernard Glick provided a rejoinder to this judgment in the heated days of 1971: "Consider: in universities and other centers of intellect a sociologist, social psychologist, or psychiatrist who studies crime is usually called a criminologist; he is never called a criminal. Similarly, a lawyer who chooses to practice criminal rather than civil law is called a criminal lawyer and not a criminal.... Yet the same social critic who can remain rather unemotional about criminologists ... often quickly exhibits great emotional bias against the military practitioner.")[49]

Though isolated, the subfield of military sociology is thriving within its own domain. In the early 1960s, the IUS had barely a dozen members. Since then, it has ballooned to over seven hundred seminarians, hosting a broad international and interdisciplinary membership. According to the present IUS chair, David Segal, a professor of sociology at the University of Maryland who is perhaps the leading military sociologist in the United States today:

> The field probably is more vibrant outside the US today than in this country. And the IUS journal, *Armed Forces & Society*, is about 36 years old and has climbed significantly among journal rankings over the last several years.... The field was truly marginal in the discipline. Now the American Sociological Association describes it as small but mainstream, and mainstream journals publish articles on the military. Military sociology has also become a major part of the public face of sociology.

That said, Segal reported that "there has never been more than one Sociology Department that was really strong in the area" in the last half-century. The tract of department leadership has followed the domicile of the leading figure in the subfield, passing from Michigan and Chicago (Janowitz) to Northwestern (Charles Moskos) to Maryland today (Segal). However, "more people are coming out of other departments having written doctoral dissertations on the military, and calling themselves military sociologists, and more departments are seeking to hire faculty who have some competence in the field among their

[48] Eric Ouellet, "New Directions in Military Sociology," in Ouellet, ed., *New Directions in Military Sociology* (de Sitter, 2005), p. 10, quoting James Burk, "Morris Janowitz and the Origins of Sociological Research on Armed Forces and Society," *Armed Forces & Society* 19, 2 (1993): 177.

[49] Edward Bernard Glick, *Soldiers, Scholars, and Society: The Social Impact of the American Military* (Goodyear, 1971), p. 7.

specialties."[50] The situation of military sociology appears to be mixed: vibrant among its adherents, but largely marginal in the discipline as a whole.

Military anthropology is a long-standing discipline that we will touch on very briefly later when we discuss military history at length. A controversy within anthropology (and other social sciences to a lesser extent) has raged in recent years regarding the legitimacy of anthropologists participating with the Army in its counterinsurgency (COIN) efforts, in particular the Human Terrain System (HTS), in Afghanistan, Iraq, and other countries afflicted with terrorism. Scholars are concerned about compromising their contacts and their academic neutrality. It is one thing to study the military, another thing to actually work with it. The American Anthropological Association (AAA) issued a resolution opposing such cooperation pursuant to an AAA commission investigation and report in late 2009. The Executive Summary of the report concluded, "In summary, while we stress that constructive engagement between anthropology and the military is possible," the commission "suggests that the AAA emphasize the incompatibility of HTS with disciplinary ethics and practice for job seekers and that it further recognize the problem of allowing HTS to define the meaning of 'anthropology' within DoD [the Department of Defense]."[51] While the AAA's concern about academic integrity must be respected and adhered to (no one could argue that anthropologists should sacrifice intellectual integrity for a cause without violating their fiduciary responsibility to society), its across-the-board dismissal of cooperation with HTS struck critics as overly broad and biased, and as a sign of the discipline's alienation from the military. Such alienation can create its own scholarly problems. Based on her own extensive field work in Afghanistan, political scientist Jennifer Brick Murtazashvili has argued that her interaction with military personnel *enhanced* the quality of her academic work, suggesting the need for greater consideration of military perspectives to understand conflicts such as that in Afghanistan.[52]

THE DIFFERENT QUESTION WE ASK: CIVIC-LIBERAL EDUCATION AND POLITICAL/MORAL REALISM

This book takes the traditional citizen-soldier rationale seriously, but it also looks at an opposite effect: *How does military presence in universities affect the prospects for civic and liberal education of non-military students?* This question has both empirical and normative dimensions. Empirically, to what extent does

[50] E-mail exchange with David Segal, University of Maryland Professor of Sociology, October 2010. See also Segal, "Current Developments and Trends in Social Research on the Military," pp. 46–66.

[51] AAA Commission on the Engagement of Anthropology with U.S. Security and Intelligence Communities (CEAUSSIC), "Final Report on the Army's Human Terrain System Proof of Concept Program," submitted to the Executive Board of American Anthropological Association, October 14, 2009, p. 3: http://www.aaanet.org/cmtes/commissions/CEAUSSIC/upload/CEAUSSIC_HTS_Final_Report.pdf. For a defense of the Department of Defense (DoD) program, see Montgomery McFate, "Anthropology and Counterinsurgency: The Strange Story of Their Curious Relationship," *Military Review*, March–April 2005.

[52] Jennifer Brick Murtazashvili, "Armed with Practice: Learning to Engage with the Military," *Forum* 8, 3 (2010): Article 3: http://www.bepress.com/forum/vol8/iss3/art3.

a gap exist between the military and the university in terms of ROTC and the availability of military and strategic security courses? Second, to what extent does the presence of such programs have an impact on the knowledge and attitudes of non-military students, and in what ways? The normative dimension leads us into the realms of political theory, citizenship, and pedagogy. Theoretically speaking, in what ways might exposure to military-related studies and presence contribute to civic and liberal education? And the normative question has its own empirical dimension: Is there any evidence that such education is taking place when such exposure is present?

We will define liberal education and civic education more fully in the next chapter. Suffice it here to say that civic education entails knowledge of key aspects of citizenship, while liberal education embraces a greater breadth of knowledge as well as the development of the capacity to pursue truth with critical and discerning reason. These forms of education stand in tension in some important respects (for the pursuit of truth can be at odds with the demands of tradition in the political community); but they can also coexist in a constructive dynamic sense that we will discuss further in the next chapter. For the purpose of this introduction, let us just very briefly mention the four basic ways that exposing students to ROTC students and military-related studies can enhance non-military students' education. We will then discuss our methods and provide a brief outline of the book's chapters.

One useful way of thinking about all of these potentially propitious effects is through the lens of what Hans Morgenthau called the "higher practicality" in a 1966 essay. (We are indebted to MIT international relations scholar Stephen Van Evera for pointing out the importance of Morgenthau's essay.) Decrying what he construed as political science's retreat into a kind of professional scholasticism, Morgenthau strove to reinvigorate the discipline by reintegrating it with historical reality and the highest level of engaged thought – a coming together of empirical knowledge and the humanities. In a manner that echoes Ortega's thoughts, Morgenthau entreated political scientists to emulate the "lasting contributions to political science, from Plato, Aristotle, and Augustine to *The Federalist*, Marx, and Calhoun," which were "responses to such challenges arising from political reality." The "higher practicality" entails studying the ways in which the efforts of major political thinkers' were "responses to [fundamental] challenges arising from political reality."[53] As anyone who has studied Morgenthau's works knows, his conception of international politics was steeped in a political philosophy that strove to have ethical commitment and realism about the human condition inform one another.[54]

[53] Hans J. Morgenthau, "The Purpose of Political Science," in James C. Charlesworth, ed., *A Design for Political Science: Scope, Objectives, and Methods* (American Academy of Political and Social Science, 1966), pp. 73, 77–8. Political scientist Lawrence Mead revived this claim and call for greater relevance in 2010. Lawrence M. Mead, "Scholasticism in Political Science," *Perspectives on Politics* 8, 2 (2010).

[54] For an incisive intellectual biography that delves deeply into the ethical, philosophical, and empirical aspects of Morgenthhau's theory of political realism, see Christoph Frei, *Hans Morgenthau: An Intellectual Biography* (Louisiana State University Press, 2001).

Morgenthau's model is firmly rooted within the liberal arts tradition; it entails not simply applying the concepts and principles attendant to the best political thought to pressing problems of politics and public policy, but also stepping back and thinking about what this interaction teaches us about history, politics, ethics, and humankind. The higher practicality "responds to political needs not by devising practical remedies, but by broadening and deepening the understanding of the problems from which the practical needs arose."[55] In other words, by studying political thinkers and others struggling with fundamental questions of social life, we can gain greater understanding of the nature of humanity and political existence. Such understanding comprises the very essence of liberal and civic education.

Morgenthau's brand of moral or ethical realism – which echoes that of such thinkers as Reinhold Niebuhr and Max Weber – is also relevant to the pedagogical model we embrace. We will discuss this theory more fully in our later chapter on the field of security studies, but let us give an inkling of it here. But first, we clarify our understanding of the term "realism," which is the leading traditional school of thought in international relations (IR) and foreign policy.

In IR study, realism refers to a deeply held perspective that emphasizes the centrality of force or the threat of force in domestic and international politics. We accept this perspective, but offer our own somewhat more subtle point of view based on the concepts of political realism and moral realism. "Political realism," in its simplest sense, understands the presence and utility of force as an omnipresent reality in international relations. Ignoring this fact is both empirically wrong and a recipe for ineffectual action under certain circumstances. National interests and ideals cannot be achieved in the real world unless they are backed by a sufficient form of power that is cognizant of reality and its attendant circumstances. (What form such power should take is a normative and instrumental question based on each case, as in "just war theory" and other theories of forceful action.) Might does not make right, but in international relations – especially those involving conflict – right must often be backed by might in some form.

"Moral realism," in contrast, deals more broadly with human nature. It has two components. First, moral realism agrees with political realism in acknowledging the moral complexity and ambiguity of political action (magnified in power politics) and the concomitant ethical obligation to sometimes engage in conduct that challenges the norms of everyday life; for example, the use of deadly force is usually a crime and a sin, but it is justified and even mandatory to protect innocent life when such life is in imminent peril of death or serious bodily harm. Similarly, just war theory justifies the appropriate killing of enemy combatants under the rules of war. Second, moral realism accepts the fact that human nature and political orders are unavoidably imperfect and flawed, so human action (including political and moral action) is fraught with self-interest, moral tension,

[55] Morgenthau, "The Purpose of Political Science," p. 78.

and the possibility of unintended consequences. We use the term "realism" and its political and moral variants to refer to this sort of sensibility and understanding. It is an understanding that accepts the importance of appropriate exercises of military and political power while appreciating the moral tensions that accompany resort to such force. Our primary concern is with the status of realism in the academy, including the political and moral versions that we articulate in the pages that follow.

Our understanding of realism is not that states, groups, and individuals never act altruistically, against their self-interest, or ethically according to independent standards of ethics, but rather that it would be naïve to assume that they will do so consistently. Realism requires first and foremost that we face the unappealing and uncomfortable aspects of human reality, which include self-interested behavior, conflict, and the possibility of violence. As Niebuhr wrote in *Moral Man and Immoral Society*, even if individuals can attain moral perfection in their own lives – a proposition Niebuhr understood to be purely hypothetical – conflicts and injustices inevitably beset, even characterize, any social organization. A "man" might achieve the moral heights as an individual, but no "society" can.[56] This is so for at least three reasons. First, experience and observation of human nature confirm that self-interest and conflict play a significant role in much of human action, for better or for worse. Self-interest has served as a spur to great deeds, but also as a cause of evil. And, as John Jay wrote in the first *Federalist* paper, "So numerous indeed and so powerful are the causes which serve to false bias to the judgment, that we, upon many occasions, see wise and good men on the wrong side as well as on the right side of questions of the first magnitude to society."[57] Second, statesmen and other leaders have a moral responsibility to protect the interests of the states and citizens whom they lead, and this duty often clashes with the interests of other countries. Basic theories of accountability and political obligation point in this direction. Third, as some theorists of political and international systems teach us, systemic pressures often push in the direction of making the interests of the state the primary motive of statesmanship, for to do otherwise would lead to one's nation being taken advantage of in the world of international politics, sometimes disastrously.[58]

Our concept of realism attempts to avoid mere cynicism and the crasser applications of Machiavellianism by striving to support ethical values in a manner that takes account of this intractable aspect of reality. We do not eschew idealism, but rather idealism divorced from realistic understanding. The Framers

[56] Reinhold Niebuhr, *Moral Man and Immoral Society* (Scribner's and Sons, 1932).

[57] John Jay, *Federalist #1*, in *The Federalist Papers*, edited by Clinton Rossiter (New American Library, 1961), p. 34.

[58] This position has been labeled "neorealism" by IR scholars because it supposedly shares similar concerns with realism, although as we shall see, it offers much less insight into the contradictions and conflicts inherent in international politics. See, e.g., Kenneth N. Waltz, *Theory of International Politics* (McGraw Hill, 1979).

of the U.S. Constitution epitomized the type of tension and balance at stake. They strove to construct a legitimate democratic state (to be sure, with the sin of slavery remaining in place, to be dealt with later) that acknowledged and took account of the self-interest and aggression that permeate the world, and which threaten the existence and purposes of the political order. In their complex view, self-interest is essential to liberty, but also the cause of faction and injustice, as James Madison famously articulated in *Federalist #10*. Throughout the *Federalist Papers*, the authors were at pains to defend the need for a legitimate and adequately powerful government to preserve liberty and justice against those domestic or foreign enemies bent on harming or destroying these goods, while also accentuating the necessity of provisions to protect the citizens from that very authority. "If men were angels," Madison wrote in another famous passage of the *Federalist*, "no government would be necessary. If angels were to govern men, neither external nor internal controls on government would be necessary."[59]

Morgenthau's tragic understanding of politics captures the meaning of moral realism well. In *Scientific Man vs. Power Politics* (a work in which he critiqued social science's fetishism with scientific detachment), he reflects:

> We have no choice between power and the common good. To act successfully, that is, according to the rules of the political art, is political wisdom. To know with despair that the political act is inevitably evil, and to act nevertheless, is moral courage. To choose among several expedient actions the least evil one is moral judgment. In the combination of political wisdom, moral courage, and moral judgment man reconciles his political nature with his moral destiny. That this conciliation is nothing more than a *modus vivendi*, uneasy, precarious, and even paradoxical, can disappoint only those who prefer to gloss over and distort the tragic contradictions of human existence with the soothing logic of a specious accord.[60]

Our understanding of moral politics is premised on this type of reasoning: Responsibility in the real world of action requires facing and dealing constructively with the "tragic contradictions of human existence." The practice and psychology of national defense are embedded in this consciousness. With this pedagogical and philosophical background in mind, let us now look at more specific ways in which military exposure can enhance civic and liberal education.

CONTRIBUTIONS OF MILITARY EXPOSURE TO CIVIC AND LIBERAL EDUCATION

The first potential contribution of military exposure to education is straightforward: Knowledge of the military is an essential part of citizenship because of that institution's importance in national life. The decision to go to war is perhaps the most momentous decision that a political community can make, and national security is the primary obligation of the state. Furthermore, however much we

[59] James Madison, *Federalist #10* and *#51*. In *The Federalist Papers*.

[60] Hans Morgenthau, *Scientific Man vs Power Politics* (University of Chicago Press, 1946), pp. 195, 202–3.

rightly rely upon such foreign policy tools as diplomacy, soft power (power based on such non-military tools as economic and social pressures or inducements), and international law to achieve ends, the fact remains that there are times when military force (or the credible threat of such force) is necessary to protect legitimate national interests or to protect human life. A legacy of the late diplomatic giant, Richard C. Holbrooke, for example, lay in his understanding of when to employ softer forms of power and when to use or threaten force. Among many achievements, Holbrooke was instrumental in the strengthening of NATO in the mid-1990s, and his ability to persuade President Clinton to use military force was indispensable in leading to the Dayton Accords in 1995 and in liberating the Kosovars from the predations of Slobodan Milosevic in 1999. Without this presence, Milosevic's genocide would have continued.[61] Military force remains one tool in the battle against terrorism, even though other, "softer," forms of power are also important. As philosopher Michael Gelven observes, "People do violent things. Under civil agreement, the uses of violence are restricted and organized. But as long as it is possible for people to violate the property and peace of a civil person, the latter must rely on some ultimate arsenal of violence if civility is to be maintained."[62]

More broadly, the propitious organization and restriction of violence are perhaps the primary task and obligation of any social order. In *Violence and Social Order*, three distinguished social scientists and economists delineate the ways in which the control and organization of violence comprise the foundation of any social order. We discern three major tenets in this work: Violence is omnipresent in the fabric of human reality; social organization is predicated upon controlling and structuring violence; social, political, and economic changes are also propelled by the social and political effort to deal with violence constructively. (Sadly, as George Santayana said, "Only the dead are safe; only the dead have seen the end of war.")[63] The authors' theory is germane to international relations and military power, as well as domestic politics. "All societies face the problem of violence. Regardless of whether our genetic makeup predisposes humans to be violent, the possibility that some individuals will be violent poses a central problem for any group. No society solves the problem of violence by eliminating violence; at best, it can be contained and managed. Violence manifests itself in many dimensions."[64] Accordingly, responsible citizens should have a basic grasp of basic military-related issues.

[61] See Richard C. Holbrooke, *To End a War* (Random House, 1998).

[62] Michael Gelven, *War and Existence: A Philosophical Inquiry* (Pennsylvania State University Press, 1994), p. 77. See also Philip Bobbitt, *Terror and Consent: The Wars of the Twenty-First Century* (Random House, 2008).

[63] George Santayana, *Soliloquies in England and Later Soliloquies* (Charles Scribner's Sons, 1922), p. 102.

[64] Douglass C. North, John Joseph Wallis, and Barry R. Weingast, *Violence and Social Orders: A Conceptual Framework for Interpreting Recorded Human History* (Cambridge University Press, 2009), p. 13. For a prodigious realist and evolutionist perspective on the presence of war in history, see Azar Gat, *War in Human Civilization* (Oxford University Press, 2006).

More broadly, the second contribution of studying war and related topics is that it can be an excellent vehicle by which to learn more about human nature, society, and the meaning of life – traditionally cardinal issues of liberal education. War is an extraordinary event that raises profound questions of morality, life and death, and character. Third, studying the ethics and obligations of war can be an excellent vehicle for thinking about moral problems and tensions relating to citizenship. One moral dilemma concerns the ambiguities inherent in the use and abuse of power and organized violence in liberal democracies – matters that citizens of liberal democracies often have difficulty navigating because of the moral and intellectual presuppositions of liberal society, which are oriented toward well-being, comfort, and the pursuit of happiness.[65]

Finally, an appropriate military presence on campus can contribute to the intellectual and moral diversity of campus life, which, in turn, can enhance the civic culture of the university. Universities are very committed to "diversity," but such diversity does not always include hospitality toward thought related to the military. Intellectual diversity is an indispensable ingredient of civic and liberal education. As Martha Nussbaum has remarked, liberal education "liberates the mind from the bondage of habit and custom, producing people who can function with sensitivity and alertness as citizens of the whole world."[66] Liberally educated individuals engage in a continuous process of self and societal examination. Nussbaum's primary meaning is the critical examination of one's own society and traditions; but her theme can also be applied to institutions. Like any institution, universities are not immune to their own versions of groupthink, consensus, and conventional wisdom, and need to be challenged along Socratic grounds. (Socrates is a model for Nussbaum's study.) Nussbaum's analysis is helpful to our question in important ways. But it does not quite convey a deeper way in which civic and liberal education take us into the heart of conflict and the agonistic struggle of beliefs. To get there, let us turn to Samuel P. Huntington.

As we will see later in this volume, the debate over ROTC in the Ivy League is not simply a dispute over instrumental consequences for the national interest, but also a passionate quarrel over deeply held moral values on both (or all) sides. As such, this debate is one chapter in the broader historical *agon* of the United States, which has often called forth struggles regarding the fundamental values and principles that define America's promise. To truly comprehend citizenship in America, students must not simply know facts; they must also fathom the normative controversies that have made us what we are and that have forged our national character. (And they must strive to *understand* these competing forces before they seek to *judge* them.) A university is supposed to expose students to the wonders and problems of the wider world that lies beyond the

65 On modernity's growing rejection and intolerance of suffering, see Joseph A. Amato, *Victims and Values: A History and a Theory of Suffering* (Praeger, 1990).

66 Martha Nussbaum, *Cultivating Humanity: A Classical Defense of Reform in Liberal Education* (Harvard University Press, 1997), p. 8.

horizons they bring to campus, and part of this wider world is the disharmony that historically has accompanied moral disputes over justice and the meaning of America – what Huntington calls battles over "creedal passion":

> The history of American politics is the repetition of new beginnings and flawed outcomes, promise and disillusion, reform and reaction. American history is the history of the efforts of groups to promote their interests by realizing American ideals. What is important, however, is not that they succeed but that they fail, not that the dream is realized but that it is not and never can be realized completely or satisfactorily.[67]

In many telling respects, the debate over the military and the university is a debate over national character and purpose – a debate that has long been of central concern for institutions of higher education. And, as Huntington shows, this debate is riveted with the kind of conflict and disagreement that makes us stronger as a nation, not weaker. To be meaningful, civic and liberal education should include a Socratic appreciation and understanding of the creedal passions and conflicts that have gone into building our nation; and an appropriate military presence on campus can contribute to this education in citizenship in distinctive ways that we will explore in the next chapter and beyond, especially in our portrayal of ROTC politics at Columbia University in Chapters 5 through 7. By opening its intellectual and moral horizons to fully face the creedal passions of the American polity, the university would be honoring a principle that is itself a creedal passion for many of us: the First Amendment and the tradition of free speech and inquiry. As the Supreme Court has declared in an important free speech case, though "the air may at times be filled with verbal cacophony is, in this sense, not a sign of weakness but of strength."[68] This cacophony is part of the civic culture of the United States; and as we will see, the politics of ROTC at Columbia contributed to this agonistic aspect of American civic culture at the same time that it constituted an effort to heal the elite–military divide that Allan Silver and others have depicted as a civic scandal.

A NORMATIVE AND THEORETICAL FRAMEWORK

As noted, one of our tasks is to provide a normative and theoretical framework that helps us conceptualize the relationship between the military and universities as institutions. To accomplish our task, we offer a theoretical framework that emphasizes the following: (1) the military is one of several clusters in society with a distinctive perspective; (2) integration of these clusters improves the ability to formulate public policies through a process we describe as "productive friction"; and (3) the university is a microcosm of civil–military relations that can improve citizenship and public reason by encouraging productive friction between the military and non-military spheres of American society. In turn, this friction can

[67] Samuel P. Huntington, *American Politics and the Promise of Disharmony* (Harvard University Press, 1981), pp. 11–12. See also Jose Ortega y Gassett, *Concord and Liberty*, translated by Helene Weyl (Norton, 1963).

[68] *Cohen v. California*, 403 U.S. 15 (1971).

strengthen civic culture by lessening the civil–military gap. We briefly introduce each of these dimensions, which we consider more fully in the following chapter.

First, our theoretical framework presupposes that there are distinct clusters in American life. The "clusterization" of society can present problems for the balance between the military and civilian institutions, especially when groups become polarized on creedal issues.[69] But at the same time, our argument for integration of diverse perspectives, specifically a distinctly military perspective, *requires* (or at least accepts the fact) that there are clusters in society. If there were no gap in knowledge and perspectives between those in the military and others in society, then nothing would be lost by excluding a military perspective.[70] In our framework, the problem for society is not the existence of clusters but rather the degree of integration and communication among clusters, each of which brings its own perspective to the table.

We are most interested in the military cluster. For our purposes, it is not essential to define all the features of the military perspective in developing our theoretical framework. We simply posit the military as a distinct cluster – although our empirical studies and those of others show that military students and military historians, in particular traditional military historians, do present different perspectives. Unlike most studies of the military gap, our concern is not with ideological differences among clusters but rather in different expertise in the cluster. The military cluster may have an ideology similar to that of the general public, yet our concern is less with their politics than with their expertise. In particular we are less concerned with the defining features of clusters than in discussion of the degree to which these clusters are integrated, for as we shall argue, it is not the existence of different perspectives but rather their integration that is a key to civic and liberal education.

The second component of our theory is that diverse perspectives can help people and societies solve complex problems, particularly issues involving war and national security. We draw especially on the insights of diversity theorists who have shown that inclusion of individuals from diverse perspectives can improve the ability of a group to solve problems. This is the general point of Scott E. Page's book *The Difference: How the Power of Diversity Creates Better Groups, Firms, Schools, and Societies*. Page emphasizes that diverse groups are

69 What sociologists call "social clusters" are broad social groupings that share their own distinct worldviews and possess their own systems and networks of cultural assumptions and norms. Clusters have proliferated in modern America. As cluster theorist Michael Weiss remarks, "Today, the country's new motto should 'E pluribus pluriba': 'Out of many, many.'" One of these clusters is the military. Michael J. Weiss, *The Clustered World* (Little, Brown, 2000), pp. 10–17, quoted in Adrian R. Lewis, *The American Culture of War: The History of the U.S. Military Force from World War II to Operation Iraqi Freedom* (Routledge, 2007), p. 10.

70 Our argument about clusters is an assumption that happens to be supported by our evidence. Through our surveys and interviews (which we discuss throughout this book), we found that ROTC students offer contrasting perspectives. Our evidence also strongly supports the hypothesis that military historians typically draw lines between traditional and new military history. For our purposes, this evidence suggests that there are indeed different clusters.

usually better at solving problems in all walks of life.[71] We apply Page's perspective on learning in arguing that integration of a military perspective improves public policy – in particular, policies involving war or national security – because the military offers one of the most distinctive and diverse perspectives that students can encounter in their academic life.

The third component of our framework is emphasis on the university as a microcosm of civil–military relations. Much of the literature on the civil–military gap emphasizes civilian control of the military, a concern that has much to do with the rise of fascism and militarism in the twentieth century. As Michael Desch has argued, this negative result is more likely if civilian and military leaders do not forge sufficient common ground on policy. Fascism is not a realistic threat in America, but problems associated with an unhealthy relationship between these two sides should be taken seriously. Two reasons the Russian military became less amenable to civilian control during the 1990s, for example, were (1) that the end of the Cold War led to the unraveling of military and civilian consensus regarding military policy and (2) that new civilian leadership had less experience and education in military matters.[72] The seminal statement of the necessity of civilian control of an increasingly professionalized and institutionalized military is Huntington's *The Soldier and the State*. The university is a microcosm of these relations, but one in which the practitioners of security policy and the voters and politicians that govern policy have opportunities to see the other. These interactions promise to reduce the threat of a widening civil–military gap, so it is critical to encourage balance and understanding between these different institutions.

Our framework thus integrates the concepts of military clusters and productive friction, applying them in order to better understand the nature of interactions within the university. The university is one of the key institutions in society that can either encourage or discourage productive friction. We posit that the university does best for students by encouraging productive friction. In the pages that follow, we evaluate how well the university does in encouraging this process.

To be clear, we are not advocating a military perspective. We offer a less controversial claim: The best state of affairs, as far as pedagogy is concerned, is to integrate the military perspective, not to promote it; the *process* itself is the key, not the particular answers that arise from it. In this respect, our approach to knowledge is decentralized in that it prescribes a struggle among competing

[71] See Scott E. Page, *The Difference: How the Power of Diversity Creates Better Groups, Firms, Schools, and Societies* (Princeton University Press, 2007), as well as his more recent, more theoretical, and equally impressive work, *Diversity and Complexity* (Princeton University Press, 2010). Page does not consider the military directly, and tends to rely on formal theoretical arguments. Our work emphasizes the significance of integrating a military perspective, both theoretically and empirically, which is a missing element in Page's informative study.

[72] Desch, *Civilian Control of the Military*, pp. 39–40.

views. It is the lack of the facilitation of interaction of diverse perspectives with which we disagree.

Empirically speaking, we are cautiously optimistic about the degree of integration of diverse perspectives within universities – and about the future of civil–military relations within universities – but we stress that our conclusions often lead us to a gray area. With respect to military history, for example, we find that there is often support of newer forms of military history, which may be cause for optimism, and limited evidence of a decline in military history in current course offerings. However, our evidence suggests that *traditional* military historians are less likely to be replaced by traditionalists, which bodes less well for productive friction in the future because traditional military history takes the military's conducting of war more seriously. Similar to the current status of military history, we find that security studies programs often are highly effective in integrating not only military history but the military itself (officers in residence, ROTC, and so on) into their programs. At the same time, there are some programs with little or no emphasis on military history – a finding that is at odds with our model of productive friction.

In terms of ROTC, our findings also require interpretive care. Historically speaking, we find that there has been an auspicious balance between the military and the university. The concept of an Ivory Tower free from the military is an idea that came about relatively recently, so we can reject the idea that the university is inherently inconsistent with the presence of the military. On the other hand, protest movements of the 1960s and 1970s were often highly effective in removing the military, especially in the Ivies. While this change suggests cause for pessimism, there is hope for productive friction because of the "return of the soldier," at least in the movement to reestablish ROTC at the nation's elite institutions and in the waves of veterans who are swelling the student ranks on campuses across the land. Moreover, opposition to the military as "militaristic" appears to have waned, though not disappeared, as have accusations that torture by some American troops is enough to keep the military off campus. The opposition appears to be rooted in policy, in particular to the now discarded DADT policy. As such, we often find a great deal of *contingent* support for a true return of the soldier to campus – a far more productive situation than has prevailed in recent decades as far as our framework is concerned. The vote to bring ROTC to Columbia in some form in April 2011 vindicated the widespread contention that DADT was the first and foremost impediment to the program's return.

A BRIEF STATEMENT REGARDING METHODS

As mentioned, this work has both normative policy and empirical dimensions. In the normative policy aspects of the book, we will proceed in the spirit of political theory, presenting an analytical framework that includes drawing on the thought of prominent thinkers whose thoughts are relevant to the topic at hand. In the next chapter, we will theoretically lay out the ways in which an appropriate exposure to a military presence on campus can contribute to both civic and liberal education.

But the analysis will ultimately depend upon some empirical findings. We are interested in how the theory fits the facts. Our empirical inquiry is divided into two parts. First, our book considers the status of the military and ROTC on campus, as well as the influence of ROTC students on non-military students. We begin our empirical discussion of the status and impact of the military on campus by tracing the historical evolution of the relationship between the university and the military, with a focus on the Ivy League, which has witnessed the most intense and dramatic conflicts over ROTC. We begin by examining the role of the Ivies in the nation's wars. We then recount the importance of the military in the Ivies in most of the nation's wars prior to Vietnam, an account that suggests that the Ivory Tower was not at odds with military presence for much of American history. Most importantly, we present a rationale or normative principle for military presence that gauges what types of military presence are appropriate and under what circumstances.

Our historical and archival analysis then shifts to the status of ROTC on campus – ROTC's origins, the demise of the program, and the current politics of DADT. This inquiry will include examining secondary material on this evolution, as well as original interview and archival research material pertaining to the ultimately successful efforts to bring ROTC back to Harvard and Columbia, which are, in effect, "ground zeros" for this movement. In particular, we were able to interview many of the major players in the effort to reinstitute ROTC at Columbia, an effort that succeeded just before this manuscript entered the production process. In addition, studying this effort furnishes insight into the politics of ROTC on campus. The case study focus on Harvard and Columbia (especially the latter) is both intrinsically interesting and indicative of the cultural conflict on campus over this issue.

After considering military presence, we offer additional quantitative evidence to evaluate our pedagogical model. We conclude the discussion of ROTC by presenting the findings of surveys we conducted at the University of Wisconsin, Madison – the institution with which we are most familiar, and which is a useful campus to study. These surveys allowed us to obtain information from students on the potential impact of exposure to military-related programs – including ROTC and military-security courses – on their thinking. We sent the survey to three sources: (1) ROTC commanders and their staff; (2) ROTC cadets; and (3) all political science majors at the junior-senior level. In addition, we gathered information from a focus group of veterans. We elicited responses from two directions: student observations of the potential impact of such exposure on themselves, and ROTC cadet observations of the impact of their exposure on other students in classroom contexts and outside of class. For our sample of non-ROTC students, we selected political science majors because political science is the largest major on campus (declared by about one thousand students) and because of our interest in the relationship between the military and politics. And we picked the University of Wisconsin (UW) as a primary source because of our proximity to the institution, and because ROTC programs there are strong but not as prominent as those at such institutions as Texas A&M or even Notre Dame. Most students at Wisconsin have had little exposure to the military before coming to campus, and ROTC has sufficient presence here to make it likely that a relatively high percentage of students have encountered someone in the program. Students we interviewed at Harvard and Columbia reported that such exposure was very limited in comparison to what is likely the case at Wisconsin. In addition, Wisconsin is famous for being a left-progressive institution, and it is well known for having had a long history of efforts to both reform and abolish ROTC.[73] At the same time, Wisconsin is home to all four ROTC programs (Navy, Army, Air Force, and Marines), and recent chancellors have remained steady in their commitments to the programs. Thus, a variety of viewpoints and experiences prevails on the campus. And as mentioned, ROTC's presence in Madison is neither overwhelming nor miniscule, making the school a good source for the survey.

Second, we are concerned with the status of military history and strategic studies in the university. To get at the status of military history and security studies, we will look at some existing literature as well as at evidence from our own inquiries. Our evidence includes the following: (1) interviews with key faculty to assess the status of military history and security studies; (2) surveys of department chairs in history, political science, and security studies; and (3) quantitative evaluation of the presence of military history in terms of course offerings and faculty teaching military history.

Our first source of evidence regarding the status of military history is interviews conducted with experts in military history and security studies. Our interviews with experts in the field of military history helped us to understand the nuances of military history – in particular, the differences between "traditional" and "new" military history. Briefly, the former concerns primarily the military as an institution, as well as details of major battles and strategies, while the latter investigates the social, cultural, and psychological dimensions of war and military institutions. These interviews provided myriad information about the status of various types of military history within universities, information that suggests that it is very difficult to make unconditional general statements about the status of military history. In particular, we found that where one stands on the issue of the potential decline of military history is contingent upon where one sits: Depending on the university and the person asked, the glass appears to be either "half empty" or "half full."

Our second source of evidence is from several surveys. First, we sent a survey to hundreds of department leaders and directors of programs in both history and political science departments. Our survey was innovative in that it is the first such survey to carefully distinguish between traditional and new military

[73] See, e.g., James Piereson, "The Left University: How It Was Born; How It Grew; How to Overcome It," *Weekly Standard*, 11, 3 (2005): 20–30. http://www.weeklystandard.com/Content/Public/Articles/000/000/006/120xbklj.asp. Piereson argues that the University of Wisconsin is the preeminent example of the "Left University."

history. In addition, we are the first to our knowledge to consider quantitatively the status of military history and military-related study in political science departments. Our interest in the degree to which military history is integrated into political science departments reflected our belief in the importance of Clausewitz's thesis that war is politics by other means, the carrying out of "policy" in the martial realm. As such, we viewed it as important to consider the status of military history in departments that emphasize the study of politics.

We surveyed department leaders for several reasons: (1) They have some agenda-setting power; (2) they know department course offerings and personnel; and (3) they likely have some idea of institutional trends. Perhaps most importantly, leaders of departments provide insight into the status of military-related study in terms of departmental priorities. That seemed to us to be the key question among military historians debating the status of their craft.

Our final source of evidence concerning the status of military history involves detailed inspection of course offerings and department faculty rosters to determine which types of military history are represented. We define several "orbits" of military history, examining whether or not each of the nation's top history programs has faculty that are "in the orbit." We also considered recent course offerings at the nation's top twenty programs in history to determine what percentage of courses are within the orbit of military history. Our findings complement existing studies of the status of the field conducted by military historians, which have not yet considered differences between traditional and new military history in any systematic way or actually catalogued course offerings and faculty teaching at the major universities (rather, they tend to focus on a few high-profile cases, such as failure to hire a military historian at the University of Wisconsin for almost two decades after the retirement of a prominent military historian, or the number of articles on traditional areas of concern to military historians). While there will be some disagreement with the specifics of our counts, we can present some conclusions with fair confidence regarding the status of military history in terms of faculty and course offerings, information that complements our surveys and interviews.

We do not claim that the findings of these surveys and interviews are in any way definitive or conclusive. They are, however, suggestive, and we hope they provide food for further thought. In addition, they afford a quantitative dimension that allows us to assess our normative and theoretical framework. For these reasons, we believe the empirical component advances our understanding of the status of the military in universities in substantial ways – although we emphasize that there remains more work to be done if we hope to understand the relationship between institutions as complex and important as the military and universities.

CHAPTER OUTLINE

Part I consists of this introductory chapter and Chapter 2, entitled "Education in the Regime: How a Military Presence Can Enhance Civic and Liberal Education." Chapter 2 presents the theoretical and normative framework that guides our inquiry into civil–military relations, introducing the ways in which exposure to military-related programs and courses can enhance civic and liberal education. Here we discuss the meaning of civic and liberal education and examine the ways in which military-related exposure can contribute to these pedagogical aspirations.

In Part II, we consider the physical presence of the military on campus in depth, with particular emphasis on ROTC. Chapter 3, "ROTC and the University: An Introduction," considers the issue of ROTC with respect to our normative model. This chapter sets up our subsequent analysis of ROTC. Chapters 4, 5, and 6 consider the historical emergence, decline, and renewal of ROTC, respectively, with a focus on the Ivy League. Chapter 4, "ROTC and the Ivies: Before the Storm," provides a historical framework for understanding the role of ROTC in the university. Then in Chapter 5, "ROTC and the Ivies: The Divorce," we detail the forces that led to the purge of ROTC from many of the nation's elite universities in the 1960s, giving special attention to Columbia University, which confronted the most explosive politics of protest. Chapter 6 describes the forces that gave rise to ROTC's renewal, again looking most closely at Columbia, where the most significant action has taken place. In Chapter 7, we consider history being made at Harvard and Columbia, which in March and April of 2011 welcomed ROTC to campus after decades away in the wake of the abolition of Don't Ask, Don't Tell. Lastly, we present and analyze our surveys to consider the impact of ROTC on one of the nation's largest, most respected public institutions. Chapter 8 provides particular insight into the relationship between liberal and republican motivation for military service, as well as a detailed case study of the experiences of student-soldiers and their impressions of their impacts on non-military students. Chapter 9 then looks at the effect of exposure to ROTC on non-military students. In addition, we present some tentative evidence of the impact of two military-oriented UW-Madison courses on students: a military history course and a humanities course entitled "The Romance of War."

Part III considers military history and its intellectual compatriot, political realism, in the university. Chapters 10 and 11 consider the status of military history. Chapter 10 is entitled "Military History: An Endangered or Protected Species?" In this chapter, we discuss different meanings of military history before turning to a quantitative assessment of the status of military history in various disciplines. Our reading of the literature suggests the profound importance of how we define military history when assessing its status on campus. Chapter 11, "Half Empty or Half Full: Military Historians' Perspectives on the Status of Military History at the Leading Departments," introduces the focus on the nation's elite history programs, discussing the method we used to analyze the twenty highest-ranked history departments and presenting general findings from our analysis. It also considers the status of military history at the nation's elite top-twenty history programs in detail. In terms of evidence, we present the findings from surveys and from interviews – evidence that allows us to offer a preliminary assessment of the status of military history. We conclude our discussion of military presence in the university in Chapters 12 and 13. Our emphasis shifts from military history per se to political realism, the intellectual foundation of security studies. The influence of political realism signifies, perhaps more than any other intellectual tradition in international relations, a concern with war, and so we consider realism to reflect military presence. Chapter 12, "Military Presence in Security Studies: Political Realism (Re)Considered," discusses security studies as a field, depicting the proliferation of approaches in recent decades. Security studies programs are the arm of the university where integration of military perspectives and knowledge of war is perhaps most important – indeed, the security studies programs are most likely to train practitioners in the field of national security. Chapter 13 then looks at a sampling of actual security studies programs that represent what we consider constructive integration of military study and security analysis. In particular, we consider whether or not universities, in responding to the challenges regarding the Cold War University from the perspective of academic integrity, have gone too far in the direction of creating barriers between universities and the nation's policy makers. In addition to our consideration of security studies programs, we present the results of our surveys of political science and history departments. Our findings indicate that the nation's leading security studies programs are in many ways models of productive friction because they strive to and succeed in integrating military perspectives, broadly defined, into their curriculum.

In Part IV, which consists of our conclusion, we offer some implications of the analysis and provide some suggestions that we believe would improve the prospects for effective civic and liberal education. Our purpose in writing this book is not simply to describe the military, but also to offer suggestions about how to organize the university to encourage more productive interactions. Furthermore, we believe such interactions are ultimately important to the conduct of policy. We conclude by arguing for the importance of the integration of the military – not the adoption of a military mindset, but rather the importance of including diverse perspectives.

It is fitting and appropriate to conclude this introductory chapter with a disclaimer: We are not military historians, nor members of the military. As such, we make no pretense that we can offer the insights of a military historian, or the practical knowledge of members of the armed forces. However, we have extensive experience in university matters and the politics of free speech on campus. But what we offer regarding the military is a more detached perspective, one that we hope allows us to make observations about the status of military history and the military without taking sides.

2

Education in the Regime

How a Military Presence Can Enhance Civic and Liberal Education

> It caused us to forget that man has to earn his security and his liberty as he has to earn his living. We came to think that our privileged position was a natural right, and then to believe that our unearned security was the reward of our moral superiority. Finally, we came to argue, like the idle rich who regard work as something for menials, that a concern with the foundations of national security, with arms, with strategy, and with diplomacy, was beneath our dignity as idealists.
>
> – Walter Lippmann, speaking of the national mentality in the 1930s[1]

> The inquiry into war, initiated with a profound realization of its paradoxical nature, thus becomes an essential task for all honest self-knowledge. If we are to know ourselves, the supreme commandment of the philosopher, we must know how to think through this paradox. To understand war is to thus to understand ourselves.
>
> – Michael Gelven[2]

In this chapter, we provide a theoretical framework to help us consider how an appropriate military presence on campus can contribute to the civic and liberal education of non-military students. This discussion has a dual character. On the one hand, it is hypothetical in nature, as it lays out the pedagogical possibilities that we consider the most likely to arise in exposing students to a military presence along the lines that we have delineated. These hypotheses will then be compared with the empirical findings that we will address in later chapters. On the other hand, this discussion is unavoidably normative in nature, as it necessarily comprises a theory of what education in this domain can or should accomplish. The normative side of this equation deals with the ways in which understanding national defense and military matters enhances citizenship in a constitutional democracy. Accordingly, this chapter proposes ideas (hypotheses) that we will compare in later chapters with the information we have gathered from archives, interviews, and surveys; at the same time, this chapter constitutes

[1] Walter Lippmann, *U.S. Foreign Policy: Shield of the Republic* (Little, Brown, 1943), p. 49.

[2] Michael Gelven, *War and Existence: A Philosophical Inquiry* (Pennsylvania State University Press, 1994), p. 18.

a political theory of citizenship respecting the military and national defense. Like any such theory, the pedagogical theory we present in this chapter is imperfect, subject to limitations and normative disagreement. We offer it in order to initiate discussion about the important matters that are the subject of this book.

CIVIC AND LIBERAL EDUCATION: BASIC ASPECTS

We should begin by recognizing the distinction between *liberal education* and *civic education*. In *Liberal Purposes*, political theorist William A. Galston distinguishes between "philosophical education" and "civic education." "Philosophical education," as Galston uses the term, is identical to what we call liberal education. Philosophical education is concerned primarily with "the disposition to seek truth, and second, the capacity to conduct rational inquiry." Such inquiry can actually conflict with narrow, restricted notions of civic education. As Galston relates, the "pursuit of truth – scientific, historical, moral, or whatever – can undermine structures of unexamined but socially central belief." Meanwhile, civic education concerns itself with "the formation of individuals who can effectively conduct their lives within, and support, their political community."[3] Civic education is about citizenship within a particular regime. But the American case is subtle, even paradoxical in this respect, for the American regime is largely liberal in inspiration, regardless of how much dispute exists over public philosophy in the United States.[4] By "liberal" we mean a limited state dedicated to rule of law, the legal equality of citizens, and the protection of individual liberty, which includes a commitment to freedom of thought and speech. This means that civic education in the American political tradition necessarily entails the freedoms that liberal education presupposes. Later in this chapter, we will discuss a form of education that synthesizes liberal and civic education. Before turning to that model, let us look at the two core aspects of civic education: knowledge relevant to citizenship and engagement in public affairs.

Civic Education as Knowledge

Civic education is a complex phenomenon, but we can glean some core aspects of it from the literature. The first component is what we will call *knowledge relevant to citizenship*. Any model of education in citizenship must begin with the simple concept of *cognitive knowledge*. Civically educated citizens need to know basic facts regarding the principles, institutions, and processes of the political system. E. D. Hirsch convincingly argues that a proper education requires sufficient "cultural literacy" in citizens, which entails a basic knowledge

[3] William A. Galston, *Liberal Purposes: Goods, Virtues, and Diversity in the Liberal State* (Cambridge University Press, 1991), pp. 242–3.

[4] See, e.g., Louis Hartz, *Liberal Tradition in America: An Interpretation of American Political Thought since the Revolution* (Harcourt, Brace, and Jovanovich, 1955).

of important cultural facts.[5] A similar proposition applies to civic education: To be civically educated, citizens need to be familiar with basic civic facts. Countless surveys have revealed a stunning lack of such knowledge among the citizenry (especially the young) about the political and constitutional system, and a number of organizations have dedicated themselves to alleviating this embarrassing national problem.[6] The Pew Research Center for People and the Press has consistently found Americans lacking in pertinent knowledge of national and international affairs, concluding that education and political engagement provide antidotes to this condition.[7] Constructive citizenship certainly requires adequate knowledge of basic political and social institutions and affairs as a necessary, if not sufficient, condition of civic attainment.

Knowledge related to citizenship also involves understanding basic values that are necessary to sustain democratic life and legitimacy. Political scientists have written about the importance of understanding the "rules of the game" and the character traits that provide an adequate foundation for democratic order.[8] In 1987, for example, the American Federation of Teachers (AFT) issued a statement supporting the proposition that democracy's survival depends upon a fundamental commitment to certain core values that need to be taught. Each generation must be taught "the political vision of liberty and equality that unites us as Americans. ... Such values are neither revealed truths nor natural habits. ... Devotion to human dignity and freedom, to equal rights, to social and economic justice, to the rule of law, to civility and truth, to tolerance of diversity, to self-restraint and self-respect – all these must be taught and learned."[9]

[5] E. D. Hirsch, Jr., *Cultural Literacy: What Every American Needs to Know* (Vintage, 1988).

[6] See the list of organizations cited in footnote 13, ch. 1, p. 180, in Stephen Macedo et al., *Democracy at Risk: How Political Choices Undermine Citizen Participation, and What to Do About It* (Brookings Institution, 2006). The military remains at the top of national esteem for institutions, although knowledge regarding it is not high. See the discussion of public opinion of the military in PEW Survey Reports, "Federal Government's Favorable Ratings Slump," May 14, 2008: http://people-press.org/report/420/federal-governments-favorable-ratings-slump. The public gave the military an 84 percent approval rating. The military has been at 75 percent or above since 1990, making it the most respected institution in the nation.

[7] Pew Research Center for the People and the Press, Survey Reports, "Public Knowledge of Current Affairs Little Changed by News and Information Revolutions," April 15, 2007: http://people-press.org/report/319/public-knowledge-of-current-affairs-little-changed-by-news-and-information-revolutions.

[8] Agreement on rights may also be critical to preserve democratic political order. Barry Weingast argues that agreement on basic rights is necessary to overcome a coordination problem that, if unresolved, can lead to transgressions by a sovereign against the rights of citizens. Some basic agreement on constitutional rights, provided through civic education, can have a focal character that enables citizens to resist transgressions by a sovereign. See Barry Weingast, "The Political Foundations of Democracy and the Rule of Law," *American Political Science Review* 91, 2 (1997): 245–63.

[9] American Federation of Teachers, "Education for Democracy: A Statement of Principles" (1987). Quoted in Galston, *Liberal Purposes*, pp. 244–5.

To be sure, philosophical and cultural disputes erupt once we leave the realm of abstraction and venture into the realm of application and practice. (For example, what the AFT calls "social justice" is notoriously open to interpretation, and considered a code word for left-wing activism by many conservatives.) Most of the national institutions devoted to higher education make racial, gender, and sexual diversity a first priority, while critics think that limiting diversity to such categories undermines the individualistic constitutional foundations of the American regime.[10]

Resolving this dispute is not necessary for our analysis, for our position regarding a military presence on campus is predicated on expanding the meaning of diversity, not replacing one notion with another notion. Expanding the meaning of diversity in the way we will suggest does entail tolerating perspectives and orientations that challenge the worldviews that prevail on many American campuses today – a matter we will discuss at the end of this chapter. True diversity in education necessarily embraces *intellectual and moral diversity*, which can foster a *clash of ideals and ideas*. What we call "productive friction" is an important ingredient of education and personal growth.[11] And to truly fathom citizenship in America, students must not simply know facts; they must also understand at least two other matters: the moral struggles and conflicts that have forged the creedal beliefs and tensions in our national character, as we stressed in Chapter 1; and the processes through which these struggles and conflicts are debated and adjudicated. The Supreme Court has captured this civic logic in its seminal free speech cases. In one such case, the Court declared there is a "profound national commitment to the principle that debate on public issues should be uninhibited, robust, and wide-open."[12] In another case, the Court said the classroom possesses a special status under the Constitution because, "Our Nation is deeply committed to safeguarding academic freedom, which is of transcendent value to all of us and not merely to the teachers concerned. That freedom is therefore a special concern of the First Amendment, which does not tolerate laws that cast a pall of orthodoxy over the classroom."[13]

Civic Education as Engagement

Knowledge of political and civic facts is a necessary, but not sufficient, condition for civic education. Experience and direct exposure to civic engagement are also

[10] Compare, for example, American Association of Colleges and Universities (AAC&U), *To Form a More Perfect Union: Campus Diversity Initiatives* (C. McTighe Musil et al., 1999), which celebrates diversity defined as a form of identity politics, with Bradley C. S. Watson, ed., *Civic Education and Culture* (ISI, 2005).

[11] See, e.g., Richard Sennett, *The Uses of Disorder: Personal Identity and City Life* (Vintage, 1970); and Richard Sennett, *The Fall of Public Man* (Vintage, 1976).

[12] *New York Times v. Sullivan*, 376 U.S. 254 (1964). On the cardinal significance of creedal passion, see Samuel P. Huntington, *American Politics and the Promise of Disharmony* (Harvard University Press, 1981).

[13] *Keyishian v. Board of Regents of the University of the State of New York et al.*, 385 U.S. 589 (1967).

important. The American Political Science Association study *Democracy at Risk* takes this approach. The authors eschewed looking at education and knowledge presented in schools, focusing instead on "civic engagement," which the group defined as "any activity, individual or collective, devoted to influencing the collective life of the polity."[14] Such activities include engaging in the political process, performing public service, and working with various voluntary and community groups.[15] Focusing on experience is important because knowledge comes alive when it is linked to our emotions, which are triggered by action and commitment. Emotion can lead reason astray, but emotion and reason nourish each other in healthy individuals and citizens.[16] At its best, civic engagement can make one more efficacious in life (both subjectively and instrumentally), and also help one to be more sensitive to the complexity and nuance of the world, expanding one's consciousness beyond the narrow sphere of solipsism that Alexis de Tocqueville and others have portrayed as a realm of anxiety and threat. The problem is that the acts of engagement and commitment are normatively empty in themselves, and the legitimacy of what one does depends upon the ends that one pursues, and the character with which one pursues those ends; indeed, some forms of engagement can be detrimental to the character traits that the proponents of civic engagement celebrate. So the project of civic education must not simply encourage action, but also concern itself with the character of citizens and their actions.[17]

Nevertheless, the political theory of civic engagement suggests that tangible, palpable experience is educative in a way that book learning is not; ideally, the two forms of knowledge nourish each other. This assumption is relevant to the ROTC question, for we hypothesize that actual exposure to ROTC students – especially if sufficient interaction takes place – can contribute to the education of non-military students in a way that simply reading about ROTC does not. Such interaction also can enhance another important aspect of civic education implied but not expressly endorsed in the AFT statement: a commitment to common citizenship and its obligations. By embodying debate over military obligation and the university, the ROTC politics that we examine in Chapters 5 through 7 contributed to bringing

[14] Similar definitions are found in Robert Putnam, *Bowling Alone: The Collapse and Revival of American Community* (Simon and Schuster, 2000).

[15] Macedo, *Democracy at Risk*, pp. 6–7.

[16] See, e.g., Antonio R. Damasio, *Descartes' Error: Emotion, Reason, and the Human Brain* (Avon, 1995). Indeed, psychiatry uniformly depicts mental maturity as the proper synthesis of emotion (or "affect") and rationality. Psychopathy and other mental disorders are linked to a severing of these two mental capacities.

[17] A major criticism of Hannah Arendt's otherwise enlightening notion of action in *The Human Condition* (University of Chicago Press, 1958) and other works is that she did not establish criteria for what constitutes legitimate action. To what ends should we act? Hitler, after all, called a nation to "action." For a nonsanguine theory of political participation, see Eric Hoffer, *The True Believer: Thoughts on the Nature of Mass Movements* (Harper and Row, 1951).

military and elite campus cultures into dialogue, thereby confronting nonmilitary students with concrete evidence of military sacrifice and the concept of civic duty. The surveys that we conducted of University of Wisconsin students, which we present in Chapters 8 and 9, also consistently showed this effect.

EDUCATION IN THE REGIME: CIVIC AND LIBERAL EDUCATION DIALECTICALLY COMBINED

Galston's analysis of the friction between civic and liberal (what he calls "philosophic") education leaves us suspended in a state of tension, as the critical inquiry espoused by the latter can undermine the former's foundations. (Recall that Galston spoke about "unexamined" central beliefs.) This is not a new tension, for it began long ago with the famous case of Socrates. On the one hand, Socrates accepted death by hemlock rather than agreeing to forsake the practice of critical philosophy, which threatened to undermine respect for Athens' corrupt regime; on the other hand, Socrates refused to escape the judgment of the Athenian laws, to which he paid due homage and respect. Socrates possessed a subtle, dialectical understanding that balanced critical philosophy with a commitment to citizenship.[18] He had one foot in the potentially radical state of philosophic truth and discourse, and one foot in the political community where convention reigned. Of course, when forced to choose, Socrates chose philosophical thought.[19]

Political theorist Peter Berkowitz provides an alternative model of education that helps to reconcile the fundamental tension between civic and liberal education in a Socratic fashion. Building on the thought of Aristotle, Berkowitz observes that the tendency of all regimes is to educate their young citizens to embody the character of the regime (reproduction), typically including the regime's virtues and vices.[20] The problem, Berkowitz points out, is that a complacent or unquestioning method of reproduction leads to overproducing the regime's vices because the reproduction discourages sufficient corrective criticism of those vices. Without their central vices being

[18] See, e.g., Darrell Dobbs, "Choosing Justice: Socrates' Model City and the Practice of Dialectic," *American Political Science Review* 88, 2 (1994): 263–77. According to Dobbs, perhaps the fundamental problem of education is being able to see how the individual relates to the community. Dobbs describes this process as synopsis. We also emphasize the relationship between the parts (such as the military as an institution) and society as a whole (such as national security) and the importance of encouraging participation of each of the parts in order to enhance the character of the regime.

[19] On Socrates' relentless questioning and how it is a model for citizenship, see Dana Villa, *Socratic Citizenship* (Princeton University Press, 2001). On the relationship between philosophic truth and politics, see Leo Strauss, *The City and Man* (University of Chicago Press, 1964).

[20] All societies that believe in themselves adopt measures to reproduce the types of character they believe in. Psychologists maintain that even early childhood training strives to do this. See, e.g., Erik H. Erikson, *Childhood and Society* (Norton, 1950).

challenged, such regimes become decadent and decline.[21] American history illustrates this point. The American regime has historically tossed and turned between its enlightened and darker sides when it comes to inclusion and citizenship. The venerable constitutional ideals of liberty, equality, inclusion, and tolerance (what Gunnar Myrdal called the principles that constitute the "American Creed") hold sway during certain eras, only to succumb to intolerance during certain periods of social tensions. Some theorists and historians argue that this tension is embedded in the psyche of the American regime.[22] At the same time, however, Berkowitz's theory of regime virtue contains a further wrinkle, for it entails a critique of an unreflective acceptance *of the liberal creed itself*. Enlightened citizens critically evaluate not only deviations from the regime's creed, but aspects of that very creed that undermine its sustenance.

The most vibrant and enlightened regimes strive to instill intellectual and moral capacities that challenge the conventional wisdom of the regime in a way that also preserves the deeper principles for which the regime stands. (Martin Luther King, Jr., is an outstanding example of this balance: His moral critiques of American hypocrisy and racism were ultimately profoundly conservative in character, grounded in the basic constitutional principles of the American regime. Huntington's theory of creedal passion also portrays this type of discursive-political process.)[23] One thinks of the difference between thoughtless patriotism and the more enlightened form of this sentiment or commitment. From this perspective, critical thought can afford a remedy to regime decline, and even reinforce the regime. Education in the regime, Berkowitz claims, "must in significant measure cut against the dominant tendency of the regime," which is to mold citizens into enthusiastic embodiments of its "guiding principle." But

> the guiding principle ceases to be an effective guide if it is allowed to become the regime's sole guide. Effective governance of oligarchies, for example, requires citizens who look beyond wealth and property to questions of honor and also to the claims of freedom and equality. And stability in democracies depends on citizens who can discipline the democratic inclination to do as one pleases so as to defer immediate

[21] The problem can be described as "positive feedbacks," which are features of a social system that are self-reinforcing. In the context of institutions, these are situations where the existence of ineffective institutions creates incentives for behavior that further undermine institutions. Positive feedbacks have increasingly been emphasized in theories of institutional change. See, e.g., Avner Greif and David D. Laitin, "A Theory of Endogenous Institutional Change," *American Political Science Review* 98, 4 (2004): 633–52; and Douglass C. North, *Institutions, Institutional Change, and Economic Performance* (Cambridge University Press, 1990).

[22] See, for example, Rogers M. Smith, *Conflicting Ideals: Conflicting Visions of Citizenship in U.S. History* (Yale University Press, 1997); and Gunnar Myrdal with the assistance of Richard Sterner and Arnold Rose, *American Dilemma: The Negro Problem and American Democracy* (Harper and Brothers, 1944).

[23] See King's classic "Letter from a Birmingham Jail," in Hugo Adam Bedau, ed., *Civil Disobedience: Theory and Practice* (Pegasus, 1969).

gratification in the interest of long-term benefits. . . . The makers of modern liberalism failed to provide adequately for the sustenance of the virtues necessary to liberalism's preservation.[24]

Liberal democracies tend to celebrate individual freedom, self-interest, and equality over other values, and to neglect or downplay the tragic limits and aspects of life, as well as the ways in which other virtues are also necessary to support viable regimes. Reinhold Niebuhr, for example, made a career out of warning liberal democracies of the pitfalls associated with their failure to face tragedy, which can lead to either childish idealism or undue cynicism.[25] Consequently, education in the regime in Berkowitz's terms should not only support the values of freedom, self-interest, and equality, but also cast a wary eye on some of the applications or extensions of these principles. Liberal regimes should also heed such virtues as duty, sacrifice, responsibility, excellence (not all individuals and actions are of equal virtue), and a tragic sense of the world. Failure to balance the demands of individuals with the requirements of community – and the emergence of institutions that nourish the former without losing sight of the latter – threaten to undermine a political regime.

THE WAYS IN WHICH AN APPROPRIATE MILITARY PRESENCE ON CAMPUS CAN ENHANCE EDUCATION

As mentioned in Chapter 1, we discern at least four ways in which an appropriate exposure and study of military-related matters can enhance civic and liberal education. Let us now examine each possibility.

Civic Education: Understanding the Military and National Defense

First, knowledge of the military is an essential part of citizenship because of that institution's importance in national life. The decision to go to war is perhaps the most momentous decision that a political community can make, and national security is the primary obligation of the state.[26] In recognition of the primary concerns of national defense, the Constitution's war powers allow for a stretching of congressional and executive powers in making war, especially in the executive branch. However much controversy rages over the proper extent and allocation of war powers, the fact remains that such powers exist in the

[24] Peter Berkowitz, *Virtue and the Making of Modern Liberalism* (Princeton University Press, 1999), p. 177.

[25] See, e.g., Reinhold Niebuhr, *The Children of Light and the Children of Darkness: A Vindication of Democracy and a Critique of Its Traditional Defense* (Charles Scribner's and Sons, 1945). On the sometimes ethereal idealism of liberal democracy, see Eric Voegelin, *The New Science of Politics* (University of Chicago Press, 1952).

[26] See John Hart Ely, *War and Responsibility: Constitutional Lessons of Vietnam and Its Aftermath* (Princeton University Press, 1993).

text, and they are essential aspects of sovereignty.[27] Accordingly, civic responsibility requires citizens to have an adequate understanding of such things as the nature of the military and war, the constitutional balance between the military and society, and the needs and contours of national security. And arguably the best way to prevent wars is to understand their causes, an understanding that is enhanced by the study of military history, diplomacy, and strategic security.[28] Those who fail to understand or remember the past, to draw from Thucydides and Santayana, are bound to repeat it.

In the spirit of education in the regime, this knowledge should be duly appreciative of the military as well as duly critical. Knowledge of the military should afford a remedy to both militarism (a mentality that runs counter to democratic character and is a recipe for disastrous ventures) and a thoughtless antimilitary attitude. The military is a cardinal institution in protecting the nation, and its members deserve deep respect for placing their lives in jeopardy on behalf of their fellow citizens. But history is replete with examples of the misuse of military power by civilian leaders, sometimes after being prodded by military leaders; furthermore, the military and its members are as human and political as the rest of us, so its institutional nobility exists alongside the usual aspects of self-promotion and self-interest. Self-interest is the reason we ask, "Who will guard the guardians?" Careerism and the managerial ethic exist side by side with the ethic of service and heroism; and individuals join the military for a variety of reasons, including (but certainly not limited to) a sense of duty and service; the seeking of adventure; the desire to see the world; family tradition; the opportunities the military provides for personal advancement; the scholarship money available in ROTC; and much more. (We will see these and other motives espoused by ROTC cadets later in this volume.) In addition, the branches are notorious for promoting their own interests in the congressional funding process and in interbranch rivalry. The considered distrust that the Framers counseled citizens to harbor toward government should apply to the military, as well.[29]

As we will encounter later in the book, our survey respondents expressed views that were both critical and appreciative of the military and its presence on campus. Some of these views were presented dogmatically, but many were more subtle, suggesting a more realistic and objective perspective, depending on the degree of exposure. One ROTC commander's observations stressed several themes that we touch upon in this chapter and will return to later, including the civic duty to understand the proper relationship between the military and civilian leadership, as well as the special sacrifice that soldiers are prepared to make:

[27] There is a copious literature on this question, of course. Two good recent works are Daniel Farber, *Lincoln's Constitution* (University of Chicago Press, 2003); and Jack L. Goldsmith, *The Terror Presidency: Law and Judgment Inside the Bush Administration* (W. W. Norton, 2007).

[28] See, e.g., Donald Kagan, *On the Origins of War and the Preservation of Peace* (Doubleday, 1995).

[29] For the ways that the services' visions of their interests influence the making of military strategy, see Carl H. Builder, *The Masks of War: American Military Styles in Strategy and Analysis* (Johns Hopkins University Press, 1989).

For ROTC members: exposure to a more traditional college experience (something not possible at a military academy) as a reminder that the military serves as an extension of the political will of the nation and that we need to learn how to communicate with, and work effectively for, the civilian branches of our government. For non-ROTC members: the program serves as a reminder that freedom is not free, that the future of our military is working hard every day to ensure that they are properly trained to lead the youth of this country into battle. In addition, college campuses tend to be slightly homogeneous, liberal, and anti-military. The presence of the ROTC units on the campus serves as a reminder that there are other points of view on "Main Street," not just the ones you hear every day on State Street. [State Street is a main street leading into the University of Wisconsin campus.]

More broadly, thinking about the military and the necessities and applications of defense strategy and politics can contribute to "the higher practicality," the conception of Hans Morgenthau that we discussed in Chapter 1. The average political scientist is "oblivious of his moral commitment" to teach students and the society how to grapple intellectually with fundamental questions confronting the political order. To remedy this situation, Morgenthau counseled political scientists to emulate the "lasting contributions to political science, from Plato, Aristotle, and Augustine to *The Federalist*, Marx, and Calhoun," which were "responses to such challenges arising from political reality."[30] Such study could link civic and liberal education by combining engagement with societal problems with an understanding of the best responsible thought of the past. In a much talked about recent essay addressing the problem of "scholasticism" in political science, Lawrence Mead carried on in Morgenthau's tradition by observing that, "Scholars are focusing more on themselves, less on the real world. That has harmed the realism of their work and the audience for it."[31] Jeffrey Isaac's recalling of political theory's "deafening silence" in response to the dissolution of the Soviet Union and the end of the Cold War supports Mead's critique.[32]

Morgenthau's reflections foreshadowed other more recent critiques of higher education's retreat from meaning and citizenship in favor of a research ideal that divorces faculty members from both undergraduates and the real world. Harry R. Lewis, former dean of Harvard College, laments a process that relegates undergraduates to being "subordinate, unworthy novices," while training graduate students to become professors who "acquire contempt for 'the world of affairs' from which they will be cut off." Lewis advocates establishing a core

[30] Hans J. Morgenthau, "The Purpose of Political Science," in James C. Charlesworth, ed., *A Design for Political Science: Scope, Objectives, and Methods* (American Academy of Political and Social Science, 1966), pp. 73, 77–8.

[31] Lawrence M. Mead, "Scholasticism in Political Science," *Perspectives on Politics* 8, 2 (2010): 453–64. Specifically, Mead argues that political science is characterized by specialization, methodologism, nonempiricism, and literature focus – each contributing to a largely policy-irrelevant political science. We would add that the exclusion of the military is a more general problem of the academy and its unwillingness to embrace the "other" when it comes to practical considerations.

[32] Jeffrey C. Isaac, "The Strange Silence of Political Theory," *Political Theory*, 23, 4 (1995). Isaac is also the editor of the journal in which Mead's critique appeared; and his stated editorial policy in *Perspectives on Politics* clearly echoes the thought of Morgenthau and Mead.

curriculum that restores a common educational background and experience for all students. He also champions teaching leadership qualities. Though Harvard (like other Ivy League schools) has traditionally prided itself (sometimes to a fault) on being a fountainhead of leadership for the nation, in practice Harvard College (the liberal arts school) has disdained teaching leadership because such teaching is considered marginal to the new research ideal that disavows responsibility for such things. Harvard's abolition of ROTC in 1969 – and its steadfast refusal to bring it back for decades before the abolition of Don't Ask, Don't Tell – is emblematic of this situation in Lewis's estimation. Its "indifference to leadership has contributed to Harvard's disenfranchisement of one of its most powerful leadership training programs: the Reserve Officers Training Corps (ROTC)." Harvard students who have been compelled to take ROTC at other campuses in the Boston area are motivated by several things, but especially by "the desire for leadership training." In Lewis's eyes, "The balance of principles is among the most troubling issues confronting universities, and the future of ROTC is visibly fought on this high ground. … ROTC is a hard sell at Harvard because professors undervalue the life skills it teaches."[33] Students who replied to our surveys at Wisconsin – especially ROTC cadets and their commanders – emphasized leadership again and again in their responses, as we will see later in this book. We will have more to say about this issue elsewhere in this chapter.

As Galston and other political theorists have emphasized, appropriate military service has historically been considered a central aspect of citizenship. "From Greek and Roman times down to the present, the allocation of the burden of national defense has been at the heart of citizenship."[34] Ignoring or dismissing the reality of national security interests – broadly defined, of course, for disagreement does and should reign regarding its meaning and application, especially in liberal democracies – is a sign of political *immaturity*, as those inclined to such dismissal are akin to children who leave the security of the home to their parents. Machiavelli captures this logic in his book *The Art of War*, in which he portrays a conversation in Cosimo Rusellai's beautiful garden among a group of leading Florentine citizens and Fabrizio Colonna, a general in the Hapsburg army who is visiting their city state. In narrating this fictional conversation, Machiavelli teaches that these men are able to enjoy the conversation in the bounty of this garden because, lurking unseen over the horizon, the city state's military defends the citizens' security:

[33] Harry R. Lewis, *Excellence Without a Soul: Does Liberal Education Have a Future?* (Public Affairs, 2007), pp. 42, 88–90, 68–9. For similar views, see Anthony Kronman, *Education's End: Why Our Colleges and Universities Have Given Up on the Meaning of Life* (Yale University Press, 2007).

[34] William Galston, "The Challenge of Civic Engagement: An Introduction," in *Community Matters: Challenges to Civic Engagement in the 21st Century* (Rowman and Littlefield, 2005), pp. 2–3. See also Richard B. Sher, "Adam Ferguson, Adam Smith, and the Problem of National Defense," *Journal of American History* 61, 2 (1989): 240–66.

For all the arts that have been introduced into society for the common benefit of mankind, and all the ordinances that have been established to make them live in fear of God and in obedience to human laws, would be in vain and insignificant if they were not supported and defended by a military force. ... [For] the best ordinances in the world will be despised and trampled under foot when they are not supported, as they ought to be, by a military power; they are like a magnificent, roofless palace which, though full of jewels and costly furniture, must soon moulder into ruin since it has nothing but its splendor and riches to defend it from the ravages of the weather.[35]

Machiavelli could have been describing an academic in the Ivory Tower who, while contemplating knowledge, forgets the reasons that he or she has the freedom to contemplate such matters. Machiavelli's insight was echoed in an interview we conducted with Harvard comparative literature and Jewish Studies professor Ruth Wisse, who has long favored the return of ROTC to Harvard. When we asked her why the actual presence of ROTC was needed given the fact that Harvard also has many courses dealing with security issues, she replied with words worth quoting at some length. Actually *seeing* students in the military is

a constant reminder. The very presence of the students who are in the military becomes a reminder and perhaps even a source of conscience to recognize that a price needs to be paid for democracy, and someone is paying that price. That there are people who have to take on their share of responsibilities and ... this is the one thing that one has to ask of people of that age ... and its always sad to demand of people who are just entering life to defend our country, but they are the ones who can do it ... this is something that the young must do for the old. This is their responsibility before they become parents. This is what they have to shoulder. And if we, the adults, don't have the courage to say this to them, then we are failing both ourselves and them. But if we fail to say this to them, it seems to me that they at least ought to have the guts to say it for themselves.[36]

Wisse's observation leads us to another aspect of citizenship that we will address more fully in a moment: how the sustenance of liberal regimes depends upon the presence of virtues that are not typically construed as "liberal," such as discipline, sacrifice, and the willingness to do certain things that are difficult and unpleasant, yet necessary (within the constraints of morality) in order to protect the very society that makes the practice of liberal values possible.

Machiavelli's position on the necessity of a military is valid four hundred years later, even though liberal democracies are generally less warlike than pre-Enlightenment polities. Though the headlines might indicate otherwise, the world is considerably less plagued by war than in the past, even if we take international terrorism into consideration. The "democratic peace" thesis provides one explanation for this progress, holding that liberal democracies are less

[35] Niccolo Machiavelli, *The Art of War*, translated by Neal Wood (Bobbs-Merrill, Library of Liberal Arts, 1965), p. 4.

[36] Interview with Ruth Wisse, October 2007. See also Ruth R. Wisse, *Jews and Power* (Schocken, 2007), which is predicated on the recognition of the need for *power* to protect what one holds dear. Jews died in the Holocaust and in other oppressions when they lacked the power to defend themselves.

inclined to fight one another than are other types of political regimes. (This thesis has not gone without challenge, but it has to be weighed in the balance.) Another reason is modernity's increasing sensitivity to suffering, which makes military thinking seem barbaric or inappropriately cruel. Before the principles of the Enlightenment took hold, most polities were either predicated on warrior virtues or held such values in very high esteem. But as polities become more liberal in inspiration and practice, the martial spirit tended to move to the margins of society – especially in countries that have suffered much at the hands of constant wars, as Europe did between the Napoleonic era and the Cold War. And in recent years, more and more scholars and foreign policy participants have begun stressing the efficacy of "soft power" (economic, social, cultural, and so on) over the deployment of military force.[37]

We need to heed all of these arguments about the lesser importance of military force in the contemporary world, especially because the unwise resort to war leaves disaster in its wake. But these arguments do not negate Machiavelli's fundamental thesis, for at least two reasons. First, situations still arise – and will probably always arise – in which force is necessary to achieve valid ends such as the self-defense of nations or people. Even many people who are skeptical of military force have found themselves siding with its use to protect human rights in Kosovo and other areas of the world where such humanistic intervention can save lives.[38] Second, however much we revise our assumptions about human nature as history unfolds, it would be imprudent to dismiss the claims of some realists that aggression is built into human nature and political orders due to evolutionary processes and a host of situational and structural factors that have been analyzed in a vast literature. To be sure, altruism and care for others are also woven into our genetic heritage, so we must be wary of overemphasizing humanity's aggressive instincts. (Soldiers feel altruism in war, especially regarding their fellow warriors. Loyalty based on bonding is one of the essential ingredients of successful war making.)[39] But just as it would be cynical to ignore the altruistic roots of human nature, so would it be naïve to disregard the aggressive aspects of human nature. One of Niebuhr's greatest contributions to our understanding of human nature is his insight that our moral propensity

[37] On democratic peace and related questions, see John E. Mueller, *Retreat from Doomsday: The Obsolescence of Major War* (Basic, 1989). On the martial spirit of the pre-liberal world, see Paul A. Rahe's remarkable series on republicanism, *Republics Ancient and Modern* (University of North Carolina Press, 1994). On the growing intolerance of suffering in modernity, see Joseph A. Amato, *Victims and Values: A History and a Theory of Suffering* (Praeger, 1990). On the marked decline of martial spirit in post–World War II Europe, see James J. Sheehan, *Where Have All the Soldiers Gone? The Transformation of Modern Europe* (Houghton Mifflin, 2008). On soft power, see Joseph S. Nye's influential book *Soft Power: The Means to Success in World Politics* (Public Affairs, 2004).

[38] On how European idealists who disdained the use of interventionist military power in international relations reconsidered their positions in light of Kosovo and similar cases, see Paul Berman's fascinating account in *Power and the Idealists, or, The Passion of Joschka Fischer and Its Aftermath* (Soft Skull Press, 2005).

[39] See James Q. Wilson, *The Moral Sense* (Free Press, 1993), ch. 2, "Sympathy."

contains conflicting, contradictory capacities: what is best in us, and what is worst in us. This is a fundamental aspect of his conception of original sin, which he applied to social analysis and foreign policy. Similarly, Freud's greatest challenge to the Enlightenment was not simply in demonstrating how our ethical impulses are *in conflict* with our aggressive instincts, but rather in teaching how our ethical impulses are actually *rooted* in our aggressive instincts.[40]

One of the best articulations of this perspective is Azar Gat's 2006 masterpiece, *War in Human Civilization.* Gat's book is nothing less than a history of human civilization, and of the ways in which war has both reflected and influenced human nature and political development. Gat does not disavow the schools of democratic peace and soft power, but is very skeptical that war can be eliminated because of what evolutionary science and historical experience suggest about who and what we are as individuals and organized societies. The causes of war are complex and hardly limited to "human nature," covering the gamut of such phenomena as honor, prestige, conflicts over resources, security dilemmas, and conflicts embedded in the structures of international relations, and technological developments.[41] One is reminded of the debate between Alfred Einstein and Sigmund Freud over war and peace during World War II. When Einstein advocated international institutions that would eliminate or at least mitigate the possibility of war, Freud (who harbored a tragic belief in the permanence of human nature) replied that the problem was not just a product of culture and institutions, but something woven into the nature of humanity and the conflicts of states.[42] Until universal justice might reign, at the very least power and organized force will be occasionally necessary to protect democratic interests and principles, whether these involve fighting terrorism or intervention to protect human rights. In 1911, Norman Angell wrote in his enormously popular book *The Great Illusion* that war would eventually be outdated by the rational self-interest of world citizens. Three years later, World War I erupted. Francis Fukuyama's memorable book *The End of History*, which forecasted the end of ideological warfare a decade before 9/11, is another work of this flawed utopian genre.[43]

[40] See Paul Ricour, *Freud and Philosophy: An Essay on Interpretation*, translated by Denis Savage (Yale University Press, 1970). In the language of Freud's typological understanding of the psyche, the super-ego (the moral force) derives its instinctual energy from the id. Freud, *The Ego and the Id*, translated by James Strachey (Norton, 1962).

[41] Azar Gat, *War in Human Civilization* (Oxford University Press, 2006). See also the classic University of Chicago project on the causes of war written by Quincy Wright, *A Study of War* (University of Chicago Press, 1942), for these and other causes.

[42] See the famous exchange between Freud and Einstein on war and human nature, "Why War?" in "The Einstein-Freud Correspondence (1931–1932)," in Otto Nathan and Heinz Norden, eds., *Einstein on Peace* (Schocken, 1960), pp. 186–203.

[43] Sir Norman Angell, *The Great Illusion: A Study of the Relation of Military Power in Nations to Their Economic and Social Advantage* (W. Heinemann, 1911); Francis Fukuyama, *The End of History and the Last Man* (Free Press, 1992). In contrast to the utopian perspectives, Samuel P. Huntington, in *The Clash of Civilizations and the Remaking of World Order* (Simon and Schuster, 1996), argues persuasively that conflicts of values will continue to undermine the promise of peace.

Can international law ride to the rescue? Surely it can ameliorate the problem of violence. In most situations, laws are effective because citizens find them morally binding; when this sense of obligation fails, it helps that laws are also backed by power and that those in power have self-interested reasons to enforce the laws.[44] But these characteristics of self-enforcing institutions do not typically characterize international law. The international system lacks any formal enforcers, those capable of being enforcers often lack will to be so, and the international system itself is subject to a formidable collective action problem.[45] Once again, this does not mean that international law is a chimera or a quixotic endeavor, but rather that experience shows that it is not always a reliable instrument in itself to support justice and achieve valid ends. It requires power to actualize its rules and norms. This conclusion also points to a normative point that we will address later in this chapter: Though always tragic, sometimes war is an expression of our moral integrity rather than simply a sign of our aggressive and predatory instincts. The venerable distinction between just and unjust wars – of ancient heritage in our legal and moral culture – is a testament to a potential normative defense of some wars.[46]

In *A Theory of Justice*, philosopher John Rawls analyzes the basic liberties and social goods that rational individuals would agree to adopt under a "veil of ignorance," in which no individual knows what skills and characteristics he or she will possess in the game of social life. Though he stresses the non-militaristic mentality of rational democratic citizens, Rawls is also clear about two things: that there is a commonly shared interest in "reasonable regulations to maintain public order and security," including "collective efforts for national defense in a just war"; and that the duties of national defense be "more or less evenly shared by all members of society."[47] National defense is so fundamental that Rawls treats it as a "primary good" that all rational citizens will demand under the

[44] The more general point is that institutions have to be self-enforcing in that all the relevant actors have incentives to abide by these rules and norms. See Randall L. Calvert, "The Rational Choice Theory of Social Institutions: Cooperation, Coordination, and Communication," in eds. Jeffrey S. Banks and Eric A. Hanushek, *Modern Political Economy: Old Topics, New Directions* (Cambridge University Press, 1995), pp. 216–68.

[45] See Eric A. Posner, *The Perils of Global Legalism* (University of Chicago Press, 2009). This does not, of course, preclude cooperation. Nation-states can cooperate provided they expect to interact in the future through reputation mechanisms. The seminal statement on international cooperation is Robert Axelrod, *The Evolution of Cooperation* (Basic, 1984). There are also a variety of commitment devices that can facilitate international cooperation. See, e.g., Lisa L. Martin, *Democratic Commitments: Legislatures and International Cooperation* (Princeton University Press, 2000); and Randall W. Stone, *Lending Credibility: The International Monetary Fund and the Post-Communist Transition* (Princeton University Press, 2002). Our point is that international law is a much weaker, less reliable system of law that, by its deficiencies, places a premium on military force to resolve fundamental conflicts in the international system.

[46] See, e.g., Michael Walzer, *Just and Unjust Wars: A Moral Argument with Historical Illustrations* (Basic, 2006); and Jean Bethke Elshtain, *Just War Against Terror: The Burden of American Power in a Violent World* (Basic, 2003).

[47] John Rawls, *A Theory of Justice* (Harvard University Press, 1971), pp. 97, 381. See, generally, pp. 90–100, 377–82.

conditions of the veil of ignorance or social contract – and to which all citizens should contribute in one form or another. In a world replete with conflict and a lack of definitive knowledge about human nature, two universal, fundamental rights or goods are self-defense and national defense. Though some have argued for unilateral disarmament, no responsible polity has ever done so, and with good reason. International relations scholars call this situation the "security dilemma," which means that arming for national defense has often led to an escalating arms race on each side that results in less, rather than more, security all around.[48] But the problem of the security dilemma counsels the more prudent policy that each side work to downsize arms mutually, rather than that one side disarm on its own.

There is a final aspect of this form of civic education that we draw, once again, from Berkowitz. Because American liberal democracy takes individual rights and liberty so seriously, liberal theorists are often reluctant to acknowledge or discuss the virtues that are necessary to sustain the regime. Consequently, critics accuse liberalism of lacking values beyond individualism and self-interest.[49] However, liberalism unavoidably assumes the preexistence of certain virtues that either stem from outside of liberalism (family, religion, community) or are implicitly embedded in the very logic and practice of liberalism itself. For example, the very institutionalization and preservation of freedom depend upon discipline, commitment, and due respect on the part of citizens – virtues that constitute an "achievement" according to John Stuart Mill and some of the more thoughtful founders of the modern liberal tradition. Mill "recognizes the need to limit individual choice so as to preserve the institutions that form individuals capable of exercising choice skillfully, responsibly, and indeed boldly ... autonomy is an *achievement*, one that crucially involves cultivation of particular qualities of mind and character." And one of the most important qualities of character that sustains the regime of individual autonomy is discipline. "The achievement of autonomy, or what Mill sometimes called individuality, like spontaneity in athletic competition and improvisation in musical performance, requires the most exacting sort of discipline."[50]

Liberal theory has to recognize the intimate connection that exists between freedom and discipline. Liberal regimes properly protect the freedom to live an undisciplined life; in fact, such freedom could serve as the very operational definition of liberalism. But someone has to be willing to assume responsibility for maintaining and protecting the regime itself. Such discipline has two dimensions: individual and systemic. Regarding individuals, liberal freedom

[48] See, e.g., Gat, *War in Human Civilization*.

[49] See, e.g., Alisdair MacIntyre, *After Virtue: A Study in Moral Theory* (University of Notre Dame Press, 1981).

[50] Berkowitz, *Virtue and the Making of Modern Liberalism*, p. 138, emphasis added. See also pp. 138–40, 170. Galston makes similar arguments in *Liberal Purposes*. On how the regime of rights constitutes a systemic social "practice" that must be sustained by effort, see Richard E. Flathman, *The Practice of Rights* (Cambridge University Press, 1976).

presupposes that individual citizens possess the capacity to be "self-governing." Indeed, the capacity to be *self*-governing is what makes a *limited* government possible in the first place. (If we do not govern ourselves, then we will be governed more extensively by others. As Tocqueville observed, the principle of authority will be manifested somewhere.) Alexander Meiklejohn, a leading philosopher and practitioner of free inquiry and education, maintained that the practice of self-government "does not mean the absence of self-control. It *is* self-control."[51] At the macro or systemic level, citizens entrusted with responsibilities for maintaining such important institutions as the rule of law, the market, and basic social welfare (including domestic defense and national security) must be disciplined to act for the welfare of other citizens and the community. Freedom and free institutions are not manna from heaven; their sustenance depends upon the sustained commitments of others to sacrifice themselves through duty to the public good. Consider what happens when authorities allow bullies to shout speakers down in the public forum: Illegitimate power tramples on the rights of speakers and listeners because legitimate authority has failed to defend and uphold liberal norms of freedom. (Weimar Germany's inability to prevent the Nazis' barbarization of the public forum is an extreme example of this surrender or deterioration.) What Thomas Emerson calls the "system of freedom of expression" prevails only if legitimate power is brought to bear to sustain and defend that system. Such recognition was paramount in the minds of America's founders, who understood that the liberty they staked their lives and honor on necessitated a Constitution that allocated sufficient power to the state to enable it to defend liberty.[52] We will have more to say about the question of power in a moment.

In many respects, the military is one of the purest examples of the professionally specific elevation of duty over rights. (Such institutions as police, the foreign service, and the intelligence services are other good examples.) In Berkowitz's terms, the military's presence can contribute to "education in the regime" by providing a vivid example of sacrifice and duty in a polity dedicated to rights. Appreciating such a normative posture enriches liberal democracy in the dialectical sense discussed earlier in this chapter. In the language of legal theorist Mary Ann Glendon, this appreciation complements "rights talk" (the predominant talk of liberal democracy) with talk about duties.[53] As one Madison student told us in a response to one of our survey questions, knowing someone in ROTC "has shown me that there are still people that go to this school [who] can aspire to do things with their lives that affect much more than

[51] Meiklejohn, "Free Speech and Its Relation to Self-Government," in *Political Freedom* (Oxford University Press, 1965). On discipline, obedience, and civic education, see William Desmond, "Autonomy, Loyalty, and Civic Piety," in Watson, ed., *Civic Education and Culture*, pp. 15–28.

[52] Thomas I. Emerson, *The System of Freedom of Expression* (Random House, 1970). Perhaps the best treatment of how power is necessary to protect rights, and how constitutionalism is the best effort to bequeath and limit power, see Stephen Holmes, *Passions and Constraint: On the Theory of Liberal Democracy* (University of Chicago Press, 1995).

[53] Mary Ann Glendon, *Rights Talk: The Impoverishment of Political Discourse* (Free Press, 1993).

themselves." As we will see later, military discipline can be very trying, as it can require the making of difficult, courageous decisions in the face of danger, but in a manner that respects the rules of war. Machiavelli's thesis of state defense in *The Art of War* is premised on this understanding: The discipline of the military is one important reason that civilians can go about their business and enjoy their freedom.

In later sections of this book, we will see that many ROTC cadets and non-military students offered reflections that affirm some of the points under discussion. To pick just one example among the many we will present later, one student echoed Wisse's perspective, stating that, "Seeing ROTC members on campus reminds me of the sacrifice and dedication so many people have made in protection of our country, which allow me to attend college. Their presence on campus reminds me that the opportunities I have should not be taken for granted." This is education in the regime.

Liberal Education: Human Nature, Society, and the Meaning of Life

A second reason for studying the military, war, and related topics is that such study can be an excellent vehicle by which to learn more about human nature, society, and the meaning of life. James Madison wrote in *Federalist #51*, "What is government itself but the greatest of all reflections on human nature?"[54] The same can be said about studying war. Thucydides, for example, teaches us that crisis and war often reveal a person's and a state's true characters. Soldiers have written many moving (and often disturbing) essays and books about the philosophical, psychological, and normative implications of war, which range from nobility to debasement and from glory to tragedy. J. Glenn Gray's *The Warriors: Reflections on Men in Battle* is a noteworthy example of this genre, as is Hannah Arendt's penetrating introduction to the book. Gray wrote his book many years after his grueling soldiering in World War II, after he had had time to place his experiences in perspective. He analyzes the moral paths that different types of soldiers traveled during the war, and how the pressures of war brought out the best or the worst in individuals, or something in between. In so doing, Gray reflects upon the philosophical implications of soldiering in war, in particular the different ways in which the strains of war affect moral character in different individuals. In but one of many remarkable passages in this book, Gray contemplates the emotions soldiers experience in combat situations in words that echo Thucydides' insight:

> In such an emotional situation there is often a surge of vitality and a glimpse of potentialities, of what we really are or have been or might become, as fleeting as it is genuine. In these situations some are able to serve others in simple yet fundamental ways. Inhuman cruelty can give way to super-human kindness. Inhibitions vanish, and people are reduced

[54] James Madison, "Federalist #51," in *The Federalist Papers*, edited by Clinton Rossiter (New American Library, 1961).

to their essence. . . . Again and again in moments of this kind I was as much inspired by the nobility of some of my fellows as appalled by the animality of others, or, more exactly, by both qualities in the same person. The average degree, which we commonly know in peacetime, conceals as much as it reveals about the human creature.[55]

Gray included chapters on such topics as the appeal of battle, love as "war's ally and foe," soldiers' relations to death, guilt, and the images soldiers have of the enemy. Each chapter examines how soldiers' postures toward these phenomena reveal or illuminate the universal human potential for good or evil, virtue or corruption.

In his recent critique of higher education in *The End of Education*, Yale professor Anthony Kronman argues that liberal education and the humanities have forsaken their historical obligation to help young adults inquire into the most fundamental questions of life, such as the meaning and mystery of existence, the meaning of mortality, and the question of how they should live (the fundamental question of political philosophy). Kronman attributes this abnegation of pedagogical responsibility to trends that have taken over the humanities since the 1960s, including political correctness, which inhibits robust inquiry into sensitive matters; the rise of the constructivist tenets of postmodernism and poststructuralism, which teach that asking such questions is meaningless and that there are no truths beyond those established by power; an overemphasis on narrow agendas of research; and the rewarding of research over good teaching. Though he wrestles with many problems abounding in higher education today, Kronman pays special attention to two shortcomings: the flight from questions of mortality and tragedy, and the lack of vibrant discourse due to political correctness. In many interesting respects, military-related studies can help to fill this void. To restore meaning to the understanding of man, we need to restore the traditional understanding of "the connection between mortality and meaning," which necessitates the overcoming of "the devaluation of mortality that defines the powerful but pointless age we inhabit." Restoring mortality and true discourse to humane studies would be part of a broader project of revitalizing the humanities by encouraging spirited inquiry that challenges reigning orthodoxies on campus. Kronman's approach echoes Morgenthau:

It would compel students to consider whether justice is a higher good than beauty, whether democracy has room for nobility, whether our reverence for human beings should be qualified by recognition of original sin. It would force them to confront a wider and more disturbing diversity of opinion than the one they now do in their college and university classrooms. It would disrupt their confidence and deepen their doubts. Today, just the opposite is the case.[56]

Thinking about the nature of war and military matters can provide one way to struggle with all of these questions, and it is perhaps no accident that the

[55] J. Glenn Gray, *The Warriors: Reflections on Men in Battle* (Harper and Row, 1967), pp. 14–15.
[56] Kronman, *Education's End*, pp. 235–6, 255–6.

marginalization of the military and military-related studies on many campuses is one manifestation of the problems that Kronman discerns. Some of the most profound ruminations on the nature of good and evil and the meaning of life have come from serious reflections on war and military obligation, as is evident in Gray's reflections on the moral impact of war. In some of the most moving passages in her remarkable book on death and the Civil War, for example, Harvard president Drew Gilpin Faust portrays the ways that such writers as Ambrose Bierce, Stephen Crane, Ernest Hemingway, Emily Dickinson, and Herman Melville (to name just five out of many) ruminated on the meaning of war. Based on his war experiences, Bierce "crafted unromanticized depictions of battle that reflected his fundamental approach to both writing and to life: 'Cultivate a taste for distasteful truths. And ... most of all, endeavor to see things as they are, not as they ought to be.'" Influenced by the war, Dickinson's poetry set the stage for modernism, for it "challenges 'the whole question of linguistic meaning and of meaning in general.' This is a crisis of language and epistemology as much as one of eschatology; it is about not just whether there is a God and whether we can know him but whether we can know or communicate anything at all." A Union chaplain wrote after Fredericksburg, "A battle is indescribable."[57]

For the most part, the Wisconsin political science students we surveyed did not venture into this special sensibility of the spirit, at least not at this level; the questions we asked dealt with such things as exposure to ROTC cadets and security studies (at the time, Wisconsin did not have a military historian), and such courses and questions are not so likely to elicit such reflection. But we did receive some feedback that touched on this sensibility, such as the student who reported that being exposed to ROTC students "definitely made me see them differently. I always thought of the military as something so far from myself, but seeing them in my classes and around campus makes me wonder about their experiences like I hadn't before." Many other students mentioned how such exposure served to correct misperceptions and misconceptions, providing a factual check that helped them to "see things as they are," so to speak. (We will present a full range of responses later in the book. Not all the responses were favorable, by the way.)

A different student who took an innovative undergraduate seminar on "The Romance of War" in Integrated Liberal Studies (a program initiated by Meiklejohn in the 1930s) and the Political Science Department at Wisconsin in the fall of 2007 mirrored these possibilities in her commentary on the class. Perhaps the fact that this small course was taught in the humanities from a philosophical perspective made the responses we received distinctive. The student stressed that she learned how utterly distinct war is as a phenomenon, how it is both appalling and appealing at the same time, and that this paradoxical fact

[57] Drew Gilpin Faust, *This Republic of Suffering: Death and the American Civil War* (Alfred A. Knopf, 2008), pp. 196–7, 208–9. The other inner quotation is from Shira Wolsosky. On the uniqueness of battle, see John Keegan, *The Face of Battle* (Penguin, 1976).

tells us something almost unfathomable about human beings. The course taught her things about human nature that she had not dealt with before. "I learned about the fact that nothing is comparable to war, and how if it be sexual attraction, drug use, and ecstasy moment, nothing can come close or substitute for war. Also I learned of things that might be able to create the bonds or community that war creates, their possibilities and setbacks." The instructor "prompted the students to think and analyze for themselves. He asked for contradictions and other points of view. This is how I formed my own ideas on war, where it comes from, and what it does for the individual. I learned more from this class than almost any other I have ever taken." War is *sui generis*; there is nothing in human experience like it, and our often complex feelings toward it tell us something about what we are as human beings.[58] A different student in this class had an even more poignant impression, as the class exposed him to the breadth of human nature and to possibilities that he had not previously imagined:

> The Romance of War was truly thought provoking, because rather than analyzing the political, economic, or social causes of a phenomenon that has been a fundamental element of human existence (as most of my political science classes have), it cut under the surface to explore whether there is a more deeply rooted source ingrained within the human psyche ... while an individual engaging in war appears fundamentally irrational (as it threatens his/her survival), it also fulfills certain psychological urges and instills meaning into a person's life.[59]

The academic humanities' retreat from the question of mortality (if Kronman's estimation is correct) parallels a similar trend in modern society, as some writers have divined a more general "denial of death" in a commercial society dedicated to self-image and an emphasis upon self-fulfillment.[60] Among other things, thinking about war and the military can compel us to confront the question of mortality, for, as Elizabeth D. Samet, a professor of English at West Point, remarks in her book *Soldier's Heart: Reading Literature through Peace and War at West Point*:

> On unusually intimate terms with violence throughout their professional lives, soldiers know things that many of the rest of us do not. The most elemental thing they know, or are at least prepared to know, is death.... Soldiers, too, are bound and dignified by craft,

[58] Response of an undergraduate student who took the course "War and Romance" at the University of Wisconsin, Madison, in the fall of 2007. Neither of us was the instructor. This student's sense of the *sui generis* nature of war is congruent with the phenomenological perspective of philosopher Gelven in *War and Existence: A Philosophical Inquiry*.

[59] Statement made by a student in the "Romance of War" class at the University of Wisconsin, spring 2008.

[60] See, e.g., Ernest Becker, *The Denial of Death* (Free Press, 1973), and *Escape from Evil* (Free Press, 1975). See also Christopher Lasch, *Culture of Narcissism: America In an Age of Diminishing Expectations* (Norton, 1978).

and they speak a language that announces their membership in it. Yet there are times, and this is one, when what soldiers end up with is less a common craft than, to borrow a phrase from Shakespeare, a royal fellowship of death.[61]

As we will see, our survey findings tended to confirm Samet's distinction between soldiers and nonsoldiers in this regard. ROTC cadets (who have not served yet) exhibited more concern about the sacrifices (including the risk of life) they were preparing to make than non-ROTC students, who (though many did mention this aspect of service) paid more attention to the way exposure "humanized" the military. One ROTC cadet reflected, "There are some secondary benefits that accrue to the university and student body, but these are not ROTC's purpose for existence. Regardless, these secondary benefits are a greater awareness among the student body of the sacrifice involved with military service, and thus a greater respect for military members." ROTC commanders were also sensitive to this notion of fellowship, with one remarking, "ROTC reminds us of service before self, and at this particular time it also means sacrifice. We are at war and kids in ROTC know that and are not swayed by the thought they will have their turn to serve overseas. With the presence of future officers on campus, it also reminds us of past sacrifices."

In *Purity and Danger: An Analysis of Concepts of Pollution and Taboo*, her classic work of anthropology, psychology, and social theory, Mary Douglas analyzes the ways that different cultures and societies draw normative and psychological lines that separate the sacred from the profane, pollution (dirt) from cleanliness, the acceptable from the transgressive.[62] To some in liberal society, soldiering and the conduct of war constitute a kind of transgression into the realm of pollution and dirt, as David Gelernter intimated in his observation recounted in Chapter 1 that his colleagues at Yale in the mid-2000s seemed "determined to turn American soldiers into an out-of-sight, out of mind servant class who are expected to do their duty and keep their mouths shut."[63] A few of our student respondents appear to have embraced this posture of "out-of-sight." For example, one proclaimed, "These interactions (though few) only further convinced me that the military has no place on a college campus. Period!" (Perhaps these postures are more aptly captured by Thorstein Veblen's classic, *The Theory of the Leisure Class*, in which Veblen portrays elite classes snobbishly looking down upon the dirty work that lower classes perform in order to sustain the

[61] Elizabeth D. Samet, *Soldier's Heart: Reading Literature Through Peace and War at West* Point (Farrar, Straus and Goroux, 2007), p. 25. See also Dave Grossman, *On Killing: The Psychological Cost of Learning to Kill in War and Society* (Little, Brown, 1995). Grossman, a former army lieutenant, maintains that American society refuses to confront the implications of war because of its more generalized fear of dealing with death.

[62] Mary Douglas, *Purity and Danger: An Analysis of Concepts of Pollution and Taboo* (Routledge & K. Paul, 1966).

[63] David Gelernter, quoted in Kathy Roth-Douquet and Frank Schaeffer, *AWOL: The Unexcused Absence of America's Upper Classes from the Military – and How It Hurts Our Country* (Harper Collins, 2006), pp. 48–9

society.)[64] Douglas reveals how such taboo-like bifurcation is natural to social order and individual psychology; but it can also come at the price of repression and the sacrifice of truth. Friedrich Nietzsche's advocacy of the retrieval of tragic consciousness in *The Birth of Tragedy* is relevant in this regard, as he construed this effort as the replenishment of something troubling yet vital to intellectual integrity and the human spirit: an awareness of the deeper and often darker aspects of life that transcend the comforting confines of conventional rational calculation and social acceptance. Tragic consciousness expands the intellectual and moral horizon, revealing disturbing yet profound truths.[65] Moral education to Nietzsche entailed the stretching of the mind to acknowledge and confront this dimension of reality.

The thoughts presented by the commentators in this section respecting the enormity and mortality of war suggest that studying war can acquaint us with a tragic sensibility. Tragic sensibility has traditionally been an important aspect of liberal education, and we will discuss it further later in this chapter when we talk about the question of intellectual diversity in higher education.

Moral Difficulties in Liberal Democracy

A third reason for exposing non-military students to war and military matters is that studying the ethics and obligations of war is an excellent vehicle for thinking about moral problems relating to citizenship in liberal democracy. The most important moral dilemma for our purposes concerns the ambiguities inherent in the use and abuse of power and organized violence. Reinhold Niebuhr perceived that liberal societies are reluctant to confront the unavoidable yet difficult relationships among power, force, justice, and national interest. When America became a world power in the aftermath of World War II, "We never dreamed that we would have as much political power as we possess today.... We were, as a matter of fact, always vague, as the whole liberal culture is fortunately vague, about how power is to be related to the allegedly universal values which we hold in trust for mankind."[66] But power and force are sometimes necessary to protect security and justice in a hostile world, though these forces can be abused; and they stand in tension with liberal democracies' commitment to the Enlightenment's aspirations of peace and reason. But even liberal regimes require a willingness to use force if necessary. As Michael Gelven writes in *War and Existence*, "The ethical ideas of a Socrates, of a Christ, of a Kant, are not beneficial without the spirit to defend them against those who would eliminate them. On the other hand, militarism by itself brings about nothing of worth. The fact remains, however: who I am is determined as much

[64] Thorstein Veblen, *The Theory of the Leisure Class: An Economic Study of Institutions* (Macmillan, 1912).

[65] Nietzsche, *The Birth of Tragedy*, in *The Birth of Tragedy and The Case of Wagner*, edited by Walter Kaufman (Vintage, 1967).

[66] Reinhold Niebuhr, *The Irony of American History* (Charles Scribers and Sons, 1952), p. 69.

by those who have fought for the ideas as by those who have thought the ideas."[67]

The phenomenon that throws the question of power into the starkest relief is violence, for violence is always morally challenging and an ultimate resort of state power. The modern state emerged as the norm in the international system in part because it provides economies of scale in violence. The sovereign state replaced other forms of organization historically because it was more efficient in monopolizing authority.[68] And the justifiable threat and use of violence is sometimes necessary for legitimate power to prevail. At the very least, those in power must be willing to use violence when necessary, or their claim to legitimate power will lack credibility and respect. (Accepting this point does not discredit the usually wise position that softer means of power should be exhausted if at all possible.)[69]

Democracies tend to be uneasy or uncomfortable with violence. In his perceptive study of the different types of police officers, for example, William Ker Muir analyzes the strategic and moral implications of officers' struggles with the question of how properly to grasp and use violence. Many officers suffer anxiety dealing with violence because it poses a moral dilemma in liberal democratic regimes in which human rights and the peaceful resolution of conflict constitute the norm. Cognitive dissonance is a constant companion of many officers. The worst officers come in two forms: those who resolve the dissonance by avoiding violence at all costs, regardless of the situation (and therefore shirk their duty to the public they serve); and those at the opposite extreme who revel in violence without moral qualms. Take your pick: children of light or the children of darkness. The best officers are those who are able to think this tension through and resolve it in a manner that enables them to exercise violence in a principled, limited manner consistent with their duty. (In a Socratic or Hegelian sense, they resolve the tension by dialectically raising their thought to a higher level of synthesis.)[70]

[67] Gelven, *War and Existence*, p. 54.

[68] Hendrik Spruyt, *The Sovereign State and Its Competitors: An Analysis of Systems Change* (Princeton University Press, 1994). See also Douglass C. North, John Joseph Wallis, and Barry R. Weingast, *Violence and Social Orders: A Conceptual Framework for Interpreting Recorded Human History* (Cambridge University Press, 2009). Spruyt's perspective is essentially an economic rationale for modern states, as it is based on economies of scale in the provision of violence. For a more general theory of state formation that makes the role of economies of scale explicit, see Yoram Barzel, *A Theory of the State: Economic Rights, Legal Rights, and the Scope of the State* (Cambridge University Press, 2002).

[69] Of course, power without constraint undermines commitment to individual liberties, which ultimately undermines a liberal state. See, e.g., David Stasavage, *Public Debt and the Birth of the Democratic State: France and Great Britain, 1688–1789* (Cambridge University Press, 2003); and Douglass C. North and Barry R. Weingast, "Constitutions and Commitment: The Evolution of Institutions Governing Public Choice in England," *Journal of Economic History* 49 (1989): 803–32.

[70] William Ker Muir, *Police: Street Corner Politicians* (University of Chicago Press, 1977). This theory is similar to cognitive dissonance theory in social psychology. See, e.g., Joel Cooper, *Cognitive Dissonance: Fifty Years of a Classic Theory* (Sage, 2007)

Glenn Gray's psychological and phenomenological analysis in *The Warriors* of the ways that soldiers cope with the *sui generis* strains of war parallels Muir's treatment in many respects. Based on his observations of colleagues, Gray constructed character types that reflect how his different comrades dealt with the experiences of force, love, friendship, and ethics under the extraordinary pressures of war. As mentioned previously, some fellow soldiers caved into debasement or depravity, while others managed to transcend their circumstances and arrive at a deeper understanding of war and life that they had not previously possessed. Others simply struggled, falling in between these two poles, or became psychological casualties. Muir maintains that the best police officers implicitly understand Max Weber's concept of the "ethic of responsibility," which accepts the fact that the world is tragic in nature, and that those with responsibilities to others must sometimes act in ways that support some values while simultaneously challenging or compromising other values. Principles and values must be prioritized, and moral maturity requires developing the capacity to exercise responsible judgment in the face of tension and doubt. Weber contrasted the ethic of responsibility with the Christian-Kantian ethic of ultimate ends, which holds that moral virtue is an end in itself regardless of the empirical consequences, and that tragic clashes of values can be avoided by absolutist thinking.[71] Good officers recognize that moral tension comes with the territory. Muir insists that education in the uses of power is essential to developing the knowledge and character needed in good officers.

Because violence is central to soldiering and war – however much soldiers' duties have expanded in the modern military – military-related studies and exposures can place the question of violence in especially stark relief, raising a host of moral questions and insights into how human beings should act under trying circumstances. In his effort to reconceptualize and justify military sociology, for example, Eric Ouellet has argued that the study of organized violence is what truly distinguishes the subfield:

> Another important opportunity for military sociology, in the expansion of its epistemological reach, is the possibility of defining a specific social realm for study, rather than a specific formal institution. . . . The central construct, which appears to me as already latent in military sociology, is violence or, more accurately, organized violence. Military sociology is the sociology of organized violence.[72]

[71] See the analysis of these two ethics in Max Weber, "Politics as a Vocation," in *Max Weber: Essays in Sociology*, edited by C. Wright Mills, translated by Hans H. Gerth (Oxford University Press, 1946). Those who rely exclusively on international law belong in the camp of ultimate ends (best represented by Kant's notion of perpetual peace and his commitment to moral duty based on ultimate ends), while others downplay international law and focus more on the role of power in achieving international justice and national interest. See, e.g., Robert Kagan, *Of Paradise and Power: America and Europe in the New World Order* (Alfred A. Knopf, 2003).

[72] Eric Ouellet, "New Directions in Military Sociology," in Ouellet, ed., *New Directions in Military Sociology* (de Sitter, 2005), pp. 22–3. This distinctive aspect of the military profession is also a theme in Samuel P. Huntington's *The Soldier and the State: The Theory and Politics of Civil-Military Relations* (Harvard University Press, 1957).

Leadership decisions in ROTC and actual military practice pivot around moral dilemmas involving violence and the ethics of conducting war. Leadership courses – the core of ROTC – stress the types of moral dilemmas that are inherent to the ethic of responsibility as envisioned by Weber and Muir: How should I act under pressure? How do I resolve moral and legal conflicts? When should I obey orders and when not? When is decisive violent action necessary? The seminal ROTC text, *Ethics and the Military Profession: The Moral Foundations of Leadership*, for example, is a tour de force in readings about the complexities and vicissitudes of moral judgment in the trying circumstances of military life. The text supports those who claim that the military has perhaps the most distinctive and meaningful professional responsibility code of any occupation. The extensive six hundred–page work is meant to be read alongside separate classic texts, and contains numerous writings of philosophers and military thinkers, treating a host of important topics. The text's major sections include the following topics: "Why Study Ethics?"; "The Moral Framework of Military Service"; "The U.S. Constitution and the Moral Foundations of Military Service: Conflicts of Principles and Loyalties"; "Religion and Military Ethics"; "Traditions of Moral Reasoning" (for example, Hobbesian mutual advantage, Kantian duty, utilitarianism, natural law, Aristotelian virtue, and so on); "The Moral Role of the Military Professional in International Relations"; "The Moral Code of the Warrior (*Jus in Bello*)"; "Upholding Truth, Enforcing Justice, and Defending Liberty and Rights"; and "Moral Leaders and Moral Warriors." Themes that recur throughout the text are the importance of military ethics as a distinct code that intersects yet also differs from other ethical systems; the contingency and difficulty of exercising judgment in sometimes trying circumstances; and the importance of synthesizing general knowledge of ethics, philosophy, and human nature with insights gained from practical experience. The first major reading, "Why Ethics Is So Hard," by Navy Captain Thomas B. Grassey, concludes:

> The bottom line of our profession's ethics is that we may have to lay down our lives in the service of our nation. No discussion of military ethics should lose sight of that fact. It is a hard truth, one not to be obscured by banal assurances. ... What is true is that our profession's ethics compels every service member's attention because its implementation is his or her responsibility, and nothing about it is easy.[73]

As mentioned, our survey respondents often accentuated the significance of leadership. One interviewee, Ted Graske, a graduate of Columbia University and its Naval ROTC program in 1959 and the alumni leader of Columbia

[73] Captain Thomas B. Grassey, U.S. Air Force Academy, "Why Ethics Is So Hard," in George R. Lucas and Captain W. Rick Rubel., eds., *Ethics and the Military Profession: The Moral Foundations of Leadership*, Second Edition (Pearson, Longman, 2007), p. 17. This book is used in ROTC leadership courses in all branches. See also Interview with Captain Scott Mobley, Naval ROTC Commander, University of Wisconsin, Madison, October 2007.

Advocates for ROTC, had this to say about how ROTC complemented the excellent liberal education he received at Columbia College:

> Made you think as well, made you face issues that, "Oh, I didn't think about that." And so, on the one hand, you'd think about what Plato meant, and on the other you'd think about what would happen if you were in the middle of the ocean and there was a tremendous storm and you were in charge. "What would you do?" So you had to think. I would call it, not critical thinking, but approaching critical thinking – practical thinking, more responsibility.[74]

As we discussed previously, Harvard dean Harry Lewis considers ROTC one of "most powerful leadership training programs."[75] Nonetheless, many universities exclude ROTC and, where ROTC programs and leadership programs exist on campus, there is often little effort to coordinate programs.[76]

In addition, the willingness to use legitimate violence when necessary can be a sign of one's acceptance of the obligation to honor serious commitments – a cardinal aspect of integrity. If we believe in something that matters, we must be willing to defend it by appropriate means – however difficult – or we risk throwing our commitment into question. Meaning can be more important than life itself.[77] Of course, integrity can also mean *not* using violence if doing so would undermine one's core beliefs and integrity. Shannon French convincingly maintains that the internalization of ethical limits regarding the use of violence is part of the *very definition and meaning* of the "code of the warrior."[78] This is why some people risk their lives to avoid doing something that would not allow them to live with themselves afterward. In *The Warriors*, Glenn Gray presents examples of soldiers who risk a great deal – including death and

[74] Interview with Ted Graske, Columbia Advocates for ROTC, April 2008.

[75] Lewis, *Excellence Without a Soul*, p. 42.

[76] We would be interested to quantify the degree of integration of ROTC into the hundreds of leadership programs, departments, and institutes in the United States. Our casual observation suggests that there is not much integration of these programs despite the fact that the military has programs that help universities set up leadership programs. For example, an ROTC instructor from the Three Rivers Battalion at the University of Pittsburgh pointed out to us that Duquesne University recently created a new leadership studies program without any consultation of ROTC. We also spoke with a director of a leadership studies program at the University of Pittsburgh who could not recall whether they had any input from ROTC in formulating their program (our investigation revealed they did not) despite a substantial military presence at the university in terms of ROTC and a nationally recognized outreach program for veterans. In Chapter 11, we discuss how such integration has occurred at Duke.

[77] Michael Gelven presents a penetrating analysis of war and integrity in *War and Existence*. According to Nietzsche, man would rather die than have no meaning whatsoever. Gelven draws on Nietzsche often in his work.

[78] Shannon E. French, *The Code of the Warrior: Exploring Warrior Values Past and Present* (Rowman and Littlefield, 2003).

execution in the case of Nazi soldiers – by refusing to obey orders to commit atrocities in war.[79]

George Fletcher and Jens David Ohlin's book on domestic and international self-defense law affords an interesting angle from which to think about war, law, and ethics. These authors maintain that lawyers and philosophers have consistently entertained different perspectives regarding the principles and rules of warfare: Philosophers deduce their guiding principles abstractly, whereas lawyers are much more interested in how rules pan out in application. Philosophers tend to be less understanding of military necessity than lawyers, and Fletcher and Ohlin even go so far as to suggest a subtle bias on philosophers' part against the military. They also claim that philosophers and lawyers seldom interact in this domain, nor read one another's work.[80] Clearly such interaction could lead to a positive friction between the two approaches that could be pedagogically productive. (One could even claim that pedagogical responsibility *requires* serious consideration of both approaches.) Though Fletcher and Ohlin do not do so, one could add military history and studies dealing with war from soldiers' perspectives to the mix. Students then would have to grapple with the question of how to reconcile the need for rules and principles with the urgencies and necessities of actual war. As the noted military historian John Keegan remarks in *The Face of Battle*, war is fraught with danger and contingencies that create their own necessities. "'Battle,' for the ordinary soldier, is a very small scale situation which will throw up its own leaders and will be fought by its own rules – alas, often by its own ethics."[81]

Grappling with all of these perspectives and tensions could deepen and sharpen moral reasoning, demonstrating the difficulty of moral choice in trying circumstances. The tension between ultimate moral ends and specific applications involving competing responsibilities is a central conundrum in moral reasoning. As the ROTC leadership text previously discussed affirms repeatedly, acknowledging the complexity, difficulty, and contingency of ethical judgment *is not the same thing as moral relativism* – indeed, quite the opposite. Moral relativism is tiresome and complacent, seeing only complexity but not the moral truth that shines behind the shadows of historical existence. It does not inspire the tension of the soul that is the sign of moral seriousness, the maturity of which accepts the reality of objective contingency in an imperfect world. As Grassey remarks after discussing the beliefs of Aristotle, St. Paul, and Jefferson that "nothing in 'the heavens' could crash to earth, and that slavery is morally acceptable.... If even the greatest thinkers of any age can be in error about such important facts, we must be humble about the possibility – the inevitability – of errors about science and ethics. But this is intellectual honesty, not relativism."[82]

[79] Gray, *The Warriors*, ch. 6. See also the path-breaking work on shooting to miss by S. L. A. Marshall, *Men Against Fire* (Peter Smith, 1978). Dave Grossman builds on Marshall's findings in *On Killing: The Psychological Cost of Learning to Kill in War and Society* (Little, Brown, 1995). Shooting to miss can constitute a dereliction of duty, of course.

[80] George P. Fletcher and Jens David Ohlin, *Defending Humanity: When Force Is Justified and Why* (Oxford University Press, 2008), ch. 1.

[81] Keegan, *The Face of Battle*, p. 47.

[82] Grassey, "Why Ethics Is So Hard," p. 14.

Hans Morgenthau also taught students that moral judgment in international politics is complicated by two realities: the intellectual obligation to acknowledge the obvious differences among the moral codes of different political regimes and militaries; and the concomitant ethical obligation to render moral judgment that transcends such relativity. Facing such tension in an ethically responsible way could be an example of the "higher practicality":

> Nobody knows with absolute certainty what absolute justice requires in a particular situation. Which is exactly the Aristotelian point of view. I have convictions about what justice requires, and I have convictions about the objective validity of my convictions. But since I am not a party to the councils of providence, I can only make judgments with a limited outlook. . . . I can only hope that I approximate objective and absolute justice.[83]

In Part II, we will report some examples of soldier-students correcting the uninformed moral judgments of non-military students in some interesting instances. One example is of a veteran student who countered the inexperienced class consensus that using deadly force to protect ones' self is an easy thing to do emotionally; other examples entail enlightening students of the difference between justifiable and nonjustifiable force.

Intellectual and Moral Diversity on Campus

Finally, an appropriate military presence on campus can contribute to intellectual and moral diversity. In many respects, the military mind contrasts with the conventional wisdom and assumptions of much campus life today. Many universities tend to be more hospitable to such things as peace studies and non-military approaches to international problems, as the questionable status of military history suggests. Whereas some scholars now question the degree to which the military mind differs from the civilian mind, our research has constantly shown us that a gap does prevail between military and university sentiments and thinking.[84] For example, the frequency of instances of campus harassment that we chronicle in the next section of this book almost certainly exceeds the frequency of such indignities taking place in the general society. Our commander/cadet and non-military student survey respondents often underscored the way in which ROTC presence contributed to campus diversity.

In *The Soldier and the State*, Samuel Huntington devotes an interesting chapter to depicting an ideal type of "the military mind." In addition to being shaped by standards of professionalism that make the military a distinctive career, the professional soldier is patriotic and a supporter of tradition and

[83] Morgenthau to a student in *Political Theory and International Affairs: Hans J. Morgenthau on Aristotle's The Politics*, edited by Anthony F. Lang (Praeger, 2004), pp. 100–1. See generally Chapter 4, "Ethics and Politics." This book consists of transcripts of Morgenthau's seminars (1970–3) on Aristotle's *The Politics* conducted at the New School in New York City.

[84] For a study that questions the split, see Darryl W. Driver, "The Military Mind: A Reassessment of the Ideological Roots of American Military Professionalism," in Suzanne C. Nielson and Don M. Snider, eds., *American Civil-Military Relations: The Soldier and the State in a New Era* (Johns Hopkins University Press, 2009), pp. 172–93.

community. He or she also believes that the nation-state is the central institution of political reality and legitimacy. Beyond these features, the so-called military mind is characterized by "conservative realism," which lies at the heart of the "professional military ethic." Conservative realism is a deeper state of mind than conservatism in a partisan sense; it shares a lot in common with a tragic sense of the world, which is perhaps one reason that soldiers and observers of war have written so much noteworthy literature and poetry. (This point is ours, not Huntington's.) Nor is the military mind the same thing as "militarism," which endorses a polity dedicated to military virtues and pursuits. (Indeed, the military mind in Huntington's portrayal is reluctant to resort to force – a portrayal we encountered often in our interviews of ROTC officers and cadets, and which is consistent with the views of many military officers in history.)[85] Nevertheless, the military mind believes that human nature, social order, and international life are such that conflict can never be fully eliminated from the world. Furthermore, the all-pervasive reality of human weakness and self-interest means that the successful resolution of conflict sometimes requires "organization, discipline, and leadership." But despite the highly developed organization of modern warfare, the conduct of war remains highly uncertain, riveted by chance. Uncertainty and chance

> make the military man skeptical of the range of human foresight and control. As between reason and irrationality in man, the military ethic emphasizes the limits of reason. The best schemes of men are frustrated by the "friction" existing in reality. "War is the province of uncertainty," Clausewitz said; "three-fourths of the things on which action in war is based lie hidden in the fog of greater or less uncertainty."...
>
> Man has elements of goodness, strength, and reason, but he is also evil, weak, and irrational. The man of the military ethic is essentially the man of Hobbes.[86]

Huntington and others have contrasted the so-called military mind with the values that characterize civilian society generally. Civil society, in this view, is marked by the Lockean values that Louis Hartz articulated in his classic book *The Liberal Tradition in America*: individual freedom, self-fulfillment, political representation, free markets, and equality under the rule of law. The mentality of liberalism is further dedicated to the amelioration of the human condition through the pursuit of reason, happiness, and individual fulfillment.[87] The tension between the military and civilian minds is perhaps a manifestation of the broader historical friction that has persisted throughout American history between civil society and the standing military.

[85] One example is the so-called Powell Doctrine, which General Colin Powell espoused, restricting the resort to war to situations of true necessity or total force and likelihood of success.

[86] Huntington, *The Soldier and the State*, p. 63. See also all of ch. 3.

[87] Huntington, *The Soldier and the State*, p. 63; see also all of ch. 3. Louis Hartz, *The Liberal Tradition in America*. See also the comparison of Hartz and Huntington in Michael Desch, "Hartz, Huntington, and the Liberal Tradition in America," in Nielson and Snider, *American Civil-Military Relations*.

Many students we know would find the depiction of the world that Huntington portrays to be unsettling; but being unsettled is an important part of the educational process. Many other students would find it fascinating, partly because it contrasts so vibrantly with everyday life and conventional wisdom on campus. As we will see in Part II of this book, many non-military students at Wisconsin underscored the ways that exposure to ROTC broadened their minds and the intellectual diversity of the campus.

And then there is the matter of student lifestyles. Like conscientious athletes, ROTC students must act according to special norms of discipline and conduct. They must follow disciplined routines, and they often have to get up early in the morning to perform tasks while most of their fellow students remain asleep. There are also norms of appropriate behavior in class and elsewhere, especially when in uniform. Several of our survey respondents mentioned observing the tasks and responsibilities to which ROTC students commit themselves; most students related that they had not realized such commitment was necessary, and that they respected these efforts, though a few were less respectful.

Many individuals we have encountered in the course of this study assert that the military should have no presence on campus because its values are inconsistent with those of the university. This position is problematic in two senses. First, it ignores the nuances that exist in the phenomenology of command and obedience in the military. Soldiers' primary oath is to the Constitution, not the military, and they are expected to appropriately question orders that are ill-conceived or unlawful, albeit within strict guidelines.[88] Second, following orders is not necessarily a sign of a personal surrender of integrity, but often quite the opposite. If we commit ourselves to duties or meanings beyond ourselves, then we necessarily assume the responsibility to obey the command of what must be done to honor that commitment. In *War and Existence*, philosopher Michael Gelven goes so far as to proclaim that the dialectic of command and obedience is a cardinal aspect of an authentic existence. Gelven quotes from a fascinating passage in Nietzsche's *Thus Spoke Zarathustra*, "On Self-Overcoming," in which Nietzsche "pierced to the very core of his inquiry into the meaning of existence." Zarathustra remarks:

> Wherever I found the living, there I heard also the speech on obedience. Whatever lives obeys.
>
> And this is the second point: he who cannot obey himself is commanded. That is the nature of the living.
>
> This, however, is the third point that I heard: that commanding is harder than obeying: and not only because he who commands must carry the burden of all who obey, and because this burden may easily crush him.... It must become the judge, the avenger, and the victim of its own law.

[88] See, e.g., *Ethics and the Military Profession: The Moral Foundations of Leadership*. Interview with Mobley, October 2007.

Gelven observes that the making and obeying of laws are part of what give meaning to life. "For Nietzsche, who is seeking the meaning of human existence, the power of law giving is indeed awesome and wonderful, for through it we transcend our simple particularity; we become no longer merely men but are now able to go beyond such limits, to go beyond ourselves."[89]

In an essay comparing military education at West Point to education at Harvard, Patrick Hoy (a West Point graduate and former Army officer who has taught English and writing at West Point, Harvard, and New York University), makes an observation that builds on Gelven's insight. Hoy agrees with those who claim that military education and civilian education differ. Soon after he came to Harvard, he realized how much more Harvard valued individual intellectual freedom than did West Point, which emphasizes routine and efficiency. Cadets are more concerned with the application of knowledge than the "sheer thrill of thinking," which reflects the pragmatic character of the military. But after teaching at Harvard a while, Hoy came to realize that Harvard's individualism came with its own liabilities:

> Most here [at Harvard] wouldn't be able to fathom the mystery of command that binds people together in those benevolent hierarchies, creating what my friend Roy Reed calls the "throngs of community." Harvard can pay respect to such an idea, but it's an idea that doesn't take root here. The reality of shared responsibility and teamwork is as hard to experience at Harvard as unfettered freedom is at West Point.... At West Point, from day one – even as cadets are learning to stand up under the most grueling individual tests – they are always investing themselves in each other's lives.

Interestingly, Hoy also found that while Harvard esteemed individual intellect, it paradoxically lacked a truly vibrant exchange of ideas. "To challenge someone's ideas at Harvard is to challenge the person. Within this loose federation of brilliant individuals, I do not find a free and open marketplace of ideas. I find instead that people cling quietly, and sometimes desperately, to their own ideas. Yet if their organizational work – the real work of the university itself – is to be effective, it must challenge the known."[90] Hoy concludes his essay by imagining an appropriate synthesis between the two models. A creative coexistence of the two modes of learning could enhance intellectual and moral insight and responsibility. Hoy's thoughts offer a fertile ground for our own inquiry. Jose Robledo, a veteran student in Columbia University's School of General Studies, enunciated a similar notion of productive friction in an interview in October 2010:

89 Nietzsche, *Thus Spoke Zarathustra*, "On Self-Overcoming," in Gelven, *War and Existence*, p. 36. Nietzsche's portrayal of the burdens of command is similar in many respects to Clausewitz's depiction of the burdens of commanding officers in warfare. See Clausewitz, *On War*, especially Book I, Chapter 3, "The Genius for War."

90 Pat C. Hoy, "Soldiers and Scholars: Between Harvard and West Point, a Deep – and Dangerous – Cultural Chasm," *Harvard Magazine* 98, 5 (1996). See also Oliver Wendell Holmes, Jr., "The Fraternity of Arms," in Richard A. Posner, ed., *The Essential Holmes: Selections from the Letters, Speeches, Judicial Opinions, and Other Writings* (University of Chicago Press, 1992), pp. 73–4.

> [T]he way I look at it is, the way the military thinks, the way the military wants you to think, is very much dependent on a very rigorous, methodical decision-making process much like an engineer would require. But there is still an element of military thinking that is critical analysis of unknowns. That's the liberal arts tradition, to be able to critically analyze the unknown. To call into question and find solutions to things that have never been thought of before, [things] that are in the abstract. So I think the military is a nice straddle between these two worlds that already exist at Columbia. The problem is that we have not figured out how to make these two cogs at Columbia [work together].[91]

Another value that a military presence can provide on campus is courage. Plato and other thinkers have portrayed courage as the preeminent virtue of the military class, and Aristotle places it at the center of the human virtues. (He said it is the virtue that guarantees all the other virtues.) But what is courage? Gelven discerns two aspects in it: acting despite the fear of the threat that one confronts, and "the counter-fear that I shall not have the courage to confront it honorably." Courage is ultimately about honoring or holding up one's sense of self-worth in the face of danger or pressure. "Without the second fear all courage becomes mere prudence; I should simply get out of the way of the first threat. To sustain one's own courage, then, requires an appeal to one's sense of one's own worth. Cowardice is simply not worthy of me."[92] In other words, courage is a matter of personal integrity.

Courage can also mean extending oneself beyond the security of what one thought was one's limit of endurance, discovering previously untapped capacities. Such stretching entails risk, exposing the old self to a kind of death. An example of instruction in this process is the pedagogical mission of Lieutenant Colonel Timothy A. Slauenwhite, former commander of the Air Force ROTC at the Massachusetts Institute of Technology (MIT). Slauenwhite told us in an interview that one of his major goals in field exercises and operations is to challenge his cadets to test their limits so that they discover inner strength and ability that they had not imagined they had.[93] Among the virtues that Slauenwhite stresses are courage and the willingness to go beyond the limits of one's sense of endurance. Every experienced soldier with whom we have spoken expressed thoughts compatible with those of General Dwight Eisenhower in the aftermath of World War II., when he remarked, "I hate war as only a soldier who has lived it can, only as one who has seen its brutality, its futility, its stupidity."[94] (In his First Inaugural Address, Eisenhower also said, "History does not long entrust the care of freedom

[91] Interview with Jose Robledo, Columbia University Student, October 2010.

[92] Gelven, *War and Existence*, p. 121. See, generally, pp. 119–24.

[93] Interview with Lt. Col. Timothy A. Slauenwhite, Commander of the MIT Air Force ROTC., October 2007.

[94] General Dwight D. Eisenhower, Speech at Canada Club, Ottawa, Canada, January 10, 1946: http://www.eisenhowermemorial.org/speeches/19460110%20Speech%20at%20Canada%20Club%20Ottawa%20Canada.htm. See also John Keegan's critique of political theories and models of citizenship dedicated to martial values and war (e.g., Clausewitz, Samurai, the Mamelukes, and other "cults of the sword," p. 45) in *A History of Warfare* (Vintage, Random House, 1993), ch. 1. "War truly has become a scourge" (p. 59).

to the weak or the timid." As Gelven notes, war is profoundly paradoxical.) The reluctance to resort to arms can even be considered part of the Soldier's Creed. That said, war – like courage – can also be a reflection of one's integrity and willingness to stand up for one's beliefs. If you believe in something, if you stand for something, you must be willing to defend it in a world of conflicting forces:

> An artist who dedicates his life to beauty, a philosopher who dedicates his life to truth, or a saint who dedicates his life to God's will – all repudiate the ranking of life itself as the highest goal. The warrior also rejects such hierarchy. Not only is he willing to forfeit his own life for the sake of his country, he is willing to forfeit the lives of the enemy to ensure that this institution is not eclipsed by foreign control. ... For a man to take up arms in defense of his country, then, can be seen as stemming from the more original meaning of a man affirming the worth of his own being.[95]

A final aspect of diversity should be mentioned. Universities today have correctly been busy promoting international and cosmopolitan perspectives, and programs dedicated to this purpose dot the higher education landscape. In some cases, however, the perspective of American citizenship and values is given less emphasis. Jeff Kwong, an undergraduate ROTC activist at Harvard to whom we spoke in the fall of 2007, observed that ROTC's marginal status at Harvard was partly a function of its identification with Americanism and patriotism as opposed to internationalism. He talked about the controversy that arose in 2006 and 2007 over instituting the new General Education Program because one of the areas of inquiry focused on America. After sometimes acrimonious objections were raised, this area was named "The United States *in* the World" as opposed to such designations as "America *and* the World." Even then, discomfort remained in some quarters. According to Kwong, "On campus there's a feeling of internationality. It's very much an international institution. ... If you walk down Harvard Yard, the likelihood of hearing English being spoken is really low; usually I hear Korean or Chinese. So we are an international university, so I think that's part of it." Former Harvard dean Harry Lewis expressed a similar concern in his book critiquing higher education at Harvard. Regarding the new program:

> There seems to be nothing in particular Harvard wants its graduates to understand about the United States, other than what comes in proportion to its wealth and military influence within the global society. Perhaps Harvard no longer thinks of itself as an American college at all but is looking to become a global college in same way that during the last century it became a national rather than regional college.

In Chapter 4 we will examine the rise of Harvard and other institutions as preeminently American institutions during the course of the twentieth century.[96]

[95] Gelven, *War and Existence*, pp. 92, 213.

[96] Interview with Harvard student Jeff Kwong, November 2007; Lewis, *Excellence Without a Soul*, p. 63. See, generally, pp. 62–70. Huntington's model of the "military mind" also includes an emphasis upon the nation-state over internationalism. A good book on the "Americanization" of Harvard is Richard Norton Smith's *The Harvard Century: The Making of a University to a Nation* (Simon and Schuster, 1986). We will draw on Smith's book in Chapter 4.

During the Senate debate at Columbia University in April 2011 that led to the vote to return some form of ROTC to the campus, this tension arose. A graduate student speaker argued that ROTC and the military were inconsistent with Columbia's new mission regarding world outreach, global presence, and internationalism. Her comments received applause. Her views were countered by two faculty members (one from India), who said that ROTC was needed to expose the military to this mission, as well as to add diversity of viewpoints to the campus. Internationalism and Americanism are not always distinct; and when they do differ, such difference is good for the university. Our point here is not to trumpet Americanism over internationalism, but rather simply to emphasize the importance of both perspectives in the contemporary university. It is ironic that a movement designed to increase diversity in the form of global perspectives can actually lead to less diversity, as Lewis and Kwong suggest in their preceding comments. We discuss this fundamental tension again in Chapter 7.[97]

CONCLUSION

These are just some of the ways in which an appropriate military presence on campus can broaden the intellectual and moral diversity of today's campuses. In later sections of the book, we will examine the ways in which our interviewees and respondents represented, or did not represent, these ideas. Because many of the ideas presented here have been drawn from the thoughts of thinkers who have spent considerable time reflecting on these matters, they have a certain universal appeal. Accordingly, we should not be surprised to find many aspects of them reflected in the thoughts of our respondents, though in individuated forms.

Let us now turn to a discussion of the history, presence, and reform of the university–military gap, beginning with the status and history of ROTC on campus.

[97] Columbia University Senate meeting, April 1, 2011, based on notes taken by coauthor Downs.

PART II

ROTC AND THE UNIVERSITY

3

ROTC and the University

An Introduction

> First comes the courage of the citizen-soldier; for this is the most like true courage. Citizen-soldiers seem to face dangers because of the penalties imposed by the laws and the reproaches they would otherwise incur; and because of the honours they win by such action; and therefore those peoples seem to be bravest among whom cowards are held in dishonour. This is the kind of courage that Homer depicts.
>
> – Aristotle[1]

> The most successful tyranny is not the one that uses force to assure uniformity, but the one that removes awareness of other possibilities.
>
> – Allan Bloom[2]

As we have stressed in the first two chapters, a liberal or civic education involves a process of conflict between an individual's preconceived beliefs and the beliefs of others as they update their views based on their exposure to competing and contrasting ideas. Some of the greatest contrasts are between student-soldiers and civilians on campus. The university often involves an active, physical presence of the military on campus in the form of ROTC – a presence that has often engendered tensions, as we will discuss in the following chapters. It also raises questions that we will seek to answer. What are the benefits of physical presence of student-soldiers – primarily through ROTC – for a university? Are there conflicts between civilians and student-soldiers? What explains the emergence, decline, and resurgence of ROTC on campus? These questions are critical to understanding the relationship between arms and the university – ones to which we hope to offer preliminary answers in the chapters that follow.

To motivate our inquiry, we return to the insights of Samuel Huntington, who argued that the emergence of effective civil–military relations requires appropriate autonomy of the military. A critical aspect of this autonomy is the

[1] Aristotle, *The Nichomachean Ethics of Aristotle*, translated by William David Ross, Book III, Chapter 8 (CreateSpace, 2011).

[2] Allan Bloom, *The Closing of the American Mind*, 1st Touchstone Edition (Simon and Schuster, 1988).

professionalization of the military;[3] but the constitutional scheme also calls for a sufficient connection between the military and civil society, lest the military become alienated from the general citizenry. Concern about the dangers posed to republican government by a professional standing military is deeply woven into the fabric of the American political tradition, and the All-Volunteer Force represents the first time in American history that a purely voluntary military is the norm in fighting the nation's wars. So the military must be effectively controlled by the public; but for this to happen, the public must sufficiently understand the military perspective. As theorists of institutional design maintain, institutions with separate missions (as in the constitutional system of checks and balances) must still speak to each other in order to attain public interest out of the mesh of their differences.[4] The public do not need to be in the military, but neither should they be entirely alien to the political culture of the military if we hope to formulate effective public policies and mutual understanding. Effective control requires political institutions to understand military ones, and vice versa.

One of the most prominent and traditional methods for achieving this auspicious dialectical balance is to promote integration of the university and the military, thereby providing benefits that go beyond professional discipline. The rationale for such integration is typically the benefit that the university brings to the military. In 1970, for example, when ROTC confronted peril because of controversy generated by the Vietnam War, the Association of State Universities and Land-Grant Colleges declared in a report that ROTC was "one of the best guarantees against the establishment in this country of a military caste or clique." A year later at the Continental Army Command's annual ROTC Conference, Dr. Lee S. Dreyfus, president of Wisconsin State University at Stevens Point and chair of the Army Advisory Panel on ROTC Affairs, proclaimed that the ROTC "is not the presence of the Army on the campus," but rather "the presence of the university in the Army." He went on to express his fear of the "elitism" that would tighten its grip on the officer corps if ROTC were abolished, for ROTC is "the key anti-militaristic check balance in the Army."[5] Concern about the elitism and separateness of professional officers trained at the academies has existed throughout American history and was the leading impulse behind three important milestones in the history of military education: the formation of civilian military colleges (including Norwich University, the Citadel, and Virginia Military College) in the first decades of the nineteenth century, which spawned military education programs at other institutions;

[3] Samuel P. Huntington, *The Soldier and the State: The Theory and Politics of Civil–Military Relations* (Harvard University Press, 1957).

[4] See, e.g., David L. Weimer, ed., *Institutional Design* (Kluwer Academic, 1995).

[5] Quoted in Arthur T. Coumbe, "Why ROTC? The Debate over Collegiate Military Training, 1969–1973," *Air & Space Power Journal Chronicles Online Journal*, September 30, 1999: http://www.airpower.maxwell.af.mil/airchronicles/cc/coumbe.html, quoting Robert L. Goldich, *The Senior Reserve Officer Training Corps: Recent Trends and Current Status* (Congressional Research Service, 1974), p. 2; and "Educators and Cadets Address ROTC Conference," *Army ROTC Newsletter* 5, 5 (September–October 1971): 1.

the passage in 1862 of the Morrill Act, which required "military training" in the land grant institutions established or affected by the act; and the 1916 National Defense Act's creation of ROTC as the preeminent form of "military education" in civilian institutions. Michael S. Neiberg, reports that, "The army's General Staff saw the creation of ROTC as the 'only foreseeable option ... to a greatly expanded military academy.'"[6]

There is also a competing view of ROTC: that it serves to militarize the university and the young. Lance C. Buhl presented this view in an article written in the *Harvard Bulletin* in May 1970, when antiwar sentiment was at a peak on college campuses. According to Buhl, General Leonard Wood, an "intellectual father" of ROTC, intended ROTC to be a vehicle for militarizing and regimenting the young in the name of national service – a process at odds with the individualism for which liberal democracy properly stands. "Concerned in 1916 with building a mass army, he [Wood] forcefully misstated the purpose and nature of democracy itself: 'Manhood suffrage means manhood obligation for service in peace or war.'"[7] Buhl further argued that ROTC had failed to provide meaningful civilian influence over the military. Buhl's position echoed the earlier allegations of the national Committee on Militarism in Education (1925–40), which strove to eliminate ROTC.[8] Buhl did not provide thorough empirical validation of his claim, and the validity of such claims is historically contingent. The ROTC of the late twentieth and early twenty-first centuries is a different creature from the ROTC of the 1910s and 1920s. As we will see in this and subsequent chapters, universities now maintain much more meaningful academic control over ROTC programs, making them considerably more subject to civilian academic influence and control than in the 1920s and even when Buhl wrote his article. That said, Buhl's perspective merits due respect. As we will see in this chapter, the citizen-soldier model has not always lived up to its ideals, and it would be naïve and foreign to the philosophy of this book to think that ROTC's influence is invariably positive or unidimensional. The question is whether ROTC on balance promotes a more propitious relationship between military and civilian values. Even if one concludes that it does – as we do – it is prudent to bear Buhl's concerns in mind in order to check any militaristic tendencies that might be attributed to ROTC's influence.

In this chapter, we provide the conceptual framework that will guide our inquiry into the relationship between *physical* military presence and the university. We begin by providing an assessment of the citizen-soldier ideal. After delineating issues surrounding the citizen-soldier ideal, we refine the theoretical

[6] Michael S. Neiberg, *Making Citizen Soldiers: ROTC and the Ideology of American Military Service* (Harvard University Press, 2001), pp. 23–4. See also Eugene M. Lyons and John W. Masland, *Education and Military Leadership: A Study of the R.O.T.C.* (Princeton University Press, 1959).

[7] Lance C. Buhl, "The Military–Civilian Complex," Part 2, *Harvard Bulletin*, May 25, 1970, p. 23.

[8] See, for example, Roswell P. Barnes, with an introduction by John Dewey, *Militarizing Our Youth: The Significance of the Reserve Officers' Training Corps in Our Schools and Colleges* (Committee on Militarism in Education, 1927).

framework that we introduced in the first two chapters. In particular, we articulate why the physical presence of the military is necessary for productive friction and hence for civic and liberal education. There will certainly be those who may object to military presence on campus. Our theoretical argument simply serves to illustrate the costs, as far as civic and liberal education are concerned, of such a stance toward the military – as well as the benefits of an appropriate military presence on campus. To state our thesis for the following chapter simply, we argue that ROTC *is* the presence of the military on campus, which is precisely why ROTC is important for civic and liberal education.

THE CITIZEN-SOLDIER IDEAL

To assess the status of ROTC on campus for our purposes, it is essential that we consider the "citizen-soldier" ideal that has been an important part of the American military tradition since the nation's inception and a cornerstone of the rationale for ROTC. Recognizing the ideal of the military will help us to avoid romanticizing military presence. But what is this ideal? At root, the citizen-soldier ideal is a product of distrust of a standing military, coexisting with a belief in the obligation of citizens (at one time only males) to defend themselves, their communities, and the nation with arms. According to Walter Millis, "The problem [of early American military policy] was to provide for an effective defense against both foreign war and domestic upheaval without trenching too far upon the jealous sovereignty of the states or rousing the universal fear and loathing of irresponsible standing armies."[9] The widely publicized near–coup d'état by senior military officer veterans of the Revolutionary Army in the Newburgh revolt of 1783 presented alarming evidence of the danger.[10] The Constitution dealt with this concern by distributing military power and policy among the president, the Congress, the states, and the citizenry. It granted the national government the power to maintain standing armies, but within constitutional limits. Meanwhile, states retained their power to control their citizen militias, which were considered the bulwark of national defense; and the people maintained their right to bear arms in the Second Amendment. In effect, the Constitution established (or, more appropriately, affirmed) three tiers of national defense: the standing Army and Navy; the states; and the citizenry.[11]

9 Walter Millis, *Arms and Men: A Study of American Military History* (Mentor, New American Library, 1956), pp. 41–2. For important documentary evidence of this concern, see the essays of Madison and Hamilton regarding standing armies and national defense, nos. 8, 16, 24–6, 29, 41, 45, 85, in *The Federalist Papers*, edited by Clinton Rossiter (New American Library, 1961).

10 On this unsuccessful revolt, see Neiberg, *Making Citizen Soldiers*, pp. 14–15.

11 Millis, *Arms and Men*, pp. 41–2. On the individualist intent of the Second Amendment, see Sanford Levinson, "The Embarrassing Second Amendment," 99 *Yale Law Journal* 637 (1989); *District of Columbia v. Heller*, 128 S.Ct. 2783 (2008). William H. Riker emphasizes the importance of the states in the development of an American military force. See William H. Riker, *Soldiers of the States* (Public Affairs Press, 1957).

We could call this rationale for the citizen-soldier ideal the "negative theory": The citizen-soldier exists as a check against the negative potentials of a standing military. A "positive" theory also exists based on the political theory of republicanism. Before the advent of the All-Volunteer Force (AVF) in the early 1970s, Americans acted upon their distrust of a standing military by accepting (to varying extents) the common obligation to share in the duty and burden of national defense, as epitomized by the Minuteman or the "embattled farmer" of Ralph Waldo Emerson. Andrew Bacevich contends, "For the generations that fought the Civil War and the world wars, and even those who served in the 1950s and 1960s, citizenship and military service remained intimately connected. Indeed, those to whom this obligation to serve did not apply – including at various times the poor, people of color, and women – were thereby marked as ineligible for full citizenship." Bacevich laments the decline of the connection between citizenship and a shared sense of military obligation that emerged after the Vietnam era and the rise of the All-Volunteer Force.[12] The retreat by elites from this burden is most pronounced, constituting a prime example of what critical historian Christopher Lasch decried as the "revolt of the elites" against civic-democratic obligations.[13]

Bacevich's defense of a more commonly shared military burden is supported by a distinguished historical lineage. Many political theorists have pronounced the ways in which military obligations and virtues have comprised building blocks of citizenship. Political theorist William A. Galston, for example, remarks, "From Greek and Roman times down to the present, the allocation of the burden of national defense has been at the heart of citizenship." In the early liberal era, such prominent liberal thinkers as Adam Ferguson and Adam Smith also touted the importance of martial ability in the citizenry at the same time that they warned of giving too much power to the state and standing armies. In their eyes, such ability is necessary to preserving republican values – not simply to protect the public good of defense, which is the purely economic rationale for national defense.[14] It is not surprising that women and racial

[12] Andrew J. Bacevich, *The New American Militarism: How Americans Are Seduced by War* (Oxford University Press, 2005), pp. 26–7.

[13] Christopher Lasch, *The Revolt of the Elites: and the Betrayal of Democracy* (W. W. Norton, 1995). A most poignant treatment of this particular problem is Kathy Roth-Douquet and Frank Schaeffer, *AWOL: The Unexcused Absence of America's Upper Classes from the Military – and How It Hurts Our Country* ((Harper Collins, 2006). For a broader critique of elites' reneging on their obligations to the general polity, see Thomas E. Ricks, "The Widening Gap Between the Military and Society," *Atlantic Monthly*, July 1997. Ricks turned this provocative and influential essay into a book: Ricks, *Making the Corps* (Scribner, Simon and Schuster, 1997). See also William H. McMichael, "Most U.S. Youth Unfit to Serve, Data Show," *Army Times*, November 5, 2009. See also the hundreds of "Comments" to the *USA Today* story on this report, "Pentagon: A Third of U.S. Youth Too Fat, Sickly to Serve," November 4, 2009.

[14] William A. Galston, "The Challenge of Civic Engagement: An Introduction," in Verna V. Gehring, ed., *Community Matters: Challenges to Civic Engagement in the 21st Century*, (Rowan and Littlefield, 2005), pp. 2–3; Richard B. Sher, "Adam Ferguson, Adam Smith, and the Problem of National Defense," *Journal of American History* 61, 2 (1989): 240–66.

minorities historically have pressed for inclusion in the military, for service is a means of credentialing claims of equal citizenship.[15] For example, when the country and Congress debated the reintroduction of peacetime military conscription after World War II, African American leaders "campaigned for a draft that would give black inductees equal treatment and combat training opportunities."[16] These claims boil down to a powerful contention: *We are as capable of bearing the burdens – including the ultimate burden – of citizenship as anyone else.*

Some military scholars maintain that the ideal of the citizen-soldier is obsolete, having disappeared in the post–World War II era for several reasons. Eliot A. Cohen, for example, has argued that the concept is dependent upon the realistic need for mass mobilization, which creates a common obligation shared by all strata of society. This condition began to wane after World War II for numerous reasons, including the growth of technological warfare (nuclear weapons and more sophisticated conventional weaponry, which called for enhanced professionalism) and the concomitant downsizing of military organizations. The rise of the All-Volunteer Force after Vietnam then exacerbated the separation of the military from the general society, rendering the citizen-soldier ideal a "sentimentalized view" of soldiering. However much the AVF strives to be representative of American society (representativeness being a precondition of the citizen-soldier ideal), the fact remains that recruiters "pay no heed, however, to socioeconomic, religious, or other kinds of ethnic diversity in the ranks. That the children of millionaires almost never serve or that a bare handful of Ivy League graduates don a uniform is not even a matter for comment." In the decades leading up to 9/11, Charles Moskos maintained that the AVF changed the primary motive for joining the military, marginalizing republican-based models of citizen obligation in favor of *homo economicus*.[17] Research conducted after 9/11, however, has shown a resurgence of

[15] See, e.g., James Burk, "Citizenship Status and Military Service: The Quest for Inclusion by Minorities and Conscientious Objectors," *Armed Forces & Society* 21, 4 (1995). Burk traces the historical significance of the link between service and equal respect, but also the changes in society that have weakened this connection. On women's equality and military education, see Phillipa Strum, *Women in the Barracks: The VMI Case and Equal Rights* (University Press of Kansas, 2002). For a clear statement of the constitutional issues, see *United States v. Virginia, et al.*, 518 U.S. 515 (1996).

[16] Edward Bernard Glick, *Soldiers and Scholars: The Social Impact of the American Army* (Goodyear, 1971), p. 17. In recent years, however, the Army has encountered significant difficulties in recruiting African Americans into combat positions. See Arthur T. Coumbe, Paul N. Kotakis, and W. Anne Gammell, *History of the U.S. Army Cadet Command: Second 10 Years, 1996–2006* (New Forums Press, 2008), pp. 224–48.

[17] Eliot A. Cohen, "Twilight of the Citizen-Soldier," *Parameters* 31 (Summer 2001): 24. Charles Moskos, "The Marketplace All-Volunteer Force: A Critique," in William Bowman, Roger Little, and G. Thomas, eds., *The All-Volunteer Force After a Decade: Retrospect and Prospect* (Pergamon-Brassey's, 1986). See also James Burk, "The Military Obligation of Citizens Since Vietnam," *Parameters* 31 (Summer 2001).

such value-oriented motivations as patriotism.[18] The rise of a "warrior ethic," discussed in Chapter 1, perhaps reflects this revival, and it is certainly present in the survey findings of ROTC cadets we present in Chapter 8; yet alongside this motivation, we also find that for many of the cadets, money matters when it comes to joining ROTC.

Ralph Peters, a retired Army lieutenant colonel who is a frequent media commentator on the military and foreign policy issues, presented what could be considered another – highly controversial – critique. In a broadly cited 2007 article published in the *American Interest* that was juxtaposed with an essay by General David H. Petraeus praising the military's contemporary emphasis on broadly educated officers, Peters asseverated that too much education can dampen the warrior spirit that makes for a good soldier. This argument has negative implications for ROTC, as it implies that too much exposure to liberal arts students and courses can eviscerate the warrior spirit:

> Hamlet thinks too much. Chewing every side of the argument to mush, he lacks the courage to swallow hard and kill an assassin at prayer – a philosophical "war crime." The archetypal academic, theory-poisoned and indecisive, Hamlet should have stayed at the university in Wittenberg, where his ability to prattle without resolution surely would have gained him early tenure.[19]

Skeptics further argue that the citizen-soldier model has never been adhered to as faithfully as its advocates imagine, as evidenced by the myriad ways that citizens have managed to avoid military service since the days of the Revolutionary War. Yet this perspective simply reminds us that the model is an *ideal*, and as such it does not necessarily embody (at least not invariably) the reality of the situation. Others believe that the ideal is useful primarily in recruiting, helping to ameliorate the tendency of the AVF to become an "occupational" or mercenary-type force. Ronald R. Krebs, for example, conceives the model as embracing a set of rhetorical devices that helps to adjust present military realities to democratic norms. That is, the citizen-soldier model remains important as a cultural ideal because such ideals can influence identity and behavior.[20] This perspective is consistent with the cultural turn in military history scholarship that we will discuss in

[18] See Todd D. Woodruff, Ryan Kelty, and David R. Segal, "Propensity to Serve and Motivation to Enlist Among American Combat Soldiers," *Armed Forces & Society* 32 (2006): 353–66.

[19] Ralph Peters, "Learning to Lose," *American Interest* (July–August 2007); David H. Petraeus, "Beyond the Cloister," *American Interest* (July–August 2007).

[20] On the role of cultural norms in politics, see Murray Edelman, *The Symbolic Uses of Politics* (University of Illinois Press, 1964). In the same vein, Michael Chwe emphasizes that cultural norms and values are sociologically, politically, and economically significant because they coordinate individuals in the game theoretic sense. Taking this a step further, one sees that mass mobilization for war involves a formidable coordination problem, one that involves much of society. As such, cultural beliefs, such as the citizen-solider ideal, are particularly important to encourage participation in these efforts. See Michael Suk-Young Chwe, *Rational Ritual: Culture, Coordination, and Common Knowledge* (Princeton University Press, 2001).

Chapter 10. "By reconceptualizing the citizen-soldier tradition in this fashion, we become open to the ways in which it remains vibrant in the United States."[21]

This said, we must admit that the ideal is challenged by present realities, including the fact that there is far less need for mass mobilization in the United States, as indicated by the very rise of a professional volunteer military itself – for the mere existence of such a force suggests there is no need for mass mobilization. Cohen, Adrian R. Lewis, Russell F. Weigley, and others have addressed the importance of the rise of "limited wars" in the post–World War II era and how this trend has created deep contradictions for the ideal. The citizen-soldier ideal makes most cultural and strategic sense in the context of wars that engage all of society, calling forth commonly shared commitment and sacrifice. In such wars, the citizenry generally accepts significant sacrifice because so much is at stake for the nation. The Civil War, World War I, and World War II are key examples. But with the advent of the Cold War, the nation became committed to a different grand strategy that called for a defense posture manned by technological elites (the deterrence strategy based on nuclear weapons) and the fighting of smaller wars around the globe, the objectives of which were the containment of Communism or other aggressive movements rather than the total defeat of the enemy. Because limited wars are broadly deemed less "necessary," the citizenry is less willing to make the direct sacrifices necessary to fight them, especially if the wars grow in scale and last a long time – hence confronting society with the contradiction of great sacrifice required to fight a war with limited objectives. The Korean War's objective was limited, but it required the reinstitution of the draft and the calling up of the reserves and the National Guard, compelling significant sacrifice. Though restless about the war, the populace accepted that burden because the sense of citizen duty remained strong in the aftermath of World War II (the Cold War Consensus remained strong), and the conflict ended in three years. Vietnam was another matter, exposing the tensions embedded in the citizen-soldier ideal in an era of limited warfare and cultural change.[22] Lewis puts the matter clearly:

> The demise of the citizen-soldier Army began at the end of World War II when the United States became a superpower and took on new political objectives, strategies, and doctrines for war. The new role of the United States created cultural conflicts that were most evident during the Korean and Vietnam Wars, but were prevalent throughout the cold war as well. The Vietnam War caused the cultural conflict to

[21] Ronald R. Krebs, "The Citizen-Soldier Tradition in the United States: Has Its Demise Been Greatly Exaggerated?" *Armed Forces & Society* 35, 1 (2009): 154.

[22] The Cold War Consensus entailed agreement among policy elites, political elites, and the general citizenry that resistance to the Soviet Union was in the national interest. See, for example, Arthur M. Schlesinger, Jr., *The Vital Center: The Politics of Freedom* (Houghton Mifflin, 1949). The Cold War Consensus began unraveling in the 1960s, especially with the onset of the Vietnam War.

emerge into a full-blown domestic war, which ended with defeat in Vietnam and the end of the citizen-soldier Army in 1973. However, the cultural conflict is still present.[23]

Another trend that is germane to this discussion involves economics. As the nation's economy expanded in the post–Cold War era, citizens were asked to bear less financial burden, per capita, when it came to funding the military, thus disencumbering them yet further from the consequences of war. (The ongoing economic crisis that erupted in 2008, involving multiple layers of debt, is complicating the financial side of this equation as of this writing.)[24]

The debate over the contemporary relevance of the citizen-soldier model is embedded in a broader, long-standing contest over the meaning of citizenship in America. From its inception, the American political tradition has embraced both republican-communitarian and liberal-individualist political theories. Republicanism accentuates the communal obligations of citizenship as a necessary support for liberty, whereas liberalism stresses individual rights and the pursuit of happiness. Some have argued that the polity has migrated over time in the liberal direction, relegating the sense of communal obligation to secondary status and therefore weakening the sense of military obligation in the process.[25] Bernard Rotsker, a former director of the Selective Service who played a pivotal role in establishing the AVF, portrayed the AVF in decidedly individualist terms in his book on the process that led to the force's creation. "Today the all-volunteer force is one that values the individual, and through increased levels of retention, individuals signal back that they value the all-volunteer force."[26] Indeed, the AVF was inspired by the logic of such Chicago School free market economists as Milton Friedman and Martin Anderson, whose views convinced presidential candidate Richard Nixon to make the AVF an important part of his presidential platform.[27] This trend wounded the hopes of such republican

[23] Adrian R. Lewis, *The American Culture of War: The History of the U.S. Military Force from World War II to Operation Iraqi Freedom* (Routledge, 2007), p. 36. See also Eliot A. Cohen, *Citizens and Soldiers: The Dilemmas of Military Service* (Cornell University Press, 1985); and Russell F. Weigley, *The American Way of War: A History of United States Military Strategy and Policy* (Macmillan, 1973).

[24] On the changing citizen financial obligations of war, see, e.g., Robert D. Hormats, *The Price of Liberty: Paying for America's Wars* (Times Books, 2007). Hormat's book deals primarily with how the need to finance wars is an important part of warfare, and how innovations in this area have had significant impacts on future financial practices. He also shows how military expense has decreased over time per capita.

[25] See, e.g., James Burk, "Theories of Democratic Civil–Military Relations," *Armed Forces & Society* 29, 1 (Fall 2009): 9–15; and John P. Diggins, *The Lost Soul of American Politics: Virtue, Self-Interest, and the Foundations of Liberalism* (Basic, 1984).

[26] Bernard Rostker, *I Want YOU! The Evolution of the All-Volunteer Force* (Rand, 2006), p. 10. Krebs points out the significance of Rostker's emphasis on the individual, as well as his words that indicate loyalty is to the force, not the nation. Krebs, "The Citizen-Soldier Tradition in the United States," p. 156.

[27] See Beth Bailey, *America's Army: Making the All-Volunteer Force* (Harvard University Press, 2009), esp. ch. 1.

theorists as Morris Janowitz, who aspired to sustain the citizen-soldier ideal by coordinating the professional training of soldiers with a national system of voluntary service and political education. But as James Burk observed in 2002, Janowitz's hope was "not realistic" because there was little support for national service, and because "Janowitz never explains how the ideal can be sustained in the absence of mass mobilization."[28]

Lewis takes this analysis further, drawing on sociological theory about culture to conclude that American society has become more fragmented and pluralized since World War II, leading to a society of distinct "clusters," each of which possesses its own network or seamless web of cultural assumptions and norms. As national culture fragments, clusters proliferate. (As cluster theorist Michael Weiss, remarks, "Today, the country's new motto should be 'E pluribus pluriba': 'Out of many, many.'")[29] One of these clusters is the military. As Lewis observes, "The American war effort in Iraq in 2003 was not a national effort. The military cluster fought the war."[30] The military cluster has preserved the martial spirit of sacrifice and selflessness in a culture that is becoming less martial in terms of citizens' personal lives. What we could call the "clusterization" of society and the military has had an effect on ROTC. Military scholar Michael Desch, for example, claimed in 2001 that ROTC cadets were growing less connected to the general society because of the neglect of elite schools and the Northeast. "The net effect was to produce an ROTC cadet pool that was more Southern and more likely to produce career officers than before. There is abundant evidence that graduates of ROTC programs are very different from the rest of civilian society."[31]

A couple of other critiques of the citizen-soldier ideal merit brief attention before we proceed. First, history shows that citizen-soldiers (originally the militia) have generally, though not invariably, performed less well in war than their professional colleagues; second, warfare requires expertise, conditioning, and hardship that non-military citizens are progressively less capable of bearing. The citizen-soldier ideal has too often blinded us to the importance of maintaining a core of regular forces that is usually most responsible for winning wars.[32] ROTC, of course, is one answer to these concerns, for it trains students in civilian universities to be professional soldiers. Nevertheless, some critics claim that ROTC is too amateurish to be a bulwark in the national defense. It prepares cadets for service, but the "real" training comes with the assumption of active duty. The student veterans we interviewed in a small focus group set up at the

[28] Burk, "Theories of Democratic Civil–Military Relations," p. 14; Morris Janowitz, *The Reconstruction of Patriotism* (University of Chicago Press, 1983).

[29] Michael J. Weiss, *The Clustered World* (Little, Brown, 2000), pp. 10–17. Quoted in Lewis, *The American Culture of War*, p. 10.

[30] Lewis, *The American Culture of War*, p. 10.

[31] Michael C. Desch, "Explaining the Gap: Vietnam, the Republicanization of the South, and the End of the Mass Army," in Peter D. Feaver and Richard H. Kohn, eds., *Soldiers and Civilians: The Civil-Military Gap and American National Security* (MIT Press, 2001), pp. 290–324, at p. 295.

[32] Lewis discusses these points throughout *The American Culture of War*.

University of Wisconsin in the fall of 2009 offered this critical assessment, as did a couple of veterans who responded to our survey questions about ROTC (these are recounted later in this chapter). A veteran at Columbia University was also critical, though not without ambivalence:

> I think [ROTC is] a couple of miles back from what I've done. There are some great people in ROTC, and there are also a lot of people I don't think are going to make great officers at all. . . . it's really "military light" and some of the officers who have instructed the ROTC know that, and they're just kind of pushing them through knowing that once they get to their unit they will be trained properly.[33]

The primary duty of the military, after all, is to win wars and related objectives, not to serve as laboratories for social relations – however important the military has been as a force of civic equality. That said, as the Columbia veteran acknowledged, compensating factors must also be recognized. First, there are "some great people in ROTC." Indeed, ROTC constitutes a blend of professionalism and the ideal of citizen-soldiering, for its cadets are regular college students who also engage in pre-professional training. Second, cadets receive further training once they obtain commissions, instruction that is supplemented and enriched by their undergraduate preparation. Third, though the military's primary duty is to fight, it properly incorporates certain social concerns because fostering and sustaining salutary military–civil relations are an element of its institutional environment and professional obligation. Indeed, this aspect of the military is intrinsic to the revolutionary democraticization of the military – the rise of a citizen army – that began in the Napoleonic era. The Napoleonic revolution meant that the military would now embody not only traditional martial values but also the norms of democratic society.[34] President Truman's decision to integrate the military by executive order (an act he knew would challenge his reelection in 1948) properly considered both military effectiveness and social relations and justice;[35] likewise, the movement to repeal the Don't Ask, Don't Tell policy regarding homosexuality takes both of these concerns into consideration, striving to reconcile homosexual presence with military effectiveness.[36] The military, in effect, balances the interests and perspectives of military and

[33] Interview with Columbia University veteran and ROTC student, April 2008; Focus Group interview with UW-Madison Student Veterans, November 2009; UW-Madison ROTC Survey, 2008.

[34] A large literature discusses this democratization phenomenon. Brian M. Dowling places it in the context of democratic revolution, a historical development as significant as the earlier "military revolution" of the sixteenth and seventeenth centuries. Dowling, *The Military Revolution and Political Change: Origins of Democracy in Early Modern Europe* (Princeton University Press, 1992), ch. 5, "France," esp. pp. 135–9.

[35] See Department of Defense, "60 Years of Military Integration": http://www.defense.gov/home/features/2008/0708_integration/.

[36] See the Department of Defense working group created to study repeal of DADT: U.S. Department of Defense, "Report of the Comprehensive Review of the Issues Associated with a Repeal of 'Don't Ask, Don't Tell,'" November 30, 2010: http://www.defense.gov/home/features/2010/0610_gatesdadt/DADTReport_FINAL_20101130(secure-hires).pdf.

liberal clusters in society, contingent upon the overarching stipulation that any balance struck furthers national security.

An interesting, if imperfect, analogy is the jury. The jury's primary function is to find the truth in a case as best it can. This is so even if the truth is shrouded in gray; in such cases, the jury must do its conscientious best. But the jury also has a role relating to democratic theory: As Tocqueville and many other democratic theorists have maintained, the jury is meant to be an important incubator and laboratory for citizenship, bringing a cross-section of the community together to fulfill the obligation of community judgment bounded by law. Because of this democratic and republican function, the Constitution forbids counsel from excluding jurors simply because of their race or gender. Critics of the jury system allege that amateur jurors are too often incompetent to understand the legal issues at stake adequately, holding that panels of experts would do a better job – and juries do often provide grist for such critics' mills.[37] But taken too far, this position would undermine the democratic and republican functions of juries. Courts weigh all of these concerns, striving to preserve the objective responsibilities of juries with their capacity for republican participation.[38] We can envision ROTC and the citizen-soldier ideal in a similar light, although ROTC cadets undergo extensive training in their roles that jurors do not receive. ROTC is intended to balance democratic and republican values with military training designed to increase professionalism and effectiveness. As with juries, the synthesis may weave in and out of proper balance, but the system strives to maintain the optimum arrangement. In both cases, however, the primary mission is objective: to find the truth and achieve military effectiveness, respectively. But these primary missions coexist with important secondary objectives.

One of our tasks is to cast light on the status of the citizen-soldier ideal; and our surveys revealed an awareness of this republicanism/liberalism tension. Non-military students and ROTC cadets and commanders often referred to the military's emphasis on duty and sacrifice in contrast to the liberal university's individualist and rights-based orientation. Perhaps these comments are simply manifestations of a kind of false consciousness, the lingering residue of a dying citizen-soldier ideal. But many respondents also pointed to factors that provide some tangible basis for supporting this assessment. How deeply such awareness or appreciation had sunk in is something we cannot assay, yet our survey results provide suggestive evidence that should occasion further work.

The debate over the meaning and relevance of the citizen-soldier ideal is an important element of the larger dialogue regarding civil–military relations,

[37] See, e.g., Stephen J. Adler, *The Jury: Trial and Error in the American Courtroom* (Times Books, 1994).

[38] The best book on the tensions and dilemmas regarding the functions of the jury is Jeffrey Abramson, *We, the Jury: The Jury System and the Ideal of Democracy* (Basic, 1994). Lee C. Bollinger maintains that the duty of jurors is paradigmatic of constitutional liberty more generally, as in the theory and aspiration of free speech. Lee C. Bollinger, *The Tolerant Society: Freedom of Speech and Extremist Speech in America* (Oxford University Press, 1986).

pedagogy, and military policy. *Nevertheless, our central thesis is not affected by the debate's resolution.* If the ideal is healthy, ROTC can help to keep it so. If the ideal is diminished, ROTC can contribute to its strengthening. Even Krebs, who downplays the historical vitality of the ideal, discerns that it helps to alleviate the negative effects of the AVF, such as the tendency toward separation from society and excessively economic-occupational motivations for enlistment. The ideal *citizen-soldier* will undoubtedly differ from the ideal *warrior*, but it is this difference that is simultaneously a constraint on the military and a source of productive friction. As such, the concept of the citizen-soldier is especially relevant to our book.

THEORETICAL MOORING

Our theoretical argument is that ROTC is useful because it brings the military to the university – benefiting students as well as benefiting student-soldiers. We hypothesize that the integration of ROTC student-soldiers with nonstudents will create friction that is conducive to understanding of the other, and that this integration can in principle improve pedagogical understanding and public policies governing national security. Though our main concern is the effect of military presence on non-military students, the model of productive friction works in the other direction as well, as the models of citizen-soldier and constructive civilian–military balance maintain. In what follows, we provide a more complete theoretical justification for an appropriate military presence on campus.

The ultimate foundation of our argument concerns the production of knowledge. The seeking of truth is a complex and sometimes mysterious process that defies simple classification. There is merit to the image of the lonely figure following his or her own path in the manner of the monastic thinker or Nietzsche's *Zarathustra*. And even in settings of communal intellectual interchange, such as the university, productive retreat into the intimacy of one's own mind is necessary in order to be thoughtful.[39] But no thinker can be entirely private (Aristotle called the isolated individual a fool), especially in *institutions* designed to teach and foster thought. It is in such settings that democratic theories of knowledge become pertinent. Though individual genius and creativity are essential to the development of knowledge, truth, and aesthetic excellence, the interchange of ideas in a communal process is also essential, especially in the domains of education and social policy. And diversity of germane ideas is central to this quest. As John Stuart Mill taught in his classic work, "On Liberty" – a work that celebrates the contributions of individual freedom and heroic individual thought to the precarious attainment of truth – no human being can possibly grasp all of truth. Each of us is inescapably fallible. Free speech and a diversity of ideas is, therefore, absolutely necessary (if not sufficient) in the grope toward truth. And even if truth is

[39] Indeed, classic First Amendment theory celebrates both the lonely thinker and the dissenter who engages and contests conventional wisdom. See Steven Shiffrin, *The First Amendment and Romance* (Harvard University Press, 1990).

ever absolutely grasped, it needs to be challenged in order to be understood and defended, and in order to have life.[40]

Other theories of collective knowledge are also germane to our discussion. The simple version of Condorcet's jury theorem contends that larger groups are more likely to reach correct answers in a jury context so long as each member has a greater than 50 percent chance of being correct and so long as each vote is made independently and is not the product of group-think or strategic calculation. (If the average probability of being correct for each member is less than 50 percent, then the opposite hypothesis holds.) Condorcet's theorem applies to the correctness of judgments and votes, but it is related in certain respects to the notion of the "wisdom of crowds," which holds that aggregations of individuals have stronger predictive success than individuals acting alone. (Stock prices are one example.)[41] These theories are relevant to our discussion because it is evident that exposure to diverse sources of knowledge contributes to the wisdom of crowds and success in Condorcet-like conditions, and a core mission of universities is to foster the collective pursuit of truth and knowledge. Because a diversity of ideas is so helpful in this context, there is a natural connection between Condorcet's theorem and freedom of speech principles.[42]

In his book *The Difference*, Scott E. Page builds on these and related theories in crafting a careful, measured, yet ultimately strong case for the importance of intellectual diversity in optimizing knowledge, efficiency, and collective wisdom. Diverse tools, critically assessed, lead to better problem solving and prediction. Page's understanding of diversity includes "identity" (race, gender, religion, sexual orientation, and so on), but it ventures broadly beyond this one-dimensional aspect. Identity diversity can contribute to positive outcomes (especially in more economically advanced countries; in less developed countries it can be the basis of unremitting conflict), but mainly because it is linked to cognitive differences and other important differences mentioned later in this chapter. Universities are especially in need of diversity broadly defined because they are constituted by the "cross-fertilization of ideas."[43]

For Page, diversity consists of key "frameworks": "cognitive differences," which include diversity of perspectives (solutions to problems); diversity of interpretations (categories we use to classify events, outcomes, and situations); diversity of heuristics (the different tools we use to solve problems); and diversity of predictive models (how we construe causal relationships between objects or

[40] John Stuart Mill, "On Liberty," in J. S. Mill, *"On Liberty" and Other Writings* (Classic Books International, 2010). On the fallibility principle and knowledge, see Jonathan Rauch, *Kindly Inquisitors: The New Attacks on Free Thought* (University of Chicago Press, 1993).

[41] See, e.g., James Surowieki, *The Wisdom of Crowds* (Doubleday, 2004). See also Jon Elster and Helene Landemore, eds., *Collective Wisdom: Principles and Mechanisms* (Cambridge University Press, 2012).

[42] See Krishna K. Ladha, "The Condorcet Theorem, Free Speech, and Correlated Values," *American Journal of Political Science* 36 (1992): 617–34.

[43] Scott E. Page, *The Difference: How the Power of Diversity Creates Better Groups, Firms, Schools, and Societies* (Princeton University Press, 2007), p. 17.

events). Diversity of values or "preferences" is another key aspect of diversity that interacts with these frameworks.[44] Page also discusses two types of value or preference differences: fundamental values and instrumental values. Fundamental values concern one's position regarding substantive outcomes and positions, whereas instrumental values pertain to the means employed to achieve these ends. Conflict over fundamental values can be good for society and groups, as it sharpens thinking and perhaps even certain character traits, but it can also be destructive if it goes too far and undermines the common ground upon which differences can thrive.[45] The debate over military presence on campus can entail both forms of values/preferences. (Recall our previous discussion of the relevance of Huntington's notion of creedal passion.) To some, the military's presence raises fundamental concerns, pro and con. To others, the military question is about means to an end: national security. In some minds, the military question involves both types of values.

Value and preference disagreement (friction) and diversity can be productive so long as they are accompanied by sufficient common ground, in which the basic humanity of the other (what we could call a presumption of existential and normative validity) is recognized. In our surveys of student soldiers and civilian students (which we discuss in Chapters 8 and 9), we will encounter many examples of cadets and civilian students who believe that ROTC's presence helped to create such common ground. Some respondents spoke of how interaction served to bridge "different worlds," thereby humanizing the other side and creating greater tolerance. This process mirrors one indicated by the Defense Department's survey study of the implications of rescinding the Don't Ask, Don't Tell (DADT) policy, conducted in late 2010. Among other things, the extensive survey of about 400,000 active and reserve service members (115,052, or 28 percent, responded) indicated that those who had had actual exposure to gays in the service were the most tolerant, as such exposure eliminated or mitigated preexisting negative assumptions and stereotypes. Seventy percent believed that repeal of DADT would not have a negative effect (positive, mixed, or neutral) on work effectiveness, while 92 percent of those who have served with service members they know are gay had no negative feelings about their gay compatriots (69 percent reported having worked with gay service members).[46] If these findings are accurate, they suggest that maintaining

[44] Page, *The Difference*, Part One, "Unpacking the Toolbox." On preferences and values, see Part Three, "Diverse Values: A Conflict of Interests (or Is It?)."

[45] An excellent classic discussion of the tension between constructive and destructive conflict is Ortega y Gassett, *Concord and Liberty* (W. W. Norton, 1963). Thinkers who celebrate the potentially constructive uses of conflict compose a long lineage, including Machiavelli, Georg Simmel, Lewis A. Coser, and Richard Sennett. See, e.g., Richard Sennett, *The Uses of Disorder: Personal Identity and City Life* (Yale University Press, 2008).

[46] U.S. Department of Defense, "Report of the Comprehensive Review of the Issues Associated with a Repeal of 'Don't Ask, Don't Tell,'" November 30, 2010: http://www.defense.gov/home/features/2010/0610_gatesdadt/DADTReport_FINAL_20101130(secure-Report_FINAL_2010 1130(secure-hires).pdf.

ROTC on campus even with DADT would help change the culture of the military because the soldiers would be exposed to different ideals and values, as well as sexual orientations.

At the same time, our survey responses also show how many persons have indeed relegated campus military personnel to a kind of shadow life, neglecting to recognize their presence and credibility, questioning their normative validity, or simply fearing their presence. What emerges is a complex picture of alienation, constructive interaction, and/or lukewarm recognition – what we might expect in a polity grappling with the problem of the civil–military gap.[47]

Our experience, research, and surveys have shown us that military presence on the campus does indeed entail fundamental value conflict for a minority of students, involving such concerns as militarism, an idealized notion of the university, or opposition to DADT. Value conflict also exists for many of the majority who favor ROTC's presence, but they appreciate being exposed to a different set of values that they also consider important and legitimate. For the clear majority of students surveyed, ROTC exposes them to something distinctive that differs in some profound ways from what they commonly experience. As for those who feel that ROTC exposes them to values that lie beyond the pale of their value systems, one response is that a university – more so than a business enterprise, interest group, or organization with a narrower mission – is defined by the commitment to intellectual challenge and exposure. Universities should be more open to fundamental value conflict than almost any other institution.

One concern is the degree of exposure. The type of dynamic that Page elucidates requires the type of serious engagement that university interaction does not always provide. For this reason, we look at the historical and current status of ROTC on campus, as reflected in battles over military presence that have beset American campuses. We also asked non-ROTC students about the extent of their exposure and found that a substantial majority had some, but not considerable, exposure. But even some exposure can be useful, for the mere awareness of the presence of alternative experiences, ideas, and values on campus can expand horizons. Allan Bloom made an astute observation in this regard in his classic book *The Closing of the American Mind*, while lamenting the ways in which the contemporary American university has too often (in his estimation) closed its mind to certain traditions and discourses that challenge the tenets or presumptions of contemporary liberalism: "Freedom of the mind requires not only, or not even especially, the absence of legal constraints but the presence of alternate thoughts. The most successful tyranny is not the one that uses force to assure uniformity, but the one that removes awareness of other possibilities."[48] As Page points out, all institutions are prone to "group-think,"

[47] One wonders whether or not such feelings will persist or diminish now that DADT has been repealed, especially at places such as the University of Wisconsin, where those who oppose the military often have an interwoven set of objections that go beyond the discriminatory stance of DADT.

[48] Allan Bloom, *The Closing of the American Mind* (Simon and Schuster, 1987), p. 227.

which limits the range of thought. Group-think is a product of many things, including the valid need to narrow alternatives in order to be efficient, but also such less-valid forces as the social pressure to conform.[49]

The negative aspects of group-think are strengthened by the nonpresence of meaningful alternatives, as Bloom implies. Sometimes persons are aware of alternative preferences or ideas, but are reluctant or afraid to express openly their honest thoughts or feelings about the subject; at times they even repress their true feelings from themselves – a self-negating process, to say the least. (Intellectual dishonesty is bad enough when communicating with others, but it borders on the clinical when it is perpetrated against oneself.) In such situations, the liberation of intellectual honesty is often facilitated by the rise of a critical mass of supporters who publicly express their minority or dissenting preference, thereby providing legitimacy and "cover" for others to follow in a kind of "bandwagon" effect.[50] The sheer presence of the alternative preference can help to set the stage for this legitimizing process. Banning ROTC from campus, or channeling ROTC to particular regions, in contrast, facilitates group-think – and limits the breadth of liberal and civic education while reducing the potential of society to reach the best outcome in terms of policy. As such, the presence of ROTC enhances prospects for meaningful deliberation on a variety of issues.

Of course, those who equate ROTC and recruiters with militarism or intolerance will view their contributions as negative. This perspective borders on a theory of contagion – bad ideas should be cut off from campus. Needless to say, this perspective is inconsistent with the concept of the marketplace of ideas, and it is likely incorrect in any event. There is no legitimate reason to associate ROTC with militarism. (Indeed, the very purpose of ROTC is to counter militarism.) The debate over DADT posed a different question. As we will see in Chapter 6, debate has raged on campus over two questions respecting DADT: whether having ROTC on campus will help to influence the military to be more tolerant of gays; and whether the benefits of maintaining ROTC outweigh the negative effects of the discriminatory policy. We argue that it is morally defensible to have strongly opposed DADT while also favoring the presence of ROTC on campus. As Professor Allan Silver articulated during the drive to return ROTC to Columbia University in 2004–5, "The military's policy on homosexuality means that the decision to have an ROTC program is a tragic choice. Put bluntly, one good must override another."[51]

More broadly, such exposure to the military "other" can enhance liberal and civic education. Friction is necessary for learning; and, as discussed in Chapter 2,

[49] The definitive work on group-think is Irving L. Janis, *Victims of Groupthink: A Psychological Study of Policy Decisions and Fiascos* (Houghton Mifflin, 1972).

[50] One of the best treatments of this process of replacing false public preferences with true public preferences, and the bandwagon effect, is Timur Kuran, *Private Truths, Public Lies: The Social Consequences of Preference Falsification* (Harvard University Press, 1995).

[51] Allan Silver, "Emails Sent to the ROTC Task Force," Columbia University Senate ROTC Task Force, February 9–24, 2005, p. 12: http://www.columbia.edu/cu/senate/committee-pages/rotc_folder/rotcemails.htm

liberal education presupposes the friction of ideas as a precondition for learning. Civic education is also strengthened because student-soldiers are civic-minded and deal with matters that are of fundamental importance to all citizens.

Of course, conflict regarding the military, military policy, and national security is – and should be – prevalent. While the vast majority of citizens agree on the fundamental importance of national defense, intense disagreement reigns over what it means and how to achieve it. Such conflict can be beneficial because it sharpens understanding, and because it is only through the appropriate conflict of ideas that good policy and truth emerge.[52] This very conflict and friction of ideas also constitutes what Jonathan Rauch, in his classic book on the centrality of free speech to liberal democracy, has called the "moral charter" of universities.[53] An appropriate military presence is especially useful to universities today for reasons associated with these points. First, the military is unique on campus, providing a special opportunity for productive friction. (See the discussion in Chapter 2 on the *sui generis* nature of the military and its mission.) This is especially the case for liberal or left-oriented campuses, for the friction between the military and civilian worlds is most pronounced at such institutions. Second, by virtue of its central role in the service of national defense and its pioneering role in diversifying the workforce – obligations that embody both common purpose and vibrant disagreement – the military represents the values of both unity and diversity, the core components of the very concept of the "uni-versity." The military cluster thus brings a distinctive perspective to the university.

The type of balance and friction at stake is dialectical. That is, it entails the appropriate blend of difference and commonality, which can lead to mutual due respect and recognition. Equal citizenship and respect are premised on due recognition of each other's worth. The drive for recognition is a primordial human motive, but it involves struggle because of the differences that separate us and which are rife in social life.[54] Without sufficient interaction and the recognition that comes from it, the members of the other side become the "other," something alien that inspires either inauthentic regard or fear. Among other things, the alleged civilian–military "gap" is a manifestation of a breakdown of the dialectical interaction or commonality between the military and civilian society, a situation that was exacerbated by the Vietnam War and the advent of the All-Volunteer Force. Such books as *AWOL* disclose the disregard that many elites have for the thought of actual military service, while the work of

[52] In their recent book on the making of national military policy, Harvey Saplosky, Eugene Gholz, and Caitlin Talmadge argue that institutional and legal arrangements that weaken the competition of ideas are a recipe for bad military and national security policy. For example, the coauthors maintain that the Goldwater-Nichols Act of 1986, which increased the control of the Joint Chiefs of Staff over the different services, has led to logrolling and a lack of competition, ultimately to the detriment of security policy. See Harvey Sapolsky, Eugene Gholz, and Caitlin Talmadge, *U.S. Defense Politics: The Origins of Security Policy* (Routledge, 2009).

[53] Rauch, *Kindly Inquisitors*, p. 86.

[54] On the primordial nature of the drive for recognition, see G. W. F. Hegel, *The Phenomenology of Mind*, translated by J. B. Baillie (Macmillan, 1955).

such journalists as Thomas Ricks chronicle the disrespect that many in the military harbor for civilian society.[55]

Appropriate exposure and interaction are preconditions for bridging such a gap. Interestingly, many of the cadets in our survey reported in Chapter 8 stressed how ROTC helps, in the words of one cadet, to "humanize" the military, revealing that members of the military "are not inherently bad people." Or, as another ROTC cadet put it, "By incorporating ROTC into public colleges, it gives people a chance to understand what life is like on the 'other' side, since military life and civilian life are two segregated societies." We will see that numerous non-ROTC students concurred with precisely this point, often using similar language.[56] And our own survey responses indicated that the primary benefit of exposure and interaction with ROTC students dealt with the psychology of recognition, as students stressed the way that such exposure humanized or gave a "human face" to ROTC. Many students referred to other benefits of exposure and interaction (such as knowledge of the program and military matters), but these consequences were clearly secondary to the more personal ones relating to the psychology of recognition and respect. Students also cited such matters as gaining more appreciation of the risks and burdens that the military bears, matters which also relate to personal qualities. For those concerned with strengthening the bridge between the military and the civilian orders, one of the best places to begin is at this level.

In the chapters ahead, we provide examples of how the outspoken presence of an alternative military position can change a class discussion. For example, a cadet described what happened in a philosophy class dealing with just war theory:

> It was a philosophy class and Madison is a fairly liberal campus, so needless to say I was the only one defending certain aspects of war. The teaching assistant in that class knew that I had no problem defending that side of the argument and frequently counted on me to further the discussion of a topic by adding the opposite view. There have been several other instances where I have changed someone's opinion [of] the military by [the classmate] getting to know me in class before they knew I was in the ROTC program.

Students in this course presumably benefited from a different perspective. It takes courage for students to defend even "certain aspects of war" (as Thomas Aquinas and others have within the just war tradition) because, in our experience, such students with a more nuanced perspective are often (unfairly) branded as militaristic.

A couple of other examples – not involving fundamental value disagreements, but one touching on a serious matter of life and death – from one of the author's own teaching experiences also illustrate the process at stake. In 2004, Downs taught an upper-level undergraduate honors seminar on criminal law and jurisprudence. One of the students was a Naval ROTC cadet who wore his uniform to class periodically. In addition to being one of the outstanding students in the

[55] Roth-Douquet and Schaeffer, *AWOL;* Ricks, "The Widening Gap Between the Military and Society"; McMichael, "Most U.S. Youth Unfit to Serve, Data Show."

[56] Respondents to ROTC Survey, University of Wisconsin, Madison.

high-achieving class, this student's understanding of military law (which he had studied in ROTC) provided a distinctive perspective on regular criminal law, especially when the class studied issues of self-defense and "necessity." The "necessity defense" pertains to a situation in which a person is permitted to violate the written law in order to prevent a greater harm – so-called legitimated disobedience.[57] The obligation of obedience is tighter in military law than in the criminal law, so the class gained a clearer understating, by contrast, of what legitimated disobedience means in the civil criminal law system than it would have obtained without this input. In a similar seminar a couple of years later, an Iraqi veteran dramatically changed the nature of the discussion about self-defense when he informed the civilian students how emotionally and existentially difficult it is to actually deploy deadly force against others, even in a case of clear self-defense. All of the other students assumed it would not be difficult, so they were speculating and hypothesizing about something they had never experienced. This student had dealt with many deadly force situations in Iraq, and the authenticity of his experience countered the arm-chair quality of the class's reasoning. Downs now uses this example whenever he teaches self-defense policy and law.[58]

We must recognize that the theory of productive friction does not mean that students must emerge with *positive* views of the military. In our chapters in which we present results from our ROTC surveys, we will encounter several examples of students for whom exposure to ROTC led to negative views, as well as some whose preexisting negative views were buttressed by such exposure. The theory of productive friction requires no particular normative conclusion. Indeed, one of the pedagogical effects of exposure that we accentuated in Chapter 2 entailed "understanding the military and national defense." Surely such exposure requires understanding the less noble and idealistic aspects of the military, including its political and more prosaic features as well as its problems, shenanigans, and transgressions. The military is just as self-interested as any other prominent American institution, and the politics within which it is embroiled often conjure images of Bismarck's famous observation about the making of laws and sausage.[59] Our only normative consideration involves process, not substantive outcomes, yet our theory also provides us with ideas about productive friction that we can evaluate to better understand the consequences of military presence. In this spirit, in our later chapters presenting survey responses to our questions about ROTC, we will consider several critical responses good examples of productive friction.

[57] See Mortimer R. Kadish and Sanford H. Kadish, *Discretion to Disobey: A Study of Lawful Departures from Legal Rules* (Stanford University Press, 1973).

[58] These are just two examples among others that we could offer from our own experience. Significant research on the psychological effects of war has shown that many soldiers are reluctant to shoot at the enemy and must be trained to overcome their natural disinclination to kill. See, e.g., Dave Grossman, *On Killing: The Psychological Cost of Learning to Kill in War and Society* (Little, Brown, 1995). Grossman builds on the pioneering work of S. L. A. Marshall. See Marshall, *Men Against Fire* (Peter Smith, 1978).

[59] See, e.g., Carl H.. Builder, *The Masks of War: American Military Styles in Strategy and Analysis* (Johns Hopkins University Press, 1989); Sapolsky, Gholz, and Talmadge, *U.S. Defense Politics*.

OBJECTIONS TO ROTC

Beyond questions raised regarding the contemporary validity of the citizen-soldier ideal, others have simply argued that the military should not be part of the university. Opponents generally raise four objections to the presence of the military on campus. First, they claim that military presence is at odds with the civil virtues of liberal education. A prominent example of this posture is the statement presented to the Columbia University Senate by the Union Theological Seminary of Columbia University opposing the return of ROTC to that campus during the universitywide debate in 2005:

> We, the Executive Committee of the Student Senate of Union Theological Seminary, strongly oppose ROTC's return to Columbia University. We believe ROTC's war-making and policy against homosexuals are violations of the sacredness of human life. While the current debate in Columbia's Senate has focused almost exclusively on ROTC's "Don't Ask Don't Tell" policy, the rationale provided below pays particular attention to the violence of militarism.[60]

For our purposes, the key word in this statement is *militarism* – the Union Theological Seminary equates the military with militarism. But, as we have seen, there is a distinction between militarism and appropriate, critical appreciation and understanding of the military as an institution. By equating ROTC with militarism, the Seminary paradoxically precludes moral theorizing about war. This point is made clear by A. J. Coates:

> One of the great strengths of the pacifist tradition is its keen awareness of a common propensity or cultural bias in favor of war, upon which the war-maker is continually able to draw and with which any peacemaker has to contend. It is to this phenomenon, which first precipitates war and then dictates its ruthless prosecution, that the term militarism is applied here. The weakness of the pacifist understanding lies in its tendency to regard *any* defense of war and *any* resort to arms as manifestations of militarism. The associations of all things military with militarism suppresses real and important distinctions and undermines any attempt to subject war to moral limitation.[61]

The key is to distinguish among the militarist, realist, and proponent of just war, or else we risk losing any meaning of these concepts (as well as losing the ability to devise a moral theory of war):

> The hallmark of militarism is the lust for war. Unlike the realist, who opts for war on pragmatic grounds, or the just war theorist, whose grudging acceptance of the moral permissibility of war stops well short of moral enthusiasm, the militarist is an enthusiast for war, a "happy warrior" who shares none of the moral anxiety rightly associated with

[60] Union Theological Seminary of Columbia University, "Statement of the Student Senate Executive Committee," April 14, 2005: http://www.law.georgetown.edu/solomon/Documents/UTSStatement.pdf.

[61] A. J. Coates, *The Ethics of War* (Manchester University Press, 1997), p. 40.

the just recourse to war. ... Militarism sweeps aside these essential moral hurdles, allowing an unobstructed path to war.[62]

To equate ROTC with militarism is clearly an error – as is equating the United States armed forces with militarism, when militarism is properly understood. Indeed, some of the least militaristic persons are military officers themselves, as they appreciate the profound consequences of going to war. (General Dwight D. Eisenhower remarked in a famous 1946 speech in Ottawa, Canada, "I hate war as only a soldier who has lived it can, only as one who has seen its brutality, its futility, its stupidity.") To oppose *any* form of military presence on campus amounts to committing the university to a position of pacifism. Though pacifism is an honorable and often courageous position, it is outweighed by such classic traditions as those that distinguish "just war" from "unjust war," the international laws of war that legitimate the proper use of deadly force in combat, and the domestic laws in every jurisdiction that authorize police officers and even citizens to use deadly force under the appropriate circumstances.[63]

A deeper threat is that pacifism paradoxically removes a constraint on militarism by equating all aspects of war with militarism. One of the key aspects of civil–military relations is ensuring civilian control of the military. By putting the university into the military, ROTC is one of these checks. Equating the military with militarism so as to remove all traces of the military from the university facilitates the clusterization of society that is likely to *increase* rather than mitigate the threat of militarism – a point made by Huntington in *The Soldier and the State*.

A second argument is that military education's emphasis on discipline and obedience is inconsistent with the intellectual freedom of liberal education. Yet, as discussed in Chapter 2, this argument amounts to a stereotype, especially after the extensive reforms of the ROTC curriculum that have been incorporated over the last four decades, which we discuss in Chapter 6. In addition, as argued in Chapter 2, duty, obedience, discipline, commitment, and leadership are important values in life generally, and it is beneficial for non-military students to be exposed to these virtues on campuses that often emphasize self-realization and the pursuit of happiness over duty. As Patrick Hoy remarked in Chapter 2, it is good to expose students to the "mystery of command" and the "throngs of community" that military service entails.[64] A third argument maintains that

[62] Coates, *The Ethics of War*, p. 43.

[63] On just war and self-defense theory, see George P. Fletcher and Jens David Ohlin, *Defending Humanity: When Force Is Justified and Why* (Oxford University Press, 2008); Michael Walzer, *Just and Unjust Wars: A Moral Argument with Historical Illustrations* (Basic, 2006); and Jean Bethke Elshtain, *Just War Against Terror: The Burden of American Power in a Violent World* (Basic, 2003).

[64] Pat C. Hoy, "Soldiers and Scholars: Between Harvard and West Point, a Deep – and Dangerous – Cultural Chasm," *Harvard Magazine* 98, 5 (1996). See also Oliver Wendell Holmes, Jr., "The Fraternity of Arms," in Richard A. Posner, ed., *The Essential Holmes: Selections from the Letters, Speeches, Judicial Opinions, and Other Writings* (University of Chicago Press, 1992), pp. 73–4. See also Michael Gelven, *War and Existence: A Philosophical Inquiry* (Pennsylvania State University Press, 1994).

ROTC is not intellectually rigorous enough to justify inclusion on campus. According to this contention, course content is rote, and instructors lack the credentials of regular faculty. This argument is stronger than the previous two, and we have encountered several observers (including ROTC students) who concur with this assessment. But course content has been improved in recent decades, partly due to the very criticisms and challenges that have arisen in this vein. In addition, universities now have the power to veto instructor assignments, and military officers today typically have more educational opportunity and training than in the past.[65] Many ROTC commanders have advanced graduate degrees from military and civilian institutions.[66] Furthermore, ROTC is not a major, amounting to an elective minor or less. Higher education today offers similar programs attached not only to professional schools, but also to liberal arts programs. These programs increasingly call for internships, service, and other extracurricular experiences, many of which provide academic credit. Given higher education's growing emphasis on real-world experience and outreach – coupled with the reforms that have improved the programs and eliminated credit in courses that faculty deem below par – it would be discriminatory to target ROTC as a program unsuited to the intellectual standards of universities.[67] A related objection is that ROTC is ultimately controlled not by the university but by the military and the government. Once again, this is a valid concern; however, it should not be dispositive, because universities are exercising more control over the program than they have in the past, and many other programs on campus have quasi-independent status.

The fourth objection is the most serious: ROTC's complicity in the military's DADT policy. We have strongly agreed that DADT should be rescinded and supported its repeal in December 2010.

Maintaining and returning ROTC to campuses where it has suffered exile can be justified on both normative and pragmatic/utilitarian grounds. The normative position relates to the duty and honor of serving the country in this capacity, whereas the utilitarian justification deals with the beneficial consequences, which have been noted by many scholars and commentators over the years. But the normative and pragmatic benefits of keeping ROTC are many:

- ROTC is cheaper than the academies, though more expensive than the Officer Candidate School system.
- On the whole, ROTC has contributed more educated, reflective officers to the military than those who did not come from civilian university backgrounds.

[65] We will discuss the substantial improvement in ROTC courses in the ensuing chapters. In general, see Neiberg, *Making Citizen Soldiers*; and Arthur T. Coumbe and Lee S. Harford, *U.S. Army Cadet Command: The 10 Year History* (Office of the Command Historian, U.S. Army Cadet Command, 1996).

[66] For a detailed account of the history of ROTC, emphasizing the reforms of recent decades, see Neiberg, *Making Citizen Soldiers*. On advances in military education, see Gregory Kennedy and Keith Nielson, eds., *Military Education: Past, Present, and Future* (Praeger, 2002), p. 151.

[67] See Richard M. Freeland, "The Third Way," *Atlantic Monthly*, October 2004.

This need was pressing because many observers attributed the poor performance of the military in Vietnam (including the perpetration of such atrocities as the My Lai massacre) to the lack of proper training and education. The military sought better-educated officers for at least three reasons. First, the modern military needed officers capable of dealing with the increasingly complex organizational and administrative aspects of the military as an institution. Second, the military had lost a great deal of prestige and respect after Vietnam, and it needed officers whose educations would help to revive the morale and capacity of the military and regain the respect of the citizenry. Third, the military believed that the loss of respect was leading to its marginalization in the eyes of civilian policy makers, thereby tilting the balance of civilian–military relations against it. "If they hoped to preserve their institutional prerogatives and effectively defend their interests, the armed forces needed educated officers – officers with the knowledge and intellectual skills requisite for countering the ill-conceived schemes of civilian defense analysts, many of whom, it was felt, lacked an appreciation of the unique requirements of military service."[68]

- The military believed that ROTC was a major vehicle for educating the public about the military. Public outreach was a motivation behind the foundational 1862 Morrill Act, which made military instruction mandatory at land grant institutions. In ensuing decades, universities crafted a mishmash of programs across the nation, and ROTC did not come into being as an official, specific form of military education until the 1916 National Defense Act. ROTC units and instructors were, in effect, "instruments with which the services told their story to America's educated classes and, it was hoped, gained their support and understanding."[69] Many of the ROTC students we surveyed indicated that they believed one of the most important purposes of ROTC was to educate those in the university community about the program and the military.
- Adhering to a traditional assumption, universities, students, and the public believed that ROTC provided educational benefits to students. Financial opportunity mattered (we have interviewed many ROTC students who joined because of the scholarships), but so did character development and, first and foremost, leadership.
- ROTC was a primary vehicle for promoting the proper concept of civil–military relations. "ROTC officers, it was often suggested, were particularly accepting of and sympathetic to 'civilian values.' Their 'essentially civilian

[68] Arthur T. Coumbe, "Why ROTC?" p. 6. For further discussion of the reasons presented here, see Neiberg, *Making Citizen Soldiers*, pp. 131–3. On the politics of military–civilian military policy making, see Peter J. Roman and David W. Tarr, "Military Professionalism and Policymaking: Is There a Civil–Military Gap at the Top? If So, Does It Matter?" in Feaver and Kohn, eds., *Soldiers and Civilians*, ch. 11.

[69] Coumbe, "Why ROTC?" p. 9. On the military's successful effort in restoring morale and public respect, see David C. King and Zachary Karabell, *The Generation of Trust: How the U.S. Military Has Regained the Public's Confidence Since Vietnam* (American Enterprise Institute Press, 2003). See also Bacevich, *The New American Militarism.*

> social, educational, and cultural' backgrounds supposedly inoculated them to some degree against what one study labeled 'the prevailing military ethos' – an ethos that, some believed, was not completely attuned to the norms and values of the larger society."[70]

To these benefits we would add a point germane to the now retired Don't Ask, Don't Tell controversy and to our model of constructive friction. In a panel discussion on homosexuality and the military held at the Lavender Law Conference in Washington, D.C., in 2006, University of Florida Law Professor Diane H. Mazur – a former Air Force officer and now a scholar of civil–military relations and constitutionalism, and an advocate of gay rights – argues that the military's clinging to the DADT policy is partly a function of the ways in which universities have separated themselves from the military in recent decades. Her comments about the lack of military education in law schools today parallel our discussion in Part III, "Military History Examined," of the disappearance of veterans in history departments in recent decades. Mazur's main focus is law schools, which played the key role in an attempt to ban military recruiters from campus because of DADT. We quote her at some length:

> People tend to view the military as this monolithic, unchanging institution. ... This is not true at all. The character and the nature of the military are very much shaped by the forces that civilians bring to bear on it. The military, in fact, has changed dramatically since the Vietnam War. ... In distancing themselves from the military, law schools are only joining in a larger trend of the last thirty years, since the end of the Vietnam War, in which institutions of law across the board are abdicating their responsibility for civilian control of the military. Courts have already deemed themselves incompetent to understand military issues, and so they defer to congressional and military judgment. Law professors have completely lost interest in legal control of the military, seemingly afflicted with a bad case of deference themselves. ... We have an institutional obligation to participate in civilian control of the military. ... There was a time when law school faculties carried enormous expertise about military law and military legal reform, and they were actually the first call that would be made when the military was sitting down and beginning to think about how it was going to reform its laws. Today, that would be the last call the military would make, because that expertise, over the last generation, really has evaporated.[71]

Accordingly, a strong case can be made for maintaining and strengthening ROTC on campus – regardless of the status of the now-dead DADT. Opponents of ROTC seek to redefine ROTC as inconsistent with the concept of the Ivory Tower. We simply observe that opponents of ROTC often obfuscate the benefits of ROTC (or ignore them) while pointing to vaguely defined costs of ROTC on campus. Even if ROTC tarnishes the Ivory Tower – a cost of ROTC – the relevant calculation is whether the benefits of ROTC, as we have outlined

[70] Coumbe, "Why ROTC?" p. 10.

[71] Diane H. Mazur, quoted in "'Rum, Sodomy, and the Lash': What the Military Thrives on and How It Affects Legal Recruitment and Law Schools," panel remarks at 2006 Lavender Law Conference, September 8, 2006. In 14 *Duke Law Journal of Gender Law and Policy* 1143 (2007): 1160–3.

them in this chapter, exceed these costs. In addition to a failure to consider benefits of ROTC, there are far too few efforts to consider the perspectives of the student-soldiers themselves.

ROTC AND THE UNIVERSITY: THE PATH AHEAD

We have suggested the importance of ROTC on campus, but how can we evaluate our claims? That is the task of the remainder of this part of the book. Our analysis of ROTC proceeds as follows. First we describe institutional conflict over ROTC in American universities. Our purpose is to articulate the historical rationale for ROTC, to describe the objections to it, and to consider the reasons that proponents are advocating its return to the campuses from which it was either banished or encouraged to leave. Our discussion suggests the importance of ROTC in universities as well as the creedal passions that the issue can evoke. A historical look at the relationship among ROTC, the military, and higher education teaches us much about the culture of higher education today, as well as the politics of constitutional citizenship. This examination comprises the next four chapters.

We conclude the discussion of ROTC by presenting results from surveys of commanders, cadets, and students at the University of Wisconsin. Our surveys provide us with additional insight into the importance of ROTC and the military on campus. Taken together, our evidence suggests that ROTC is important because it brings the military to the university – and in doing so, enhances the possibility of liberal and civic education. All told, our evidence suggests the importance of welcoming rather than rejecting an appropriate military presence if one hopes to improve prospects for a liberal and civic education.

4

ROTC and the Ivies

Before the Storm

> What the radicals did not understand, according to John Updike, is that, in a world indelibly stained by Original Sin, peace "depends upon the threat of violence. The threat cannot always be idle."
>
> – Janet Tassel, discussing and quoting Harvard graduate John Updike[1]

It is fitting to begin our empirical sojourn with the most politicized dimension of the relationship between the military and the university: the historical movement against ROTC and the subsequent efforts to bring it back from institutions that drove it away in the 1960s. Our focus is the Ivy League in general and Columbia University in particular. The reasons for this focus are threefold. First, Columbia and the Ivies offer the most prominent examples of the campus war truces that led to the abolition or abandonment of ROTC in the late 1960s and early 1970s. As we will see, there is some confusion as to the actual motives that lay behind this process, so the best way to express what happened has been offered by Columbia sociologist Allan Silver, who says that such universities "effectively barred" ROTC at the time.[2] Second, the Ivies have emerged as a key home front for what we could call the "return of the soldier" to higher education in terms of both physical and mental presence. Columbia is a veritable ground zero for this movement. Third, because of their elite and self-proclaimed status as America's most prestigious schools of preparing future leaders, Ivy institutions represent the most interesting and telling examples of the abandonment of the military by the nation's elites – the "absent without leave" (AWOL) phenomenon that has occasioned the justifiable consternation of citizens committed to a common civic order.

This chapter has two primary objectives. First, we present a sketch of Ivy institutions' contributions to war before the late 1960s, which witnessed "one of the great generational divides in American history," in the words of a historian

[1] Janet Tassel, "The 30 Years War: Cultural Conservatives Struggle with the Harvard They Love," *Harvard Magazine*, September–October 1999.

[2] We have had numerous discussions with Silver, and this phrasing is but one manifestation of such interaction.

of Columbia University.[3] This sketch will underscore the profundity of the changes of that period. Second, our portrayal ultimately helps us to draw some important analytic distinctions regarding our thesis of civic-liberal education. We will see that the world wars of the twentieth century brought the military into great involvement in the affairs of universities. Yet few – including critics of the military-university connection in more recent times – question these particular involvements. One reason is that those wars were "total wars" in which the national interest required broad mobilization. Absent clear emergency situations in which the "public necessity" calls for the military's deep involvement with the university, the role of the military on campus must not be dominant, taking special care to respect and preserve the autonomy, academic freedom, and intellectual diversity that constitute the moral charters of civilian universities. Accordingly, this chapter will assist us in refining our normative and empirical theory of the military's place in civic-liberal education.

THE RETREAT

ROTC's retreat from several Ivy League schools in the late 1960s and early 1970s was both telling and ironic. It was telling because it reflected broader trends in American society, including a widening gap between civil society and the military in reaction to Vietnam and changes in American culture, a movement that included the relegation of the burdens of war to a smaller percentage of the public in an era of limited war fought by the All-Volunteer Force. It also signified the process of "clusterization" that we discussed in previous chapters, as the Ivy League and other elite bailiwicks began to separate themselves from direct exposure to the military. As Tom Ricks, who possesses one of journalism's most acute understandings of the military and its relationship to civil society, said regarding President Obama's Afghanistan War "surge" during a *Meet the Press* panel discussion on June 23, 2010: "The U.S. military is one percent of this country, and it's carrying 99 percent of the burden of the war."[4] The Ivies' retreat was ironic because before the late 1960s the Ivy League had prided itself on being in the forefront of military service and leadership during war, periodic campus pacifism and antimilitary movements notwithstanding. Recall also that the military itself is partly responsible for this retreat, concentrating "in the South and Midwest at the expense of more populous and diverse metropolitan

[3] Robert A. McCaughey, *Stand Columbia: A History of Columbia University in the City of New York* (Columbia University Press, 2003), p. 356.

[4] For a full-fledged discussion of this cultural and political trend, see Adrian R. Lewis, *The American Culture of War: A History of Military Force from World War II to Operation Iraqi Freedom* (Routledge, 2006); *Meet the Press* transcript for June 27, 2010: http://www.msnbc.msn.com/id/37943252/ns/meet_the_press-transcripts/. Andrew Bacevich maintains that this disproportionate burden lurks behind the alienation between military and civil leadership unveiled by the infamous McChrystal interview in *Rolling Stone* that led to the general's resignation. See Bacevich, "Endless War: A Recipe for Four Star Arrogance," *Washington Post*, June 27, 2010; Michael Hastings, "The Runaway General," *Rolling Stone*, June 22, 2010.

areas," according to a *Washington Post* story in July 2010. As critic Steve Trynosky observed in this article, "This is not about the 'bad Ivies. This is about the military's capricious decision, supported by questionable analysis, that students from these regions – at state schools as well as the Ivies – are not as willing to serve in the officer corps, and are not as desirable, as those from the 'favored' regions."[5]

In the following sections, we will take a capsule look at the involvement of Ivy institutions in previous wars. Two important trends or themes stand out. First, few citizens question a deep penetration of the military into the halls of academe when the nation is engaged in a total war that the citizenry believes poses an existential threat to the nation. Though they typically wrestled with pacifism and neutrality in the stages leading up to war (viewpoints that are themselves honored parts of the American political tradition), universities extended a strong helping hand once the First and Second World Wars became inevitable. More recent wars – such as the Cold War, Vietnam, and the War on Terror – have been more controversial, being less existential and, in the case of the confrontation with terror, having no foreseeable end. The university–military relationship should be adjusted accordingly.[6]

Second, though some critics of higher education's involvement with the military depict the process as an imperial aggrandizement by the military of the university, a more plausible interpretation portrays the process as symbiotic.[7] Despite the military and the university being fundamentally different institutions, each has benefited from a relationship, and both have been deeply affected by the rise of science (physical and social) and technology to preeminence during the course of the twentieth century, nourishing a common intellectual ground. World War II was a key catalyst in this regard. As historian Richard M. Abrams points out, President Franklin Roosevelt's creation of the Office of Scientific Research and Development in 1941 "endorsed, essentially, for the first time, the view that the proper function of government included support for basic research by university scientists."[8] Although the symbiosis would encounter rough waters in the 1960s and thereafter, it has managed to stay afloat.

[5] Steve Trynosky, quoted in John Renehan, "Army ROTC Needs More Boots on More Campuses," *Washington Post*, July 4, 2010. Trynosky expressed similar views in an interview with us in May 2008. He is one of the main sources of this side of the issue. He is a reserve officer who once served in the famous Tenth Mountain Division and a former active-duty Army medical professions recruiter, and "has tussled with Army ROTC's chief demographer."

[6] Bacevich and Lewis both maintain that "endless" and less definable war has contributed to the alienation between the military and society. See Bacevich, "Endless War"; Lewis, *The American Culture of War*.

[7] See, e.g., David Engerman's review essay of leading literature on the Cold War University, "Rethinking Cold War Universities: Some Recent Histories," *Journal of Cold War Studies* 5, 3 (2003): 80–95.

[8] Richard M. Abrams, "The U.S. Military and Higher Education: A Brief History," *Symposium: Universities and the Military. Annals of the American Academy of Political Science and Social Science* 502 (March 1989): 20.

The 1916 National Defense Act was a landmark piece of legislation that brought the overall structure of the American military into the modern, more nationalized era, establishing the three major components of today's military system: the active-duty forces, the organized reserves, and the National Guard. It also created the ROTC. According to Michael Neiberg, ROTC was designed to "absorb and build on military training programs already in existence at land-grant schools and many other large universities." Students and university leaders leaped to take advantage, lest they miss out on the opportunities the fledgling program offered. "Students at Bowdoin, Williams, Harvard, Princeton, Yale, and Dartmouth all circulated petitions asking to have an ROTC unit. All were approved."[9] Indeed, most of the Ivy League institutions have a long and distinguished military tradition. Let us take a peek at this history. For the sake of brevity, we will portray only selected institutions for each time period before the 1960s, referring to others as necessary to provide the proper perspective.

Revolutionary and Civil Wars

The war legacy of most Ivy schools extends back to the Revolutionary period. Only nine institutions of higher education existed in the country at the time, and they had very small enrollments. Cornell University did not come into existence until the close of the Civil War, and Dartmouth College wasn't founded until 1770, enrolling only a handful of students at the dawn of war. But other Ivy schools participated in the Revolutionary War, and most of them had some impact on the Civil War.

In the Revolutionary War, for example, Harvard's Massachusetts Hall offered shelter to soldiers of the Continental Army, and numerous Harvard graduates and students participated in the war effort, especially during the Battle of Boston.[10] During the Civil War, the Twentieth Massachusetts Volunteer Infantry distinguished itself in most of the Army of the Potomac's major battles; the unit was known as the "Harvard Regiment" because of the large number of Harvard men who fought in its elite force, including future Supreme Court justice Oliver Wendell Holmes, Jr. Richard F. Miller, the author of a book about the regiment, presented figures of Harvard's overall participation in an essay in the *History News Network* entitled "Why Don't Harvard Graduates Join the Military Anymore?" Five hundred and seventy-eight officers and men with Harvard connections served in the Federal Army, and about 30 percent were killed in action or mortally or seriously wounded. "The best

[9] Michael Neiberg, *Making Citizen Soldiers: ROTC and the Ideology of American Military Service* (Harvard University Press, 2000), pp. 24–5, citing Eugene M. Lyons and John W. Masland, *Education and Military Leadership: A Study of the R.O.T.C.* (Princeton University Press, 1959), pp. 42–3; and Clyde W. Barrow, *Universities and the Capitalist State: Corporate Liberalism and the Reconstruction of American Higher Education, 1894–1928* (University of Wisconsin Press, 1990), pp. 135–6.

[10] See, e.g., Samuel Elliot Morrison, *Three Centuries of Harvard: 1636–1936* (Harvard University Press, 1936), ch. 7: http://www.news.harvard.edu/guide/to_do/to_do2.html.

indication of Harvard's commitment to the war is found in the percentages of the eve-of-war graduating classes that served in the Federal army and navy: 42 percent of the Class of 1859, 55 percent of the Class of 1860, and 68 percent of the Class of 1861."[11] According to James M. McPherson, Harvard's elite (its "Brahmins at War") fought because, "Strong convictions of duty and honor grew from [their] heritage – the duty to serve, and the dishonor of failing to serve. ... Closely related to these values of duty and honor was an ethic of sacrifice, the noblesse-oblige conviction that the privileged classes had a greater obligation to defend the country precisely because of the privileged status they enjoyed."[12] The names of Harvard's soldiers killed in action are famously honored on plaques in Memorial Hall.

The president of Princeton (then the College of New Jersey), John Witherspoon, was the only college president to sign the Declaration of Independence; and during the Revolutionary War and the Battle of Princeton, Nassau Hall sheltered American and British troops, depending on which side held sway.[13] Princeton mobilized for the national cause during the Civil War, and in response, all the southern students left campus. Princeton soldiers comprised a significant measure of the first four regiments from New Jersey, and over seventy with direct ties to Princeton lost their lives in the fratricidal affair. Yale's contributions to the nation's first two major wars were also noteworthy. During the Revolution, student David Bushell invented the submarine torpedo, after which he built the first submarine deployed in war. And, of course, there was the renowned Nathan Hale, executed by the British for spying. According to historian Brooks Mather Kelley, "Hale may have been the first hero of the Revolution." A statue of Hale stands to this day in two prominent locations: outside of Yale's oldest standing campus building, and in front of the Central Intelligence Agency's (CIA) headquarters in Langley, Virginia. During the Civil War, 19 percent of Yale's graduates served in the military, 35 percent between 1851 and 1863.[14]

The Ivies' "Big Three" were not alone in contributing to our first two major wars. As the Revolution was waged, Brown University (then called the College of Rhode Island) quartered troops of our key ally, France, and made a military hospital available to troops, while several of its graduates served as leading officers in the war effort. In the Civil War, according to an incomplete

[11] Richard F. Miller, "Why Don't Harvard Graduates Join the Military Anymore?" *History News Network*, October 24, 2005: http://hnn.us/articles/16884.html. See also Richard F. Miller, *Harvard's Civil War: A History of the Twentieth Massachusetts Volunteer Infantry* (University Press of New England, 2005).

[12] James P. McPherson, *This Mighty Scourge: Perspectives on the Civil* War (Oxford University Press, 2007), p. 147; see chapter 12, "Brahmins at War." See also James F. McPherson, *For Cause and Comrades: Why Men Fought in the Civil War* (Oxford University Press, 1997).

[13] Henry Lyttleton Savage, *Nassau Hall, 1756–1956* (Princeton University Press, 1956).

[14] Brooks Mather Kelley, *Yale: A History* (Yale University Press, 1974), pp. 87–8, 198. See also M. William Phelps, *Nathan Hale: The Life and Death of America's First Spy* (St. Martin's Press, 2008).

compilation published in 1920, 417 Brown graduates or students fought on the Union side, 39 of whom died. At the dedication of the Civil War Memorial Tablet in Brown's Manning Hall in 1866, Professor D. L. Diman compared Brown to the Athens that Pericles praised in his famous Funeral Oration on the eve of the Peloponnesian War. "[Pericles] proudly proclaimed that Athens had lost none of that cultivation of those arts to which she owed her highest fame; and we, too, looking back on our record, remembering the readiness with which so many of our educated youth made sacrifice of the hopes of years . . . bewailing, alas, what might not even now be mentioned without renewing in the hearts of some here present a grief too sacred and too recent to be disturbed, may repeat with added emphasis the words of the great Athenian orator, 'We have not been enfeebled by philosophy.'"[15] At Columbia, several students in King's College (the name of the school then) served in the Revolutionary War, including Alexander Hamilton. And during the Civil War, 45 percent of the Class of 1861 enlisted for service – with many becoming high-ranking officers.[16]

World War I

Cornell University's experiences were typical of Ivy institutions and other schools as the country embarked on a mass mobilization for war. Founded in 1865 with assistance from the Morrill Act, which "transformed the concept of higher education in America," Cornell embodied the spirit of the modern research university, whose mission is the wide dissemination of knowledge and research in service to the public good. Incorporating the Morrill Act's requirement of "military instruction," Cornell was "at its beginning organized as a military school," according to Cornell historian Morris Bishop, hosting a school of military science designed to instill martial virtues in the students. Yet Andrew Dixon White (a pioneer in American higher education who served as Cornell's first president) was ambivalent about military education; he believed it worthwhile to impart certain virtues and to prepare Cornell students to "lead in repressing civil discord," but "his faith in human reasonableness, his detestation of social and intellectual discipline, his impatient utopianism, made him instinctively antimilitarist."[17]

As in most universities, the military science program at Cornell waxed and waned in its popularity and quality before the advent of ROTC with the National Defense Act (NDA) of 1916. In 1917, ROTC nationwide was folded into the Student Army Training Corps (SATC), run directly by the War Department. Consequently, "Cornell became in 1918 a military school." The

[15] See Forward, *Civil War Record of Brown University*, compiled by and forward written by Brevet Major Henry S. Burrage (n.p., 1920), esp. p. x.

[16] See Columbia University, "Report of the Task Force on Military Engagement," March 4, 2011, p. 6: http://www.columbia.edu/cu/senate/militaryengagement/docs/20110304%20-%20TFMEReport.pdf.

[17] Morris Bishop, *A History of Cornell* (Cornell University Press, 1962), pp. 57, 170.

university also hosted a variety of war programs, including: a school of military aeronautics; radio engineers and aerial photographers; a Naval training unit of 310 men; a Marine unit of 170 men; and an Army trade school. The Cornell Medical College in New York City became headquarters of a School for Military Roentgenologists.[18] According to Cornell's Army ROTC webpage, the university supplied more commissioned officers to the war effort than any other institution in America, including West Point (4,598). Two hundred and sixty-four Cornellians met their deaths in the war.[19] The war left a mark on Cornell, enhancing the status of the sciences and leaving administrative reorganization in its wake.

Other Ivy schools followed the Cornell pattern in the World War I period. Yale, for example, initiated a military program after the passage of the Morrill Act, and with the later passage of the NDA, it "immediately became involved [in ROTC] and because of its previous experience, it became the sole college to give field artillery training." When ROTC folded into the SATC, Yale faculty voted thirty-eight to zero to grant credit to the courses.[20] The university also pioneered the development of the Naval Aviation Force. At least 9,000 students and graduates served in the war effort, with 227 giving their lives. Overall, "Nearly the entire student body was enrolled in an informal military training course." At the same time, noted historian Gaddis Smith maintains that "ROTC was a problem from its inception in 1917" because of the less-than-stellar quality of its courses and instructors – a problem nationwide, according to other scholars of ROTC.[21] "A skeptical Yale College faculty acquiesced in granting course credit because President Arthur Hadley said it was the right thing to do."[22] Like Cornell, Yale also underwent administrative change after World War I, moving toward greater centralization. This pattern mirrors national developments, for war and military policy needs have been important catalysts in the trend toward greater administrative centralization in American history, albeit continuously checked by the proponents of libertarianism and federalism.[23]

[18] Bishop, *A History of Cornell*, pp. 425–36.

[19] Cornell University, Excelsior Battalion U.S. Army ROTC, Commissioning: http://armyrotc.cornell.edu/prospective_commissioning.shtml

[20] Kelley, *Yale*, pp. 349–51; Marc Lindemann, "Storming the Ivory Tower: The Military's Return to American Campuses," *Parameters* 44 (Winter 2006–7): 46–7.

[21] See, e.g., Arthur T. Coumbe and Lee S. Harford, *U.S. Army Cadet Command: The 10 Year History* (Office of the Command Historian, U.S. Army Cadet Command, 1996).

[22] Gaddis W. Smith, "Yale and the Vietnam War," paper presented at University Seminar on the History of Columbia University, October 19, 1999, pp. 12–13: http://beatl.barnard.columbia.edu/cuhistory/yale.htm; Coumbe and Harford, *U.S. Army Cadet Command: The 10 Year History*.

[23] This is a major theme in Stephen Skowronek, *Building a New American State: The Expansion of National Administrative Capacities, 1877–1920* (Cambridge University Press, 1982). Skowronek devotes an ample section to military administrative development and its effect on the nationalization of administration. The theme is one of national advance, constantly checked by blowback from local and state interests. A similar theme (although with a stronger emphasis on libertarian philosophy) is found in Aaron Friedberg, *In the Shadow of the Garrison State: America's Anti-Statism and Its Cold*

World War I impacted Harvard, Princeton, and Columbia in much the same way. At Princeton, historian James Axtel writes, "The two world wars were considered by most students worth fighting and their causes even worth dying for. ... They prepared patriotically in upper class ROTC units, classes and summer camps. ... Student opposition to the war was minimal before America signed on in the spring of 1917; after that, it vanished."[24] Columbia was one of the first universities to adopt a Naval ROTC unit in 1916, and it joined the military effort during the mobilization for war. (According to the webpage of the Columbia Alliance for ROTC, "Columbia's dedication to the service was profound – at one point in its history the university was producing more officers per year than even the U.S. Naval Academy.")[25] Like the country as a whole, Columbia struggled with reconciling patriotism and free thought throughout the war period and in its aftermath, but it strove to learn from these travails and to reassert its commitment to academic freedom after the war.[26] Some students and faculty opposed the war, leading to clashes with the administration (historian Charles Beard being perhaps the most famous example); but overall, Columbia dedicated itself to the war effort. Hundreds of students enlisted or served in the SATC, and dozens of faculty members "enthusiastically joined the war effort, either in uniform or in one of the many war agencies." According to a 2011 Columbia University Task Force on Military Engagement that we will discuss in Chapter 7, more than 2,600 Columbians served in World War I. Most were students or alumni, but more than 350 were faculty members or administrators. Nearly a third of the Class of 1918 missed commencement due to service obligations.[27] Interestingly, an SATC course on "War Aims" (which Robert A. McCaughey describes as a course in "Applied Apologetics") evolved into the path-breaking "Core" course on "Contemporary Civilizations" after the war, making Columbia the birthplace of the "general education movement in the United States."[28]

The involvement of other Ivy schools in the war effort mirrored that of Cornell, Princeton, and Columbia. At the University of Pennsylvania, for example, "the campus became militarized," forming a volunteer student battalion and

War Strategy (Princeton University Press, 2000). See also Richard Franklin Bensel, *Yankee Leviathan: The Origins of Central State Authority in America, 1859–1877* (Cambridge University Press, 1990). Bensel argues that the demands of the Civil War contributed to development of a centralized American state.

[24] James Axtel, *The Making of Princeton University: From Woodrow Wilson to the Present* (Princeton University Press, 2006), p. 345.

[25] ROTC Advocacy at Columbia: http://www.advocatesforrotc.org/columbia/index.html.

[26] The literature on the violations of free speech and civil liberty during World War I is voluminous. See, e.g., Geoffrey Stone, *War and Liberty: An American Dilemma, 1790 to the Present* (W. W. Norton, 2007). John Dewey, Columbia's famous pragmatist philosopher, was lukewarm about free speech before the war, but emerged as an advocate of free thought after witnessing the violations at Columbia and in the nation. See David Rabban, *Free Speech in Its Forgotten Years, 1870–1920* (Cambridge University Press, 1997).

[27] Columbia University, "Task Force on Military Engagement," p. 6.

[28] McCaughey, *Stand Columbia*, pp. 253, 290–3.

instituting special programs for aviation and government service. The university also initiated a four-year program in military science toward the end of the war. With war's arrival, "the population of Penn students and alumni answered the call." As of commencement exercises in 1918, 6,012 Penn students and alumni were reported to be serving in one of these capacities, most in the Army.[29]

World War II

World War II presented ROTC with its first major test as an organization. Between August 1940 and the end of 1941, eighty thousand Organized Reserve Corps officers, most of whom hailed from ROTC, stepped up to duty, forming what Army Cadet Command historians Arthur T. Coumbe and Lee S. Harford call the "nucleus around which General [George C.] Marshall built the war-time Army." (However, the abilities that these officers gained were mostly derived from real war experience and training, not ROTC itself. Officers from Officer Candidate School proved to be superior.)[30] We devote our attention in this section to Harvard, Yale, Dartmouth, and the University of Pennsylvania, as they represent what took place throughout the Ivy League.

After the attack on Pearl Harbor, the government lowered the draft age to eighteen, and university employees and students left campuses in droves to serve. Their exit posed a problem for universities and the military, both of which confronted a dearth of students and qualified officers, respectively. In response, the military branches formed new programs in 1943 to replace ROTC that combined college education with military service, such as the Navy's "V" Training Programs, the Naval Indoctrination Training School, and Army programs under the umbrella of the Army Specialized Training Program, turning universities into veritable military instruction institutions.[31]

Harvard was the most noteworthy example of the World War II university among a competitive Ivy group. To its president, James Bryant Conant, winning the war against fascism did not just mean surviving a national existential threat: It was also a matter of preserving the mission of liberal democracy in a hostile world. As the world situation worsened in the late 1930s, Conant, a highly regarded chemist before ascending Harvard's administrative ladder, began crafting a political philosophy of normative realism that reflected the thought of Reinhold Niebuhr and Winston Churchill. In an address to the Harvard community at the commencement of the new school year, he challenged the thought of those who sought to appease Hitler: "War is not the worst possibility we face;

[29] University of Pennsylvania, "A Brief History of Global Engagement at the University of Pennsylvania, International Crises: World War I": http://www.archives.upenn.edu/histy/features/intrntnl/crises/ww1.html.

[30] Coumbe and Harford, *U.S. Army Cadet Command: The 10 Year History*, pp. 18–19.

[31] See, e.g., Jennifer Seaton, "Dartmouth During World War II": http://www.dartmouth.edu/~library/rauner/archives/oral_history/worldwar2/history.html; adapted from an article by Seaton in *Dartmouth Engineer*.

the worst is the complete triumph of totalitarianism. Such a triumph might conceivably include this republic among the victims as a result of military reversals. Or we might become in essence a dependent state through a policy of appeasement under the coercion of a Nazi system which controlled the seas."[32]

As America moved into war, Conant assumed national leadership and helped to enlist Harvard and other institutions as partners with the government and the military. In another speech in the midst of the war, he articulated a vision of civic education that was reminiscent of the Periclean speech that Professor Diman delivered for Brown's honored dead in the Civil War: "Once it is clear in a man's mind that the demands of war are one thing and those of a free society another, the virtues which are developed on the battlefield reinforce the natural talents. And this education may prove as valuable in the postwar world as years of study in academic halls." Historian Richard Norton Smith elaborates regarding the speech:

> He needn't remind [the students], Conant went on, that the silencing of guns would not eliminate men's problems. All in common would require courage, endurance, and patience – above all patience – if the coming peace were not to be more than an empty husk, a mere pause in the shooting and slaughter. For the youths seated before him, sacrifice would impart its special brand of knowledge. Freedom won through risk would assume an almost holy significance.[33]

The political enslavement and Gulags that engulfed Central and Eastern Europe after the withdrawal of the Allies sadly gave substance to Conant's forebodings in that unfortunate region of the world.[34]

Carrying his philosophy into the realm of action, Conant presided over institutional transformation at Harvard (creating what was known as "Conant's Arsenal") at the same time that he advanced on the national front. In 1940, he became a top assistant to the redoubtable Vannevar Bush in setting up the National Defense Research Committee (NDRC), which "would license the marriage of bureaucrat and professor that would so color postwar education";[35] he was also instrumental in setting up the Manhattan Project. Though many Harvard students vocally opposed war before 1941, they "flocked to war

[32] Conant Harvard address, quoted in Richard Norton Smith, *The Harvard Century: The Making of a University to a Nation* (Simon and Schuster, 1986), p. 144. Control of the seas had become a preeminent strategic and tactical assumption of military policy in America and the world. Its most famous exponent was Alfred Thayer Mahan, whose book *The Influence of Sea Power upon History, 1660–1783* (Little, Brown, 1890) is one of the most influential books on naval power ever published.

[33] Smith, *The Harvard Century*, p. 157.

[34] See Timothy Snyder's remarkable *Bloodlands: Europe Between Hitler and Stalin* (Basic, 2010). As is well known, and as Snyder tirelessly documents, mass slaughter also took place during the war, as well, and before in the case of Soviet areas.

[35] Smith, *The Harvard Century*, p. 143. On the vital role of the NDRC in military and scientific research, see Roger L. Geiger, *Research and Relevant Knowledge: American Research Universities Since World War II* (Oxford University Press, 1993), ch. 1.

courses" once war became inevitable. Numerous professors redirected their campus research toward the war effort, while others joined the government and the military, including J. Robert Oppenheimer, a father of the atomic bomb. In a letter to his Board of Overseers, Conant wrote that, "It is time for war, therefore, and not for peace that we must now lay our immediate educational plans." As the war went on, almost eighty university laboratories lent a hand in military research projects, involving such matters as radar, napalm, explosives, and various medical treatments. By the last year of the war, the university's share of government research reached $33.5 million, third in the nation behind MIT and Cal Tech. "Almost 27,000 University alumni, students, employees, and faculty members served in the armed forces; 697 lost their lives. The war had a lasting impact on Harvard and American higher education. It brought universities, government, and industry into a powerful and continuing partnership." According to one dean, the university "became in large measure a military and navy training school."[36]

Yale also contributed in notable ways. Its president, Charles Seymour, declared that "the justification of a university is to be found in the service which it gives to the nation."[37] Yale professor Paul Kennedy relates that Yale became a "military camp" for the second time in its history during the war. A total of 18,678 alumni performed military service, 514 of whom died in action.[38] "The students were members of the armed services first and Yale students second."[39] Yale researchers worked on radar and the atomic bomb, and many faculty members served in the armed forces or taught courses to more than twenty thousand soldiers in all the services. Moreover, "Yale faculty members worked all over the world in the war effort."[40] Yale was also a wellspring for the Office of Strategic Services (OSS), created in 1942 to engage in intelligence gathering. The predecessor of the CIA, OSS's membership for many years consisted of disproportionate numbers of Ivy students and graduates (especially in its research and analysis branch), with Yale heading the list. By the summer of 1942, according to Robin W. Winks, Yale "was on a full war footing."[41] During the war, Yale's Institute for International Studies (founded in 1935 with a grant from the Rockefeller Foundation) worked closely with the State Department on many projects, and the university's Institute for Human Relations handled intelligence matters. Winks, whose book *Cloak and Gown* is a leading (and highly entertaining) source on Yale, the Ivies, and the OSS-CIA,

[36] John T. Bethell, *Harvard Observed: An Illustrated History of the University in the Twentieth Century* (Harvard Magazine, 1998), pp. 137–8.

[37] Kelley, *Yale: A History*, p. 396, quoted in Lindemann, "Storming the Ivy Tower," p. 47.

[38] Kennedy quoted by Jeremy Kutner, "Panel Urges Ties Between Yale, Military," *Yale Daily News*, April 10, 2003. Cited in Lindemann, "Storming the Ivy Tower," p. 47. On the number of Yale alumni serving and dying, see Lindemann, "Storming the Ivy Tower," p. 47.

[39] Smith, "Yale and the Vietnam War," p. 13.

[40] Kelley, *Yale: A History*, p. 403.

[41] Robin W. Winks, *Cloak and Gown: Scholars in the Secret War, 1939–1961* (Yale University Press, 1986), p. 31.

sums up the relationship between the universities and the intelligence agencies by the end of the 1940s: "The urgencies of the wartime campus simply extended, with hardly the hiatus of 1946, into the cold war and, at most universities, through the war in Korea, not to be questioned until the early 1960s." Winks proceeds to describe the political philosophy that undergirded these enterprises: It was a time when Yale and the upper-middle class

> thought of themselves as having a mission to the world, enjoying "the blessings of liberty," able to reshape the world to its benefit and, not incidentally, to America's. They had health, knowledge, power. One enemy would be replaced with another, but the continuity of purpose, the conviction that to apply one's education in the service of the state was an appropriate thing to do, the certainty that civic virtue grew from the broadly liberalizing study of the humanities, of cultures other than one's own, and of the languages that framed those cultures, these convictions remained, from World War II, across the arch of the cold war, in Korea, into the 1960s.... Pride in one's culture, one's history, like pride in one's work, or in one's university, was the glue that gave coherence, and force ... to a society that, perhaps, had lacked the good grace to be confused, as it would be by the 1960s.[42]

Dartmouth, about which we have said little thus far, was also profoundly affected by World War II. The Thayer School of Engineering found space in each of its several laboratories for two hundred students, and the college opened its gates to the Navy, hosting the largest Navy V-12 unit in the nation. Jennifer Seaton writes, "Run on military time, with reveille at 6 a.m. and taps at 10 p.m., Dartmouth operated like a naval base for the rest of the war." By mid-July, about 2,000 enlisted men and an officer staff moved to the college, with 300 Dartmouth students and 74 students enrolled at Thayer. One veteran commented that "the campus was really a naval station."[43] According to Sarah Hartwell, a reference researcher at Dartmouth, 11,091 members of the Dartmouth community (alumni, students, and staff) served in the military in World War II, and 301 died.[44]

World War II may have had more of an effect on Columbia than any other Ivy school, if only because Columbia had lagged behind most of the league in the reception of federal funding before the war. Its main source of federal funding at this time was a $30,000 grant received from the Office of Scientific Research and Development (OSRD) to build magnetrons. At war's end, however, "that initial $30,000 contract had grown to two hundred contracts with fourteen different government agencies, totaling $43 million. At the height of the war, Columbia

[42] Winks, *Cloak and Gown*, pp. 55, 59.

[43] Jennifer Seaton, "Engineered for Service: World War II Vets on the War Years at Dartmouth," *Dartmouth Engineer* (Winter 2008). See also Rauner Library, "Oral History: World War Two at Dartmouth"; "About the Project": http://www.dartmouth.edu/~library/rauner/archives/oral_history/worldwar2/about.html.

[44] Statistic provided by Sarah Hartwell, Reading Room Supervisor, Rauner Special Collections, Dartmouth College, July 15, 2010. Hartwell checked internal memos in the World War I and II files.

employed twenty-six hundred individuals in war-related research and teaching." Nationally, Columbia ranked fourth in the country in wartime funding, trailing only MIT, Cal Tech, and Harvard. The university also set up three foreign-area studies programs, making it a national leader in this realm.[45] In addition, Columbia staff conducted significant research. The Manhattan Project began at the university in 1940, and faculty members performed important work relating to radar. More than 15,000 Columbia alumni and students served during the war, with as many as 450 dying in uniform. Soon after Pearl Harbor, the campus became a training center for the Navy, with twelve of its buildings housing a Midshipman's School that trained over 20,000 officer candidates. Meanwhile, a Navy V-12 program prepared dentists and doctors for service, while the university and military established the Military Government School under the aegis of government professor Schuyler Wallace. The Military Government School taught administrative skills to Naval officers who would be administering occupied territories. "These contributions to the war effort gave the military a strong presence on the Columbia campus."[46] At one point during the war, Columbia's Midshipmen School "rivaled the United States Military Academy in size."[47]

THE WORLD WAR I AND WORLD WAR II UNIVERSITY CONSIDERED

The pattern traced thus far reveals increasing involvement of higher education in military matters in successive wars. This trajectory paralleled broader national trends that fostered centralization of political power, the internationalization and globalization of the world and of the American interest, and the growing influence of scientific expertise in national life. Modern research universities now conceived their missions to lie in service to society, which included, for better or worse, providing assistance in the national defense and in the study of the world.

Much attention has been given to what we will look at in the next section of this chapter: the "Cold War University," which ultimately provoked the powerful dissent of the 1960s that engendered the demise of ROTC at many elite schools, including several in the Ivy League. But the cursory presentation in this section reveals that two other war-related models of the university existed before the Cold War University: the World War I and World War II universities. Interestingly, few of the many critics of the Cold War University have turned their critical sights on these incarnations of the university. But, as historian David Engerman informs us, new scholars of the Cold War are now considering the university that preceded the Cold War University. "Demonstrating the tremendous value of historical perspective, these books show that the symptoms

[45] McCaughey, *Stand Columbia*, pp. 329, 357, 425.

[46] Columbia University, "Columbia University Roll of Honor: World War II": http://www.warmemorial.columbia.edu/wars/world-war-ii.

[47] Columbia University, "Task Force on Military Engagement," p. 6.

of the Cold War University – political interference in faculty appointments, depoliticized social sciences that emphasized the scientific over the social, federally sponsored research, and the ascent of faculty members more connected to research communities than to their own institutions – predated the Cold War. World War II was the watershed moment for the involvement of federal agencies in university-based research."[48]

Many reasons for these different assessments could be proffered. Some academics objected to the strategic, tactical, and human aspects of the Korean War; the nuclear standoff with the Soviet Union; and, later, the Vietnam War. Others simply objected to the continuance of a strong military presence on campus after World War II ended: Accepting such presence in a total war is one thing, but extending it into an era of limited yet indefinite wars is another matter. Others may have felt less hostility toward Communist aggression and expansion than toward fascist enemies.[49]

A related factor was the way in which the Vietnam War solidified a growing concern regarding the growth of American influence in the world over the span of the twentieth century. Some scholars and critics have argued that America acquired an empire based on imperialism and domination, whereas others have entertained the more sanguine view that the American empire was essentially economic and democratic in nature – a different, more benign form of imperialism, American style. Critics of the Cold War University generally took the more pessimistic view.[50]

We can glean one lesson from the World War I and II universities regarding the military-university relationship: Substantial governmental/military intervention into university affairs can be justified when the nation is fighting a total war that necessitates such action. This is no doubt one reason that critics of the Cold War University have been reluctant to turn their ire upon this university's predecessors. Of course, basic academic freedom must be preserved even in these circumstances, lest the university lose its integrity by violating its moral

[48] Engerman, "Rethinking Cold War Universities," p. 81.

[49] On how many intellectuals harbored more moral condemnation for Nazism than Communism, see Anne Applebaum, *Gulag: A History* (Random House, Anchor, 2003), Introduction. On how many American historians turned a blind eye to Soviet espionage, see John Earl Haynes and Harvey Klehr, *In Denial: Historians, Communism and Espionage* (Encounter, 2003). See also Snyder, *Bloodlands*.

[50] William Appleman Williams, a well-known and rightly highly regarded American foreign policy historian at Wisconsin and Oregon State, is an interesting example of this logic. Williams became a leading critic of the Cold War University and also viewed American empire through darker lenses. See *The Tragedy of American Diplomacy* (Dell, 1962). On Williams' view of the Cold War University, see Matthew Levin, "Cold War University," presented at the William Appleman Williams Conference: 50th Anniversary of the Tragedy of American Diplomacy; Panel One: William Appleman Williams and Staughton Lynd, "Scholar Activists and the Cold War University," October 9, 2009, University of Wisconsin, Madison: http://eucenter.wisc.edu/WAW%20Conference%20Color%20Copy.pdf. A more sanguine view of the effects of American diplomacy and foreign policy is found in Thomas F. Madden, *Empires of Trust: How Rome Built – and America Is Building – A New World* (Dutton, 2008).

charter. But in times of war and other emergencies, official and informal codes of conduct may properly yield to the demands of public necessity, so long as a publicly justified reason or set of reasons meets the test for exceptions.[51] The criminal law, for example, provides a "necessity defense" in extreme cases that authorizes the breaking of law; and the Third Amendment prohibits the quartering of soldiers in homes, *except* when emergencies justify such normally unconscionable action.

In a similar vein, presidents in wartime have often relied upon their executive powers (explicit or implicit in Article II of the Constitution, or in the very nature of sovereignty) to enact measures that would not withstand the scrutiny of law in peacetime. Such ambiguity comes with the very territory of statecraft.[52] The claim that the ends *never* justify one's means in *any* way is naïve and wrong: Though the ends can never absolutely or unreflectively justify the means, such absolutist separation of means and ends defies moral obligation. Would not trespassing be legitimate to save a drowning child? As Lincoln wrote in an April 1864 letter to Albert G. Hodges in defense of his frequent invocation of the doctrine of "public necessity" in the Civil War:

> I [understood] my oath to preserve the Constitution to the best of my ability, imposed upon me the duty of preserving, by every indispensable means, that government – that nation – of which that Constitution was the organic law. Was it possible to lose the nation, and yet preserve the Constitution? I felt that measures, otherwise unconstitutional, might become lawful by becoming indispensable to the preservation of the Constitution, through the preservation of the nation.[53]

A similar logic applies to the university and the military: The greater the emergency, the more intervention may be justified, so long as it preserves the basic academic freedom that is the defining attribute of higher education.

But what about less-than-total wars, such as the Cold War? In such cases, we should think of a sliding scale, calibrated to measure or reflect the extent of the emergency. And in conceiving emergency, we must take into account that emergency and crisis are the constant state of humanity and its history. We return to this question in our concluding chapter.

[51] This obligation lies at the heart of Socratic moral reasoning. Positions we take, especially those that appear counterintuitive, require careful and thoughtful justification. See, e.g., Dana Villa, *Socratic Citizenship* (Princeton University Press, 2001).

[52] A recent book-long articulation of this historical truth is Charles Hill's *Grand Strategies: Literature, Statecraft, and World Order* (Yale University Press, 2010). See also Isaiah Berlin's influential essay on Machiavelli's teaching that political leadership is obligated to practice an ethical system that is sometimes different from the ethics of everyday civil life. Isaiah Berlin, "The Question of Machiavelli," *New York Review of Books*, November 4, 1971.

[53] Abraham Lincoln, "Letter to Albert Hodges," April 4, 1864: http://teachingamericanhistory.org/library/index.asp?documentprint=423. On the necessity defense and legitimated disobedience in criminal law, see Sanford Kadish and Mortimer Kadish, *Discretion to Disobey* (Stanford University Press, 1973). On Lincoln's embrace of the public necessity doctrine in war, see Daniel Farber, *Lincoln's Constitution* (University of Chicago Press, 2003). A penetrating recent discussion of the intimate relationship between means and ends is Philip Bobbitt, *Terror and Consent: The Wars for the Twenty-first Century* (Random House, Anchor, 2009).

THE COLD WAR UNIVERSITY

World War II wrought monumental change in higher education, including the rise of the Cold War University on the heels of the World War II University. Massive amounts of government defense-related funding began flowing into university coffers at the same time that institutions reaped benefits from the return to campus of millions of veterans. Among the returning veterans, 2,200,000 (51 percent of total returning veterans) took advantage of the opportunities provided by the G. I. Bill of 1944 (the Servicemen's Readjustment Act) by entering or returning to college, while another 5,600,000 attended vocational schools or undertook on-the-job training. Interestingly, civic engagement and awareness (defined as participation in civic and public interest groups and electoral behavior) of those who participated in the program increased markedly after the war, according to a seminal study conducted by Suzanne Mettler. One of Mettler's most interesting findings was that the bill's impact on civic engagement was due in part to the fact that veterans construed the opportunity not as a "right" but rather as a privilege and reward for having taken on the *obligation* or *duty* of military service in a time of national need. They felt thankful, not entitled, and returned the favor by becoming more involved in community and national affairs.[54] This sense of duty and engagement fueled a portion of the national support for the Cold War national defense policy that the United States forged after the war (what scholars have called the early Cold War Consensus).

Following World War II, the nation underwent the process of demobilization that had followed previous wars. But America's new international commitments as the emergent leader of the Free World and the onset of the Cold War and the war in Korea thwarted this hope. International problems erupted like a whirlwind across the globe: The Soviets detonated an atom bomb in mid-1949, and governments inspired by Stalin-style Communism usurped power across Eastern Europe, including a coup in Czechoslovakia, followed by the blockade of Berlin. In 1949, Mao led the Communist takeover of China, and the Communists of North Korea invaded South Korea the following year.[55] The Cold War posed serious challenges to America's military manpower policy. Such events and situations unnerved a nation that had expected history to repeat itself by allowing the citizenry to turn their backs on war and military concerns in the aftermath of major war. As Arthur Schlesinger, Jr., wrote at the very beginning of *The Vital Center*, in which he made the case for a foreign policy consensus to resist Communism, "Western Man in the middle of the twentieth century is tense,

[54] Suzanne Mettler, "Bringing the State Back In to Civic Engagement: Policy Feedback Effects of the G. I. Bill for World War II Veterans," *American Political Science Review* 96, 2 (June 2002). Mettler expanded her quantitative and qualitative analysis in a subsequent book, *Soldiers to Citizens: The G.I. Bill and the Making of the Greatest Generation* (Oxford University Press, 2005).

[55] See, e.g., Ronald E. Powaski, *The Cold War: The United States and the Soviet Union, 1917–1991* (Oxford University Press, 1998), ch. 3.

uncertain, adrift. We look upon our epoch as a time of troubles, an age of anxiety."[56]

Before 1948, the country was moving toward restoring its traditional policy of relying on volunteers, accompanied by occasional limited drafts. The draft ended in 1947, but the new threats, especially Korea, reversed the hopes of limited mobilization, leading President Truman, the Congress, and the military to call for the enactment of Universal Military Training (UMT), which required all able-bodied eighteen-year-olds and high school graduates to perform two years of service. (Harvard's Conant was a leading advocate of UMT, which led to it being labeled the "Conant Plan.") Though a UMT bill did pass Congress, it fell short of implementation due to widespread opposition; the nation finally settled on a compromise policy, the Selective Service Act of 1948, which offered a host of exemptions.[57] When the Korean War broke out in mid-1950, America was still maintaining six hundred thousand troops around the world, "enervated by the precipitous postwar demobilization, the temporary suspension of the draft, and the labors of occupation duty."[58]

Responding to the need for better-trained officers, the military strove to restore ROTC's status in the military establishment. A survey of college students in 1950 found that 90 percent favored making ROTC available, even though most programs were compulsory at that time at both land grant and private institutions. The early Cold War ushered in an era of "fusion" between civilian and military expertise in order to bridge military and scientific knowledge, bringing pressures on ROTC to change its curriculum by making it less careerist and more educational in orientation.[59]

Despite its growth, ROTC's effectiveness languished. But the program was buttressed by growing awareness that the new age of international obligations, complex technology, and military administrative complexity required officers with better educations in the physical and social sciences.[60] In addition, the national-level Gray Commission recommended that the Army ROTC become the leading source of active officers. "These developments reflected the growing feeling that the ROTC was, given prevailing conditions, the best available means of producing enough officers of the right type to lead America's Cold War Army."[61] The

[56] Arthur M. Schlesinger, Jr., *The Vital Center: The Politics of Democracy* (Houghton Mifflin, 1949), p. 1.

[57] An excellent treatment of the blowback from libertarian forces on the right and the left to the call for UMT is Friedberg, *In the Shadow of the Garrison State*, ch. 5.

[58] Eliot A. Cohen, *Citizens and Soldiers: The Dilemmas of Military Service* (Cornell University Press, 1985), p. 103.

[59] The information in the paragraph is drawn largely from Neiberg, *Making Citizen Soldiers*, ch. 3, "The Origins of Postwar Dissatisfaction." The concept of fusion is from Samuel P. Huntington, *The Soldier and the State: The Theory and Politics of Civil–Military Relations* (Harvard University Press, 1957), p. 351.

[60] This is a major theme in Lyons and Masland, *Education and Military Leadership*. See also Morris Janowitz, *The Professional Soldier: A Social and Political Portrait*, 2nd Edition (Free Press, 1971).

[61] Coumbe and Harford, *U.S. Army Cadet Command: The 10 Year History*, pp. 21–2.

Selective Service Act produced an incentive for students to join ROTC, for the program offered an exemption from the draft, as well as an officer position upon graduation. According to Neiberg, the expansion of ROTC in the 1960s and early 1970s reflected, to an extent, fear of the draft and a desire to join the military on one's own terms.[62]

Universities strove to accommodate ROTC for several reasons, including their belief in the normative commitment to the national defense during the Cold War and their concurrence with the findings of a 1950 presidential committee that cautioned that military dominance of American society could be avoided only by striving "to preserve within the military as much of [the soldier's] civilian life as possible."[63] ROTC was one tool for maintaining military preparedness in a new era of enhanced commitments without falling prey to the usurpations of the "Garrison State." Universities became integral partners in the emerging Cold War Consensus, the "Vital Center."[64]

All Ivy League schools remained committed to ROTC during the Cold War, although the tensions that sprouted in those institutions tended to be more prominent than at many other schools. In a dress rehearsal of the conflicts that would erupt in later years, Harvard, Yale, and Princeton protested a Navy peacetime program that would have given the service the power to select the schools' students and to govern the living conditions and details of cadet lives. In the end, the Navy acquiesced to the trio's concerns. During the 1950s, Harvard maintained programs in all three of the services, but the programs were small, with only a dozen or so graduates in 1957. According to a recent history of modern Harvard, as faculty power waxed in the postwar period, "Meritocracy began to put strains on the Harvard-ROTC relationship well before Vietnam."[65] Faculty members had historically been more suspicious of ROTC than had university leadership, so the shift toward greater faculty power and the faculty-oriented standard of merit after the war contributed to the steady marginalization of the program that would soon take place.[66] Naval and Army programs returned to Yale after the war, as well, along with an Air Force unit in 1949 (although it lasted only a few years). ROTC membership at Yale crested during the Korean War, falling steadily afterward for several years. During the 1950s, "faculty members began to express doubts about the inclusion of ROTC in a liberal education."[67]

62 Michael Neiberg, "The Irony of an All Volunteer Force," Conference on Civil-Military Relations in American Universities, Pittsburgh, Pennsylvania, April 2010.

63 Neiberg, *Making Citizen Soldiers*, p. 42, quoting from Mark Grandstaff, "Making the Military American: Advertising, Reform, and the Demise of an Antistanding Military Tradition," *Journal of Military History* 60 (April 1996): 299–324, quoting p. 315.

64 Schlesinger, *The Vital Center*..

65 Morton Keller and Phyllis Keller, *Making Harvard Modern: The Rise of America's University* (Oxford University Press, 2001), p. 208.

66 On the rise of meritocracy and professional autonomy and power as a major feature of faculty life, see Christopher Jencks and David Riesman, *The Academic Revolution* (Transaction, 2001).

67 See Smith, "Yale and the Vietnam War," pp. 13–14; Lindemann, "Storming the Ivory Tower," pp. 47–8.

Princeton reactivated its Army ROTC unit immediately after the war, adding a Naval unit in 1946 and an Air Force detachment in 1951. According to Alexander Leitch, ROTC assumed a "significant presence" on campus during this period, partly due to the Cold War, the draft exemption offered to ROTC cadets, and the promise of a commission. In 1951, campus units contained 1,107 members, coming replete with annual reviews, military balls, and commissioning ceremonies. "But even with the support given ROTC by Presidents [John Grier] Hibben and [Harold Willis] Dodds, there were always some who questioned the presence of a military training unit on a liberal arts campus. As early as 1927, an article in the *Alumni Weekly* had foreshadowed the principal arguments later put forth against ROTC when it declared not only that ROTC courses are not properly a part of a university curriculum, but also that they are "detrimental to the furtherance of permanent peace, toward which the University ... should constantly strive."[68]

Cornell also renewed its relationship with ROTC units; and Brown reactivated its Naval unit at war's end while opening its doors to a detachment of the Air Force ROTC, one of seventy-seven such programs nationally.[69] Reflecting the Cold War Consensus, Brown president Henry Merritt Wriston declared his support for the new program, which enrolled seventy freshmen and sophomores the first year: "Under the circumstances, it is a public service the University can render, and I am delighted that the Air Force has given Brown this opportunity."[70] For its part, Dartmouth maintained its Army and Naval units after the war, adding an Air Force detachment soon thereafter. Ivy school graduates and students also participated in the Korean War, although at what appears to have been a significantly lesser rate than in the two world wars, even considering that the war was smaller and "limited."[71]

The Cold War University, Research, and Active Policy Making

ROTC was just one facet of the Cold War University. Another prong involved dynamic relationships among universities, the government, private foundations, and corporations, each of which supplied large-scale funding through a complex web of interactions. An array of government agencies provided federal funds

68 Alexander Leitch, *A Princeton Companion* (Princeton University Press, 1978): http://etcweb.princeton.edu/CampusWWW/Companion/reserve_officers_training_corps.html.

69 Brown University, Office of Communications, "From Martha Mitchell's Encyclopedia Brunoniana": http://www.brown.edu/Administration/News_Bureau/Databases/Encyclopedia/search.php?serial=W0410.

70 Brown University, Office of Communications, "From Martha Mitchell's Encyclopedia Brunoniana": http://www.brown.edu/Administration/News_Bureau/Databases/Encyclopedia/search.php?serial=M0330.

71 See, e.g., "Memorial Honors Cornellians Who Served Their Country," *Cornell News*, February 11, 2003: http://www.news.cornell.edu/releases/Feb03/memorial.rededication.lgk.html; Dartmouth information provided by Sarah Hartwell, Reading Room Supervisor, July 13, 2010. Hartwell obtained the information from Charles Wood's pamphlet "The Hill Wind Knows Their Name; A Guide to Dartmouth's War Memorial."

relating to defense, including the Department of Defense (DoD, which replaced the War Department in the 1947 reorganization of the national defense bureaucracy), the Office of Naval Research (ONR, established in 1946), the Atomic Energy Commission (AEC, founded in 1946), and the National Aeronautics and Space Administration (NASA). The National Science Foundation (NSF, established in 1950) and the National Institutes for Health (NIH, founded in 1887) had broader missions, but their funding was "correlated with the Cold War." The NSF budget, for example, mushroomed from $100,000 in 1950 to $100 million in 1960, most going to university-related research. According to historian Matthew Levin, "By the late sixties, the numbers were even more dramatic, with universities spending three billion dollars on research in 1968, seventy percent of it funded by the federal government. . . . More than half of this came from defense-related agencies, including the AEC ($110,000,000), NASA ($129,000,000), and the Department of Defense ($243,000,000)." Another signal act was the National Defense Act of 1958, precipitated by the Soviet Union's launching of Sputnik in 1957. Although most other outside funding went to natural scientists and language programs, social scientists also received support for interdisciplinary studies that had implications for the Cold War. The Rockefeller and Carnegie Foundations disseminated funds for the first area-study programs, which dealt with the Soviet Union, and the Ford Foundation supplied funds for multidisciplinary studies of world regions. After Sputnik, the federal government unveiled the Title VI program, which furnished funds for area-studies programs.[72]

Beyond the cold monetary facts, the Cold War University stood for an idea of citizenship and a related conception of the university. Historian Jeremi Suri analyzes the constellation of ideas that comprised the Cold War University in his book on Henry Kissinger, whose ultimate rise to eminence began at Harvard, a paragon of the Cold War University. The "intellectual and institutional transformation from traditional scholarly detachment to contemporary political empowerment created the 'Cold War University,'" Suri observes. "The intentional blurring of the lines between academic and policy analysis, as well as scholarship and national defense, constituted the Cold War University." Drawing on the historical experiences of Jews such as Kissinger and other outsiders who had suffered oppression at the hands of power that they could not counter, many practitioners of the Cold War University underscored the values of liberal democracy at the same time that they valued the role of the state in protecting the freedom and rights they cherished. (Kissinger himself embodied an uneasy balance between Kant and Hobbes.) The group of policy scholars Kissinger helped to assemble at and around Harvard "identified themselves as defenders of the United States against extremes at home and abroad. For all their intellectual expertise they pursued research explicitly designed to serve practical

[72] Much of the information in this paragraph is from Levin, "Cold War University," pp. 57–8, 64–5; and Engerman, "Rethinking Cold War Universities." See also McCaughey, *Stand Columbia*, p. 365.

and immediate government purposes, in the process protecting a liberal capitalist world. This was the overriding ethos of the Cold War University."[73] Kissinger drew inspiration from his Harvard mentor William Yandell Elliott, who lent him a hand in setting up the famous International Seminar in 1950, which connected students and an extraordinary number of leading foreign policy analysts and practitioners. The seminar was a thread in the complex web of "Cold War networks" forged by Cold War University practitioners. Enjoying exceptional ties to the Cold War policy community, Elliot construed the Cold War as "a struggle for national survival" that called for a stronger national defense. In Elliot's words, "the most elementary lesson of history: No power retains friends which is too weak to defend itself in will or war potential." Elliot's foreign policy realism called for political will to counter "the great mistake of liberalism," which is the belief "that there was [an] automatic character about the rights of people without an affirmation of values or a dedication to duty."[74] Liberal democracy's freedoms are not manna from heaven.

Elliot's vision paralleled the mission of ROTC, as articulated in a 1960 Army pamphlet. "From the privileged sanctuary of our campus quadrangles, laboratories and study halls, dare we forget for whom the bell tolls? It tolls not for the murdered students of Prague, Riga, and Warsaw, but for those now bent to the task of the extinguishment of man's hopes. . . . It tolls for all who fail to realize the nature of this supreme contest of our times." A similar vision was echoed by the famous statement NSC-68, a 1950 National Security Council policy document written by Paul Nitze, the director of policy planning for the State Department (1950–3). NSC-68 presented the moral and prudential case for accepting the duty to engage the Soviet Union, shaping American foreign policy and strategy for the next twenty years.[75]

[73] Jeremi Suri, *Henry Kissinger and the American Century* (Harvard University Press, 2007), pp. 93, 97. For an interesting account of Jews' historical relationship with power as a means of survival, see Ruth Wisse, *Jews and Power* (Schocken, 2007). This logic is consistent with the very foundation of statecraft in the modern era and with the logic of the American constitutional Founders. On the Founders, see Stephen Holmes, *Passions and Constraints: On the Theory of Liberal* Democracy (University of Chicago Press, 1995); on statecraft as state-oriented, see Hill, *Grand Strategies.*

[74] Elliot to Paul Nitze, Policy Planning Staff, U.S. State Department, December 11, 1950; and Transcript of William Elliot and Henry Kissinger in Elliot's Contemporary Political Theory Seminar 204 at Harvard University, March 21, 1955. Quoted in Suri, *Henry Kissinger and the American Century*, pp. 112–3. Nitze was one of the leading national architects of Cold War containment and nuclear deterrence and often engaged in a love-hate relationship with Princeton's George Kennan, the father of the containment policy who became more dovish in later years. See Nicholas Thompson, *The Hawk and the Dove: Paul Nitze, George Kennan, and the History of the Cold War* (Henry Holt, 2009).

[75] Army ROTC 1960 pamphlet, quoted in Neiberg, *Making Citizen Soldiers*, p. 41. National Security Council, *NSC-68: United States Objectives and Programs for National Security. A Report to the President Pursuant to the President's Directive of January 31, 1950*, April 14, 1950: http://www.fas.org/irp/offdocs/nsc-hst/nsc-68.htm. See the discussion of NSC-68 in Thompson, *The Hawk and the Dove*. For a critique of this type of "military metaphysics," see Andrew Bacevich, "The Tyranny of Defense," *Atlantic Monthly*, January–February 2011.

Although the Cold War University was buttressed by the Cold War Consensus, it planted seeds that would later sprout into outright tension. By creating new centers, institutes, and programs that relied on outside funding and members whose ties to traditional departments and undergraduate teaching were often tenuous, the Cold War University weaved a quasi-alien institutional structure into the fabric of the traditional university. Suri, for example, notes Kissinger's indifference to Harvard's Government Department and to faculty members who were "less prominent, middling figures."[76] Even Vannevar Bush expressed discomfort with the potential militarization of the university – a position that reflected Eisenhower's later famous warning about the military-government-industrial complex.[77] ROTC and the research arm of the Cold War University raised similar questions regarding the quality of the product and the respective programs' independence from the normal institutional rules and obligations to which more traditional faculty members and programs had to adhere. At the same time, ROTC and Cold War research provided benefits to universities and to the nation. The relationship between these two institutions entails a "paradoxical" balancing of two themes. As David A. Wilson observes:

> One is that the essential character or purposes of a university and that of a military organization are contradictory, so that the soul of a university cooperating with the military is threatened. The second is that finding ways of sustaining an effective civilian influence on the military – for example, in the form of Reserve Officers' Training Corps and academic scientists in the picture – is a good, American thing to do.[78]

McCarthyism was a major problem in the 1950s, but, according to Engerman and other new scholars of the Cold War University, most of the government programs under discussion were relatively unaffected by this disease and tolerated surprisingly spacious breathing room for academic and intellectual freedom. But McCarthyism did affect the AEC, especially in its treatment of J. Robert Oppenheimer, the lead scientist in the Manhattan Project, who was accused of Communist sympathies;[79] when campus rebellion erupted in the 1960s, the lingering toxins of McCarthyism may have helped to further poison the military–campus relationship.

Not surprisingly, Ivy League institutions were leaders on the Cold War University front, along with such other institutions as MIT, Cal Tech, Stanford, Berkeley, Chicago, Michigan, Illinois, and Wisconsin.[80] We encapsulate some of

76 Suri, *Henry Kissinger and the American Century*, pp. 133–4.

77 Dwight D. Eisenhower, "Military-Industrial Complex Speech, Dwight D. Eisenhower, 1961," *Public Papers of the Presidents, Dwight D. Eisenhower* (U.S. Government Printing Office, 1961), pp. 1035–40: http://www.h-net.org/~hst306/documents/indust.html.

78 David A. Wilson, Preface, *Universities and the Military* (Annals of the American Academy of Political Science), p. 14.

79 Engerman, "Rethinking the Cold War University"; Carl Kaysen, "Can Universities Cooperate with the Defense Establishment?" *Universities and the Military*, p. 34.

80 On the relationship between the Cold War and academic science at other institutions, especially MIT and Stanford, see Stuart W. Leslie, *The Cold War and American Science: The Military-Industrial-Academic Complex at MIT and Stanford* (Columbia University Press, 1993). Leslie's first chapter, on MIT, is entitled "A University Polarized Around the Military."

the activities of three representative Ivy institutions – Cornell, Harvard, and Columbia – to illustrate the Cold War University's research agenda in action.

Cornell made a smooth adjustment to the Cold War University out of the ashes of World War II. Bishop captures the spirit of the time nicely: "The war made research respectable in the general view. What had been the peculiar passion of unworldly professors became a necessity in international and industrial warfare, and its practitioners the darlings even of the vast *profanum vulgas*." Before World War II, Cornell's research expenditures amounted to about $2 million a year; the sum jumped to $12 million in 1947–8, three quarters of which were enabling funds from the government, the rest flowing from corporations, trade associations, foundations, individuals, and the Cornell budget. To handle the new load, Cornell created the new position of vice president of research. The Department of Chinese Studies (launched in 1944–5) broadened its scope, becoming the program in Far Eastern Studies, which drew on social anthropology to produce knowledge of cultures. The dean overseeing the program stated that this knowledge along with knowledge of languages constituted "a form of national power." Rockefeller funds supported foreign language studies, and other funds backed research in theoretical and applied physics.[81]

Perhaps the most controversial Cornell project was emblematic of the "paradoxes" posed by the Cold War University. In 1946, Cornell obtained an aeronautical laboratory from the Curtiss-Wright Corporation. The pioneering project became the Cornell Aeronautical Laboratory, connected to Cornell's new School of Aeronautical Engineering and various military projects.[82] By incorporating the lab, Cornell tightened the knot tied by the Cold War University paradox. Bishop's portrayal is portentous. "This was a solemn moment in Cornell's history. The University assumed the direction of a great research institution far from its own campus. It took the chance of financial troubles which might conceivably overwhelm the University. And it accepted implicitly a bold new principle: that research divorced from education is part of the proper business of a university." Much of the Cornell lab's research was secret, raising further questions. But this activity enhanced Cornell's prestige and involvements. Not long after it obtained the Aeronautical Lab, Cornell (on behalf of its Nuclear Studies, Chemical Engineering, and Electrical and Mechanical Engineering units) entered into another extramural activity, the Associated University, Incorporated, a consortium of leading universities committed to working in the nuclear field. This project obligated faculty members to leave Cornell to assume eighteen-month stints on Long Island. On February 17, 1947, Cornell held a banquet at the Waldorf-Astoria Hotel in New York City

[81] Bishop, *A History of Cornell*, p. 578. The information in this and the next paragraph on Cornell is drawn from pp. 560–85.

[82] See Virginia Li, "From the Archives: Controversy and Innovation at the Cornell Aeronautical Laboratory," *Cornell Daily Sun*, April 29, 2001: http://cornellsun.com/node/37281.

honoring five Cornellians who had won Nobel Prizes. Under the pressure of student protests, Cornell sold the lab in 1972.[83]

Harvard was second to none in the Ivy League in the Cold War University stakes. In 1953, the university managed over a hundred funding contracts with twenty government agencies worth $8 million. By 1963, the value of such contracts ballooned to $30 million (the same figure as during World War II), concentrated in medicine, public health, and arts and sciences. A lengthy 1954 faculty committee report on "The Behavioral Sciences at Harvard" related that, "Large scale research projects, centers, and laboratories flourished, well watered by grants from the National Institutes of Health (NIMH) and other Croesian founts."[84] These institutions featured burgeoning area studies centers, such as the Russian, East Asian, Middle East, Urban Affairs, International Affairs, and Kissinger's Center for International Affairs. President Nathan Pusey, who replaced Conant in the early 1950s, declared that these institutions were key tools in "Harvard's mission in the world."[85] This mission was crowned in 1947, when Secretary of State George Marshall announced the momentous Marshall Plan at Harvard's commencement. In 1962, as the Cold War University's nemeses began assembling on the horizon, the university founded the Harvard Institute for International Development. By this point, "The tensions between teaching departments and research centers, the problems of balancing scholarship and activism, and of dividing grant money among a flock of clamoring claimants, paled beside the hubris of 'Harvard in the World'. ... [Harvard] zestfully took on the challenge of area and international studies." Nevertheless, "old timers regretted the loss of a once strong sense of community."[86] As at Cornell, excessive federal funding engendered tensions. A 1961 "Institutional Self-Study" posed the dilemma that was now besetting higher education:

> The university no longer expects to avoid involvement in public affairs, for it is by now all too clear that free universities and free politics are interdependent and their futures intertwined. But it will serve society well only as it remains true to its essential nature – a university is not an agency of government. It is entitled to demand complete intellectual freedom. To this end it must ask for a measure of detachment from current crises and routine procedures as necessary conditions for fulfilling its fundamental purpose in civilized society.[87]

Columbia also garnered its share of Cold War University laurels. The Columbia Radiation Lab employed 1,200 workers, and the university's president, Grayson Kirk, placed fewer limits on research than the leaders of such competitors as Harvard and Chicago. The university also joined the Institute for Defense Analysis (IDA), a nonprofit research organization consisting of "highly

[83] Bishop, *A History of Cornell*, pp. 581–5.
[84] Keller and Keller, *Making Harvard Modern*, p. 217.
[85] Bethell, *Harvard Observed*, p. 209.
[86] Keller and Keller, *Making Harvard Modern*, p. 218.
[87] Bethell, *Harvard Observed*, p. 202.

trained scientists" dedicated to studying defense and security problems; it was created in the mid-1950s by the secretary of defense and the Joint Chiefs of Staff and placed under the auspices of a national consortium of major universities.[88] Columbia also reaped the beneficence of such major philanthropic institutions as the Ford and Rockefeller foundations, which supported its numerous esteemed foreign area–studies programs, including the Russian Institute and the East Asian Institute, both funded by the Rockefeller Foundation, and the Near and Middle Eastern Institute. Columbia also had an array of "area" programs in Latin American Studies, South Asian Studies, and the Soviet System, the latter of which competed with the Russian Center. In 1954, the Council on Foreign Relations and the federal government supplied money to establish the East Central Europe Institute, headed by Zbigniew Brzezinski; and in 1965, the Ford Foundation endowed five professorships in area studies and "to help with the construction of a building for the School of International Affairs," which would become a landmark among higher education international affairs programs. Corporate funding also played its part, funding the Business School and the Bureau of Applied Social Research (BASR), run by the noted sociologist Paul E. Lazarsfield. For three decades, the BASR provided the tools for data analysis to graduate students, including such eminent figures as James Coleman, Seymour Martin Lipset, Nathan Glazer, and Juan Linz.[89]

CLOUDS ON THE HORIZON

By the early 1960s, the cracks in the foundation of the Cold War University had begun to widen. What McCaughey calls "one of the great generational divides in American history" loomed on the horizon, with the nation's involvement in war lying at the heart of the coming tempest.[90] The first inklings of trouble emerged in the later 1950s, as students began to agitate against such issues as nuclear arms, racial injustice, alienation in society, and assorted problems in the academy, including the state of student and academic freedom, the reign of *in loco parentis*, the weakening sense of campus community, and the faculty's emphasis on research over teaching. These and related concerns were echoed in the 1962 Port Huron Statement of Students for a Democratic Society (SDS) and the manifestoes of the 1964 Free Speech Movement at Berkeley – two shots heard around the university world.[91] ROTC and the Cold War University's connection

[88] See Institute for Defense Analyses, "About Us," "History and Mission": https://www.ida.org/aboutus/historyandmission.php.

[89] Most of the information for this discussion of Columbia is drawn from McCaughey, *Stand Columbia*, pp. 356–90.

[90] McCaughey, *Stand Columbia*, p. 356.

[91] See, for example, Donald Alexander Downs, *Cornell '69: Liberalism and the Crisis of the American University* (Cornell University Press, 1999), chaps. 1 and 2; Students for a Democratic Society, *Port Huron Statement of the Students for a Democratic Society, 1962*: http://www.h-net.org/~hst306/documents/huron.html; Seymour Martin Lipset and John H. Schaar, eds., *The Berkeley Student Revolt: Facts and Interpretations* (Doubleday Anchor

to the government-military-industrial complex turned into targets of student discontent, especially after Vietnam took center stage on campus.

As we have mentioned often, the relationship between ROTC and the campus had been fraught with underlying tension from the beginning, however much university leaders and faculty have shared a commitment to national defense. The pressures that threatened ROTC in new ways in the 1960s were the product of at least two forces.

The first force was a manifestation of the inherent tension between military and civilian educational institutions. This tension deepened during the 1950s and 1960s as universities became more concerned about the academic quality of ROTC courses and instructors and about institutional control. At the same time, the military began to place more emphasis on ROTC as a source of officers and strove to make the program even more compatible with military needs. Something had to give. Responding to these concerns, the military and universities enacted reform measures during the early 1960s, culminating in the ROTC Vitalization Act in 1964. To attract more high-quality students into programs, the Act incorporated some major reforms after extensive congressional debate and horse trading that confirmed, yet again, Bismarck's famous observation about legislation and the making of sausage. Among other things, the Act created a new scholarship program, enhanced subsistence for cadets in the advanced course, and created a modified curriculum option for students who decided to enroll in ROTC after their first or second year in school. This option allowed junior and community college students to join upon entering four-year colleges.[92]

Sponsors of the Act hoped that it would revitalize ROTC and universities' commitment. But, according to Neiberg, it fell considerably short of achieving this objective. It preserved visible forms of drill, for example, at the military's behest, and its reduction of contact hours came not from technical military subjects (which many pro-reform advocates in both academe and the military wanted consigned to summer camp), but rather from liberal arts courses, signaling the evisceration of "substitution." Instead of improving matters, the Revitalization Act

> underscored ROTC's growing divergence from the general trend in higher education.... It reduced time spent in the cognate academic courses that civilian officials saw as central to the mission of higher education and maintained the emphasis on the technical military showpiece courses that the universities saw as most antithetical to their mission. Moreover, the act did not address some important abiding concerns, such as instructor qualification and credit for ROTC courses. Nor did it address the widely held perception that ROTC was so out of step with the new American university that it could not attract men and keep them interested long enough to convince them to pursue military training.[93]

Original, 1965). This latter volume, consisting of original source material, is one of the most interesting compilations on the rise of the student revolt.

92 Much of the discussion in this section is drawn from Neiberg, *Making Citizen Soldiers*, chaps. 2 and 3. Other sources include Coumbe and Harford, *U.S. Army Cadet Command: The 10 Year History*, ch. 1.

93 Neiberg, *Making Citizen Soldiers*, pp. 98–100.

The other force, of course, was the radical student activism just mentioned, which strove to drive the program from campus. Which force was most responsible for the fate that ROTC met at several Ivy League institutions? One reason it is difficult to determine the causal relationship is that ROTC's retreat was in reaction to faculty-promulgated conditions that the program could not, or would not, meet. Accordingly, one interpretation is that the program left many schools voluntarily because the military refused to accept conditions set by the schools. Another interpretation is that these conditions were largely pretexts, at least in some cases, and that the faculty members strategically endorsed them knowing – and even hoping – that the conditions would not be met. Setting new standards was a way to rid the campus of a troubling program without appearing to cave in to student pressure – a constant theme during the 1960s campus wars.[94] We will see that some of the faculty committees at stake made their decisions within shouting distance of tumultuous events that shook their respective institutions to the core, suggesting that their motivations may not have been as conventional or nonpolitical as they claimed. Because of the fog that accompanied this campus war, Silver's preference for concluding that some campuses "effectively barred" ROTC is apt.

Of course, 1964 was also the year that President Lyndon Johnson, armed with Congress's Tonkin Gulf Resolution, committed America to the defense of South Vietnam. In other words, the problems that clung to the heels of the Revitalization Act could hardly have come at a less propitious time. The Cold War Consensus had already begun to unravel by the late 1950s and early 1960s, with critics – ranging from the radical sociologist C. Wright Mills to retiring President Dwight D. Eisenhower, a hero of the Second World War – sounding alarms about the "military-industrial complex" and the "Garrison State." Meanwhile, embryonic campus opposition to the Vietnam War was sprouting in a few portentous places by 1965, such as the University of Michigan, which held one of the first "teach-ins" on the war, and Columbia University, which witnessed the first known aggressive protest against ROTC.[95]

Our discussion of the historical relationship between the military and universities suggests that the notion of an irreconcilable conflict between the Ivory Tower and the military is a recent phenomenon. Opponents of ROTC often talk about the need to *preserve* the idea of the Ivory Tower when arguing against ROTC on campus. A more accurate statement is that opponents of ROTC want

[94] Downs's *Cornell '69* portrays faculty members' agonizing over having to choose between standing by principle or conceding to enormous pressure. Such dilemmas were widespread in higher education at the time.

[95] C. Wright Mills, *The Power Elite* (Oxford University Press, 1956), esp. p. 217. Eisenhower, "Military-Industrial Complex Speech, Dwight D. Eisenhower, 1961," pp. 1035–40. See also Neiberg, *Making Citizen Soldiers*, pp. 84–5. On Mills, Eisenhower, and Michigan, see Neiberg's discussion of these nascent forces in *Making Citizen Soldiers*, pp. 84–6.

to *construct* the Ivory Tower in ways that preclude cooperation with the military. Historically, a military presence was viewed as important to the university and to students from the Revolutionary War to the 1960s. The Ivory Tower was alive and well even with a great deal of integration of the military on campus – indeed, the rise of the great American universities, and the Ivory Tower ideal itself, was intertwined with the military. Let us now turn our attention to the campus politics of the 1960s.

5

ROTC and the Ivies

The Divorce

> In the years around 1968, a utopian exhilaration swept across the student universe and across several adult universes as well, and almost everyone in my own circle of friends and classmates was swept up in it. ... Four enormous revolutions were roiling the world, at that one moment. ... And from each of those revolutions, and from the combination of all four, radiated an intense excitement, which came beaming down on us and on people like ourselves in scattered university towns all over the world ...
>
> [In later years] it was obvious that those long-ago efforts to change the shape of the world were a young people's rehearsal, preparatory for adult events that only came later. Suddenly it was obvious that the authentic political revolution of our era was now, not then; liberal and democratic, not radical leftist in the '68 style; real, not imaginary.
>
> – Paul Berman[1]

> Stupidly, we thought revolution was imminent. Our rage blinded us. I now believe that the war in Vietnam drove us crazy.
>
> – Mark Rudd, former leader of Students for a Democratic Society, Columbia University, speaking at the university's twentieth anniversary of the 1968 crisis[2]

In this chapter, we examine ROTC's exodus from the Ivy League in the late 1960s, preparing us to look in the next two chapters at the movement to bring the program back after September 11, 2001, including the major steps taken at Harvard and Columbia in early 2011 to recall ROTC after a decades-long exodus. We begin by considering trends in the Ivy League and the nation, focusing later on Columbia University, where the major action took place.

[1] Paul Berman, *A Tale of Two Utopias: The Political Journey of the Generation of 1968* (W. W. Norton, 1996).

[2] Mark Rudd, quoted in David B. Truman, *Reflections on the Columbia Disorders of 1968* (unpublished manuscript, 1995), p. 94.

RIDING THE STORM: ROTC, THE IVY LEAGUE, AND THE 1960S

"The undeclared war in Vietnam entangled the ROTC in a controversy of an intensity unparalleled in the program's history," according to two ROTC historians.[3] As a visible symbol of the military on campus, ROTC was often a target of student antiwar protest. But it hardly stood alone. Antiwar activists opposed all aspects of the Cold War: the Vietnam War University edifice, including research centers and contracts; military, intelligence (mainly CIA), and corporate recruiting; and campus organizations that provided information to the Selective Service.

In reading the sections that follow relating to the Vietnam era, the reader should bear three things in mind. First, the hostilities surrounding the war remind us of General George C. Marshall's observation that democracies cannot endure long wars, especially wars that do not have clear objectives backed by sufficient consent. The type of limited war fought in Vietnam threatened to unravel the cords of union. But our purpose here is not to judge the validity of the Vietnam War, only to acknowledge its impact on American politics and higher education's feelings about the military. In assessing the strategic ambiguities of the war, Adrian R. Lewis (a historian and retired Army major) captures the feelings of much of the public. "The Vietnam War never should have been fought. And this is not an assessment that is a function of hindsight, it is an assessment based on an understanding of geography, history, culture, the nature of American military power, and relative, potential combat power."[4] And unlike the public today, which appears to separate its feelings about particular wars from its sentiments about the military, many citizens lumped these two attitudes together during Vietnam, holding the military – all the way down to the "grunts" – to be as morally accountable as the civilian leaders who made the ultimate decisions.[5] Second, the antiwar movement comprised part of a broader critique of American society that embraced the status of race relations, the nature of economic institutions and arrangements, and the prevalence of societal alienation in general. The 1960s were a period of intense social and political critique that continues to shape and influence American political and cultural development.

Third, the war provoked powerful passions on many sides, unleashing moral furies that often exerted great pressures on university faculty and administrators. Acknowledging these pressures, it is difficult to distinguish between rational decision making by faculty and administration and simple reaction to pressure and fear. More generally, the pressures and demands of the time simply defied

[3] Arthur T. Coumbe and Lee S. Harford, *U.S. Army Cadet Command: The 10 Year History* (Office of the Command Historian, U.S. Army Cadet Command, 1996), ch. 1, p. 33.

[4] Adrian R. Lewis, *The American Culture of War: The History of U.S. Military Force from World War II to Operation Iraqi Freedom* (Routledge, 2007), p. 220.

[5] See, e.g., Charles R. Figley and Seymour Leventman, *Strangers at Home: Vietnam Veterans Since the War* (Praeger, 1980). "They felt the initial shock of confusion and disappointment upon return ... and the sting of recognition that their actual homecoming was nothing like the one they dreamed about in 'Nam" (p. 4).

conventional approaches to problem solving. As David B. Truman wrote in his unpublished memoir of the crisis at Columbia University in the spring of 1968 (after which he resigned his position as vice president and provost), the campus upheavals of the late 1960s

> confronted most college and university presidents with a sharply altered set of conditions and a collection of problems not readily susceptible of solution through the methods of consultation, discussion, and reason that are the established norm in such institutions.... [Leaders'] customary modes of operation did not work, and in some instances were woefully inadequate. ... Some were confronted with circumstances so intractable to any rational handling that they were bound to lose no matter what methods they attempted to use.[6]

College leaders, previously accustomed to the respect rendered duly constituted authority, were suddenly thrust into the plight of Bob Dylan's "Mr. Jones," the character in the song, "Ballad of a Thin Man," who personified America's educated and enlightened liberal leaders who now struggled to grasp the confounding claims and passions suddenly unfurled their way. "Ah, you've been with the professors and they've all liked your looks/ With great lawyers you have discussed lepers and crooks/ You've been through all of F. Scott Fitzgerald's books/ You're very well read, it's well known/ But something is happening here and you don't know what it is/ do you, Mister Jones?"[7] Nor is it evident that the student vanguards of change truly fathomed the full measure of the wave they rode. As one of the authors of this book wrote in a book on the Cornell crisis of 1969, "Marx made a statement in the *Eighteenth Brumaire of Louis Napoleon* that history is lived twice, the first time as tragedy, the second time as farce. Cornell appears to have been both at the same time."[8] This perspective is perhaps pertinent to the narratives presented in this chapter.

A turning point on campus arose in 1967. From 1965 to 1967, the antiwar movement remained "largely respectful, its tactics designed to build an antiwar consensus." But the Johnson administration's continued buildup of troops in Vietnam and the Tet offensive of 1968 brought an end to this strategic mentality on the part of many movement leaders. "The emphasis of dissident strategy turned from an attempt to influence key policy-shapers to the mobilizing of massive demonstrations." Antiwar leaders went from harboring hope to being "afflicted with despair" – from "protest" to "resistance."[9] Worldwide, student

[6] David B. Truman, *Reflections on the Columbia Disorders of 1968* (unpublished manuscript available at the Columbia University Rare Book and Manuscript Collection, Butler Library). Henceforth, we will refer to this archive as Butler Library.

[7] Bob Dylan, "Ballad of a Thin Man," on *Highway 61 Revisited* album (Columbia Records, 1965). Legend has it that "Mr. Jones" was modeled after a journalist and professor, Jeffrey Owen Jones, who had interviewed Dylan for *Time* in 1965. Jones died in early November 2007. See "Bob Dylan's 'Mr. Jones' Dies at 63," *Spinner*, November 28, 2007: http://www.spinner.com/2007/11/28/bob-dylans-mr-jones-dies-at-63/.

[8] Donald Alexander Downs, *Cornell '69: Liberalism and the Crisis of the American University* (Cornell University Press, 1999), p. 188.

[9] Charles DeBenedetti and Charles Chatfield (assisting author), *An American Ordeal: The Antiwar Movement of the Vietnam Era* (Syracuse University Press, 1990), pp. 391–2.

protest power influenced the foreign policy and strategic thinking of governments in ways both subtle and overt, from pressuring for the withdrawal from Vietnam to contributing to the emergence of the grand strategy of détente between the United States and the Soviet Union under President Richard Nixon.[10]

ATTACKS ON ROTC

The first known major physical confrontation against the programs took place at Columbia University in May 1965, when a group of students disrupted the Naval ROTC's year-end awards ceremony. The following fall, anti-ROTC rallies erupted at Kent State, meeting intense opposition from fellow students.[11] The main crisis escalated in the aftermath of the Tet offensive, which, in Michael Neiberg's words, "created psychological collapse in the United States and a dramatic shift in attitudes toward the war." ROTC commanders began to feel that they were living in an alien world – "an embassy on foreign soil," as one professor of military science put it.[12] As their radicalization deepened, many movement leaders began connecting the dots demarking the array of Cold War University institutions and activities, composing a picture of imperialistic power bent on unjust world domination. At the State University of New York at Buffalo, for example, the Radical Faculty Caucus in 1969 espoused a familiar refrain, calling for "the U.S. military withdrawal from South Vietnam, the abolition of ROTC, and the termination of all university-military research projects." The hostility to the military and its actions was inspired by a variety of motives, including political, moral, and religious. The first anti-ROTC demonstrations at Michigan State, for example, were motivated by religious and pacifist concerns.[13]

ROTC headquarters suffered attacks on numerous campuses, ranging from acute verbal harassment to vandalism, arson, and firebombings. Slighting (if not outright ignoring) such subtleties as the need to preserve civilian influence on the military, militant critics now viewed ROTC as a cog in the war machine. By late 1969, "bombings and burnings of ROTC buildings were increasing

[10] On how protest movements influenced foreign policy, strategy, and détente, see Jeremi Suri, *Power and Protest: Global Revolution and the Rise of Détente* (Harvard University Press, 2003). The student protests and other events in the 1960s also engendered a conservative counter-revolt, ultimately leading to the election of Ronald Reagan in 1980. See Rick Perlstein, *Before the Storm: Barry Goldwater and the Unmaking of the American Consensus* (Hill and Wang, 2001). Reagan rejected détente in favor of confrontation that led to the eventual rapprochement with Mikhail Gorbachev.

[11] On the early Kent State protests, see Kenneth J. Heineman, *Campus Wars: The Peace Movement at American State Universities in the Vietnam Era* (NYU Press, 1993), pp. 177–8.

[12] Michael Neiberg, *Making Citizen Soldiers: ROTC and the Ideology of American Military Service* (Harvard University Press, 2000), p. 113.

[13] Heineman, *Campus Wars*, pp. 65, 186–7; Murray Polner and Jim O'Grady, *Disarmed and Dangerous: The Radical Life and Times of Daniel and Phillip Berrigan, Brothers in Religious Faith and Civil Disobedience* (Basic, 1997).

dramatically," relates movement historian Tom Wells. A couple of weeks before President Nixon provoked explosive campus reactions by publicly acknowledging the secret bombing of Cambodia on the last day of April 1970, thousands of Berkeley students marched on the campus's ROTC headquarters, "sparking a five hour battle with police." The next day, the administration closed the campus, declaring a "state of emergency." After Nixon's disclosure, Kent State protesters torched the campus's wooden ROTC building; when first responders arrived, the protesters threw rocks at the National Guard and sliced the hoses of firefighters. This action ignited the chain reaction that soon led, seemingly ineluctably, to the infamous National Guard shooting of thirteen students – four fatally – on May 4. Kent State was not alone in suffering fiery attacks on ROTC that week. "During the first week of May nation-wide, ROTC buildings were exploding or igniting at the rate of more than four a day."[14] The Air Force presented the following figures in incident reports for the academic year of 1969–70: major damage or injury to Air Force detachments, 55; minor damage or injury, 138; disruptive demonstrations, 37; official studies, 175; threats of disruption or violence, 90; and nonviolent demonstrations, 180. Incidents in 1970–1 amounted to fewer than half these figures, but they were still substantial.[15] Theorists of cascades emphasize that social movements can spread like a forest fire once ignited. The movement against ROTC had all the key elements of a cascade, with the first attacks setting off a movement that would culminate in institutional change. The integration of military "culture" may itself have been a trigger for conflict. Arguing theoretically, economists Timur Kuran and William H. Sandholm show that cultural integration can trigger a backlash to impose cultural cohesiveness under certain conditions.[16] The struggle over ROTC provides an example that illustrates the economic logic of cultural integration and disintegration. In this case, students of the left represented a culture that came in conflict with, and perhaps even precluded, the military culture, the byproduct of which was sustained violence.

The pedagogical, political, and physical attacks on ROTC placed two policy prescriptions on the table: abolition or reform. According to Neiberg, the services terminated eighty-eight programs nationwide during this period, but only one termination was expressly due to an overt abolition decision by a college or university (Dartmouth).[17] The other schools that lost programs

[14] Tom Wells, *The War Within: America's Battle over Vietnam* (University of California Press, 1994), pp. 400–1, 406, 421, 426.

[15] "AFROTC/Host Institutional Activities" (1972), in University of Illinois Archives, President John Corbally Papers, Box 33. ROTC–Air Force, quoted in Neiberg, *Making Citizen Soldiers*, p. 120.

[16] See Timur Kuran and William H. Sandholm, "Cultural Integration and Its Discontents," *Review of Economic Studies* 75, 1 (2008): 201–28. On cascades more generally, see Timur Kuran, "Sparks and Prairie Fires: A Theory of Unanticipated Revolution," *Public Choice* 61, 1 (1989): 41–74; and Suzanne Lohman, "The Dynamics of Informational Cascades: The Monday Demonstrations in Leipzig, East Germany, 1989–91," *World Politics* 47, 1 (1994): 42–101.

[17] See Neiberg, *Making Citizen Soldiers*, p. 171. The Army terminated nine programs; see Coumbe and Harford, *U.S. Army Cadet Command: The 10 Year History*, p. 33.

enacted conditions that often had unpromising prospects of being accepted by the military, amounting, in effect, to abolition or something close to it. Nevertheless, ROTC still enjoyed the basic support of most students, faculty, and administrative leaders, according to several polls, and this support was reflected in the actions that universities took. Contesting the claim that academics promulgated conditions as a pretext for abolition, Neiberg avers:

> Instead, the faculties issued reports that challenged ROTC to reform itself to become more a part of the university according to the same criteria applied to other programs. When the dean of Rutgers College reviewed the report of the Rutgers faculty in 1968, he did not describe it as the first step of a program to eliminate ROTC; rather, he said that the "faculty did everything it could *to bring ROTC into the mainstream of Rutgers College as a regular department*."[18]

From this perspective, the university as an institution changed, and the faculty was caught up in these changes – they were a product of social forces beyond the faculty's control, lacking agency. As such, the choice was left to the military, not to the faculty. At the same time, we have to remember that the story can also be a convenient cover. All we know for certain is that the conditions given to ROTC facilitated its retreat from campus.

Neiberg is certainly right about the national scene in general. ROTC would emerge as a better and more legitimate enterprise in the 1980s, strengthened by academic reforms and the institution of more uniformity through the establishment of Cadet Commands to oversee programs nationwide. But the upheavals of the 1960s did leave some negative legacies. First, the program vanished for good at several institutions (or for the foreseeable future, as the first domino in ROTC's return, Harvard, had already fallen), including four in the Ivy League – five if we include Dartmouth, which brought it back over a decade later, albeit in a substantially watered-down form. Second, even where programs remained, many were shells of their former selves. Third, this period witnessed the beginning of ROTC's geographical redistribution toward the South and parts of the Midwest and West. Furthermore, as we will see in the case of Columbia University, it is often difficult to separate the pedagogical from the political at many of the institutions that set academic and programmatic standards that the military ultimately refused to accept.

On the positive side, universities compelled ROTC to accept basic changes in the curriculum and crediting of courses that brought the program more into harmony with the general mission of higher education. Between 1968 and the early 1970s, numerous universities engaged in serious reviews of ROTC programs as the pressures exerted by protesters coincided with preexisting institutional concerns about the quality of the programs and their consistency with university standards. Many schools withdrew credit for courses that did not pass academic muster (something engineering schools had done previously), while others reclassified the titles and status of ROTC instructors, subjected the crediting of courses to standard university operating procedures, and/or changed

[18] Neiberg, *Making Citizen Soldiers*, p. 123, emphasis added.

ROTC from "department" to "program" or extracurricular status.[19] As we will see in our presentation of ROTC politics at Columbia University, by the early 1970s the Department of Defense had come to accept noncredit status for ROTC programs if that meant holding on to units at top-ranked institutions in the Ivy League, the Big Ten, and other major conferences. Unfortunately, the scopes and political contexts of some of these reform efforts precluded reasonable expectations of ROTC's continuance at some institutions.

These efforts were encouraged by a national committee initiated by Secretary of Defense Melvin Laird and concerned military leaders to address the problems. The Benson Committee, named after its chair, George Benson (former president of the Claremont Colleges), issued a sixty-one-page report in September 1969. Refusing to concur with the proposition that ROTC did not belong in higher education, the Benson Report presented twenty-one recommendations that served as a boilerplate for educational institutions to mold their own reforms. Many institutions adopted more meaningful reforms. The report's substantive changes included calling on institutions to take on more responsibility for the hiring and firing of instructors; promoting the creation of faculty-administrative committees to oversee ROTC programs; and advancing the cause of non-ROTC course substitution for regular ROTC courses. Laird then instituted the office of assistant secretary of defense (education), selecting Benson for the position. "Through the Benson Report, the DOD made a commitment, as the universities had, to work to save ROTC."[20] Meanwhile, the Army had already begun acting on its own, launching the Military Science Core Curriculum, known as Option C. Option C lowered the number of contact hours in the advanced course and allowed almost half of the program's 390 hours to be "filled with regular academic subjects believed to be of value to the future officer." Most institutions adopted Option C, but it left a bad taste in the mouths of many Army officers, who believed it inadequately prepared cadets to be real soldiers.[21]

On the negative side, the abolition of ROTC at elite schools introduced the trend toward geographic and institutional underrepresentation, as the move away from such schools "was more than offset, quantitatively at least, by the creation of additional detachments at state institutions in the South and West."[22] This trend contributed to the eventual overrepresentation of

[19] To learn more details, see the in-depth discussion of the reforms in Neiberg, *Making Citizen Solders*, pp. 123–50. Much of the following discussion draws on Neiberg's account.

[20] Neiberg, *Making Citizen Soldiers*, pp. 130–1. At the University of Wisconsin, for example, three different committees worked on reforming ROTC in response to a movement on campus to remove it. The Cleland Committee drew from the Benson Report, ended up strengthening the curriculum through substitution and other measures, and established a faculty committee to oversee the program, as the Benson Report advised. See Report of the Ad Hoc Committee on ROTC (Cleland Committee), University of Wisconsin Faculty Document 38, April 5, 1971.

[21] See Coumbe and Harford, *U.S. Army Cadet Command: The 10 Year History*, pp. 33–5. Lyons and Masland presented their ideas in *Education and Military Leadership: A Study of the R.O.T.C.* (Princeton University Press, 1959).

[22] Coumbe and Harford, *U.S. Army Cadet Command: The 10 Year History*, p. 33.

conservative and Republican ideology among military officers, which is a key component of the "gap" problem now facing the nation. More broadly, although these reforms helped to "save" ROTC in higher education, they did not prevent serious shortfalls in ROTC from befalling the program in the 1970s; ROTC enrollments fell by 75 percent between the 1967 and 1972–3 academic years.[23]

Before we turn to the Columbia ROTC story, let us look briefly at how the programs fared in Ivy schools at the hands of the 1960s protests. The nature of the protests varied with each institution; extreme pressure reigned at such schools as Columbia and Harvard, while more civil pressure was the order of the day at Yale. Other institutions fell somewhere between these poles. Full programs exist today at Cornell, Princeton, and Penn, but their present enrollments are typically modest. Each of the schools without ROTC on campus do permit their students to take courses at other institutions, although without credit and at often significant inconvenience. However, since September 11, 2001, Ivy campuses have witnessed a renaissance of favorable student *press coverage* that is part of the broader phenomenon of the "return of the soldier." Thus far, however, there is not much evidence that this revival of favorable campus opinion has led (or will lead) to increased elite student *participation*, although the return of ROTC to Columbia, Harvard, Stanford, and Yale in the first half of 2011 certainly bodes well on this dimension.

Dartmouth

All three of Dartmouth's ROTC programs retreated from campus in the wake of political movements in 1969. A student vote against ROTC "virtually shut the school down," according to one observer. This initiative was followed by a faculty committee vote to abolish ROTC. These votes compelled the administration to announce the termination of its contracts with the military; and the Army and Air Force programs left campus in 1971, followed by the Navy program in 1973.[24] In defending the exodus in 1969, one student remarked, "There were students who felt the ROTC was incompatible with a liberal arts education" – a position backed by the American Civil Liberties Union in the name of academic freedom. Other students believed ROTC constituted an "instrument of the U.S. military." One student reported widespread campus opposition to the military per se: "the College should not have been in support of the U.S. military at a time when so many students saw it as 'morally reprehensible.'"[25] The Dartmouth Army program did return in 1985, although in a limited form: An Army instructor from Norwich University (where the predecessor of ROTC was first conceived in the early-nineteenth century) drives to

[23] Coumbe and Harford, *U.S. Army Cadet Command: The 10 Year History*, p. 36.

[24] "A Survey of ROTC's Status in the Ivies," *Harvard Crimson*, September 28, 1973; Neiberg, *Making Citizen Soldiers*, p. 127.

[25] "Dartmouth College ROTC," History: http://www.dartmouth.edu/~rotc/history.htm.

Dartmouth several times a week to teach courses. Only a handful of students belong to the present program.

Penn

In December 1968, the College of Arts and Sciences at Penn voted to withdraw academic credit from courses taught by ROTC instructors, but not to abolish the programs, despite demonstrators' demands to do so. The Navy program elected to remain on campus because it was able to work out arrangements for other departments to teach relevant courses in such areas as technology, military history, and diplomacy. Penn's School of Engineering and Applied Sciences is a major partner in this enterprise. (See also the discussion of military history and Penn's programs in diplomatic history in Chapter 11.) In addition to the Engineering School, the College for Women and the Wharton School opted to allow credit for certain ROTC courses. Writing at the time of the Arts and Sciences decision, the editors of the *Daily Pennsylvanian* observed, "No one says the action was taken on moral grounds. The vote only discredited the military science department – not ROTC itself – on the academic grounds of direct control from Washington."[26]

Cornell

As the Ivy's only institution with land grant schools, Cornell held on to all three of its ROTC programs in the face of sometimes strident student protest between 1968 and 1971. The one negative action was a vote by the faculty of the College of Arts and Sciences to eliminate accredited ROTC courses in the college, relegating ROTC to "program" status. (The college is private, not part of the land grant system at Cornell.) Cornell also set up a joint faculty-student-military "watchdog" committee to oversee the programs for a three-year trial period.[27] According to a 1973 *Harvard Crimson* summary of the status of ROTC in the Ivies in the aftermath of the 1960s protests, the College of Arts and Sciences later accepted credit for a course in 1973, encountering no student opposition. In 1973, about two hundred students participated in ROTC, twenty-five in the College of Arts and Sciences.[28]

Princeton

Protests at Princeton broke out in earnest in 1968, when about 1,100 protesters marched on a campus building to "protest the exclusion of students and faculty

[26] See "ROTC Can Stay on Penn Campus Despite Loss of Academic Credit," *Harvard Crimson*, December 6, 1968: http://www.thecrimson.com/article/1968/12/6/rotc-can-stay-on-penn-campus/.

[27] See "NROTC Committee Report in an Ivy League Context," Memorandum to Dr. Andrew W. Cordier from Harvey C. Mansfield, Columbia University, p. 2. This memorandum is in the "University Protest and Activism Collection, 1958–1999," Butler Library.

[28] "A Survey of ROTC's Status in the Ivies."

from university decision-making" and to demand the university sever its ties to the Defense Department. Student groups and a faculty committee also advocated that the university drop credit for ROTC courses and faculty status for program instructors. The 1969 Ad Hoc Committee on ROTC contended that "the ROTC courses of instruction are prescribed and conducted under procedures incompatible with those which normally govern the establishment of courses and the selection of faculty at Princeton." The faculty as a whole then "overwhelmingly" approved the committee's proposal that turned ROTC into a "program" with noncredit, extracurricular status. Princeton also banned drill and lethal weapons from campus.[29] In a March 4 letter to Secretary of Defense Laird, Princeton president Robert F. Goheen wrote, "Contrary to the impressions created by some of the national press on this action by the Princeton faculty, I hope you will note the report's strong affirmation of the importance of continuing programs designed to train civilian reserve officers for service in the armed forces of our country."[30] After President Nixon went public about the invasion of Cambodia in May 1970, the ROTC armory was firebombed. Then, at an "unprecedented seven-hour session" attended by over a thousand people, the University Council voted to "determine ways to sever any association whatsoever" with ROTC. A month later, the trustees agreed to end all three of Princeton's programs by June 1972; the Army and Air Force units departed immediately, while the Navy unit remained until the expiration of its contract in June 1972. Interestingly, a year later, 57 percent of the students voted in a referendum sponsored by the Undergraduate Assembly to bring ROTC back, subject to the conditions that the faculty established in 1969. Affected by both alumni and student pressure, and by new evidence that ROTC courses provided sufficient open discussion and debate, the trustees then followed suit, offering contracts to the military. The Air Force and the Navy declined the invitation, but the Army accepted it in June 1972. "That fall ROTC quietly returned to Princeton – not as field artillery and not for course credit, but as a non-credit elective program of officer education. Thereafter, growth was modest but sustained. By 1976, seventy-four students (thirteen of them women) were enrolled, with the prospect of the first coed being commissioned in 1978." Noncredit for ROTC courses remains the policy to this day.[31]

29 Neiberg, *Making Citizen Soldiers*, pp. 126–7. See Columbia University, Report of the Ad Hoc Committee on ROTC to the University Faculty, March 3, 1969, in "University Protest and Activism Collection, 1958–1999," Butler Archive.

30 Letter from President Robert F. Goheen to Secretary of Defense Melvin R. Laird, March 4, 1969, Butler Archive.

31 "Reserve Officers Training Corps (R.O.T.C.)," in Alexander Leitch, *A Princeton Companion* (Princeton University Press, 1978): http://etcweb.princeton.edu/CampusWWW/Companion/reserve_officers_training_corps.html;

Jennifer Epstein and Matt Davis, "CAP's ROTC Advocacy Died Down in 1980s," *Daily Princetonian*, January 13, 2006; Mark F. Bernstein, "ROTC Seeks Course Credit," *Princeton Alumni Weekly*, May 13, 2009: http://paw.princeton.edu/issues/2009/05/13/pages/7302/.

Brown

Although less intense than at other Ivy institutions, anti-ROTC politics did succeed in driving the program from Brown. The Air Force detachments at Harvard, Princeton, and Brown had been averaging only seven graduates a year in the early 1960s, although enrollments increased in response to the draft. In the spring of 1967, thirty-five members of the Brown Committee to Abolish ROTC picketed the annual ROTC spring review. Later in the year, Brown's Cammarian Club passed a resolution declaring ROTC "incompatible with the academic integrity of the university," a position affirmed by Brown's chapter of the American Association of University Professors. On March 18, 1969, the faculty considered the position taken by the Ad Hoc Committee on ROTC (submitted March 12), which said the program should be retained in some form "so that it will be possible for the services to continue to recruit future officers with a liberal arts education." But the committee did recommend eliminating academic status for the programs' departments, credit for ROTC courses, and faculty status for instructors. The faculty accepted these recommendations, with a few amendments. Yet in 1971 the university determined that the military was not meeting these conditions, so it decided – pressured by weeks-long student protests – to terminate the programs. Within a year, ROTC departed Brown for good. Like the other Ivy schools that dropped ROTC, Brown today allows its students to take Army ROTC at another school, Providence College. During the 2009–10 academic year, only one student (out of six thousand undergraduates) was involved in this program, and no credits earned in the program transfer back to Brown.[32]

Yale

Yale's ROTC politics were also relatively mild compared to Harvard's and Columbia's. SDS began targeting the university's Army and Navy units in the fall of 1967, but it was only after the Tet offensive in 1968 that a committee on courses undertook a serious review of the programs. According to Gaddis Smith, Yale's examination of ROTC was driven by three main concerns: academic standards; the recent reduction of overall credit hours required of undergraduates independent of ROTC, which meant that ROTC would now take up a greater percentage of students' academic loads; and an elitist reaction to the

[32] Report of the Committee on the Curriculum Concerning ROTC Programs at Brown University, March 12, 1969; and Faculty Vote, March 18, 1969. Both contained in Letter to Ivy Group Presidents from Ray L. Heffner, Brown University, March 25, 1969. All three of these documents are in the Butler Archive, Columbia University. Office of University Communications, Brown University, "From Martha Mitchell's *Encyclopedia Brunoniana*, Military Education": http://www.brown.edu/Administration/News_Bureau/Databases/Encyclopedia/search.php?serial=M0330; "Reserve-ing Judgment for ROTC: Forty Years After ROTC's Eviction, Attitudes Soften on Campus," *Brown Daily Herald*, April 29, 2010; "A Survey of ROTC's Status in the Ivies"; Neiberg, *Making Citizen Soldiers*, p. 171.

programs' inclusion of the University of New Haven and Southern Connecticut College as partners. There were also the typical concerns about the incompatibility of ROTC with the philosophy of the university. In January 1969, the course committee recommended the end of credit and faculty status for instructors. The faculty then supported the recommendations by a four-to-one ratio, and called for an ad hoc committee to review the programs further. At least one dissenting faculty member accused the majority of "yielding to political pressure," while another claimed that newly conducted seminars authorized for Yale's colleges were no more rigorous than ROTC courses. In negotiations with the Yale Corporation over the matter, President Kingman Brewster, Jr., argued against abolition, citing the opportunities provided to students and the contribution of ROTC to the services. But then Harvard protesters occupied University Hall in April – an explosive event that "alarmed" the administration, "excited students, [and] was followed by a month of political theater." Responding to the movement, Brewster called a mass meeting in the hockey rink that culminated in an amazing tie vote (1,286 to 1,286) over the question of abolition. The next day the faculty adopted the ad hoc committee's recommendations: to end course credit and faculty status for instructors; to allow cadets to major in subjects in the humanities and arts that the military did not authorize; to allow students to resign from ROTC without penalty; and to require the government to bear the full costs of the programs. A few months later, the military pulled the programs from Yale after negotiations with the Yale Corporation failed to reach an agreement.[33]

Harvard

The demise of ROTC at Harvard followed on the heels of tumultuous and famous protests in the spring of 1969. According to Harvey C. Mansfield, the professor of government who chaired the key committee on ROTC at Columbia University in 1968–9 (described later in this chapter), "The Harvard faculty vote (207–145) was the most hostile to ROTC."[34] Harvard, Columbia, and Cornell were home to some of the most radical and active SDS factions in the country, and Harvard's chapter focused its sights on ROTC in the "war against the war, against racism, against Harvard." In declaring the reasons for their occupation of University Hall on April 9, 1969, activist leaders proclaimed, "We consider the ROTC as a life and death issue for the people of the world whose lands are occupied by U.S. troops." Harvard's faculty first addressed ROTC in the fall of 1968, after which activist pressure escalated. At another meeting in February 1969, the faculty voted by a seven-to-one margin to maintain ROTC, but by a

[33] The information in this paragraph is based on Gaddis W. Smith, "Yale and the Vietnam War." University Seminar on the History of Columbia University, October 19, 1999, pp. 14–16; Marc Lindemann, "Storming the Ivory Tower: The Military's Return to American Campuses," *Parameters* (Winter 2006–7): 48–9; "A Survey of ROTC's Status in the Ivies."

[34] "NROTC Committee Report in an Ivy League Context," p. 1.

two-to-one ratio to deny credit for courses, to withhold faculty status from instructors, and to end the provision of free facilities to the programs. President Nathan Pusey (who supported ROTC despite the mounting discontent among students and faculty) and the Harvard Corporation then strove to fashion a mutually acceptable compromise, but this effort was superseded by a faculty committee that disclaimed any compatibility between ROTC and other extracurricular programs. They proposed instead that ROTC be wound down in two years. Nevertheless, the failure to recommend immediate abolition precipitated the semiviolent takeover of University Hall by several hundred students on April 9. Two days later, Pusey called in the police, who forcefully removed the occupiers. In response, activists called for a student strike that lasted several weeks. Tensions mounted as the faculty wrestled with issues that would define the character of the university, including sanctions against the students who had broken the law. On April 17, the faculty reaffirmed its earlier vote establishing stringent guidelines for ROTC, and these were accepted by the Corporation. "Without the status of regular academic programs, Harvard's ROTC units withdrew."[35]

Noted journalist Roger Rosenblatt, an instructor in English at Harvard during the tumult, published a scintillating memoir of these and related events in 1997 entitled *Coming Apart: A Memoir of the Harvard Wars of 1969*. Rosenblatt narrates and analyzes the array of issues that beset the university, including the ROTC wars. Among other things, he decries the failure of many faculty members to stand up for the university as "the one place in American society where the country's defining freedoms were not only protected, but also nurtured and celebrated." And he linked the fate of ROTC to this failure:

> When I reached into the caves of this belief, I was even in favor of maintaining the presence of ROTC on campus – not to give ROTC academic credit, but to allow it to remain as an option for anyone seeking the military life or needing it to complete an education. What Jim Watson [Professor James Watson] had said to the faculty about ROTC being useless was nonsense to me. In a worthwhile war, who would not wish to be led by a more thoughtful and educated first lieutenant?

Rosenblatt acknowledges his own complicity in this failure in words that suggest Harvard's decision regarding ROTC stemmed from more than purely academic considerations. (In fact, Rosenblatt acquitted himself well during the crisis, especially compared to many of his colleagues.) "I would never say such a thing, however, and that was the trouble with me. I knew that I could have my opinion two ways, or three, or four. ... But I was just playing it safe, for as long as I could, in the interests of being loved." This failure to stand up to moral and political pressures was widespread in the campus conflicts of the time, and it has lived on in the campus wars over free speech and academic freedom in our time.

[35] See Morton Keller and Phyllis Keller, *Making Harvard Modern: The Rise of America's University* (Oxford University Press, 2001), pp. 313–29; John T. Bethell, *Harvard Observed: An Illustrated History of the University in the Twentieth Century* (Harvard University Press, 1998), pp. 224–36; "A Survey of ROTC's Status in the Ivies."

(The failure, alas, is universal, although not absolute: In situations of political and moral pressure, one's public position is often at variance with one's true beliefs – a process economist and sociologist Timur Kuran labels "preference falsification" in a fascinating book.)[36] Rosenblatt's belated confession suggests that the motivations behind the setting of standards for ROTC during this period sometimes went beyond being "purely academic" concerns.[37]

COLUMBIA UNIVERSITY: "UP AGAINST THE IVY WALL," ROTC

ROTC's retreat from Columbia followed in the wake of what was very possibly the most explosive campus upheaval of the late 1960s. A de facto revolutionary situation seized the campus in April and May of 1968, as a cadre of perhaps one hundred hard-core members of SDS instigated a virtual takeover of the university that was ultimately supported by several thousand students. To some, the events augured the advent of a new, more just order – or, at least, the rejection of what leading activists considered a fundamentally illegitimate society and political order. As Robert Friedman wrote in his introduction to the *Columbia Daily Spectator*'s authoritative history of the Columbia crisis (*Up Against the Ivy Wall: A History of the Columbia Crisis*), student agitators suffered "disillusionment," objecting to the war, the status of social justice, the moral state of the university, and other matters. In respect to Columbia, he remarked, "Columbia offers an education which lacks what education at most other large universities lacks – spirit."[38] To others, the crisis was tragic in nature. In his history of the 1960s, historian William L. O'Neill wrote that Columbia "was hurt in ways that would not be fully known for years.... That so experienced a man as [Columbia professor] Dwight Macdonald could be swept along by them [the rebels] was, perhaps, only a further sign of how advanced national pathology had become. ... It was a mixture of living theater, cowboys and Indians, the Russian Revolution, and nursery school."[39] Our purpose in this particular

[36] Timur Kuran, *Private Truths, Public Lies: The Social Consequences of Preference Falsification* (Harvard University Press, 1997). Kuran provides a theory and model of the processes of preference falsification and liberation with sociological, psychological, and economic elements.

[37] Roger Rosenblatt, *Coming Apart: A Memoir of the Harvard Wars of 1969* (Little, Brown, 1997), pp. 182–3. In *Cornell '69*, Downs illustrates at length how the faculty's capitulation to student demands was motivated in substantial part by fear and guilt, not just principle. He extends this type of critical inquiry to recent times in *Restoring Free Speech and Liberty on Campus* (Independent Institute/Cambridge University Press, 2006).

[38] Robert Friedman, "Introduction," in Jerry L. Avorn and Members of the Staff of the *Columbia Daily Spectator*, *Up Against the Ivy Wall: A History of the Columbia Crisis* (Atheneum, 1968), p. 5; Cox Commission, *Crisis at Columbia: Report of the Fact-Finding Commission Appointed to Investigate the Disturbances at Columbia University in April and May of 1968* (Vintage, Random House, 1968), pp. 4–10. The Cox Commission was the fact-finding commission established by Columbia's Executive Committee of the Faculties to investigate, report on, and make recommendations regarding the upheavals of spring 1968.

[39] William L. O'Neill, *Coming Apart: An Informal History of America in the '60s* (Ivan R. Dee, 1971), pp. 64, 291.

book is not to judge which side is correct, but rather to portray and assess how the 1968 crisis and related events affected the eventual departure of ROTC from Columbia's gates. The rebellion included week-long takeovers of five different buildings the last week of April, followed by a campuswide strike in response to the forceful police actions that evacuated the buildings. As the spring term ended, the campus reeled in a state of shock.

Constitutional law scholar Alan Westin, who played a leading, yet ultimately futile, role in mediating among the student factions, the faculty, and the administration during the crisis (à la Yeats, the liberal center could not hold), described a meeting between a faculty group and the trustees held shortly after the ejection of the students from the buildings. "Professor [Lionel] Trilling spoke to them eloquently of revolutions and explained that we are in the midst of one.... The world they had known and had expected to continue is no longer intact, and we had to provide them with a fantastic amount of information, attitudes, and perspectives that they normally do not get." A few days earlier, during a tense moment in the heat of the crisis, sociology professor Allan Silver – a member of the liberal-minded Ad Hoc Faculty Group, which Westin chaired – asked SDS leader Mark Rudd a simple yet fateful question: "Doesn't the University have any redeeming features that merit your saving it before leading it to disaster? The fabric of the University must be preserved ... and SDS must bear the consequences of its actions." Momentarily stunned, Rudd could not answer Silver's penetrating question, remarking later, "We were really up tight. We had no answer to this huge question."[40] In a rendering of this confrontation written shortly after the 1968 upheaval, Rudd wrote, "Had I been as sure then as I was several weeks later, after much study, experience, and discussion, the answer NO would have come readily. As it was, neither I nor any of the six or so SDS people present had any answer. We had to decide what is the value of a capitalist university, what is its function in society, and what are the contradictions which can possibly make it useful to a revolutionary movement?"[41]

There were three overarching issues in 1968. The first was race relations with the local community, epitomized by opposition to the university's plan to build a new gymnasium in Morningside Park. Second was disagreement with the way the administration was handling the discipline of SDS leaders who had violated a new rule forbidding indoor demonstrations – opposition that was magnified as disciplinary actions expanded with events, leading to what amounted to disciplinary chaos (528 individuals were arrested in the aftermath of the takeovers). Finally, there was resistance against Columbia's relationship with the military,

40 Westin, Silver, and Rudd, quoted in Avorn et al., *Up Against the Ivy Wall*, pp. 232, 106. According to David B. Truman's compelling unpublished memoir of the crisis, the Ad Hoc Faculty Group strove to mediate, but in effect facilitated the radical factions. See Truman, *Reflections on the Columbia Disorders of 1968*, pp. 126–37.

41 Mark Rudd, "Columbia: Notes on the Spring Rebellion," in Carl Oglesby, ed., *The New Left Reader* (Grove Press, 1969), p. 300: http://platypus.uchicago.edu/ruddmark_columbia 1968_rebellionnotes1969.pdf; link provided to authors by Allan Silver.

in particular the Institute for Defense Analysis (IDA), which "symbolized complicity in the war in Vietnam." As mentioned in Chapter 4, Columbia was one of a dozen universities with an institutional relationship with IDA, which included providing expert advice and research.[42] The IDA and military controversies occupied center stage, for, as the *Columbia Spectator*'s history pointed out, SDS was able to garner broader campus support over time by wrapping various military-related issues into a single package. "The primary political issue then [1966, when SDS became a force on campus], as it was in 1968, was the University's involvement with the 'military establishment' and with the burgeoning war in Vietnam."[43] SDS and other antiwar activists targeted the major aspects of the Cold War–Vietnam War University: the war itself; war research (including secret/classified contracts) and relationships with the military; and campus recruiting by organizations linked to the war, especially the CIA, the military services, and certain corporate interests. According to the Cox Report, IDA became SDS's "bread and butter issue."[44] Looking back twenty years later as the keynote speaker at Columbia's twentieth anniversary of the upheaval, Rudd remarked, "Stupidly, we thought revolution was imminent. Our rage blinded us. I now believe that the war in Vietnam drove us crazy."[45]

Fears regarding the fate of the university (and higher education in general) abounded in the aftermath of spring 1968. Columbia's president, Grayson Kirk, resigned in August, and the once-glittering career of Kirk's would-be successor, Provost–Vice President David B. Truman, had suffered near-irreparable damage. Truman joined Kirk in resigning not long after the crisis. One cannot read the extensive archival materials on the 1960s protests at Columbia (collected in the "University Protest and Activism Collection, 1958–1999," at Columbia University Rare Book and Manuscript Library, located in Butler Library) without being struck by the profound emotions, concerns, and fears that animated those who cared about the university.

Nevertheless, although tensions remained intense in the face of continuing protests (the war, after all, was still being fought), the regenerative process of healing the university began to sprout as the spring term mercifully gave way to summer. (The refrain of "healing" was bandied about often in the aftermath of the crisis.) In a nutshell, "revolution" conceded to "reform." Although most – though hardly all – students supported SDS's positions on the war and the bureaucratic and undemocratic nature of university authority, the vast majority disapproved of the group's highly uncivil methods – paradoxically mixed with utopian radicalism – and believed that the university, as well as the nation, were worth saving. (Indeed, just a year before the 1968 crisis, two-thirds of the

[42] Cox Commission, *Crisis at Columbia*, p. 75.

[43] Avorn et al., *Up Against the Ivy Wall*, p. 9.

[44] Cox Commission, *Crisis at Columbia*, p. 94. The Cox Commission was the fact-finding commission established by Columbia's Executive Committee of the Faculties to investigate, report on, and make recommendations regarding the upheavals of spring 1968.

[45] Rudd, quoted in Truman, *Reflections on the Columbia Disorders of 1968*, p. 94.

student body had voted in a referendum to support open recruiting by the military and CIA on campus – a position echoed by a committee chaired by Silver.)[46] Despite its efforts to perpetuate its leadership position, SDS marginalized itself by splitting into yet more factions and by maintaining an unconstructive posture. It was either not able to answer Silver's defining question, or it answered it the wrong way (in the negative). Meanwhile, new alliances of students, faculty members, and administrators filled the vacuum left by the disintegration of administrative authority, a process augmented by the failure of the University Council – Columbia's seventy-eight-year-old version of a faculty senate – to command allegiance and by the concomitant emergence of a new group constituting itself as the Executive Committee of the Faculty to speak on the faculty's behalf.[47] The Executive Committee was the de facto heir of the Ad Hoc Faculty Group, which dissolved after its efforts at compromise had fallen short.

The new alliances rolled up their sleeves and initiated the "restructuring" of the university. Restructuring led to the creation of a University Senate – consisting of faculty (tenured and nontenured), students, and administrators and staff – in 1969 to replace the tired and now irrelevant University Council. It also entailed greater student participation on committees, including the committees that adjudicated the cases of students charged with violating campus rules during the upheaval. To its dismay, SDS discovered in the fall that Columbia was not quite the same university that it had dismantled the previous spring. As early as September 1968, the *Washington Post* reported in a headline that "Reforms at Columbia Deflate SDS Sails." The new interim president, Andrew W. Cordier, was more open to student input than Kirk had been, and SDS "was now faced with what appeared to be a new and unprecedented attitude of conciliation and most open to change on the part of the administration." In addition, many of the major demands of the 1968 leaders had been met or were on the way to being met, including the severing of the university's connection to IDA, rejection of the Morningside Heights gymnasium, and reform of the procedures for disciplining miscreants. "A modest mood of optimism" now prevailed.[48]

We mention these matters because they offer pertinent background information regarding the reasons that Columbia dropped ROTC. One interpretation is

[46] See "Students at Columbia Support Recruiting," *New York Times*, November 2, 1967. Silver's committee did not hold that the principles of academic freedom and the open university required openness to all recruiting, only that there was no principle on either side of the issue, rendering the default position of freedom advisable. Most student rebellion movements were led by a minority faction that fomented upheaval through vanguard action that spawned a broadening of support through a process of "contagion." See Michael W. Miles, *The Radical Probe: The Logic of Student Rebellion* (Atheneum, 1971), p. 36.

[47] See the discussion of the Executive Committee of the Faculty's rise to power in the denouement of the crisis in Truman, *Reflections on the Columbia Disorders of 1968*.

[48] "Reforms at Columbia Deflate SDS Sails," *Washington Post*, September 23, 1968; "Columbia's Radicals Face a Changed Foe," *New York Times*, September 22, 1968.

that the relevant decision makers (the respective ROTC committees, the University Council in its last meeting, and the trustees) were overwhelmed by pressure still emanating from 1968. And it is evident that this force loomed over the campus throughout this period. The other interpretation is more nuanced. As we have just seen, the university had managed to recollect itself to some meaningful extent and had succeeded in winning the majority of students over to its reform agenda. The broader pattern of events at Columbia was very similar to that of other campuses that underwent rebellions in the late 1960s: fervent eruptions of revolutionary politics, followed fairly quickly by quasi-restorations based on restructuring and reform.[49] This meant that the final deliberations over ROTC took place in less emotional circumstances, freeing the decision makers somewhat to concentrate more on academic, not political, concerns; at the same time, keeping ROTC on campus could have jeopardized the fledgling consensus of reconciliation that the university had achieved – however precariously – and political pressures had hardly departed. So it might be naïve to downplay the politics surrounding the decision. Complicating matters is the fact that Columbia had already been grappling with the ROTC question on academic grounds for several years. In fact, this examination had begun in earnest at the same time as serious protest against ROTC first appeared. From the very beginning of the process, antiwar pressure and academic concerns, like Tristan and Isolde, coexisted in an inseparable embrace.

These events were foreshadowed by demonstrations against perceptions of American militarism at Columbia that began in the early 1960s, including protests against Naval Reserve Officers Training Corps (NROTC) in 1963 and 1964. But the "breakthrough" confrontation took place on May 7, 1965, when a group of forty to fifty students, led by the Independent Committee on Vietnam, planned to disrupt the annual NROTC awards ceremony by throwing custard and lemon meringue pies at the cadets. Their purpose was to protest the war in Vietnam, President Lyndon Johnson's recent invasion of the Dominican Republic, and NRTOC's presence on campus. (Other groups, such as the Progressive Labor Movement, the May 2 Movement, Youth Against War and Fascism, and SDS, joined the fray.) The number of protesters soon swelled to about two hundred. Due to rain, the proceeding moved to the Rotunda of Low Library, a traditional space for ceremonies, where protesters locked arms to block entry to the area. According to the Cox Commission Report, the demonstration "rapidly got out of hand." Unable to restore order, the university called in the police, but also postponed the ceremony. A perusal of newspaper and university accounts of the incident reveals an institution recoiling in shock over what had transpired. The incident "was the first occasion of major police action, within recent memory, on Columbia's campus." The next year, the Navy requested that the year-end review of the program be canceled, and the

[49] Cornell and Harvard are good examples, but the model could be broadly applied. See, e.g., Downs, *Cornell '69*; Rosenblatt, *Coming Apart*.

administration called off the awards ceremony in 1967. Then, in 1968, "upon the Navy's initiative, the ceremony was permanently abandoned."[50]

Astute observers fathomed the ominous import of the 1965 NROTC disruption. Four days after the incident, President Kirk issued a "Memorandum to the University Community" addressing the situation, in which he stressed the "danger of extreme violence" that could have erupted had police used their power to allow the ceremony to proceed. He also warned that such disruptions of a "regularly scheduled academic function of the University ... could not be tolerated." A subsequent report to Kirk authored by David Truman and two deans began by stating, "We have fully shared your view that the implications of this incident for Columbia are profound, that the values at stake extend far beyond this campus, and that further dishonor to these values should not occur as a result of any action or inaction by us. ..." In a term paper on the incident available in the Columbia archives, a student applied novelist Reverend Andrew Greely's description of the nation's new generation of protesters to the May 7 demonstrators at Columbia: They represented "a new breed" of student resistance. Letters to Kirk from angry alumni and others conveyed deep misgivings and discontent over the postponement of the ceremony, which had handed a victory to the protesters. One letter from the national chief of Naval personnel expressed "grave concern within the Department of the Navy," and warned that "additional efforts can be expected as a result of the success of the past endeavor." Two weeks later, the university "censured" fifty students for their actions in this incident. Censures are warnings that students could be expelled in the event they recidivated.[51]

Like many other universities at the time (see the preceding sections), Columbia was simultaneously engaged in an evaluation of the ROTC program on campus. The original contract with the Navy for an NROTC program had been signed in mid-1945, as World War II was winding down. In a letter to the chair of the University Council, Associate Dean N. M. McKnight affirmed the university's intention to maintain common standards for cadets and regular students: "The relationship of the Naval ROTC students to the University will closely resemble that of our civilian undergraduate students."[52] The seas of the relationship remained relatively calm until the storm of Vietnam hit, but they did encounter some rough waters along the way. An undercurrent of congenital concerns about the academic status of the program rippled throughout the

[50] Cox Commission, *Crisis at Columbia*, pp. 63–4.

[51] President Grayson Kirk, "Memorandum to the University Community," May 11, 1965; Report on May 7, 1965 NROTC Disruption Submitted to President Grayson Kirk by Ralph S. Halford, Wesley J. Hennessy, and David B. Truman, May 17, 1965; Irving DeKoff, "May 7th Conflict Between Students and Administration," October 7, 1965; Letter to Kirk from Vice Admiral B. J. Semmes, Chief of Naval Personnel, May 19, 1965; Letters to President Kirk on May 7, 1965 incident; "Censures Issued to 50 at Columbia," *New York Times*, May 21, 1965. All of these documents in Butler Archive.

[52] Letter from N. M. McKnight to Dean George B. Pegram, Chair, University Council, June 6, 1945, in Butler Archive.

university during this time, with some activities of the program raising eyebrows. For example, the university intervened in 1962 when an instructor was alleged to have engaged in indoctrination and brainwashing while giving classes on the nature of Communism.[53]

On the academic front, in late 1964 (the year of the national ROTC Vitalization Act), the Student Academic Affairs Committee submitted a report to the dean of Columbia College (the main undergraduate school) calling for revision of the ROTC curriculum, which the students considered "too technical" and at odds with the intellectual spirit of the liberal arts school. Another problem was that the program required twenty-one credit hours of work, making it difficult for the cadets to complete their normal course loads and limiting their ability to take a broader selection of liberal arts offerings. The student committee, which advised the faculty-based College Committee on Instruction, considered different recommendations, including limiting the program to summer school, reducing the number of ROTC credits allowed, and even abolishing the program. Its final recommendation (accompanied by a "strong dissenting group" that favored abolition), issued two weeks before the May 7 demonstration, called for lowering the number of credits that ROTC could offer. The committee said that "ideally" the program should be abolished, but it was reluctant to recommend this step because of the impact it would have on scholarship opportunities for fellow students.[54] This report launched a serious reconsideration of ROTC that was to last for over three years.

So the fledgling attack on ROTC in 1965 now operated on two flanks: academic and moral/political. On September 27 of the following school term, Columbia's student newspaper, the *Columbia Daily Spectator*, reported the release of a memorandum from Kirk. Responding to the claims of both the student report and the anti-NROTC demonstrators in May, Kirk affirmed the university's support for ROTC on academic grounds and because of the program's contribution to the military and the university.[55] But a mere day after reporting Kirk's affirmation, the *Spectator* published an interview with David Truman in which the (then) dean of Columbia College informed readers that the college might engage in a review of the NROTC program. The article cited faculty concerns that had arisen in reaction to the report by the Student Affairs Committee the previous spring. The commander of NROTC at Columbia responded by defending the program, but agreeing that appropriate modifications of the program could be accommodated. In his unpublished memoir of the crisis, Truman admitted that he had always been lukewarm, at best, about

[53] "Controversial Talk to ROTC Spurs Columbia Policy Inquiry," *New York Times*, January 11, 1962. See also "ROTC Has Had Tumultuous Career at Columbia," *Columbia Spectator*, October 20, 1965.

[54] See "Student Group Asks Revision for NROTC," *New York Times*, November 25, 1964; "Student Group Seeks to Cut NROTC Credit," *Columbia Spectator*, April 23, 1965. On file in Butler Archive.

[55] "Kirk Says NROTC Ties Will Be Maintained at CU," *Columbia Spectator*, September 27, 1965.

ROTC. In conveying his thoughts about the disruption of May 7, 1965, he admitted, "I held no strong brief for this program and had grave doubts about its academic quality, despite the fact that the courses were subject to the review of the Committee on Instruction, like all courses in the College, and despite the fact that the credentials of the officers nominated to the program by the Navy were subject to our review and approval."[56] The program would need more commitment than this given the escalating pressures that it would confront in ensuing years.

Shortly thereafter, the *Spectator* disclosed that an assistant professor in the NROTC program had recently charged in the United States Naval Institute's *Proceedings* that ROTC courses were below par because "the average officer's teaching abilities are insufficient ... being on a level equivalent to physical education."[57] Similar concerns percolated throughout higher education, leading to the changes endorsed by the Benson Report, issued in 1969. But the Benson Report's purpose was to encourage constructive reform in order to fend off abolition. What course would Columbia take?

As Truman intimated, Kirk had indeed commissioned a committee – the President's Committee to Examine the NROTC Curriculum – to review the academic status of ROTC. In November 1965, this committee asked the Columbia College Committee on Instruction, in conjunction with representatives from the Committees on Instruction in the School of Engineering and Applied Science and the School of General Studies (the school for adult students) to examine the curriculum of the Department of Naval Science. This committee then set up a subcommittee of eleven members, chaired by Truman, to conduct the lion's share of the inquiry. The subcommittee worked with the NROTC commander at Columbia and with the Bureau of Naval Personnel in the Department of the Navy to craft a position. The subcommittee issued its recommendations in June 1966, calling for substantial curricular reform. It concluded that many of ROTC's technical courses were of "trade school" quality, and that the program would be strengthened by requiring cadets to take a sequence of regular mathematics and physics courses. In addition, courses dealing with indoctrination were often one-sided and unsophisticated, and the military history component that was prominent in most nontechnical military science courses was often "narrow, at best, and texts for the most part naïve and unscholarly." On the instruction front, the subcommittee reported that ROTC teachers were not well prepared as scholars, and that their terms of employment were too limited to facilitate professional development. The subcommittee issued several recommendations to address these findings. They boiled down to strengthening the intellectual quality of the program; limiting the credits

56 Truman, *Reflections on the Columbia Disorders of 1968*, p. 85.

57 "School May Review NROTC's Program," *Columbia Spectator*, September 28, 1965; "NROTC Leeway Seen by Paulsen," *Columbia Spectator*, October 5, 1965; "Dean Labels Navy Demands 'Reasonable,'" *Columbia Spectator*, October 14, 1965; "Dispute Competence of NROTC Faculty," *Columbia Spectator*, October 19, 1965.

cadets could earn for technical military courses, while eliminating credit for indoctrination; and giving the university more say over the hiring of instructors. The President's Committee worked on the matter from 1966 to 1967, going back and forth with the Navy on matters of concern.[58]

While the university pursued the NROTC curriculum issue, political pressure against the war was also building across the nation and on the campus. In February 1967, a new group, ROTC-Off-The-Campus, announced its formation for "the purpose of forcing the Columbia unit [of the NROTC] off the campus." A group leader told the *Spectator* that targeting NROTC "is one way people around here can have an effect on the war." Within days of its inception, the group began attending and disrupting ROTC classes as a form of protest, later moving on to other measures after the administration cracked down on this action.[59] Antiwar demonstrations became fixtures of the university's landscape over the next few years, featuring the ROTC protests; resistance to recruiting by such organizations as the CIA, the Marines, and Dow Chemical Company; agitation against the new gymnasium and university plans for expansion; and major demonstrations against IDA in the days leading up to the 1968 crisis.[60]

After the subcommittee on the NROTC curriculum released its report in June 1966, the university began conferring with the Navy over reforms. Negotiations suffered a setback in February 1967 when the Navy adopted a policy of requiring cadets to take three new courses in computer science, sea-to-land ballistics, and techniques of propaganda. This requirement went against the entire grain of the Columbia subcommittee's recommendations, leading the College Committee on Instruction to declare, "The addition of another course without compensatory reduction in the Department offerings is not debatable." For its part, the Navy said, "We simply could not meet the demands that the University set forth."[61]

But the Navy was reluctant to lose representation at Columbia and other prestigious institutions, and was disconcerted by Columbia's canceling of the May 1967 NROTC awards ceremony due to political pressure. Consequently, exploratory discussions "covering 'the whole matter' of the NROTC program on the Columbia campus" took place in the summer of 1967. The Navy seemed willing to bend, leading Truman to report that the Navy might be amenable to using Columbia as "testing grounds for changes in the NROTC national curriculum."[62] Indeed, at the national level, the Navy and the other armed services

[58] See "The Final Report of the Subcommittee of the President's Committee on the NROTC Program, June 24, 1966," in "Report on the N.R.O.T.C.," December 10, 1968, in Butler Archive.

[59] "Group Wants ROTC to Leave Columbia," *Columbia Spectator*, March 1, 1967; "College Warns Nine Students to Discontinue NROTC Sit-In," *Columbia Spectator*, March 7, 1968.

[60] On the series of protests leading up to the 1968 crisis, see Cox Commission, *Crisis at Columbia*. See also the extensive media coverage of the recruiting wars in the Butler Archive. See, e.g., "Columbia Ends Campus Ban on Recruiting by Military," *New York Times*, January 11, 1968.

[61] "NROTC Unit Will Be Removed from Campus Within Five Years: Navy to Phase Out Program Gradually After CU Rejects Increase in Courses," *Columbia Spectator*, March 30, 1967.

[62] "CU, Navy Discuss Future of NROTC," *Columbia Spectator*, August 10, 1967.

were struggling earnestly with the question of academic credit in the last few years of the decade. The Navy threatened to remove its units from schools that withdrew credit, but this could mean sacrificing outposts at some Ivy League schools and at some major state universities. This concern was heightened after the six Ivy institutions dropped ROTC programs at the end of the decade. Would Big Ten schools follow suit? None of the sixty schools on the waiting list for programs was, in the words of a top administrator at the University of Michigan, "an equivalent to ... any one of the institutions in the Big Ten with NROTC units."[63] Most importantly, Secretary of State Melvin Laird and Assistant Secretary of Defense Theodore Marrs feared adding Big Ten units to their string of losses. Nevertheless, in 1971 the Navy adopted a policy of not allowing a scholarship student to enroll in a program that did not provide credit; but it lifted the policy a mere year later under pressure from the Association of NROTC Colleges and Universities. According to Neiberg, "This debate over credit indicates that the services – even in the navy, which fought hardest on this issue – preferred having no-credit programs at schools like Michigan and Illinois to having full-time credit ones at less visible, less prestigious schools."[64]

Striving to find common ground as the university entered the 1967–8 academic year, the two sides reached what proved to be a precarious rapprochement. On January 24, 1968, the Committee on Instruction of Columbia College approved a new curriculum proposed by the university's Department of Naval Science, which incorporated many of the curriculum revisions recommended by the subcommittee of the President's Committee. The new curriculum, which went into the college bulletin for 1968–9, substituted courses in government and history for the previous two terms of Naval history; relegated the more rote aspects of Naval science courses to an increased number of summer cruises; eliminated Naval science study in the sophomore year "to give NROTC students greater latitude in their academic programs"; required Naval students to take two regular math courses plus a course in a physical science; and reduced the credit points for ROTC courses from nineteen to nine. A university report on this agreement stated, "By implication, the whole tone of the subcommittee report supported the idea of giving the chairman of the Department of Naval Science far more flexibility to use the curriculum of the host school in his program than was heretofore the case."[65]

63 Robert Williams to Robben Fleming and Allan Smith, November 5, 1970, University of Michigan Archives, Bentley Historical Library, President's Papers, Box 23, ROTC Folder, cited and quoted in Neiberg, *Making Citizens Soldiers*, p. 148.

64 Neiberg, *Making Citizen Soldiers*, p. 148. The University of Wisconsin, Madison is another Big Ten school that struggled mightily with this issue, forming its own set of committees whose work paralleled the work of the Benson Committee. See University of Wisconsin, Faculty Council Recommendation on All-University ROTC Policy Committee, Report and Recommendations, UFA Document 51, June 2, 1971.

65 "Actions Taken by the University in Response to the Report of the Subcommittee of the President's Committee to Examine the NROTC Curriculum," October 29, 1968, in Report on the N.R.O.T.C., December 10, 1968, Butler Archive.

Meanwhile, antimilitary fervor began reaching a fever pitch in 1967–8, with orchestrated antiwar demonstrations and numerous agitations against recruiting and the IDA dominating the campus scene. Antiwar activists held a day-long series of programs protesting the war and the draft on March 13, 1968. The *West Side News* reported on March 21 that, "At Columbia University, protest against the draft is picking up. Almost every week the Resistance, an organization concerned with opposition to the war in Vietnam, sends out a statement about a Columbia student opposing the draft."[66] ROTC's future at Columbia was precarious enough as it was, but then came the revolutionary crisis of the spring.

A few months before the outbreak of the crisis, Truman established on January 10, 1968, the Columbia University Committee on Relations with Outside Agencies. Chaired by noted foreign affairs law scholar Louis Henkin, the committee's charge was to examine the nature and propriety of Columbia's relationships to outside entities (corporate and governmental). The Henkin Committee scrutinized a healthy portion of Columbia's vast network of outside associations, including many of the crown jewels of the Cold War University. It issued its report at the end of May, a month after the revolution. Aware of allegations that naturally would accompany their conclusions under the circumstances, committee members attested in an introductory letter to the president to "having made every effort to insulate ourselves" from the havoc of the 1968 crisis. The report recommended guidelines for the university's relations with outside organizations, the most important of which dealt with the IDA. Affirming that most such relationships were beneficial to all concerned, the committee also stipulated that such arrangements should be consistent with "the university's principal purposes of instruction and research." This meant that the university should guard against its authority being surrendered or unduly transferred to outside agencies and that such enterprises as secret research should not be undertaken except in very special cases, subject to approval by the institution. Regarding IDA, the report found "nothing sinister" in the university's arrangement with the institute. "Only on the assumption that our society and our government are irredeemably corrupt, that national defense is immoral, that all who serve the nation's military purposes are unspeakable, can IDA be condemned; we do not accept those assumptions." But citing the feelings of "a substantial spectrum of campus opinion" that holds that "the purposes of a University and of the military services are essentially incompatible and that the University should not be formally affiliated with organizations serving a predominantly military purpose," the committee went on to conclude that the university in its corporate capacity should discontinue its formal relationship to the IDA. Researchers could maintain ties, but only in their individual discretion.[67] Although the Henkin Report surprisingly never mentioned

[66] "Columbia: Draft Protest Quickens," *West Side News*, March 21, 1968 (in Butler Archive).

[67] Report of the Columbia University Committee on Relations with Outside Agencies (Henkin Committee), May 31, 1968, Butler Archive, Introductory Letter and pp. 3, 17–18.

NROTC by name – it was, after all, a prime example of an "outside agency" or organization with a "military purpose" posing challenges to the university's autonomy – the implications of the report's basic principles and its reasoning pertaining to IDA could not have boded well for the program.

The Henkin Committee's efforts did not placate SDS and its allies. "The announcement of this 'disaffiliation' outraged, rather than satisfied, the critics," the Cox Commission concluded. "In terms of the IDA connection, they not unnaturally saw the change as a rather disingenuous attempt to assert severance while continuing the substance of the relationship."[68]

So the institution of the new curricular arrangement for NROTC in January of 1968 now confronted two contrary forces: the widely accepted principles articulated in the Henkin Committee Report, which had severed the university's official ties to the IDA; and the broader implications of the 1968 crisis. The task of overseeing what would be the deciding appraisal regarding NROTC in the aftermath of the 1968 crisis would fall to another group that had helped to spearhead the reform movement. On October 9, 1968, the newly empowered Executive Committee of the Faculty – the faculty group that had stepped into the vacuum of authority left by the demise of the Kirk administration and the delegitimizing of the University Council – announced its own plans to "investigate the role and purpose of the Naval Reserve Officers Training Program at Columbia." Then on October 28 – a day before the final report of the old President's Committee confirming the NROTC curriculum reform's entry into the college catalogue – the Executive Committee of the Faculty established yet another committee, whose charge made explicit the possibility of abolition of the program. The Executive Committee of the Faculty Joint Committee on NROTC was charged to review previous reports and actions respecting NROTC, and "after a full consideration of the present situation and arguments in favor of and opposition to the continuance of the NROTC at Columbia, the Committee will present its recommendations for continuation, change, or abolition to the faculties concerned."[69] The new NROTC committee, which included student members, was chaired by Harvey C. Mansfield, professor of government. At the time, NROTC at Columbia had fifty-five regular cadets, twenty-six in the college and twenty-nine in the engineering school.

About a month before the Mansfield Committee issued its report on March 14, 1969, all of the presidents of Ivy League institutions received letters from Secretary of Defense Laird, expressing, in the words of the March 24 minutes of the Columbia University Board of Trustees, "concern over the actions contemplated by some leading universities in the withdrawal of credit for certain NROTC courses ... and stating his concern that such actions would tend to degrade career military service as an honorable profession." Fearing these actions would "have a detrimental effect on the future of the officers corps and

[68] Cox Commission, *Crisis at Columbia*, p. 94.

[69] Executive Committee of the Faculty Joint Committee on NROTC, Report of the NROTC Committee, March 14, 1969, Butler Archive (henceforth Mansfield Committee Report), pp. 1–2.

on national security," Laird stated that unilateral action taken by such institutions would be "premature and unwise." President Cordier of Columbia informed Laird that the university was proceeding deliberately, and that the Department of Defense would be informed of any university action.[70]

The thirteen-member Mansfield Committee's Report issued on March 14 carefully considered all sides of the argument, and its members disagreed on a number of points. "I transmit herewith the hard-fought report of the NROTC Committee," Mansfield wrote in a prefatory note to the report to the faculty.[71] The committee interviewed numerous individuals and studied a vast array of material, including the ways other Ivy League institutions were dealing with ROTC. It discussed the claim that ROTC contributed to the national interest and to national service, as well as the thoughts of those who considered it contrary to the university's proper purposes. In a pivotal move, the report acknowledged drawing inspiration from the Henkin Committee's principles regarding institutional autonomy:

> The key issue concerning NROTC is the degree of control of a university program from outside the University and the freedom of the University to set its own academic standards. The position of this committee (and of the Henkin Committee) reflects a sense of a new direction in official University policy since former President Kirk's statement of the University's relations with outside organizations.

Kirk's position, as stated in the *Cox Commission Report*, was that the university should refrain from letting its "value judgment about any of the organizations concerned" influence its decisions respecting outside agencies.[72] Divorcing itself from this standard liberal position, the Mansfield Report seemed to inch toward the more partisan or value-laden notion of the university. Kirk's "statement does not provide the answer when that autonomy is said to be jeopardized by either the continuance or the abolition of NROTC on campus." But rather than expressly taking a side, the report simply presented ideal-type articulations of the pure neutrality position and the more partisan position. In articulating the latter, the committee wrote, "If the military is regarded as an institution that thrives on unquestioning discipline and discourages the questioning of basic assumptions, it is clear that the (ideal) university stands in direct contrast to this attitude."[73]

Like the Henkin Report, the Mansfield Report addressed the question of political pressures. But the six-member minority that recommended overt abolition admitted the difficulty of insulating academic judgments from political judgments:

[70] Minutes of Columbia University Board of Trustees Meeting, March 24, 1969, Butler Archive, pp. 383–4.

[71] Mansfield Committee Report, p. 1.

[72] See Cox Commission, *Crisis at Columbia*.

[73] Mansfield Committee Report, pp. 4–5.

Throughout the deliberations of the NROTC Committee a genuine effort was made to separate the issue of NROTC from the issue of the Vietnam War. It was felt that the major questions were academic ones. Nonetheless, it should be admitted that the academic arguments against NROTC on campus have been as valid for over twenty years as they are today. Why, then, are they causing such controversy that one university after another is considering basic alterations of the program?

In the end, however, the group simply said, "We do not consider this an act of political defiance of the government but merely the reassertion of normal academic control over the university curriculum."[74]

A slight majority (seven to six) opposed direct abolition, but the committee enjoyed "near unanimous acceptance" of four recommendations that would be difficult for the military to accept: (1) credit should be allowed only if a course "is also listed in the offerings of a regular academic department;" (2) professorial rank for ROTC instructors should be dropped unless such individuals are "appointed according to regular procedures;" (3) office space for drill or instructional purposes should be withdrawn, even for courses that might achieve credit status; and (4) ROTC scholarships should be modeled on loans under the National Defense Education Act (NEDA) of 1958, which allows for withdrawal from the funded program by virtue of repayment of the sums that the government laid out, but without the further requirement of punitive service liabilities.[75] In effect, these policies would render the program extracurricular.

Six days after the presentation of the Mansfield Committee Report to the university, the University Council dealt with the report as well as two resolutions from the Columbia College faculty. According to a report of a Board of Trustees meeting on March 24, these resolutions declared opposition to "the external control exercised over faculty appointments, curriculum, and student conduct by the NROTC program, but also affirmed respect for the right of the individual students to enter into agreements with the armed services, and support for a program which enabled students to make arrangements to their own advantage."[76] At this meeting, the Council voted to recommend that the university "terminate the present arrangements with the Navy Department for the NROTC program" in order to establish a new relationship based on the Mansfield proposals.[77] After some further discussions, the Navy informed the university that it would not be possible to meet the University Council's conditions because federal statutes at that time precluded making ROTC programs extracurricular. (This situation changed, but only after it was too late for Columbia.) The stage was set for abolition.

While all this was transpiring, Roger T. Kelley, assistant secretary of defense for manpower and reserve affairs, mailed packages to the professors of military

[74] Mansfield Committee Report, p. 10.

[75] Mansfield Committee Report, p. 2.

[76] Minutes of Columbia University Board of Trustees Meeting, March 24, 1969, p. 379.

[77] Columbia University Office of Public Information, Notice of University Council Approval of Mansfield Committee Recommendations, Butler Archive, March 20, 1969.

science across the country and to the presidents of colleges and universities that had ROTC units. Kelley was the Defense Department's point man for discussions with college and university leaders over the fate of ROTC. The package, dated April 29, contained the transcript of a press briefing that Kelley had given earlier that day. Laird had introduced that meeting by stating, "The issues on those few campuses where opposition to ROTC has been manifested go further [than reform], however. Those schools are threatened by denial of the opportunity to provide a portion of our future national leadership. The Nation and the military services would suffer a loss if any part of the civilian academic community declined that opportunity."[78]

On May 13, Columbia's University Council met again in a "special session" called by President Cordier to address NROTC's situation in light of the Navy's position. The Council dealt with a resolution dissolving NROTC. A summary of the minutes of that meeting reported President Cordier as observing "that this proposal is more radical that the previous resolution of the Council in that it provides for the complete termination of N.R.O.T.C. activities as soon as presently enrolled students have completed their courses." Arguments for and against the measure were presented, but the desire to terminate prevailed. The final vote was forty-four to zero. During discussion, however, Professor William T. R. Fox, a pioneer in international conflict studies, raised the specter of political pressure. The notes to the meeting reported:

> It has been a principle of our democracy [Fox remarked] that the officer corps of the military services should not be staffed solely by graduates of the military academies. To eliminate the program completely is an impulsive response to an emotional situation. Indeed, in his view there is an implicit hypocrisy in the sudden discovery that the presence of a Naval training unit is inappropriate on a university campus.... Professor Fox urged that the resolution be modified so as not to preclude the possibility of means being devised in the future to make some kind of military training available to those who wish it.[79]

The Council's resolution then went to the trustees for final approval. Within ten days of this vote, the Council dissolved itself after having rendered seventy-nine years of service. It passed its authority to the University Senate, which held its first meeting on May 28 in order to constitute itself formally.[80]

The trustees then met on May 13, the same day of the Council's vote, and affirmed the resolution to remove NROTC from campus in light of the Navy's position, becoming effective by June 1971. They also officially authorized the establishment of the University Senate that day. The official notes of the meeting

78 Department of Defense Press Briefing, Honorable Roger T. Kelley, Assistant Secretary of Defense Manpower and Reserve Affairs, April 29, 1969, Butler Archive, p. 2.

79 University Council, Summary of Minutes, Columbia University, May 13, 1969, Butler Archive.

80 Minutes of the First Meeting of the Columbia University Senate, May 28, 1969: http://www.columbia.edu/cu/senate/information/40th_anniversary/senate_minutes_1969.pdf. See also "Here Are Some Important Documents from the Years 1968–71, About the Founding and Early Operations of the Columbia University Senate": http://www.columbia.edu/cu/senate/information/40th_anniversary/40th_anniversary_page.htm.

suggest that the substantive discussions had already taken place in previous meetings or other venues, for the main point of concern was how to deal with the four incoming students who had accepted ROTC scholarships to attend Columbia. They voted that no new students would be enrolled in the remaining program. No debate over termination was reported in the notes. But the previous meeting on April 7 had witnessed some interesting exchanges. A faculty representative, Professor Polykarp Kusch, a Nobel Laureate in physics in 1955, sternly presented the radical position on ROTC. "He said that he had come to the conclusion that NROTC contributes nothing to the University. If it were not already here, he said, no one would demand it. Its very existence at the University, and not credit for its courses and academic rank for its instructors, is the issue." Then he issued a warning: "He noted that substantial numbers say that NROTC is an affirmative evil, and that some are willing to do horrible things in support of that view."[81] The trustees voted to sever Columbia's relationship with NROTC. In the eyes of the *Spectator*, the university's resolution on ROTC constituted the "strongest move by [a] major university against ROTC."[82]

The trustees' decision triggered an avalanche of letters to administrative leaders, mostly expressing anger and dismay. One letter came from the one new student in Columbia College who could not enroll in the fall because of the withdrawal of his ROTC scholarship. (His uncle also wrote on his behalf.) In a letter replying to another angry alumnus, Dean Carl V. Hovde countered the alumnus's claim that the decision was made at the point of a political gun. "I can understand that the phasing-out of ROTC may look like a collapse before pressure. Certainly there are others who feel as you do. But as I mentioned when we had lunch at the Columbia Club, there is a difference between the reason why a particular issue is raised and the principles in accord with which the issue is resolved."[83]

CONCLUDING THOUGHTS

The most important question relating to the departure of ROTC from Columbia is whether this result was merited under the circumstances. The answer is not as clear as partisans on either side of the debate claim. On the one hand, even the leading historians of Army ROTC maintain that that program was not strong until the 1980s, when the military as a whole began recovering from its post-Vietnam funk. The programs of the other services also needed improvement. Furthermore, the number of students joining ROTC began to decline after the Nixon administration turned to the draft lottery in 1969–70. Only four

[81] Minutes of Columbia University Board of Trustees Meeting, April 7, 1969, pp. 405–6.

[82] "Columbia's Trustees Abolish R.O.T.C.," *New York Times*, May 14, 1969; "Resolution Represents Strongest Move by Major University Against ROTC," *Columbia Spectator*, May 14, 1969.

[83] Letters from Alumni in Response to the Abolition of ROTC, Butler Archive.

incoming freshmen had NROTC scholarships in the fall of 1969 at Columbia, a number that could not sustain a viable program. As Roger T. Kelley stated after being queried about the Ivy League in the Department of Defense press briefing previously mentioned, "I don't think it is an either-or proposition. The judgment has been made that we wish to continue ROTC at any of our fine colleges and universities if, No. 1, the university finds the essence of ROTC in accord with its own educational philosophy, and, No. 2, it produces at least the minimum number of ROTC graduates."[84] There were legitimate academic reasons to be wary of ROTC's presence at Columbia, although it is also clear that the Navy was attempting to find common ground.

On the other hand, the evidence also strongly suggests that disagreement with the Vietnam War and the remarkable political pressures that accompanied this discontent were omnipresent throughout the decisive stages of deliberation. As Neiberg demonstrates so well, other schools where antiwar sentiment raged maintained their programs, and even Princeton brought an Army program back two years after its decision to effectively bar it. The Ivy schools considered themselves the nation's intellectual and moral vanguards in higher education, and the *Zeitgeist* of the intellectual classes had turned decisively against the war, dragging disrespect for the military into this change of heart. For decades, the military would not hold an honored place in the intellectual and moral spirit of many of the nation's elite higher-education institutions. It is evident that this new spirit played a major role in what went down at Columbia and other Ivy schools. Perhaps we should leave it at that.

[84] Department of Defense Press Briefing, Roger T. Kelley, April 29, 1969, p. 6.

6

ROTC, Columbia, and the Ivy League

Sisyphus Renews His Quest to Renew a Troubled Relationship

> Law professors have completely lost interest in legal control of the military, seemingly afflicted with a bad case of deference themselves. ... We have an institutional obligation to participate in civilian control of the military. ... There was a time when law school faculties carried enormous expertise about military law and military legal reform, and they were actually the first call that would be made when the military was sitting down and beginning to think about how it was going to reform its laws. Today, that would be the last call the military would make, because that expertise, over the last generation, really has evaporated.
>
> – Diane H. Mazur, professor of law, and former captain, United States Air Force[1]

In this chapter, we look at the "return of ROTC" movement at Columbia and other Ivy schools. The chapter presents illustrative evidence of the gap that exists between elite universities and the military, and of a struggle to bridge that gap through the reintegration of ROTC with the campus. The story of the ROTC movement at Columbia highlights the tensions that exist between the value systems of the military and the university, as well as the potential for the finding of common ground that can hold its own amid differences.

Although the renewed politics of ROTC involves tangible benefits and consequences – offering scholarship and career opportunities for cadets, providing a fresh and different voice to campus discourse, bridging the civil-military gap, improving the officer corps, and so on – it is also an example of the "creedal passions" we talked about in Chapter 1 – the fundamental values and principles about which we, the people, feel most passionate. The ROTC debate pivots around such principles as civic equality, equal respect and dignity, freedom and diversity of thought, self-sacrifice and community, and commitment. It is partly a symbolic politics, which entails groups and

[1] Quoted in "'Rum, Sodomy, and the Lash': What the Military Thrives on and How It Affects Legal Recruitment and Law Schools," 14 *Duke Law Journal of Gender Law and Policy* 1143 (2007): 1160–3.

individuals seeking policy goals in order to secure validation or recognition of their beliefs and values.[2]

The decade-long Columbia ROTC movement consisted of three major stages: (1) the 2001–5 movement, in which activists made ROTC a major public issue on campus, only to fall short in the University Senate because of a new objection to military presence that had replaced the antimilitary attitudes of the 1960s and 1970s as the primary reason to oppose ROTC: the presence of Don't Ask, Don't Tell (DADT); (2) 2006–8, in which a more modest movement kept the issue alive, but continued to fall short; (3) 2008–11, which culminated in the Sisyphean ROTC movement finally managing to roll its pebble to the top of the academic mountain soon after the death knell of DADT sounded. By the end of the process, ROTC advocates had succeeded in fostering a paradigm shift in campus opinion and attitudes regarding the military, bringing that institution more within the ambit of intellectual, moral, and professional legitimacy. On the one hand, this shift entailed further assimilating the military to preexisting campus mores and norms, such as diversity (a status that necessitated the ending of DADT), tolerance, equal respect, and leadership. On the other hand, the shift reflected a stretching of the university mind to embrace a set of perspectives and values that lie beyond the ken of most campus citizens these days, such as military conceptions of duty, patriotism, and the use of force in justifiable circumstances. In so doing, this shift in the politics of ROTC presented a case study in institutional change.

Interestingly, some of the strongest arguments on behalf of ROTC in all three movements embraced the same discourse of diversity and equality that called for protecting the rights of homosexuals: Military students (ROTC and veterans) should be given the same respect, tolerance, and opportunities as other students. The principles of diversity and equal respect should apply to military students as well. Advocates also appealed to classic arguments for ROTC (the citizen-soldier ideal) as well as to traditional university principles trumpeting diversity of thought and Ivy institutions' historic pride in producing students dedicated to service and leadership.

Perhaps surprisingly, the mutual use of the politics of recognition intimated that an alliance could be had if the contradictory knot of DADT were untied. Interviews we conducted with Columbia cadets, and a reading of the copious public commentary in campus forums revealed the intensity of the politics of recognition at stake on both sides. Gays were fighting hard to achieve the status of equal citizenship and the recognition of worthiness that comes with it. And in American history there has been an intimate link between the recognition of equal citizenship and the opportunity and ability to serve in the military, the institution most likely to ask for the ultimate sacrifice. Recall historian Andrew Bacevich's observations in Chapter 1:"For the generations that fought the Civil

[2] Samuel P. Huntington, *American Politics and the Promise of Disharmony* (Harvard University Press, 1981). On the nature of symbolic politics, see, e.g., Murray Edelman, *The Symbolic Uses of Politics* (University of Illinois Press, 1964).

War and the world wars, and even those who served in the 1950s and 1960s, citizenship and military service remained intimately connected. Indeed, those to whom this obligation to serve did not apply – including at various times the poor, people of color, and women – were thereby marked as ineligible for full citizenship." Political theorist William A. Galston echoes this understanding. "From Greek and Roman times down to the present, the allocation of the burden of national defense has been at the heart of citizenship." It is no accident that civil rights and equality movements have often included equal access to military service in their claims, for being asked to defend the nation is an ultimate sign of trust.[3]

Interestingly, this link meant that some gay activists who opposed ROTC for antidiscriminatory reasons were also very *open* to ROTC's return in the event of DADT's repeal. Indeed, one of the key student leaders in the final drive of Columbia's ROTC movement was Learned Foote, the student government president (2010–11) and a leader of gay politics on the campus. Accordingly, the Columbia case represented what a Marxist or Hegelian might call a paradox of history, the unraveling of which propels meaningful change: The gay politics that comprised the new center of opposition to ROTC also held a key to opening the door for ROTC's return.[4] Winston Churchill once quipped, "You can always count on Americans to do the right thing – after they've tried everything else." While the evidence in this book indicates that the "gap problem" we discussed in Chapter 1 remains alive, it also suggests that American society is groping toward a solution. And, as we will soon see, numerous students and faculty in the Ivy League support bringing more substantial versions of ROTC back to their respective campuses. This movement was given a big boost in the arm with Congress's repeal of DADT in late December 2010. Following this historic vote, several schools have made meaningful efforts to restore their relationships with ROTC and the military, with Columbia, Harvard, Stanford, and Yale deciding in their respective ways to bring NROTC back. Soon after the repeal of DADT in December 2010, legal scholar Diane H. Mazur cautioned that the military might not take this Ivy bait, "because it is expensive to operate

[3] Andrew J. Bacevich, *The New American Militarism: How Americans Are Seduced by War* (Oxford University Press, 2005), pp. 26–7; William A. Galston, "The Challenge of Civic Engagement: An Introduction," in Verna V. Gehring, ed., *Community Matters: Challenges to Civic Engagement in the 21st Century* (Rowan and Littlefield, 2005), pp. 2–3. See also James Burk, "Citizenship Status and Military Service: The Quest for Inclusion by Minorities and Conscientious Objectors," *Armed Forces & Society* 21, 4 (1995). Burk traces the historical significance of the link between service and equal respect, but also the changes in society that have weakened this connection. On women's equality and military education, see Phillipa Strum, *Women in the Barracks: The VMI Case and Equal Rights* (University Press of Kansas, 2002). For a clear statement of the constitutional issues, see *United States v. Virginia, et al.*, 518 U.S. 515 (1996).

[4] Hegel, it should be remembered, was also the leading philosopher of the phenomenon of recognition, as well as the preeminent theorist of how self-respect and the respect of others reside in the willingness to confront the fear of death, which happens to be a signal aspect of military service. G. W. F. Hegel, *The Phenomenology of Spirit*, A.V. Miller, trans. (Oxford University Press, 1977), pp. 104–19 (the discussion of the "self-certainty" and the "lordship and bondage" phenomenon).

there, particularly for the relatively few number of students the services are likely to recruit."[5] But as we report in Chapter 7, the military (especially the Navy) began making overtures to some schools that had effectively barred ROTC in the late 1960s. The process is in flux as this book was sent to production in August 2011, although the next chapter suggests the tide has indeed turned in ROTC's favor – although the story of ROTC continues to be written.

The return of ROTC to Harvard and Columbia reinforces another development: the efforts of campuses across the country to accommodate and welcome veterans, whose numbers on campus swelled to three hundred thousand in the spring semester of 2010. In January 2010, the *New York Times* published a lengthy article on the growing prominence of veterans in the Ivy League, reporting that Columbia and other Ivy schools have opened their arms to veterans for a variety of reasons. Universities welcome the money provided by the new, more generous, G. I. Bill (the Veterans Educational Assistance Act of 2008, as part of the Yellow Ribbon Program), and they increasingly appreciate the real-world diversity of experiences that the veterans bring to campus:

> Perhaps nowhere is this new wave more striking than at Columbia, which more than any other Ivy League institution has thrown out a welcome mat for returning servicemen and women. There are 210 veterans across the university, integrating a campus whose image-defining moment in the past half-century was of violent protests against the Vietnam War.... The campus still tilts heavily to the left, with many students displaying the arty, jaded aura befitting their Manhattan surroundings. But now, students largely welcome the vets, who are both admired and considered something of a curiosity.[6]

Peter Awn, the dean of Columbia's School of General Studies, agreed heartily with this depiction in an interview in the fall of 2010. As nontraditional, adult students, the veteran students matriculate in this school, and Awn has developed a constructive relationship with them. Unlike at most universities, nontraditional students at Columbia take all of their courses with traditional students, so there is extensive interaction:

> The level of acceptance the veterans have found on campus – and they have some heated debates with fellow students – but there isn't hostility toward them because they represent the military. So it's a very, very different climate. And more often than not, the traditional students find them really interesting.... I think this is good for Columbia undergraduate education. It adds something unique to the intellectual discourse in the classroom that we have not had for decades.... The skills that they bring to this really come to the fore. You may find this amusing, but I frequently compare them to the dancers in the [School of General Studies'] population: people who at a fairly young age have made some choices to put themselves into a clearly disciplined environment. And by making that choice, they have excluded a whole range of other activities that are age appropriate.... If they've got the intellectual goods, and they've really done some interesting things in the military, and

5 "Colleges Rethink R.O.T.C. After 'Don't Ask' Repeal," *New York Times*, December 21, 2010.

6 "From Battlefield to the Ivy League, on the G. I. Bill," *New York Times*, January 8, 2010. On the Yellow Ribbon Program and the new G. I. Bill, see United States Department of Veteran Affairs: http://www.gibill.va.gov/gi_bill_info/ch33/yellow_ribbon.htm.

they frequently end up in some elite service or other – they transfer that to their work here in ways that are astonishingly productive.[7]

The "return of the soldier" theme in the Ivy League emerged out of the shadows a day after September 11, 2001. Its major focus from the beginning was on the institution that antiwar and antimilitary forces had made their main target in the late 1960s: ROTC. Let us now turn to that story. We begin by looking briefly at an area often neglected by the commentary on ROTC and the Ivies, as well as the commentary on the antiwar movement more generally: the (partial) reversal of the antimilitary mood – in particular, the "quasi-comebacks" of the programs in the fifteen years or so after their banishments. As a headline in the *Harvard Crimson* article read in the mid-1970s, this development represented reconnecting with ROTC "through the back door."

THROUGH THE BACK DOOR

As the smoke settled from the campus fires of the late 1960s, numerous ROTC programs had vanished, including programs from six Ivy League schools.[8] Programs remained at Cornell and Penn, albeit in lesser forms. But hope of ROTC's second coming simmered beneath the ashes. As soon as October 1971, the *Harvard Crimson* reported George S. Benson (deputy assistant secretary of defense for education) relating that Princeton, Brown, and Stanford were "negotiating with the Pentagon for the possible restoration of ROTC."[9] In fact, student and alumni advocates had sponsored a referendum at Princeton in the spring of 1971 in which a majority of undergraduates voted to bring a program back as an extracurricular activity. According to Doug Lovejoy, the leader of Alumni and Friends of Princeton University ROTC, a "group of alumni led by BG, USAFR (Ret) Jack Bitner '38 mobilized sufficient alumni support in general to lead the trustees to reverse their position."[10] After some political to and fro, the administration, University Council, and trustees determined in the fall of 1971 that the proposal for an Army battalion satisfied relevant conditions that the university had stipulated for its acceptance – the pressures exerted by 200 demonstrators and the presentation of a petition signed by 1,154 members of the Princeton community opposing ROTC and the war notwithstanding.[11] This was

7 Interview with Peter Awn, Dean of the School of General Studies, Columbia University, October 2010.

8 The figure of eighty-eight is from Michael S. Neiberg, *Making Citizen Soldiers: ROTC and the Ideology of American Military Service* (Harvard University Press, 2000). In a widely cited essay, military historian Peter Karsten reported that twenty-nine schools drove ROTC away between 1966 and 1970. The difference between these accounts is partly explained by the fact that some schools lost multiple programs. See Peter Karsten, "Anti-ROTC: Response to Vietnam or 'Consciousness III?'" in John P. Lovell and Philip S. Kronenberg, eds., *New Civil-Military Relations: The Agonies of Adjustment to Post-Vietnam Realities* (Transaction, 1974), p. 114.

9 "ROTC May Return to Ivy Schools," *Harvard Crimson*, October 15, 1971.

10 E-mail exchange with Doug Lovejoy, Alumni and Friends of Princeton ROTC, September 2010.

11 "Princeton Students Protest Return of ROTC," *Harvard Crimson*, January 13, 1972.

a rather extraordinary result given that antiwar fever continued to grip campuses, and that such events as the Kent State killings remained fresh in memories. Over at Brown and Stanford, however, similar agitations foundered on the shoals of opposition.

But hope lingered even in such redoubts as Harvard and Columbia, which had been beset by more revolutionary upheavals than most schools, although it took slightly longer to surface there. At Harvard, the 206-member Harvard Republican Club (HRC) launched a campaign in March 1973 to call ROTC back from its exile. Grabbing the baton from the HRC, Harvard's new president, Derek Bok, made a pitch for ROTC at a meeting of the Harvard Alumni Club in June 1973. Bok struck a still raw nerve by stating that many disconcerted alumni "sensed" that "Harvard had not opposed ROTC solely for academic reasons but had behaved expediently in the face of pressure."[12] Bok's comments, coupled with controversial maneuvers at nearby Boston University that summer that led to the return of ROTC there, provoked attention. William F. Buckley praised Bok in his national "On the Right" column in June 1973, and the following September the *Crimson* ran a lengthy story by Peter M. Shane entitled "ROTC: Is It Coming Back?" Providing rather telling examples of the simplistic intellectual content of some ROTC exams in the paper's possession, Shane challenged – rather ambiguously – Bok's claim that Harvard's faculty had broken under pressure. "Bok may simply have underestimated the sensitivity of the nerves he touched by making even an offhand reference to bringing Harvard ROTC back to life – especially by suggesting that ROTC was a casualty of excessive political pressure and not of genuine academic, *moral, and political* concerns of the Faculty and students." The controversy unleashed by Bok evoked interesting exchanges on both sides of the debate, including a letter to the *Crimson* in support of ROTC by a former student who had been suspended by Harvard twice in the late 1960s for occupying buildings in protest against ROTC and the war.[13]

Bok's initiative, which presaged a similar statement in the aftermath of 9/11 by Harvard president Lawrence Summers, did not lead to the reinstitution of ROTC, but his actions did clear the road for more minor reform. In October 1975, the Department of Defense rescinded a policy it had adopted that banned graduate students funded by the department from attending Harvard and thirteen other schools that had dropped ROTC in the late 1960s. Two months later, Harvard's Committee on Undergraduate Education recommended that the faculty allow two Harvard students to cross-register in MITs' noncredit program. (MIT was participating in the program in which certain schools served as "host" centers that drew cadets from associated satellite schools.) By mid-1976, the

[12] "Harvard Republicans Campaign to Reinstate ROTC Program," *Harvard Crimson*, March 19, 1973; "Bok Urges Reconsideration of ROTC, Wants Programs to Meet Harvard Ideals," *Harvard Crimson*, June 14, 1973.

[13] "Buckley Commends Bok for Position on ROTC," *Harvard Crimson*, July 2, 1973; Peter M. Shane, "ROTC: Is It Coming Back?" *Harvard Crimson*, September 1, 1973 (emphasis added); "Changed Minds," *Harvard Crimson*, February 16, 1974.

Harvard faculty had sanctioned the arrangement, leading to a *Crimson* story written by future editor-in-chief Gay Seidman with the headline "ROTC Slips Through the Backdoor."[14]

The acceptance of this watered-down alternative approach to ROTC raised hopes for a more meaningful breakthrough. In 1981, a *Crimson* headline read "ROTC: Making a Comeback." Cross-registration was beginning to bear fruit at Harvard and nationally, and ROTC enrollments were recovering from their 1970s blues. Forty-one and twenty-nine Harvard students were enrolled in the Army and Navy programs at MIT, respectively, at that time. The story registered optimism about a regular program returning to Harvard itself. "[O]n the 12th anniversary of the occupation of University Hall, some ROTC officials are confidently predicting that Harvard will have its own detachment again within six years."[15] But no detachment would come to Harvard. It was one thing to let Harvard ROTC students travel down the "T" (the subway) to nearby MIT while Harvard eschewed supplying any resources or credit, but another to reopen Harvard's gates to a full-fledged program. Furthermore, after a fitful start, the military was now growing more pleased with the financial efficiency of cross-registration programs, which provided remote ROTC access to students in elite schools while avoiding the cost (and potential irritation) of running programs at those institutions. The services were now reconciled to the loss of elite institutions; such units were deemed more costly and less productive, and the Army made up for these losses (at least in quantitative respects) by extending programs to other schools – suggesting that the Army cared more about substance than symbol. "Most of the schools that gained new ROTC units during the late 1960s were small to medium-sized state institutions located in the South or Mid-west. These were, in the main, schools without a tradition of political activism and, according to some worried Defense Department officials, without a reputation for academic excellence."[16] The growth of cross-registration programs provided a way for some Ivy schools to reach out and touch ROTC students at a distance, rather than having to abide their actual presence.

Other Ivy schools replayed the same act. Pro-ROTC sentiments resurfaced at Columbia in 1975, and in January 1976 the University Senate held a lengthy debate, after which it voted thirty-three to nine against a proposal that "would have left the door open for possible future ROTC implementation."[17] In 1980,

[14] "ROTC Students Can Now Attend Harvard," *Harvard Crimson*, October 8, 1975; "CUE Recommends ROTC Clarification," *Harvard Crimson*, December 2, 1975; "Faculty Moves to Allow Students to Take ROTC," *Harvard Crimson*, May 5, 1976; Gay Seidman, "ROTC Slips Through the Backdoor," *Harvard Crimson*, May 7, 1976.

[15] "ROTC: Making a Comeback," *Harvard Crimson*, April 8, 1981.

[16] Arthur T. Coumbe and Lee S. Harford, *U.S. Army Cadet Command: The 10 Year History* (Office of the Command Historian, U.S. Army Cadet Command, 1996), pp. 123, 221–2.

[17] "University Senate Passes Resolution Opposing ROTC," *Columbia Daily Spectator*, January 16, 1976; "Report of the Special Committee to Study R.O.T.C. Amended Resolution – Adopted," January 23, 1976, in Columbia University Senate Archive: http://www.columbia.edu/cu/senate/archives/resolutions_archives/resolutions/old_resolutions/reslist1.htm.

Columbia sanctioned a compromise of sorts by allowing students to take Army ROTC at Fordham University, Air Force ROTC at Manhattan College, and Marine ROTC (the Marine Corps Platoon Leaders Class) in six-week summer training sessions for freshmen and sophomores at the Marine Corps Officer Candidate School in Quantico, Virginia, or a ten-week session at Quantico for juniors.[18] These programs remain in effect.

The back-door inching back of ROTC in the 1970s and 1980s was accompanied by broader background trends. After dips in the 1970s, enrollments began rising in the 1980s as public respect for the military revived, the memory of Vietnam lost some of its tenacity, and the military began implementing policies designed to increase the number of cadets by augmenting scholarships, improving the curriculum, and buffeting recruitment. It also began reaching out to racial minorities and women. Congress set the stage for this growth in 1967 by rescinding the 2 percent ceiling and promotion restrictions for women officers stemming from a 1948 law. Women responded favorably, citing the thrill of the challenge, the chance to serve, and the provision of equal pay. "In a 1980 survey, four in five female ROTC cadets said that ROTC gave them more opportunities for personal growth than any other campus activity."[19] The women's movement was gathering support in national politics (the "second wave of feminism," mounting the steps laid by the suffragists), and many young women grasped the historical and psychological relationships among military service, equal citizenship, and equal respect.[20] Another factor in ROTC's comeback in the 1980s was the mid-decade establishment of Cadet Command centers to oversee and systematize ROTC programs nationally. Although beset by conflicts and problems endemic to the program (budget limitations, tensions with universities, the ebbs and flows of enrollments and the propensity to serve, and so on), Cadet Commands provided better regulation and oversight and strengthened the programs academically, making it easier for universities and colleges to accept a relationship in some form.[21]

A key factor in these background developments was the diversification of the military and the ROTC. But there was one major exception: gays and lesbians. The emergence of the gay rights movement would prove to be the most important obstacle to the full-fledged return of ROTC to elite campuses.

18 Reserve Officers Training Corps at Columbia University: http://www.columbia.edu/cu/rotc/hist.htm.

19 Michael S. Neiberg, *Making Citizen Soldiers*, p. 164. Of course, the survey consisted of women who joined ROTC, presumably because they believed it afforded them good opportunities, so there is a selection effect with such statistics. Nonetheless, it appears clear that the vast majority of women who joined ROTC believed that it was an excellent option for them.

20 For a thorough portrayal of these motives in the drive for equal opportunity at Virginia Military Academy, see Philippa Strum, *Women in the Barracks*..

21 On the rise and administration of Army Cadet Command, see Coumbe and Harford, *U.S. Army Cadet Command: The 10 Year History*; and Arthur T. Coumbe, Paul N. Kotakis, and W. Anne Gammell, *History of the U.S. Army Cadet Command: The Second 10 Years, 1996–2006* (New Forums Press, 2009).

THE GAY RIGHTS MOVEMENT AND THE MILITARY

As we have seen, the major objections to ROTC on campus in the late 1960s centered on the war and on militarization, with academic standards thrown in for good measure. One looks almost in vain for references to homosexuality in the historical materials pertaining to the ROTC conflicts of this period. The reason is simple: Although it had been brewing for many years, the modern international gay rights movement did not burst into prominent public attention until the night of June 28, 1969, in Greenwich Village, New York – a month after Columbia's University Senate had exiled ROTC from campus up at the other end of Manhattan. It was in Greenwich Village that a group of homosexuals, prostitutes, and transvestites inspired a riot by resisting arrest after police busted the Stonewall Inn in Sheridan Square. From this explosive-yet-modest beginning, the movement spread from lower Manhattan to the world, confronting the usual achievements and pitfalls of such undertakings as it wound its tortuous path toward greater equality.[22]

It was only a matter of time before the issue would thrust itself into the ROTC debate, although this did not happen until the 1980s. In March 1983, for example, Harvard considered a proposal to give official university recognition to a student group supporting ROTC. The main issue was the name of the club. The name – the Harvard-Radcliffe ROTC Club – furrowed many an academic brow, for it implied that Harvard would be hosting actual ROTC units. So a tentative agreement called for the name to be modified to the less suggestive Harvard-Radcliffe *Friends* of the ROTC Club (emphasis added). But the *Crimson* report of the controversy also alluded to homosexuality, referring to members of the Undergraduate Council (UC) who "could not endorse the proposal because military and ROTC policies against hiring and recruiting homosexuals and handicapped students would be in conflict with the council's constitution."[23] In April, the UC approved the new group. Although the name change satisfied those for whom a word paints a thousand pictures, some ROTC foes were less mollified. Two weeks after approving the "Friends," the UC sanctioned two other groups: Enemies of ROTC and Opponents of ROTC. In the spirit of academic freedom, the Opponents pledged that their first event would be "a debate with 'Friends' over the merits of ROTC."[24]

The concerns of some members of Harvard's Undergraduate Council prefigured the ascendancy of a new objection to ROTC that signified a paradigm shift in the public philosophy of higher education. The new paradigm was the "civil rights" paradigm, which stands for nondiscrimination and equality. Indeed, the drive for equality and equal rights comprised the most important agenda of the

[22] See the characteristically fascinating account in Paul Berman, *A Tale of Two Utopias: The Political Journey of the Generation of 1968* (W.W. Norton, 1996), ch. 4, "The Gay Awakening."

[23] "New Name May Gain Approval for Proposed ROTC Group," *Harvard Crimson*, March 15, 1983.

[24] "Divide and Conquer," Short Takes, *Harvard Crimson*, April 26, 1983.

Supreme Court and legal mobilization in the United States in the post–World War II era, as well as the core of the human rights movement that gained authority in the domain of international law and theory.[25] Allan Silver, a leading participant in the politics of ROTC at Columbia, expressed the power of this paradigm in a talk delivered at a 2009 conference of the National Association of Scholars:

> To be sure, the civil rights frame – sincerely or not – may cover hostility to any program educating officers in the armed forces. However, cast as a civil rights issue, the question of ROTC ignites the hegemonic culture celebrating equality of rights, nowhere more intensely than at universities. As Tocqueville seminally understood, equality is an appetite that – like its aristocratic predecessor, honor – grows by what it feeds on. Moreover, military service has long and conspicuously validated equality in civic status and dignity. Homosexuals are making a claim as have, earlier, Japanese-Americans, blacks, women, and today, less conspicuously, Hispanics. Despite obvious differences among these cases, all are driven by demands for equality of respect and by military necessity. In today's America, that necessity includes legitimizing the military as an exemplar of democratic equality.[26]

The civil rights paradigm became the centerpiece of new objections to ROTC – ironically, at the same time that general attitudes toward the military were leavening around the country. The ROTC movement at Columbia and elsewhere appropriated the same language and logic of civil rights and identity (in the form of the politics of recognition) that its opponents deployed. The case for gays in the military represents a traditional, classic civil rights claim against discrimination: Gays want to be eligible to serve, and are not asking for special treatment or dispensation of any sort. They asked only to be given the opportunity to meet the multiple challenges and responsibilities for which military service calls.[27] A classic example of this emphasis is the movement's successful drive in 1973 to compel the American Psychiatric Association (APA) to declassify homosexuality as a mental disorder or disease. This effort entailed asserting that gays are not the objects of therapeutic rescue, but rather individuals whose capacities for responsibility are equal to those of all mature citizens.[28]

[25] On the paradigm shift to civil rights and liberties in American constitutional law and the parallel rise of human rights in international law, see Richard Primus, *The American Language of Rights* (Cambridge University Press, 1999).

[26] Allan Silver, talk delivered on panel on "The Changing Landscape of American Higher Education – Panel on the Military and the Academy," National Association of Scholars, Washington, D.C., January 9–11, 2009. Copy provided to authors by Silver.

[27] On the civil rights movement's devolution into a therapeutic logic and practice, see Elizabeth Lasch-Quinn, *Race Experts: How Racial Etiquette, Sensitivity Training, and New Age Therapy Hijacked the Civil Rights Movement* (W.W. Norton, 2001). On the rise of therapeutic politics and thinking, see Philip Rieff's classic book *The Triumph of the Therapeutic: Uses of Faith After Freud* (University of Chicago Press, 1966).

[28] Ronald Bayer provides a compelling portrayal of the movement to reform the APA's position on homosexuality in *Homosexuality and American Psychiatry: The Politics of Diagnosis* (Princeton University Press, 1987). See also Donald Alexander Downs, *More Than Victims: Battered Women, the Syndrome Society, and the Law* (University of Chicago Press, 1996), ch. 7; and Evan Gerstmann, *The Constitutional Underclass: Gays, Lesbians, and the Failure of Class-Based Equal Protection* (University of Chicago Press, 1999).

Although it was long a matter of concern, the military did not make the presence of gays a preoccupation until World War II, when it instituted psychiatric screening in induction procedures. Whereas homosexual *conduct* was previously seen as the problem, now simply *being* a homosexual could get one discharged. In 1981, the Department of Defense promulgated a policy explicitly stating that homosexuality is irreconcilable with military service. Thousands of discharges followed.[29] In reaction, individuals began bringing legal challenges against the policy; and the gay rights movement forged inroads on campuses, with more and more institutions adding homosexuality to their lists of prohibited forms of discrimination.

Accordingly, the late 1980s and early 1990s witnessed the second major wave of legal challenges to ROTC, this time in the name of equal rights. Numerous campuses held referenda and votes or engaged in other forms of public debate over the validity of hosting ROTC programs that discriminate.[30] Almost all universities retained their programs, but often made continuance of the program contingent upon the military rescinding its antigay policies in a specified number of years. As the government adopted rules making it more difficult to eliminate programs (discussed later in this chapter), recruitment emerged as a more prevalent policy response than abolition, especially after the advent of Don't Ask, Don't Tell.

DON'T ASK, DON'T TELL: RECRUITING, THE SOLOMON ACT, AND 9/11

Universities that had broken ties with ROTC still had to grapple with the question of how much cooperation to allow between the university and the military, in particular in the matter of recruiters. Law schools made themselves the center of resistance to DADT because of their long commitments to equality and because the military was especially concerned about recruiting law students to serve in the Judicial Advocate General's (JAG) Corps. The Association of American Law Schools added sexual discrimination to its nondiscrimination policy in 1990, making bans on recruiting by organizations that discriminate a linchpin of the policy.[31] In 1992, presidential candidate Bill Clinton committed

[29] Department of Defense Directive 1332.14, Part 1, Section H, January 28, 1982. See, e.g., Gregory M. Harek, Jared B. Jobe, and Ralph M. Carney, eds., *Out in Force: Sexual Orientation and the Military* (University of Chicago Press, 1996); and the useful online overview, Gregory M. Herek, "Lesbians and Gay Men in the U.S. Military: Historical Background": http://psychology.ucdavis.edu/rainbow/html/military_history.html.

[30] See, e.g., Harvard president Derek Bok's response to a Harvard student being removed from ROTC in 1990 after disclosing his homosexuality. Bok wrote a letter to Defense Secretary Richard Cheney protesting discrimination on the basis of sexual orientation, not only because it was unfair but because it would be "likely to weaken the national R.O.T.C. program by creating an increasing amount of antagonism toward the R.O.T.C. on university campuses." Tamar Lewin, "Harvard Protesting R.O.T.C Rejection of Homosexuality," *New York Times*, June 15, 1990.

[31] Marc Lindemann, "Storming the Ivory Tower: The Military's Return to American Campuses," *Parameters* 44 (Winter 2006–7).

himself to reforming military policy respecting gays. Once he assumed office, however, Clinton confronted blowback by the military and congressional leaders on both sides of the aisle who opposed fundamental change.

The Clinton administration's compromise in the end was Don't Ask, Don't Tell. DADT allowed people to serve in the military regardless of their sexual orientation as long as they did not openly discuss or reveal their sexual orientation. DADT constituted the first time that federal legislation (as opposed to nonlegislated military policy) prohibited open homosexuality in the military.[32] When universities – especially law schools – reacted to DADT by limiting recruiting even more, Congress retaliated by passing the Solomon Amendment in 1994 as part of its annual defense appropriations bill. The Solomon Amendment denies federal funding for failure to allow military recruiters on campus or for dropping ROTC programs that existed at the time without the military's consent.[33]

Law schools typically banned military recruiters from participating fully in recruitment, but often allowed student groups to facilitate communication between the military and interested students in separate meetings and locations. Elite law schools also began requiring all groups engaging with their law students to sign a nondiscrimination pact. DADT was interpreted to violate these pacts. Law schools believed that by allowing private coordination between the military and interested students, they were in compliance with the Solomon Amendment and contended that that it was their right to impose these requirements on recruiters because their First Amendment right to freedom of association protected their right to enforce their own expressive values, which they linked to the academic freedom of the institution.[34] Harvard Law School, for example, prevented the military from being listed on its regular recruiting schedule and from using the Office of Career Services. Making a concession to the freedom of speech of students, the school did allow military recruiters on campus when specifically invited by student groups; but recruiters were effectively banned from 1979 to 2002 and from 2004 to 2005.[35]

The events of 9/11 changed the political and legal landscape. It unleashed pro-military feeling and thought on campus, but it also escalated the commitment to the civil rights paradigm because of the continuation of DADT and the government's strengthening of the requirements regarding access for military recruiters.

[32] 10 *U.S.C.* § 654. For thorough and balanced analyses of the issues pro, con, and intermediate regarding DADT, see Melissa Sheriden Embser-Herbert, ed., *The U.S. Military's Don't Ask, Don't Tell Policy: A Reference Handbook* (Praeger Security International, 2007).

[33] 10 *U.S.C.* § 983. For a discussion of the issues surrounding the Solomon Amendment, see Lindemann, "Storming the Ivory Tower," pp. 44–57.

[34] See Brief *Amicus Curiae* of Law Professors and Law Students in Support of Petitioners (*Rumsfeld v. FAIR*), in the Supreme Court of the United States, no. 04–1152, July 18, 2005: http://www.law.georgetown.edu/solomon/documents/amicusLawProfs.pdf. On expressive values as the core of freedom of association, see *Roberts v. United States Jaycees*, 468 U.S. 609 (1984).

[35] Art Pine, "The Few. The Proud: The (Harvard???) Marines," *Proceedings*, U.S. Naval Institute, 133 (2007): 40–4.

Several factors merged to create a perfect storm of sorts. First, in response to the new recruitment needs and the new interpretation of the Solomon Amendment, the Department of Defense boldly declared that the government would not tolerate diminished access for recruiters, and threatened substantial losses of university funding for failure to abide by rules. Second, Advocates for ROTC gained steam as an umbrella organization after 9/11, coordinating various groups in the Ivy League and at Stanford dedicated to reinstalling ROTC on campuses that had once pushed its programs away.[36] Third, student sentiment began to favor more military presence. A survey of Harvard undergraduates after 9/11 indicated that 62 percent of students favored returning ROTC to campus. Many Harvard faculty members suggested that perspectives had changed, with historian Ernest May observing that antimilitary fervor is a relic of the past. Several business school professors at Harvard also expressed their belief that military students were better prepared, were more articulate, and demonstrated better leadership than those with civilian backgrounds.[37] The editorial boards at student newspapers at elite institutions also relaxed their anti-ROTC stances.[38]

One of the most notable administrators to support ROTC was former Harvard president Lawrence Summers. Early in his tenure, and shortly after 9/11, Summers stated that military service is noble and that the university should be careful about adopting any policy reflecting nonsupport for those defending the country.[39] He later remarked that the post-Vietnam cleavage between coastal elites and certain mainstream values carries real costs, and that the war in Afghanistan offered potential for constructive change because the conflict lacked the moral ambiguity of Vietnam, providing an opportunity for a reconciliation of values.[40]

One day after a federal appeals court blocked the Pentagon in the name of academic freedom from cutting federal funds to universities that limited the recruiting process in 2004, Harvard Law School moved to reinstate its policy that barred regular access of the armed services to students.[41] Law School Dean (and future Supreme Court Justice) Elena Kagan said the school would require all recruiters to pledge not to discriminate on the basis of sexual orientation. In this case's appeal to the Supreme Court in September 2005, forty Harvard Law School professors filed a brief opposing the Solomon Amendment, arguing that law schools should be able to deny military recruiters access to campus unless the Pentagon pledges to end DADT.[42]

[36] See http://www.advocatesforrotc.org/.

[37] Pine, "The Few. The Proud."

[38] Michael Winerip, "The R.O.T.C. Dilemma," *New York Times*, October 26, 2009.

[39] William M. Rasmussen, "Summers Expresses Pride in ROTC," *Harvard Crimson*, October 9, 2001.

[40] David H. Gellis and Catherine E. Shoichet, "Summers Speaks Out on Patriotism," *Harvard Crimson*, November 16, 2001.

[41] *Rumsfeld v. FAIR*, 390 F. 3d 219 (2004).

[42] Javier C. Hernandez, "Professors Stand Up to Recruiters," *Harvard Crimson*, September 22, 2005.

Meanwhile, the Law School at Yale had since 1978 required recruiters to sign a pledge of nondiscrimination. The school complied with the Department of Defense after it threatened to withhold hundreds of millions in funding from Yale, but forty-five members of the faculty joined the suit over the Solomon Amendment, alleging that the government action violated academic freedom (and freedom of association).[43] Although the anti-Solomon movement represented the views of most law professors, some important voices among the ranks of the elite professoriate voiced their dissent. Yale law professor Peter H. Schuck, for example, charged that the school disserved both students and the military, as it failed to

> treat students as mature adults who can weigh the evidence and make their own choices among employers without the universities' thumb on the scales. They supposedly cherish diversity, but then reduce students' exposure to a world view – opposition to gays in the military – that is the law of the land and is preached by some of the great religions to which many of the students subscribe. ... A university's moral and pedagogical duty to its students is to cultivate their capacity for independent thinking, explain its own view (if it has one) and then get out of the way.[44]

Resistance to the Solomon Amendment met its Waterloo before the Supreme Court in 2006. In September 2003, a group of thirty law schools launched the litigation process under discussion by forming the Forum for Academic and Institutional Rights, Inc. (FAIR), and petitioning the federal courts to overturn the Solomon Amendment as a violation of the schools' freedom of speech and academic freedom. (The right of free speech entails the right to choose with whom or what one is associated.) The coalition included elite law schools such as Columbia, New York University (NYU), Penn, Harvard, and Yale, each of which had been pursuing a policy of noncooperation with military recruiters. In reversing the Court of Appeals, the Supreme Court unanimously concluded that Congress had a legitimate interest in providing military recruiters with equal access, and could have mandated access even without tying funding to the schools' decision. Furthermore, universities' academic freedom rights were not compromised because reasonable observers would not associate recruiters' views with those of the university, and because such institutions enjoy ample avenues to make their dissent from government policy known.[45]

Conceding legal defeat, many law schools also took advantage of the First Amendment rights to which the Supreme Court referred by proclaiming their opposition to military policy regarding homosexuals. The official website of Columbia University Law School, for example, contains a statement by the dean affirming the school's respect for the military as well as its disagreement with DADT:

[43] Thomas Kaplan, "Yale Law, Newly Defeated, Allows Military Recruiters," *New York Times*, October 1, 2007.

[44] Peter H. Schuck, "Fighting on the Wrong Front," *New York Times*, December 9, 2005.

[45] *Rumsfeld v. Fair*, 547 U.S. 47 (2006).

As a community, we are mindful of the military's status as an institution that protects the nation. We admire the courage and self-sacrifice of our troops and appreciate the particular contributions of military lawyers in an age when national security and personal liberty must be balanced in difficult new contexts.... This very certitude renders it even more troubling that our gay, lesbian and bisexual students are discouraged from doing so, due to the "Don't Ask, Don't Tell" statute.

This statement is accompanied by a letter signed by over seventy Columbia law professors attesting their opposition to DADT.[46]

9/11 AND THE DRIVE TO REINSTATE ROTC AT COLUMBIA, 2001–2005: INTRODUCTION

The legal actions just discussed transpired while another movement was brewing at many institutions that had banned ROTC during the throes of the Vietnam War. Movements that had sputtered for years were rejuvenated by the terrorist attacks on America on September 11, 2001. ROTC advocacy revived across the Ivy League, especially at Columbia, residing in the northern reaches of the island whose southern flanks had suffered those historic blows. As Yoni Appelbaum, a liberal Columbia undergraduate who edited the *Columbia Political Review* and contributed to the movement at Columbia, related in an interview, "The campus changed on September 11, 2001."[47]

The first Columbia movement in this new era was engineered by a vanguard coalition of military and non-military students who reached out to the campus through a referendum drive that led to a vote on ROTC's reinstatement in the University Senate in May 2005. Although it fell short in the end, this movement's story (2001–5) is nonetheless one of unexpected success. The politics of the movement reveals both the alienation of the military from a major elite campus at the same time that it portrays a dialectical struggle to bridge that alienation. The politics was creedal: It is the story of the university living up to its own ideals of dialogue and the pursuit of truth, for the public debates over ROTC often witnessed eloquent public arguments about such important matters as the meanings and obligations of the university, the military, citizenship, moral commitment, national defense, and civil rights and liberties. It also compelled many Columbians and others to wrestle with the tensions and trade-offs of strongly held values that such controversies often entail. As Allan Silver articulated in an e-mail to the Columbia Task Force on ROTC in February 2005, the university's decision in the matter was "tragic" in nature. Although Silver did not mention Max Weber by name, Silver's conception of tragedy in this instance resembled one of Weber's uses of that term in "Politics as a Vocation": In applying the ethic of responsibility in the real world, citizens and leaders must sometimes make difficult decisions that necessitate giving priority to some cherished values over

[46] Columbia University Law School webpage: http://www.law.columbia.edu/careers/military-recruiting.

[47] Interview with Yoni Appelbaum, Columbia student, November 2007.

others. Columbians had presented forceful arguments about homosexual rights and the rights of ROTC aspirants, creating a clash of principles and commitments:

> These [rights-oriented aspects of the issue] are authentically moving and, in human terms, serious. But they do not define the fundamental issue, which is at the level of high democratic politics and institutional responsibility in this phase of American history. The requirement to take responsibility for the consequences of our preferences applies also to those advocating an ROTC program. The military's policy on homosexuality means that the decision to have an ROTC program is a tragic choice. Put bluntly, one good must override another.[48]

The two-year process witnessed often emotional debate and – although sometimes honored in the breach – a concerted effort to maintain civility. In many respects, this control of passion by reason epitomized the mental process that free speech scholar Lee C. Bollinger contends lies at the heart of First Amendment and constitutional citizenship. Respecting the rights of those whose views we disparage, fear, or even hate – within the constitutional limits that a sane society must impose – compels us to control our passions, thereby making us more thoughtful and mature, and able to carry out our responsibilities as citizens in the face of adversity, which is when such virtue matters most.[49] In this sense, the debate over ROTC at Columbia afforded a living example of the creedal practice of constitutional citizenship. Incidentally, Bollinger was president of Columbia University at the time, and he cast one of the votes in the University Senate against bringing the program back to campus in 2005. His role in April 2011 would be quite different.

Although the debate embodied what amounted to a creedal constitutional moment, it also exposed the underlying alienation between the university and the military. ROTC advocates were sometimes the targets of stereotyping and ignorance of military professional responsibilities (in particular, the ultimate authority of civil authorities for the making of military policy) and the nature of ROTC. Sean Wilkes, an ROTC student who helped lead the movement to reinstate ROTC, depicted the problem in words that echo the views of many other interviewees: "Our thought process . . . started with my initial want or need to have a leadership program, and then it sort of developed to where we were looking at the issue more broadly. And as we experienced at Columbia, the ignorance that people had about the military, about military life, why people joined the military – 'They just want to kill people, you know' – it was a little jarring to me."[50]

48 Allan Silver, "Emails Sent to the ROTC Task Force," Columbia University Senate ROTC Task Force, February 9–24, 2005, p. 12: http://www.columbia.edu/cu/senate/committeepages/rotc_folder/rotcemails.htm. On the "ethic of responsibility," see Max Weber, "Politics as a Vocation," in *Max Weber: Essays in Sociology*, edited by C. Wright Mills, translated by Hans H. Gerth (Oxford University Press, 1946).

49 Lee C. Bollinger, *The Tolerant Society: Freedom of Speech and Extremist Speech in America* (Oxford University Clarendon Press, 1986).

50 Interview with Sean Wilkes, Columbia ROTC student, October 2007. The desire of ROTC students to demystify the military is also a theme in our chapter on soldier-students at the University of Wisconsin.

We also interviewed seven students involved in ROTC programs at Columbia in the spring of 2008 (a small number, admittedly, but it was almost all of the ROTC students at that time). Their views differed on many matters, including such things as political loyalties, the appropriateness of American military policy, the nature of Columbia's obligations to military students, and the degree of hostility toward the military that pervaded the campus. But they concurred that a gap of experience and knowledge abounded between military students and a majority of non-military students and faculty. Brief profiles of each cadet provide context for the ensuing discussion. Although we conducted these interviews three years after the 2005 vote, the issue was still alive, and most of the cadets had been at Columbia at that time.

Riaz Zaidi was an international relations and computer science major enrolled in the Army ROTC program at Fordham and the president in 2007 of the Hamilton Society, Columbia's society of military students. His family came to America from Pakistan, and he is a Democrat who believes deeply in the principles of liberal democracy and internationalism. He was slated to go to Iraq a few months after our interview. Our discussion covered a number of issues, ranging from the conditions under which a nation may defend itself and its interests with force to the movement toward more international governance and oversight of military actions. Zaidi said that he had never encountered a seriously negative reaction at Columbia; but he lamented the relative paucity of military programs in the New York area, the geographic underrepresentation of the Northeast in ROTC, and the inability of his fellow students to fathom his chosen path. "Actually, most people [at Columbia] are supportive, but it's just totally incomprehensible, the idea of someone joining the armed forces. It's just outside their experience."[51]

Austin Bird, a participant in the summer Marine program at Quantico, was also a leader among military students at Columbia. He was very committed to the "warrior ethic" of the Marines and was proud to stand up for his beliefs at the university. He was more critical of his fellow students than Zaidi, who had a more stoical attitude about the student gap. In Bird's view, the biggest problem at Columbia is that most students "don't care" one way or the other. "They don't feel attached to it [military service]. They don't feel a need for it because our society no longer acts, no longer demands that all levels of society serve, especially the elite." Columbia "touts leadership, but [students] don't have any respect for the fact that that's the military's goal in the officer corps.... In a basic sense, what you hear from people at Columbia is 'We don't want you militarizing our campuses.'" In classroom encounters, he said, he often finds himself countering misconceptions. Students will retort that your view doesn't matter unless you are in the military, he related, so you let them in on your secret. "And then all of a sudden there's that barrier between you and them, it's you versus them, not 'the class.' And that happens all the time."[52]

[51] Interview with Columbia student Riaz Zaidi, April 2008.

[52] Interview with Columbia student Austin Bird, April 2008.

John McClelland had served as a medic for four tours in Afghanistan and Iraq before coming to Columbia as a student in general studies and as an ROTC student in the Army program at Fordham. (He spent some time working in the famous special operations group led by General Stanley McChrystal.) In 2010, he assumed the command of the Army ROTC battalion at Fordham, the program hub for twenty schools in the New York City area, including Columbia. He "loved" his courses in international relations in the international studies program. "The image of Columbia being a bunch of bleeding hearts may hold true in the media, but there's a wide diversity of opinions. There's a bunch of veterans here, of all different stripes. . . . I haven't met anyone who isn't willing to listen to me." In the spirit of General David Petraeus and the other Columbia student interviewees, McClelland stressed the importance of education and intellectual sophistication in military leadership today.[53] He believed that Columbia is too inward-looking in an elitist sense, an attitude reflected in its dismissal of ROTC. "ROTC is just another facet of the world that Columbia doesn't see." He told a story of how exposure to an actual soldier changed the thinking of a woman he knew. She had a low view of the military, "But then she met me and realized, 'Okay, we're both liberals.'. . . But that to me kind of illustrates what Columbia's like with ROTC. So it just showed her that a soldier can love literature just as much as she could, and she kind of stereotyped. She didn't believe when I came up to her that I was in the military because I said, 'Your glasses are very Joycean.' And she's like, 'That's my favorite author,' and I was like, 'Mine, too.'" In the end, McClelland questioned Columbia's negative attitude toward ROTC. "I think it's undercutting its own prestige to cause positive change in the world. ... The institution [military] is not going to change by us ignoring it. . . . You have to have people to actively go in it and change the policy [DADT]."[54]

Joe Naughton was a graduate student in the School for Environmental and Public Affairs (SEPA) on an Army ROTC graduate student scholarship. (He was slated to join the Reserves upon graduation.) Naughton graduated from the University of New Hampshire with a degree in Russian and international affairs, having switched from animal science after the terrorist attacks on 9/11. He considered military service the "purist form of public service" because soldiers cannot resign at their discretion and because they must follow orders from civilian leadership. Although he respected the students and instructors in his international security concentration, he felt that they did not always adequately grasp military reality. They are not antimilitary, "but they don't really understand, even at their level studying these issues, why they would actually enter the military. So there's this disconnect even among that group of people." He gave the example of a fellow student who was frustrated by his lack of fortune with recruiters for the national clandestine intelligence services. When Naughton

[53] See, e.g., General David Petraeus, "Beyond the Cloister," *American Interest*, July–August 2007: http://www.the-american-interest.com/article.cfm?piece=290.

[54] Interview with John McClelland, Columbia student and ROTC commander, April 2008.

informed him that there were also many such opportunities in the military, the student was incredulous at the thought of joining the military. "So that concept is just so foreign to him that he couldn't even really comprehend that." He also mentioned how an Army major made several contributions to a class on terrorism because "he really added to the discussion ... from an operational level as opposed to a theoretical level given by the academics. ... In academia, they spend a lot of time thinking about the cause of and the solutions to wars, but don't spend a lot of time thinking about the preparations, which is where most military activity is conducted. It's where the officer makes his money."[55]

Elizabeth Feldmeier, the leader of the Hamilton Society in 2008 who was working with alumni on the ROTC issue, considered gaining recognition an important matter, and was working to get her group recognized as an official campus group:

> In terms of recognition, I just think it'd be nice if other students on campus realized there were students on campus who were in officer admission programs. Because they might not think of themselves as so disconnected from the military, especially at Columbia, where we have kind of a core curriculum, where everyone has a similar base in the same intellectual background, so there are people with the same intellectual background as you who are also in the military.[56]

Another student who asked for anonymity presented the bleakest picture of the civilian–military gap at Columbia that we encountered. His views appear to jump right out of the pages of Thomas Ricks' book *Making the Corps* or Kathy Roth-Douquet's and Frank Schaeffer's book *AWOL: The Unexcused Absence of America's Upper Classes from the Military – and How It Hurts Our Country*:[57]

> The military would not be welcomed here if DADT wasn't real. They kicked ROTC off in '69, so the issues are so deep-seated when it's talked about. ... And then there's the students' relationship being here in New York. They come here to go to the law school and get rich, and that's really the way America is headed now ... they don't really understand, they can't even balance that idea of service or anything besides themselves. And there is someone out there doing it, but it's not going to be them. ... When I was in Russia, I said to my friend, "I think I want to join the Army after I graduate." And he said, "People like us don't join the Army, we don't join the military." He went to Brown, which doesn't have ROTC. It's a huge problem for the country as a whole.[58]

[55] Interview with Columbia student Joe Naughton, April 2008.

[56] Interview with Columbia student Elizabeth Feldmeier, April 2008.

[57] Thomas Ricks, *Making the Corps* (Scribner, Simon and Schuster, 1997); Kathy Roth-Douquet and Frank Schaeffer, *AWOL: The Unexcused Absence of America's Upper Classes from the Military – and How It Hurts Our Country* (Harper Collins, 2006).

[58] Anonymous comments from Columbia ROTC student, April 2008. Available on tape in the authors' possession.

THE RISE OF THE NEW ROTC MOVEMENT

The rumblings of discontent that emanated from Columbia's ROTC alumni in the years after the program left campus in 1969 were heartfelt, yet unorganized. This situation would change when the ROTC Class of 1951 convened for its Fiftieth Reunion on September 7, 2001. As former Marine Philip Bergovoy reported in materials accompanying an April 2002 program on ROTC held at Columbia:

> We were surprised to discover how many of us had written, individually, to the various university presidents since the fateful day of 1969 when it was decided that the college would terminate its relationship with naval service. After dinner ... Admiral Jim Lowe and I circulated amongst our brother officers to sound them out about the possibility of joining together in a concerted effort to bring ROTC back to Morningside Heights. The group was almost unanimous in its belief that both Columbia and the nation at large would gain from an ROTC presence on campus. Furthermore, almost all of them pledged their best efforts to work together to accomplish that goal.[59]

Thus was born Columbia Alumni for a Strong America. This group – the offspring of the Columbia group inspired and led by Admiral Lowe – would later become an integral part of the Columbia Advocates for ROTC, the Columbia branch of Advocates for ROTC, an umbrella organization uniting advocate groups of alumni, students, and other friends of ROTC at the individual Ivy League campuses, as well as Stanford and MIT. (Today the group calls itself the Columbia Alliance for ROTC.)[60] The attacks on lower Manhattan just four days after this fiftieth reunion presented an opportunity amid tragedy. Soon alliances began forming among pro-military and conservative student groups, including Students for a Strong America, Students United for Victory, the Columbia College Conservatives Club, and Columbia College Republicans. On Sunday, April 28, 2002, these groups sponsored a program at Columbia entitled "Should ROTC Return to Columbia?"

In the autumn of 2001, the *Columbia Political Review* – the journal of the Columbia Political Union, a nonpartisan student organization dedicated to fostering vibrant and inclusive political discourse on campus – featured an article on the new ROTC movement in its first edition. Drawing on the new alumni group, the article was entitled "Revisiting the ROTC: Is It Time to Bring the Reserve Officers' Training Corps Back to Columbia?" Yoni Appelbaum, an original member of the *Review*, used the story to promote awareness of the

[59] Philip Bergovoy, "A Note on the Founding of Columbia Alumni for a Strong America," in materials for "Should ROTC Return to Columbia?" Panel-forum held at Columbia University, April 28, 2002. See also interview with Philip Bergovoy, April 2008.

[60] See http://www.advocatesforrotc.org/. This website is the link to extensive national and local coverage of ROTC-related media and events at Ivy League schools, as well as links to the separate Advocate groups at Harvard, Columbia, Princeton, Yale, Brown, Dartmouth, Stanford, and MIT. The website is run by Michael (Mickey) Segal, a physician and medical researcher at Harvard, who was also interviewed for this book.

ROTC issue. Appelbaum was deeply affected by the events of 9/11, which caused him to take the responsibilities and commitments of national defense more seriously and to think of American nationality in universal, nonpartisan terms. The CPU's receptiveness to the movement typified what was transpiring on other campuses after 9/11. In November 2001, for example, the *New York Times* mentioned Columbia and the Students United for Victory in a story on how students were reconsidering their feelings about the military nationwide. "At Columbia University, where students have for decades shared a liberal disdain for all things military, some students say they have had a change of heart. A small group has even formed a new, pro-military organization."[61]

Students United for Victory was led by a small group of students, including Lovinsky Joseph, Alfred Zaragoza, and Eric Chen. In a short essay included in the materials of the April 2002 forum cosponsored by the new alumni group and conservative student groups, Zaragoza and Chen presented the case for ROTC's return to Columbia by accentuating the importance of the military tradition and ROTC's contributions to student opportunities and diversity on the campus: "It is the noble duty of an academic institution of Columbia's magnitude to provide its students with diverse enough opportunities so that they can discover and then pursue the fields in which they can flourish and nurture their talents. ... Today's Columbia students are denied sufficient exposure to the military as an art, a science, and a possible career choice."[62] In an interview with us, Chen highlighted two other motives for becoming an activist. First, Columbia has a duty to the nation to provide high-level military leadership. Second,

> My motivation as a Columbia ROTC advocate begins with 9/11. I didn't come to Columbia to be a civil–military reformer. But the enemy that attacked us represents an existential evolutionary challenge to our nation.... The cleavage of the Columbia ROTC partnership damaged our nation. We need to regain our footing to face the new challenges from a changing world; an element to revitalize America is restoring the Columbia ROTC partnership.... We organized as students dismayed by the tepid campus response to 9/11. For example, my first class after 9/11 was a political science TA [teaching assistant] section on 9/13. The professor led the discussion and asked how the US should react to the attack. Two Israeli students and I responded that a military response was necessary; the rest of the section thought the proper response by America to 9/11 was self-blame and self-correction.[63]

[61] Matt Continetti, "Revisiting the ROTC: Is It Time to Bring the Reserve Officers' Training Corps Back to Columbia?" *Columbia Political Review* (Autumn 2001); "On Campuses, Seeing the Military with New Eyes: After September 11 Attack, Students Reconsider Old Opinions," *New York Times*, November 26, 2001. Interview with Appelbaum.

[62] Alfred Zaragoza and Eric Chen, "Time for America to Return to Campus," in *Should ROTC Return to Columbia?* pp. 6–8.

[63] E-mail response by Eric Chen, September 2008. Chen provided us with a twenty-page single-space response covering a range of points.

Concerned after a while about being labeled "conservative," the movement undertook efforts to broaden its appeal beyond the narrower base of the previous year. In the fall of 2002, Sean Wilkes arrived as a freshman, enrolling in the Army ROTC program held at Fordham. A neurobiology major from a military family, Wilkes joined Chen to lead the student movement for ROTC's return. As part of the broadening project, Students United for Victory (SU4V) renamed itself Students for a United America. Meanwhile, Chen began writing editorial pieces in the *Spectator*, and he and Wilkes formed the Independent Committee for ROTC Advocacy (ICRA), the predecessor of Columbia Advocates for ROTC. In his short history of the Columbia movement, Wilkes wrote that they created the Advocates "in order to expand ROTC advocacy beyond SU4V's organizational constraints."[64]

Wilkes and Chen formulated a three-pronged plan targeting students, the institution and its administration, and alumni. As a liberal activist conversant with Columbia's extensive network of student groups, Chen manned the grassroots part of the operation, developing relations with other campus groups and ideas for public outreach. Wilkes concentrated on the institutional side of the effort, which included convincing the university to acknowledge completion of ROTC courses on transcripts, improving the quality of instructors, and developing channels to connect with students (for example, creating a website for the movement, www.columbia.edu/cu/rotc). Their strategic objective was to be "slowly chipping away at the antagonisms."[65]

Implementing the third prong, the students reached out to ROTC alumni as members of a shared community and in order to put pressure on the university from outside. Admiral Lowe and Philip Bergovoy headed the alumni effort at first, followed in 2004 by Ted Graske, NROTC 1959. By then, the organization became known as the Columbia Alliance for ROTC (CAR). By the spring of 2008, CAR had a mailing list of about nine hundred supporters (95 percent of whom are alumni); as is usual for such groups, between ten and twenty individuals handled most of the work. A retired corporate human relations executive and former Columbia football player, Graske strove to put a more diplomatic face on the alumni component of the Advocates, making it less adversarial and combative in order to persuade rather than antagonize. As quoted in Chapter 2, Graske valued both the liberal education he received at Columbia and the way that ROTC supplemented this education with practical ethics and leadership. Members of CAR span the gamut in terms of politics and the way they approach their alma mater. Some members want to "crucify" the university, whereas others simply yearn to restore ROTC in order to provide more student opportunities and to compel Columbia to live up to its service obligation to society.

[64] Sean Wilkes, "The Movement to Restore ROTC to Columbia: Historical Background," August 31, 2006: http://advocatesforrotc.org/columbia/history2006.html; Eric Chen, "Changing Times at Columbia," *Columbia Daily Spectator*, September 17, 2002.

[65] Interview with Columbia student Sean Wilkes, October 2007; Wilkes, "The Movement to Restore ROTC to Columbia," p. 1.

Graske himself does "not think Columbia is unpatriotic. I think they are misguided – extremely misguided – about the military, not so different from the culture, so they are perhaps playing a little too hard at political correctness."[66] In addition to publishing a biannual newsletter, the *Wounded Lion*, CAR undertakes other efforts, including lobbying Columbia's trustees and administrative leaders as well as the Department of Defense to encourage its receptivity to ROTC's return to elite schools; supporting campus commissioning ceremonies, military balls, and other relevant official events; and conducting media outreach on several fronts.

Advocate groups exist on several other campuses. One of the most active is at Harvard, headed by Paul Mawn, Captain USN (Ret.), a graduate of Harvard's NROTC. Mawn took great pride in his service and ROTC work. "Being in the military transforms the way you grow up 'American.'... there's no substitute for the leadership you have to have to hack it [in the military] ... you're doing something beyond yourself, you don't get paid much, it can be very uncomfortable at times, but there's adventure and you get friends that last the rest of your life." As of 2008, Harvard's Advocates had 2,200 members, about 80 percent of them veterans. Mawn pinpointed three major objectives of his group: "To take down these barriers [between the military and the university] and promote diversity, and ... to promote the history and tradition of Harvard students serving their country ... not necessarily as career military, but at least doing their service. And also to help increase the number of Harvard students that participate in this program." When coauthor Downs visited Mawn at his Concord, Massachusetts, office in October 2007, Mawn began the interview by taking Downs to Monument Square in downtown Concord, underscoring how Harvard students were among the Civil War soldiers honored there. The Harvard Advocates engage in a similar array of activities as Columbia's group.[67] Alumni and Friends of Princeton ROTC is another very active group. The group was formed in 2003 as a successor to the ROTC Advisory Council, which originated when Princeton brought ROTC back in 1971. According to Doug Lovejoy, the group's leader who came to Princeton in 1985 as commander of the Army program, "In essence there has been a group of alumni who have worked with the University for nearly forty years." Alumni and Friends' board currently has twenty members, with ten members serving on the Executive Committee; overall membership numbers over four hundred. Because it does not have the burden of restoring a vanquished program to campus, the group's main strategy is to work with the administration to strengthen the existing program. In Chapter 10, we will mention the impressive input that the program has had in the broader sphere of campus pedagogy.[68]

Like Graske and Mawn, Wilkes expressed dismay at Columbia's position regarding ROTC while also appreciating its need to maintain standards and

[66] Interview with Ted Graske, Columbia Alliance for ROTC alumni leader, April 2008.
[67] Interview with Harvard Advocates for ROTC leader Paul Mawn, October 2007.
[68] E-mail exchange with Doug Lovejoy, September 2010.

institutional control; and he acknowledged that the military life is not for everyone:

> There are fewer opportunities to bridge the so-called civil–military gap, with Iraq happening and the consolidation of bases into larger units with less geographic representation. So ROTC is one of those few areas of direct civilian–military interaction where you can have an everyday interaction.... And it's good for both sides because you get the broad range of ideas from academia and the broad range of experience.... There's less alienation.

The employment of the language of civil rights, including diversity and recognition, was pivotal to the inroads the movement made. "Our main goal, I think that's another reason why we were so successful to a large degree, is because we were speaking their language. We didn't come at it from the perspective that we are a bunch of conservative students ramming this down their throats.... We wouldn't have gotten anywhere. We set ourselves up for success because we used this language."[69] Nonetheless, some opponents questioned both the use of the civil rights model and the sincerity of the effort to reach out across partisan lines. One law professor told us that he and his colleagues perceived some of the pro-ROTC advocacy as too adversarial and disrespectful to be persuasive, especially in the forum of the University Senate. Others simply did not accept the use of the language of civil rights and equal opportunity given the reality of DADT. However much the pro-ROTC movement strove to seek common ground based on universal principle, its followers could not completely transcend their feelings of discontent and alienation.

Once Wilkes and Chen had constructed a plan of action, they embarked on an advertising campaign with the assistance of such allies as Jennifer Thorpe (president of S4UA by then), Eric Gutman, and Shane Hachey. They forged working relationships with students and the student press, as well as with several deans and assistant deans in the spring of 2003. Dean of Student Affairs Chris Colombo suggested "that the best way to gain the support of Student Affairs and the Administration was to demonstrate student support for the issue."[70] Responding to this advice, student ROTC activists worked with several students in the Columbia College Student Council to place a nonbinding referendum on ROTC in the Student Council elections in the spring. On April 16, 973 students voted in favor of the pro-ROTC questions posed, with 530 against (65 percent in favor). The unusually high turnout (aided by general interest in the elections for Student Council) and unexpectedly strong support encouraged ROTC advocates, and undoubtedly enabled the subsequent political process. But the referendum was marked by some controversy. Rather than asking students directly whether ROTC should return, the referendum asked whether "ROTC should be prohibited." As opponents were quick to point out, one could oppose ROTC's return as a matter of policy without endorsing paternalistic prohibition of such a

[69] Interview with Wilkes.

[70] Wilkes, "The Movement to Restore ROTC at Columbia," p. 2; and interview with Wilkes.

return. The student ROTC supporters defended their role in the referendum by disclosing that the word change had been made by a polling expert in the Office of Student Affairs, not them; they also pointed out that the strong favorable vote made further campus consideration advisable regardless of the wording.[71]

In the 2003–4 academic year, the ICRA reorganized itself as the Advocates for Columbia ROTC. Working with deans and other administrators behind the scenes, the student leaders persuaded Columbia to allow "registration credit" ("R") for ROTC on students' transcripts, and convinced the Financial Aid Department to provide information about ROTC online and in the Columbia publications. As the year progressed, they met with more influential administrators, including Dean Zvi Galil of the School of Environmental and Public Affairs, Dean Austin Quigley of Columbia College, and President Lee Bollinger. Bollinger declined to offer his substantive support, maintaining that the ultimate decision resided with the Senate, which had instituted the ban back in 1969 (see Chapter 5). Bollinger maintained a modest posture throughout the multiyear process that led to the the April 2011 Senate vote in favor of ROTC; in the vernacular of national politics in 2011, he chose to "lead from behind," as it were. But early on, he offered the resources of the Senate and its secretary, Tom Mathewson, a legendary institutional resource unto himself with a long and respected record as Columbia's Senate authority. With the help of Mathewson and others, the Advocates made connections with other governing bodies and individuals, including the Student Affairs Committee and the Executive Committee – committees with supporters of the movement, such as Professor Paul Duby of the School of Engineering and Applied Science (SEAS) and Professor Eugene Galanter (the latter being openly critical of the student revolt in 1969).[72]

THE TASK FORCE ON ROTC: TOWN HALL MEETING AND ON TO THE SENATE

As a result of these and other activities, the Advocates were able to present a proposal to the Senate for ROTC's return. The proposal discussed historical matters and changes that ROTC had undergone since 1969 and contrasted the benefits of the programs with arguments against it: lowering the wall separating Columbia's "Ivory Tower" from the country; the role of the "citizen-soldier"; educating the armed forces; providing an example of discipline, leadership, and "pragmatic skills" to the campus; and enriching the "diversity" of the campus.[73]

[71] See "High Turnout Decides CC Student Council Election," *Columbia Daily Spectator*, April 17, 2003; Wilkes, "The Movement to Restore ROTC at Columbia," p. 2; and interview with Wilkes.

[72] Wilkes, "The Movement to Restore ROTC at Columbia," pp. 3–4. See also interview with Wilkes.

[73] Sean Wilkes and Jennifer Thorpe, "Advocates for Columbia ROTC and Students United for America Brief: Proposal to Return ROTC to Columbia's Campus": http://www.columbia.edu/cu/senate/annual_reports/03-04/rotc/html.

In March 2004, the Student Affairs Committee agreed to authorize a special Task Force on ROTC, which the Senate approved. The establishment of a task force is Columbia's main vehicle for addressing major policy proposals. As is usually the case in forming such a lead group, selecting the membership of the Task Force became political and controversial, and its recommendations would be influential. The Task Force eventually consisted of six students, five faculty members, and one alumni representative. (Two members had to withdraw later, leaving the number at ten.) Wilkes was chosen as a student representative, and the ROTC Task Force began meeting in the fall of 2004.[74]

The group solicited and received over 120 e-mail messages on both sides of the ROTC controversy, as well as a dozen letters, the latter mostly from pro-ROTC alumni. They also received three formal resolutions from student governments representing general studies, the Law School, and the Union Theological Seminary. The Law School's resolution (adopted on April 20, 2005) stated its "appreciation" of the "dedication" of the U.S. armed forces, but opposed ROTC until the ending of DADT. The General Studies Student Council's resolution stated its support of the military and the idea that ROTC would add a new, diverse voice to campus life, but nonetheless opposed ROTC because of DADT. Meanwhile, the Union Theological Seminary opposed all things military:

> We, the Executive Committee of the Student Senate of Union Theological Seminary, strongly oppose ROTC's return to Columbia University. We believe ROTC's war-making and policy against homosexuals are violations of the sacredness of human life. While the current debate in Columbia's Senate has focused almost exclusively on ROTC's "Don't Ask, Don't Tell" policy, the rationale provided below pays particular attention to the violence of *militarism*.[75]

The Task Force also received a petition on April 15, 2005, opposing ROTC on antidiscrimination grounds written by a professor in the School of Public Health and signed by over six hundred faculty members, students, administrators, staff, and alumni of Columbia.[76]

The faculty chair of the Task Force was astronomy professor James Applegate, who ultimately favored the return of ROTC to Columbia. Applegate is a gregarious, libertarian-oriented man in his fifties who over the years has attained the

[74] Wilkes, "The Movement to Restore ROTC at Columbia," p. 2; and interview with Wilkes.

[75] "Resolutions on ROTC by Columbia University's General Studies Student Council, Union Theological Seminary, and Law School Student Senate," in Appendix 6, Columbia University ROTC Task Force, Final Report, May 6, 2005 (hereafter Final Report), pp. 48–9; Appendix 7, emphasis added: http://www.columbia.edu/cu/senate/committeepages/rotc_folder/0505rotcreport.htm. As we discussed in previous chapters, UTS equates the military with militarism. As such, they rule out the possibility of "just war." Sufficient to say that we believe that such equivocation fails to appreciate differences between militaristic societies where war is an end in itself and societies in which the use of military force is constrained by deliberative institutions with the hope that war is a means to other ends or a justifiable response to militarism.

[76] "Resolutions on ROTC by Columbia University's General Studies Student Council, Union Theological Seminary, and Law School Student Senate," in Appendix 7, University Petition with over 600 Signatures, p. 50: http://www.columbia.edu/cu/senate/committeepages/rotc_folder/0505rotcreport.htm.

status of being a "university citizen" faculty member at Columbia. (He played a major role in opposing Columbia's notorious sexual misconduct policy in the early 2000s, which captured national attention.)[77] His recollections of the antiwar sentiments of the 1960s remained fresh in his mind when he chanced upon the ROTC table on College Walk manned by Wilkes. "I was walking through campus one day and I passed this guy sitting at a table that said, 'Bring back ROTC.' It was Sean Wilkes. And I thought, 'Now I'm getting old. I've seen everything.'" The student chair was Nate Walker, a thoughtful, gay religion student from Nevada who respected the military, yet opposed ROTC because of DADT. In an interview, Applegate said the ultimate failure of the movement in the Senate could be summed up "in four words: Don't Ask, Don't Tell."

The Task Force endured many "long and arduous" deliberations dealing with a variety of ROTC-related issues, such as the nature of the program, credits and instructor titles, costs, university control, space for the program, scholarships, the nature of the obligation to serve after accepting a scholarship and completing time in the program, and the normative question of the compatibility of such a military program with the mission of the University. But DADT dominated the discussion, constituting 90 percent of the discussion, in Applegate's estimation:

> [The Task Force] ... met about once a month, and 90 percent of those meetings was about DADT.... Now of the committee there were five students on it, and three of them were openly gay ... and that was the [key] issue. That was it. So now you've got four out of the ten votes going no, you've got a woman who's rather unsympathetic to the military.... But the thing that made me change my mind on the ROTC issue is you say, "Okay, I can make this decision looking inwards at Columbia and if you do that, you vote no because of the discrimination." If you make the decision looking out[ward], at what the university or the United States or the world at large should be, you say, "Our world is education, the world's not perfect, DADT is a bad law, but we as an institution should be strong enough to rise above that law," and you vote yes.[78]

The Task Force presented an interim report to the Senate and held a town hall meeting on February 15, 2005, at which about fifty-five speakers lined up to address the issue, pro and con. About one hundred people attended the event, which received considerable publicity. The Task Force had planned the meeting to run two hours, but it ended up lasting three. The Task Force then invited e-mail comments, which were organized into two batches, February 9 through 24 (about fifty pages of e-mails) and February 25 through March 28 (sixteen pages). The transcripts of the town hall meeting and the e-mails present the full range of thinking, emotion, and commitment regarding the issue. No one at the town hall meeting or in the e-mails spoke in favor of DADT, and the propriety of the policy per se was never at issue in the politics. The question was whether ROTC could

[77] See Donald Alexander Downs, *Restoring Free Speech and Liberty on Campus* (Cambridge University Press, 2006), ch. 3.

[78] Interview with Columbia professor James Applegate, April 2008; Wilkes, "The Movement to Restore ROTC at Columbia," p. 4; interview with Wilkes.

be justified *in spite of* DADT, and pro-ROTC forces bore the burden of meeting this standard of proof.

For brevity, we will present just some of the representative arguments and statements made at the town hall meeting. For those interested in the e-mails (which were sometimes more detailed and more passionate), they are available online as well. We calculate that thirty-one speakers at the town hall meeting opposed bringing ROTC back to Columbia, while twenty-three favored return. The e-mails were about fifty-fifty in terms of balance. Our figures are based on what we considered clear pro or con statements. Some speakers simply asked questions or provided information rather than staking a position, so we did not include them in the count. Some questions or comments were posed in a way that indicated a position, but we did not count them as registering a position unless the question or comment "clearly and convincingly" demonstrated a stance.

Pro-ROTC speakers at the town hall included veterans, ROTC students, professors, alumni, and other supporters. The anti-ROTC side consisted of similar voices, including some gay veterans and a former junior ROTC student who had been expelled from the program for being gay. Resistance was based largely on opposition to DADT, although some vociferous antimilitary views were also proclaimed.[79]

The main pro-ROTC positions stressed the opportunities and choices that ROTC provides students; the contributions that ROTC would make to the campus, especially in terms of diversity and offering a "different voice" to the public discourse; the ways in which bringing ROTC back would honor Columbia's self-conscious commitment to national leadership and service; the need for inclusion at such schools as Columbia in order to help bridge the gap between civilian society and the military, especially in respect to elite educational institutions; the ways in which reestablishing ROTC at Columbia would signify that a military career is worthy of intellectual respect; and the ways in which a Columbia program could help to influence the military "from within" to change its discriminatory policy. Another argument was more "negative" in nature: ROTC is not the only organization on campus that discriminates. So does a whole college: Barnard College, Columbia's "sister college" just across the street on Broadway, does not admit men. (Men may take courses there, but gays can also take ROTC courses. In neither Barnard nor ROTC programs may they receive a diploma or commission.) In effect, "You let them discriminate, so why can't ROTC?" A better twist on the position is more positive: On balance, we accept Barnard's discrimination because we conclude that such institutions make important contributions to society. A similar case could be made for

[79] Proceedings of the University Senate: Should Columbia Restore ROTC? A Town Hall Meeting Moderated by the Senate Task Force on ROTC (hereafter Town Hall Meeting), February 15, 2005: http://www.columbia.edu/cu/senate/archives/hearings/rotc_hearings05.html. For the e-mails, see "Emails Sent to the ROTC Task Force," February 9–24: http://www.columbia.edu/cu/senate/committeepages/rotc_folder/rotcemails.htm%20February%2025-March%2028: http://www.columbia.edu/cu/senate/committeepages/rotc_folder/rotcemails2.htm.

ROTC. Mark Xue made this point at the town hall meeting. "If you are a man, Barnard College does not want you. But Columbia College has made an exception to its nondiscriminatory policy because it believes that the greater good for the university and for society as a whole is served by having Barnard College than by not."[80]

As mentioned earlier, Allan Silver presented one of the most penetrating arguments for ROTC, which he portrayed as a "tragic" decision at the town hall meeting and in a subsequent e-mail. His emphasis was "civic": No responsible society can tolerate having the burden of military obligation bypass the privileged classes. The military,

> love it or leave it, is a permanent, major institution in the American polity ... it would be irresponsible on a political level, using the word politics in its higher sense, not in its, let us say, colloquial sense, for Columbia to refuse having ROTC on the campus. ... It makes Columbia as part of civil society a free rider, a free rider on an institution, like it or not, which is both indispensable and permanent as far as we can tell, a free rider in which you are not – none of us anymore – forced to serve. And I think that is a professionally and politically irresponsible and unacceptable situation.[81]

Jake Bennett, a business student who served three years in the Israeli military, emphasized the importance of having a military that is representative of the society, including its educated elite, as in Israel, which requires universal service. (He did not mention that gays are a part of the representative society.) "I think that when you have a democracy where the military is also representative of all the aspects of society, you get the best out of your military. And when you have an institution such as this [Columbia], which is an elite intellectual institution, denying the military a place here, you are in effect denying the intellectual elite of Columbia from part in the military." Another student, Iman Bhullar, accentuated Columbia's special opportunity to reform the military from within. "[I]f you actually want to effect change in policies, like against the gays, and policies ... you'd want people from Columbia to be there. You don't want to plug your ears, close your eyes and shout and say, 'Thank God we aren't contributing to that stuff. Oh, but let it go on anyway. ... You know, that's just lack of bravery, lack of faith in Columbia." (Applause followed this remark.) Lyman Doyle, a former Army officer from West Point, also drew applause with his five-point defense of ROTC. Pointing to the growth of red-state representation in the military, Doyle said the military needs "more guys like Sean Wilkes." He also strove to dispel myths about military rigidity and the military's inconsistency with higher education's mission. "[T]he face of America in many parts of the world is the American soldier, sailor, airman, and marine. Essentially they are the face of the people in this room. Let's make that a good face. Let's make the mind behind that face an intelligent, educated mind."[82]

80 See, e.g., comments by student Mark Xue, Town Hall Meeting.

81 Comment by Professor Allan Silver, Town Hall Meeting.

82 Comment by students Jake Bennett, Iman Bhullar, and Lyman Doyle, Town Hall Meeting.

A representative of the General Studies Student Council (the school for adults and nontraditional students) presented a resolution that reflected the mainstream position against ROTC. The organization acknowledged that ROTC "would provide a new alternative voice on campus," but nevertheless opposed the program's return until the termination of DADT.[83] One student attacked ROTC advocates' employment of the language of civil rights, which included a claim that an "affirmative action" case could be made for ROTC. "I find that terribly insulting," Monique Dols remonstrated. Moez Kaba, a third-year law student, employed the psychology of identity politics. "It's hard to be civil because of lot of the discussion sort of attacks you at the core. So I'm going to maintain civility as much as possible. [Applegate asks whether discrimination is] sufficient grounds to exclude them from campus. I would suggest that the question is itself offensive and the answer simply is, 'yes.' It is sufficient grounds."[84]

One twist on the civil rights position dealt with alleged *economic* discrimination in the military, claiming that military service is attractive primarily to the economically disadvantaged. Failing to fathom the argument of ROTC supporters that ROTC's presence at an elite school such as Columbia would actually *lessen* the overrepresentation of the economically disadvantaged in the military, one student remarked, "You know, it's not an issue of discrimination. It's an issue of Columbia endorsing this relationship between the military and higher education that to me is very harmful both to higher education and to the poor and working class who are being bribed to join into a type of service that they don't know the full extent of when they're young and impressionable."[85]

Some anti-ROTC positions were simply manifestations of antimilitary views and/or profound disagreement with U.S. foreign and military policy. One speaker was blunt: "To me, I don't see how we can support part of this community, this group that tortures, that kills. It's difficult for me to see how we can allow them on campus and not actually be supporting those things." This student's comments were met with applause from the audience. At one point, Applegate, who ran the meeting, had to ask the audience to refrain from applause because it was politicizing the proceedings too much. Kendall Thomas, a gay law professor and a member of the Task Force who opposed ROTC, underscored the need for civility. Later, he said, "I do think that it's worth marking that civility aside, this discussion places us all in a political situation. That is to say, this town hall discussion is taking place against the backdrop of a number of developments, both inside the university and outside of it."[86] The objections of a graduate student member of the Spartacus Youth Club

[83] Comments by student Matan Ariel, Town Hall Meeting: http://www/columbia.edu/cu/senate/archives/hearings/rotc_hearings/rotc_hearings05.html.

[84] Comments by students Monique Dols and Moez Kaba, Town Hall Meeting.

[85] Comments by student Dylan Stillwood, Town Hall Meeting.

[86] Comments by student Joshua Spodek, Town Hall Meeting; law professor Kendall Thomas, Town Hall Meeting.

were "primarily based on the role of the military in general. One can look anywhere from Abu Ghraib to interventions in places like Haiti and Panama and so forth, and with the history major I could give you a long list."[87]

A student in the Mailman School of Public Health also referred to the "torture of defenseless detainees," concluding, "For me it's a moral and ethical issue." Interestingly, this argument could actually play into the hands of ROTC defenders, for their position is premised on the claim that fewer such atrocities would be inflicted if better-educated officers came out of ROTC. Many military scholars maintain that the atrocities committed at My Lai in Vietnam were at least partly due to the fact that the officer in charge, Lieutenant William Calley, had not received sufficient ethical education in his expedited officer training course at Officer Candidate School. Among other things, ROTC and the academies are designed to provide the ethical training that is essential to the making of professional officers. Although no one made this point explicitly in response to the public health student at Columbia, it is an implication of this reasoning.[88] Similar to some other critics, a student in the School of Engineering and Applied Science linked ROTC to the disfavored Iraq War, which he said typified what is wrong with the military. "The military is an organization that trains people to kill and to be violent and to follow orders. It doesn't train them to be active within it and change things."

Another student worried that there has been "a greater right-wing force that's taken over Columbia." Yet another student asserted that the military is incompatible with university life, and that allowing ROTC back would represent approval of U.S. foreign policy. "[E]ven if the military did not discriminate, ROTC still has no place on this campus because universities should not be training grounds for the military ... that is really the core issue. The decision that Columbia makes on this is going to be seen as a decision and a reflection of the university's approval or disapproval of U.S. foreign policy and the use of U.S. military power."[89]

One of the most powerful voices in opposition was that of Ilan Meyer, an associate professor at the School of Public Health and gay man who had served in the military in Israel. Meyer pointed out a paradox at the heart of ROTC

[87] Comments by student Quincy Leh, Town Hall Meeting, p. 10.

[88] For an interesting discussion of the debate over ROTC and ethical training in relation to Vietnam atrocities, see Ed Berger et al., "ROTC, My Lai, and the Volunteer Army," *Foreign Policy* 2 (Spring 1971): 135–60. Since Homeric times, professional soldiering has consistently included commonly accepted norms of ethical limits to war and combat. See Shannon E. French, *The Code of the Warrior: Exploring Warrior Values, Past and Present* (Rowman and Littlefield, 2003). In his influential book on the psychological impact of war, Dave Grossman maintains that much of the traumatic reaction to combat stems from the existential loss of self-respect that follows from violating ethical norms that comprise the self-image of being a warrior. Dave Grossman, *On Killing: The Psychological Cost of Learning to Kill in War and Society* (Back Bay, Little, Brown, 2009).

[89] Comments by students Tim Frasca, Quincey Lehr, Margaret Yardley, David Judd, Yi-Sheng Ng, and Amy Offner, Town Hall Meeting.

advocates' positions: The stronger the arguments *in favor* of ROTC, the greater the harm to those who are excluded from participating because of their sexual orientation. "[T]he better your claim is about ROTC, the greater the evil of this discrimination is, because it's saying basically we are withholding something that is really great, not just anything that is unimportant."[90]

THE TASK FORCE REPORT AND THE SENATE

The completion of the town hall meeting and the scrutiny of the e-mails and related input set the stage for the Task Force to promulgate its conclusions and for subsequent deliberations in the Senate. Previous Senate meetings in 2004 and early 2005 had dealt with introductory matters, so the April 1 meeting was more substantive, with Applegate summarizing the ideas presented at the town hall meeting.[91] The April 1 discussion was cut short, however, so Bollinger set up a special plenary session for April 15 for a full discussion of ROTC. The April 15 meeting proved to be a full dress rehearsal for the final Senate meeting on May 6. The "Executive Summary" of the Task Force reported six committee votes to the Senate on April 15, the first two of which were the most important: (1) The Task Force split five to five on the question of "whether or not ROTC should return to Columbia University in the 2006–7 academic year"; and (2) a supermajority (nine for, zero against, and one abstaining) voted "in favor of returning ROTC *if there is no longer discrimination against lesbian, gay, and bi-sexual service members* in the military." The other resolutions dealt with strengthening the existing relationship with the Fordham and City College of New York (CCNY) programs, university control in the event that DADT came back, and administrative matters.[92]

At the April 15 meeting, Applegate and other Task Force members acknowledged that the critical second resolution (to welcome ROTC back "if there is no longer discrimination") was the product of a misunderstanding based on ambiguity concerning the word "if." (Perhaps with President Bill Clinton's adventures with the word "is" dancing in his mind, Applegate confided to the Senate that, "I can't believe I'm saying this in the senate.") As the Task Force defined the problem in its final report, "The clause 'if there is no discrimination' could be understood as a hypothetical, counterfactual statement or as a necessary condition (as in, *if and only if* there is no discrimination." Task Force members entertained different understandings of the meaning of these words. So a week later, the Task Force presented a compromise version of the second resolution to

[90] Comments by Professor Ilan Meyer, Town Hall Meeting.

[91] Minutes of March 26, 2004, February 25, 2005, and April 1, 2005 Columbia University Senate Meetings:http://www.columbia.edu/cu/senate/archives/plenary/03-04/SenMins032604.htm; http://www.columbia.edu/cu/senate/archives/plenary/04-05/mins012805.htm; http://www.columbia.edu/cu/senate/archives/plenary/04-05/minsfeb.htm.

[92] Final Report, Appendix 8, "Task Force Report to the Senate," April 15, 2005: http://www.columbia.edu/cu/senate/committeepages/rotc_folder/0505rotcreport.htm, emphasis added.

the Senate that garnered six votes in its favor. This resolution boiled down to the following: "that *in the event* that gay, lesbian, and bisexual service-members are permitted to serve openly in the military, Columbia should establish an on-campus ROTC program."[93]

Despite the Task Force's earnest efforts, the Executive Committee of the Senate refused to accept this resolution at its separate meeting on April 25, saying that it exposed the university to legal risks under the terms of the Solomon Amendment. To settle and get to the heart of the matter, the Executive Committee then voted to replace the Task Force resolution (seven votes for, two against, and one abstaining) with its own stark choice: "*a straight up-or-down resolution to restore ROTC as soon as is practical, despite DADT.*" Executive Committee Chair Paul Duby said that the intent was "to offer a clear, unambiguous choice."[94]

Task Force members presented the Senate with statements of their own positions on April 25. Applegate's statement spoke of the complexities of the contemporary world that have placed new, subtle demands on the military, including peacekeeping missions and local wars:

> America's military leaders need to be well-educated in the history, culture, politics, and sensibilities of the world's diverse population in order to do their jobs and to represent our nation abroad.... The opponents of ROTC argue that the armed forces are "just another discriminating employer." I cannot think of more powerful evidence of the erosion of the idea that the maintenance of our Armed Forces is the collective responsibility of all Americans, or demonstration of the depth and breadth of the civilian–military gap at Columbia than the fact that this statement is made so frequently and has gone unchallenged so long.

Walker offered several responses: that only a few Columbia students are in ROTC; that there is no evidence of hardship for these students; that a Columbia program could hurt the regional programs that already existed; that military leadership does not require a program at Columbia, for Columbia students can join other programs; DADT violates Columbia's antidiscrimination policy; and Columbia is powerless to influence the military, in any event.[95]

One of the strongest arguments against the program during the actual discussion at the April 15 meeting came from Professor Kendall Thomas of the law school, whose words resonated with the civil rights commitment of Columbia. His words no doubt foretold ROTC's doom at the next Senate meeting. Critiquing Applegate's reference to affirmative action as a form of discrimination that Columbia accepts for the greater good, Thomas pointed to

[93] Final Report, p. 13.

[94] Final Report, p. 14, emphasis added.

[95] Final Report, pp. 16–19. "Representative Statements by Task Force Members of Pro and Con Positions on Resolution to Restore ROTC"; James H. Applegate, "The Case for ROTC at Columbia"; Nathan C. Walker, "The Case Arguing Against the Immediate Return of ROTC." See also "Other Recent Statements by Task Force Members," pp. 20–3.

a distinction that I very often make in my constitutional law class between invidious and non-invidious discrimination. There's a very real difference between a helping hand and a slap in the face. As far as I'm concerned, the reinstatement of ROTC on the Columbia campus is a slap in the face which will make Columbia complicit not simply in the everyday and ordinary incivilities that characterize life in the military, but in a pattern, a well-documented pattern, of harassment, violence and indeed death for persons whose sexuality has been revealed when they have served in the U.S. military. And I think the members of the University Senate ought to think hard and long about taking action that would make this university an accessory to that culture of discrimination, of violence, and indeed death.

Task Force Co-Chair Nate Walker also spoke in words that reverberated with the civil rights priority of the campus. Walker found the arguments of the pro-ROTC forces so convincing that he had given serious consideration to becoming a military chaplain. But as a gay man, he could not take the plunge:

Some of you know I'm a candidate for Unitarian Universalitist ministry and that I come from Nevada, where many of my friends with whom I grew up near the Army base and the Air Force base are currently in Iraq. This has compelled me to consider potentially serving for a year as a chaplain. But the fact is, I cannot. The United States of America denies openly gay citizens their right to serve their country. It is self-evident that this is the ultimate betrayal of patriotism. An equal betrayal would be if this university turns a blind eye to a non-discrimination policy that we have upheld.

A long discussion ensued in which arguments similar to those brought up at the town hall meeting were raised once again. In addition, there was much discussion over the meaning of the Task Force's nine-to-zero-to-one recommendation to reinstate ROTC if and when DADT and similar policies are abandoned by the government. Although the arguments of such senators as Thomas and Walker would prove most telling at mid-decade Columbia, some countercommentary at this meeting could have left an impression, making the Senate aware that this debate was far from over. For example, the words of alumnus Steve Brozak, a former Marine, played on the guilt that some Columbians felt at keeping the military at arm's length. Columbia's embrace of ROTC would send a message that the military should change:

I am that military face. I retired after 22 years in the Marine Corps, serving in places like Bosnia on the peacekeeping missions, Haiti, and the year before last in Iraq. I left the Marine Corps after twenty-two years to run for Congress. I'm sure if I were to ask for a show of hands in this room how many people would support Don't Ask, Don't Tell, not a hand would go up. But I'm equally sure that if I asked for a show of hands of how many people in this room had active U.S. military service, not many more hands would go up either. Right now I ran for Congress because the U.S. military is literally on its last legs. There are not that many people that understand what the problems are and are willing to challenge those problems.[96]

[96] Professor Kendall Thomas, student Nate Walker, and alumnus Steve Brozak, Columbia University Senate, Transcript of Special Meeting on ROTC, April 15, 2005: http://www.columbia.edu/cu/senate/committeepages/rotc_folder/transcript415.htm.

While the discussions were ensuing in the Senate, opponents and proponents were busy engaging in networking, garnering publicity, working at tables on College Walk, and participating in public forums, including events at Teachers College, Barnard, and the School of Journalism.[97] On April 25, the Advocates for Columbia ROTC held a panel discussion open to the public. The panel consisted of eight speakers, including Applegate, Silver, and Brozak, each of whom has been quoted in this chapter. Only one member of the panel opposed ROTC: Professor Lewis Cole, who had been one of the student leaders opposing ROTC in 1969. Critics were quick to point out the unbalanced nature of the panel. According to an e-mail exchange provided to us by a law professor who voted against ROTC in the Senate, the Advocates asked Cole to join the panel after being criticized for not including a countervoice.[98] But the anti-ROTC forces had held an even more one-sided panel discussion on April 6 in the form of an anti-ROTC "teach-in" organized by Kendall Thomas at the law school. The three-hour event was sponsored by the Law School's Center for the Study of Law and Culture and a student group called "Outlaws." Thomas moderated the event, which featured professors from other law schools in the New York City area. According to the *Spectator*, "All of the speakers were firmly against the return of ROTC to Columbia's campus, and several stated that the University should never compromise its non-discrimination policy."[99]

THE FINAL SENATE VOTE

The final Senate vote took place on May 6. As mentioned previously, the "Resolution to Establish a Reserve Officer Training Corps Program at Columbia University" promulgated by the Executive Committee called for a simple up or down vote on returning ROTC as soon as possible, rather than "if" such discriminatory military policies as DADT were terminated. Unfortunately, the complexity of the Task Force's votes on resolutions, coupled with the Executive Committee's substitution of its own resolution, wreaked chaos in the Senate meeting, as senators jostled with the implications of what was at hand. The lion's share of the meeting was devoted to parliamentary matters rather than substance. Bollinger, who presided over the meeting, began the deliberations by reflecting on the "very thoughtful and careful" two-year process that had led to this point.[100]

[97] Wilkes, "The Movement to Restore ROTC to Columbia," p. 5.

[98] E-mail exchange with Jeffrey Fagan, Columbia Law School, April 2008.

[99] "Panel Examines ROTC Conflict: Clash Between CU Non-Discrimination Policy and Military's 'Don't Ask, Don't Tell' Stressed," *Columbia Daily Spectator*, April 6, 2005: http://www.columbiaspectator.com/2005/04/06/panel-examines-rotc-conflict.

[100] Columbia University, Proceedings of the University Senate: Transcript of the Plenary Meeting of May 6, 2005: http://www.columbia.edu/cu/senate/archives/plenary/04–05/transcript050605.htm. All quotations and paraphrases that follow are based on this transcript unless otherwise stated.

After Bollinger thanked the participants for the thoughtful process they had fostered, Applegate and Walker began the substantive discussion with strong statements that were similar in kind to the remarks they made in April. Perhaps sensing the motion's poor prospects, Professor Samuel Silverstein, an ROTC supporter, then criticized the motion for not allowing a vote based on the condition of DADT's removal. "As worded, the Executive Committee's resolution, if voted down, requires that we say to ROTC, You're not welcome here. I don't have any feelings that ROTC shouldn't be welcome here. As far as I'm concerned, this is an opportunity for Columbia students. ROTC ought to be welcome on this campus. The military is an essential part of this country, and we need a strong defense." Sensing that his amendment welcoming ROTC so long as it complied with Columbia's antidiscrimination policies would not pass, Silverstein called for tabling the main resolution. Extensive discussion followed, leading to a debate about Silverstein's motion. The discussion became so procedurally confusing that one senator (Jay Mohr) joked, "Are there any rules that pertain to how many times the issue of tabling can be raised?" [Laughter] "I thought we voted on this. We do have to be alert to serial tablers," Bollinger replied to laughter.

After further lengthy parliamentary squabbling and to and fro with the parliamentarian, the Senate voted on Silverstein's original amendment, which was to restore the Task Force's position on ROTC and DADT: "In the event that gay and lesbian and bisexual service members are permitted to serve openly in the military, Columbia would reconsider the establishment of ROTC on the Columbia campus." After yet more procedural wrangling mixed with substance, however, the Executive Committee's original motion was all that was left standing on the table – no pun intended. The ensuing substantive discussion was brief. Provost Alan Brinkley set the tone early in words that not only highlighted the ultimate priority of the civil rights paradigm, but also relegated the pro-ROTC position to the status of a "policy," not a "principle." (In contrast, recall that Silver had discerned a "tragic choice" "at the level of high democratic politics and institutional responsibility in this phase of American history.") Brinkley expressed "great respect" for the military and the ROTC choice of students, but declared:

> We are weighing two social goods. One social good is presumably to strengthen the military by our presence in it and giving opportunities to our students to participate openly and easily in military training, receiving money for scholarship. And the other social good is defending our own principles of discrimination. And the question is, Are those two goods equal? I believe they are not. One is essentially a practical good, and the other is to me a moral good.
>
> Would we, would we, if faced with a similar situation, agree to form a formal association with an organization that said, African Americans can join this organization only if they pass for white? [Laughter] Jews can join this organization only if they pretend to be Christians? Women can join this organization only if they appear to be men? Clearly we would not accept an organization that has those qualifications for a formal university affiliation.

Applause erupted in response to these words. Several other senators spoke, including Kendall Thomas (also applauded). Alumnus Bradley Bloch was hissed more than once as he strove to defend ROTC by talking about the military obligation in the shadow of 9/11. But Senator Mohr received applause when he beseeched the Senate to stop demonizing the other side and simply to vote up or down. "Can I just say that I disagree with the comment about doing what is right as if we're supposed to vote against ROTC? There might be some who think it is to do right to vote *for* ROTC. So how about let's [inaudible] and stop trying to intimidate each other on right or wrong. Why don't we decide whether we would like it to come back or not like it to come back, and vote?" Applause followed. Shortly thereafter, debate was closed, setting the stage for the vote, which was fifty-one against, eleven for, and five abstaining.

Defeat in the Senate closed the door on the ROTC question at Columbia, but did not lock it. Other efforts to revive the issue would arise in the latter years of the decade, culminating in the climactic period of the spring of 2011, when the politics of ROTC were radically altered in the wake of the demise of DADT. We discuss this final drive in the next chapter. One question loomed large after the repeal of DADT: Was that policy truly the predominant reason that Columbia and its sister institutions refused to bring ROTC back, or was it merely a pretext masquerading other reasons, such as antimilitary ideology or simple discomfort regarding military presence on campus?

7

Post-DADT

Sisyphus Ascends the Mountain

> Four years ago, Harvard chose you, and four years ago you chose military service. You chose military service in 2003, in a time of war. You chose military service, knowing that you could be sent by your country in harm's way. You did not choose the peacetime military, but, rather, the life of a warrior. Harvard honors public service, but is uneasy with national military service, because it is uneasy with war, and with warriors, and it is no longer comfortable with the idea of Harvard as an American university, as opposed to an international university. We all wish to avoid war, none more so than the men and women who must confront the face of war directly. We welcome students and faculty from around the world. But the United States is our country. Without the United States, there would be no Harvard, and we should never forget that. And our country is still at war, and so I salute your courage, your commitment to national service, and the sacrifices you have made and will make.
>
> – Professor Stephen Rosen, "Remarks at the Harvard ROTC Commissioning Ceremony," 2007[1]

> "Naval ROTC was an obvious symbol of Columbia's involvement in the war in Vietnam," says Mark Rudd, one of the student leaders of the 1968 revolt. "Attacking the ROTC became a useful way to attack the war itself." Moreover, with the current officer corps "very heavily conservative Republican," Rudd wonders if perhaps training future officers at Columbia might not be a bad thing after all. "They'll have been exposed to both liberals and the liberal arts," he says. "Perhaps they'll moderate the right-wing officer caste mentality a bit."
>
> – Fahmida Y. Rashid[2]

This chapter is the product of an unusual yet exciting experience that few writers of books encounter: historically significant change taking place regarding the authors' very topic just as the book is being prepared to go to production. Our editors allowed us to put these events to pen at the last minute, so to speak, and this chapter is the result. We wrote most of it in later March and early April of

[1] Stephen Rosen, "Remarks at the Harvard ROTC Commissioning Ceremony," 2007: http://www.advocatesforrotc.org/harvard/rosen_2007.html.

[2] Fahmida Y. Rashid, "The Return of ROTC to Columbia," *Village Voice*, April 6, 2011.

2011, shortly after the repeal of Don't Ask, Don't Tell (DADT) in December 2010 and the responsive actions undertaken by some institutions we have discussed. The repeal of DADT spawned a surprisingly rapid reaction among many academic institutions that had effectively barred ROTC in the late 1960s. Given our policy and pedagogical predilections, this reaction has been in the direction we favor; it is also something that we did not foresee when we embarked on this project of research and writing in late 2007. Readers should bear in mind that the story of ROTC's revival is still a work in progress, as practical, political, and legal hurdles remain. But as of this writing in April 2011, the major initial obstacle to ROTC's return has been overcome at four signal institutions –Harvard, Yale, Stanford, and Columbia – as we will relate. Sisyphus appears to have rewritten his own myth. This chapter is the story – admittedly bare-boned and abbreviated – of this reversal of fortune.

INCREMENTAL REFORM: 2005–2010

Given the power of the civil rights/human rights commitment, the final Senate vote against ROTC at Columbia in 2005 was not surprising. The referendum had shown substantial campus support, but the Senate consisted of active members of the Columbia community who were more likely to be committed to the university's institutional worldview. Four factors appear to have been decisive: powerful opposition to Don't Ask, Don't Tell; lingering strands of discomfort or outright opposition regarding the military and especially its presence on campus; enduring concerns about academic standards and institutional control; and the prevalence of more negative faculty sentiment over generally more favorable student sentiment, as we will illustrate in this chapter. Until these concerns and obstacles were met or ameliorated, the prospects for ROTC's return would remain dim.

Columbia graduate Yoni Appelbaum had one of the more insightful (and, as we will see, prescient) perspectives on the Senate and the culture of the higher reaches of the university. Bringing ROTC back was largely an undergraduate cause, and the movement collided with the culture of the graduate students, faculty, and administration. "On the issue of ROTC, the undergrads were particularly more welcoming to ROTC than the grad students ... the politics changes dramatically [in the Senate]. It wasn't unusual for things the undergrads wanted to die a slow and painful death in the Senate. It's not a body rigged to respond to undergrad wishes, which is ironic [given its origins]."[3] Eric Chen attributed the defeat to a broader problem: the civil–military divide that has beset the campus since the 1960s:

> For Columbia, the civil–military divide has caused the military to be removed from the life experience of many Columbians. No students, and increasingly fewer alumni, administrators and faculty, remember when ROTC was on campus. To many, the civil-military

[3] Interview with Yoni Appelbaum, November 2008.

divide problem is esoteric and abstract. They view the ROTC program as marginally relevant to Columbia, on the approximate level of the Julliard dance classes some take. However, it's important to note . . . to them, the military is not a villain; it is simply outside their experience.[4]

The struggle at Columbia illustrated the tensions that riddled the university and the military, but also the striving to find common ground within those differences. According to James Applegate, the principle of civic duty did not receive as much explicit attention in the politics of 2003–5 as it could have. "There was very, very little discussion of civic duty, the kind of stuff that Allan Silver would talk about. It was a few months into it before I even started thinking about it in those terms."[5] But civic duty was clearly implied by the very presence of the debate and became more prominent in the later politics. In addition, civic duty does indeed entail equal protection of the law and equal citizenship, as the critics of DADT knew so well. Repeal of DADT could breathe real life into the civic duty position.

In the years following the 2005 Senate vote, minor progress continued on both the DADT and ROTC fronts, although a broad consensus settled in across most of the board: The program's return was inextricably contingent upon the fate of DADT. Indeed, the 2005 Task Force voted nine-to-zero-to-one in support of ROTC only in the event that DADT was overturned. This understanding was important, for the adoption of ROTC under the shadow of DADT would expose the program to relentless criticism that would continuously threaten to undermine ROTC's legitimacy. After all, one of the strongest arguments for ROTC's return was its contribution to the diversity of the campus – a claim not exactly in harmony with the fact that gays could not get commissioned as ROTC officers. Applegate grasped this reality as Columbia approached the Senate vote in 2005. He believed in the sincerity of most of those who claimed to oppose ROTC because of DADT, and he divined that the end of DADT would pave the road to ROTC's return. After the April 1, 2011, vote he recollected, "The opposition to DADT was real, but it was hard to tell who would either support ROTC or be indifferent once DADT was gone, and who was ideologically antimilitary and found DADT a convenient cover. My hunch was that the ideologues were a minority, and that turned out to be correct."[6]

Chen and his allies such as Sean Wilkes worried that the issue would die after the 2005 defeat and their subsequent graduation. But new student activists would fill their shoes, including Learned Foote (a treasurer for the Columbia Queer Alliance who became president of the Columbia student body in 2010–11), John McClelland, Jose Robledo, Kate O'Gorman, Tao Tan, and Nico Barragan, among several others. These individuals, along with their faculty and Columbia Alliance allies, would keep the movement alive, changing their strategy and tactics along the way. But broader fortuitous forces and events were

[4] Eric Chen, e-mail interview, September 2010.

[5] Interview with James Applegate, April 2008.

[6] E-mail exchange with James Applegate, April 6, 2011.

also poised to enter the picture, effectuating a tailwind that would assist the movement in the coming years. Along with the continued activism of a few individuals, these forces would lead Columbia to a climactic vote on ROTC on April 1, 2011. In the end, a combination of entrepreneurial individual/group mobilization and broader political and historical forces contributed to the result. Sidney Hook has touted the importance of individual "heroes" as agents of historical change, whereas Leo Tolstoy has emphasized the indispensability of multiple, mysteriously interacting forces.[7] The politics of ROTC appears to have vindicated both viewpoints, depending on where one stands or looks.

BIDING TIME BEFORE DADT'S REPEAL

On September 11 and 12, 2008, Columbia hosted a "Service Nation Presidential Candidates Forum," which the university described as a "Two-day Summit on Civic Engagement and Public Service." At this event, presidential candidates John McCain and Barack Obama took turns advocating the return of ROTC to Columbia and similar institutions.[8] Inspired by this propitious turn of events, a couple of student senators strove to introduce another resolution to bring ROTC back. This action led to the four undergraduate student governments arranging another referendum regarding the return of ROTC. The vote aroused controversy after it was discovered that one person had cast multiple votes, and because the tabulations were not broken down according to school (a normal practice for such votes). After making the necessary adjustments, the eventual vote was extremely close: Overall, 49.2 percent favored returning ROTC to campus, with 50.6 percent opposed, and 0.2 percent abstaining.[9] According to McClelland, "The Senate was radioactive-like in 2005," so supporters walked the issue over to the student councils of the colleges, which sponsored a nonbinding referendum. With half of the student body voting, the referendum lost by fifty votes, with the large deficit at Barnard accounting most for the narrow defeat. Opponents were better organized this time around than the Alliance and its allies, deploying a sophisticated network that included such groups as Students Against Imperialism, Students for Indigenous Groups, Columbia Queer Alliance, Everyone Allied Against Homophobia, Pride, and College Democrats.[10]

[7] Compare Sidney Hook, *The Hero in History: A Study in Limitation and Possibility* (Humanities Press, 1950), with Leo Tolstoy, *War and Peace*, translated by Richard Pevear and Larissa Volokhonsky (Alfred A. Knopf, 2007), esp. the Epilogue.

[8] See Columbia University, New York Stories, "Service Nation Announces Columbia University to Host 'Service Nation Presidential Candidates Forum'": http://www.columbia.edu/cu/news/newyorkstories/servicenation.html.

[9] See Columbia University, "Report of the Task Force on Military Engagement," March 4, 2011, p. 11: http://www.columbia.edu/cu/senate/militaryengagement/docs/20110304%20-%20TFMEReport.pdf.

[10] Interview with John McClelland, October 2010; "Students Roughly Split on NROTC Return," *Columbia Daily Spectator*, December 2, 2008: http://www.columbiaspectator.com/2008/12/02/students-roughly-split-nrotc-return.

Despite this setback, pro-military forces continued to engage in what Robledo, a general studies major and university senator who has served as a staff sergeant in the Army in Iraq and Afghanistan, described as an "incremental" approach to reform. On December 12, 2008, for example, a longstanding campaign involving students, alumni, some faculty, and trustees was finally rewarded by the erection and official recognition of a War Memorial Plaque in Butler Library honoring all Columbians who had fought or suffered injury in the nation's wars. As *Columbia College Today* reported, President Lee C. Bollinger affirmed the importance of the memorial to the Columbia community. "We think of public service in the University as something that is deep in our mission," he said. "There is no greater public service than that which is honored by the event this evening."[11] The year 2008 was also when veterans began their benign colonization of Columbia and other campuses pursuant to the Yellow Ribbon Program, bringing the changes to the campus military climate that General Studies Dean Peter Awn described in Chapter 6. U.S. Military Veterans of Columbia University (Mil-Vets), founded in 2002, grew in prominence on campus with this immigration, working alongside the Alliance, ROTC, and the Hamilton Society to keep the ROTC torch burning.

The presidential election in November 2008 also bore promise for ROTC because the U.S. president-elect had expressed his desire to end DADT. Although President Obama did not proceed with the dispatch that anti-DADT forces desired once assuming office, an anti-DADT position was consistent with his own beliefs and his political advantage vis-à-vis his base, so change appeared in the cards once other pressing political projects such as healthcare reform were addressed. Obama named his old Harvard Law School pal Ray Mabus secretary of the Navy, and Mabus had good relations with Harvard, which would be the first Ivy institution to bite at the Navy ROTC apple after DADT's repeal in December 2011. Indeed, Navy officials began to hold discussions with the leaders of several universities in late 2010 and early 2011 to confer about ROTC and prepare the ground for the program's revival.

Meanwhile, the defeats of 2005 and 2008 convinced the new cadre of student leaders at Columbia that the strategy instituted by Chen and Wilkes – to mobilize broad student support – was no longer feasible. One of the first and most difficult tasks of any policy movement is to cross the line that separates public invisibility and public visibility – political irrelevance from political relevance; so by placing the issue of ROTC so prominently on the stage of the public agenda, the first movement had accomplished much.[12] But a new strategy

[11] "University War Memorial Dedicated," *Columbia College Today*, March/April 2009: http://www.college.columbia.edu/cct/mar_apr09/around_the_quads2; interview with Jose Robledo, Columbia University student, October 2010.

[12] For an illuminating political and sociological analysis of the factors that contribute to crossing this crucial threshold, see Joseph R. Gusfield, *The Culture of Public Problems: Drinking-Driving and the Public Order* (University of Chicago Press, 1981).

was called for in a new time. In a strategic shift, new student leaders of this third ROTC movement decided to focus on the major internal roadblocks that had proved to be decisive in 2005, including key administrative, faculty, and student groups rather than the general student population. They operated on the assumption that general student opposition would wane or be marginalized in the event that DADT met its end. Although such professors as Silver and Applegate continued to make major contributions along with the alumni Advocates/Alliance group led by the likes of Ted Graske and Mickey Segal, the campus movement had always been mainly an undergraduate student initiative that had fallen short in the Senate and the myriad institutions with which the Senate was connected in Columbia's labyrinth of committees. The new strategy would prove to be propitious.

Part of this strategy in the last two years of the decade entailed promoting more minor reforms designed to nudge Columbia closer to the ultimate goal of reinstitution of ROTC in some meaningful form. One initiative involved persuading the university to allow ROTC physical activities to count as credit toward the general physical education requirement – an effort that was implemented in the spring of 2011. Another project was convincing the university to allow the handful of ROTC cadets to conduct color guard flag ceremonies on special occasions on campus. Robledo described the significance of this exercise in words that echo Ruth Wisse's comments in Chapter 2 about the symbolic value of ROTC on campus, as well as Robledo's understanding of the need for ROTC and Columbia to share some common ground. Such ceremony would constitute

> a visible and positive force of the military and students on campus, one that no one is willing to commit political suicide to protest, one. But two, is that a lot of the ROTC cadets don't feel that pride of being ROTC and at Columbia at the same time. There are two strands of pride. Their parents are very proud they are Columbia students. Their parents are very proud that they are ROTC cadets. But the two don't merge.[13]

These efforts bore fruit when Columbia authorized color guard participation on Veterans Day, November 11, 2010. As the *Spectator* wrote, "Breaking from a 42-year ban on military activities on campus, students raised the American flag over Low Plaza Thursday morning in a traditional ceremony in honor of Veterans Day."[14]

Meanwhile, another breakthrough of sorts took place at Harvard on November 17, 2010. In introducing Admiral Mike Mullen, chairman of the Joint Chiefs of Staff, at Harvard's Institute of Politics, Harvard president Drew G. Faust denounced DADT, but also declared that Harvard would "fully and formally" welcome ROTC back in the event of DADT's repeal. As the *Crimson* reported:

> Faust has previously conditioned ROTC's return to Harvard upon the policy's repeal, but yesterday marks the first time that she has explicitly said that her administration would

[13] Interview with Robledo, October 2010.

[14] "ROTC Members Raise Flag, Break Ban," *Columbia Daily Spectator*, November 12, 2010: http://www.columbiaspectator.com/2010/11/12/student-veterans-raise-flag-break-ban.

welcome ROTC back to Harvard's campus. "As a further embodiment of that tradition [of service], a ROTC program open to all ought to be fully and formally present on our campus," Faust said to a ringing round of applause.[15]

The vicissitudes of DADT were also getting interesting on legal and political fronts as the decade unwound. In September 2010, a federal district court in California ruled the policy a violation of the Fourteenth Amendment's equal protection clause in a suit brought by the Log Cabin Republicans, and an appeal was winding its way through the federal courts at the end of the year. But the big political breakthrough, on December 18, 2010, rendered the legal route moot: The Senate joined the House in voting to repeal DADT, to be phased in over a period of several months. President Obama signed the repeal act on December 22.[16] After an investigatory period, on July 22 Defense Secretary Leon Panetta and Joint Chief of Staff Chairman Admiral Mike Mullen certified that the military was ready to accept openly gay and lesbian soldiers and that their presence would not harm military readiness; the repeal is slated to take full effect sixty days after this certification.[17] The end of DADT placed the ROTC question at center stage at schools that had abandoned or effectively barred the program in the later 1960s. Would they bring it back? Had their opposition to ROTC really been due to DADT, or was DADT just a pretext for an antimilitary posture that had feared to show its true face? If the latter, the bluff could now be called. In anticipation of DADT's repeal, Columbia's Senate established another Task Force shortly before December 22 to consider the next step. (That they acted so precipitously signified the institution's proclivity regarding the outcome.) ROTC's fate hung in the balance as the decade retired into history.

TOWARD RENEWAL

As promised by many sources, the repeal of DADT reopened the door to ROTC in the Ivy League and other elite institutions. As of this writing, Harvard, Yale, and Columbia have signed contracts establishing new formal ties to NROTC and some are considering agreements with the other services. Similar efforts are percolating at some of the other institutions that had exiled programs at the height of the opposition to the Vietnam War.

At Stanford, the Ad Hoc Committee on ROTC had already been meeting during the year pursuant to a Faculty Senate authorization to explore the

[15] "Drew Faust Endorses Return of ROTC," *Harvard Crimson*, November 18, 2010: http://www.thecrimson.com/article/2010/11/18/dont-harvard-military-rotc/.

[16] See "Military Policy on Gays to Stand, Pending Appeal, *New York Times*, November 1, 2010; "Colleges Rethink R.O.T.C. after 'Don't Ask' Repeal," *New York Times*, December 21, 2010.

[17] "Don't Ask, Don't Tell Repeal Certified," CNN Politics, July 22, 2011: http://politicalticker.blogs.cnn.com/2011/07/22/breaking-dont-ask-dont-tell-repeal-certified/; see "Committee 'Schooled' on ROTC, Seeking More Input from Faculty and Staff," *Stanford University News*, January 12, 2011.

financial and pedagogical implications of the program. The committee held numerous meetings and presented studies on a variety of related topics.[18] In the spring of 2011, Stanford had fourteen students taking ROTC courses at Berkeley (Navy and Marine), Santa Clara University (Army), and San Jose State (Air Force). Opposition to ROTC centered on the continued exclusion of transgendered and transsexual students from ROTC. Nonetheless, in late April, the Stanford Faculty Senate voted twenty-eight to nine in favor of bringing ROTC back.[19] At Yale, a survey conducted by the Yale College Council in late December 2010 found surprisingly strong student support for ROTC: Almost 40 percent of the 1,346 respondents favored bringing ROTC back *even in the absence of DADT's repeal*, while 30 percent said they would support ROTC in the event of repeal; 16.5 percent of the respondents opposed return. According to the *Yale Daily News*, these students "cited moral opposition to the United States military or the military's 'War on Terror.' Others said military culture would not fit into Yale's campus culture." The Yale College Council then asked the Yale administration to contact the Department of Defense to consider "the feasibility of establishing a unit on campus."[20] Yale president Richard C. Levin then spoke with U.S. Secretary of Defense Robert Gates and another senior military official about bringing ROTC back to the school, and asked Yale's general counsel and the dean of Yale College to initiate discussions with officials in Washington. In January 2011, Dean Mary Miller pointed out that any unit would have to conform to the guidelines that Yale established in 1969 regarding ROTC, and called for an open forum to discuss the matter. The process led to opening the gates, and in late May, Yale signed an agreement with the Navy "that establishes the Naval ROTC's formal presence at Yale for the first time since the early 1970s."[21]

But the first major breakthrough took place at Harvard, where Faust made good on her promise to initiate a serious move after the demise of DADT. On March 3, 2011, the *Boston Globe* reported, "Upholding a promise to welcome ROTC back to campus following Congress' repeal of a ban on gays and lesbians serving openly in the military, Harvard University will officially recognize the Naval ROTC in an agreement to be signed Friday, university officials said."[22] Faust formally announced the agreement the next day, declaring "Our renewed

[18] See "Committee 'Schooled' on ROTC, Seeking More Input from Faculty and Staff."

[19] "Stanford Faculty Votes to Bring Back ROTC," UPI.com, April 29, 2011: http://www.upi.com/Top_News/US/2011/04/29/Stanford-faculty-votes-to-bring-back-ROTC/UPI-76121304132592/.

[20] "Yalies Support ROTC Return, Survey Says," *Yale Daily News*, December 22, 2010: http://www.yaledailynews.com/news/2010/dec/22/yalies-support-rotc-return-survey-says/.

[21] "Yale Announces Return of ROTC After 4 Decades," Mercury News.com, May 26, 2011: http://www.mercurynews.com/breaking-news/ci_18145117?nclick_check=1. See also "ROTC Discussions Underway Between Yale and Defense Department," *Yale Daily Bulletin*, January 10, 2011: http://dailybulletin.yale.edu/article.aspx?id=8146.

[22] "Harvard to Officially Recognize ROTC," *Boston Globe*, March 3, 2011: http://www.boston.com/news/local/breaking_news/2011/03/harvard_to_offi.html?p1=News_links.

relationship affirms the vital role that members of our armed forces play in serving the nation and securing our freedoms, while also affirming the inclusion and opportunity as powerful American ideals."[23] Although opposition to ROTC resurfaced on campus after DADT's repeal (for example, some activists protested the military's continued discrimination against "trans-identified and intersex individuals"), Faust's move was supported by the editorial board of the *Harvard Crimson*, which invoked antidiscrimination – this time *in support* of the military – in a January 31 editorial. "Just as DADT represented an outdated prejudice directed toward gay American citizens, the absence of ROTC now stands as a relic of an outdated bias against the American armed forces." As Robledo told us in the aftermath of Columbia's vote on April 1, most Columbians were now ready to cut the military slack regarding transsexuals, for it had now demonstrated its openness to reform and was now largely in sync with American society regarding gays. Discrimination against transsexuals might indeed be the next important civil rights issue in America, but it was not enough to undermine the pro-ROTC cause at this point in time.[24] Harvard Naval cadets will continue to take ROTC at the consortium at MIT, as the Navy concluded that this is the best way to maintain the "efficiency and effectiveness of MIT's 'Old Ironsides Battalion,'" according to Harvard officials. But Harvard will appoint a director of Naval ROTC, pay for the students' participation, and provide office space, access to classrooms, and athletic fields for program exercises. Some form of physical presence will exist.[25] These actions reflect the fact that renewed participation in ROTC need not take the form of restarting full programs.

As mentioned in Chapter 6, consortium or "host" arrangements have proved practical over time, and the military has financial, pragmatic, and even philosophical reasons to be wary of returning to Ivy institutions from which it had been effectively banned. And there are a variety of ways that official recognition can make a difference, such as providing financial support, granting credit, and providing other resources. Harvard's participation in the host program accommodates the interests and values of the university, the students, and the military, and does not disrupt the MIT host program that has existed many years. Harvard also appointed Kevin "Kit" Parker, an

[23] "Harvard Brings Back ROTC," *Bostonist*, March 4, 2011: http://bostonist.com/2011/03/04/harvard_brings_back_rotc.php.

[24] The July 14, 2011 cover of *The New Republic* was about transgender rights: "Welcome to America's Next Great Civil Rights Struggle." See the story inside by Eliza Gray, "Transitions: What Will It Take for America to Accept Transgender People for Who They Really Are?"

[25] See, e.g., Samuel Bakkhila and Jia Hui Lee, "Continued Discrimination in ROTC," op-ed in *Harvard Crimson*, January 28, 2011: http://www.thecrimson.com/article/2011/1/28/transgender-individuals-military-rotc/; "ACTA Advocates for ROTC Recognition," *Harvard Crimson*, March 1, 2011: http://www.thecrimson.com/article/2011/3/1/rotc-university-harvard-military/#; "The Return of ROTC: It Is Time for Harvard to Spearhead a Rapprochement with America's Military," *Harvard Crimson*, January 31, 2011: http://www.thecrimson.com/article/2011/2/3/rotc-harvard-military-dont/.

associate professor at the School of Engineering and Applied Sciences, as chair of a newly created ROTC implementation committee. Parker said that Harvard is going to be "aggressive" about reaching out to the other services as well.[26]

According to sources we contacted at Harvard, the process essentially bypassed the faculty.[27] A special university ROTC committee had been working on the matter for quite some time, and Harvard alumni associated with the Advocates maneuvered behind the scenes, pressuring and interacting with Faust. Paul Mawn, the leader of Harvard Advocates for ROTC, maintains that the administration's decision to recognize ROTC is an important step, but still only a "beachhead." For a substantial relationship to develop, Harvard would have to take further action. Such steps include providing meaningful office space and beginning to pay for the overhead involved in running the consortium arrangement with MIT. The ultimate goal is "getting Harvard to be proactive about eventually hosting the best units in the country." Mawn is skeptical of the latter happening because of the culture at Harvard, which is not antimilitary anymore, but rather indifferent. He provided several examples of how the military is left out of consideration in career and related programs. "It just isn't on their radar scope. They are all for the Peace Corps and public interest work, but say nothing about the military, 'That's for someone else.'"[28]

The road to ROTC at Columbia covered different terrain from that of Harvard. Achieving the agreement or consent of multiple constituencies is important at Columbia, and President Bollinger had eschewed taking a leading role for many years, devoting himself to encouraging the involvement of several constituencies while holding his cards close to his vest. In effect, he chose, in contemporary parlance, to "lead from behind." But Harvard's move was another external event that exerted some influence on Columbia. Alumni began contacting Bollinger in larger numbers after DADT's repeal and Harvard's action, and the broader political winds began blowing more favorably in ROTC's direction. Opposition to ROTC still existed as of mid-March 2011, centered in the faculty among anthropology, Middle East studies, and cognate fields. And anti-ROTC student groups remobilized.[29] Nevertheless, the March 2011 edition of the pro-ROTC faculty support petition directed by Silver was broadly based and growing. As of March 25, there were seventy-four

[26] "Harvard to Officially Recognize Naval ROTC," *Harvard Crimson*, March 3, 2011: http://www.thecrimson.com/article/2011/3/3/university-program-rotc-returns-harvard/#.

[27] E-mail exchange with Harvard professor Ruth Wisse, March 2011; interview with Paul Mawn (Captain, USN Ret.), Harvard Advocates for ROTC, March 2011.

[28] Interview with Mawn. Requests for interviews with other Harvard sources were not returned.

[29] In February, a group of professors signed a statement opposing the return of ROTC under any circumstances. See "Faculty Statement Falls Short," *Columbia Daily Spectator*, February 28, 2011: http://www.columbiaspectator.com/2011/02/28/response-professors.

signees – compared to only a dozen in October 2010.[30] Meanwhile, the student press remained favorable. To paraphrase a line from Bob Dylan, "the times, they were a changing."

Columbia: ROTC's Reversal of Fortune

Two days *before* President Obama signed the repeal of DADT, the executive committee of Columbia's Senate reconstituted a new task force: the Task Force on Military Engagement. The mandate of the Task Force was to reconsider the place of ROTC at Columbia in the wake of the repeal of DADT. The Task Force consisted of nine members, including General Studies Dean Peter Awn and Professor James Applegate, five students, and two other faculty members. It was co-chaired by law student and student senator Ron Mazor and Roosevelt Montas, associate dean of the Center for the Core Curriculum. Critics alleged that the leading members were already pro-ROTC, and that a kind of "fix" was in. In fact, the members did lean in favor, but their position reflected an underlying reality: A consensus was emerging that Columbia was now ready to take the fateful step. The Task Force focused on three main avenues of opinion gathering: hearings (open to all Columbia University ID holders); a survey of students; and statements from all Columbia University affiliates, including alumni. On March 4, 2011, the Task Force on Military Engagement presented its findings to the University Senate.[31] The Task Force's summary of the survey findings indicated widespread support:

- Sixty percent of students favor return of ROTC to Columbia's campuses, while 33 percent were not in favor.
- Seventy-nine percent of students support participation of Columbia students in ROTC, whether on or off campus.
- Thirty percent of students surveyed believe a relationship between Columbia and the military supports or somewhat supports Columbia's identity, principles, and policies; 35 percent believe that the relationship detracts or somewhat detracts; and 24 percent believe it neither supports nor detracts.
- Forty-two percent of students surveyed believe that military engagement will increase or somewhat increase academic freedom on campus; 28 percent believe it will decrease or somewhat decrease academic freedom; and 27 percent believe that it neither increases nor decreases academic freedom.
- Fifty-eight percent of students surveyed believe that military engagement on campus will increase or somewhat increase intellectual diversity on campus;

[30] See "Faculty for a Reserve Officers Training Program, March 25, 2011," Columbia University. This petition was handled by Columbia professor Allan Silver and was not published in the *Spectator* or other sources, but rather simply presented to numerous members of the Columbia community. It is in Downs' possession. Another petition, dated February 16, 2011, had fewer signatures and was published in the *Spectator* along with another petition signed by opponents of ROTC. This petition is not available online, but is also in Downs' possession.

[31] Columbia University, Final Report: Task Force on Military Engagement, March 2011.

18 percent believe it will reduce or somewhat reduce intellectual diversity on campus; and 22 percent believe it will neither increase nor reduce intellectual diversity.

- Sixty-six percent of students surveyed believed that an ROTC program that leads to more Columbia-educated officers would be a positive development; 18 percent believed it would be a negative development; and 11 percent were neutral.

The Task Force also collected 113 statements from individuals with a valid Columbia ID between December 20, 2010, and March 2, 2011. Of these, 65 were from current students, 28 from faculty and staff, and 20 from alumni. Eighty-eight statements were in support of ROTC and 25 in opposition.

Three hearings or town hall meetings were held in February 2011. On the eve of the last hearing, the newly formed Coalition Against ROTC held its first major meeting, a panel discussion attended by one hundred people that excluded pro-ROTC voices. The meeting was designed to counter what the organizers considered inaccurate media portrayals of them "as rude and unpatriotic." According to the *Columbia Daily Spectator*, "The exclusively anti-ROTC environment was necessary, coalition member Feride Eralp said, because the town halls 'do not provide a safe space' to discuss ROTC's return. 'We feel that the administration is biased in favor of ROTC, and that we cannot discuss our opinions without being portrayed as being unpatriotic or harassing veterans,' Eralp, CC [Columbia College] '14, said."[32] A faculty group opposed to ROTC also issued a statement in late February. Its position was countered by an editorial in the *Spectator* by Learned Foote and Sean Wilkes.[33]

As we will see, Eralp was probably onto something, for by now the administration appeared to be in favor of ROTC for several reasons. For starters, university leaders had always proclaimed that DADT was the penultimate reason to hold ROTC at bay. With DADT now on the official road to extinction, continued resistance would make Columbia appear blatantly antimilitary – a black eye that the administration no doubt wished to avoid. Indeed, Bollinger was now under pressure from alumni and public opinion to get on with it. Equally important, Columbia's trustees began making their views felt for the first time. Unlike at Harvard, where the Corporation is actively involved in many matters, Columbia's trustees typically play a more reserved role – but not now, as we will reveal later in this chapter. In addition, the issue had become a festering aggravation, and many thought it was time to end procrastination with a favorable vote.

More generally, a few other key factors on campus – along with external events – were paving the way for a vote to restore ROTC:

32 "Anti-ROTC Coalition Holds Own Discussion," *Columbia Daily Spectator*, February 23, 2011: http://www.columbiaspectator.com/2011/02/23/anti-rotc-coalition-holds-own-discussion.

33 "Faculty Statement Falls Short," *Columbia Daily Spectator*, February 28, 2011: http://www.columbiaspectator.com/2011/02/28/response-professors.

- Opposition had dwindled to a smaller faction of students and faculty, while support among faculty was increasing, as evidenced by the growing number of names on Silver's petition.
- Key members of the faculty who are prominent for their left-oriented views either came out in support or made it evident that they would not oppose ROTC. In effect, doubts or criticism on the Left were neutralized. The former group included the well-known historian Todd Gitlin, a scholar of the student left and a signer of the original SDS Port Huron Statement, while the latter group included historian Eric Foner. The opposition was simply unable to garner a critical mass of serious leftist scholars.
- ROTC supporters to whom we spoke underscored the fact that most of the campus population (80 percent, they alleged) had not mobilized and were largely indifferent to the issue. They could live with ROTC, but were not committed to its presence. (If true, this reality suggests that the AWOL attitude still haunts certain halls of academe.) Accordingly, anti-ROTC forces found it hard to build coalitions. At a forum held a couple of nights before the final vote on April 1, for example, only a few anti-ROTC activists attended. And although anti-ROTC leaders called for a "city-wide" protest to take place outside the Law School building in which the climactic vote was held on April 1 – security guards were spread outside and inside Jerome Hall, not letting anyone without a Columbia ID inside – only a small number showed up.[34] Anti-ROTC forces would go out with more of a whimper than a bang.

In addition to the hearings, other meetings took place in various venues around the campus in anticipation of a University Senate vote on April 1. One noteworthy event on March 8 was entitled "'Perspectives on ROTC at Columbia': A Panel Discussion Featuring Columbia Faculty," held at the School of International and Public Affairs. On the pro-ROTC side were political scientist Richard K. Betts (also director of the Saltzman Institute for War and Peace Studies) and emeritus sociologist Allan Silver. The anti-ROTC side consisted of English and comparative literature professor Bruce W. Robbins and David J. Helfand, professor of astronomy. Silver reiterated his civic culture theme: The "great divide" between the military cluster and the civil society "ruptures the Republic." Robbins, on the other hand, accused the military of engaging in unjust wars and militarism. "I almost vowed not to bring up the Nazis. I didn't quite vow to do it. I'll just say, since the Nuremberg trials, it seems to me that just doing your job, or just following orders, has not cut it." Betts countered this position by critiquing what he considered the three underlying fallacious assumptions behind the negative position: (1) that the United States

[34] Coauthor Downs was a guest of the Senate at this meeting, and had to arrive before 11:30 A.M. – the meeting started at 1:15 P.M – in order to be able to enter the building before the security restrictions went into effect. Security guards told him that they would not have allowed him to enter – even with an escort from the Columbia faculty – had he arrived later than that.

should not have a military at all; (2) that if there must be a military, officers should not come from schools like Columbia, but rather from the academies and other schools; and (3) if Columbia graduates must be officers, the university should do nothing to assist them. For his part, Helfand underscored the common refrain that "there is a fundamental disjuncture between the military culture and the university culture, and between the military's mission, and the university's mission in society." Unlike the open-mindedness of the university, the military entails "the abdication of independent thought and moral reflection, and submission to authority."[35] The question and answer period was also lively.

The Task Force divided the comments at the public hearings along several dimensions. Because the comments largely reiterated those made during the hearings in 2005, our treatment here is rather truncated. A couple new arguments were presented: (1) DADT had been appealed, but not yet implemented, so the university should wait to ensure that the military is no longer discriminating against gays; (2) even if DADT is fully implemented, unacceptable forms of discrimination remain in effect, in particular against transsexuals and the physically handicapped. The other arguments included old standbys:

- Views on the military. Opponents offered several reasons why they believed ROTC would be detrimental: The military preys on low-income individuals; endorses a relatively high level of sexual abuse among women; and is a tool for killing and destruction. Proponents responded with the following perspectives: ROTC would provide the military with effective and nuanced leadership; the military is an apolitical implementer of U.S. policy, so it is wrong to blame it for the political leadership's sins or mistakes; and the military aids in humanitarian and noncombat operations.
- Opportunity and diversity. Proponents emphasized opportunity for career and educational choice and the importance of intellectual diversity.
- Financial considerations. Many proponents emphasized additional scholarship opportunities, while opponents believed that offering scholarships for military service was coercive.
- Intellectual diversity and academic freedom. Opponents argued that the military promotes deference to authority that cannot be reconciled with academic freedom, while the proponents of ROTC emphasized that a liberal arts education is an asset to potential military officers and leaders, and that greater presence of ROTC cadets contributes to diversity of opinion and positive academic interactions.[36]

Based on these findings, the Task Force presented its own resolutions. The resolutions supported ROTC, yet stated that the decision lay in the hands of

[35] "'Perspectives on ROTC at Columbia': A Panel Discussion Featuring Columbia Faculty," John H. Coatsworth, Dean, School of International and Public Affairs (SIPA), moderator, Columbia University, March 8, 2011.

[36] See "Report of the Task Force on Military Engagement," Columbia University, Transcripts of Public Hearings, February 7, 15, 23, 2011, pp. 108–228.

the democratic process that led to the Senate. First, the Task Force declared that Columbia's current relationships with the military enrich the Columbia community; second, having received a wide and complex range of views on the issue, the Task Force proclaimed that the appropriate time to consider the matter conclusively had arrived; third, Columbia should actively support the endeavors of individual students to participate in ROTC programs, whether on or off-campus; fourth, if ROTC returns, the program must meet academic standards set by the university, not the military; and finally, regardless of ROTC's fate, the nondiscrimination policy of Columbia is deeply important to Columbia's identity and expresses the shared value of fostering a tolerant and open community.

FINDINGS FROM THE HEARINGS

Much is learned about the culture of ROTC politics by considering the substantive comments at the hearings, many of which reinforce our argument that ROTC contributes to "productive friction" on campus. Although important in themselves and to the almost excruciatingly democratic process to which modern Columbia is committed, the hearings were less important in 2011 than in 2005, for the campus was by now sufficiently educated in the arguments pro and con, and the most important politics were being conducted behind the scenes in ways we will examine. Accordingly, we present only a handful of comments that we believe are most indicative of the respective sides, and are interesting to boot.

Pro-ROTC Return

While many important perspectives were offered, we were particularly interested in the perspectives offered by veterans and ROTC cadets present at the hearings. Dan Morosani, a former Marine Corps officer, offered insight into the importance of university education to responsible military leadership. After alluding to publicized failures of military leadership that a previous speaker had addressed, he said:

> Failures of leadership ultimately originate in bad leaders. And the way to reduce and ultimately eliminate these leadership failures is to give our young war fighters the best leadership they can have. . . . I respect the fact that a lot of people here are against war in general, but America will fight wars a lot in the future. It's just a fact, and given that fact, I think we should give our young war fighters the best leadership they can have.

After more debate, Morosani "set the record straight":

> You mentioned [referring to another speaker's comments] that the people who will be recruited by ROTC will not be ones in the front lines getting shot at. You could not make a more factually inaccurate statement than that. You know, love it or hate it, I am a combat veteran of the Iraq war. As a lieutenant in the Marine Corps I was always in the first vehicle, the first one out of the helicopter, the first, or one of the first people on patrol. The casualties statistics among platoon commanders in combat on a per capita basis are by far worse than any other demographic. So in short, I'm not sure which military you're

referring to, in which enlisted soldiers or Marines take all the casualties and officers take none. It is certainly not ours. And again, I think this is very illustrative of the misinformation and the stereotypes that persist because of a community that does not have a good amount of exposure to the military.[37]

The importance of leadership was also addressed by John McClelland, an ROTC cadet and battalion commander in charge of New York City Army ROTC:

I want people to be against war. You know, I've spent, most of my military career in Afghanistan. I've lost 11 friends in Afghanistan in the past two years. I do not like the Afghan war. I will go on record in saying that. But I will serve over there. I will lead troops over there, and I will lead them very well to make sure that they come home. I will make sure that the communities out there in Afghanistan are serviced properly, and that my little piece of Afghanistan when I go over there is going to be the safest that I can physically make it. Now, it's about everyone here because in '68 when everyone revolted against the Vietnam war, guess what, in 1972 when the all-volunteer military force came into effect, all those protests went away. . . . I want ROTC to come back to Columbia because I want people to engage with people in the military. I want people to know somebody in the military. . . . You're going to be leaders of business, and I want you to understand that the military needs to be connected with you and not disconnected.[38]

One of the most interesting perspectives, which we quote at some length, was offered by College of Arts and Science Dean Michele Moody-Adams, who gave the opening remarks at the second hearing. Before coming to Columbia, Moody-Adams had taught just war theory at West Point and Indiana University and had served as the administrator overseeing all three branches of ROTC at Cornell:

But how do we produce a military in which the service and sacrifice of its members [are] indeed ultimately subject to civilian control and best [protect] democratic institutions that ground the rights and interests of citizens? The Constitution is very wise here. I think that we must insure that military training and discipline create what we can call citizen soldiers. We should encourage the members of the military also to see themselves as such. And I think those of you who have been watching the events unfold in Egypt will understand just what it means for a military to be able to say, Maybe I'm a citizen as well as a soldier.

Of course as a consequence of their training, citizen soldiers may develop expertise and knowledge that do distinguish them in important ways from citizens who never serve and never will serve as soldiers. And without a draft we know that may include a lot of people. But if as a consequence of their training they can come to see themselves not merely as professional soldiers, which they may be, but also as citizens. If they do not come to do this, I think our society has failed at one of the most fundamental tasks at which any healthy democracy needs to succeed.[39]

37 "Report of the Task Force on Military Engagement," February 7, 2011.

38 "Report of the Task Force on Military Engagement," February 7, 2011. We also interviewed McClelland in 2008 and 2010.

39 "Report of the Task Force on Military Engagement," February 14, 2011.

Anti-ROTC Return

Many of the opponents who spoke against ROTC emphasized that the issue is no longer about discriminating against gays but rather against transgendered people, a position they argued continues to violate the university's antidiscrimination policy. Here is a representative comment on the transgender issue from a Columbia undergraduate:

Since 2005 nothing has changed. The military continues to discriminate against people, and they can discriminate against our students. They still discriminate against gays and lesbians, and though that will be overturned within the year according to our president, the military still discriminates against trans people. Trans people are a part of the Columbia community, and the debate in 2005, as it should be in 2011, was about how to make sure that we're protecting our Columbia community.[40]

Most interesting from our perspective was the opposition to the military in general, and the belief that the military is by its very nature militaristic. Matt (he identified only his first name), a grad student in the History Department, offered a militaristic interpretation of the armed forces:

I think one thing that was kind of missing from the discussion is that we've talked a lot about the impact of DADT, but it's important to remember the context in which ROTC left campus in the first place, which is actually the context of a massive student movement against the Vietnam war, and it went through a panel and many formal channels, but the environment was one in which actually students were saying, We don't think our university should have a relationship with an institution that is killing, in the case of Vietnam, ended up killing in the course of that war 2 million Vietnamese ... along with of course 60,000 U.S. soldiers who also died in that war. ... And I think as a student of history I can look back through American history and recognize that no matter what party, no matter what time, the U.S. military has been used in such a way to actually not spread democracy but many times to hinder it and to murder civilians.[41]

Several anthropology graduate students participated and spoke at each hearing. Sumayya Kassamali, a graduate student in anthropology who was "shocked" at Dean Moody-Adams' "glorifying just war theory" and ROTC (Kassamali's comments received "extended applause," according to the Task Force), accentuated militarism, exploitation, and the fact that simply reading about the military is sufficient for full understanding:

I want to respond to this notion that the military is distant from us. So first of all for those of us that read the news, it's not distant. Those of us that see and are outraged by the daily violence perpetrated by the military, it's not something that's far away. ... They're not things that we don't understand or we need a broader perspective about or we need more personal interaction with. In fact, we understand them very well.

... I want to say that the critique around DADT, which has now become around transgender individuals, that's not enough. Our opposition to the military and to

40 "Report of the Task Force on Military Engagement," February 14, 2011.

41 "Report of the Task Force on Military Engagement," February 7, 2011.

institutional ties between universities and the military needs to be unequivocal. . . . I think we need to be clear that our opposition is against militarization in general.[42]

Although other anthropology representatives agreed with Kassamali, some division reigned within even those ranks. Madeleine Elish, a graduate student in anthropology, spoke despite her fear of retribution from colleagues for expressing views sympathetic to the return of ROTC to Columbia:

I'm afraid that when I express an opinion which I know is not the dominant one in the environment where I am, I am going to be somehow judged in a certain way. And I'm afraid of those repercussions because I am in support of the return of ROTC to campus. Do I agree with the U.S. military as an institution? I've been to protests that are against all of our wars. I do not believe in the military's, well, the imperial wars that we're waging right now. . . . I think that really protesting ROTC in this way demonizes the individuals who will be serving in our military and who have served in our military. Someone raised the excellent point that Columbia wouldn't discourage students from joining Congress or becoming president, and it should be noted that those are the bodies that actually authorized the wars that we're currently engaged in. . . . Columbia is a part of academia, and I think that when there is the widespread resistance of institutions such as at Columbia to not allow ROTC on campus, it says academia has checked out of the picture and we will not engage with views that are not like our own. And so I think, I believe that having ROTC on campus would lead to our principles of inclusion and diversity of values.[43]

ON TO THE SENATE

The Task Force sent its report and resolutions to the Executive Committee of the Senate, chaired by Sharyn O'Halloran, on March 4. The Executive Committee then hammered out a four-part resolution that was derived from seven background "Whereas" observations, which included acknowledgment of the existence of Columbia's other relationships with the military (for example, the Yellow Ribbon Program and the armed forces scholarship program in the health sciences); the repeal of DADT; the long-standing participation of Columbia students in ROTC at other host campuses; Columbia's historical commitment to leadership beyond the borders of the campus; the broad and extensive process fostered by the Task Force; and the importance of Columbia's antidiscrimination policy.

Based on these "Whereas" acknowledgments, the Committee "resolved" the following:

- That it is in Columbia's interest "to continue to constructively engage with the Armed Forces of the United States to educate future military leaders"

[42] "Report of the Task Force on Military Engagement, Columbia University, February 7, 2011.

[43] "Report of the Task Force on Military Engagement, Columbia University, February 7, 2011.

- That the university "welcomes the opportunity to explore further mutually beneficial relationships with the Armed Forces of the United States, including participation in the programs of the Reserve Officer Training Corps"
- That the university maintain authority over academic standards, including academic credit, faculty appointments, academic governance, and space
- That the Executive Committee "periodically review" all further relationships with the military[44]

This four-part resolution is what the Senate considered on April 1.

Considerable work was conducted behind the scenes in the run-up to the Senate vote on April 1, both before March 4 and especially thereafter. Student ROTC supporters had one major strategic objective: in Jose Robledo's words, "to keep the faculty from hijacking a student issue, as they had in 2005." As seen, this meant focusing on faculty and key student identity groups, not the general student body. Because he is the leader of student ROTC advocates, Robledo took the initiative in talking with forty-six faculty senators one on one (out of sixty or so). Many straddled the fence, so he informed them of the reasons to be supportive. He succeeded in gaining the support of most.[45]

Meanwhile, as soon as DADT was repealed, Tao Tan, chair of the Senate's Student Affairs Committee (SAC), put together a team to work on appointing the Task Force. The SAC named law student Ron Mazor the student chair and Roosevelt Montas as faculty co-chair. (They considered naming Applegate to this position, but his well-known and strong pro-ROTC position caused them simply to appoint him a regular member of the Task Force. The Task Force was supposed to be neutral at the inception.) As related, the Task Force was responsible for setting up the process of campus deliberation (hearings, survey, and so on) and for writing an extensive report on the process and issues. After receiving the Task Force Report, the Executive Committee of the Senate worked on fashioning resolutions to carry out the Task Force's recommendations. On March 25, its members voted nine to nothing to sponsor the resolutions. Soon thereafter, the Faculty Affairs Committee voted eight to one to support the resolutions – a vote Tao Tan called "incredible." The Student Affairs Committee then met (twenty-three of its twenty-four members attended) and voted seventeen for and five against, with one abstention, in support after a ninety-minute discussion. A quorum then voted to send a letter to the full Senate, asking it to vote on the question by the end of the spring semester. "Our reasoning," Tan related, "was that 13/24 student Senators would turn over, and over 11,000 students would graduate. A case would be made that the process needs to start over, and that would undermine the work the Task Force had selflessly devoted to the process." During the next week, advocates

[44] "Resolution on Columbia University's Relationships with the Armed Forces of the United States of America," Columbia University Senate, Proposed April 1, 2011. Copy given to Downs at the April 1 Senate meeting.

[45] Interview with Robledo, April 2011.

engaged in nonstop interactions with faculty senators.[46] In addition to the desire to fend off faculty cooption, a major student objective was to prevent the vote from being dragged out any longer.

Robledo related that strategists acted on four fronts. The first front was the trustees, who wanted more engagement with the military. Right after classes resumed in January, Robledo and two other veterans met with Dean Awn and the trustees. When Robledo told the trustee chair, William V. Campbell, that ROTC advocates had already prepared a curricular plan based on the Princeton model, this information cemented trustee support. (At Princeton, ROTC professors are assigned "a rank equivalent to the senior academic rank of professor" in order to stay within the law. The program operates as an extracurricular program, so academic credit is not given. Currently most of the cadets' physical work takes place at Rutgers University, although the instruction of ROTC classes is given on Princeton's campus.) Second was the alumni front, which had two prongs. Although Graske did not do anything to change Bollinger's mind at this point, he and Columbia graduate Mickey Segal (whose Advocates website kept flowing with articles about ROTC and the politics of renewal), along with others, continued their pro-ROTC efforts.[47] A second front opened up through the Alumni Affairs Committee of the Senate, reaching a broader swath of alumni who registered support for ROTC.

A third mobilization was led by such professors as Silver and Applegate, who were involved in the faculty petition and a series of one-on-one meetings discussed previously in this chapter. The fourth front was directed at getting the *Spectator* on board. Student advocates met with the paper's leaders and made sure that they did not miss any important event. In addition to widespread reporting and the publication of several opinion editorials by ROTC advocates and critics, the *Spectator* editorial board strongly supported ROTC's return. In a key editorial during the last week of February, the *Spectator* called for the end of ideological politics over the issue and for greater Columbia influence over the military in the name of broadening the military mind. It concluded by declaring:

> Our academic experience at Columbia that instills us with values of honesty, justice, mercy, and truth can be practically applied in military service. To deny students who seek ROTC membership the chance to pursue military service, regardless of their reasons, is itself ideologically flawed. So Columbia students, we urge you to peek your heads out of our ivory tower and consider what ROTC has to offer. Vote yes to ROTC.[48]

The common thread among these fronts, in Robledo's words, "was always to win the Senate vote."[49]

[46] Tao Tan, "ROTC at Columbia University: An Advocate's Path," April 2, 2011. Tan sent a copy of this ten-page memoir – composed soon after the April 1 vote – to the authors.

[47] See, e.g., the page on the Advocates webpage that Segal constructed, "Issues and Myths About ROTC": http://www.advocatesforrotc.org/issues/.

[48] "Vote Yes," *Columbia Daily Spectator*, editorial, February 21, 2011: http://www.columbiaspectator.com/2011/02/21/vote-yes.

[49] Interview with Robledo, April 2011.

A fifth front, which took place beyond the purview of Robledo and the student movement, was initiated by the military itself. High-level ROTC officials began making contact with Bollinger in January and February 2011, focusing on issues regarding credit. Similar interactions took place with Harvard and other schools. A key point is that the military took the initiative. The Princeton arrangement has been given consideration: open the campus to physical ROTC presence, treating it as an extracurricular program subject to "appropriate" credit on a course-by-course basis. The Navy desires to enhance the relationship, and a number of New York area schools are poised to vie to be a new host school.

Beyond working on the faculty, student activists engaged major student groups who were well known as skeptical, such as the Latin United Community Housing Association (LUCHA) and the Columbia Queer Alliance (CQA). Student Nico Barragan lobbied the CQA, asking the organization to refrain from taking an official position against ROTC. Lucha and the International Socialist Organization continued to press for ROTC's defeat, but CQA – widely considered to have the most important horse in the race – maintained official neutrality. CQA's retreat from the battle constituted a major coup for Barragan and his pro-ROTC allies, further marginalizing opposition.

THE SENATE VOTE ON APRIL 1

As mentioned, anti-ROTC activists called for a massive rally at Jerome Hall to influence the vote.[50] Only about twenty protesters showed up, and they could not be heard inside the Senate meeting room. As Tao Tan relates, "An angry e-mail had gone out to an umbrella organization of left-wing groups across New York City urging them to turn up with 'instruments, signs, megaphones, banners, or whatever you want to make as much noise as possible' to 'create a disturbance' so that presumably the Senate would 'acknowledge student resistance,' since 'students' voices have been silenced throughout this whole process.'"[51]

Regardless, by the time of the Senate vote, the proverbial ducks had been lined up. Bollinger opened the meeting with words that foreshadowed the result. He spoke about how he had been around long enough to see the world change. The implication was that Columbia was now ready to reverse what it had done back in 1968–9 with respect to ROTC. Indeed, Bollinger had sat in the back of the

[50] Note that the minutes of the April 1 Senate meeting were not available when this book was sent to production. Consequently, we rely on notes that author Downs took during the meeting, which he attended as a guest of the Senate. Quotations from Downs are not exact, but rather honest approximations of what was said. Silver and Applegate made this arrangement, along with Tom Mathewson, the secretary of the Senate. We stress only the highlights here.

[51] Tan, "ROTC at Columbia University," p. 7. See also "Senate Votes for ROTC's Return," *Columbia Daily Spectator*, April 2, 2011.

University Council (the predecessor of the Senate; see Chapter 5) as a law student in the late 1960s, and he recalled that he had never imagined back then that he would be presiding over such a meeting as president of the university over forty years later. He pointed to Columbia's influence around the world, and to the importance of reaching a decision on the merits through civility and respect. He said that the vote bore significance for the institution as a whole, and that it was appropriate to deal with it now. He concluded his introductory remarks by stressing the importance of the process, however arduous it had been. Unlike other schools – the reference to Harvard was unmistakable, although he did not mention it by name – a tortuous process was emblematic of the institution.[52]

O'Halloran then spoke about the Task Force and the process it had shepherded ("this is anything but a rushed process") and dispelled some prevalent misconceptions about ROTC. She then introduced four speakers who addressed the issue, pro and con. Tan and Applegate spoke in favor of ROTC, while Bette Gordon (adjunct professor of professional practice) and Liya Yu (Ph.D. student) spoke against. "For many students, and particularly those from countries where the military, whether American or not, is associated with the destruction of civil life, the presence [of ROTC] would be inhibiting, if not traumatizing," Gordon declared.[53]

In addition to raising standard objections, Yu underscored a very important point that had not often surfaced in public debates: that Columbia's growing "worldwide mission" would be severely compromised by ROTC's presence if America were to engage in controversial wars such as the Vietnam War in the future. "What's in it for us? Columbia's global vision is radically reshaping our identity. Bringing back ROTC contradicts our vision for the future. Many international students are now in our Global Centers. What if there is another Vietnam? Columbia's internationality is a new symbolism of global peace and stability. Graduate students and faculty have not been polled. We need more time."[54] Yu's comments – which met loud applause from supporters – struck to the heart of crosscurrents that have hurtled beneath the surface of the ROTC debate: ROTC and the military represent patriotism and a primary commitment or orientation toward national interest, whereas much of the contemporary university – beholden to internationalism, international law, and the like – leans toward cosmopolitan notions of citizenship. (See our discussion of this tension near the end of Chapter 1.) In our view, this tension is all the more reason to open the door to ROTC, for three reasons: because it enhances productive

[52] See Donald Alexander Downs, "Notes of Columbia University Senate Meeting, April 1, 2011." These notes are in the personal possession of Downs. They closely resemble the official transcript minutes now available online at Columbia. We quote from Downs' notes because the official minutes are not verbatim, so there is no reason to rely on this version over Downs' own notes. Readers are certainly welcome to check the official minutes as well. Columbia University Senate Meeting Minutes, April 1, 2011: http://www.columbia.edu/cu/senate/archives/plenary/10–11/plenary_minutes_10–11/plenary_mins_4–1–11.html.

[53] "USenate Votes for ROTC's Return," *Columbia Spectator*, April 1, 2011.

[54] Downs, "Notes of Columbia University Senate meeting, April 1, 2011."

friction; because it adds to the diversity of viewpoints on campus; and because it would make little sense for a major American university to adopt an *exclusively* international identity. Regardless, Yu's point merited attention.

Yu's comments were countered by two senators. Chemistry professor Ronald Breslow highlighted student choice, opportunity, and diversity of opinion. "If faculty could join ROTC, would you say 'no'? Should conservatives have to go to Fordham instead of Columbia? Will we tolerate only ideas we like? As a liberal university, we need to be open to other ideas." Sheena Iyengar, a business professor from India, added, "We need ROTC precisely because we are global. We need to broaden. This is precisely in line with globalization; and we want the military to engage in the dialogue. If we shut them out, we undermine this mission."[55]

The ensuing lively discussion involved a familiar motion to table the vote until a later date, which was defeated. A second motion pushed by philosophy professor Lydia Goehr would have changed the language of the key resolution to call on Columbia to "continue to discuss a relationship with ROTC" rather than make a stronger commitment that signaled real change. This motion failed after intense discussion. There were also friendly motions designed to more pointedly ensure the university's adherence to academic standards and non-discrimination. Debate became more heated, with some senators asserting their desire to eschew yet more parliamentary maneuvering in favor of taking a direct vote on the substance of the matter at hand. As often happens in such faculty meetings, parliamentary entanglements began to descend upon the proceedings after close to an hour and a half of discussion and debate.

It was at this point that Bollinger began to take over the meeting, leading from the front at long last – authoritatively, yet with velvet gloves. Responding to senators who wanted a simple, clean motion that cut to the heart of the matter, Bollinger led the Senate toward motions that would remove three of the four resolutions presented to the Senate by the Executive Committee: the resolution concerning the university's continued control over academic standards, faculty appointments, and the allocation of space; the provision calling for "periodic review" by the Senate Executive Committee of any new relationships forged with the military; and the clause that asserted Columbia's interest in continuing to engage the armed forces constructively and to "educate future military leaders." The Senate voted in favor of this move, leaving only one resolution – the pivotal one – in place for a vote: "That Columbia University welcomes the opportunity to explore further mutually beneficial relationships with the Armed Forces of the United States, including participation in the programs of the Reserve Officers Training Corps."

When Bollinger asked for a vote on this last standing resolution, some senators vociferously called for yet more debate and clarification. The president responded with further boldness. He began by reminding the room that the

[55] Downs, "Notes of Columbia University Senate meeting, April 1, 2011."

ROTC discussion had been exhaustively extensive and that all viewpoints had been given an opportunity to be heard. "There is a change in this world that we must consider," he intoned. He then took a risk that was uncharacteristic of the way he had dealt with the issue since 2004–5: He challenged the Senate to trust that he would uphold the university's integrity regarding the antidiscrimination policy; institutional control, standards, and the provision of physical space for ROTC classes and exercise were other matters to work out. The passage of further resolutions would be, in effect, an insult to his conscientious leadership, which had been so careful to honor democratic process and inclusion. If passed, the resolution meant that "there is a general understanding that there is a desire to pursue the interest of setting up ROTC programs on campus. This is a powerful vote here, in my mind." A senator then spoke. "We should trust the president" in this matter, he averred.

Despite some disgruntlement, the Senate decided to take the leap of faith – even though it meant, in effect, that upholding the core conditions the Mansfield Committee had set for ROTC back in 1969 were to be relegated to the considered discretion and judgment of the president (see Chapter 5). The vote was at hand at 3:15 P.M.: fifty-one in favor, seventeen in opposition, and one in abstention. It was an historical moment not only in Columbia's history, but in higher education in America.

CONCLUDING THOUGHTS

The vote made national news. The *New York Times'* coverage captured how many felt:

> In the popular eye, and in history texts, Columbia's relations with the military have been more or less defined by the decision in 1969 to ban R.O.T.C. The move came at the end of a period of pitched student activism – the Spirit of '68, as it was known – that included student strikes and the occupation of Hamilton Hall, a main academic building. On Friday, the sense of generational turnabout in the Senate vote was not lost on the students of today.[56]

Like many individuals who have led movements that succeed against stiff odds, many student, faculty, and alumni leaders of the Columbia ROTC movement looked back with a sense of satisfaction and even amazement.[57] The extent of the victory – fifty-one for, seventeen against, and one abstaining – almost a mirror opposite of the vote in 2005 – added to the strength of these feelings. Leaders

[56] "Decades After Ban, Columbia Opens Door to ROTC Return," *New York Times*, April 2, 2011: http://www.nytimes.com/2011/04/02/nyregion/02rotc.html?_r=1&scp=1&sq=columbia%20rotc&st=cse.

[57] On the feeling of "amazement" after such success, see Timur Kuran, *Private Truths/Public Lies: The Social Consequences of Preference Falsification* (Harvard University Press, 1997). One difference is that Kuran describes situations of rapid transformation, whereas the Columbia movement won after a laborious and drawn-out process. But the feeling of "wow" is similar for both types of success.

also placed the vote in a broader historical and institutional context. To Allan Silver, the Army veteran with liberal arts credentials who had labored for a long time in the pro-ROTC trenches, the vote showed that that the campus wars that have pitted left against right – often in an exaggerated way – were perhaps subsiding. Silver took pride in the fact that liberals were just as involved in the campus movement as conservatives. "The campaign on campus has been waged by liberals no less than conservatives," he wrote in *The Wounded Lion*. "We all need to engage Washington no less than Morningside Heights."[58] Maybe common ground – the "uni" part of the concept "university" – was slouching toward Alma Mater (the famous statue on the steps of Low Library), waiting to be reborn, however tenuously. The vote could also represent an important step in overcoming the military–civil society divide, which has been of such concern to Silver and others. Applegate also interpreted the vote as a potential watershed for the institution. First, the Senate's placement of trust in the president signified a historical turn. The Senate's origin, as we saw in Chapter 5, lay in distrust of the central administration. True to this core character, Applegate had never witnessed the Senate vesting such trust in the president or central administration. Time might prove Applegate's anticipation misguided or even naïve, especially given the politics of higher education and the nation today; but clearly something new had appeared under the sun at Columbia on that day at least:

> Yesterday's meeting may have done more than vote 51–17 in favor of Columbia ROTC. The Senate may have redefined its relationship with the President of the University. I have been attending faculty meetings and participating in governance for more than 25 years here, and I have never heard a body like the Senate or the faculty tell the president or other senior administrator that we trust them to negotiate in good faith on our behalf . . . by Lee Bollinger asking us to trust him to act in good faith with regards to the implementation of DADT repeal and the Senate agreeing to that, and then the Senate reciprocating by offering and accepting a friendly amendment removing the explicit statement of the Mansfield conditions in favor of trusting him, we redefined the relationship as more of a partnership than has ever existed previously.

In addition, the vote could have represented a generational shift. Applegate credited student, faculty, and alumni activists for the success, but he gave main credit to the students:

> This was a team victory by a group of volunteers with no clear leader. Everyone did what they were particularly suited for. We were each center stage when it was our turn, and we all knew when to get off or play a supporting role when someone else was in the spotlight. Having said that, the students were the inspiration, soul, and infantry that got this done. This was a generational passing of the torch and they are the future. It was a victory of an idea whose time had come over an idea whose time had passed. In the 1960's students kicked ROTC off the Columbia campus, and in 2011 students invited them back.[59]

[58] Allan Silver, "It Takes Two to Tango," *Wounded Lion* 7, 1 ("Navy Reconciliation Issue") (2011): 7.

[59] E-mail exchanges with Applegate, April 2011.

Eric Chen chimed in with a similar take. In addition to describing how "personal" the issue had been with him, he stressed how dealing with the civil–military divide had been "his baby" from the start. Furthermore, the lengthy movement that led to the vote epitomized the spirit of Columbia:

> What stands out most about the outcome is that Columbia didn't endorse ROTC by fiat, but rather with the unimpeachable legitimacy of an exhaustive democratic process. The ROTC movement started nine years ago from grassroots when most people perceived our cause to be quixotic. Since then, the issue has been debated and discussed at all levels of the Columbia community, including 3 student surveys and 2 senate votes. After this long introspection and important events along the way ... Columbia finally arrived at a consensus to welcome ROTC.[60]

Jose Robledo echoed this understanding. As he engaged the administration on such issues as physical education credit, space allocation, and raising the flag, he found an increasing openness to ROTC. "But they waited for the Senate. The faculty and the Senate really wanted to be part of the process." The outstanding feature was the "total engagement this conversation entailed. No one felt excluded. People felt this was an organic process. No one felt manipulated."[61] Learned Foote was in the same camp:

> Both the Senate vote and the student vote [the surveys conducted by the Task Force] revealed a substantial majority in favor of ROTC. These majorities were especially meaningful because similar efforts had failed in previous years. The pro-ROTC side worked very hard to convey its views for many years, and clearly people were listening and engaging during the substantive town halls and media debates. The moment was right for all of these universities to reconsider ROTC, but at Columbia the process was more messy and dramatic than at any other school. It was wonderful to see Columbia engage with the issues so deeply and finally come to the right conclusion by significant margins.[62]

To some critics, especially among the older generation of alumni, Bollinger's consensus-oriented approach to the ROTC question was lamentably Hamlet-like in its lack of decisiveness. Garnering consensus behind ROTC at a place such as Columbia seemed akin to herding cats, or asking Sisyphus to roll that pebble up the mountain with his nose. But perhaps Bollinger was vindicated in the end, not only because of the vote on April 1. By having laboriously (even torturously) come to a consensus on ROTC, Columbia established the most promising foundation for bridging the military–civil society gap, which has been especially pronounced at places such as Columbia. Premature adoption of a pro-ROTC position would have been cursed with accusations of illegitimacy, especially before the repeal of DADT. And persuasion is always preferable to ramming something through by coercion or on the heels of a bare majority vote over a deeply contested issue.

[60] E-mail exchanges with Chen, April 4, 2011.

[61] Interview with Robledo, April 2, 2011.

[62] E-mail exchange with Columbia student Learned Foote, April 9, 2011.

The ROTC vote was the product of two things that are especially propitious for bridging the civil–military–university gap. First, as we have stressed at length, it was the product of a broad, hard-fought consensus. Second, some of the most persuasive arguments for ROTC were based on applying the university's core values to the military itself: diversity of thought and nondiscrimination. With the demise of DADT, the anti-ROTC position was now seen as closed-minded and discriminatory in its own right. In other words, ROTC was now being accepted on the basis of the core value system of the university, while its opponents now wore the mantel of close-mindedness and discrimination. (Being opponents is one thing, but being critics is another: No institution should be considered beyond criticism.) Such acceptance could provide the background condition to make productive friction most effective. As we argued in Chapter 3, diversity works best when sharp differences coexist with basic consensus about core institutional values.

Perhaps no response to the vote symbolized the historical turn more than that of Mark Rudd, the militant leader of Columbia's student revolt in 1968. He and his allies targeted ROTC as a cardinal example of the military's presence on campus, succeeding in driving it from the university in 1969. After the Senate vote on April 1, 2011, Rudd reminded the *Village Voice* of this history, but then offered a conciliatory observation that resembled the classic rationale for ROTC discussed in our previous chapters. As Fahmida Y. Rashid reported, "with the current officer corps 'very heavily conservative Republican,' Rudd wonders if perhaps training future officers at Columbia might not be a bad thing after all. 'They'll have been exposed to both liberals and the liberal arts,' he says. 'Perhaps they'll moderate the right-wing officer caste mentality a bit.'"[63] It is hard to imagine a more poignant example of the pendulum's return in matters military on campus.

Of course, the ROTC saga at Columbia, Harvard, and other institutions is far from over. As we have discussed, how such schools will reintegrate with the military remains an open question that is dependent upon resources in troubled financial times, the degree of institutional support and resistance, the availability of space (a special concern at Columbia), and other factors. Indifference and benign neglect remain threats to productive friction. For such ROTC advocates as Silver, true engagement with ROTC will come only when there is a meaningful physical presence on campus, which would include a visible space for operations. As of this writing, Silver and other activists had concerns about how thorough Columbia's carry-through would be. As Ted Graske wrote in his "Chairman's Message" in *The Wounded Lion*, "While welcoming the return of the Navy to Columbia has great symbolic value, there is much to be done. Some say, 'Columbia has done itself proud.' Other, more skeptical alumni say, 'they threw us a bone.' Yet another group says, 'what exactly happens now.'"[64]

[63] Fahmida Y. Rashid, "The Return of ROTC to Columbia," *Village Voice*, April 6, 2011: http://www.villagevoice.com/2011-04-06/news/the-return-of-rotc-to-columbia/.

[64] Graske, "Chairman's Message," *The Wounded Lion* 7, 1 (2011): 2.

Furthermore, the ROTC that might return to schools such as Columbia will be a different program from the one that left in the late 1960s in terms of such things as resources, organizational structure, and standards.

The last hurdle for meaningful engagement is the military itself. As Robledo remarked, "The hardest part now is to convince the military that they need Columbia as much as Columbia needs them. That's the real hurdle now."[65]

[65] Interview with Robledo, April 2, 2011.

8

Pedagogy and Military Presence

The Educational Influence of Student-Soldiers in Their Own Words

> Since we are of the opinion that the military is going to be with us in the U.S. for some time, we feel that any "reform" that makes it difficult for a Princeton English major or a Pittsburgh philosophy major to become an officer is most undesirable.... Which brings us to our third conclusion. If you don't like the way the military functions, you can't expect it to improve by insulating yourself from it.
>
> – Ed Berger et al.[1]

> It is easy for people to become detached from things that they have no interaction with.
>
> – Anonymous ROTC cadet[2]

In Chapter 2, we considered theoretically the various ways in which military presence can contribute to liberal and civic education, focusing on four ways in particular. First, military presence can be a means of empirically "understanding the military and national defense," which includes, among other things, "education in the regime." The latter entails understanding the responsibilities necessary for the sustenance and protection of the regime and its fundamental principles. Second, students have opportunities to learn about "human nature, society, and the meaning of life" by encountering or studying the institution that is most closely associated with the conduct of war. Third, appropriate military presence can confront students with "moral difficulties in liberal democracy," such as the moral conundrums regarding the use of force and the relationship between the threat or deployment of legitimate violent force and the public good. (The theory of moral realism best captures this theme.) Finally, military presence can be a source of "intellectual and moral diversity on campus." Based on these reasons, we construed military presence as a source of productive friction and as an example of what Hans Morgenthau and his progeny consider the "higher practicality," which entails applying philosophical and ethical thought to

[1] Ed Berger, Larry Flatley, John Frisch, Mayda Gottlieb, Judy Haisley, Peter Karsten, Larry Pexton, and William Worrest, "ROTC, Mylai, and the Volunteer Army," *Foreign Affairs* 2 (1971): 131–60.

[2] Interview, University of Wisconsin, 2009.

historical and contemporary problems that reflect fundamental human, social, and political dilemmas.

In the last two chapters of this section, which to this point has dealt with the politics of excluding ROTC from campus, we consider more explicitly the hypotheses we set forth in Chapter 2 regarding the productive contribution of student-soldiers and military presence to non-military students. We do this by asking ROTC students and non-ROTC students about their experiences with each other on campus; furthermore, we examine the reactions of several students to humanities courses dealing with the military and with war. Through surveys and focus groups, we were able to gain insight into the self-reported contribution of ROTC students to campus learning.[3] In particular, we asked cadets how they themselves have contributed knowledge of the military and created opportunities to engage students regarding matters of war. We also asked them about how their presence might have led to discussion or debate about some of the moral ambiguities of war, as well as their contributions to diversity on campus. We found that ROTC presence often does improve prospects for civic education, provides a different perspective on matters of war, and contributes to intellectual diversity. Yet we needed additional insights to consider the deeper philosophical and moral issues involving war and university education. The last dimension of learning – how military presence contributes to our understanding of human nature, society, and the meaning of life – did not receive significant attention from either cadet or civilian student respondents. This lack was probably due to the fact that the aspect of exposure treated in these surveys – to ROTC cadets – did not lend itself to such reflection. Such reflection is more likely to stem from exposure to humanities courses dealing with such subjects as military history and philosophical thinking about the military and war. For this reason, we consider the impact of a couple of such courses in the next chapter, which focuses on civilian student responses.

In this and the next chapter, our emphasis is on the perspectives of student-soldiers – in particular, how their military presence on campus has provided non-military students with knowledge of the military, and more importantly, whether it caused them to think about human nature, morality of war, and related matters. Here too we found that presence of ROTC was a source of productive friction. In particular – and this is especially the case for the students in the two humanities courses – we found many non-military students struggling to come to terms with their feelings and thoughts about the military and war.

[3] One of the seminal studies of ROTC is Berger et al., "ROTC, MyLai, and the Volunteer Army." Their contribution lay in examining the impact of the university on the officer, finding that well-educated officers (in particular, those trained in humanities) are less likely to engage in what would now be considered war crimes – one of the strongest rationales for including ROTC on campus is indeed to prevent the types of actions that ROTC opponents associate with ROTC. Our perspective differs in that we consider ROTC as a two-way street: we not only consider how the university contributes to the military but also what the military can do for the university.

This state is to be expected for several reasons that we discuss at the beginning of the next chapter. In essence, it boils down to the fact that the military and war are *sui generis*, as we discussed in Chapter 2: These topics deal with morally difficult responsibilities that go against the grain of common ethics, and with uncomfortable aspects of existence. But facing such truths is itself a form of productive friction. All told, the findings reinforced our theoretical argument: The presence of ROTC is important because it brings a military perspective to the university.

Although we contacted cadets and their commanders in the surveys for the present chapter, we concentrate on the experiences of cadets because of our primary interest in what student-soldiers bring to the university. To gain insight into the experience of ROTC cadets, we begin by presenting the quantitative findings for each set of respondents based on how responses fell into categories according to the questions we asked. We did not choose these categories ahead of time, but rather selected them after reading the responses provided by cadets in order to ensure that cadets were free to explain the diversity of their experiences. Although open-ended surveys are desirable because they impose few constraints on respondents, such surveys require judgment in presenting findings. The categories we constructed represent our best effort to encapsulate the most prevalent types of responses. After each chart, we present and discuss some of the actual qualitative comments.

The surveys of cadets offer insight into the status of the military on campus as well as one of the great questions of civil–military relations – namely, liberal and communitarian rationales for participation in the military forces. Liberal and communitarian perspectives on participation in the military – the former emphasizes economic and/or individualistic motivation, whereas the latter accentuates service in the republican ideal – furnishes a framework that guides our inquiry in this chapter.[4] Our findings suggest that student-soldiers tend to join ROTC based on a combination of self-interested and republican motivations. The information we received allows us to get a feel for how cadets view their contribution to the university, as well as a sense of their positive or negative experiences on campus.

We conducted three surveys of students and soldiers for this project, including ROTC commanders and staff at the University of Wisconsin–Madison (UW-Madison), ROTC alumni, and political science majors. Commanders provided additional insight into the importance of ROTC on campus, as well as their experiences over the years at UW-Madison and at other universities. For brevity, we present only a few illustrative comments by commanders, and leave the ROTC alumni responses aside for future research. One thing we can say about alumni: Those who were cadets during the Vietnam era reported more

[4] See Charles Moskos, "The Marketplace All-Volunteer Force: A Critique," in William Bowman, Roger Little, and G. Thomas, eds., *The All-Volunteer Force After a Decade: Retrospect and Prospect*, (Pergamon-Brassey's, 1986). On republican and liberal values and the citizen-soldier ideal, see James Burk, "Theories of Democratic Civil-Military Relations," *Armed Forces & Society* 29, 1 (Fall 2009).

significant negative experiences on campus. These unsurprising responses comport with what we have reiterated in the preceding: Because ROTC is usually the most visible sign of the military on campus, attitudes toward ROTC are a function of broader attitudes toward the military. Given today's more sanguine view of the military, we would expect fewer antimilitary encounters on campus.[5]

One of the most important sections for our purposes is the section on non-ROTC student responses, for the impact of military exposure on them comprises the central focus of this book. Student perspectives provide insight into their awareness of ROTC, as well as their perceptions of the military on campus. That said, we think it is instructive to look at what ROTC cadets and instructors have to say about their interactions with non-military persons in order to paint a more complete picture. This juxtaposition casts some light on the nature and status of the military/university "gap."

Madison is a good case to study because it is one of about ninety institutions that host ROTC units for all three branches of the military (the Marines are housed in Navy ROTC), and because it also has a large student body, which means that we could expect a wide variety of responses. ROTC is noticeable on campus, but it is not omnipresent. The programs are larger and more conspicuous than those at such schools as Cornell and Princeton, but not nearly as prominent as programs at such places as Texas A&M. The Navy ROTC battalion at Wisconsin had 65 students enrolled in its Navy and Marine Corps programs at the beginning of the academic year in which we conducted the survey (2008–9). The Army's Department of Military Science had 149 cadets pursuing a commission, while the Air Force's Department of Aerospace Studies hosted 53 students. These numbers include students from smaller institutions in the broader area who attend the "hub" Madison programs.[6]

In addition, UW-Madison's history is laced with commitment and opposition to ROTC. Although administrative leaders have generally strongly supported ROTC, some students, faculty, and citizens have periodically opposed it, most recently on account of the Vietnam War and DADT. Wisconsin was the first land grant institution to end the mandatory status of ROTC, and forces sought outright abolition in the late 1960s to the early 1970s and in the late 1980s and early 1990s.[7] While tensions had waned by the 2008–9 academic year, concerns about ROTC still had some currency on campus. More broadly, UW-Madison is famous for being on the left and progressive side of the political scale.

5 The survey responses of our ROTC alumni survey are available upon request.

6 University of Wisconsin, Madison Faculty Senate, *Officer Education Committee Annual Report for 2008–2009*, Faculty Document 2105 (March 2, 2009): http://www.secfac.wisc.edu/senate/2009/0302/2105.pdf.

7 See E. David Cronon and John W. Jenkins, *The University of Wisconsin: A History, 1925–1945, Politics, Depression, and War*. Volume III (University of Wisconsin Press, 1994), pp. 130–1, 287–91, 385, 402–4, 633, 673; E. David Cronon and John W. Jenkins, *The University of Wisconsin: A History, 1945–1971, Renewal to Revolution*. Volume IV (University of Wisconsin Press, 1999), chs. 7, 8.

During the Vietnam War, the campus was a national leader in radical – and at times violent – opposition to the war. In a 2005 cover article in the *Weekly Standard* entitled "The Left University," conservative commentator and activist James Piereson chronicled the rise of left-progressive universities in the United States during the course of the twentieth century and their impact on higher education and national policy. He selected UW-Madison as the "paradigm" example of such an institution.[8] Accordingly, UW-Madison is a good laboratory to test the theory of productive friction and its contribution to diversity and the pursuit of knowledge. Numerous ROTC and non-ROTC students were acutely aware of the tension between the ROTC and what they called "the liberal" or "left-wing" campus. Interestingly, many of them considered ROTC presence important for this very reason.

So UW-Madison offers a rich and varied context in which to field our questions. Students have encountered ROTC cadets in various contexts, including in class, housing, student activities, and the public domain. Likewise, the effects of exposure differ. Some students gain knowledge and respect from exposure, whereas others are turned off – a distinct minority, according to the responses we received. Effects, of course, depend upon the personal characteristics, values, and experiences that students bring to their encounters, as does the degree of interaction between military and non-military students. Students who are more sympathetic to ROTC may be more likely to interact with students who participate in the program. We were not able to treat these aspects, as our purpose was simply to attain insight into the impact of ROTC on non-military students in a sample of students who are most likely to be engaged in or interested in politics (political science majors).

We asked cadets, ROTC alumni, commanders, and non-cadet political science majors several questions designed to cast light on the impact that ROTC exposure can have on non-ROTC students. Our results are suggestive, not definitive, for our survey was limited. Readers will note some differences between the cadet and civilian student responses, as well as significant areas of agreement. It is not surprising that cadets have a more positive overall take on ROTC and that they are more uniformly sanguine about the program's impact. ROTC is a form of military education that includes indoctrination in the military's mission and ways and the instilling of *esprit de corps*. Hence, it is only natural that cadets will have more positive feelings about the program and its influence. Lest one be inclined to disparage the military for engaging in indoctrination, remember that all professions engage in this practice, for inculcating a

[8] James Piereson, "The Left University: How It Was Born, How It Grew, How to Overcome It," *Weekly Standard* 11, 3 (2005): http://www.weeklystandard.com/Content/Public/Articles/000/000/006/120xbklj.asp. On UW-Madison's history of radical opposition to the Vietnam War, see, e.g., David Maraniss, *They Marched into Sunlight: War and Peace in Vietnam and America* (Simon and Schuster, 2003). The book juxtaposes the takeover of the Commerce Building in October 1967 – the nation's first illegal takeover of a building on campus to protest the Vietnam War – with a crucial battle in Vietnam that took place at the same time.

sense of identity and distinctiveness is essential to the achievement of all professional missions.[9]

Not all of the interactions between the military and non-military spheres were productive, as one would expect. A quarter of our cadet respondents reported witnessing acts of hostility toward ROTC and the military, and a large number also related student apathy or ignorance. Thus, our survey results present a complex picture: Many examples support our hypothesis of positive dialectical interaction, whereas others reflect the alienation of recognition. Of course, this mixed picture could actually support our thesis, for the evidence shows not only a gap of recognition, but also many examples of interactions that have helped to bridge the gap.

The responses to our surveys help to paint a picture of the ongoing, dynamic relationship between the military and the campus. In previous chapters, we have found it useful to describe various clusters in society, in particular military and civilian clusters. Taken together, these surveys provide us with insight into the perspective of several different clusters within the university and different groups within the military cluster. As such, they present a glimpse into civil–military relations from the perspective of students and student-soldiers.[10] It is a complex and subtle tapestry, as one might expect. Social reality consists of the countless subjective and intersubjective experiences of individuals who are complex beings.[11] Accordingly, it is impossible to fully capture the social meaning of an important event or institution, for such meaning exists to a significant extent in the minds of countless individuals, most of whom harbor conflicting and even contradictory impressions and attitudes. (As Nietzsche wrote, the will is not monolithic, but a "parliament.") We simply hope that our presentation provides an instructive portrayal of the status and impact of ROTC on campus.

[9] On this and other aspects of military education, see Charles Shrader, "Education, Military," in John Chambers, ed., *Oxford Guide to American Military History* (Oxford University Press, 1999), p. 243. See also the essays in Gregory Kennedy and Keith Nielson, eds., *Military Education: Past, Present, and Future* (Praeger, 2002), p. 151. Many works have dealt with professionalism's instilling of a distinct sense of mission and identity as well as power. See, e.g., Burton Bledstein, *The Culture of Professionalism: The Middle Class and the Development of Higher Education in America* (W. W. Norton, 1976).

[10] Other studies of the civil–military gap emphasize the gap in attitudes between military personnel/veterans and the general public on policy issues. See, e.g., Peter D. Feaver and Christopher Gelpi, *Choosing your Battles: American Civil-Military Relations and the Use of Force* (Princeton University Press, 2004). Our surveys emphasize the experience of student-soldiers and their reasons for membership in the armed forces rather than a comparison of their attitudes to the non-military public. Our questions about their experience in the classroom provide us with insight into the diversity of perspectives that they offer.

[11] See, e.g., Peter L. Berger and Thomas Luckmann, *The Social Construction of Reality: A Treatise in the Sociology of Knowledge* (Anchor, 1967). Although social construction is a fact, this does not mean that there is no such thing as objective reality beyond such mental construction. On the relationship between construction and objectivity, see John R. Searle, *The Construction of Social Reality* (Free Press, 1995). This tension between objectivity claims and construction mirrors the debate between realism and constructivism in international relations theory. See Chapter 11 in this book.

Two final points should be stressed before we consider our surveys. First, as we have underscored often, productive friction does not require that students emerge with *positive* views of the military. Indeed, criticism of the military is *good* for a liberal democracy on several fronts because critical intelligence is a hallmark of a free citizenry, and undue respect would threaten proper civil–military relations in the other direction. As we said in Chapter 3, the military is just as self-interested as any other prominent American institution, and the politics within which it is embroiled often conjures images of Bismarck's famous observation about the making of laws and sausage.[12] In Chapter 9, we will encounter several examples of students whose negative views of the military came about because of exposure to ROTC cadets, as well as some whose preexisting negative views were confirmed or solidified by such exposure. Such results can be consistent with the theory of productive friction, for the theory requires no particular normative endpoint. To be sure, it does envision the overcoming (or at least partial overcoming) of the alienation attendant to "othering," and it entails understanding the sacrifice that soldiers make to defend the country in some general sense (education in the regime). So some normative perspective attends the theory, but this does not require approval or disapproval of ROTC and all aspects of the military. Indeed, as stressed previously in this book, the military is as flawed as any other institution. As a retired officer told us in Chapter 1, "The military can have a significant bullshit problem."[13] One of our most impressive student responses in Chapter 9 was by a self-described "anarcho-syndicalist" who disparaged the need for a military at the same time that he or she advocated military presence on campus because it is an important part of our reality and because such presence contributes to intellectual and normative diversity on campus. What our theory *does* call for is constructive engagement and consideration rather than dogmatism. One of John Stuart Mill's central theses in "On Liberty" is that free speech and exposure to contrary opinions and ideas are necessary even for those who stick to their cherished truths, for such truths are given life and greater significance by the process in which they are defended against counterpoints and arguments. "However unwillingly a person who has a strong opinion may admit the possibility that his opinion may be false, he ought to be moved by the consideration that, however true it may be, if it is not fully, frequently, and fearlessly discussed, it will be held as a dead dogma, not a living truth."[14]

Second, the process of productive friction is a two-way street involving both military and non-military personnel. Although our main focus is on the ways in which non-military students can learn from military perspectives, it is equally

[12] See, e.g., Carl H.. Builder, *The Masks of War: American Military Styles in Strategy and Analysis* (Johns Hopkins University Press, 1989); Harvey Sapolsky, Eugene Gholz, and Caitlin Talmadge, *U.S. Defense Politics: The Origins of Security Policy* (Routledge, 2009).

[13] Interview with Rob Sayre, Army Lt. Col., October 2010.

[14] John Stuart Mill, *On Liberty*, in *J. S. Mill, On Liberty and Other Writings* (Classic Books International, 2007), p. 38.

important for military students to learn from civilian students and instructors – for example, universities would benefit from ROTC in the Ivies because it exposes future officers to perspectives (often through protest) on DADT and defense policy that they might not experience at programs located in the South. Both sides of the dialectic are vital to the model of the citizen-soldier and the achievement of a propitious civil–military relationship. We will come across several examples of this two-way street in this and the next chapter.

THE EXPERIENCE OF ROTC STUDENT-SOLDIERS

We began by contacting several ROTC commanders to ask permission to survey their cadets, to which they agreed. We received responses from eighty-seven cadets from the Air Force, Navy, and Navy/Marines ROTC detachments at the University of Wisconsin of the nearly two hundred cadets on our e-mail list.

Question 1: Why They Joined

We first wanted to understand **why students join ROTC**, so we asked cadets to relate the major reasons for their signing up, ranking them if they could. The reasons cited are consistent with other findings regarding what motivates individuals to join the military.[15]

This question is perhaps most relevant to understanding how well the ideal of the citizen-soldier holds up. In his essay analyzing the contemporary viability of the citizen-soldier ideal, Ronald J. Krebs argues that the ideal has never been honored in practice as much as its advocates claim. Numerous eligible citizens have managed to avoid military service even during wars of mass mobilization, beginning with the Revolutionary and Civil wars. Furthermore, the motivations for joining the military have evolved over time as liberal-individualist concepts of citizenship have gained greater currency in comparison to more traditional, republican-communitarian motives based on the ideals of public service and sacrifice. Such liberal values as self-interest and personal advancement have permeated the culture, affecting the motivations for military service as well (Charles Moskos' *homo economicus*).[16]

Despite this broad secular and objective trend, the citizen-soldier ideal has nevertheless continued to maintain its normative status in our cultural

[15] See, e.g., Morris Janowitz, *The Professional Soldier: A Social and Political Portrait* (Free Press, 1964).

[16] Moskos, "The Marketplace All-Volunteer Force: A Critique." Philip Bobbitt provides a broader historical context in which to think about the tensions between the civic republican and economic models of military motivation. Taking a broader historical view, he argues that the era in which the "nation-state" was the predominant political unit in international relations has given way (albeit in an imperfect, complex way) to the era of globalization in which the "market state" is the predominant or competing model of political organization. See Bobbitt, *The Shield of Achilles: War, Peace, and the Course of History* (Alfred A. Knopf, 2002); and Bobbitt, *Terror and Consent: The Wars of the Twenty-First Century* (Random House, 2008).

understanding – especially in the military, whose self-image and normative justification are so intimately tied to the idea of sacrifice for the nation. As a result, Krebs observes that liberal-individualist and republican-communitarian images of the military coexist in the minds of soldiers and the public. "In other words, the citizen-soldier tradition might be reconceptualized as a set of rhetorical conventions to which social and political actors, both claimants and authorities, give voice.... What are these rhetorical conventions? Occupying the discursive space opposite the citizen-soldier is the *employee*-soldier whose political allegiances are flexible and whose fighting skills can be bought."[17] Given the tension between liberal and republican (self-interest/patriotic duty) principles in American political culture, one would expect military and non-military citizens to emphasize both self-interested and self-sacrificing motives when asked about soldiers' reasons for joining the services. Krebs considers the following questions:

1. Do soldiers and veterans narrate their own service in terms of patriotism (altruism/voluntarism)? Obligation (coercion)? Self-interest (egoism)?
2. Are soldiers and veterans praised (criticized) as paragons (negative models) of patriotism (treason)? Obedience (disobedience?) or as high-performing employees (incompetents)?
3. Are special rights claimed on the basis of special obligations performed (e.g., battlefield sacrifice)? Are claims granted on that basis? If they are turned aside, on what basis?

Applying these questions, Krebs poses the key hypothesis: "Cultural practices are typically laced through with contradictions and tensions, and thus it would not be surprising to find representations consistent with both models."[18]

Our survey responses are clearly in line with Krebs' expectations. Based on the answers given, we were able to construct several response categories to organize the information provided by cadets. While there is always some subjectivity in coming up with these types of categories, we are confident that these categories capture most of the responses given, and we are also confident in the ranking of answers given – although where percentages are close, we would consider the response a tie. The categories we came up with, and the percentage of cadets listing that response, are given in Table 8.1 (the percentages add up to more than 100 percent because each cadet could list more than one reason).

After service and scholarship support, the next three highest motives for joining ROTC were, respectively, future career prospects or promise of employment; interest in a particular branch; and development of leadership skills. The promise of a job was one of the important reasons for joining ROTC, which is also consistent with liberal-individualist motivation. In contrast, interest in particular features of one of the branches of the armed forces and development of leadership skill reflect republican or communitarian motivation.

[17] Ronald R. Krebs, "The Citizen-Soldier Tradition in the United States: Has Its Demise Been Greatly Exaggerated?" *Armed Forces & Society* 36, 1 (2009): 161–2. Emphasis in original.

[18] Krebs, "The Citizen-Soldier Tradition in the United States," p. 162.

TABLE 8.1. *Cadets' Reasons for Joining ROTC*

Response Category	Percentage of Cadets Listing Response
To serve county, the cause of freedom, duty, be part of the military, etc.	57.6
Scholarship money to further education	56.4
Future career prospects or promise of employment	27.1
Interest in particular branch (fly jets, be a Marine officer, etc.)	25.9
To gain leadership ability	21.1
Build character/self-improvement/take on a challenge	12.9
Tradition (family, other)	7.1
Experience something other students may not experience	5.9
N = 85	

Several other reasons were offered, although these reasons appear to have weighed less heavily in the decision to join ROTC. Building character was mentioned by several cadets as an important reason for joining, as was family tradition. Several cadets believed that honoring their parents and grandparents who served was a reason to join, as was the desire to network. Some of the cadets believed that ROTC was a way to experience something other students did not get a chance to experience.

Only a few cadets did not offer at least one liberal and one republican reason for joining ROTC, which suggests that the decision to become a citizen-soldier reflects a complex set of motivations, neither simply communal nor individualistic. The importance of republican/communitarian motivation suggests that the citizen-soldier ideal is alive and well.

As there were eighty-five responses in this category, the categories listed in Table 8.1 present only a snapshot of the reasons given for joining ROTC. Most of the responses involved a mix of motives, and they differed from one another mainly in terms of the ranking of motives and the eloquence (and terseness) of the responder. We simply quote some representative responses because the comments speak for themselves. What is distinctive about this set of responses is the importance of duty and leadership. "R" denotes an answer from a single respondent.

R: (1) Fearless leaders have defended this country so I can observe my freedom today, and I feel that I am capable of maintaining this freedom for years to come. (2) I have always valued my education, and I enjoy great challenges. ROTC presents an opportunity for both. (3) My grandparents served in the military, and it is an honor to serve after them.

R: (1) Great opportunity to serve. (2) Offers a lot more challenging and unique career options than I would otherwise have available as an engineer. (3) Pays for my school.

R: (1) I wanted to serve my country and do my civic duty. (2) I wanted to have a sense of adventure in my life after college. (3) I wanted to develop my leadership skills as well as my ability to work within a team structure. (4) Job security.

R: From most important to me to least important: serving America, protecting our freedoms, discipline, leadership development, building character, seeing the world, desire to do something great, keep in shape, declaring independence from parents, job security, chance to excel.

R: (1) To serve my country (2) To receive a high quality education with an emphasis on leadership (3) To surround myself with motivated people of good character.

R: (1) Help protect my country and our way of life. (2) Long term career benefits and job opportunities. (3) Financial support. (4) What other job lets you fly supersonic jets?

We can also say something about the civil–military gap by comparing the perspectives of student-soldiers and their non-ROTC counterparts (the evaluation of the responses of non-cadets is presented in the next chapter). We did not ask non-cadets what they think motivated cadets to join ROTC, but their answers to our questions about exposure to ROTC often contained information that was pertinent to this question. In this regard, both cadets and non-cadets emphasized duty-sacrifice–based *and* self-interested motives for military service. Interestingly, non-cadets gave less weight to self-interested motives than cadets, perhaps because their separation from the military put them in a position to idealize that service. (Idealization is partly a function of distance or unfamiliarity.) This difference suggests that the civil–military "gap" can lead not only to negative alienation and suspicion, but also to an opposite effect: an idealization of the other that is unrealistic in the other direction.[19] On the other hand, some civilian students – a clear minority – reported that their concrete exposure to cadets decreased their respect for the military for a variety of reasons, including the fact that the cadets' conduct and attitudes fell short of the citizen-soldier ideal. These responses reflect the continued power of the citizen-soldier ideal *for non-military students*. One non-cadet, for example, related, "I have attended many of the ROTC social functions with friends who are members. It was my experience that most were there to get their education paid for, and I felt they did not take their responsibilities seriously." This negative assessment appears to be based on two concerns: The primary motivation of ROTC students is self-interest, not service; and the training is not rigorous enough, thereby compromising the citizen-soldier ideal and jeopardizing the national interest in a dangerous world. The latter concern reflects a commitment to "realism," which we will discuss in a moment. Similarly, one of the soldiers who was not a member of ROTC commented that ROTC does not add much to the university because the

[19] See, for example, Andrew J. Bacevich, *The New American Militarism: How Americans Are Seduced by War* (Oxford University Press, 2005).

cadets do not have much experience with actual war – a perspective that also suggests a thorough commitment to realism.

Question 2: Why ROTC Is Important for the Country and University

We then asked the cadets **why, in a general sense, they felt that ROTC is important for the country and for university education, for both members of ROTC and for non-members.** The cadets themselves reflected on their purpose in the university. Table 8.2 lists the percentage of cadets listing each response category. Responses are divided into benefits for the military and benefits for the university.

A plurality of cadets identified training and preparing future officers as the primary reason for ROTC on campus. Several cadets also highlighted diversity within the officer corps, stating that ROTC provides a different education than the military academies and Officer Candidate School. (These responses reflect the Huntington and Janowitz perspectives on civil–military relations, respectively, suggesting the coexistence of these perspectives in the citizen-soldier ideal.)[20] Many cadets also remarked that ROTC helped students understand what they are getting into before receiving their commission, and several emphasized the importance of interacting with civilian students.

TABLE 8.2. *Cadets' Views on the Importance of ROTC to the Military and University*

Response Category	Percentage of Cadets Listing Response
Benefits for the Military	
Training and preparing future officers/need for more officers	38.8
Increasing diversity of office corps relative to academies and Officer Candidate School	14.1
Opportunity to experience military life before commission	10.6
Officers have opportunities to interact with citizens	8.2
No benefits to the military	1.1
Benefits for the University	
To actually see and interact with members of the military "bridges the gap" between soldiers and civilians	45.9
Good example to students, such as discipline, leadership, or morals	26.7
Symbolic reminder of those who are willing to defend this country and those who have sacrificed for this country	16.5
ROTC is not directly relevant for non-ROTC students	2.4
N = 85	

20 Samuel P. Huntington, *The Soldier and the State: The Theory and Politics of Civil–Military Relations* (Harvard University Press, 1957); Janowitz, *The Professional Soldier*.

Cadets spent more time discussing the relevance of ROTC to the university. Nearly half of the cadets mentioned that ROTC is important to "bridge the gap" between soldiers and civilians. The cadets appeared to be well aware of controversy over the military on campus, and they believed that their presence helped students to see what the military is really like. Several cadets mentioned that ROTC allows students to see that military officers are just like them in many respects.

Over a quarter of the cadets mentioned setting a good example as one of the reasons that ROTC is important on campus, and several alluded to the importance of symbolic reminders of the military on campus. Cadets offering these benefits of ROTC reflected the belief that service is a republican virtue. Symbolism matters, for as one student stated, "it is important to let them know that there are people out there fighting a war." The cadets understood the value of diversity of opinion, perhaps because they are aware of controversy over the military. Regardless of the reason, it seems evident that the members of ROTC believe in the value of productive friction and seek to encourage it on campus. Less than 2 percent of the cadet respondents believe that there are no benefits to ROTC on campus.

The qualitative responses were very interesting, offering greater nuance and precision than simple numerical calculation can convey. Perhaps the most important contribution pertains to the growth of mutual respect and recognition based on actual exposure. Many respondents also underscored the inability of the service academies and Officer Candidate School to make a sufficient number of officers available. In addition, many of the cadets believed that ROTC adds to the diversity of the corps of officers because students who are in the universities bring different perspectives to the military from those in the service academies.

In harmony with our thesis, cadets also offered several reasons that they believed ROTC is important for the university, not just the military. The strongest reasons were to dispel myths about the military and to educate non-military students to see that military members are not so different from themselves. (ROTC dispels the notion of the military as the "other.") Most importantly, ROTC can "humanize" the military on campus. Humanizing the ROTC allows the program, as it were, to enter the "diversity process" of engagement and interchange that Scott E. Page and cognitive diversity theorists discuss, for it brings the program within the ambit of moral legitimacy and recognition.[21] A similar process of humanization appears to have taken place in the military regarding homosexual service members, as high levels of tolerance were reported by soldiers who had had actual exposure to gays among their ranks.[22] One student in the ROTC program at Wisconsin said, "ROTC can help reduce

[21] See Scott E. Page, *The Difference: How the Power of Diversity Creates Better Groups, Firms, Schools, and Societies* (Princeton University Press, 2007).

[22] U.S. Department of Defense, *Report of the Comprehensive Review of the Issues Associated with a Repeal of "Don't Ask, Don't Tell"* (2010): http://www.defense.gov/home/features/2010/0610_gatesdadt/DADTReport_FINAL_20101130(secure-hires).pdf.

ignorance and dispel myths about the military and its culture," while another cadet spoke of how ROTC "personalizes the military for those who feel we are only present in foreign places." A third cadet observed that many non-ROTC students "are familiar with ROTC/military people and thus have firsthand experience with them and don't have to rely on stereotypes and rumors." Recall the student quoted in Chapter 2, whose words point to the theme of "recognition" that we discussed in Chapters 3 and 6 : ROTC "gives people a chance to understand what life is like on the 'other side,' since military life and civilian life are two segregated societies."

A related major belief concerned building a bridge between the military and civilian society, comprising another important component of the citizen-soldier ideal. Two representative comments capture this perspective: "ROTC is important because it provides our nation's military with well-educated and well-rounded officers"; "Without it, all officers would come from military academies and prior enlistment programs. ROTC gives normal citizens a chance to interact with those who will become the leaders of the future."

Knowledge conveyed through exposure consists of both factual and what we could call "existential" truths. Factual knowledge deals with technical military matters (what the military does, what cadets do on campus, the military's role in wars, and so on), whereas existential factors concern such matters as sacrifice, effort, challenge, and bearing the responsibilities of leadership. These factors – especially the latter – are also related to what we called the "moral difficulties of democracy" in Chapter 2: Despite the civil and peaceful aspirations of liberal democratic orders, legitimate violence is sometimes necessary to maintain and secure the order, and certain attributes of character are necessary to reconcile the legitimate use of force with democratic norms (courage, intellectual grasp, ethical training, and such).[23] One cadet remarked, "Through the years, people who have consistently been in class with me eventually learn a lot about the military and are always asking questions, whether it be something they saw in the news, a question on my uniform, what kind of training we do, etc." Another respondent framed his or her answer in the light of what Samuel Huntington calls "conservative realism": "The military, like it or not, is necessary for any nation."[24] Another opined further on a realist theme:

Some cadets will go on to be high ranking, decision making commanders who might have life and death decisions handed to her/him daily. ROTC also helps non-members understand that even though some may not think the applications of the military are the greatest, the military is still needed for now. I think it helps people understand the role

[23] ROTC leadership courses involve ethics as much as anything. See, e.g., George R. Lucas and Capt. W. Rick Rubel, eds., *Ethics and the Military Profession: The Moral Foundations of Leadership*, 2nd Edition (U.S. Air Force Academy, Pearson, Longman, 2007). On how being a warrior entails strict ethical strictures and limits, see Shannon E. French, *The Code of the Warrior: Exploring Warrior Values Past and Present* (Rowman and Littlefield, 2003).

[24] See Huntington, *The Soldier and the State*, p. 63. See also Chapter 11 of this book.

of the military more, and lets people know we are just normal guys/gals who made the choice to be in the armed forces.

Non-ROTC students also referred often to the theme of realism. Realism differs from the citizen-soldier theme because it is less an ethical ideal and more an attitude and understanding of the nature of the world. To be sure, as we discussed in Chapters 1 and 2, and will see in our discussion of realism in Chapter 11 on security studies, the most profound forms of realism are ultimately steeped in such normative theories as moral realism and republican *virtu* (facing the harsh realities and truths of the world is a matter of character).[25] In this sense, we would make a distinction between moral realism and realism per se. At the same time, both moral realism and realism also make universal claims about the nature of the world that transcend normative models of citizenship and soldiering. Indeed, the most austere version of realism is indifferent, in principle, to the model of soldiering that happens to prevail in any particular society, unless that model has an impact on the polity's ability to act in a realistic manner. In theory, austere realists might prefer a mercenary military force if it enables the nation to act more effectively in the international arena – effectiveness is praised over virtue. In a sense, the debate posed by the citizen-soldier ideal constitutes a domestic politics version of the tension in American foreign policy and international relations theory between idealism and realism – a tension with deep roots in the American political tradition.[26] Idealism is based on America's commitment to democratic norms and principles of freedom in the world, principles related to the citizen-soldier ideal as well. Realism accepts the fact that there are limits to these principles in the international field, and that the nation sometimes has to accept nondemocratic regimes as partners. And, as Huntington avers, realism is historically an aspect of the "military mind." (As we discussed in Chapter 1, the realism of Hans Morgenthau that we endorse is more complex, embodying a tension between austere realism and idealism that is truer to statesmanship and the American regime.)

The tension between realism and idealism in foreign policy coexists with the related, yet different, tension between self-interest and republicanism that Krebs posits at the heart of the citizen-soldier dilemma. Our respondents had clashing perspectives on this tension. Some construed ROTC and realism as consistent, whereas others considered ROTC an ineffective tool to defend the nation. In the latter cases, the commitment to realism outweighed the commitment to the citizen-soldier ideal. A member of the National Guard who attended some ROTC physical training exercises provided a good example of a realism critique:

[25] See, e.g., A. J. H. Murray, "The Moral Politics of Hans Morgenthau," *Review of Politics* 58 (1996): 81–107; on the political virtue (*virtu*) of facing hard truths about the world, see J. G. A. Pocock's classic book, *The Machiavellian Moment: Florentine Political Thought and the Atlantic Republican Tradition* (Princeton University Press, 1975).

[26] For a detailed historical overview of the dialectical influences of realism and idealism in American foreign policy history, see Norman A. Graebner, "Realism and Idealism," in *Encyclopedia of American Foreign Policy* (Gale, 2002).

"I ... found them completely unorganized and arrogant. Junior Officers have just as much to learn about the military as the lowest enlisted soldier, if not more. I think veterans on campus are a better asset, we have real-world experience. ROTC cadets are just playing soldier." Each of the five veterans in our Veteran Focus Group offered very similar observations.[27]

The "existential" survey responses were among the most interesting, and closely related to variables that Krebs associates with the citizen-soldier ideal. After relating how ROTC is the most "efficient" means of training officers, a cadet discussed the "secondary benefits" of the program in existential terms: "These secondary benefits are a greater awareness among the student body of the sacrifice involved with military service, and thus a greater respect for military members." In a related vein, another respondent observed, "It is equally important that non-military members be informed about what the ROTC units have done, are doing, and what they are preparing to do to better appreciate the effort the military is exerting. ROTC at a university personalizes the military. ... ROTC members can be an example of the proud heritage the military carries."

Several cadets emphasized something that Harvard professor Ruth Wisse – one of the few outspoken faculty advocates for ROTC at Harvard – underscored in an interview: how having ROTC on campus is a visible, tangible reminder of the military and its role in defending liberal democracy. (See the discussion in Chapter 2 regarding "education in the regime.") Wisse, we have seen, emphasized that ROTC is a constant reminder that democracy has a price and that the military bears that cost.[28] A representative example of this position among our respondents is the following comment: "I think it is important for members of the University to actually see members of the military, instead of just hearing about them. It is easy for people to become detached from things that they have no interaction with." Another respondent concurred: "It is good to have military presence on campus to remind students of what people have done and are still doing to defend our country and our way of life."

Finally, several military students referred to how ROTC contributes to the diversity of experience and knowledge on campus. (This theme is also implicit in many of the statements already quoted.) One student, for example, observed, "For the University, particularly here in Madison, it provides a more balanced view of our military amidst a strongly anti-war population."

Questions 3 and 4: Negative and Positive Experiences

The next set of questions **asked cadets about positive and negative experiences with ROTC**. A majority of cadets did not experience negative repercussions, but nearly 40 percent said that they had (see Table 8.3). We divided negative experiences into several categories. Conflict with student protesters or particular students groups was the most common negative response. Encountering

[27] Veterans Focus Group interview, UW-Madison, November 2009.

[28] Interview with Harvard University Professor Ruth Wisse, November 2007.

TABLE 8.3. *Negative Experiences of Cadets*

Response	Percentage of Cadets Listing Response
None	63.8
Conflict with student protesters or particular student groups	12.1
Negative comments from civilians	9.6
Problems with faculty or TAs, including generalizations about the military	7.2
Feeling of antimilitary sentiment on campus, including vandalism expressing hostility toward the military	6.0
N = 83	

protests is not in itself a negative experience, as our theory of productive friction (linked to free speech) teaches. Indeed, being exposed to protests against war and the military constitutes a valuable part of the productive friction process, as some of our cadet respondents acknowledge in comments that are recounted later in this section. Encouraging protest is part of productive friction, provided it is not violent, and it is a reason that ROTC should be on campus even if people disagree with it – otherwise, such fledgling soldiers will probably never be exposed to protests, especially with ROTC's retreat to southern redoubts. But many of the experiences reported by our cadets were not of this "Millian" nature, but rather more personal and acrimonious. Whether such interactions are part of productive friction is a question we will let readers resolve. The other relevant categories included negative comments from civilians, problems with faculty or teaching assistants (TAs), and a feeling of antimilitary sentiment. Several cadets mentioned that they felt that the Madison campus was hostile to the military without experiencing any negative repercussions directly. One student, for example, remarked about antiwar graffiti.

In considering the responses provided in this section, the reader should bear in mind three facts: (1) Nearly two-thirds of our respondents reported having no negative experiences whatsoever; (2) a larger percentage mentioned positive experiences, which we present shortly; and (3) being exposed to criticism can be good for productive friction – indeed, there can be no friction when thoughts and preferences are in perfect harmony. Accordingly, we must not necessarily judge such encounters as purely negative.

If we had to identify a key feature of the responses, it was the perception that the military on campus is "different." The military is often viewed as the "other," something strange and discomforting, eliciting fundamental value/preference conflict. Once again, this fact can be constructive for the reasons mentioned. It becomes negative when the gap is so great that it disallows productive friction. The following responses illustrate how reaction to the visibility of the military evokes the military's *sui generis* status on campus, sometimes causing special notice or awkwardness. These comments are evidence of the "gap" thesis, but they are also indicative of the importance of appropriate exposure in compelling citizens to confront this tension. Several responses suggest there is some disconcerting friction: "Some people give us some trouble about the military when in uniform, but, very rarely, sometimes I feel awkward in class and some professors treat me differently when I'm in uniform than when I'm not." In one of the most thought-provoking comments, another cadet reflected on how his or her presence provoked silence in others:

> I know of people in my unit who have had negative comments made to them or have been spit on. The worst I have had to deal with are the many stares from people on the streets or in class. One time, I was walking to a joint service dinner in my SDBs [service dress blues, or formal uniforms] and there was a group of girls moving towards me. They were laughing, joking, and having a good time. The annoying yet humorous part is that when they saw me, they immediately fell silent.

Many students referred to the difference between being in uniform and out of uniform. The uniform is a visible display of the military, and it symbolizes the military's special status, its discipline, and, perhaps, its potential for violence. (Similarly, many commentators have observed the special symbolism of a police officer in uniform as opposed to being out of uniform.) During the 1960s, the issue of drill and uniform display generated considerable debate on campuses and in the military, for drill and the wearing of the uniform comprised the public face of ROTC on campus, accentuating the contrast between military training and civilian educational practices. In response, the military loosened requirements for drill and the wearing of uniforms during the 1960s and 1970s in order to quell campus hostility, which was severe at many schools.[29] But such practice has made a comeback with the return of military pride and its contributions in the age of the All-Volunteer Force. (Cadets attaining the rights to perform color guard and flag ceremonies at Columbia are another good example of such symbolism, as we discussed in Chapter 7.) Cadets and commanders are now counseled to feel honor in the uniform and drill. This pride is consistent with the institutionalization of a new "Warrior Ethos" program and "Soldier's Creed" adopted by the Army Chief of Staff in late 2003. The previous creed, which had prevailed since Vietnam, emphasized the uniform and training as they related to commitment to the country and the military as an institution. The new Warrior Ethos preserves this commitment, but emphasizes commitment to one's fellow soldiers and warrior values more

[29] See the extensive discussion of this issue in Michael Neiberg, *Making Citizen Soldiers: ROTC and the Ideology of American Military Service* (Harvard University Press, 2000), esp. p. 121. Several works, in addition to Neiberg's, have chronicled the verbal and physical attacks on ROTC during this period; see, e.g., Kenneth J. Heineman, *Campus Wars: The Peace Movement at American State Universities in the Vietnam Era* (NYU Press, 1993). On anti-ROTC protest, including the firebombing at the University of Wisconsin, see Cronon and Jenkins, *The University of Wisconsin: A History, 1945–1971, Renewal to Revolution*, chs. 7, 8.

than the previous creed.[30] The Army defended the new ethos by citing the need to reaffirm a shared Army identity in an age of military specialization and fragmentation. Critics worry that the new ethos widens the gap between civilian and military values by downplaying the commonality of soldiers and citizens.[31] At the same time, the new Army creed reflects the tenets of realism – that the military is a fighting force that consists of *warriors*.

Regardless, wearing the uniform has become a matter of pride, although it still can evoke uncomfortable reactions, as more than one cadet and commander recounted. One UW-Madison ROTC commander who responded to our survey questions was especially upset at disrespect for the uniform, calling it a

> great shame that ROTC students cannot walk around on this campus in their uniforms with a sense of pride and accomplishment, free from the concern that they will be viewed negatively by their non-ROTC peers, will face ridicule for their opinions, or silent persecution for their commitment to our country. I've been to many college campuses with ROTC programs – they are not all like this place. The general support that you see from the American people is not echoed here at UW.[32]

Some cadets reported similar experiences. "With students, they mostly will ignore me if I am in uniform," one cadet remarked. "If I say something to one of them, they appear shocked, as if they're surprised I am talking to them. Their

[30] See Vernon Loeb, "Army Plans Steps to Heighten 'Warrior Ethos,'" Washington Post, September 8, 2003. The new Creed reads: "I am an American Soldier: I am a Warrior and a member of a team. I serve the people of the United States, and live the Army Values/ I will always place the mission first/I will never accept defeat/ I will never quit/ I will never leave a fallen comrade/ I am disciplined, physically and mentally tough, trained and proficient in my warrior tasks and drills/ I always maintain my arms, my equipment and myself/ I am an expert and I am a professional/ I stand ready to deploy, engage, and destroy, the enemies of the United States of America in close combat/ I am a guardian of freedom and the American way of life/ I am an American Soldier." The previous Creed said: "I am an American Soldier: I am a member of the United States Army – a protector of the greatest nation on earth/ Because I am proud of the uniform I wear, I will always act in ways creditable to the military service and the nation it is sworn to guard/ I am proud of my own organization. I will do all I can to make it the finest unit in the Army/ I will be loyal to those under whom I serve. I will do my full part to carry out orders and instructions given to me or my unit/ As a soldier, I realize that I am a member of a time-honored profession – that I am doing my share to keep alive the principles of freedom for which my country stands/ No matter what the situation I am in, I will never do anything, for pleasure, profit, or personal safety, which will disgrace my uniform, my unit, or my country/ I will use every means I have, even beyond the line of duty, to restrain my Army comrades from actions disgraceful to themselves and to the uniform/ I am proud of my country and its flag/ I will try to make the people of this nation proud of the service I represent, for I am an American Soldier."

[31] Interview with Stephen Tynosky, U.S. Army. May 2008. For a very thoughtful discussion of the costs and benefits of the new warrior ethos of "leave no fallen comrade behind," see Leonard Wong, "Leave No Man Behind: Recovering America's Fallen Warriors," *Armed Forces & Society* 31, 4 (2005): 599–622.

[32] See our commander/staff survey, from which we draw illustrative examples. Space considerations prevented presenting this survey in the same detail as the cadet and student surveys, but it is available from the authors.

first reaction is that of being intimidated. It is something I don't get out of uniform, only while in uniform." Another detailed,

> The only negative repercussions I have seen [are] when we wear our uniforms around campus once per week. The [non-military] staff has responded well and unbiased towards me, but people along the street will slander you by saying remarks out loud at you. One such example was walking down State Street in Madison, WI, and having a well-dressed, mid/upper-class white male call me a baby killer as I walked past and spit on the ground next to me.

Other respondents provided a range of negative examples, from being ignored or taken for granted to being treated in a hostile fashion. One complained of the campus's general "apathy" regarding the program and its students, while another expressed dismay at the "indignation" too many students feel, which "stems from their ignorance," especially their blaming the military for military actions that are ultimately promulgated by political leaders. ("I hate the Iraq War, therefore I hate you.") This theme came up more than once among both cadets and our student respondents. It is important because it shows that some students are ignorant of a central tenet of the military–civilian relationship and the constitutional order: distinguishing the military from military policy fashioned by political leaders (or worse, such students understand the distinction, yet let their emotions over policy override their judgment).[33] Students who reacted to ROTC cadets in this fashion represent a failure of civic education. Another cadet recoiled at the stereotyping of a professor in the humanities. "The only really bad incident that I have had was with a humanities faculty member. She thought that she could generalize about the military and say things that she did not know about, so I had to correct her. It was pretty unpleasant."

More overtly negative experiences include being called a "baby killer," being "spat upon" by antiwar or antimilitary students, and observing "U.S. Troops Are War Criminals" painted on the outside of a building on campus. One student has had to endure many negative experiences. "I have experienced a range of reactions from individuals on this campus and in the surrounding community. The negative behaviors have included, but are not limited to: dirty looks, name-calling, heckling, open hostility, unwillingness to participate in conversation, and more physical responses. The worst physical incident involved having a hot beverage dumped on me while in uniform."

We then asked about **positive repercussions from belonging to ROTC on campus**. Despite the campus's traditional wariness of the military, well over 90 percent of cadets benefited from expressions of gratitude for their service. Such encounters are good, but they can also amount to flattery, which would undercut productive friction. Interestingly, non-military students (in the eyes of cadets) appear considerably more interested in learning about cadet life – lifestyle

[33] We acknowledge that sometimes political leaders are pressured by military leaders to make certain decisions, for better or worse, depending on the situation. It is not evident that such is the case in the Iraq War or the War on Terror.

issues – than asking cadets about military policy and war. (We were disappointed at this finding, but the concern about lifestyle is a good start.) Cadets were often asked about the nature of ROTC, and how ROTC students navigate or balance the two worlds of the military and civilian life on a liberal campus. As we discussed in Chapter 3, in order for value/preference conflict and friction to be productive, sufficient common ground must exist in the first place. Perhaps the best way to build such common ground lies in this process of humanization and personalization taking place in the context of campus activities and campus life. In this vein, one cadet reported that, "People are just generally impressed that we are able to function simultaneously in two very different environments." Another remarked, "I have had many people (students, professors, random adults) walk up to me while I am in uniform and thank me for what I do and also others who show keen interest in what all is involved in the ROTC program. Many are curious what life is like as a cadet at a liberal school." The response categories we identified, and the percentage of cadets listing this response, are provided in Table 8.4.

Previously we saw how wearing the uniform can be an occasion for derision. But the flip side of the coin appears to come up more often, as several respondents wrote about specific incidents of praise. One cadet testified:

> There have been a few times when people have stopped me on the streets or seen me in lines and have thanked me for what I do.... And not only that, but the people respect the uniform and therefore respect my brothers in arms overseas and around the world protecting their freedoms. People that I am closer to are always asking me about what ROTC is like and several friends have decided to join the Navy or Marine Corps after graduation partly because of this.

Even bus and car drivers have gotten into the act while pursuing their routines, according to two students. "Bus drivers will stop and ask if I need a ride early in the morning, some people on the streets will thank me for my service, and others just ask lots of questions, mostly why I joined," said one. Another described how, "Two years ago I was walking with some friends down the road, and a car pulled off the side of the road, the guy got out, and shook all of our hands and thanked us for our service. I have also had several students ask about the service or the ROTC program."

TABLE 8.4. *Positive Experiences of Cadets*

Response	Percentage of Cadets Listing Response
None	6.0
Positive feedback about service	48.2
Questions/interest about ROTC	32.5
Ask opinion about war	10.8
N = 83	

Some of the respondents pointed out that others on campus treat them with special respect because of their membership in ROTC. One recounted that "people expect more of me (hold me to higher standards) and are often interested in my political views. I can't count how many times my roommates/friends have introduced me as a Marine." Another cadet stated that, "My roommate in particular likes to 'brag' that I am in the Navy and admires my dedication and strength when it comes to any activities we may have. When other students find out that I am in the ROTC unit, they act very surprised and then ask me a lot of questions about the activities we do and how physically demanding the program is."

Questions 5 and 6: Other Positive Effects on the Campus

We also asked two related questions about possible positive effects that ROTC and its cadets might have had on campus. These are the cadets' perceptions of the benefits of ROTC. We recognize that a more "objective" measure of the benefits of ROTC would be desirable. For example, future research should strive to identify more precisely the impact of ROTC or interactions with ROTC members on outcomes such as support for the military on campus. We would hypothesize that more interactions with ROTC would lead to greater understanding of the military or a more open mind when it came to such matters. Our surveys, because they emphasize perceptions and beliefs of cadets, do not allow us to make causal claims about the effect of ROTC units or interactions with ROTC on objective outcomes. Nevertheless, we believe it is important to understand the reasons the cadets themselves entertain for ROTC on campus. In a way, this is *their* statement of their purpose on campus.

The first such question was more general: We asked the cadets about **what they felt were the major benefits of ROTC for the UW campus that they have experienced.** The second question asked more specifically about **the positive impacts that their belonging to ROTC has had the learning process and understanding on campus.** We asked about experiences in a classroom or in interpersonal relations with other members of the community. The results for the first question appear in Table 8.5.

Cadets believed that ROTC enhanced the quality of the student body by educating people to do "the right thing" as moral leaders or exemplars. Many cadets said that they are strongly encouraged to undertake volunteer contributions, including community service, blood drives, and various forms of philanthropy. As just mentioned, sharing in the various activities of the campus appears to be one of the most effective ways to bridge differences. Such tasks can be considered part of the new military's broader world mission, which includes cultural and developmental tasks.[34] Setting examples of leadership

[34] See "Ivies and the Military: Toward Reconciliation," Conference at Harvard Divinity School, Cambridge, MA, April 3–4, 2009, esp. Panel 5, "Sea Changes in the Military Mission," Major General Tom Wilkerson (USMC, Ret.), moderator: http://hopetending.org/; General David H. Petraeus, "Beyond the Cloister," *American Interest* (July–August 2007).

TABLE 8.5. *Cadets' Perceptions of Benefits of ROTC on Campus*

Response	Percentage of Cadets Listing Response
Volunteering at campus events	26.3
Demonstrates or showcases leadership and virtue through various ROTC activities	14.1
Constructive interactions between military students and civilian students and faculty	10.0
Increased awareness of the contribution of the military to the nation	8.8
Adding to the diversity of viewpoints and values on campus	8.8
Providing role models for other students	7.5
Enhancing the reputation of the military on campus	7.5
No benefits or negative effects	2.5
N = 80	

was also stressed. "We do some great volunteer work and try to set the example for leadership and academics at UW." (The focus group of UW student veterans also stressed *leadership* as the single most important impact they have on non-military students. They gave examples of taking the initiatives to lead in class exercises and in extracurricular activities. Indeed, their feeling about this impact seemed even stronger than that of the ROTC students.)[35] Another student referred to the "discipline, respect, and leadership" that ROTC provides. Cadets' emphasis upon leadership extended beyond ROTC to the classroom and student organizations. In a similar vein, cadets cited moral leadership. "[ROTC] teaches me to do the right thing when no one else is looking," one student stated, while two others spoke about cadets being models of discipline: "It teaches discipline, respect, and leadership." ROTC provides "Presentation skills, demonstrating leadership, attaining higher levels of ethics." "My campus gets high-performing and disciplined individuals added to its student body."

As we saw previously, ROTC students also espouse the citizen-soldier idea of bridging civilian and soldier worlds. Thus, one student said, "I believe that the presence of ROTC has made other students aware that the people fighting for their freedom are normal, everyday people, young adults included, and that this realization has helped bring them to a higher level of respect for those serving in the military." One aspect of unique perspectives is diversity of opinion and information. In the eyes of one student, ROTC "Assists in the diversity of the campus because it exposes the fact that there are many different institutions that one can be a part of on campus." In addition to citing moral and physical fitness, another cadet accentuated the following contribution to the campus: "ROTC involves people who bring about a different mindset and attitude to campus,

[35] Focus group interview with University of Wisconsin student veterans, November 2009.

TABLE 8.6. *Cadets' Self-Described Impact on Campus*

Response	Percentage of Cadets Listing Response
Correct or demystify stereotypes or setting the record straight	52.4
Provide a "go-to" person on war-related issues	22.0
Give the military a human face	18.3
I do not have enough experience to set the record straight	11.0
Prior experience adds to the classroom	9.8
N = 82	

therefore diversifying [the campus] even more than it already is. There are a lot of antimilitary people around, so we counterbalance that."

The second question pertaining to contributions to the campus was directed at the classroom and interpersonal encounters in the campus community. The results appear in Table 8.6. More than half of the cadets provided a response that could be described as "correcting or demystifying stereotypes or setting the record straight." Many of the cadets said that they had at some point presented information to fellow students about what they do. According to these cadets, many people on campus did not really understand what ROTC did. A good number of cadets (nearly a fifth of respondents) believed that they gave the military a human face.

These responses deal with both the classroom and interactions outside of class, and involve such things as providing specific knowledge of ROTC and military matters, furnishing more general knowledge of such matters, attitudinal factors, and personal attributes or characteristics. More than one student told us that his or her commanders have told the group not to represent the military in classroom situations, or, in the words of one respondent, "not to 'set the record straight' nor to talk about military policy" in class, lest others get the impression that the student is speaking for the military. Yet others related that they had indeed at times straightened the record, so the picture in this regard is mixed. Based on our samples, many of the discussions between student-soldiers and others in the university community take place outside the classroom, but some reported interesting instances inside the classroom as well.

General Knowledge Inside and Outside of Class

As in other domains of response, cadets emphasized how exposure to non-military students helped, in the words of one, to "demystify the military for my friends and other students that I meet." This student's comment poignantly captured the importance of establishing sufficient common ground to ameliorate the alienation that threatens civilian–military relations. Exposure to him or her outside of class (as an engineering student, he or she has had little impact inside the classroom) helped students to "realize that Marines are people who come from similar backgrounds and have similar hopes/aspirations as them and not a completely different population of our society which longs for combat and violence. I feel that I have helped to reduce some misconceptions regarding the Marines which some people hold due to the wars in Iraq/Afghanistan and also due to 'Don't Ask, Don't Tell' and the Solomon Amendment." One respondent reported that he or she has been able to "educate my friends about some aspects of the military that they find hazy," while another related that most people he or she encounters "did not know anything" about the program, but became "very impressed with what we do and the level of commitment we have towards it."

The notion of diversity of thought and unique perspective arose often in the responses to this question. Being an ROTC student "allows one to give the people around one a different perspective on the military and the people involved in it and possibly eliminating/clarify stereotypes and prejudices against the military." This different perspective can be especially useful on a liberal campus. "There are several instances where more liberal friends of mine have talked about the military, and I was able to simply 'set the record straight' and tell them that simply wasn't true to squash any biases that might have grown from the discussion."

Another aspect of diversity on a liberal campus in the era of the All-Volunteer Force is influencing non-military students to remember that soldiers are fighting real wars on behalf of the country. Such recognition is an important aspect of civic education, as articulated in Chapter 2, for it entails fathoming the reality of military force and sacrifice in service of the nation. In his book *In a Time of War: The Proud and Perilous Journey of West Point's Class of 2002*, *New York Times* reporter Bill Murphy, Jr., chronicles the stories and travails of several West Point graduates and their families as the new officers assumed duties overseas, mainly in Iraq and Afghanistan. Several of the officers died or were seriously wounded, irreparably affecting their families and loved ones. Murphy concludes the book by lamenting the fact that many such soldiers feel that the greater society has forgotten or downplayed the sacrifices they and their families have made for the country – a problem that appears to be endemic to war itself, as Paul Fussell and other keen observers have discussed in their treatises on war and society.[36] Other thinkers maintain that the alienation between warriors and nonwarriors has been growing in the decades since World War II because the way that we fight wars has had a declining impact on the rest of society. For both personal and structural reasons, as we have elucidated at several junctures in this book, the fighting of war is relatively more segmented from the rest of American society than it was in the past, changing the cultural meaning of war for citizens and the

[36] Bill Murphy, Jr., *In a Time of War: The Proud and Perilous Journey of West Point's Class of 2002* (Henry Holt, 2008). In his classic book on memory, literature, and World War I, Paul Fussell repeatedly reports soldiers lamenting in literature and in practice the inability of civilians to fathom the reality of the front. Fussell, *The Great War and Modern Memory* (Oxford University Press, 2000 [1975]).

cultural meaning of citizenship.[37] The confusions associated with the struggle against terrorism reflect this state of affairs. We are unsure whether the struggle constitutes war, law enforcement, or something else; and the vast majority of citizens have not been personally affected by the war on terror in a major way. (In our view, the struggle involves all forms of power: war; law; soft power.)[38]

Whatever its causes, the sense of betrayal that results from civilians' failure to share in the sacrifice of war is poisonous to civil–military relations, for obvious reasons. Several of the respondents to our questions focused on this problem. We have already read responses that spoke about "reminding" non-ROTC students of the efforts and sacrifices of the military. Another cadet broached this point in response to our "positive effects" question. "Some positive impacts are reminding the students that there is still a war going on overseas because people do not think about it as much as they used to." Yet another cadet put the matter more simply: "Wearing my uniform helps show college students that you can go to school and be a part of something that most people aren't a part of."

More Specific Knowledge

A few cadets referred to situations in which their ROTC backgrounds contributed to more specific knowledge, or expertise, in the classroom. (We had expected more such responses. Cadets were either reluctant to relate such stories or had few such stories to convey in specificity.) One student who had worked overseas said that his or her presence in the political science classroom added to knowledge because "we have firsthand experience" in foreign countries. Another said that his or her "more realistic understanding of the military" corrected the views of "those whose knowledge is based purely on stereotype." Two students provided more vivid, detailed examples of how their backgrounds added to the subtlety and complexity of a class in a manner highly reflective of Scott Page's notion of cognitive and value diversity. We quote them at some length because each shows how cadet input can offer a distinctive contribution to the complexity and diversity of the discussion at hand, such as that reflected in the observations of another cadet: "My unique experience and point of view provided a viewpoint that most people never heard or understood. But having them know that I am also a normal student helps them connect to what happens in the military and how that connects to their lives."

First Student: In Contemporary Moral Issues, the first topic we discussed was just war theory. It was a philosophy class and Madison is a fairly liberal campus, so needless to say

[37] On this issue, see Robert D. Hormats, *The Price of Liberty: Paying for America's Wars* (Times Books, 2007); Adrian R. Lewis, *The American Culture of War: The History of US Military Force from World War II to Operation Iraqi Freedom* (Routledge, 2007); James Burk, "The Changing Moral Contract for Military Service," in Andrew Bacevich, ed., *The Long War: America's Quest for Security Since World War II* (Columbia University Press, 2007), p. 444.

[38] On how the War on Terrorism blurs old boundaries on a variety of levels and fronts, see Philip Bobbitt's magisterial *Terror and Consent*. Bobbitt concludes that it is indeed a "war," but is acutely aware of the complexities involved.

I was the only one defending certain aspects of war. The teaching assistant in that class knew that I had no problem defending that side of the argument and frequently counted on me to further the discussion of a topic by adding the opposite view. There have been several other instances where I have changed someone's opinion on the military by getting to know me in class before they knew I was in the ROTC program.

Second Student: In classroom settings, I have been asked a couple times to give my opinion due to my military background. In philosophy, I was asked what my opinion was about the death sentence for military persons, as it is different from the civilian. More often, though, I am asked by students, maybe in a team setting, about my views on things as a military member. I have had more talks outside of classes with class members about my views on political situations, wars, presidential candidates, etc., than anywhere else. Some people are confused why the war is going on now, and I will explain that it has never stopped and has been going on for years with our involvement, and centuries between the inhabitants.

Of course, it is important to note that we are not arguing that the student-soldiers are necessarily correct when they "set the record straight." Indeed, we could go back and find some examples in our interviews where the student-soldiers are incorrect in their reading of history, their inferences, or their knowledge of different cultures. Yet to criticize them for mistakes is not our purpose. Rather, our point is that they bring a different perspective grounded in genuine experience – one that, by necessity, will sometimes be incorrect. Cadets do not hold a monopoly on truth any more than professors, non-military students, or student protesters. Our perspective suggests that bringing those into the intellectual fray who *believe* that they can set the record straight and who have a *legitimate* claim to expertise will do more to improve prospects for civic and liberal education, as well as to improve discourse regarding national security and military policy, than the crafting of institutional barriers that inhibit such interactions. In underscoring the importance of setting the record straight, we remain committed to the idea that the truths of the student-soldiers must also be challenged in order for productive friction to obtain because their knowledge is also of an imperfect sort.

Question 7: Non-ROTC Students

Our interest in interactions among various clusters emphasizes the relationship between soldiers and students, including how non-cadets influence the perspectives of cadets. To help us understand the nature of interactions between ROTC and non-ROTC students, we asked **how many non-ROTC students take part in their courses, and the benefits that non-ROTC students might bring to such courses**. The results are shown in Table 8.7. Most of the cadets stated that all ROTC courses are open to civilian students, and most knew that there were civilian students in the courses. Several cadets mentioned that there were civilians in the courses addressing leadership, which we believe reflects the

TABLE 8.7. *Influence of Non-ROTC Students in the ROTC Classroom*

Response	Percentage of Cadets Listing Response
Unaware of non-ROTC students	4.7
Do not bring that much to the table	31.7
Positive impact because of alternative perspectives	18.8
Former enlisted personnel (veterans who were enlisted) or cadets from other branches provide an alternative perspective in ROTC courses	9.4
N = 85	

recognition of the ability of the military to provide leadership skills.[39] Many of the cadets valued such students' opinions, although not without exceptions. Three cadets praised the presence of *veterans* in their classes because of the real-world experience and knowledge that they conveyed, but this relationship is intramilitary, as it were.

Some respondents felt that non-ROTC students' presence was either unhelpful or negative. One said that they are most prominent in the naval history and weapons classes, and that they "tend to be annoying, so I haven't particularly enjoyed their presence." Another observation points to two themes we have discussed previously: the intimidation that some non-military students feel in the presence of military students and the distinct senses of professionalism and *esprit de corps* to which military personnel are acculturated. The non-ROTC students "really do not bring anything to the class, and I personally think it is because they are a little intimidated because they don't know other people like battalion members know each other."

Other respondents (less numerous) offered more positive assessments that appeared more thoughtful. Some simply referred rather generically to the significance of the "civilian point of view" or "different perspectives," while others went further and presented more poignant points that directly addressed the tensions between civilian and military viewpoints. One related how students from outside of ROTC are more prone to be critical of the government: "Having the non-ROTC students definitely provides a different perspective to classes. Many of us cadets are set on the U.S. military being the greatest in the world and forget that the U.S. government makes mistakes." Another stressed how outsiders challenged the relative group-think of ROTC students: "They do bring benefits to the class because since we are all ROTC members, we have many of the same values and ideals. As non-ROTC members, they may have very

[39] A research question that we leave open is how much the non-military leadership programs are integrated with leadership courses taught by the military. There are many leadership institutes on campus, but we suspect that there would be many opportunities to build bridges between leadership institutes on campus and leadership skills taught by ROTC faculty.

different perspectives on situations that we [the cadets] all have the same opinion on." Another cadet added to this point in words directly relevant to the concept of productive friction, relating that having two or three non-ROTC students in class is important because it helps cadets to see how the civilian world views them. They "bring an outside prospective to the discussions, especially once we have been in the ROTC for a couple of years, or if we have grown up with a military background. Sometimes, having someone without a military understanding or inside knowledge helps us to understand how we are viewed by society, and even to help change some of the fallacies." One student discussed civilian and military perspectives on specific foreign policy issues, mentioning a "Colombian student in her thirties who really offered quite an interesting perspective, especially since it was during the class that we discussed foreign policy and we did regional studies, including South America. I think we all helped each other get a much better understanding of how our countries view the other. It was very helpful." Another cadet referred to the non-ROTC students who made up 10–20 percent of the students in naval/marine history courses. "Non-ROTC students do bring a different perspective to analyzing historical events/policies because they are not as familiar with naval history/customs/courtesies. I think they gain a deeper understanding of what the Marine Corps/Navy stands for and how they accomplish their missions." Finally, a cadet opined that it would benefit the program to have more non-ROTC students in the program: "I think it would be more beneficial to see greater advertisement of these classes, and incorporate a broader 'civilian' base."

Question 8: General Observation of Status on Campus

Finally, we asked the cadets in the sample if there was **anything they wanted to comment on regarding the status of the military on campus, based on their own experiences and perceptions**. The numbers indicated 65 percent of students had a good experience, 20 percent had a bad experience, and 15 percent described it as both good and bad.

The qualitative responses were very interesting, and differed in degree and intensity. Some mentioned how complex the situation is, especially now that so many military-related students are present at campuses across the country, including National Guards, veterans, ROTC, and military personnel pursuing degrees – a development that occasioned a lengthy story in the *New York Times* in early 2010.[40] A respondent praised the University of Wisconsin for providing new offices serving veteran students, including a new post in the Dean of Students office.[41] Given the sheer number of military-related students on campus, experiences are bound to be varied.

[40] Lisa W. Foderaro, "From the Battlefield to Ivy League, on the G. I. Bill," *New York Times*, January 9, 2010.

[41] See Dean of Students, UW-Madison, Veterans: http://students.wisc.edu/veterans/veterans.html.

Among positive overall impressions, one student said, "Our campus is known to be very liberal, but overall I have only experienced positive things," while another noted that, "Madison is far more supportive of ROTC students then one would think. Any anger that antiwar people might have has been shifted from the military to the administration running it." Another student supported this assessment: "I honestly thought that being in the military would bring me negative attention, with Madison being as liberal and antiwar as it is. What I have experienced has been just the opposite. I am very surprised at the positive reception I have received from students and faculty."

But other cadets were less sanguine. One was very blunt, without elaborating: "This campus is horrible in the way they treat military personnel." Another lamented, "I would like to add that the military is not given much credit on this campus. Since it is so liberal there have been several times when I have been mistreated by professors, students, and other university visitors." Another student depicted a middle ground of tolerance falling short of sincere recognition: "The military seems to be regarded with tolerance instead of pride. It seems students and faculty don't really want us to be here but will tolerate our presence instead of being proud to be part of a campus with a strong military history." After mentioning pros and cons, a final student we will quote said that dealing with the tension is part of the military mission: "That's all part of the deal, though. We persevere because that follows the uniform around, too – dedication, and a type of courage that doesn't involve weapons and far-off lands."

Let us now look at the responses of non-military students.

9

Winning Hearts and Minds?

The Consequences of Military Presence for Non-military Students

Given the purpose of this book, we were very interested in the perspectives of non-ROTC students. In our survey of such students at the University of Wisconsin, Madison, we were able to obtain information about how non-military students' interactions with ROTC – inside and outside of the classroom – had impacted them, and the nature of their basic perceptions of ROTC on campus. In general, the student respondents reported even more dynamic interactions and reactions than the cadets related, as the statements quoted in this chapter will indicate. We found this difference very interesting, for our assumption was that cadets would be more inclined to exaggerate positive effects than regular students. If such student reports are to be trusted (and there is no reason not to trust them), the presence of ROTC on this campus has had a meaningful impact on students, although it is not as strong or poignant as the ideal model of interaction would hope.

In addition to surveying numerous ROTC and civilian students concerning their interactions, we also report the responses of some students in two humanities courses that dealt with military and war themes. One course was a small seminar entitled "War and Romance," which was taught in Integrated Liberal Studies and Political Science. The other was a lecture course entitled "Military History of the United States to 1902," taught in the History Department. Although we received a low percentage of respondent returns for these courses, the responses that we received provide suggestive evidence of the thinking that such courses can inspire.

As mentioned briefly in the previous chapter, it was also evident that these students sometimes struggled to reconcile their feelings and knowledge regarding the military with their everyday beliefs. They did not often express this discomfort in explicit language; rather, it can be inferred from the way that they portray ROTC or the military as fundamentally different from themselves, even as they strive to understand (and, in some cases, appreciate) it. In Chapter 2, we discussed how the responsibilities of the military are *sui generis* in key respects, calling for the legitimate uses of force (or the threat of force) that often stand in tension with the more peaceful norms and expectations of liberal civil society. We portrayed this tension as "moral difficulties in liberal democracy." This difficulty can be articulated in conscious thought (for example, "although I disavow the use of violence, I came to understand why it might be legitimate in certain cases"; "although I could not join such an organization, I understand why the job must be done"; and so on), or it can be experienced or handled more existentially or emotionally, expressed in the juxtaposition of conflicting worldviews or experiences. We will see this difficulty in action in some of the responses depicted in this chapter, especially in the responses of students in the humanities courses that we consider.

ROTC AT WISCONSIN: CIVILIAN-STUDENT SURVEY RESPONSES

To get a handle on the impact of ROTC, we surveyed University of Wisconsin (UW) political science majors to determine their interactions with ROTC students and their knowledge of ROTC. Nearly two hundred students responded from a list of approximately eight hundred juniors and seniors majoring in political science. We began by noting their political views. About 65 percent identified themselves as somewhat or very liberal, 20 percent as moderate, 12 percent as somewhat conservative, and 3 percent as very conservative. These findings affirmed the perception of many of the student-soldiers we surveyed, who remarked how "liberal" the campus is. Our survey certainly supports this assessment. When forced to choose ("if you had to choose one party ..."), 75 percent identified as Democratic, 25 percent as Republican.

We asked how important students thought having ROTC was on a college campus. Of the students surveyed, 13.5 percent replied they felt it is extremely important, and 44.9 percent said that it is somewhat important, whereas 29 percent remarked it is not very important. We also allowed students to state that "universities should be separate from the military." Only 13 percent of students chose that response, which may be surprising given the reputation of the University of Wisconsin as a liberal, antiwar university. However, these findings are quite consistent with previous surveys or polls measuring student support for ROTC nationwide or on various campuses. Despite periodic controversies surrounding the military and the program, overall student support for ROTC has held steady in the post–World War II era, even during the Vietnam War crisis – although not without dissent.[1]

We then asked the students a series of questions about their exposure to ROTC and how it has influenced their thinking. We asked how much knowledge of ROTC they possessed and how much exposure to ROTC they have had. Among those who have had at least some exposure to ROTC, we asked **how such exposure influenced their thinking about the military as an institution or regarding the legitimacy of the military on campus**. We found some evidence of productive friction, with nearly 30 percent of students who have been exposed to

[1] This theme is stressed repeatedly in the definitive account, Michael Neiberg's *Making Citizen Soldiers: ROTC and the Ideology of American Military Service* (Harvard University Press, 2000).

TABLE 9.1. *Student Interactions with ROTC*

	How much knowledge of ROTC do you have? (%)	How much exposure have you had to ROTC? (%)	(Among students who have had at least some exposure to ROTC) How much has exposure influenced your thinking about the military? (%)
A great deal	5.2	8.3	4.0
Some	26.9	17.2	25.3
Not much	61.1	56.3	40.7
None	6.7	16.1	27.3
	N = 193	N = 185	N = 155

ROTC stating that ROTC influenced their thinking a great deal or somewhat (see Table 9.1).

These findings suggest that ROTC impacts students despite its small size relative to the student body. Although cadets and commanders felt that they had had a meaningful impact on the non-military students with whom they interacted, those students did not indicate widespread impact; in addition, many also offered stories of broader campus indifference, with one-quarter reporting direct negative experiences. Given the large size of the student body (forty thousand) and the relatively small size of ROTC, we did not expect a great deal of interaction. At the same time, a quarter of our respondents stated that they experienced some or a great deal of interaction, and only 16 percent reported having no interaction with ROTC. This suggests that even a small presence of ROTC leads to interactions with the military cluster, which would be a precondition for productive friction.

We then asked students the extent to which exposure to ROTC influenced their educational experience. Of students who had at least minimal exposure to ROTC, nearly 16 percent conveyed that having ROTC on campus influenced their educational experience a great deal or somewhat. In contrast, only 2 percent of students surveyed stated that ROTC was detrimental to their experience (only 3 students of 146 who answered this question). Of course, this leaves 82 percent of students who felt it did not impact them. Naturally, we cannot assume that students will always be influenced. It is perhaps most relevant that far more students contended that they had productive interactions rather than negative interactions with ROTC.

Open-ended questions allow us to probe more deeply into how interactions with ROTC influenced student perspectives. We asked the students to explain **how their interactions, if they had any, with ROTC influenced their beliefs about the role of the military on campus.** If the interactions had no effect, we asked the students to explain why. ROTC appears to have had a moderating effect on many students who remarked that they would have been more hostile toward the military if not for productive interactions with cadets.

The most common responses given were that exposure to ROTC increased the students' respect for military members; that ROTC students offered a different, interesting perspective; and that these interactions gave the military a more personal face. Several students said ROTC increased their support for the military, while a smaller number of students viewed ROTC as a "reality check" that led them to overcome stereotypes.

We also received several negative reactions. Some students believed ROTC interactions compelled them to feel that the program was unnecessary on campus; others said that ROTC made them feel that they did not want the military on campus. A few students believed that recruiters prey on college-age students. We estimate that approximately 85 percent of responses were positive, with the remaining 15 percent negative in terms of attitudes toward the military. Recall, once again, that a negative attitude can be conducive to productive friction, and that negative attitudes about the military are to be expected and respected in a liberal democracy.

For the most part, non-ROTC students' comments indicate that ROTC's impact is more *symbolic*, *attitudinal*, *normative*, and what we could call *existential* than purely informational or intellectual. That is, students often alluded to what we could call the "whom I know" phenomenon. A common wisdom counsels that it is not always "what you know, but whom you know" that matters; beyond meaning that personal connections are helpful in getting what one wants, this maxim points to a broader human reality: Truths and values often mean more to us when we link them to human beings whom we like or respect. (A similar claim is that facts come alive when presented in stories. Narratives in the courtroom convey facts – although we must remain on guard not to fall into the intellectual and moral quicksand of believing that narratives are all there is to truth.)[2] Our worldviews are significantly shaped by those with whom we associate, by what sociologists call our reference groups. (Recall the perhaps apocryphal story of the denizen of Manhattan's Upper West Side who exclaimed after the 1980 presidential election, "How could Ronald Reagan have won? I don't know anyone who voted for him!?") One reason for this reality is the fact that mental health consists of the appropriate balance of reason and emotion. We are not rational machines, but rather embodied minds, and our reason is influenced by our emotions, including our biases and self-interest.[3] Our survey responses lend some support to this "human, all too human" interpretation of human reality, as numerous students emphasized how exposure to ROTC humanized the cadets, whom they had previously viewed as objects of either suspicion or as curiosities.

[2] On the role of narrative and rhetoric in the courtroom, see W. Lance Bennett and Martha S. Feldman, *Reconstructing Reality in the Courtroom: Justice and Judgment in American Culture* (Rutgers University Press, 1981). For a strong critique of those who let "narrative" seduce them from seeing the actual truth, see Jeffrey Toobin, *The Run of His Life: The People v. O. J. Simpson* (Random House, 1996).

[3] See Antonio R. Damasio, *Descartes' Error: Emotion, Reason, and the Human Brain* (Quill, 2005).

Similarly, the responses of many students reflected educational effects relating to what we called "understanding the military and national defense," "education in the regime," and (to a lesser extent) "moral difficulties in liberal democracy" in Chapter 2: Exposure made them more tangibly aware of the sacrifice entailed in military service and how this sacrifice protected national security. In Allan Silver's terms, this understanding could contribute to a greater appreciation of civic duty and equal obligation. One student related how exposure to cadets made him or her more aware of national security concerns, and how such matters "may affect someone that I know." Another student reported how being exposed to cadets in classes significantly changed his or her view of them as human beings. "It definitely made me see them differently. I always thought of the military as something so far from myself, but seeing them in my classes and around campus makes me wonder about their experiences like I hadn't before." Thus, *perhaps the single most significant finding of this survey is that the most important impact of exposure to ROTC from the perspective of non-ROTC students is emotional, attitudinal, and normative in nature, rather than technical or intellectual.* Students were more prone to stress personal qualities and what ROTC represents than to delve into informational detail.

Personal exposure can also contribute to factual knowledge, of course. A good example was provided by Columbia University professor James Applegate, who chaired the Task Force on ROTC in 2004–5. At a hearing in 2008 on the second Columbia ROTC initiative (discussed in Chapter 7), Applegate witnessed a conversation/debate in which some student critics of ROTC were asserting that the military is replete with sexual harassment and harassment of gays. A woman veteran was present and corrected them by saying that she had not witnessed such behavior in her many years in the military, that it was far from prevalent, and that it was punished when known. The students immediately retracted their allegations, saying that they had had no interaction with military personnel, and that they appreciated learning something firsthand from an actual military person that ran counter to their views. Applegate said that this was the first time he realized how important the presence of veterans was on campus in providing knowledge of the military.[4]

Of course, this anecdote reminds us that we have to be aware of the problems that may arise because of deference to the military. Is the fact that the students *immediately* retracted their view a good thing for productive friction? If students capitulate to those in the military simply because of their status, it would not be very productive as far as the educational experience – and citizenship – is concerned. Some students may also want to impress those in the military, or at least be held in high regard by them. While we believe Applegate's example is the type of productive friction we envision, we still have to recognize the complexities that arise when people interact with a member of the military. Productive friction must work in more than one direction.

[4] Conversation with Columbia University professor James Applegate, October 2010.

As we discussed previously, bridging the gap between the military and civilian society (on campus or elsewhere) involves both personal and intellectual aspects. Those who harbor concerns about the gap often stress the lack of presence and tangible exposure between the two sides. Recall Ruth Wisse's observation in Chapter 2 respecting the importance of being tangibly exposed to military personnel and the uniform. Military historians of the post–World War II generation believe that the declining number of veterans among the ranks of historians is partly responsible for the decline of military history, an issue we consider at length in Chapters 10 and 11. And other students of military–civilian affairs have lamented how the lack of exposure to military members or veterans has alienated many elites from the military. In many ways, there is no substitute for actual personal exposure, for personal interactions contribute mightily to individuals' social assumptions and worldviews.[5] This said, exposure to ROTC also contributed to more technical knowledge, but this impact was secondary to the more existential and normative impacts just discussed.

We can place our responses in this section into three overarching categories. One category is respondents who had *positive* views about ROTC's contribution to the campus, but whose thoughts were *not due to exposure* to the program or cadets they had encountered. These students – most of whom were quite thoughtful – had formed their thoughts before any interactions with ROTC. The large number of students who indicated that their positive thoughts about ROTC derived from exposure supports our thesis that exposure helps bridge the gap of alienation and ignorance between the civilian and military sectors – although we will meet with some examples of students whose negative thoughts and feelings were confirmed or made worse by exposure. These responses suggest that the presence of ROTC encourages students to think about the military even if they themselves have limited interaction with cadets.

Some of our longest and most reflective responses were favorable to ROTC's presence on campus, but not necessarily because of the exposure that the respondents had to the program or to cadets. One student stated that ROTC's presence contributes to understanding the military and national defense, stressing that while the university is not a place for exposure to pro-military propaganda, it is a place for all discussion, "especially those [issues or phenomena] that affect us as directly as military presence and wars overseas. As long as those discussions remain open and thoughtful, I think ROTC presence can allow for both sides of the discussion to continue these conversations in a respectful and enlightened manner." Another student said that he or she has long entertained a realistic appreciation of society's need for military service. "Somebody has to do the country's fighting. They have to be recruited from somewhere. State universities seem like the appropriate place."

[5] See, e.g., interviews with Ruth Wisse, November 2007, and Mac Coffman, January 2008. Kathy Roth-Douquet and Frank Schaeffer, *AWOL: The Unexcused Absence of America's Upper Classes from the Military – and How It Hurts Our Country* (Harper Collins, 2006).

Two other students' comments clearly echoed our concept of productive friction and the attendant idea of intellectual diversity. One, who indicated opposition to much about the military, was nonetheless an excellent representative of these concepts. This student described himself or herself as an "anarcho-syndicalist" who opposes militarism as "counterproductive to utopian social progress" and "human potential and creativity." This same student also said that he or she has "respect [for cadets'] commitment and their perspective," that "we need a diversity of viewpoints on campus," and that "discomfort" around ROTC members is not something that compromises ROTC's legitimacy. Of course, we applaud the maturity of the student's desire to engage those of differing opinions, beliefs, and values. This student's self-described "intellectual foundation" based in political theory protected him or her from sliding into either unreflective disparagement or adulation of service members. "Some students with less fully formed political theories, alas, *do* feel uncomfortable towards ROTC members – they have no point of departure towards deeper and less personal criticism. Of course, take what I say with a grain of salt because ROTC life on campus is not a world I claim to understand completely." Another student criticized those who want ROTC

> banned from campus, which shows that they aren't willing to consider why someone would want to serve in the military or serve their country. I think people judge the military without trying to learn more about it or who serves in it. Instead I think those opposed to ROTC and the military in general just tolerate their presence on campus. Personally I support the military, but I don't think it's because I was exposed to them on campus. I formulated my opinion earlier.

From our perspective, ROTC on campus is important even for those students who formed opinions earlier because it gives them the opportunity to *change* their opinion.

The *second category* is students who said they *benefited from exposure* to ROTC and/or cadets. These responses vary across the board. Some students had significant exposure (roommates, friends, in class, and so on) whereas others had some but not much. Students also alluded to different reasons for supporting ROTC, mentioning not only such policy issues as diversity, knowledge of the military and security-related matters, and bridging the military–civilian society gap, but also such practical matters as the provision of scholarship money and career opportunity (most college students are acutely attuned to means of providing financial support in this era of unprecedentedly higher education costs). And although some derived something significant from their exposure, others experienced less impact. For example, one student "almost joined ROTC" after having met some cadets, while another (along with several others) thinks ROTC participation "is important," but can only wish he or she "had more interaction with" cadets. Another said that limited exposure in the classroom showed him or her that ROTC "involvement tends to bring a drastically different point of view on many issues." One student remarked that exposure to ROTC students in class altered his or her opinion of ROTC. "I have had a few classes with students who are part of the ROTC. I've had certain negative preexisting ideas about the ROTC and those who chose to participate in it. However after getting to know a few of them, some of those negative ideas went away." Some perceptions were more mixed. One student said exposure "made me realize the importance of dedication, honor, commitment that the military teaches," but also brought to his or her attention that a person he or she knows is in ROTC "for all the wrong reasons," which makes the program "look bad." A few other students' impressions were modified for the worse by exposure to actual ROTC cadets. One said that the handful of cadets he or she knew had negative views of the military themselves, while another student said that the cadets known to him or her had little respect for others. If true, these comments reflect non-cadets' belief that some cadets fail to live up to the citizen-soldier ideal, thereby discrediting the normative justification for ROTC. Some of the misgivings that veterans had regarding ROTC can also be traced to their belief that ROTC, at least to an extent, does not live up to the citizen-soldier ideal (although many veterans were more pragmatic, arguing instead that ROTC may not contribute much knowledge about war and relative issues because cadets have not experienced much).[6]

Several students referred to the significance of the uniform (in either positive or negative senses), as well as the related fact that cadets' presence "reminded" them of the fact of war. Here is one typical remark in this vein: "The presence of the ROTC on campus has made me more aware of issues of national security in terms of potential conflicts that my classmates may be called up to engage in, and how while international conflict may not directly affect me, it may affect someone that I know." Another student conveyed a similar impact, talking about the "human face" that the ROTC now had for him or her. This student, who came from a large suburban high school in which only 3 of 743 graduates went into the military, remarked that interacting with ROTC students, and having a "good friend" in Marine ROTC, "helped me to put a human face on the military." Another student concurred: "Being in class with ROTC students certainly makes things like the war and Iraq and Afghanistan hit closer to home. This is mostly due to the fact that I do not have any close friends in the military. Therefore, to actually see and meet students who will be serving in those conflicts does put a more human face on the war."

Exposure can also reveal that cadets are citizens like everyone else, and that the military is not monolithic in its thinking. "Interaction with ROTC has not influenced my thinking about military affairs or the role of the military on campus that much. I have a few friends who are ROTC, and listening to their experiences and outlook on topics such as the War in Iraq has given me a deeper

[6] Several cadets also pointed out that many cadets will not make it through the program (for various reasons), so some of these negative experiences may have been from cadets who will not see the program to its conclusion. More generally, whether the student is exposed to a cadet in his or her first year of the program or a cadet on the cusp of receiving his or her commission is likely to influence the kind of experience non-ROTC students have in their interaction with ROTC cadets.

appreciation for the type of diversity (both in types of people and in views) that makes up the military." Another student had a freshman woman roommate in the ROTC through whom he or she met other ROTC students. He or she observed motivations relating to both the citizen-soldier ideal and the liberal model of individual advancement: "They had some influence because I would not normally have such direct contact with ROTC students – it put a face to the program for me. It made me appreciate how important the ROTC program is because it allows students simultaneously to pursue a military career and a degree." Another related, "If anything, having ROTC students on campus (some of them with whom I am friends) has shown me a more personal face of the military. You realize they are students, just like you, and still worry about taking exams and doing homework on time." Yet another student echoed these sentiments: "Through my interactions with these friends, I have been able to see the character of ROTC members and have appreciated their different perspective [more] than that of many Madison students."

Many students echoed the themes of sacrifice and "reminding" that we encountered with the cadets. In this area, students and cadets appear to be very much on the same page. One student (already quoted earlier) said that he or she had always thought of the military as "something so far from myself," but that seeing ROTC students in class "makes me wonder about their experiences like I hadn't before." One student stressed the way that ROTC exposure reminded him of the *sui generis* nature of the military commitment – *sui generis* in the sense of the use of violence. This perspective relates to several of the impacts we elucidated in Chapter 2, including leadership, education in the regime, and the moral dilemmas of liberal democracy. "In this time of war, I think the ROTC program allows students to see that military personnel are the same people we are, but with a commitment to something potentially dangerous. When I see ROTC students on campus, I see students just like me, who are much more mature and prepared for the world than the average undergrad." Another student echoed this sentiment: "Seeing ROTC members on campus reminds me of the sacrifice and dedication so many people have made in protection of our country, which allow me to attend college. Their presence on campus reminds me that the opportunities I have should not be taken for granted."

In a similar vein, students offered observations about how ROTC presents normative and/or existential models for the campus. For example, the special theme of *duty* – a key component of the citizen-soldier ideal – as well as the theme of diversity – discussed in Chapter 2 and throughout this book – arose in some commentary. "It has shown me that there are still people that go to this school that can aspire to do things with their lives that affect much more than themselves." One student added that ROTC presented the campus with good examples of "leadership," while another was impressed at the rigors of the program. "My first-year roommate was in NROTC, and I learned from her how demanding the NROTC program is. I don't particularly agree with the missions of the U.S. military presently, but I understand that for her, NROTC was an amazing opportunity." Similarly, another student said that ROTC represented a "very strong work ethic." The theme of realism came through in some commentary. One student linked realism with the citizen-soldier ideal. "After talking with members of ROTC, I came to accept the fact that with the state of the world today, we need not only a strong military, but a well-educated military, and I think that a university education is very beneficial."

The contribution to intellectual and normative diversity on campus mattered to several students, some of whom suggest that the presence of ROTC is especially important on a left-wing campus. As mentioned in the previous chapter, we would expect the conservative realism embedded in the military mind to pose the most friction on a left-wing campus. One student referred to ROTC students' "choices to join and motivating reasons. Also their excitement to serve was refreshing in an extremely left-wing campus." Another student also referred to the liberal nature of the campus, and noted the strains that it can put on cadets. In some respects, ROTC presence exposed something disconcerting in the liberalism of some students – an interesting lesson in itself, we suppose:

> I'm a Democrat and was excited to be on a liberal campus. However, I was shocked to see how the students who are in the service are treated on campus. One member of the Army told me he always experiences snarky comments and once had food thrown on him. His textbooks were hidden from him at a local bookstore because the clerk was antimilitary! I am tired of the incessant whining by [some of the *Badger Herald*'s writers] about the troops. I am tired of the antimilitary environment. We should be proud of our student soldiers!

As with the cadets discussed previously, student responses concentrated mainly on normative and existential matters, but some also referred to more specific or technical information and knowledge in classroom settings. For example, one respondent was likely a student in the class on terrorism and just war theory, of which a cadet respondent informed us in Chapter 8. The student's observations support the cadet's assessment: "Having an ROTC student in a seminar on terrorism and just war theory gave our course another viewpoint, of someone who could be in the active-duty military fairly soon. [This] led to some areas of conversation on military matters in war that we might not have gone into without an ROTC student there."

Some of the students who benefited from interaction with ROTC also had more mixed feelings, although largely positive. One remarked:

> I have had several ROTC students in my classes, a couple of ROTC friends, and even took a military science course through ROTC as an elective. I do not come from a military background, so much of this exposure was beneficial in my personal education about the military. I do, however, possess some negative views towards the military that were formed not as a result of this exposure to ROTC on campus, but due to the military in general.

Another student had a similar reaction: "ROTC students in my political science and humanities classes in general have been able to bring a different perspective on the military into my classes. Generally they have been able to talk about how students are treated in the military, etc. They have negatively impacted my image of the military because they have talked about the hardships involved with involuntary redeployment and medical care in the military."

The *third category* in this section consists of those students whose exposure or modest exposure had had a *neutral or negative* impact on them. The comments of those who said the impact was neutral were pretty generic, simply reporting that their thinking or knowledge was not affected much one way or the other. The following comment is typical in this regard: "Honestly, it has had very little impact on me. I think rarely about the ROTC. I have heard of it and seen mention of it in newspapers or on sidewalk chalk advertisements, but other than that, I think rarely about the ROTC." One student expressed genuine respect, but said it hadn't impacted his or her thinking: "I greatly respect what these students are brave enough to do for their country."

As mentioned previously, several students expressed *negative* views of the military on campus, often in response to their experience with ROTC. One negative view appears consistent with the model of productive friction that we have articulated, as a student related how he or she had stuck to his or her original negative position regarding the military while at the same time experiencing significant interaction with ROTC students. To reiterate what we stressed in previous chapters, our hypothesis of productive friction should not be limited to cases in which non-military students agree with ROTC or modify their own views in a direction favorable to the military. One can also learn more about one's own beliefs, and – in the sense that John Stuart Mill emphasized in "On Liberty" – attain a more secure footing for one's own beliefs by defending them and exposing them to contrary positions. Indeed, this type of impact is, in principle, just as valid and important as the modification of one's views, so long as such fortification of one's existing position is based on a meaningful engagement with the other side. This student related, "As I lived with approximately nine members of an on-campus ROTC program, I found we were able to successfully separate personal relationships/beliefs [from] their personal responsibilities and beliefs about the military. I stood my ground and was not persuaded by their military beliefs as they were quite distant from my own." But most of the other negative views did not show this kind of constructive friction. One student has not had negative interactions with ROTC, but has not budged in his or her thinking. "My interaction has not changed my opinion. I have never supported the military and their presence has not changed that. I have not, however, had any bad experiences with ROTC members, which is undoubtedly why my lack of support has not gotten any more extreme."

Most negative responses were more dismissive than these comments. The following statement is representative of this position: "We are on this campus for college, not combat. The military has no place on our campus. Organizations like the ROTC are designed as a lousy PR move for the military, but by dressing up kids in uniforms to parade around our campus, they're not changing any minds about the injustice of our military. Stop trying to recruit us!" One has had several classes with ROTC students, but concluded that they "normally don't make much of an impression. Whenever I spot one, all I think is that I'm glad my parents did not manage to talk me into that." Another student had friends in ROTC, but has "always thought it was strange and inappropriate that the military has such a visible role in an educational institution." We saw previously that military uniforms discomfort many students, and we received responses representing this concern. One student remarked, "When I see students dressed in their military uniforms it makes me think that the uniforms serve as a advertisement for the military and that campus should be a military paraphernalia–free zone," while another student said, "I've always disliked the presence of uniformed ROTC students in class and on campus. Seeing individuals in military uniforms on my campus goes against my belief that the military and universities should [not] have any affiliation."

Some of the returning veterans expressed the most negative views of ROTC, several of whom viewed ROTC as amateurish compared to their military experiences. This sentiment was echoed by our student veteran focus group.[7] In fairness, it is not surprising that those who have experienced the hardships of battle would feel superior to, or judgmental toward, those who had not yet done so. At the very least, they have a superior claim to understand war in a practical sense. One student veteran who was critical of ROTC proffered an opinion that was typical of this genre:

> I've been in the military seven years and have dealt with the [new officers] on active duty fresh from ROTC. I didn't have a high opinion of them then, and don't feel the need to go out of my way to interact with them. Cadets tend to keep to themselves while in uniform outside the ROTC building and they have little impact on the campus as a whole. They are lost kittens who will need someone to hold their hand when they graduate. The only thing I got from ROTC was a few credits for completing active duty basic training and [Advanced Infantry Training].

A member of the National Guard felt the same way. When he or she attended an ROTC training event, he or she felt "like I was back in Basic Training for Boy Scouts compared to training with the National Guard and having served one tour in Iraq. ... [I] found them completely unorganized and arrogant. Junior officers have just as much to learn about the military as the lowest enlisted soldier, if not more. I think veterans on campus on are a better asset, we have real-world experience, ROTC cadets are just playing soldier." Another student considered ROTC a relic of the Cold War: "My interaction with ROTC really hasn't influenced my views of military. I personally feel ROTC is a relic of an old political/Cold War time where the government felt it important to have a military presence on campus for perhaps recruiting efforts."[8]

[7] Student Veterans Focus Group, UW-Madison, November 2009.

[8] Phil Haan, an Air Force officer studying for his Ph.D. in security studies at MIT who was an ROTC student at Harvard in the early 1980s (he took his ROTC courses at MIT), expressed a similarly low view of ROTC's academic courses in an interview. "At Harvard? I don't know. The programs that I've had with ROTC, I'll be honest with you, the academic rigor is next to nothing. It really is not education, any kind of stuff they put up as far as leadership and all is very barebones, it's not education. It's informative, there are certain things it will do. But it's not an education program and the officers they send to run those kind of programs, it would be very rare to have somebody that

WAR, HUMAN NATURE, AND HUMANITIES COURSES

The ROTC survey responses touched mainly upon three of the four civic-liberal education themes discussed in Chapter 2: understanding the military and national defense (including education in the regime); moral difficulties in liberal democracy; and intellectual and moral diversity on campus. (Of these, "moral difficulties" was less represented than the other two.) Few students mentioned anything regarding human nature and the meaning of life. We were not surprised by this lack of reflection, as simple exposure and interaction with ROTC was not likely to elicit such reflection. We did, however, gain insight into this question with responses from students in two humanities courses at Wisconsin that one might expect to have engendered deeper reflection in this regard. The courses were a lecture history course in "Military History of the United States to 1902," taught in the fall of 2010, and a small seminar course in integrated liberal studies/political science on "The Romance of War," taught in the fall of 2007 and the fall of 2010. As mentioned, the responses to these courses were modest in number. These responses were sent directly to the authors, so we were able to ascertain the gender of the respondents in all cases but one. That is why we employ gendered pronouns in the ensuing discussion, but did not in the ROTC survey discussion.

We received ten responses in the lecture course (out of over one hundred students), and only four from the seminar courses. These low rates mean that we cannot draw more general conclusions with any confidence. But we still consider it useful to discuss the responses, as they provide some indication of impact and can serve to encourage further research. We only ask that readers refrain from jumping to conclusions regarding the responses, and that we not be accused of attempting to draw more from the responses than is merited. We wish we had a larger group from which to draw, but that was not the case.

Military History Course

History 396, "Military History of the United States to 1902," taught by Assistant Professor John Hall (a retired Army major with a book recently published by Harvard University Press), is the first military history course taught in the History Department at the University of Wisconsin, Madison since the retirement of Mac Coffman in 1992.[9] (See our portrayal of this issue in Chapters 10 and 11.) The course was broad in chronological and substantive

you could compete with academically." Interview with Phil Haan, MIT graduate student, November 2007. Of course, we should note that a Harvard undergraduate and MIT security studies graduate student probably has a fairly high bar when it comes to defining "academic rigor." Yet this has historically been one of the criticisms of ROTC, a point that we have addressed elsewhere, and Haan's observations suggest the continued importance of maintaining high academic standards.

[9] John W. Hall, *Uncommon Defense: Indian Allies in the Black Hawk War* (Harvard University Press, 2009).

scope, covering the gamut of military history approaches that we discuss in Chapter 9. Indeed, it is a model of the integration of traditional and "new" military history. History 396 dealt with American military history from the early settlement of Jamestown to the twentieth century, including the military practices of indigenous peoples and the different colonial powers that vied for dominance of the continent. In addition, the syllabus states that the course "embraces the 'New Military History,' and we will examine the influence of warfare on all aspects of American society. We will not omit the traditional mainstays of the field – the study of battles and leaders – but we will consider them within the broader context of American experience. Ultimately, this course will provide an appreciation of how war has shaped America, and, in many regards, defined its interaction with the world." Hall strove to have students understand five major issues: (1) the diverse military traditions that collided in colonial America; (2) "how and why American military policies, establishments, and practices evolved over time"; (3) how concepts of identity (such as race, ethnicity, kinship, gender, and religion) affect (and are affected by) war; (4) how war is experienced and endured on the battlefield, at home, and in government; and (5) how to analyze and interpret historical process and events.[10]

We sent the questions toward the end of the course. All the student respondents were very pleased with the course and impressed with Hall's mastery of the subject. (Surprisingly, they did not mention his previous service in the military.) We asked the students four questions:

- Why did you take this course?
- In what ways has the course impacted your thinking about the military in American society?
- In what ways has the course impacted your thinking about war?
- In what ways has your inquiry into military history impacted your thinking about human nature and citizenship?

Reasons for taking the course were what we would expect. For some it fulfilled a requirement, but most of the respondents took the course out of historical interest. Several students were interested in foreign policy and considered understanding military history indispensable to understanding America's relations with other countries. One student simply remarked, "I have an interest in American history, and to me, wars have always been the most interesting part of American history." A second student enrolled in order to understand how the past has informed and shaped the present: "I think it is imperative to be firmly grounded in the United States' history to better understand the choices that are made in the present day. In many ways, the wars and conflicts that occurred in the eighteenth and nineteenth centuries help explain U.S. political and military situations today." A third student, who has several family members and friends

[10] Syllabus for History 396: U.S. Military History, The American Military Experience to 1902, University of Wisconsin, Madison: https://mywebspace.wisc.edu/groups/History/web/syllabi_archive/history396/history396_fall2010.pdf.

in the military, pointed to the military's significance as an institution: "I feel a duty as a citizen to, at the very least, have some basic understanding of the character and composition of my country's military, the experience of being a part of it, and its role (present and past) on the global stage."

The second question asked about the impact of the course on students' thinking about the military in American society. These responses suggest that what we called "understanding the military and national security" in Chapter 2 was enhanced by the course. One respondent reported a normative impact, saying the course "has helped me to truly appreciate those who fight to protect our nation and freedom." The other responses to this question were also empirical and policy-oriented, often touching on the basic issue of civil–military relations. Four students mentioned the nation's historical aversion to a standing army/military as a key aspect of this issue. One related that the course gave him "a greater appreciation of the complexity of the relationship between the U.S. military and American society. I did not realize that Englishmen, colonists, and early Americans feared a standing army. That fear seems to have had a significant bearing on military history in the U.S." Another student took a different tack in respect to the militia and standing army. The course "broadened my thinking about the military in American society, it showed me that the military shapes American society, and American society also shapes the military in return. This course altered my belief that a standing army is unnecessary, and that this is a very American belief." A fellow student also referred to the militia, yet more critically: "This class has made me reconsider my prior notions about our military, such as the myth of the militia being the primary reason for American victory in the Revolution." A student in the NROTC said the "most significant realization" from the course was the negative attitudes that the general citizenry has had over time regarding the federal military. He remarked that this realization was contrary to his own personal experience in the post-Vietnam era. (Presumably, he had in mind the high public esteem for the military in recent decades.)

Two students related that the course helped to demystify the military for them, making it more human. For one student, the demystification led to a more realistic view of the military, as the course helped her to "see the military as an institution with its own politics, whereas in the past I have thought of it more abstractly." (One thinks of Andrew Bacevich's argument about how abstractionism and separation from the military can breed militarism.)[11] As stated repeatedly previously, such critical understanding is crucial to being educated regarding the role of the military in American life. Another remarked that the course "made me think of the military as more of a living, breathing aspect than a cold distant figure that is always there." Another student was more philosophical about this question, informing us that the course "has caused me to reevaluate two fundamental philosophical questions: 'who fights?' and 'why fight?'"

[11] Andrew J. Bacevich, *The New American Militarism: How Americans Are Seduced by War* (Oxford University Press, 2005), p. 28.

One aspect of military life not mentioned was how the military differs from other institutions in American life in terms of its defining professional use of violence and the importance of command, obedience, and order (the *sui generis* point discussed in Chapter 2). Perhaps students would have raised this point had they been asked to provide longer responses; but the complete absence of this response suggests it was not a primary concern for the students or for the course, although the fourth of Hall's objectives touches on it ("how war is experienced and endured on the battlefield, at home, and in government"). It is interesting to compare this absence or omission to our student responses to the ROTC survey, which embraced this point more fully. Once again, the difference suggests the importance of exposure that is concrete, personal, or existential in nature, as we articulated previously. That said, several History 396 respondents did pinpoint the significance of soldiers' sacrifices for the defense of the country, which is an aspect of the *sui generis* nature of the military.

The third question was about how the course might have impacted students' thinking about war itself. Almost all of the students affirmed that the course contributed to their understandings of the causes and consequences of war. Reasons for this influence varied, as did the conclusions students derived from this impact. Some stressed the sheer variety of the causes and consequences of war (one mentioned that Hall warned them of the dangers attendant to the penchant for drawing sweeping lessons from history), whereas others drew more common themes from their exposure. One student began by asserting that the course had no "apparent effect" on his thinking about war, but then proceeded to outline how he learned that different periods of history had produced different reasons for going to war (for example, to protect national sovereignty before the Civil War, more to protect and promote national interest thereafter). Another student said that the course confirmed or hardened her belief that war "is an unnecessary evil and that diplomacy should be the nation's first and foremost strategy to solve conflicts." Another's views were similarly buttressed, as the course "reaffirmed my view that war is a very tragic event." A student who highlighted how the course gave him a "clearer understanding" of the causes and consequences of war also praised the reading of several memoirs written from the soldiers' points of view, which taught him "how devastating war can be for the individual as well as the society" – an impact associated with war and society scholarship. (See the discussion of Ambrose Bierce, Stephen Crane, Ernest Hemingway, Emily Dickinson, and Herman Melville in Chapter 2.) Another student registered a similar impact. The course "opened my eyes to how the soldier views war: i.e., the emotions they go through, the way a soldier leaving impacts his hometown, etc."

Several of the students referred to how the course "complicated" their previous understandings. One claimed that the course challenged his previous notions of war in a normative sense by making him more aware of the "obscurity of war. I think that war makes less sense to me now because several of the wars in early American history were avoidable." Another student took a different empirical tack in this regard, describing how he or she learned that wars do not always involve equal adversaries fighting on a grand scale, but often skirmishes between or among unequal nations, and that diplomacy is more likely to hold sway when a nation's commercial and social interests work against taking up arms.

Although several of the responses to this third question embodied implicitly philosophical understandings, one was overtly philosophical in nature. This student wrote that the course aroused Hobbesian reflections in her, although these thoughts were incidental to the actual course material. Her observations also echo some of the literature of international relations theorists, who study the causes of war in constructivist and realist terms:

> I have learned a lot about war as a lived experience (for civilians as well as soldiers), and I have an idea of some of the tensions and dissatisfactions about identity and access to resources which seem to escalate the scales of conflict between groups. But in a more philosophical way, the implications of the course are pretty Hobbesian: a lot of people are behaving badly most of the time, and desperation and poor choices regularly converge to compel people to violence. I have, for the moment, suspended disbelief and taken this assumption at face value, but I think it warrants more thoughtful reflection than a course like this has time for.

This reflection echoes, in a somewhat different sound, Charles Moskos' depiction of war in his essay, "Vietnam: Why Men Fight." After spending time accompanying soldiers in Vietnam, Moskos observed that, "War is a Hobbesian world, and, in combat, life is truly short, nasty, and brutish. ... Under fire, the soldier not only faces an imminent danger of his own death and wounding; he also witnesses the killing and suffering of his buddies."[12]

Our fourth and final question asked about the ways in which the students' inquiries into military history had impacted their thinking about human nature and citizenship. Although a couple of responses reflected little thought, overall the question elicited among the most interesting, thought-provoking answers, which covered a variety of viewpoints and topics. One student focused on intellectual and epistemological skepticism, stating that the course "probably made me more cynical" about drawing broad lessons from history – a theme Hall stressed in his lectures. "Military history seems to be one of the primary areas of historical study in which the abuse of overgeneralization is carried out."

The question addressed both citizenship and human nature. Let us treat the citizenship component first. Two students underscored how the course influenced their thinking and aroused their appreciation of the normative aspects of citizenship and service – comments that related to what we called "education in the regime" in Chapter 2. One mentioned the Revolutionary period, when citizenship and the militia "went hand-in-hand. ... It made me consider what

[12] Charles C. Moskos, Jr., "Vietnam: Why Men Fight," in Martin Oppenheimer, ed., *The American Military* (Transaction, 1971), pp. 19–20. One of the most vivid and compelling portrayals of the shocking violence and chaos of combat is Virginia senator James Webb's masterpiece novel based on his Vietnam experience, *Fields of Fire* (Prentice Hall, 1978). See also John Keegan, *The Face of Battle* (Penguin, 1976).

soldiers, today and in the past, have sacrificed for our American citizenship." The same student who stressed Hobbes said the course showed her that "responsible citizenship is very hard," and that the All-Volunteer Force is "an absolute privilege." Other students maintained that the course gave them a more realistic, concrete perspective on the military that defied their previous stereotypes. Echoing the thinking of such scholars as Adrian Lewis, who have analyzed the cultural and political implications of limited wars, especially the way such wars entail a distancing of the consequences of war from the general population, one student said she was interested in how wars that are uncontroversial or ignored by the general society "can often be very contentious within the military and among different branches/ranks within a branch." She then pondered the ways in which advancing technology creates "more literal distance between targets and actors," making it easier for the general society to downplay the consequences of war. These reflections led to a policy prescription based on the concern about civic obligation expressed by Allan Silver and others: "This is why I think a draft or some form of militia should be reinstituted (not the reserves) because it would create more consciousness on both citizenry and government."[13] In a different realist vein, the NROTC student observed that people generally act to further their own interests; accordingly, wars occur when people in power convince the populace that war is in their interest.

Not all the respondents answered the human nature part of the fourth question. Although their views about human nature and conflict varied, the students who responded to this question all disclosed that the course made them more aware of this aspect of the human condition – including one student who expressed a fervent belief in the human desire for peace. A couple of students also added a more sophisticated point: "War" as a phenomenon is not the same thing as violence per se, but rather the institution and implementation of violence through collective action, usually – although not always – in the form of the state. One student adhered to his belief that "human nature doesn't want war but rather peace," but said he now believes that war "becomes a necessity" when certain conflicts arise. The others referred to the universal nature of human conflict, which contributes to war. One student conveyed that the course confirmed his long-standing belief that war has always been "a major part of the experience through history," while another observed that conflict (not war per se) "will always" be part of life because of human nature, thereby leading to war because of citizens having to "partake in its [the state's] survival." Similarly, another student reflected, "My inquiry into military history has shown me that

[13] Allan Silver, "The Military and Academe," paper and talk presented at National Association of Scholars Conference, February 19, 2009: http://www.nas.org/polArticles.cfm?doctype_code=Article&doc_id=569&Keyword_Desc=NAS%20Conference%20Video. Silver does not advocate the return of the draft, but some other thinkers in the civic obligation vein have done so. See, e.g., James Fallows, *National Defense* (Vintage, 1982), ch. 5; William A. Galson, "A Sketch of Some Arguments for Conscription," in Verna V. Gehring, ed., *Community Matters: Challenges to Civic Engagement in the 21st Century* (Rowman and Littlefield, 2005), ch. 5.

conflict between humans is inevitable and throughout human history human conflicts only managed to become increasingly violent and brutal" as humanity devises more destructive ways of killing. Our Hobbesian student referred again to Hobbes, but learned that the question of war is more complex than the self-interest and conflict built in to the human condition. Like any profession, soldiering fosters its own professional identity and ethics, through which the practice of war is filtered, and which create their own types of tension with society. "There is also the identity and professional ethos of the soldier to contend with, and that throws a fascinating wrench into the gears. The identity-craft of the military indoctrination yields some spectacular paradoxes, including but not limited to, 'I am morally superior to you because I am your servant,' and, 'I am harmless to the United States of America because I have committed my life to the craft of killing people and breaking things.'" This observation echoed themes in the works of Thomas Ricks and other students of the civil–military gap.[14]

It is apparent from this modest set of responses that Hall's course conveyed knowledge and understanding related to the themes we discussed in Chapter 2. The one theme that was not overt was "moral difficulties in liberal democracy." However, the presence of this theme appears to have been present in the course in an implicit sense. The students evidently struggled in reconciling the lessons of the class with their preexisting beliefs, such as the student who reinforced her belief in the peaceful aspirations of human beings at the same time that she came to understand why war was necessary in certain situations: "I believe that our human nature doesn't want war but rather peace. However, when conflict arises, war becomes a necessity to solve problems." Another student learned "how devastating war can be for the individual as well as the society," but "human nature dictates that there will always be conflicts" that threaten the state, and citizens must "actively partake in its survival." And recall the student whose beliefs were that "war is an unnecessary evil" and that diplomacy should always be the route to go, but informed us that, "My inquiry into military history has shown me that conflict between humans is inevitable." Such thinking pretty clearly reveals a struggle or tension between value systems that are directly related to the moral tensions that Niebuhr and other thinkers discerned at the heart of liberal democratic orders. These thoughts are also prime examples of the productive friction that we have posited as an important element of liberal and civic education. They also point to the type of realism advocated by Ambrose Bierce in Chapter 2: "Cultivate a taste for distasteful truths. And ... most of all, endeavor to see things as they are, not as they ought to be."[15]

[14] See Thomas E. Ricks, *Making the Corps* (Scribner, Simon and Schuster, 1997); and Shannon E. French, *The Code of the Warrior: Exploring Warrior Values Past and Present* (Rowman and Littlefield, 2003).

[15] Ambrose Bierce, quoted in Drew Gilpin Faust, *This Republic of Suffering: Death and the American Civil War* (Alfred A. Knopf, 2008), pp. 196–7.

A final theme from Chapter 2 was also a subject of reflection in this course: death. A greater awareness of death, human frailty, and sin was clearly implied by many of these students' responses. The very subject of military history is infused with this sensitivity when it is well taught, as Hall's course appears to have been. The "connection between mortality and meaning" that Anthony Kronman places at the center of a revived humanities education appears to have taken place in History 396, if only by implication. As Kronman remarked in Chapter 2, such study

> would compel students to consider whether justice is a higher good than beauty, whether democracy has room for nobility, whether our reverence for human beings should be qualified by recognition of original sin. It would force them to confront a wider and more disturbing diversity of opinion than the one they now do in their college and university classrooms. It would disrupt their confidence and deepen their doubts. Today, just the opposite is the case.[16]

Although not developed, the student responses above reflect consternation and reflection regarding power, violence, the "disturbing diversity of opinion" about humanity, and the more disturbing aspects of human nature and organized society ("original sin"). This is even more the case in the next course.

Romance of War

We also sought input from students in the seminar course entitled "The Romance of War," taught by Assistant Professor Richard Avramenko. The course is a political theory course cross-listed in Political Science (PS 506) and Integrated Liberal Studies (ILS 371) at the University of Wisconsin. Avramenko's objective in the course is Socratic and critical: to arouse students' natural inclination to be swept up in the emotional appeal of war (the seeking of glory, the spectacle of violence, the appeal of collective engagement, and so on) and then to compel students to examine this feeling and commitment through the exercise of critical intelligence and analytical reasoning. In the political theory tradition, Avramenko utilizes the emotional side of the students to coax them into identifying with the romance of war and then appealing to the rational element in them to critically examine their own feelings and ideas. The objective is to achieve a deeper understanding of the subject matter, of humanity, and of themselves.[17] The 2008 syllabus stated:

> This course investigates the philosophy and psychology of war and violence. While many studies of war look to states and institutions, here we turn our attention to what might be called the "romance of war." Simply put, despite their horrible costs, both human and

[16] Anthony Kronman, *Education's End: Why Our Colleges and Universities Have Given Up on the Meaning of Life* (Yale University Press, 2007), pp. 235–6, 255–6.

[17] The psychoanalytic theory and practice of "transference" is similar in interesting respects. The therapy elicits emotional and erotic feelings in the patient toward the analyst, which the analyst then uses as a vehicle for the patient to gain greater rational understanding of himself or herself.

economic war and battle seem to have an enduring appeal that defies its rational implications. Our task here is to probe the depths of the human experience with war and violence as to better understand its appeal.

As Avramenko related to us in language drawn from classical political theory, students should learn more about the complex makeup of their "souls." He strives to achieve this objective by having the students study courage and honor in terms of ancient notions of the good warrior, proceeding to examine the actual experiences of men in battle. According to the syllabus, "With these investigations we will discuss and dispute the competing claims that man is either naturally drawn to war or naturally repulsed by it. ... Specifically, we ask whether there is a contradictory element to the experience of war and battle – an element that appeals to something fundamental in human beings yet at the same time causes humans to overlook the inhumanity of war."[18] Texts included Andrew Bacevich's *The New American Militarism*; Barbara Ehrenreich's *Blood Rites: Origins and History of the Passions of War*; Michael Gelven's *War and Existence: A Philosophical Inquiry*; J. Glenn Gray's *The Warriors: Reflections on Men in Battle*; Victor Davis Hanson's *The Soul of Battle*; Chris Hedge's *War Is a Force that Gives Us Meaning*; and Plutarch's writings on Sparta.[19]

Avramenko's closing remarks to his class in the fall of 2010 echoed the psychological and phenomenological aspects of war pedagogy that we discussed in Chapter 2, including the ways in which war evokes primal passions, emotions, and sensibilities – from what Patrick Hoy called "the mystery of command that binds people together in those benevolent hierarchies and the 'throngs of community,'" to the excitement of danger and violence in the name of a cause (Gelven, Nietzsche, and so on), to the emotional and moral agonies attendant to the brutalities of war that J. Glenn Gray elucidates. In particular, Avramenko emphasized the tensions and contradictions that should arise when one considers war as a phenomenon:

> The idea in this class has been to romanticize war. I don't think we should aim to leave it romantic, but instead to see if we can create this sensation in both our rational selves, and in our colleagues who hold dearly to the romance of peace. I hope that you all leave this class with some idea of the paradox that is war, the paradox they don't talk about in more conventional international relations classes, the paradox that is nevertheless perpetuated in our usual IR classes.

[18] Conversation with Richard Avramenko, University of Wisconsin, Madison, December 2010; Syllabus for "The Romance of War," University of Wisconsin, Department of Political Science and Integrated Liberal Studies, Fall 2007.

[19] Bacevich, *The New American Militarism*; J. Glenn Gray, *The Warriors: Reflections on Men in Battle* (Harper and Row, 1967); Michael Gelven, *War and Existence: A Philosophical Inquiry* (Pennsylvania State University Press, 1994); Barbara Ehrenreich, *Blood Rites: Origins and History of the Passions of War* (Henry Holt, 1997); Victor Davis Hanson, *The Soul of Battle: From Ancient Times to the Present Day, How Three Great Liberators Vanquished Tyranny* (Random House, 1999); Chris Hedge, *War Is a Force That Gives Us Meaning* (Random House, 2003); Plutarch, *The Lives of the Noble Grecians and Romans*, revised by Arthur Hugh Clough, translated by John Dryden (Modern Library, 1932).

In these classes, you know, they seldom talk about war being perpetuated by the will to power, by the instinctive drive for fraternity, by war's aesthetic appeal, by the idea that war creates better citizens, by the idea that war is an escape from profound boredom, by the idea that danger can be closely associated with meaningful existence, by the kinship between love and war, sex and battle.

Having said that my hope is actually to romanticize war, it is not my hope that you'll leave this class with an untutored susceptibility to the romance. In some ways, I am hoping to disabuse you of this susceptibility. But to disabuse, in many ways, is to create a reasonable defense. As you all probably know very well by know, I don't think reason is the best tool for fighting against our passions, our intuitions, our ability (or susceptibility), to be romanticized. So, I sort of regard this as an exercise in dealing with the visceral, in dealing with the emotional, by experiencing the visceral and the emotional in a self-conscious kind of way. In the end, I hope that you come away from this with a slightly more nuanced understanding of the problem of war – because it IS a problem – and hopefully you had some fun in this odd kind of class.[20]

We had only three responses from the 2007 class of twenty students. (Also, we looked at the standard evaluations for the class, which received very high scores overall. The response rate for these, too, was not high, so it is not surprising that we received a low turnout for a project that was independent of the course.) One student underscored the *sui generis* nature of war in clear terms: "I learned about the fact that nothing is comparable to war, and how be it sexual attraction, drug use, and ecstasy moment, nothing can come close or substitute for war. Also I learned of things that might be able to create the bonds of community that war creates, their possibilities and setbacks." The instructor "prompted the students to think and analyze for themselves. He asked for contradictions and other points of view. This is how I formed my own ideas on war, where it comes from, and what it does for the individual. I learned more from this class than almost any other I have ever taken."[21] War is *sui generis*, there is nothing in human experience like it, and our often complex feelings toward it tell us something about what we are as human beings. A different student in this class had an even more poignant impression, as the class exposed him to the range and depth of human nature and possibilities that he had not previously encountered:

The Romance of War was truly thought provoking, because rather than analyzing the political, economic, or social causes of a phenomenon that has been a fundamental element of human existence (as most of my political science classes have), it cut under the surface to explore whether there is a more deeply rooted source ingrained within the human psyche ... while an individual engaging in war appears fundamentally irrational (as it threatens his/her survival), it also fulfills certain psychological urges and instills

[20] Avramenko, Concluding Remarks to Students in "The Romance of War," December 9, 2010.

[21] Response of an undergraduate student who took "The Romance of War" at the University of Wisconsin, Madison, in the fall of 2007. Neither of us was the instructor. This student's sense of the *sui generis* nature of war is congruent with the phenomenological perspective of philosopher Michael Gelven in *War and Existence*.

meaning into a person's life. It also made me reflect on the state of our current society.... In the end, despite uncovering many myths regarding war and the shallowness of its appeal, I confess that I had a slight urge to visit the nearest recruiting office and sign up. I'm still trying to figure out what it's all about.[22]

We also elicited responses from students in the 2010 course. One student's comments about the *sui generis* nature of the course were typical of the respondents, and quite in line with our theory of productive friction. She said that the course "enabled me to think of War and the military in a completely different way," treating war from philosophical, psychological, and romantic standpoints, "which I had never considered prior (growing up in a liberal family and always being taught that war was bad). I learned to look at it phenomenologically, and now have a better understanding of what it feels like to actually be in the military and what that can mean for the returning soldier." Looking at war from soldiers' perspectives provided "something unique, something extraordinary, that no other endeavor can offer, and regardless of the supposed political, economical, or patriotic reasons people give for fighting a war, these other aspects (camaraderie, transcendence, adrenaline, violence) are what the soldier remembers as their experience during a war."[23] As far as human nature is concerned, this student reported that the course reinforced her belief "that violence and 'lust of the eye' for violence are innate, hardwired," and that, "Citizens rally around a war effort, and demonize the enemy, and feeling like one is part of a 'we' fighting a 'they' makes their ties to their country and their society stronger than they otherwise would be. Being a citizen and pride for your country is a huge part in the romantic vision of war." Avramenko also brought in a veteran student who had fought in Iraq, and this student had quite an impact:

[He] gave so much insight into what it's actually like to be fighting in a modern war. He literally said a lot of the things that we had read in the books, about what it feels like to fight, the emptiness when he returned, his anger, what was exciting about war, how his training enabled him to work like a machine, all of these things. ... I think that just speaking with a veteran like him who was so open and willing to answer all of our questions really impacted how I think about the war and the military, at least in modern times.

[22] Statement made by a student in "Romance of War" class at Wisconsin, spring 2008. One can see how some quarters would view with fear a course that motivated students to contemplate joining the military. Our perspective is that students should have this opportunity to make informed choices by encouraging an appropriate military presence.

[23] As many scholars of warfare have concluded, as their experiences with war progress, soldiers' commitments typically evolve from more abstract notions of patriotism and patriotic duty to the more personal sense of loyalty to one's comrades in arms – what sociologists call a loyalty to one's "primary group." Duty to the primary group of one's comrades in arms supersedes duty to country. See, e.g., Samuel A. Stouffer et al., *The America Soldier* (Princeton University Press, 1949); and J. Glenn Gray, *The Warriors*.. For a view that quasi-rejects this perspective in favor of a more dialectical understanding of the links between personal, primary group, and broader values, see Moskos, "Vietnam: Why Men Fight," pp. 16–36.

CONCLUDING THOUGHTS

The findings of the last two chapters buttress the case that exposure to the military – not simply physical presence of the military but also intellectual consideration of war in its purest sense – is beneficial to students *and* cadets on a variety of levels. The evidence provides some support for the "gap" claim; yet very many students acknowledged a gap at the same time that they observed that exposure to ROTC helped to bridge the gap, bringing two worlds or perspectives into contact (and sometimes into conflict). This was true even though a vast majority of students reported not having had major exposure to ROTC, for the symbolic presence of the military often proved sufficient to provoke deeper thought about the issues that have occupied our thoughts in this book. For most, this bridging consisted more in the realm of the personal than the realm of ideas: Exposure "gave a human face" to fellow citizen-soldiers. That said, many students also mentioned how exposure contributed to their knowledge. We also found that some students in Military History 306 and "The Romance of War" at Wisconsin gained *sui generis* knowledge that contributed to their understanding of the world and themselves in a way that other courses could not. This appears to have been especially the case with "The Romance of War," as that course was more explicitly designed to provoke critical examination of society, citizenship, human nature, and the self and the soul.

Given the limited nature of our ROTC surveys and the anecdotal nature of the responses to our queries of students in the military history and "Romance of War" classes, we believe future research could begin by broadening the survey to include other majors and by conducting more thorough qualitative interviews – as well as interviews and surveys with the same students over time to understand how their views change in regard to their interactions with various clusters within the university. One possibility is measuring the attitudes of students before and after they complete a course with other ROTC students, or to follow a cohort of ROTC students to understand how a distinctly military perspective is forged. Extensions of this sort would provide more insight into the causal relationship between exposure to ROTC and student attitudes. We hypothesize that students with more exposure to different perspectives will have better learning outcomes. Our surveys provided some insight into this question, but we acknowledge that more work remains to be done to determine the causal relationships implicit in our pedagogical model. The same points apply to our treatment of the military history and "Romance of War" courses.

Yet in the end we are convinced that there is an *understanding* gap between civilians and the military within the university and that the physical presence of ROTC serves to alleviate it. The presence of student-soldiers presents students who may never experience military life with an opportunity to learn from those who are familiar with such a life. And in many situations, the students who encounter student-soldiers better understand the military. These findings also reaffirm one of our central points, that intellectual consideration of the military and military affairs is a critical dimension of military presence. The courses discussed in this chapter were a source of productive friction, leading some students to reconsider their deeply held beliefs, and compelling some to face the inevitable discomfort that arises as they begin to better understand the darker sides of history, political life, and human nature. This journey may even have its own romance, for we believe that the discomfort that accompanies the path that these students traveled can indeed be "fun," as Professor Avramenko hoped.

PART III

MILITARY HISTORY EXAMINED

10

Military History

An Endangered or Protected Species?

> The moralist must praise heroism and condemn cruelty; but the moralist does not explain events.
>
> – Georges Lefebrve[1]

> History would be an impossible area of human reflection if there were no recurrent attributes of human nature.
>
> – Willson H. Coates[2]

Up to this point, our empirical focus has been on the physical presence of the military in universities, which is one of the most charged aspects of campus political life. Yet protests over ROTC are only one dimension of military presence, even if they involve the best-known conflicts. A second dimension of conflict over military presence is more intellectual, one in which the primary conflicts occur within the walls of departments and with various sorties coming from different departments. As we argued in Chapter 2, intellectual consideration of war is perhaps as important as physical presence in bridging the divide between civilian and military life. Intellectual inquiry into war benefits not only students but the student-soldiers on campus. In the following chapters, we consider empirically the status of military history and political realism in the academy. In particular, we are interested in the degree to which the disciplines of history, political science, and security studies facilitate an appropriate military presence, as well as broad trends in the status of the study of war in its more traditional forms within these disciplines.

This chapter and the next one focus almost exclusively on military history within its traditional abode, history departments. Our central objective of this chapter is to present a conceptual framework that informs our analysis of military history, as well as the first of the results from our surveys. Although we emphasize the status of military history in its conventional abode, we do not limit our consideration of military history to history departments, for we are also

[1] Georges Lefebvre, quoted in Ferenc M. Szasz, "The Many Meanings of History, Part II," *History Teacher* 8, 1 (1974): 58.

[2] Willson H. Coates, quoted in Szasz, "The Many Meanings of History, Part II," p. 58.

interested in military history's status in political science and security studies programs. Indeed, our theory of productive friction, which highlights diverse perspectives, suggests the importance of military history for those who are primarily interested in the study of politics and security.

We launch our analysis by discussing several of the recent perspectives offered regarding military history by military historians. One implication of these considerations is the importance of how we define military history – in traditional terms or as the "new military history." By defining the field broadly, we obtain a different picture of its status – one that suggests a much less "threatened" status for military history. After discussing various issues involved with conceptualization, we argue that the key dimension is between traditional and new military history, a conceptual distinction to which we return throughout our analysis.

After documenting the nature of the debates among military historians, we provide evidence from a survey of leaders of history departments to ascertain further the status of military history. Based on interviews with military historians and our review of the debates raging over the status of military history, we devised survey questions that address the status of both traditional and new military history. Our surveys furnish us with a greater understanding of the relative emphasis of each approach in history departments. Perhaps more importantly, our surveys offer insight into the *future* of *traditional* military history in terms of departmental priorities.

We also asked questions pertaining to the status of national security–related issues in history departments. Whereas national security is conventionally understood to be the province of political science and security studies, our perspective contends that the integration of national security issues and historical analysis can cast light on important issues. Consequently, we consider the status of security in our evaluation of history departments. In addition, we provide a brief analysis of the status of military history in political science departments, for political science and military history share a concern for national security as a subject matter. Carl von Clausewitz famously defined war as politics conducted by other means; as such, we would like to know whether political scientists consider military history a proper part of the political science curriculum. In Chapters 12 and 13, we also reflect on security studies programs at some length in order to understand the extent to which security studies programs integrate military history into their programs – finding them to be a bastion of military history within political science. At the same time, it is important to understand the role of military history in the discipline of *political science*, not simply in the narrower field of security studies. While we do not expect political science programs to emphasize military history nearly as much as history departments do, we do not believe that there should be a hard and fast disciplinary line separating history and political science. Accordingly, we seek to understand whether the type of "productive friction" discussed in previous chapters exists between history and political science departments. The discussion in this chapter will also help to set the stage for our later analysis of security studies programs per se.

Finally, while this chapter emphasizes the status of military history in the academy, we recognize that a separate issue is the *impact* of such courses on students. In our earlier chapter on the impact of the study of the military and war, we examined the impact that taking a traditional military history course had on students at the University of Wisconsin in order to better grasp the consequences of military history for university education. Those findings suggested to us that the presence of such courses is important to a university education, and we now consider more deeply the extent to which history departments create a fertile ground for consideration of such issues.

Before delving into the discussion, we reiterate our disclaimer: We are political scientists seeking to understand the status of military history, not military historians. Yet we believe our approach faithfully integrates the insights of military historians. In deciding what questions we asked in our surveys, we interviewed many of the leading military historians as well as experts on security who are knowledgeable about military history. These interviews provided us with a knowledge basis upon which to proceed. At the same time, we believe that we have touched on some empirical dimensions that have not yet been uncovered by military historians, not only in our surveys that consider the distinctions between traditional and new military history, but also in considering military history from the perspective of three disciplines: history, political science, and security studies. To fully understand the status of military history, we need to understand it inside and outside of its conventional domain.

RECENT SKIRMISHES OVER MILITARY HISTORY

In 2006, John J. Miller wrote a widely cited essay that appeared in the *National Review Digital* magazine entitled "Sounding Taps: Why Military History Is Being Retired." Miller began with a discussion of the difficulties besetting the University of Wisconsin History Department in its attempt to replace the distinguished military historian Mac Coffman after his retirement in 1992. Miller then made a sweeping indictment of the academic history profession and higher education in general, accusing them of intentionally marginalizing military history for ideological reasons. "Although military history remains incredibly popular among students who fill lecture halls to learn about Saratoga and Iwo Jima and among readers who buy piles of books on Gettysburg and D-Day," Miller exclaimed, "on campus it's making a last stand against the shock troops of political correctness." He quoted Frederick Kagan, a resident scholar at the American Enterprise Institute who taught at West Point for ten years: "Pretty soon, it may become virtually impossible to find military-history professors who study war with the aim of understanding why one side won and the other lost."[3] According to John Cooper, a University of Wisconsin historian whom Miller

[3] John J. Miller, "Sounding Taps: Why Military History Is Being Retired," NR/Digital Online, October 9, 2006: http://nrd.nationalreview.com/article/?q=YTdiMDkzZDJjYTYwOWM4YmIyMmE4N2IwODFlNWUoMjE=.

also quoted, "Sounding Taps" escalated public and alumni pressure on Wisconsin and other departments to open their arms to military history.[4]

Miller's presentation did not sit well with all military historians, however. Mark Grimsley of Ohio State charged that Miller's essay "is constructed so tendentiously, and overlooks so many relevant facts, that it is really quite misleading." In addition to castigating Miller's tone, Grimsley accused the journalist of ignoring positive developments in the discipline, such as the prominence of several distinguished programs that emphasize military history, including those at Ohio State, Duke, North Carolina, Kansas, and Texas A&M.[5] Although only one of these programs is a "top twenty" department (see Chapter 11), these are prominent institutions with strong research faculty.

Miller's essay is perhaps the most noteworthy in a recent barrage of journalistic critiques of the state of academic military history.[6] The debate has also been raging inside academia for many years, at least among military historians and their allies. The picture that emerges from professionals in the field (some of whom we will present at some length in the next chapter) is pretty dark or gray, but not black and white. Some military historians believe that military history is beleaguered, while others view the field as either flourishing or, at least, holding its own. And many opinions lie in between these poles. North Carolina military historian Richard Kohn, who has been at North Carolina twenty years, expressed a representative view in an e-mail exchange. His ambiguity is credible given the fact that he is a champion of military history, old and new:

> There is some disagreement among many of us in the field, though all of us, I think, admit to being unsure. It's a glass half full, half empty problem. Although I love the joke Bill Cosby tells about going home, and visiting his grandmother, and a 2 hour discussion of some philosophical point when he was a student at Temple. His grandmother asked what he had studied that day, and he described the ambiguous discussion of the glass problem. "That's easy," she replied. When he questioned her rather skeptically, she replied: "It depends on whether you're pouring, or getting."[7]

Military historian Donald A. Yerxa appropriately entitles his preface to a recent edited book on military history "The Curious State of Military History." Yerxa rehashes the debate over the Miller thesis and concludes that Miller's position has more support than his critics allow. "While Miller's blanket report of military history's decline in the academy is possibly overstated, the relatively few institutional exceptions to his assessment tend to support his case." At the same time, Yerxa acknowledges, "What makes this debate so interesting is that,

[4] Interview with John Cooper, University of Wisconsin History Department, April 2009.

[5] Mark Grimsley, "Crocodile Tears for the Military: An Open Letter to John J. Miller," at his blog: http://warhistorian.org/wordpress/?p=433. This site also contains many interesting responses to Grimsley's take on Miller's piece.

[6] See, e.g., David A. Bell, "Casualty of War: Military History Bites the Dust," *New Republic*, May 7, 2007.

[7] E-mail exchange with Richard Kohn, University of North Carolina History Department, June–July 2009.

from an intellectual standpoint, military history is quite robust, as the various offerings in this anthology attest."[8] Yerxa refers to the stretching of military history to include broader cultural themes as one reason for this robustness.

As with biblical exegesis, one can garner evidence to support optimistic, gloomy, and mixed views of military history's status. But the fact of complexity does not in itself relieve us of the responsibility of weighing evidence and rendering judgments about where the weight of the evidence lies. The evidence we will examine clearly supports the conclusion that military history is indeed embattled within history departments, but there are countervailing facts or factors that qualify or complicate this assessment. In addition, trends often change, and we might be witnessing a relative revival of interest in academic military history as the twenty-first century's second decade begins. Positive factors include the strength of research in military history at popular, practical, and academic levels; the meaningful presence of military history in at least some major history departments; the broadening of military history as a field of study that links it in a dynamic way to other fields within history; the rise of some innovative programs, including nondepartment-oriented campus centers that feature military history (often linking it to security studies and related endeavors); and outreach programs that bridge campus and noncampus groups. Given the demand for military history that prevails both on and off campus, it is only natural that some outlets will be found that furnish opportunities for such study. Nor should we neglect the fact that the military establishment hosts a vast array of programs that provide military history and related programs, including ROTC programs on campus.

One fact is not in dispute: Military history enjoys a large audience, and there is no dearth of writers in the area.[9] One indicator of this popularity is membership in an organization that attracts professionally oriented individuals and groups. In 1933, a band of soldiers and academics founded the American Military History Foundation in Washington, D.C., which had a membership of 199 by 1936. A year later, the foundation launched a quarterly journal, the *Journal of the American Military History Foundation*. According to the Forward of the first issue, "Thus far, our efforts to secure publication through the medium of other organizations have met with no success." The foundation would later change its name to the American Military Institute and, ultimately, to the Society for Military History; it also changed its journal's name to *Military Affairs* and,

[8] Donald A. Yerxa, "The Curious State of Military History," in Donald A. Yerxa, ed., *Recent Themes in Military History: Historians in Conversation* (University of South Carolina Press, 2008), p. 2.

[9] Many of the military historians we talked to volunteered that they teach military history in large lecture halls filled with hundreds of students, and that the courses are nearly uniformly fully subscribed, which seems to suggest the veracity of Miller's comments about the popularity of military history. Our interviews suggest that military history, at the very least, remains a very popular subject. Coffman's courses, for example, were extremely popular, as are those taught by John Lynn at Illinois and Northwestern, whose work we consider later in this chapter.

later still, to the *Journal of Military History*.[10] After 1936, membership in the organization swelled, totaling 590 individuals by 1941, and ultimately expanding to about 2,700 today.[11] These figures are but one indication of the popularity of the field.

To consider the status of academic military history, we must fashion a *definition of military history* and look at the kinds of work being done in the field. We must avoid the Scylla of an unduly narrow definition and the Charybdis of an inappropriately broad one. An overly narrow definition will lead to a bleaker assessment of the field's prospects than a broader definition, for narrow definitions exclude work that is closely related and, perhaps, deserving of inclusion as military history. An overly broad definition will have the opposite effect, making the status of military history appear more sanguine than the facts merit. Our purpose in the next sections is to find an appropriately nuanced notion of military history that permits us to evaluate its status credibly. Once we have a definition in mind, we can proceed to empirically estimate the status of military history.

OTHER APPROACHES TO THE STUDY OF WAR

Before we consider the definition of military history, we should briefly note that because of the significance of war, several disciplinary approaches to its study have arisen, many of which intersect with historical research.[12] These approaches include the following:

- *Anthropology*, which studies war from a comparative perspective that includes biological-evolutionary approaches; ecological theories (the way war mediates the relationship between society and the environment); social-cultural models that link war to specific cultural traits and practices; and hermeneutic models, which consider how the practice of war is influenced by cultural symbols, meanings, and rituals.
- *Cultural history*, which is "the analysis of the ways groups and individuals ascribe meaning to military conflict" before, during, and after war.[13]
- The new fields of *peace studies and studies in conflict resolution*, which emerged in the 1960s out of reaction to the Vietnam War, international conflict, and militarism.[14]

[10] This information is drawn from Edward M. Coffman, "Military History and the OAH," unpublished manuscript provided to the authors, pp. 5–6.

[11] See Edward M. Coffman, "The Course of Military History in the United States Since World War II, *Journal of Military History* 61, 761 (1997): 774, footnote 26.

[12] See the various essays on "Disciplinary Views of War" in John Whitclay Chambers II, ed., *The Oxford Guide to American Military History* (Oxford University Press, 1999), pp. 216–30. The discussion in this section draws a great deal from this book.

[13] Jay Winter, "Disciplinary Views of War: Cultural History," in Chambers, ed., *Oxford Guide to American Military History*, p. 218.

[14] Charles F. Howlett, "Disciplinary Views of War: Peace History," in Chambers, ed., *Oxford Guide to American Military History*, p. 225. See also David P. Barash and Charles P. Webel, *Peace and Conflict Studies*, 2nd Edition (Sage, 2009).

- *Diplomatic history*, which traditionally concentrated on the interactions that take place before or after actual military conflict. With the advent of the Cold War, however, this boundary broke down, blending diplomatic history with military history. This blending is perhaps one reason that diplomatic history (as well as "political history") has also lost status in many history departments, as many e-mail respondents from the top twenty research departments will claim in Chapter 11. H. W. Brands also mentions another reason: the increasing importance of non-elite ("social" and "peoples" history) historical analysis beginning in the 1960s:

In addition, even as the context of diplomacy was changing during the Cold War, so was the context of diplomatic history. Starting in the 1960s, the American historical profession experienced a revolt against elitism. The study of governing groups and ruling classes gave way to investigations into the lives of common people. Women and racial and ethnic minorities were judged more interesting than white males. Political historians were supplanted by social and cultural history. On nearly all fronts, diplomatic history came under attack.[15]

Other approaches to the military and war include the following:

- *Economics*, which studies such matters as the financing of war, war's impact on the economy and the society, and the institutional legacy of war.
- *Feminist and gender studies* of war, which build on the egalitarian thrust of the new social and cultural history of the 1960s and the growing prioritizing of "the study of social structures and mentalities" over the concentration on concrete events. Feminist military studies also consider "the larger phenomenon of war, which involves political structures, economic organization, and social hierarchies, and thus affects noncombatants as well as combatants, women as well as men."[16]
- The *history of science and technology*, which arose out of the disciplines of the history of science and intellectual history. Its practitioners study the impact of technology on war and the military as an institution, as well as the ways in which military technology and science have influenced forms of social organization. Included in this research are the ways in which universities became deeply intertwined with military research during World War II and its aftermath. The relationship between military research and the

[15] H. W. Brands, ""Disciplinary Approaches of War: Diplomatic History," in Chambers, ed., *Oxford Guide to American Military History*, p. 219. The egalitarian and reform theme that Brands describes is examined at length in Peter Novick's exhaustive work, *That Noble Dream: The "Objectivity" Question and the American Historical Profession* (Cambridge University Press, 1988), esp. Part IV. For a fascinating account of how this egalitarian ideology has led to a reexamination of the politics and implications of the fall of the Roman Empire at the hands of invading barbarians, see Bryan Ward-Perkins, *The Fall of Rome and the End of Civilization* (Oxford University Press, 2005).

[16] Margaret Higonnet, "Disciplinary Views of War: Feminist and Gender Studies," in Chambers, ed., *Oxford Guide to American Military History*, p. 221.

Vietnam War spawned the crisis of the military-university relationship that comprises a central theme of this book.

- *Political science and international relations*, which include the schools of realism, neorealism, and constructivism, which we will examine in Chapters 12 and 13.
- *Psychology*, which deals with such issues as the psychological origins of war, the selection of military personnel, training for combat, the use of psychological warfare, and therapy for soldiers afflicted with war-related trauma (post-traumatic stress disorder, in today's nomenclature). Today there is even the field of "peace psychology," replete with its own journal entitled *Peace and Conflict: Journal of Peace Psychology.*[17]
- *Sociology and society studies*, which traces its origins at least to Clausewitz, who taught that war represents the extension of political objectives to the battlefield. Military sociology studies war and military institutions as distinct forms of social organization and group life. According to Martin Shaw, however, "Although war is one of the most important human social activities, the study of war in its social context has remained marginal to both sociology of war and war studies. Sociology has tended to treat war as an abnormal intrusion into the regularities of social life, rather than a major social institution in its own right."[18]
- The last disciplinary approach to the study of war is *Military History*, which is the bailiwick of military historians.

We can see from this quick review that there are many perspectives on war offered by those who are not military historians, yet military history is the only disciplinary perspective that is traditionally defined by the study of actual war and combat. We now turn to conceptual distinctions within military history (for our interest is in military history rather than other perspectives on war) before considering the status of military history in greater depth.

MILITARY HISTORY: DEFINITIONAL ISSUES

One cannot assess the status of military history without a grasp of the nature of the subject as a field of inquiry. Because our focus is on the academy, we begin by distinguishing *academic* military history from the two major competing forms.

Popular military history focuses mainly on issues that appeal to the general public, including battles and the heroics of war. It tends to be less critical (in the sense of looking at all the angles and applying scholarly tools) than academic works, but it can still contribute to our knowledge – or at least stimulate inquiry by more traditional academic military historians. Some academic military

[17] Michelle Wessells, "Disciplinary Views of War: Psychology," in Chambers, ed., *Oxford Guide to American Military History*, pp. 228–9.

[18] Martin Shaw, "Disciplinary Views of War: Society Studies," in Chambers, ed., *Oxford Guide to American Military History*, p. 228; Morris Janowitz, *The Professional Soldier: A Social and Political Portrait* (Free Press, 1960).

historians cast a jaundiced eye upon popular military history, but some scholars reply that the resort to popular military history (as well as what is called "operational military history," discussed momentarily) is at least in part a product of the marginalization of academic military history. Jeremy Black, a prolific academic in the field, observes a Catch-22 quality to this game:

> Work of this type [popular military history] is validated through structures, largely, if not exclusively, commercial in character, that are outside those of the academic profession, but that does not make it less important. With the "academy" in large part closed, authors who focus on operational military history are obliged to live by their pens, and this encourages publication in a style that further marginalizes the subject in terms of the academy.[19]

Applied (or operational) military history is often more utilitarian in nature. Like popular military history, operational military history has many productive uses, but can also suffer, depending on the product, from a tendency to be pundit-like and superficial.[20] According to Wayne E. Lee, "The applied literature derives from the now long-held conviction that understanding the wars of the past will help military leaders plan for, and succeed in the future."[21] (Although history does not repeat itself, it does rhyme, as Mark Twain observed.) Applied military history has a long-standing tradition, and is practiced extensively in military circles. It also has a significant place in certain sectors of the academy. Each service branch has fashioned its own list of such works for different ranks to study; and the professional military journals are primary sources for such studies. Applied military history has obvious practical uses, and its best products are thorough and nuanced. Christopher Zenk, a freshly commissioned second lieutenant from Detachment 730 at the University of Pittsburgh summarized the operational aspects of military history based on his four years of experience in the program. We quote him at some length in order to convey the subtleties that he describes:

> Military history, heritage, and culture were presented to me almost immediately upon the outset of my military education as a Cadet. The AFROTC curriculum is broken into four distinct categories: 1) Foundations of the Air Force; 2) The Evolution of Aerospace Studies; 3) Leadership Studies; and 4) National Security Studies and Preparation for Active Duty. In each of these sections there is substantial military history. Yet it is primarily based upon the foundations and ideas put forth in Air Force specific doctrine.... We are exposed to the traditional model of lecture supplemented by written assignments and tests, yet we are engaged on a much more personal level through the use of case studies, personal accounts, Air University training videos, and an instructor who has, at least in some instances, been involved with the Air Force operations we discuss

[19] Jeremy Black, *Rethinking Military History* (Routledge, 2004), p. 39.

[20] John A. Lynn II, "Breaching the Walls of Academe: The Purposes, Problems, and Prospects of Military History," *Academic Questions* 21 (2008): 23.

[21] Wayne Lee, "Mind and Matter – Cultural Analysis in American Military History: A Look at the State of the Field," *Journal of American History* (March 2007): 1116. We derive these three types of military history from both Lee and John A. Lynn II, "Breaching the Walls of Academe," pp. 18–36.

> within the classroom. ... The class is also conducted in a military setting within our detachment, with everyone in the uniform of the day. The room is called for the instructor as he enters and exits the room, NO ONE is ever late, and if you miss class you better have a damned good reason or have a pre-arrangement with the instructor. This all facilitates a professional and highly beneficial atmosphere for not only learning but the development of officership/proper customs and courtesies in a group military environment.[22]

The operational aspects of military history are paramount in ROTC, which is expected given the nature of the program. The material may not always be purely academic, but it should not be taken lightly; the military history of which Zenk speaks is used instrumentally to train future officers to contribute to fighting and winning wars and related conflicts, as well as to understand how to avoid using force when it is not necessary.

In addition, operational military history has achieved long-standing distinction in academia in research; it deals with what Robert M. Citino calls the "province of war, of campaign, and of battle," in a 2007 review essay of military history in the *American Historical Review*. (The publication of this review itself suggests some sort of revival in the field, as does the publication of Wayne Lee's review essay, which we will discuss shortly.) Citino maintains that the broadening of operational history in recent decades reflects similar movements in the field of military history more broadly: "Once the almost exclusive preserve of 'drums and trumpets,' packed with stirring tales of glory and shame, bravery and cowardice, it benefits today from a much more sophisticated conceptual framework that includes questions of culture (both military and civic), sociology, and group psychology."[23] Thus, we may properly place this type of operational military history within the ambit of academic military history, to which we now turn.

The third type of military history, *academic military history*, concerns us most, as our focus is on the university. The broader mission of academic military history is similar to that of general academic history, as John Lynn relates: "Academic military history is much like the study of other historical specialties: its goal is to understand the past for its own sake; its standards demand the high level of scholarship, and its intended audience is, above all, the community of historians."[24]

[22] E-mail exchange with Christopher Zenk, University of Pittsburgh, November 2010. Zenk was in the final year of a BA/MA program (he completed both degress in only four years) en route to flight school, where he is now a lieutenant in the Air Force.

[23] Robert M. Citino, "Review Essay. Military Histories Old and New: A Reintroduction," *American Historical Review* 1112, 4 (2007): paragraph 21, online version: http://www.historycooperative.org/journals/ahr/112.4/citino.html. Citino names Dennis E. Showalter and Reed Browning as primary examples of excellent operational military historians.

[24] Lynn, "Breaching the Walls of Academe," pp. 22–3. At the same time, the divide is not always hard and fast, as some leading academic military historians operate in military circles to integrate the academy with scholars at military institutions. For example, the Harold Keith Johnson Chair of Military History at the Army War College is selected from the ranks of the nation's leading academic military historians, who then teach soldiers primarily interested in operational knowledge.

The definition of academic military history is less straightforward. Because the military's primary duty is to defend the country through the efficient deployment of force (even in today's more broadly defined strategic environment), the concept or phenomenon of war must be part of the definition of military history.[25] Lynn provides a good operational definition: "Military history is the study of military institutions and practices and of the conduct of war in the past." And military historians "are those who write military history, whether this work comprises their main scholarly effort or simply part of it, whether or not they define themselves as military historians."[26] Lynn also advocates

> re-conceptualizing war into the broader category of security.... Samuel Johnson wrote that "Nothing focuses the mind like a hanging," and the fact is that life and death issues trump the contemplative meanderings so dear to many cultural historians. At least in my head, one way to get back to reality is to deal with security. And by security I would include violence, illness, and economic threat. War encompasses all of these in the extreme.[27]

On the one hand, Lynn's basic definition is narrow, as it excludes those who study the *causes and consequences* of war, however much the shadow of war might hang over their work. On the other hand, Lynn's definition is also somewhat flexible because it covers scholars who are not military historians in a narrower sense. Lynn includes such historians as Geoffrey Parker and James McPherson on his list because "a significant part of their output addresses the history of military institutions and the conduct of war."[28] Although a noted member of the school of thought that believes military history is embattled, retired military historian John Shy praises the publication of several works by scholars who are not primarily military historians. He cites John Dower's *War Without Mercy* (which addresses race and the Pacific War); John Brewer's *The Sinews of Power* (about how war was a key factor in the rise of England as a world power between 1688 and 1783); Niall Ferguson's *The Pity of War* (a reinterpretation of the causes, course, and consequences of World War I); and David Bell's *The First Total War* (dealing with how the French Revolution and Napoleonic Wars helped to shape twentieth-century wars.)[29] Of course, Lynn's

[25] David Kilcullen emphasizes the importance of understanding the new security environment to win wars. See Kilcullen, *The Accidental Guerilla: Fighting Small Wars in the Midst of a Big One* (Oxford University Press, 2009).

[26] Lynn, "Breaching the Walls of Academe," pp. 18–19.

[27] Lynn, "Breaching the Walls of Academe," pp. 28–9. We could add "cyber war" to the list. See, e.g., Richard A. Clarke, *Cyber War: The Next Threat to National Security and What to Do About It* (HarperCollins, 2010).

[28] Lynn, "Breaching the Walls of Academe," p. 19. McPherson, for example, published a book in 2008 on how Lincoln came to understand that conducting the Civil War as commander in chief was his paramount duty as president. See James M. McPherson, *Tied by War: Abraham Lincoln as Commander in Chief* (Penguin Press, 2008).

[29] John Shy, "The 2008 George C. Marshall Lecture in Military History: History and the History of War," *Michigan Studies Review*, December 1, 2008; John Dower, *War Without Mercy: Race and Power in the Pacific War* (Random House, 1986); John Brewer, *The Sinews of Power: War, Money, and the English State, 1688–1763* (Harvard University Press, 1988); Niall Ferguson, *The*

definition gets blurry at the margins. It is unclear, for example, whether, Donald Kagan's book *On the Origins of War and the Preservation of Peace* would qualify under this definition, as it deals mainly with causes of war, although it does treat military practices and institutions. (Lynn does not discuss this work himself.) In our view, Kagan's book fits as military history; interestingly, Kagan does not consider himself a military historian, even though he has also published such works as *The Peloponnesian War*.[30]

Wayne E. Lee presents a broader interpretation of military history in a major review essay of the state of the field in the 2007 *Journal of American History*. According to Lee, academic military history has two "interconnected parts." The first is the more traditional form that "comprises the 'material and operational' works that focus on the nature of weapons and the activities of armies within political, economic, and technological contexts." The second is the type of scholarship that has risen to prominence since the 1960s: the "new military history," which consists of cultural studies and studies in "war and society." The new military history places the study of the military within a broader intellectual horizon, linking it to developments in history as a discipline:

> The now-old new military history has focused on the more humanistic side of war: Who was the military, and what happened to them while they were there? The tremendous success in answering those basic questions about the composition of military organizations and the experience of their members has begun to open up new and more complex questions about values, motivations, and expectations. Military historians have thus followed the trend within the discipline from social history into the so-called cultural or linguistic turn.[31]

Cultural scholarship examines the mental, psychological, and social background out of which military-related choices emerge in such areas as recruitment, training, strategy, tactics, tradition, and the like. "Cultural analysis in military history should connect that 'idea template' to wartime behavior, while recognizing that there may be different templates at different levels within the military and the political leadership." Lee cites Lynn himself as an example of cultural analysis at its best (as does Citino), for Lynn's *Battle* deals with tensions between a society's "discourse" on war and its army's actual practice in combat. "The almost unavoidable disconnect between the values found in the discourse and the actual experience of war is in turn likely to produce a new discourse."[32] (Recall the

Pity of War: Explaining World War I (Penguin Press, 1998); David Bell, *The First Total War: Napoleon's Europe and the Birth of Warfare as We Know It* (Houghton Mifflin, 2007).

[30] Interview with Donald Kagan, Yale University Department of History, 2008; Donald Kagan, *On the Origins of War and the Preservation of Peace* (Doubleday, 1995); Donald Kagan, *The Peloponnesian War* (Penguin, 2003.)

[31] Lee, "Mind and Matter," p. 1117. Citino also focuses on the new military history. For an extended analysis and defense of the cultural turn in military history, see Black, *Rethinking Military History*. Cultural military history bears a close resemblance to the "constructivism" that has become a major school of scholarship in the international relations field. As we will see when we discuss the status of strategic studies, constructivism has enriched the field; yet it also can distract us from facing the harsh realities of realism.

[32] Lee, *Mind and Matter*, p. 1119.

discussion in Chapter 2 of the poet Ambrose Bierce and other thinker-soldiers: "Cultivate a taste for distasteful truths. And ... most of all, endeavor to see things as they are, not as they ought to be," Bierce counseled.)[33] In many respects, the cultural approach (especially "war and society" scholarship) is not new, extending back to the famous work of Clausewitz and Hans Delbruck, who were among the first military historians and theoreticians to develop the important links between the military, society, culture, and politics.[34]

Lee discerns four major categories of cultural studies.[35] The first, "strategic culture," embraces the most traditional military history, addressing the culture in which individuals and relevant institutions "consciously conceived of specific military or policy choices." A classic work of strategic culture is Russell F. Weigley's *The American Way of War*, which argues that American culture limits the strategic paradigms that military leaders envision (or, at least, the effectiveness of paradigms inconsistent with the culture), making the extended fighting of limited wars difficult.[36] The second category, "societal culture," looks beyond specific military and policy choices toward the broader relationship between culture and the military as an institution and way of life. In what ways do deeply rooted cultural values affect the proneness to violence and how wars are fought? How does culture affect such things as recruitment and the factors that motivate a soldier to fight? How does culture shape the military as an institution? The list is virtually endless.

A third approach is "memory and memorization," which is the way in which war is constructed in personal and cultural memory. (Citino considers memory to be the most important component of cultural military history.)[37] This area of study has mushroomed into a cottage industry over the last twenty years, as a perusal of course offerings on department websites reveals. Finally, the "war and society" approach emphasizes "the connections between social organization, political institutions, and military activity (whether institutional activity or war making)." War and society literature is voluminous, "encompassing studies of the social and economic background of soldiers, civil–military relations, the marginalized within the military (including women, African Americans, Native

[33] Lynn discusses cultural military history in a very favorable vein in a 1997 essay otherwise devoted to sounding alarm bells about the status of military history in the academy. John A. Lynn, "The Embattled Future of Academic Military History," *Journal of Military History* 61 (1997): 777–89; John A. Lynn, *Battle: A Cultural History of Combat and Culture* (Westview Press, 2003).

[34] Carl von Clausewitz, *On War* (Penguin, 1968); Gordon Craig, "Delbruck: The Military Historian," in Peter Paret, ed., *Makers of Modern Strategy: From Machiavelli to the Nuclear Age*, 2nd Edition (Princeton University Press, 1986), pp. 326–53.

[35] The discussion of these four types is drawn from Lee, *Mind and Matter*, pp. 1119–42.

[36] Russell F. Weigley, *The American Way of War: A History of United States Military Strategy and Policy* (University of Indiana Press, 1973). For a political science version of this type of logic, see Alexander L. George's pioneering essay, "The Operational Code: A Neglected Approach to the Study of Political Leaders and Decision-Making," *International Studies Quarterly* 13, 2 (July 1969).

[37] Citino, "Military Histories Old and New," paragraphs 21–7, online version: http://www.historycooperative.org/journals/ahr/112.4/citino.html.

Americans, and Hispanics), the experience of the home front, and the impact of war on society and the state."[38] In some respects, our book is an example of war and society literature, for we are concerned with the status of the military as an institution within the university and how such integration affects education – although, as we have underscored, we are not military historians.

Lee's and Citino's reviews of the broad scope of military history reveal the richness and depth of the best scholarship in the field and counsel us to be careful about jumping to conclusions regarding the status of military history. And no one should question the significance of the broader works that Lee discusses. However, our question is not the significance of such work, but rather the status of military history as a distinctive enterprise with something to contribute to education that other forms of scholarship are not able to provide. The discussion in Chapter 2 provides the tools with which to choose a definition: *the normative and political significance of national security, war, and the military as an institution, and the practical and existential aspects of the use of violence to achieve necessary normative purposes.* Combat and the targeting of force are crucial foci in this regard. As Lynn wrote in an earlier essay, "To me, the essence of military history is combat; it is what makes our subject unique. The life and death nature of war defines attitudes and practices within militaries, even in peacetime and even in elements of the military which are not directly in harm's way. Emphasis on social history tended to move us away from that focus."[39] (Recall also Eric Ouellet's suggestion in Chapter 2 that military sociology stake out "organized violence" as its research *sine qua non*: "The central construct, which appears to me as already latent in military sociology, is violence or, more accurately, organized violence. Military sociology is the sociology of organized violence.")[40] Citino sums up the matter well in his discussion of Lynn's somewhat ambiguous relationship to cultural military history:

> [Lynn's] *Battle*, therefore, plays a dual role. It offers a promising new cultural approach to the study of war, but it also demonstrates the limits to which most military historians feel they can go without breaking faith with their subject. The truth is, as deeply as they probe the culture of war, they will still want to ground themselves in the event itself, as opposed to its later interpretation, its memory, or its instrumentalization. It is highly unlikely, therefore, that they will ever be completely comfortable with [Pierre] Nora's definition of history as being "less interested in events themselves than in the construction of events over time," or with focusing exclusively on the constructed cultural icon.[41]

[38] Lee, *Mind and Matter*, p. 1138.

[39] Lynn, "The Embattled Future of Military History," p. 783.

[40] Eric Ouellet, "New Directions in Military Sociology," in Ouellet, ed., *New Directions in Military Sociology* (de Sitter, 2005), pp. 22–3. This distinctive aspect of the military profession is also a theme in Samuel P. Huntington, *The Soldier and the State: The Theory and Politics of Civil-Military Relations* (Harvard University Press, 1957).

[41] Citino, "Military Histories Old and New," paragraph 41, online version: http://www.history-cooperative.org/journals/ahr/112.4/citino.html.

Lee's review also illustrates that one's position regarding the condition of military history is partly a function of definition and of how broadly one conceptualizes the field. Lynn's definition concentrates more intensely on the conduct of war, and it is easier to conclude that military history is "embattled" if we apply this definition rather than the orientation proffered by Lee and Citino. It is not surprising, then, that these historians appear more optimistic about the status of military history than Lynn does. (Perhaps we could say the same thing about the Miller/Grimsley dispute discussed previously, although they did not offer definitions of the field.)

Lynn's definition is more helpful for our specific purposes than Lee's approach to the field, although the approaches do overlap. (Lynn does not provide an exact definition, but it is clear that he considers broad swaths of cultural, war/society, and memorization scholarship to be part of military history, although often outside of its core meaning.) But Lynn's operational definition of military history brings us back to the centrality of war itself in the enterprise. (Also recall Lynn's emphasis on security, mentioned previously.) Definitions should stress what is distinctive about a term, and when all is said and done, the military's core function is to wage and win wars in the name of national security. As Samuel Huntington wrote, "The existence of the military profession presupposes conflicting human interests and the use of violence to further those interests. Consequently, the military ethic views conflict as a universal pattern throughout nature and sees violence rooted in the permanent biological and psychological nature of men."[42] In addition, definitions should be precise enough to give sufficient coherence to an inquiry. By broadening the definition to include such things as memorization, we risk losing the core of military history, which is about war. Black contends that the war and society movement "brought military history back into the academy through the back door, at least in America."[43] Black's terminology intimates that the academy can only tolerate or endure military history if it is sufficiently divorced from the actuality of war. This assessment can be unfair, for, as we will see in the following chapter, one valid critique of some products of traditional military history pertains to their lack of intellectual breadth and depth. For our purposes, therefore, Black's point simply cautions us not to be too sanguine about the status of military history simply because of the successes of the war society and cultural movements.

In his 2008 Marshall Lecture, John Shy praised those authors who do not avert their eyes from the actuality of war and combat. They "recall us to our main business, which is to study and write about war ... with the aim of educating ourselves, our colleagues, and ultimately our students and the public about war in all its awful complexity and perversity."[44] At its best, military history deals with the problem of war in a thoughtful, penetrating manner that

[42] Huntington, *The Soldier and the State*, pp. 62–3.

[43] Black, *Rethinking Military History*, p. 8.

[44] Shy, "The 2008 George C. Marshall Lecture in Military History: History and the History of War," p. 11. In a review of the American Military Institute's 1991 Annual Meeting, which was

compels us to face what Nietzsche called uncomfortable truths. In addressing the relevance of Sun-Tzu and Clausewitz for thinking about the war on terrorism, Robert Kaplan reflects on the significance of what these theorists of war left unsaid in their classic works: "War is a fact of the human social condition neither man wishes were so. ... Both oppose militarism, but accept the reality of war, and from that acceptance reason that any policy lacking martial vigor – any policy that fails to communicate a warrior spirit – only makes war more likely."[45] As discussed in Chapter 2, *it is this extraordinary, realistic consciousness that the study of war and security can contribute to liberal and civic education.* This perspective embraces the significance of all the works that Lee and Citino evaluate, but it persuades us to pay special attention to the focus of Lynn – especially given the pedagogical interests of this book.

BASIC HISTORICAL TRENDS

In dealing with historical trends, we must be careful to avoid falling into the "Golden Age" trap, for in reality, military history has seldom enjoyed high status in the academic field of history. As Wayne Lee remarked in an e-mail exchange, "There was no 'golden age' of military history from which we have somehow slipped. There were never piles of institutions invested in it as a major subfield of their department. In fact, quite the reverse: as an academic field it is quite young."[46] And as Gordon Craig comments in an essay on the great military historian Hans Delbruck, the military historian has "generally been a kind of misfit, regarded with suspicion by both his colleagues and by the military men whose activities he seeks to portray." Craig also points to a deeper cause: "In democratic countries especially, [suspicion] arises from the belief that war is an aberration in the historical process and that, consequently, the study of war is neither truthful nor seemly."[47] In many respects, this status parallels public attitudes toward the professional military in American history, even though that institution's status today is very high, as it was in the 1960s before the Vietnam War took its toll. Historically, the citizen-soldier ideal is partly a product of societal distrust of a standing professional military.[48] Accordingly,

dedicated to "The New Military History," John Whiteclay Chambers reported that the distinguished panelists agreed that cultural and war/society scholarship had made significant contributions to the study of the military and war. That said, "The predominant view at the conference seemed to be that the 'new' military history must not avoid the study of armed conflict; it should not try to 'escape from war.'" John Whiteclay Chambers, "Conference Review Essay: The New Military History: Myth and Reality," *Journal of Military History* 55, 395 (1991), p. 405.

45 Robert D. Kaplan, "On Forgetting the Obvious," *American Interest* (July/August 2007).

46 E-mail exchange with Wayne Lee, University of North Carolina History Department, June–July 2009.

47 Craig, "Delbruck: The Military Historian," p. 352. See also, Hans Joas, *War and Modernity* (Polity, 2003). ch. 7, "Between Power Politics and Pacifist Utopia: Peace and War in Social Theory."

48 See, e.g., Robert L. Bateman, "The Army and Academic Culture," *Academic Questions* 21 (2008): 62–4; Edward M. Coffman, *The Old Army: A Portrait of the American Army in Peacetime, 1784–1898* (Oxford University Press, 1986).

we must be realistic in interpreting the status of military history, comparing the status to the actual past rather than an idealized past that never existed.

In a seminal 1962 essay, "The Historian and the Study of War," Louis Morton pointed out that historians turned away from military history in the 1890s to concentrate on "social, economic, and intellectual problems." By the 1920s and 1930s, history textbooks either ignored wars or dealt with war in shallow ways. Consequently, the most serious military history during this period was written by military professionals, mainly as applied or operational military history.[49] A catalogue survey of thirty leading U.S. universities in 1935–6 found "virtually no courses" in military and naval history during this period.[50] Morton did not provide a succinct definition of military history, but it is evident that he construed the discipline along the lines of Lynn; for example, he remarks that the textbooks of the 1920s and 1930s "ignored wars altogether or treated them cursorily, concentrating instead on their causes and results." He also underscored the difference between studying the "impact" of war rather than "an analysis of war itself as a social phenomenon" and the military as an institution.[51]

The situation changed somewhat after World War II, but not for a while. The status of military history continued to be marginal in the mid-1950s, as an extensive 1954 survey conducted by Richard C. Brown revealed. Of the 493 colleges and universities that responded to Brown, only 37 offered courses in military history. In addition, only five schools reported supporting graduate programs, accommodating between forty and forty-five students. In a 1955 American Historical Association accounting of Ph.D. dissertations in progress in American universities, only twenty-five dissertations dealt with military subjects. Morton observed that, "There has been little or no response to the intellectual challenge of the Cold War in terms of research and training. There is no evidence that the situation had basically changed by 1960." In concluding his essay, Morton speculated on the causes for this state of affairs as of 1960: "Regarding war as an aberration, an interruption to the normal course of human progress, historians have generally avoided it as a subject unworthy of study, if not downright dangerous. It is almost as if they hoped that by ignoring war, they might eliminate it altogether."[52] We can contrast this view with realists going back to Thucydides, who have believed that history is a source of wisdom that can help us to avoid past mistakes that contributed to war. At the same time, although the number of dissertations and courses during the first decade after

[49] Louis Morton, "The Historian and the Study of War," *Mississippi Valley Historical Review* 48, 599 (1962), p. 600.

[50] Edward. M. Coffman, "The Course of Military History Since World War II," *Journal of Military History* 61 (1997), p. 763.

[51] Morton, "The Historian and the Study of War," p. 600.

[52] Morton, "The Historian and the Study of War," pp. 601, 610–12; Richard C. Brown, *The Teaching of Military History in Colleges and Universities of the United States,* Historical Studies, no. 124 (U.S. Air Force Historical Division, Research Studies Institute, Air University, 1955).

World War II seems small, an alternative possibility is that this period was poised to spawn a comparative upswing in the status of military history, especially considering its almost nonexistent status in the 1930s.

Interestingly, Mac Coffman draws a different conclusion respecting this period, partly from the same evidence that Morton cites. Perhaps Morton's assessment came at the end of an era, just as another age was about to spread its wings. According to Hegel, the owl of Minerva – the symbol of wisdom – flies at dusk, when the completeness of the day lies before its eyes. Similarly, the best historical knowledge comes at the end of an era, not at the beginning. Herein lies Coffman's advantage over Morton. Compared to the virtual nonexistence of university courses before World War II, the quarter-century following the war represented a "phenomenal increase in courses on that subject in academe." For example, by 1970, 110 schools offered courses in military history.[53] In 1961, the American Historical Association included military history in the pamphlets published by the organization's Service Center for Teachers of History and a number of distinguished scholars made military history their calling:

> From the early 1960s into the 1990s, under the leadership of such prominent historians as Russell Weigley, John Shy, Peter Paret, Allan Millet, Robin Higham, Charles Burdick, and others [Coffman's modesty prevented him from mentioning himself], military history flourished in academe. Ohio State, Michigan, Temple, Illinois, Wisconsin, Stanford, Princeton, Yale, Penn State, Kansas State, Texas A&M, and several California State University campuses were among those which offered fields in that area.

Meanwhile, the military itself began developing programs in military history. In 1969, the Air Force opened a new history office in its Air Staff, and the Army created a Military Research Collection (now the Military History Institute) at the Army War College in 1967. These and related organizations forged links with academic military historians.[54] In other words, the resources, visibility, connections, and relationships that bestow the power necessary to sustain and nourish professional knowledge and fields began to flourish.[55]

Coffman's own class in American military history at Wisconsin thrived even as Vietnam War protests raged on a campus that was an "epicenter" of antiwar activity. Class enrollment peaked at two hundred students during this time, and no one ever held a protest against what Coffman taught. Unfortunately, this was not the case for Wisconsin political scientist David Tarr, who taught national security courses. Tarr felt pedagogically obligated to inform students in his classes and in forums across the campus (often presenting outside speakers and officials) of the government's positions regarding the war. Protesters

[53] Coffman, "The Course of Military History Since World War II," p. 765. Coffman, however, did not provide a definition of the term. In the next chapter, we extend Coffman's study, and in doing so attempt to provide a clear definition of different types of military history. We consider courses offered as well as perspectives from historians on the status of various types of military history.

[54] Coffman, "The Course of Military History Since World War II," pp. 769–72.

[55] See, e.g., Michel Foucault, *Knowledge/Power: Selected Interviews and Other Writings, 1972–77*, edited by Colin Gordon (Pantheon, 1980).

repeatedly disrupted Tarr's classes and public appearances during those years, and the university did little to protect the academic freedom of Tarr and his students in the classroom.[56]

Coffman attributes the elevation of military history's status to several factors. For starters, many historians participated in the extensive governmental sponsorship of historical work on World War II, centered in the federal Office of the Chief of Military History and the Office of Production Management. Perhaps half of the professional historians in the country between the ages of twenty-five and forty interacted in some capacity in these enterprises. De facto, this office "became the school of military history that had never existed before in this country." Historians participated in many government programs during World War II, serving as soldiers and as workers in government agencies – including the Office of Strategic Services (OSS), which was the predecessor of the CIA. University involvement with the government and the military during World War II and the Cold War was deep and extensive, as depicted by a vast literature.[57] In addition, the fact that many historians had served in the war engendered an interest in military history. Meanwhile, the advent of the Cold War spawned a broad interest in national security, military affairs, technology, and social science; new security studies programs mushroomed around the country out of this fertile context.[58] When Coffman joined the history department at Madison in 1961, one-third of its thirty-five members were veterans. By the mid-1990s, when he retired, only seven of fifty had served. (The decline in the percentages of veterans serving in university departments is often cited as a major reason for the growing gap between the military and the university.) The number today is considerably smaller. As we saw in Chapters 8 and 9 regarding ROTC's presence on campus, actual contact with individuals with certain experiences is important.

Another factor assisting military history was the general explosion of funding for education in the postwar years. As Wayne Lee observed in an e-mail exchange, "As in most history departments all the sub-fields are engaged in at least friendly competition with each other for priority in hiring, comparative

[56] Interview with Professor David W. Tarr, University of Wisconsin, June 2007; Oral History Interview, University of Wisconsin Archives and Records Management, Interview 614: http://archives.library.wisc.edu/oral-history/guide/601–700/611–620.html#tarr; Interview 837 http://archives.library.wisc.edu/oral-history/guide/801–900/831–840.html#tarr.

[57] Coffman, "The Course of Military History Since World War II," pp. 763–6. On historians' participation in OSS, see Robin W. Winks, *Cloak and Gown: Scholars in the Secret War, 1939–1961* (Yale University Press, 1987). See the discussion of the World War II and Cold War Universities in Chapter 4 of this book.

[58] See Gene M. Lyons and Louis Morton, *Schools for Strategy: Education and Research in National Security Affairs* (Frederick A. Praeger, 1965); Jeremi Suri, *Henry Kissinger and the American Century* (Harvard University Press, 2007), pp. 3–99, 107–17, 122–39, 161, 191, 207. For one of the best books on defense spending and the post–World War II University, see Roger L. Geiger, *Research and Relevant Knowledge: American Research Universities Since World War II* (Oxford University Press, 1993).

prestige, graduate admissions, etc."[59] Tolerance comes naturally when there is money to share, thereby rendering less competition over limited slots in an erstwhile zero-sum game. The new military history arose on the heels of this growth. The situation remained favorable to academic military history at the dawn of the century's last decade. In 1991, Yale historian Paul Kennedy depicted the field as thriving and speculated that one of its major problems would be finding enough resources to accommodate its swelling number of practitioners.[60] But Kennedy may have been the owl of Minerva's next victim, although for a different reason from that cited by Morton. Addressing Kennedy's prediction in 1997, Coffman wrote, "Such has not been the case. While military history is certainly alive in academe, there is a question as to its wellness as two major universities – Michigan and Wisconsin – have recently virtually abandoned the field. The new generation of academics is not as tolerant as their predecessors."[61]

The status of military history, as we have seen, is hard to pin down, a fact that remains even when we consider several recent surveys of the field by military historians.

RECENT MILITARY HISTORIAN SURVEYS

In this section, we discuss some recent surveys conducted by military historians dealing with the status of academic military history and then consider evidence that we have gathered in our own national survey.

One indicator of the status of military history is the prevalence of military history articles in leading journals over time. In 2007, Mac Coffman conducted a Journal Storage (JSTOR) survey of titles and articles published in the *Mississippi Valley Historical Review*, which changed its name to the *Journal of American History* in the mid-1960s. This survey is a follow-up to a survey of thirty-four "established military historians" who responded to a questionnaire that Coffman sent them in 2001. Many of the respondents in the latter survey were "despondent," with several claiming "that colleagues considered them old fashioned, hence insignificant, and, despite interest among undergraduates who filled their courses, they would likely not be replaced when they retired." One respondent wrote, "My concern is that history is losing the capacity to teach serious military and political history to such a degree that general undergraduate comprehension of the real world, past, present, and future, will be significantly degraded."[62] We received some similarly pessimistic responses from several

[59] E-mail exchange with Wayne Lee, June–July 2009.

[60] Paul Kennedy, "The Fall and Rise of Military History, *MHQ: The Quarterly Journal of Military History* 3 (Winter 1991), p. 12.

[61] Coffman, "The Course of Military History Since World War II," p. 775.

[62] Edward M. Coffman, "Military History and the OAH," manuscript provided to the author by Coffman, p. 18. The quotation is from Jon Sumida of the University of Maryland.

e-mail correspondents in the top-twenty history departments. One particularly negative respondent requested nonattribution:

> The climate in the department is not exactly hostile to topics on security and the military. Rather, these are areas that do not strike my colleagues as "interesting" or important. Part of the reason is distaste for things military and material. [Recall Lee's juxtaposition of "Mind and Matter."] Part of it is a sense that military history and related fields do not offer insights and understanding that my colleagues find useful in their own work, though it might be said that my colleagues show little evidence of having sampled much literature in these fields ... I doubt that the department will replace me when I retire.... They have declared my position critical but not urgent. In taking this position, my colleagues reflect the history community and the larger scholarly community in the United States.... When the American Historical Association asks its members to evaluate history departments, military history is not one of the fields they count. So giving a position to military history is tantamount to relinquishing a position that might raise the department's reputation. Military history will continue to thrive at second- and third-tier schools, because there is so much student demand. But it is disappearing from first-tier schools. The story for diplomatic history and other fields that explore issues of security is much the same.[63]

The conclusions that Coffman reached in his 2007 survey furnish a basis for guardedly less pessimism about the field – as do Lynn's reflections a couple of years after he wrote his 2008 essay "Breaching the Walls of Academe" (discussed later in this section). Coffman's definition of military history in his survey of the *Journal of American History (JAH)* is intentionally broad, including applied/operational aspects of war as well as the war and society approach. His definition is modeled on Theodore Roosevelt's 1912 call for a broader, more intellectually sophisticated approach to such study: "the political, diplomatic, economic, and social aspects of war, as well as the organization, mobilization, training, planning, and the conduct of war." Over time, the content of articles that met Coffman's criteria varied with the evolving interests of contributors (for example, the war covered – Revolutionary War, Civil War, World War I, World War II, Cold War, Korean War, and so on – and the political aspects of war, economic aspects, social aspects, and diplomatic aspects). But the percentages of articles dealing with military history thus defined remained surprisingly consistent over time.

From 1914 to 1930, the *Mississippi Valley Historical Review (MVHR)* published 221 articles, 31 of which constituted military history under the ambit of military so broadly defined, or 14 percent. The 1930s witnessed a mild decrease: Of 153 articles in the *MVHR*, 18 represented military history, or a bit less than 12 percent. Although professional military history enjoyed a boost during and after World War II due to governmental efforts that we will touch on in a moment, there was no meaningful increase in the *MVHR*: 18 of 142 articles during the 1940s, amounting to 12.5 percent; and 26 of 206 articles in the 1950s, constituting 12.6 percent. The 1960s and 1970s saw the first big

[63] E-mail exchange with a prominent military historian who asked "not for attribution." June–July 2009.

boost in teachers, courses, and Ph.D.s in military history, as we will see later in this chapter. But the percentage of military articles in the *MVHR* and *JAH* remained about the same as before: 26 of 218 articles in the 1960s, or 11.9 percent; and 21 of 190 articles in the 1970s, constituting 11 percent. Coffman cites a "notable shift of interest" toward social history during this period, indicating a preference for the "new" military history over its more traditional rivals. In the 1980s, the *JAH* published 175 articles, of which 22 were military history, making 12.5 percent (the topic of the Cold War led such entries); while the percentage fell to 8.5 percent (the lowest of the decades that Coffman covers) during the 1990s – the period during which critics began discerning a crisis for military history in the academy. But the figure jumps back to the historical norm between 2000 and 2007: 31 of 240 articles, amounting to 12.9 percent.[64]

In addition to these findings, Coffman also points to two American Organization of Historians (OAH) surveys taken in 2003, which "demonstrate that the situation of military history is not as bad as some who practice it think." A 2003 *JAH Recent Scholarship Online* survey revealed that political history had more published articles, books, and dissertations than social history, and that military history ranked seventh in a list of twenty-three fields, running ahead of Women and Femininity, Urban and Suburban, Native Americans, and Labor and Working Class History. The OAH survey listed up to five interests of members in twenty-nine fields. Military history ranked fourteenth in this survey, "far behind the four leaders – Social, Cultural, Political, and Women, as well as Labor and Urban history, yet ahead of Indian, Sexuality/Gender, and Environment history." Based on these and his own findings, Coffman concludes that "the future appears to be brighter than some military historians think."[65] As we will see in the next chapter, however, the status of military history in the leading departments might not be so sanguine. And we should bear in mind that Coffman's definition is considerably broader than Lynn's.

Lynn has also conducted an informal survey of 150 issues of the bellwether journal *The American Historical Review* between 1976 and 2006, publishing his findings in *Academic Questions*. As mentioned in Chapter 1, Lynn found only a handful of articles dealing with military history throughout this period, and only four departments among the top ninety-one with graduate programs in the field as of 2007 based on his criterion of two faculty members to qualify as a field.[66] Again, Lynn's definition of *military* was narrower than Coffman's. But like Coffman, Lynn believes that the pendulum could be swinging back in military history's favor. In 2009, he retired from Illinois (which he claims has no intention of replacing him) and accepted a part-time chair as Distinguished Professor of Military History at Northwestern. In an e-mail exchange, Lynn stressed how recent developments have made him more sanguine about the field. He also

[64] These results are all from Coffman, "Military History and the OAH."

[65] Coffman, "Military History and the OAH," p. 19.

[66] Lynn, "Breaching the Walls of Academe"; see also Lynn, "The Embattled Future of Academic Military History," pp. 777–89.

articulated these views in an address he gave at the University of Illinois' Phi Alpha Theta banquet that served as his retirement address at that institution. After discussing the conclusions he reached as a result of his purview of *The American Historical Review* (up to 2006), he turned to what might be the winds of change: "*But so much for the bad old news, how about the good new news?* Perhaps we are pariahs no more! We have emerged with surprising suddenness into the full light of attention. It has been rather blinding, and I am still stunned. But I'll try to explain it." Lynn pointed to the October issue of *The American Historical Review*, which included the first review essay of the military history field to appear in its pages for decades, Robert M. Citino's "Military Histories Old and New: A Reintroduction." In addition, military subjects have begun to be represented in the journal's "Featured Reviews," which usually number about five per volume. Beginning in 2007, of the sixty-seven Featured Reviews, three dealt with classic military history books, and eight "were devoted to books dealing with conquest, organized violence, and their somber consequences – all works of central interest to historians of war, military institutions, and war and culture."[67]

Of course, the comeback would be hollow if it was not matched by a sea change in departmental priorities to reflect demand for courses, particularly at the nation's leading universities.

MILITARY HISTORY AND THE DISCIPLINES: FINDINGS FROM A SURVEY OF SCHOLARS

We surveyed historians and political scientists from leading research universities in the United States. The survey sample consists of the top fifty research and top fifty private universities.[68] We chose the survey sample to illustrate any emphases and trends prevailing in the field of military history at leading research universities, both public and private, including hiring trends and the relative emphasis of military history in courses. These research universities are some of the most influential in the United States, so we are particularly interested in the status of military history in these institutions. (We consider the top twenty programs in some depth in the following chapter.)

We sent the survey to individuals with knowledge of courses, department history, and department priorities, such as department chairs and associate chairs.[69] We initially sent the survey to two individuals from each history and

67 E-mail exchange with John Lynn, Northwestern University History Department, May 2009. John A. Lynn II, "Victories and Surrenders: Riding with the Four Horsemen of the Apocalypse," an address given at the University of Illinois at Urbana-Champaign Phi Alpha Theta banquet, April 25, 2009. Emphasis in the original.

68 We used the *U.S. News & World Report* Rankings for the "National University Rankings": http://colleges.usnews.rankingsandreviews.com/best-colleges/national-universities-rankings/. This measure may not be ideal, but it is as good as any other to get an idea of the top research universities.

69 The survey was conducted through e-mail using the Department of Political Science Survey System at the University of Wisconsin. Our surveys were in the field from late 2007 to early 2008, with some brief follow-up surveys conducted in the summer of 2008.

political science department, taking the first response if both responded (as we only were seeking one response per department). When neither responded, we sent the survey to another knowledgeable member of the department, usually a tenured faculty member.[70] Our response rate for the history department survey and the political science survey were both about 90 percent.

We selected leaders of departments because department leaders presumably have knowledge of departmental hiring priorities and also because they may have a role in setting the agenda as far as hiring priorities are concerned. They also are the ones who likely do much of the lobbying for new hiring lines to university administrators. For these reasons, their perspectives on the status of military history are particularly important for our inquiry.[71]

The surveys were conducted in 2007–8, so we acknowledge that they are slightly dated, and do not take into consideration some of the more recent developments that we address, such as Lynn's reappraisal of the status of military history and (in the next chapter) the University of Wisconsin's hiring of a military historian. But they are nonetheless indicative of recent situations and trends, so the reader should find them useful, so long as he or she takes the timing of the surveys into consideration.

In the next chapter, we consider the status of military history from the vantage point of military historians. Before considering their perspective, we set the stage by considering the perspective of historians who have only an indirect stake in the issue, such as department chairs. Of course, a trade-off is that department chairs may not be as in tune to issues in military history as military historians. For this reason, we attempted to write questions in a manner that would resonate with department chairs. Specifically, we elected to forgo a highly nuanced approach to questions regarding military history, emphasizing instead broad distinctions between "traditional" and "new" military history. Our results indicate that historians think about military history in these terms. In the next chapter, we consider in depth the perspective of military historians in their own words, which provides us with the nuance and expertise that we require to better understand the status of military history.

The survey of history departments was designed to elicit information regarding the degree of emphasis on military history in those departments and in the field more broadly. The initial set of questions asked how often specific courses on military history are taught and the extent to which courses with substantial military history content are taught. We also divided responses for courses that are not being taught into "never taught" and "taught once but no longer." The question about courses being taught once but no longer provides insight into

[70] We attempted to contact at most four individuals from each department. Using this method, we were able to secure responses from nearly all the universities in our sample.

[71] Our survey has the benefit of assessing the perspective of leaders, but such an approach sacrifices the quantity of responses. We leave to future research a broader survey to determine the status of military history among historians or political scientists more generally, focusing instead on the status in leading departments, with the perspective of the department represented by its leaders.

trends in military history. If military history is on the decline, then we would expect many of the universities to have ceased teaching military history, or for the influence of military history to be limited in terms of providing specific courses and the content of courses.

Historians may also deal with issues of national security, as suggested by Lynn's plea for a security angle to military history, quoted earlier in this chapter. In particular, we were interested in the status of *national security* courses in history departments. Taking Clausewitz's observation that war and politics are seriously interrelated, history departments may benefit from courses on national security because it can be thought of as a more explicitly political aspect of the study of conflict and war. In this spirit, we asked how often courses on national security are taught, or how often courses dealing with *some* national security content are taught. We expected there to be limited emphasis on courses with national security in history departments because the traditional division of labor places national security issues in political science departments; but we also simply did not know the magnitude of emphasis of such courses in history departments.

Initial Survey with No Specific Definition of Military History

We have explained how the definition of military history one chooses influences how much status is ascribed to it. Accordingly, our initial survey began with four questions that did not define "military" history in any particular fashion, leaving its definition to the imagination or discretion of the respondent (we were also sure to mention that respondents should not include courses that are *primarily* oriented toward military history when considering whether there are courses that have *substantial content* devoted to military history). The four primary questions in the survey are as follows:

1. To the best of your knowledge, are there courses taught in your department that emphasize military politics or military history?
2. To the best of your knowledge, are there courses taught in your department that devote substantial attention to military politics or military history (not including courses specifically on military politics or military history)?
3. To the best of your knowledge, are there courses taught in your department devoted specifically to national security?
4. To the best of your knowledge, are there courses taught in your department that cover the topic of national security (not including courses that emphasize national security directly)?

Respondents were given the option of choosing "regularly taught," "periodically taught," "once, but no longer taught," and "never taught." The survey results of these questions are presented in Table 10.1.

Several results stand out in these findings. First, there is far more emphasis on military history than on national security, as we expected. Second – as our

TABLE 10.1. *Military History and National Security in History Departments: A First Take*

	Military History Courses (%)	Courses with Substantial Military History Content (%)	National Security Courses (%)	Courses with Some National Security Content (%)
Regularly taught	58.4	49.6	14.3	35.0
Periodically taught	28.1	34.4	27.3	26.3
Once, but no longer taught	7.9	3.4	2.5	2.5
Never taught	5.6	12.6	55.9	36.2
N	89	87	84	80

preceding coverage of the field of military history prepared us to expect – there are many courses with military history *content* even if there is not a specific course on military history. (This is hardly surprising given the significance of the military in national life.) Third, there is some evidence of a decline of military history. Several departments have taught military history courses with substantial military history content, but no longer do so. However, there is still substantial emphasis on military history, at least as defined in an open-ended manner. Over 85 percent of departments teach military history regularly or periodically, and nearly 85 percent of departments teach courses with substantial military history content regularly or periodically. The claim of a severe decline of military history appears to be overstated, as military historians Lynn and Coffman ascertained – *at least based on this measure, and given our broad definition of the term in this particular survey* (and assuming that our respondents' reports are credible). Our argument here is that, while such surveys provide us with useful information, to better understand the status of military history, it is necessary to consider explicitly the status of traditional military history.

We also asked our respondents about the appropriate degree of emphasis on military history. Few of the respondents believed that there is too much emphasis on military history. Recall that as department leaders, these respondents may not be representative of the departments, but as leaders they may have agenda-setting powers that make their perspectives more influential in the process of academic hiring. As such, the following results provide insight into whether or not leaders of departments believe that there is too much emphasis on the military.

To gauge departmental support, we asked the following question: Do you feel that military politics and military history receive enough attention in your discipline? Over 60 percent of individuals believe that the emphasis on military history is "about right." Over 30 percent believed that there is not enough emphasis on military history. That almost one-third of the leaders of the top one hundred departments consider military history underrepresented was surprising to us, indicating that a substantial minority agree with those who depict military history as "embattled." Because we did not provide a narrow definition of military history in this particular survey, this 30 percent figure may be optimistic. Department chairs could have in mind additions in cultural or social approaches to military history that are viewed as new and hence may improve the department's reputation as an innovative institution. We expect that a narrower concept of military history, what is conventionally understood as "guns and bombs" military history, would have less support among historians.[72]

We also asked about hiring priorities: How much of a priority does the department place on hiring faculty who can teach military politics or military history? We wanted to know whether there are any universities that give high priority to military history. It turns out that it is not a high-priority topic, and less than 25 percent of departments have even a low to moderate demand for military history from their respective departments. Slightly over 40 percent of departments stated that military history is not a priority, even though they have few experts. However, over 30 percent of the departments do not have priorities because their department has expertise in this area.[73] These results suggest to us that the glass is "half full."

We should also note that many of these programs are on campuses that have some military presence, mainly in the form of ROTC programs; respondents from over seventy of the history departments reported having ROTC programs on campus. So some form of military history enjoys at least some presence on campus even in departments that lack military historians.

Military History Survey Refined: Traditional Versus "New" Military History

After conducting the survey just discussed, we sent a survey that specifically distinguished between traditional military history (as defined by John Lynn) and the "new military history" that Wayne Lee and Robert Citino have portrayed. As we have repeatedly asseverated, we surmised that one's assessments regarding the status of military history are dependent upon the breadth of one's definition of the field. It could well be the case that new military history is doing well while traditional military history is not. In our view, both forms of military history have something important to offer, so both should be represented in order to encourage productive friction and learning. We conducted two separate surveys: one of the history departments that we had contacted in the first survey, and another of political science departments.

[72] The specific numbers for each response were as follows: too much, 4.8 percent; about right, 62.7 percent; not enough, 32.5 percent. N=83.

[73] The specific numbers for each response were as follows: high, 3.5 percent; low to moderate, 21.2 percent; not a priority, but we have a few experts in this area, 41.1 percent; not a priority because we have expertise in this area, 34.1 percent. N=85.

We introduced the survey by discussing the difference between traditional and new military history. We defined traditional military history as "the study of military institutions and practices and of the conduct of war in the past," including "chronicles of battles and operational aspects of war; the reasoning behind the formation of grand strategy, more specific strategy, and tactics by military leaders and rulers; and the politics and operation of the military as an institution." New military history includes the study of "'war and society' and cultural approaches to the military and war. The new military history includes such things as the ways in which cultural discursive norms and assumptions shape the way war is fought; the cultural, economic, and social causes of war; the social, economic, and political consequences of war; and how war is envisioned in individual and cultural memory." These definitions were included in the introduction to our survey, and we asked respondents to keep these definitions in mind when completing the survey. We then asked six questions about the emphasis of military history in respondents' departments:

1. With these distinctions in mind, how often are courses taught in your department that primarily focus on TRADITIONAL military history, defined as the study of military institutions and practices and of the conduct of war in the past? We are interested here in courses that focus primarily on traditional military history, not a combination of traditional and new approaches.
2. How often are courses taught in your department that primarily focus on NEW military history, which emphasizes the social and cultural aspects of war? We are interested here in courses that focus primarily on new military history, not a combination of traditional and new approaches.
3. How often are courses taught in your department on military history that balance traditional with new military history?
4. How often are courses taught in your department that devote substantial attention to traditional military history, yet do not focus primarily on traditional military history?
5. How often are course taught in your department that devote substantial attention to new military history, yet are not primarily on new military history?
6. How often are courses taught in your department that are devoted primarily to military history, but that do not emphasize traditional or new military history, as we have defined these areas?

For each question, we gave respondents four options: "frequently taught"; "periodically taught"; "once taught but no longer taught"; and "never taught." Our findings are presented in Table 10.2 (TMH refers to traditional military history and NMH to new military history).

We next asked a question about emphasis in their courses offered in military history: On balance, what types of military history courses are being taught? We gave respondents the options of traditional military history, new military history, a balance between traditional and military history, or some other system of

TABLE 10.2. *Traditional and New Military History in History Departments*

	Primary Focus on TMH (%)	Primary Focus on NMH (%)	Balance NMH and TMH (%)	Substantive Attention to TMH (%)	Substantive Attention to NMH (%)	Other Military History (%)
Frequently taught	19.8	27.7	24.8	17.8	24.7	1.9
Periodically taught	41.6	56.4	45.5	38.6	53.5	22.8
Once, but no longer taught	14.8	0	3.9	12.9	1.0	6.9
Never taught	23.7	15.8	25.7	30.7	20.8	68.3
N	83	83	83	83	82	82

military history. We found that 19.8 percent emphasize traditional military history, 27.7 percent emphasize new military history, and 44.5 percent balance traditional and new military history. We found that 14.8 percent offered courses that did not fit our definition of military history, either traditional or new.[74]

Our next questions pertained to hiring priorities. We asked the following question:

If your department were to hire a new faculty member specializing in military history, do you believe [the percentage of responses is provided after each question]:[75]

1. The department would be *more likely* to hire someone specializing in traditional military history [0 percent].
2. The department would be *less likely* to hire someone specializing in traditional military history [85.5 percent].
3. Distinctions between traditional and new military history would be *irrelevant* [14.5 percent].

While traditional military history may be enjoying a good deal of representation today, it may not enjoy such robust representation in the near future. *None* of the respondents indicated that they would be *more likely* to hire someone specializing in traditional military history. In contrast, many of the departments would be *less likely* to hire such a faculty member. It is also relevant to note that the distinctions between the two approaches to military history appear relevant to departments, with the vast majority stating that the distinctions among the approaches as we have defined them come into play in hiring decisions.

[74] N = 82.
[75] N = 82.

Our next question asked about how departments would react if a traditional military historian retired from the department. Specifically, we asked:

If there was a retirement of a traditional military historian in your department, do you believe that the department would be" [the percentage of responses is provided after each question]:[76]

1. Very likely to hire another traditional military historian [0 percent]
2. Somewhat likely to hire another traditional military historian [3.9 percent]
3. Very likely to hire someone specializing in new military history [16.8 percent]
4. Somewhat likely to hire someone specializing in new military history [14.8 percent]
5. Very likely to hire someone but specialization would be relatively unimportant [12.9 percent]
6. Somewhat likely to hire someone but specialization would be relatively unimportant [8.9 percent]
7. We would be unlikely to replace a traditional military historian regardless of the approach of new hires [42.6 percent]

Clearly, the last question suggests the glass is half full if you are working in the area of new military history, but it appears empty (at least in terms of future hiring priorities) if you are working from a more traditional perspective. None of our respondents (remember, these are department leaders) view replacing a traditionalist as very likely, and nearly half would not replace a military historian regardless of how his or her research is defined. Shy's exhortation earlier in this chapter to military historians (also encapsulated earlier by Citino) – to "recall us to our main business, which is to study and write about war ... with the aim of educating ourselves, our colleagues, and ultimately our students and the public about war in all its awful complexity and perversity" – appears to be falling on deaf ears.

Our last two questions of history department leaders dealt with the percentage of historians in traditional and new military history, respectively:[77]

Of your department faculty, how many specialize in traditional military history?

1. None [59.4 percent]
2. One [27.7 percent]
3. Two [9.9 percent]
4. Three or more [2.9 percent]

Of your department faculty, how many specialize in new military history?

1. None [47.5 percent]
2. One [32.6 percent]
3. Two [13.9 percent]
4. Three or more [6.9 percent]

These findings indicated to us that there appears to be more representation of new military history, but the matter remains close. As noted previously, however, hiring priorities may tip the balance more in favor of new military history.

[76] N = 82.

[77] N = 83 for each set of questions.

As faculty with expertise in traditional military history retire, they may be more likely to be replaced by scholars working within the new military history, or at least scholars who can package their work that way. We also see that there are many departments without military historians at all, but military history courses are often taught, which suggests that there are options to take courses at many programs even if they do not have a specialist in that area. But it is one thing to have courses available, and another to have them taught by true specialists in the field.

Open-Ended Questions

We also asked several open-ended questions in this survey. With these questions, we wanted to find out if there have been many conflicts over hiring military historians. As seen in the preceding, such conflicts have received much publicity and attention in recent years. We asked the following question to determine whether we could get at this issue with a survey: "*Do you know of any conflicts over hiring of faculty that reflects the status of military history or security studies in your department? If so, can you or would you be willing to comment on the nature of the conflict?*"

We received many responses to this question. Keep in mind that a strong majority of people said there were no conflicts of which they were aware. The fact that there are no reported conflicts does not mean that military history is not embattled in a department, for there could be a solid consensus that that it is not worthy of inclusion or significant presence. We provide the lion's share of these responses in this section. We omitted those that were repetitious or which in our determination were not really responsive to the question. (The list of all responses is available from the authors.)

As might be expected, these responses reflect the difference between traditional military history and the "new" military history, as well as differences of opinion based on a respondent's departmental situation, his or her view of what constitutes military history, and his or her own ideological orientation toward military history. The responses help to paint a picture of the complex tapestry within which military history struggles for recognition. If there was a trend, these responses indicate a concern about the status of military history. Thirteen of the twenty-one respondents to this question referred to opposition to military history in one form or another, some forms more strenuous than others. (Once again, recall that the larger pool of respondents reported little or no conflict.) "R" denotes an answer from a single respondent:

R: This hasn't posed a problem. We have a consensus that these topics should be researched and taught in this department.

R: Not at present, but I can well imagine conflicts erupting over the desirability of hiring someone who specializes in the field.

R: We have a large undergraduate major in diplomatic history and we participate in a large major in international relations. Military history is a part of that but it's fair to say that we would be more likely to identify such positions in terms of diplomatic history than in terms of military history.

R: 35 years ago a proposal was made to bring in a specialist in military history, partly to supplant the military history course offered by the DoD in the ROTC program at UC-Berkeley. The proposal was shot down without a great deal of discussion. There has been no move to bring up the subject again.

R: It's clear that most of my colleagues are ignorant or dismissive of the work in this area, although my chair is an exception to that rule. They would prefer to fill other "gaps" in the roster that reflect their own self-interest.

R: My department has consensually agreed on the need to build and maintain a strong presence in these fields.

R: No such conflicts during the past nine years of hiring, which in large part reflects the types of positions we've been trying to fill. None of them are related to military/security/international studies.

R: The full time faculty in my department view military history as "old fashioned" and do not value it as necessary field in the department. Candidates that focus on military history have little chance of being hired by my colleagues, but the field is very popular with students.

R: We hired last year in 20th century U.S. military history, but had a considerable struggle in the department.

R: My colleagues have had a prejudice against the teaching of military history, believing, falsely, that it is no more than "strategy and tactics." This, in spite of the emergence of a new military history that has a much wider scope of analytical concerns. Thus, we have never been able to agree to make hiring someone in the field a priority, and the matter actually rarely comes up. In recent years, however, there has been a bit of softening of opinion on this, though it has made no practical difference in our hiring priorities. By the way, we have known for years that students want military history taught, but those who are the loudest in asserting this opinion are usually war "buffs" and hobbyists, whose lack of intellectual engagement with the subject of war doesn't give them a lot of credibility.

R: We were given funds by an outside donor to search for a position in military history and will do so next year. But some faculty were opposed to the idea, since the field has become seen by some (not a majority) as too traditional etc.

R: Opposition by individual faculty to appointments as manifesting "militarization" of the university. Such individuals in our department represent a small minority.

R: Our department currently has two specialists in military history, and in all likelihood will maintain a commitment to that subfield in the future.

R: No conflicts. It is simply that we are charged with covering a much wider geographical and topical expanse of the past with the same (or at times, fewer) faculty members. Whereas in the past a department might feel compelled to have a dedicated military historian, now this is no more compelling than having a dedicated gender historian or intellectual historian or African historians etc. This is as it should be.

R: Any conflicts in this area have as much to do with the intellectual isolation of military/security scholars from other areas of study as they have to do with conflict among faculty in my department.

R: We have a prominent medievalist who teaches popular courses in military history. In our heavily social history department, it would be next to impossible to make the case successfully that we should hire another person in military history. This is not my view as department chair, but we are a highly democratic department and I would certainly be outvoted on this issue.

R: Some faculty think that military history is passe; others think it has advanced far beyond the old guns-and-bugles schools, and now addresses cultural and political history; others believe that if we do not teach military history, ROTC will take it over and do a poor job of it.

R: Most of the members of my department believe we have too many military historians already.

R: I know of no such conflict. We appointed a senior instructor whose teaching is predominantly in the field of military history, and the appointment was unanimously supported.

Conclusions Drawn from the Second History Department Survey

These survey results allow us to draw some tentative conclusions about the status of military history in the history departments at the nation's leading research universities. As Table 10.2 shows, a course (or courses) with a primary focus on traditional military history is frequently taught in only 19.8 percent of these departments, whereas 52.5 percent have courses involving either new military history or a balance of new and traditional (27.7 percent plus 24.8 percent). The figures look better if we include courses that devote "substantial attention" to traditional military history, although not as a primary focus: 37.6 percent of the departments have courses in which traditional military history is either a primary focus or a substantial focus (19.8 percent plus 17.8 percent). Still, this figure constitutes only slightly more than one-third of all departments, which hardly suggests a renaissance of military history, especially given the broader scope of the combined categories (primary focus plus substantial content). Overall, these figures suggest marginal status for traditional military history, but considerably stronger status for new military history. This conclusion is consistent with most of the commentary on military history's state, as well as the data collected in the next chapter. The information about courses taught on balance parallels Table 10.2.

Of course, the figures in Table 10.2 tell us neither how many courses are taught in the military history area, nor what fraction of all courses they represent. If a department teaches one military history course each year out of two hundred courses, that hardly constitutes meaningful status. The next chapter will provide such counts for the top-twenty history departments.

But this survey did inquire about the expertise of existing faculty members. We found that almost 60 percent of the departments had no one teaching traditional military history (59.4 percent), with slightly more than a quarter (27.7 percent) employing one such scholar. Departments with two or more such faculty members accounted for 12.8 percent. These figures suggest that traditional military historians are overloaded in a few departments – a conclusion supported by the more specific findings in the following chapter. Interestingly, almost half of the department leaders reported having no faculty members in new military history (47.5 percent), and the percentage who indicated that they had one, two, or three or more was not at all that much higher than the percentages for traditional military history.

Perhaps the most revealing figures regarding a threat to traditional military history pertain to hiring priorities. Recall that *no one* (representing 90 percent of the top–one hundred research universities) said that his or her department would hire a traditional military historian if the department were hiring a military historian. When asked about replacing a retiring traditional military historian, *none* of the department leaders surveyed said that replacing this person with someone like him or her was "very likely," and *only 3.9 percent* revealed that such replacement was "somewhat likely." New military history fared better in this category, but only 30.6 percent reported that their department would be either very or somewhat likely to hire such a scholar. These expressions of hiring priorities suggest that any renaissance in military history will reflect new military history rather than its traditional counterpart.

Universities began to experience substantial financial contractions while we were conducting these surveys (primarily in 2007 and 2008), so it is possible that the responses were skewed by the lack of resources, which – as accentuated previously – engenders a zero-sum mentality among fields in the politics of hiring. But the wording of the questions assumed the power to hire ("*If* your department were to hire . . ."), so we hope to have mitigated this effect.

SURVEY: THE STATUS OF MILITARY HISTORY: POLITICAL SCIENTISTS' PERSPECTIVES

There has been limited attention in existing surveys to the status of military history outside of its conventional abode, the history department. To cast light on the status of military history outside the discipline of history, we asked the same set of questions about course content using the traditional/new military history questions of members of political science departments. Table 10.3 reports the results.

We also asked members of political science departments about the balance among their courses. The choices were the same as the ones offered to members of history departments. Of the responses given, traditional military history was taught by 11.9 percent, new military history by 24.2 percent, and a balance between these two poles by 19.8 percent. A majority of departments taught military history "some other way."[78]

[78] N = 87.

TABLE 10.3. *Traditional and New Military History in Political Science Departments*

	Primary Focus on TMH (%)	Primary Focus on NMH (%)	Balance NMH and TMH (%)	Substantive Content to THM (%)	Substantive Content to NMH (%)	Other Military History (%)
Frequently taught	5.3	5.4	3.6	8.1	6.3	3.6
Periodically taught	20.3	44.2	26.6	31.2	40.8	17.9
Once, but no longer taught	15.1	3.5	5.4	8.9	6.4	6.4
Never taught	59.4	47.1	63.9	50.5	45.3	71.8
N	91	91	90	90	88	88

Political science departments offer far less in terms of military history content, either traditional or new. This is not surprising, for we based our definitions of military history on distinctions gleaned from debates among military historians. Military history (however defined) clearly plays a secondary role in political science, a finding that does not bode well for productive friction. Yet it is security studies where military history may be more important within the discipline of political science. Indeed, it is in security studies where we would view knowledge of military history as even more relevant.

Knowledge of military history is also more relevant in courses in national security, which led us to inquire about courses on national security and the content of military history in those courses. National security can be taught with varying degrees of historical emphasis, which is why some of our questions asked about the integration of military history into the study of national security. We began by asking the following question: "How often are courses taught in American national security?" We found that courses were taught at most places at least periodically (57.5 percent responded that courses were taught frequently and 38.9 percent periodically). Only 1.8 percent responded that such courses are never taught, and 1.8 percent responded that courses were once taught but no longer are.[79]

As with the concept "military history," scholars have defined the term "national security" broadly or narrowly. Security studies and programs now embrace such things as environmental harms, natural disasters, poverty, and disease, not just military security. Similarly, scholars now include "soft power" as a means of promoting security in a world of conflict.[80] To narrow the focus of

[79] N = 87.

[80] See, e.g., Paul D. Williams, ed., *Security Studies: An Introduction* (Routledge, 2008).

our questions, we also asked political scientists about the military content of courses on American national security: In courses on American national security, how much emphasis is placed on traditional military history? What about new military history?[81] We found that most courses placed limited emphasis on military history, but that new military history enjoyed somewhat greater emphasis than traditional military history. For traditional military history, we found that it is emphasized "a great deal" by 6.4 percent of departments, "some" by 34.8 percent of departments, and "limited or none" by 58.8 percent of departments.[82] For comparison, the respective percentages for new military history were 9.9 percent, 43.6 percent, and 46.4 percent.[83] These results probably reflect the fact that political science courses tend to be less concerned with historical detail than history courses. The results could also reflect the fact that political science – like history – has turned away from close attention to military-related matters.

PRELIMINARY IMPLICATIONS FOR THE STATUS OF MILITARY HISTORY

What is the status of military history? Our brief inquiry in this chapter cannot answer the question definitively, but it is suggestive. We offer preliminary implications that we will refine through further study in the following chapter. First, our analysis reveals that the definition of military history that we choose influences how we view the status of military history. Military historians have identified various perspectives on military history, which we have divided into traditional and new military history. Our surveys reveal that departments tend to think about military history along these lines, and that these distinctions are relevant in departmental priorities. We could easily have found that department leaders do not think in terms of traditional and new military history, but these concepts frame the debates over departmental priorities in military history.

Second, there is evidence that, in the broadest sense, military history remains fairly well represented. Many of the nation's research institutions have military historians, broadly defined, on their faculty, and some departments are creating a niche market in military history, which one would expect because of their comparative advantage in particular areas.

Third, to fully understand the possibility of a threat or change in priorities, we must distinguish traditional and new military history. When we make this move, we see that the future of traditional military history bodes less well than that of new military history. Traditional military history is not very well represented,

81 In analyzing security studies departments in Chapter 13, we broaden our analysis to ask about the relative emphasis of various "-isms" in the program: realism, neorealism, neoliberalism, constructivism, as well as peace studies. Our interest here is in military history in national security programs rather than determining how much other approaches are represented.

82 N = 86.

83 N = 86.

and may be under greater threat in the future, in terms of hiring priorities. New military history, in contrast, is likely to receive more support than traditional military history in the future; yet we must recall that nearly half the departments would be unlikely to prioritize military history, regardless of how we define it.

Fourth, we find some evidence of productive friction in political science departments. Military history enjoys some degree of emphasis in political science, although the primary disciplinary divide is to allocate military history to history departments and national security study to political science departments. We expect there to be more integration of military history and politics in security studies programs, so we were encouraged that in a broad survey of such departments, military history had some representation. We cannot expect most political science departments to have resources committed to military historians, yet for security studies, we would expect far more integration.

Fifth, political scientists think less about military history in terms of the two poles of traditional and new history than do history departments, which we expected. Political scientists view their departments as emphasizing something different from traditional or new military history, although they construe political science as historically informed. We suspect they emphasize historical conflict in more general terms, especially among scholars of comparative politics who often recount histories of war in their courses, or courses in international relations that consider such topics as civil war, genocide, and humanitarian intervention in war-torn societies. Each field considers issues of war, yet not from the perspective of military historians. In the chapter that follows, we delve more deeply into the status of military history in history departments, utilizing what we learned so far to guide our inquiry, before turning to our consideration of military presence in security studies programs.

Some commentators have alleged that the status of military history is weaker in higher-ranked departments, which are more attuned to the "cutting edges" of the discipline of history. In the next chapter, we will look into the situation of military history in the top-twenty history research programs. If the commentators' allegations are true, such a finding would support the contention that alienation from the military is worst among elites (the "AWOL" problem of elites). It would also buttress our concern about pedagogy, for leading departments set tones for their disciplines.

11

Half Empty or Half Full?

Military Historians' Perspectives on the Status of Military History at the Leading Departments

> The subject of history is the life of peoples and of mankind. To grasp directly and embrace in words – to describe – the life not only of mankind, but of one people, appears impossible.
>
> – Leo Tolstoy[1]

In the last chapter, we did not consider explicitly the status of military history at the nation's most prestigious history departments. The top-twenty history departments are the largest and, arguably, the most diverse departments in the country in terms of faculty and course offerings. But does "diversity" include substantial representation of military history in its traditional or newer forms? To answer this question, we conducted an inquiry into the status of military history in the top-twenty history programs in the United States during 2008 and 2009. Looking at the top-twenty history departments gives us greater insight into the status of military history in the higher echelons of history departments, and also provides a comparison to the surveys discussed in the preceding chapter, which covered a broader swath of higher education.

We selected the departments from the 2008 *U.S. News & World Report* list.[2] *U.S. News & World Report* lists are notoriously subject to criticism and second-guessing, but this is not important for our purposes; where a department stands on the list is immaterial to our inquiry, for we are interested in the group as a whole, not how the respective departments rank vis-à-vis one another; and the inclusion or exclusion of a few schools does not affect our inquiry. Furthermore, if some departments on the list should be replaced by other departments, a similar claim could be made about the new list. Our only requirement is that the *U.S. News & World Report* list approximates the upper echelons of research departments, even if the list is not infallible or definitive. The schools on this list are, in rank order (some are tied): Yale; Princeton; Berkeley; Harvard; Stanford;

[1] Leo Tolstoy, *War and Peace*, Reprint Edition. translated by Richard Pevear and Larissa Volokhonsky (Vintage Classics, 2008).

[2] See http://grad-schools.usnews.rankingsandreviews.com/best-graduate-schools/top-humanities-schools.

Chicago; Columbia; Michigan; Johns Hopkins; UCLA; Cornell; Wisconsin; North Carolina; Pennsylvania; Brown; Duke; Northwestern; Rutgers; Indiana; and Texas.

Of course, this list does not include many very fine departments, and we are appropriately wary of such "top" lists. To wit, in Chapter 13 we will examine the military history–security program at Ohio State in some detail. This program, which is a national leader, is enmeshed in the History Department there, which ranks in the top twenty-five according to *U.S. News & World Report*. We will also look at the significant security program at MIT, although MIT's History Department is not ranked in the top twenty, either. (The securities program at MIT is based mainly in political science, which is ranked.)

We conducted much of this research through the Internet, so we were dependent upon what department websites provided. A major drawback with this approach is that we were not able to gather historical data that could be used to show trends in each department, for such information is simply not available online, except on a very limited basis. But we are able to offer a meaningful overview of the present status of military history in these departments. Furthermore, we gained some historical insight through the use of e-mail correspondence and personal interviews with individuals in those departments (including some emeritus faculty members) whose work bears some relationship to military history, as we asked them to reflect on historical trends in their respective departments and in the discipline as a whole.

QUANTITATIVE FINDINGS

Our quantitative assessment of the status of military history in the top-twenty departments consists of two components: counts of faculty members and counts of courses. We began by counting the total number of faculty members in each department. We did not count adjunct or emeritus faculty members, if such information was available. Second, we counted the number of faculty members whose research or teaching dealt in a meaningful way (as best we could gather from information provided online) with military history. If an individual's work was "within the orbit" of military history, we included that person in this count. We then derived percentages based on these findings. To be more precise and consistent with the survey analysis of the preceding chapter, we divided the faculty members who lie within the ambit of military history into three categories. MH1 consists of those individuals who teach military history according to the narrower, traditional, or classical definition provided by John Lynn in Chapter 10: the study of military institutions and practices and of the conduct of war in the past. MH3 includes those who deal with the broader social, cultural, and psychological aspects of war that Wayne Lee probed in his review essay in the *Journal of American History*. MH2 is an intermediate category that was more intuitive than precise. It includes those who deal with strategy in a manner that clearly reflects a security/military orientation, or which deals with war in a more direct way than those whose foci are predominantly cultural, social, or psychological. (See John Shy's discussion in Chapter 10 of the works of John Dower, John Brewer, Niall Ferguson, and David Bell.) [3] Not surprisingly, the number of faculty members diminishes as we move from MH3 to MH1 – from newer to more traditional forms of military history. We did not include such fields as diplomacy or scholars of specific war periods unless some evidence indicated that their scholarship or teaching contained some more-than-negligible military component. This was an important, yet delicate, decision because some of our respondents and other observers contend that courses treating specific wars (or a specific set of wars) comprise military history, whereas others maintain that the actual military content of many such courses is often meager. Sometimes websites provided extensive information about the content of courses, whereas other times we had to rely on either brief course descriptions or titles.

We did our best to designate these individuals properly (as well as those who did not make the broader list), but our decisions necessarily required the exercise of judgment and (we hope) considered discretion. Accordingly, our conclusions are not meant to be definitive or exact, and are, therefore, subject to disagreement. But the subject matter does not lend itself to precision, and our findings should at least be indicative of reality – at least to the extent that a survey reflects reality. We should acknowledge that our classifications were not always consistent with the observations or judgments of our e-mail correspondents. If anything, we tended to be overinclusive of individuals and courses, and sometimes we included individuals in a category whom some respondents did not consider military historians (thus, we are more likely to overstate the presence of military history). Readers are free to make their own assessments after considering the information provided in this chapter. Our hope is that our findings paint a representative picture of reality even though they necessarily fall short of ideal objectivity.

One example (among many) of the subjectivity involved in such assessments was the comment of a historian who asked to be anonymous. We found a significant number of "new" military historians in his department, so we construed his department as a source of military history, broadly interpreted. But his assessment was less sanguine:

> In general, foreign policy, military history and intelligence are poorly represented. Everyone seems to do "cultural history". . . . courses on WWII, for instance, do not deal with the military aspects but on the people's experiences or something like that ("social aspects"). Regrettably, in our department there is virtually no interest in the sorts of history you are talking about. . . . People who taught such subjects have been replaced by "cultural" historians who have pronounced disdain for such subjects.[4]

[3] Wayne Lee, "Mind and Matter – Cultural Analysis in American Military History: A Look at the State of the Field," *Journal of American History* (March 2007): 1116; John Shy, "The 2008 George C. Marshall Lecture in Military History: History and the History of War," *Michigan Studies Review*, December 1, 2008; John A. Lynn II, "Breaching the Walls of Academe: The Purposes, Problems, and Prospects of Military History," *Academic Questions* (March 2008).

[4] E-mail exchange with a professor in a top-twenty department. We decided to not mention the department as well, as such information would enable readers to identify him. He asked for

We approached courses in a similar manner, counting the total number provided during the 2008–9 academic year if this information existed online; otherwise, we took what was available. In one case (Brown University), we could not access meaningful course information, and in two cases (North Carolina and Duke) we could obtain only one semester of data. In another case (Stanford), we used the general course catalogue because the actual schedule of courses was not provided online at the time we conducted this project; we acknowledge that this source is less reliable as an indicator of what is actually taught. Regarding the other schools, one academic year does not necessarily reflect the normal availability of courses, but it is fair to assume that overestimations and underestimations will more or less cancel each other out across departments. Our experience suggests that course offerings are highly persistent, particularly over the span of a couple years.

In addition, in some cases individuals who might normally teach a course or courses within the orbit of military history were either on leave during this time or had taken on administrative duties that precluded their teaching such courses. At Johns Hopkins, for example, David Bell has become a dean and is unable to teach his courses that address military matters. Bell's comment in our e-mail exchange reflects a number of subtle points that have emerged from the responses and the general public commentary on military history:

> I have taught graduate courses on war and violence in early modern Europe, and have a more general undergraduate "History of War in the West" course that I haven't had the time to offer for a while. There is no one else in the department who deals with these issues, or who has taught military history or security issues for the past 25 years at least, although our American historians regularly teach courses on the Civil War. In our Department of Political Science, there are a couple of professors who regularly teach strategy, security, and military affairs, generally with a strong historical bent.[5]

As with faculty members, we assigned courses to the MH1, MH2, and MH3 categories based on the definitions or terms we employed previously, counting both undergraduate and graduate courses (All the departments we covered have Ph.D. programs – although we did not distinguish in our analysis between Ph.D. and undergraduate courses, or make any attempt to consider the status of military history as a field for doctoral students.) We left courses with nonspecific content out of the overall count (for example, independent studies, nonspecific research courses, Ph.D. exam preparation courses, and so on). Furthermore, as our e-mail respondents often pointed out, many courses touch on military matters to varying extents, but might or might not be considered military history courses, properly speaking. For example, one respondent stressed that a graduate course on the Civil War at his institution clearly represented military history, whereas another respondent pointed to this very course as an example of how a

anonymity because he said he needed to confront the problem "directly," not "indirectly" through quotation in this book – an admirable position.

[5] E-mail exchange with David Bell, Johns Hopkins University, History Department, June–July 2009.

course can have "war" in its title, yet not deal very much at all with the military.[6] Kenneth T. Jackson of Columbia University's History Department emphasized that it is difficult to get a handle on the status of military history because many courses have "war" in the title yet do not deal with it in a significant or satisfactory fashion. "You just can't tell a lot by that information," he said. In Jackson's view, military history is likely to be less prevalent than it appears in catalogues and web pages.[7] As mentioned previously, if the available evidence did not indicate military content, we did not count such courses as in the realm of military history. If such evidence availed, then we counted the course.

Faculty Within the Orbit of Military History

The total number of faculty members that we counted was 1,274, and we counted 94 faculty members within the orbit of military history (7.54 percent). The largest department was Michigan, with 119 faculty members, whereas the smallest was Johns Hopkins, with 30 members. The categories for the members broke down as follows:

MH1: 15 members = 1.18 percent of total history faculty; 15.95 percent of those within the orbit[8]

MH2: 21 members = 1.65 percent of total history faculty; 22.34 percent of those within the orbit

MH3: 58 members = 4.5 percent of total history faculty; 61.70 percent of those within the orbit

These general figures pretty much confirm the general impressions that emerge from reading the public commentary on the status of military history. First, traditional or classical military historians are substantially outnumbered by those who study the cultural, social, and/or psychological aspects of war (by a ratio of almost five to one). The average top-twenty history department has 64 members based on our count, but traditional military historians constitute only 0.75 members per department, or 1.18 percent of all top-twenty history faculty members. And this number is inflated by the relatively large numbers of such individuals at North Carolina and Northwestern (three MH1 members each), as Table 11.1 shows. If we take North Carolina and Northwestern out of the tabulations, we find that the remaining 18 departments have 0.5 MH1 historians each by our measure; excluding the few top history departments with

[6] This course was James McPherson's graduate course at Princeton on the Civil War. McPherson himself is not primarily a military historian, but his recent book on Lincoln's acts as commander in chief in the Civil War is clearly within the military history orbit, close to MH1. See James M. McPherson, *Tried by War: Abraham Lincoln as Commander-in-Chief* (Penguin, 2008).

[7] E-mail exchange with Kenneth Jackson, Columbia University History Department, June–July, 2009.

[8] The percentages were rounded, so they might not add up to an exact 100 percent. Also, we counted John Lynn as a member of the History Department at Northwestern, as he was to be assuming a Distinguished Chair there in the summer of 2009, right after we conducted this inquiry.

TABLE 11.1. *Faculty in Various Military History Orbits*

Department	Total Faculty Members	In Orbit	MH1	MH2	MH3
Yale	105	8	0	3	5
Princeton	51	3	1	0	2
Berkeley	74	4	0	0	4
Harvard	56	6	0	5	1
Stanford	52	5	0	1	4
Chicago	46	5	1	1	3
Columbia	93	6	0	0	6
Michigan	119	1	0	1	0
Johns Hopkins	30	3	2	0	1
UCLA	70	2	0	1	1
Wisconsin	48	3	1	0	2
Cornell	41	4	1	1	2
North Carolina	52	8	3	0	5
Penn	48	5	1	1	3
Brown	39	4	0	0	4
Duke	66	5	1	4	0
Northwestern	68	5	3	0	2
Rutgers	67	4	1	1	2
Indiana	53	8	0	1	7
Texas	95	5	0	1	4
Total	1,273	94	15	21	58

exceptional military history programs, the top history programs on average have only half a military historian. This situation looks better, however, when we include MH2 historians, those who fall in between the traditional types and the "new military history" types. Together, MH1 and MH2 comprise slightly more than a third of those historians who fall within the orbit of military history.

It is interesting to compare these findings with the two 2003 surveys that Mac Coffman addressed in Chapter 10. These surveys compared the prevalence of military history or military-related research to research in other fields and subfields within the abode of history; we have not made this comparison, so our thoughts in this regard can be only impressionistic. But recall that the 2003 *JAH Recent Scholarship Online* survey found that political history stood ahead of social history in terms of dissertations and published books and articles; and that military history ranked number seven overall, ahead of such fields as Women and Femininity, Urban and Suburban, Native Americans, and Labor and Working Class History.[9] Yet our findings among the twenty highest-ranked departments suggest a lesser status for military history – although, again, actual comparisons would have to be made to solidify this assessment. The key is MH1,

[9] Edward M. Coffman, "Military History and the OAH," manuscript provided to the authors.

which is the core of military history. While ranking seventh may sound good, one must be less enthusiastic that only about 1 percent of faculty members in the top-twenty departments fall into the traditionalist category, and the number is one-half of 1 percent of that if we exclude the two programs with strong military history programs!

Two reasons might account for the comparative optimism that Coffman derives from the *JAH* and *OAH* surveys. First, many historians deal with subjects that unavoidably involve some aspects of war. Consequently, a large number of historians might list war as among their interests, even if they should not be considered military historians in any meaningful sense of the term. Indeed, we expect most historians to be interested in war, but much more is required before one can be considered MH1.

Second, it is quite possible that higher-ranked departments are less open to military history than other departments, especially if they consider themselves to be leaders in prevailing academic thinking or fashion. After all, John J. Miller's essay on the "retirement" of military history emphasized the lack of (traditional) military historians as the University of Wisconsin and the University of Michigan, two of the largest and most prestigious history programs in the United States.[10] Scholarship involving identity politics (for example, race, gender, sexual orientation, religion) – or what Peter Novick called "particularism" in his magnum opus on the historical trends in the field of American history – has become prominent in historical analysis. The central theme of Novick's book is that the history profession historically justified its disciplinary claim to professional autonomy by virtue of a consensual dedication to ideological neutrality, objectivity, and universalism (that is, all humanity shares in the same essential truth). This consensus had weathered some meaningful challenges during the course of the twentieth century, but it persevered until the explosive political, cultural, and intellectual upheavals of the 1960s, which questioned these foundational tenets.[11] One result of this challenge was the rise of a belief in identity politics and particularism that questioned, if not rejected, assumptions of universality: Human reality is constituted not by universally shared truths, but rather by particularistic loyalties and experiences, especially those involving race, gender, and other "ascriptive" characteristics.[12] Universal forms of history – including those associated with such allegedly oppressive institutions as traditional politics and the military – fell out of fashion in favor of such forms of inquiry as women's history, black studies, sex studies, and the like.

[10] John J. Miller, "Sounding Taps: Why Military History Is Being Retired," NR/Digital Online, October 9, 2006: http://nrd.nationalreview.com/article/?q=YTdiMDkzZDJjYTYwOWM4YmIy MmE4N2IwODFlNWU0MjE=.

[11] Peter Novick, *That Noble Dream: The "Objectivity" Question and the American Historical Profession* (Cambridge University Press, 1988), esp. Part IV.

[12] In later academic jargon, the epistemology associated with this way of thinking was designated "standpoint epistemology."

Although Novick does not examine or determine which departments were more influenced by these developments, it is likely that they have been especially pronounced in the more prestigious departments, for prestige often entails striding the "cutting edge" once that edge becomes sufficiently established.[13] The Society for Military History maintains a list of military history programs in the United States, Canada, and Britain.[14] Of the twenty-eight programs that offer both master's degrees and Ph.D. degrees, only North Carolina and Duke are among the top-twenty history programs – and the program sponsored by both schools is more influenced by North Carolina's History Department than Duke's (this is discussed later in this chapter).[15] Although this list hardly constitutes sufficient evidence of major departments' marginalization of military history, it does provide some support for this claim.

Table 11.1 presents are our findings for the faculty and course counts for each of the top-twenty history departments.

Courses Within the Orbit of Military History

Altogether, we counted 4,247 courses. Of these, we found 118 to be "within the orbit of military history," as we have defined it, or 2.78 percent. There were 28 MH1 courses, accounting for 0.66 percent, and 23 MH2 courses, amounting to 0.54 percent of the total. MH3 courses accounted for 67 courses, which was 1.58 percent of the total courses. These figures are presented in Table 11.2.

QUALITATIVE FINDINGS

The figures presented in Tables 11.1 and 11.2 provide a rough sketch of the prevalence of military history within these departments in 2009, but we were also interested in utilizing the expertise offered by military historians in our assessment of the status of military history. We e-mailed each of the ninety-four individuals within the orbit of military history, and sixty-seven replied, a response rate of about 75 percent.[16] The embattled status of military history

[13] Readers will note the irony in this claim, for what is "cutting edge" can readily become what is "fashionable," thereby losing its edge. In academia, cutting edge and fashion (and, therefore, conformity) can have a way of being two sides of the same coin.

[14] Society for Military History, "Graduate Programs in Military History": http://www.smh-hq.org/degree.html.

[15] This list is Bilkent University; Brunel University; Duke University; George Mason University; George Washington University; Kansas State University; King's College London; Ohio State University; Ohio University; Penn State University; Royal Military College of Canada; Scottish Centre for War Studies; Temple University; Texas A&M University; Texas Christian University; Texas Tech University; University of Alabama; University of Calgary; University of Houston; University of Kansas; University of Nebraska–Lincoln; University of New Brunswick; University of New Mexico; University of North Carolina–Chapel Hill; University of North Texas; University of Salford; University of Southern Mississippi; and University of Tennessee.

[16] We did not e-mail the new military historian at Wisconsin because he was not on board when we compiled these figures and would not have been in a position to evaluate the Wisconsin situation.

TABLE 11.2. *Courses in Various Military History Orbits*

Department	Total History Courses	Courses in Military History Orbit	MH1	MH2	MH3
Yale	234	8	1	4	3
Princeton	100	3	0	0	3
Berkeley	240	3	1	0	2
Harvard	277	6	0	5	1
Stanford	488	14	0	6	8
Chicago	213	3	3	0	0
Columbia	488	11	3	0	8
Michigan	395	7	4	2	1
Johns Hopkins	139	3	0	0	3
UCLA	223	1	0	1	0
Wisconsin	176	5	2	2	1
Cornell	164	8	3	1	4
North Carolina	59	8	6	1	1
Penn	78	4	1	2	2
Brown	No course information provided				
Northwestern	239	10	2	1	7
Rutgers	199	5	2	0	3
Indiana	279	11	1	2	8
Texas	195	7	0	0	7

no doubt contributed to the impressive rate of response. The rates of reply varied across departments, as did the quality and depth of the responses. Nonetheless, we had a good response rate that provides a glimpse at the status of military history in the nation's leading history departments. We will have more to say about these qualitative responses later in this chapter. Here are the questions we sent to individual scholars:

1) First, is military history taught with any regularity at your university's history department? (By military history, we mean courses that deal specifically or primarily with the strategic, tactical, social, or political aspects of war per se.)
2) Second, to what extent is the matter of security and the military given attention in your department? Is this topic dealt with within history, or is it something that is done in other centers or departments on campus?
3) Third, can you say anything about how the status of military history may have changed over the course of the last 20 years? In particular, has the department replaced individuals who have retired in this area?

Since then, we have interviewed him to gain greater understanding of the status of military history at Wisconsin.

The e-mails sent our way by respondents help to flesh out the picture in at least three respects. First, they provide an additional perspective on reality, albeit an incomplete one. Second, they tell us something about the attitudinal culture of military history, as the respondents are either military historians themselves or historians who treat military issues to a meaningful extent in their work. Their comments comprise insights into the status of military history, as well as evidence of attitudes about this status. Third, the e-mails provide us with insight into trends that we could not say much about with just our snapshot view of history presented in the numbers tabulated in our statistical analysis.

The e-mails are largely consistent with the material presented in Chapter 10. Observations and opinions are indeed "all over the map" regarding the status of military history in respondents' respective departments and in the nation generally, confirming Richard Kohn's observation, drawn from twenty years of experience at North Carolina, that "all of us, I think, admit to being unsure. It's a glass half full, half empty problem."[17] Nevertheless, we were able to discern a few themes from the collective thoughts of the correspondents.

First, as we discussed in Chapter 10, whether the glass is half empty or half full is, not surprisingly, largely a function of how one construes or defines military history. Those who conceive of military history through a traditional or classical lens (MH1) perceive a greater problem for the field than those who apply a broader "new military history" lens. In our data, "new" military historians who examine the social, cultural, and psychological aspects of the military and war outnumber traditional military historians by five to one, and the commentaries indicate that their scholarship has garnered more respect from their colleagues – although there is some evidence that this situation is changing as more commentators raise concerns about the marginality of traditional military history.

Second, programs embracing aspects of military history have proliferated in innovative forms either within departments or outside the normal structures of departments – often with resources obtained from outside funding. (This is especially the case for national security programs, which often include some military history component.) Some programs have been established in institutes or centers on campus, while others involve outreach to audiences beyond the university. In other cases, such as at Wisconsin and Northwestern (two schools that hired faculty in military history in 2009), chairs within departments were created with funds received from external bequests. At Cornell, an endowment from an alumnus enabled Cornell's military historian (Barry Strauss) to introduce a new team-taught course on military history. Such efforts represent a classic strategic move by those who lack influence vis-à-vis established local power: expanding the scope of the controversy to include outside allies or

[17] E-mail exchange with Richard Kohn, University of North Carolina History Department, June 2009.

constituencies who can rebalance the scales in a more propitious manner.[18] This move is highly beneficial to the advocates of military history, for, as seen in Chapter 10, constituencies outside the university are deeply interested in the subject, as evidenced by the popularity of military history publications among the general citizenry.

Third, issues involving the military have ineluctably seeped into the work of scholars who are not military historians, even according to the broader definition of MH3. This fact is a testament to the significance of the military and war as social phenomena. As Leon Trotsky allegedly remarked, "you might not be interested in war, but war is interested in you." In other words, war and the military are an important part of the human condition, for better or for worse, and responsible scholars must account for these phenomena even if they are not devoted to them per se.[19]

The commentaries also remind us that several factors other than prejudice have influenced the status of military history in history departments. One factor is broader trends in the discipline. As Joshua Cole of Michigan commented, the lesser status of traditional military history

> ... is not because historians no longer think that the military is important, but because the methods of historical research and investigation and the styles of historical writing associated with this older model of military history have been challenged in recent decades on a number of fronts. Social and economic historians have challenged older models of narrative history, cultural historians have challenged prior assumptions about the relationship between ideology and the exercise of power in modern societies, political historians have sought new understandings of the relationship between individuals and social and political institutions, etc. These various impulses have led many historians to look for new contexts for understanding the significance of war and warfare in the modern world.[20]

Cole's point is important, although we must also bear in mind that it is not always possible to divorce method from ideology, philosophy, or more substantive concerns. In international relations scholarship, for example, the dispute between realists/neorealists and constructivists is not simply about how to study international relations, but also about assumptions regarding human nature and normative values. Realists are more committed to constants in human nature and to the state, whereas constructivists construe human nature as more

[18] James Madison exhorted such expansion of the constituency as a remedy to the "mischief of faction" in *Federalist #10*, and it was a chief tactic of the civil rights movement. In both cases, the idea was that justice could be secured by expanding the scope of politics to a national, as opposed to a local, constituency. A classic book on the strategy is Grant McConnell, *Private Power and American Democracy* (Knopf, 1966).

[19] On the universality of war, see Azar Gat's magisterial *War and Civilization*, which is nothing less than a history of war, of the social science of war, and of world civilization itself. Gat is a realist international relations scholar who incorporates evolutionary concepts into his analysis of historical constants and change. Azar Gat, *War in Human Civilization* (Oxford University Press, 2006).

[20] E-mail exchange with Joshua Cole, University of Michigan History Department, June–July 2009.

pliable.[21] Hans Morgenthau, a father of realism in international relations, held views of human nature and politics that stood in stark contrast to those of contemporary constructivists, who step out of the cultural schools of thought that influenced the study of history before moving on to political science:

> Political realism believes politics, like society in general, is governed by objective laws that have their roots in human nature. ... Human nature, in which the laws of politics have their roots, has not changed since the classical philosophies of China, India, and Greece endeavored to discover these laws. Hence, novelty is not necessarily a virtue in political theory, nor is old age a defect. ... To dismiss such a theory because it had its flowering in centuries past is to present not a rational argument but a modernistic prejudice that takes for granted the superiority of the present over the past. To dispose of the revival of such a theory as a "fashion" or "fad" is tantamount to assuming that in matters political we can have opinions but no truths.[22]

The same point applies to methodological differences in historical research; in particular, the new assumptions that Cole emphasizes are linked in various ways to Michel Foucault's concepts of power. Foucault and his many acolytes shifted the focus on power away from elites and traditional foci of power toward the manifold and mysterious ways in which power is manifested in all sectors of society. Foucault's decentering conception of power is deeply implicated in normative disputes in politics and in higher education.[23] One consequence of this influence is the move away from universal (nonparticularistic) forms of historical inquiry toward culturally specific and micro forms of inquiry. Part of this movement is the deemphasis on political and diplomatic history in favor of cultural and social historical forms of inquiry that examine the nooks and crannies of power rather than power exerted at the zenith points of the polity.[24] As H. W. Brands observed in Chapter 10 regarding the decline of diplomatic and political history, "Starting in the 1960s, the American historical profession experienced a revolt against elitism. The study of governing groups and ruling classes gave way to investigations into the lives of common people."[25] Numerous commentators have observed the decline of political and diplomatic history in the higher-ranked history departments as well as history departments in the leading research universities (there is substantial but not perfect overlap in

[21] See Alexander Wendt, *Social Theory of International Politics* (Cambridge University Press, 1999).

[22] Hans J. Morgenthau, *Politics Among Nations: The Struggle for Power and Peace*, 5th Edition, Revised (Alfred A. Knopf, 1978), p. 4. See, generally, "Six Principles of Realism," pp. 4–15. The distinction between opinion and truth is of ancient vintage, of course, extending from the classical philosophy of Socrates, Plato, and Aristotle. Morgenthau's use of this terminology signifies that his theory of international politics is grounded in philosophical understanding.

[23] Among Foucault's many works on power, one should begin with *Power/Knowledge: Selected Interviews and Other Writings, 1972–1977*, edited by Colin Gordon (Pantheon, 1980).

[24] See Novick, *That Noble Dream*.

[25] H. W. Brands, "Disciplinary Approaches of War: Diplomatic History," in John Whitclay Chambers II, editor in chief, *Oxford Guide to American Military History* (Oxford University Press, 1999), p. 219.

these categories). At Wisconsin, for example, the status of political and diplomatic history played a background role in the debate over hiring a military historian.

Finally, the place of military history in history departments is also a function of more mundane – less ideological – factors. One such factor is simple resources. As we mentioned in the previous chapter, one reason that military history fared well throughout the 1960s and early 1970s is because the availability of ample financial resources enabled colleagues to be more tolerant of its existence, even if by benign neglect. But as resources and funding diminished, hiring decisions began to resemble zero-sum games, in which the scramble for resources weakened the generosity of spirit. University of Pennsylvania historian Alan Kors pointed out that the favorable status of military history at Penn is, to a significant extent, the product of funding necessities: The university extends financial resources to departments based on undergraduate enrollments, and there is a substantial undergraduate interest in military-related courses.[26]

In these circumstances, it helps to have allies in the department. But as the trends depicted by Cole and others developed, traditional military historians lost allies, a problem exacerbated by the fact that military veterans began retiring from departments in droves. Wayne Lee stressed this point in his e-mail correspondence: "There has certainly been a de-emphasis in departments on the hiring of diplomatic and political historians who are the natural allies of military historians, and who were once much more numerically prominent. So maybe that's why military historians feel more isolated now."[27] A meaningful presence of political and diplomatic historians helps military historians in at least two ways. First, it offers them allies who will often vote with them on important issues, including hiring decisions. Second, military historians gain more respect by being linked to political and diplomatic history, for such association deghettoizes the field. We see this dynamic in play most vividly at Penn, where a strong program in diplomacy (Penn has a diplomatic history concentration) appears to have provided both cover and resources for the study of military history.

In the discussion that follows, we divide history programs into departments in which military history has relatively marginal status and those in which it has more prominence. We did this in order to determine whether the military historians in departments where they enjoy greater company have a different perspective – in other words, does where one stands on the issue of military history depend upon where one sits? Is one's assessment of the glass being "half full" or "half empty" influenced by the situation in one's immediate environment?

[26] E-mail exchange with Alan Kors, University of Pennsylvania History Department, June–July 2009.

[27] E-mail exchange with Wayne Lee, University of North Carolina History Department, June–July 2009.

We also begin to delve briefly into the issue of security studies on campus. Military historians often suggested that issues of war receive treatment elsewhere on campus, in particular within security studies programs. For this reason, we briefly touch on security studies programs when investigating the status of military history in history departments. Our findings suggest that security studies centers can be a source of productive friction involving the military and the academy. At the same time, it became clear to us that many of these centers study war as an afterthought, with conceptions of security that are stretched so broad that the programs bear little resemblance to more conventional forms of military history.

Finally, we limit our more detailed coverage to twelve departments, for two primary reasons. First, discussing twenty programs became somewhat repetitious and redundant. Although some fresh ideas were expressed by faculty members of all departments, common themes emerged rather readily. Second, capsule portrayals of twelve departments are sufficient to convey the cultural texture we wish to portray. We have selected those departments that best represent what is taking place in the major departments. In addition, we present some comments by individuals in non-covered departments if they help to illuminate the situation. With these broader and background themes in mind, let us now proceed to a discussion of our findings, drawing on the quantitative and qualitative data that we have obtained.

LESSER PLAYERS

In this section, we consider six top-twenty history programs in which military history has some, but not extensive, presence as of 2008–9.

Brown University

(National Rank: tied at number fifteen with Duke[28]) Military history offerings are sparse at Brown. Recall that we could not access any course listings for Brown, so our discussion focuses only on faculty members and their comments. All four of our respondents disclosed that military history enjoys little presence at Brown. Kurt Raaflaub, for example, told us that, "To my knowledge, my own course on War and Society in the Ancient World is the *only* course in the History Department specifically devoted to issues of war."[29]

Among Brown's thirty-nine faculty members, four can be considered MH3, but no one MH1 or MH2. Omar Bartov has famously written much about war-related issues, such as genocide, and Raaflaub addresses such matters as war,

[28] Brown University, History Department, People, Faculty: http://www.brown.edu/Departments/History/people/.

[29] E-mail exchanges with Kurt Raaflaub and Michael Vorenberg, Brown University History Department, June–July 2009. Emphasis added. Naoko Shibusa and Vorenberg were in sync with Raabflaub.

society, and peace in the ancient and medieval worlds. Nakao Shibusawa studies issues of personal identity, security, and peace, while Michael Vorenberg covers the Civil War and its effect on equality and citizenship.

A former member of the department presented the bleakest picture at Brown and elsewhere:

> Alas, military history has not thrived at Brown, where there is a general aversion to dealing with all the wars the U.S. has fought and continues to fight. ... The History Department, like many departments around the country, stereotypes military history as dull and uninteresting, ignores undergraduate interests, and adds more and more people who specialize in cultural and gender history. ... Finally, the Department has never reached out to the Naval War College, where there are many fine historians who deal with military history and strategic studies. ... [Brown, like the profession] ignores large aspects of the human experience and stands aside while independent historians fill in all the gaps.

Omar Bartov offered a somewhat brighter picture, but agreed that the interest in military matters has "greatly evolved over the last 20–30 years from 'pure' studies of strategy and tactics to social and now increasingly cultural history."[30]

As some e-mail respondents mentioned, the Watson Institute for International Studies at Brown touches on military and security subjects, as does the Political Science Department. Most of the Watson Institute's offerings are in areas other than war, including "diplomacy, war, and peace; poverty, inequality, and development; trade, globalization, and economic conflict; human rights and humanitarianism; the production and role of culture and political identities; and the environment and global public health."[31] In political science, only one of the four specialists in international relations works with military security-related issues (Ulrich Krotz).[32]

University of Michigan

(National Rank: tied for number seven with Columbia[33]) Michigan lost a renowned military historian, John Shy, to retirement several years ago, and has not replaced him with someone in the MH1 category – one of the developments that has precipitated the outcry regarding the status of military history. Of 118 faculty members on the website, none falls within the MH1 designation, and only one seemed to fall under the ambit of MH2 or MH3 (Chun-shu Chang, whom we categorized as MH2 for his work in the military and diplomacy area).

30 E-mail exchanges with Omar Bartov, Brown University, and a former member of the department, June–July 2009.

31 Watson Institute for International Relations, Brown University: http://www.watsoninstitute.org/ir/.

32 Brown University, Political Science Department, "Faculty by Interest": http://www.brown.edu/Departments/Political_Science/people/interests.html.

33 University of Michigan, Department of History, Faculty List: http://www.lsa.umich.edu/history/facstaff/; Courses: http://www.lsa.umich.edu/history/courses/.

Of 395 courses, 7 appeared within the realm of military history. Four courses fell within the MH1 bailiwick, generously construed: The Vietnam War; Referencing Iraq; Twentieth Century American Wars; The Korean War; and War Since the Eighteenth Century. Meanwhile, two courses fit the MH2 description: War in the Pacific: History, Culture, Memory; and a course on September 11. One course matched criteria for MH3, Conflict and Diplomacy in the Caucasus.

We received only one e-mail response from Michigan, but it was thought provoking and particularly informative to our study. Joshua Cole echoed the insights of the commentators we read earlier addressing new methods of historical inquiry and the place of the military in relation to these approaches:

> I think that the response depends on what you mean by military history. We have a significant number of courses in which the history of war and warfare plays a central role (individual courses on the Vietnam War, the Korean War, Europe in the age of total war – there are many others).... These courses necessarily deal with the history of the military and its connection to questions of state formation, the balance of power at various moments in history, the history of technology, and economic and social developments in various societies and cultures.

Cole also accentuated the importance of such "new military history" approaches as economic, social, and cultural history, which have brought new methods and writing styles into prominence. "Social and economic historians have challenged older models of narrative history, cultural historians have challenged prior assumptions about the relationship between ideology and the exercise of power in modern societies, political historians have sought new understandings of the relationship between individuals and social and political institutions, etc."[34] Michael Sherry of Northwestern offered an observation about the field nationally that supplements Cole's perspective, so we present it here as well:

> The fundamental changes have involved context and packaging. Much that was once called military history now gets taught under other rubrics, the boundaries around "military history" are more porous and contested, and historians are less in agreement about what constitutes "military history." Some critics see in that trend signs of the field's decline and its neglect by the academy. I don't see it that way: the boundaries around most fields are blurred, with similar results – few courses are offered explicitly as "intellectual history," but much intellectual history still gets taught. Meanwhile, strong scholarship in the field of military history still gets recognized.... Comparing now [to the 1970s], I'd say that the field gets more respect and attention in the profession as a whole than in the 1970s.[35]

Beyond the History Department, Michigan's Political Science Department houses nine scholars in the field of "World Politics/International Relations." Of these, four work in areas involving war and the military: Robert Axelrod,

[34] E-mail exchange with Cole, June–July 2009.

[35] E-mail exchange with Michael Sherry, Northwestern University Department of History, June–July 2009.

James D. Morrow, J. David Singer (Correlates of War Project), and Allan Stam.[36] Axelrod and Morrow are formal theorists, while Singer and Stam utilize quantitative approaches to understand international relations. The Political Science Department also has a Peace Research field of specialty, with Singer listed as the only professor.[37] These faculty members emphasize formal models and statistical analysis of war. The Correlates of War Project is the foundation of modern quantitative studies of war, and as such, it has a historical component, although it is clearly not within the orbit of military history.

Columbia University

(National Rank: tied for number seven with Michigan[38]) Columbia does not have an MH1 military historian, but rather several professors who incorporate military history into their work. Respondents reported that military history has not enjoyed primary status at Columbia for many years.[39] A core military history course, Military History and Policy, is now being taught by Ken Jackson, who specializes in urban American history, but is not a military historian by his own admission. But Jackson believes strongly in military history, and has been vocal in the movements extending back to the mid-1970s to bring ROTC back to campus. Jackson told us that ROTC and the military matter for at least three reasons: because of the importance of the military as an institution; because ROTC adds to the diversity of the campus; and because ROTC provides scholarship money to students. Furthermore, "the history of war is significant."[40]

As noted earlier, Columbia has ninety-three historians listed on its web page, none of whom is an MH1. In our estimation, all six historians at Columbia who are within the wide orbit of military history belong in the MH3 category: Jackson (urban, social, and military history): Volker Berghahn (Cold War and Intellectuals; Cold War in Europe); Charles Armstrong (North Korea in the Cold War); Carol Gluck (World War II and memory); Anders Stephanson (diplomacy and America in the Cold War); and Matthew Connelley (diplomatic history, primarily). As for courses, Columbia listed 488 courses in 2009–10, although very many will not be taught. Given the size of this number, we would expect to find a larger number of courses under the umbrella of MH courses, and this is indeed the case, as we located eleven such courses. Three were MH1 courses:

36 University of Michigan, Department of Political Science, Research Interests: World Politics/International Relations: http://polisci.lsa.umich.edu/research_areas/worldPolitics.html.

37 University of Michigan, Department of Political Science, Research Interests: Peace Research: http://polisci.lsa.umich.edu/research_areas/peaceResearch.html.

38 Columbia University, History Department, Faculty: http://www.columbia.edu/cu/history/lists/faculty.html; Courses: http://www.columbia.edu/cu/history/courses/main/index/index.html.

39 E-mail exchanges with Charles Armstrong, Volker Berghahn, and Kenneth Jackson, Columbia University History Department, June–July 2009.

40 Phone interview with Kenneth Jacobson, Columbia University History Department, June–July 2009.

Jackson's Military History and Policy; The Asian Pacific Wars, 1931–1975; and World War. The other eight courses were all MH3 (for example, war and society courses; specific wars; and so on). These statistics largely confirm the observations of our e-mail correspondents: Military history is taught in various ways, but classical (MH1) military history is marginal at Columbia.

Security studies are quite prominent outside the History Department at Columbia, however. The Department of Political Science employs several international relations scholars who study war and security, including Richard Betts, Jack Snyder, Michael Doyle, and Robert Jervis. And the well-known School of International and Public Affairs hosts a variety of international programs, including the Saltzman Institute of War and Peace Studies.[41]

University of Wisconsin

(National Rank: tied at number eleven with Cornell[42]) Wisconsin presents an interesting case because it has recently hired a military historian after a period of extended intradepartmental wrangling over the issue. Wisconsin is the only department among the top twenty that reported (through e-mail exchanges) hiring an MH1 historian in recent times, other than John Lynn's new half-time chair in retirement at Northwestern. The background of the Wisconsin hiring is instructive on several counts, and is worth relating at some length here.

As of spring 2009, Wisconsin had forty-seven faculty members, two of whom fall within the orbit of military history, broadly speaking. (Neither considers himself a military historian, so, once again, our tabulations err on the side of generosity.) John Cooper is an expert in later-nineteenth- and early-twentieth-century American political history and a noted Woodrow Wilson scholar. He has taught courses on "The Three Wars," the Civil War, and American foreign relations. Jeremi Suri teaches courses on international history and politics, including issues of diplomacy, foreign relations, and grand strategy. But in the spring of 2009, Wisconsin hired a true military historian to replace Mac Coffman (who retired in 1992) after an extended period of inertia and subsequent intradepartmental debate. Major John Hall is a career military officer (of sixteen years) who received a Ph.D. in history from North Carolina in 2007. He studies the long history of counterinsurgency and irregular warfare, dating back to the early-nineteenth century and up to the present. His first book, *Uncommon Defense: Indian Allies in the Blackhawk War*, was published by Harvard University Press in 2009. In addition, Hall began teaching two courses in

[41] School of International and Public Affairs, Columbia University: http://www.sipa.columbia.edu/. Arnold A. Saltzman Institute of War and Peace Studies: http://www.columbia.edu/cu/siwps/faculty.htm. See also Richard K. Betts, "Should Strategic Studies Survive?" *World Politics* 50, 7 (1997). Interview with Richard Betts, School of International and Public Affairs, Columbia University, April 2008.

[42] University of Wisconsin, Madison, Department of History, Faculty Listed by Area of Specialty: http://history.wisc.edu/people/faculty_specialty.htm; Courses: http://history.wisc.edu/courses.htm.

2009–10 that are MH1 military history. Accordingly, of Wisconsin's current forty-eight faculty members, three are within the orbit, with Hall constituting MH1 and Cooper and Suri representing MH3. In terms of courses, Wisconsin offered 176 courses (spring 2009 and fall 2009), with two MH1 (taught by Hall), two MH2, and one MH3.

The department expended little effort to replace Coffman during the decade after his retirement, the efforts of Cooper and a few others notwithstanding. Then opportunity knocked on the door in the later 1990s, when the department received an endowment for a chair in military history from Stephen Ambrose, the famous popular military historian who had earned his Ph.D. in the department decades before. Nonetheless, no serious effort materialized to fill the position. Meanwhile, Cooper kept pressing the issue, "Because I believe in military history. It is important, and I felt bad over Mac Coffman being slighted."[43]

Then John J. Miller published "Sounding Taps: Why Military History Is Being Retired" in the *National Review* in 2006.[44] Although he considered Miller's take overwrought, Cooper and his allies (now including Suri) seized the advantage that the article presented to pressure the department into action. Along with a member of the University of Wisconsin Foundation (the university's main fundraising arm), Cooper and department chair David McDonald ventured up Bascom Hill to the dean of Letters and Sciences and persuaded him to supplement the endowment with university money. In the spring of 2007, the department brought in three candidates (out of about forty applicants) for a new round of interviews. After a contentious process that merits a short story in its own right, the department defeated a motion to hire Brian Linn, a respected military historian at Texas A&M – a well-known military history redoubt.[45] According to Cooper and Suri, factions formed around different positions, and the vote (although a majority in favor) fell short of the two-thirds needed to carry the day. Some sources said Linn's approach did not fit the department's intellectual profile. According to Cooper, "a lot of people – between ten and twelve – just didn't want military history."[46] In Suri's eyes, it was a question of double standards:

> There is a presumption against military historians, not outright opposition. If you do guns and battles, you have to show something else. This is not true for those who do, say, "just slavery." When we interview someone who does race and urban life, we wouldn't hold it against them if they knew nothing about the military. But when we interview a military

[43] Interview with John M. Cooper, University of Wisconsin Department of History, May 2009.

[44] Miller, "Sounding Taps: Why Military History Is Being Retired." We discussed this article in Chapter 10.

[45] See, e.g., Brian McAllister Linn, *The Echo of Battle: The Army's Way of War* (Harvard University Press, 2007). Linn has twice won the Society for Military History's book award and had been a visiting professor at the Army War College.

[46] Interview with John Cooper, University of Wisconsin Department of History, May 2009.

historian, we ask him or her all the time about race theory, race relations, and the like. They must demonstrate knowledge in this area, not expertise. It's a double standard. The bar is set differently. Linn knew about race, but "didn't talk the talk." It's a sociological problem in departments. Many distinguished professors here just don't read military history.[47]

The department's decision was poorly received by advocates of military history around the country, and proponents within the department retreated to lick their wounds. Suri and Cooper waited a year to move again, and this time other influential members of the department decided that it was in the department's interest to make a good hire in the field. McDonald formed a search committee with Suri as the chair, and asked one of the leading opponents of hiring Linn to serve on it (this individual declined). This time around, the department ultimately voted to support Hall unanimously. Individuals with whom we spoke felt better in 2009 than they had in 2007, and hopeful that Hall's hiring augured well for the field and the department.

Suri has also played a path-breaking role in developing outreach courses at Wisconsin embracing the military, military history, strategy, and diplomacy. Among other things, he has pioneered a new Grand Strategies Program that involves grand strategy courses and multifaceted outreach programs to the public, including a variety of talks and programs at the Wisconsin Veterans Center in Madison. Pursuant to a federal grant (2009–11), Suri and retired UW-Madison history professor Stanley Schultz pioneered a program of lectures and discussions for high school teachers at the Veterans Center that focused on the military and American society. William Tischler, a media specialist in the university's Division of Continuing Studies, has assisted these programs by developing innovative methods of televising and communication. These efforts are part of the newly founded UW JASONs, an interdisciplinary group of faculty members devoted to bringing scholars, the general public, and students together to study and discuss important public problems and issues.[48] Building on the "Wisconsin Idea," which entails university outreach to the state and wider world, JASONs has two basic purposes. "First, we work together to tackle problems of significant societal importance at the state, national and/or international levels, in a collaborative fashion. Second is our educational mission: we strive to involve students in our projects, encouraging them to think about societal problems and to use multidisciplinary methods for solving those problems."[49] We discuss Suri's work more fully in Chapter 13, where we talk about strategic security programs. The work is a model of the type of synergistic, critical pedagogy and outreach regarding the military and security that we envision.

[47] Interview with Jeremi Suri, University of Wisconsin Department of History, June 2007.

[48] University of Wisconsin, Madison: A History of Grand Strategy: http://grandstrategy.wisc.edu/; and Grand Strategy Program: http://grandstrategy.wisc.edu/. Interviews with Scott Mobley and Suri, NROTC Commander, University of Wisconsin, Madison, June 2007.

[49] UW JASONs: http://jasons.wisc.edu/.

Another reason that such efforts are noteworthy is that they show how a considerable amount of teaching about the military and security-related matters is taking place outside the traditional jurisdictions of departments. Professorships, centers, and institutes on campus can be erected with alumni and other outside money that promote programs that need not rely upon support within established entities. This is one method of making the university more responsive to the society that it serves.

Wisconsin is also home to political scientists with research interests related to war. Andy Kydd emphasizes formal models of bargaining with an emphasis on diplomatic history. As a formal modeler, Kydd includes in his work important examples of military history as a framework for developing models of different bargaining situations. Like most formal modelers, Kydd uses game theory to explain the consistency (or inconsistency) of choices with formal logic, considering historical bargaining situations instrumentally in the sense that they are used to illustrate more general theoretical arguments. There has also been some collaboration or integration between scholars of international relations and members of the History Department involving issues of grand strategy. Jon Pevehouse also has expertise in national security, and works with the JASONs group. He has recently published a book with William Howell on the decision to go to war. Their book, *While Dangers Gather*, describes how institutional incentives, in particular the relationship between Congress and the president, influence the decision to declare war.[50] This type of research does not fall within the orbit of military history, yet it complements research on diplomacy and political history by utilizing insights from institutional theories.

Princeton University

(National Ranking: tied for number two with Berkeley[51]) According to Paul Miles, "Military history is taught with some degree of regularity at Princeton," including Miles' courses on the "United States and the Vietnam Wars" and "War and Society in the Modern World," which he teaches every year. Miles also alluded to James McPherson's course, "The American Civil War and Reconstruction," which McPherson taught annually until his recent retirement. "Princeton has also recently made an offer to a young historian to teach "The American Civil War and Reconstruction," and has introduced a new course on "The American Military Experience." Miles also mentioned "Between Resistance and Collaboration: The Second World War in Europe," taught by Jan Gross, who holds the Tomlinson Chair in War and Society at Princeton. Thomas J. Christensen agreed that military history "is still taught here,

[50] William G. Howell and Jon C. Pevehouse, *While Dangers Gather: Congressional Checks on Presidential War Powers* (Princeton University Press, 2007).

[51] Princeton University, History Department, People, Faculty: http://www.princeton.edu/history/people/index.xml?display=faculty; Undergraduate Courses: http://www.princeton.edu/history/undergraduate/courses/; Graduate Courses: http://www.princeton.edu/history/graduate/courses/.

following a long tradition," but mused that "the offerings are not as robust as in the past, however."[52]

Once again, what constitutes military history lies in the eyes of the definer, and whether he or she construes military history as MH1, MH2, and/or MH3. In our own calculations, we found three Princeton faculty members who lie under the umbrella of military history out of fifty-one in the department. We counted Miles as MH1 because his courses stress military history, as does his research; in addition, he is a retired Army colonel with thirty years' military experience in Vietnam and Washington (among other things, he served as aid de camp to General William Westmoreland). Miles is a lecturer in history, not a tenure-track faculty member, but we counted him because of the central role he plays in teaching. We ranked two faculty members as MH3: Jan Gross, who does work on the social and psychological consequences of war (especially World War II), and – a stretch, we admit – Sean Wilentz, whose work has encompassed some military issues. In the fall of 2009, the department also introduced a new course, "The American Military Experience," which was taught by Lieutenant Colonel John Stark, the commander of Princeton's Army ROTC unit. In addition, in 2008, the department made an offer to an assistant professor in the field of nineteenth-century United States history who studies the implications of the Civil War (Chandra Manning, who wrote *What This Cruel War Was Over: Soldiers, Slavery, and the Civil War*) to replace McPherson upon his retirement. She turned down the offer, but, according to Miles, the department is making "a 'good faith' effort to replace such faculty."

Of the one hundred courses offered during the 2008–9 academic year, three fit within the ambit of military history, all three in the MH3 category: Miles' two courses ("War and Society in the Modern World" and "The United States and the Vietnam Wars") and Gross's "Between Resistance and Collaboration: The Second World War in Europe."

Princeton's Politics Department and Woodrow Wilson Center also handle military-security issues and foster substantial interactions between students and the military. Political scientist Thomas Christensen related, "We have military officers as students, visiting lectures by military officers, and regular professional interactions between the military and the faculty." Aaron Friedberg, Gary Bass, G. John Ikenberry, Jay Lyall, and Jake Shapiro are other faculty members in these bailiwicks. For example, Shapiro and Lyall work with top military commanders and with West Point faculty on research relating to the Iraq War. Friedberg concurred: "International security and related issues are given a good deal of attention in the Politics department, though we don't really have anyone on our permanent faculty who is an expert on military history, operations etc. In general I think that the study of war and

[52] E-mail exchanges with Thomas Christensen, Paul Miles, and Aaron Friedberg, Princeton University History and Politics departments, June–July 2009; February 2011.

strategy has fared better in political science than in history departments around the country."[53] The Center for International Security Studies (CISS) was established in 2009 within the Woodrow Wilson School of Public and International Affairs. Led by Friedberg and Ikenberry (both of whom are in the Politics Department), CISS deals specifically with national and international security and strategy issues.[54]

Yale University

(National Ranking: number one[55]) At Yale, Jay Winter declared that, "Military history is taught front and center. ... Paul Kennedy, John Gaddis, Bruno Cabanes, and I are all military historians, and we deal with most aspects of European and American military history in the last 150 years. David Blight also teaches the Civil War, and is one of our premier teachers of military matters." Likewise, Cabanes, who teaches a "War and Society" course, said, "Yes, the social and cultural history of war is taught with some regularity at Yale. I give three seminars on the 'cultural history of World War One,' 'The Aftermath of War,' and 'The Body in Modern Warfare,' and a lecture course on 'The Experience of War in the 20th Century.' Next year, I plan to teach a course on 'Trauma,' along with a colleague from the department of psychiatry who is working with Iraq veterans."[56]

Donald Kagan took a more classical (MH1) view of what constitutes military history, thereby arriving at a more negative assessment: "In my view the state of military history at Yale is deplorable." Kagan found no courses offered at Yale during the 2008–9 year that he would term military history. (We discerned eight courses according to our inclusion of MH2 and MH3 courses, but only one that we considered MH1.) "As I see it, we have no proper military historian and no really professional courses in military history." Although Gaddis holds Yale's Robert A. Lovett Chair in Military and Naval History, this "splendid historian of American Foreign Policy and especially the Cold War" is "in no way a military historian," according to Kagan. Kagan reached the same conclusion about Kennedy. "Although Paul Kennedy has written some fine military history, he is really interested in international relations and diplomatic history." Kagan

53 E-mail exchanges with Christensen and Friedberg, Princeton University Politics Department, June–July 2009; February 2011. Christensen mentioned that the main individuals in the Politics Department who deal with the security side of international relations. See Princeton University, Department of Politics, Faculty, International Relations: http://www.princeton.edu/politics/people/byfield/ir/.

54 Princeton University, Woodrow Wilson School of Public and International Affairs, Center for International Security Studies: http://www.princeton.edu/ciss/.

55 Yale University, Department of History, Faculty: http://www.yale.edu/history/faculty.html; Courses: http://www.yale.edu/history/courses.html.

56 E-mail exchanges with Jay Winter and Bruno Cabanes, Yale University History Department, June–July 2009; February 2011.

pointed to the departure of such more classical military historians as Michael Howard, Geoffrey Parker, and Mary Habeck. Since Habeck left a couple of years ago, "She has not been replaced in kind and will not be. That's the sad story."[57] The differences of opinion at Yale clearly boil down to how one defines military history. Our own tabulations pertaining to Yale were slightly more generous than Kagan's, as we included Cabanes in the MH2 category – although we acknowledge that this classification might be a stretch. Ironically, we also included Kagan's course on "Thucydides and the Peloponnesian War" as the one MH1 course at Yale, mainly because such a course would deal with many military matters. MH2 courses included Gaddis and Kennedy courses on grand strategy, while MH3 courses included Blight and Winter on "War, Memory, and Identity," and Gaddis's "The Cold War in Asia." Overall, of Yale's 105 faculty members, we placed 8 in the ambit of military history because of our relatively generous MH2 and MH3 categories.

Yale is also the home of the International Security Studies (ISS) Center, which, according to its web page, "is a center for teaching and research in grand strategy and international, diplomatic, and military affairs." ISS has close ties to the history department at Yale; its director is Kennedy, and it comprises part of the flagship ISS program, the Brady-Johnson Program in Grand Strategy, which is directed by Gaddis.[58] We discuss this program at some length in Chapter 12. There are several political scientists at Yale with expertise in civil war, most notably Stathis Kalyvas and Nicholas Sambanis. Sambanis emphasizes case studies of civil war, primarily as a response to quantitative studies of civil war.[59]

In conclusion, whereas Yale does not appear to be particularly hospitable to military history as classically defined (MH1), it is more than hospitable to military history more broadly construed, especially regarding our MH2 category, which includes strategic security concerns. There are several important scholars studying civil war in the Political Science Department, but we were not able to detect much of a role of military history or historians in the project.

MORE MAJOR PLAYERS

Military history has more presence in some departments, so we place them in a different category. Once again, our choices were based on representativeness. As in the previous section, we selected six programs for further scrutiny.

57 E-mail response from Donald Kagan, Yale University History Department.

58 Yale University, International Security Studies: http://yale.edu/iss/people.html; Yale University, Brady-Johnson Program in Grand Strategy: http://www.yale.edu/iss/gs/.

59 See Nicholas Sambanis, "Using Case Studies to Expand Economic Models of Civil War," *Perspectives on Politics* 2, 2 (2004): 259–79.

University of Chicago

(National Rank: tied at number four with Harvard and Stanford[60]) According to two of our Chicago respondents, Chicago has not had a military historian, but a few of its instructors have significant knowledge of the military. Michael Geyer (who deals, among other things, with ethical and cultural aspects of violence and war) reported that, "We have never had a military historian …. [but] with [Bruce] Cumings, [Walter] Kaegi, and me, we have more knowledge of the military than ever before." Geyer also said that "war is covered pretty regularly in east Asia, the US, Europe, and the Near East." James Sparrow told us that, "Some teach it, but not on a regular basis: Walter Kaegi and Bruce Cumings teach a course on War in American Society. I have taught war in American society to date." Kaegi told us that he has been teaching courses since the 1980s on Byzantine military history that "include strategy (and Byzantine writings on military strategy and command and tactics; in fact they are among the oldest treatises on such topics) and operations, as well as some emphasis on military institutional structures and their evolution, and modern controversies about them." He also teaches a course on the "History of Strategy (Continental European)" from antiquity to 1815. Cumings teaches a course called "Asian Wars of the 20th Century" that deals with the Pacific War, Korea, and Vietnam in equal measure. "It is not a military history course, but plenty of that gets into it. I approach it from classical theory (Clausewitz) and just war theory (Walzer and others), and assign books like Dower's *War Without Mercy* from the US side, and a 'native' account on the other – Iyenaga's *Pacific War*, Ha Jin's *War Trash*, etc. So I guess it's a combination of what you list below."[61] Cameron Hawkins also teaches courses dealing with war and society in ancient Greece, Rome, and the Hellenistic era.

We counted Kaegi as an MH1 historian and Cumings as MH2. Kaegi teaches a course on "European Military History and Strategy," as well as a course on Byzantine history that has substantial military content. Meanwhile, Cumings has published a book on the origins of the Korean War and is at work on a book about American power in the Pacific. In our count, 3 of Chicago's 213 courses in 2008–9 were within the orbit of military history, all in the category of MH1: Kaegi's two courses on Byzantine military history and Cuming's course on Asian wars of the twentieth century.

Outside of the Department of History, Chicago is well known for its political science scholars dealing with national security issues – in particular, John Mearshimer and Robert Pape – and political theorist Nathan Tarcov also

[60] University of Chicago, Department of History, People, Faculty: http://history.uchicago.edu/people/index.html; Graduate Program, courses: http://history.uchicago.edu/graduate/courses.html; Undergraduate Program, courses: http://history.uchicago.edu/undergraduate/courses.html.

[61] E-mail exchanges with James Sparrow, Michael Geyer, Walter Kaegi, and Bruce Cumings, University of Chicago History Department, June–July, 2009; February 2011.

teaches American foreign policy.[62] Mearshimer and Pape are among the co-directors of the Program on International Security Policy at Chicago's Harris School of Public Policy. Topics in the program include "nuclear proliferation, theories of war and peace, American national security policy, military doctrine and organization, and terrorism."[63]

Cornell University

(National Rank: tied for number eleven with Wisconsin[64]) Cornell presents an interesting case. Out of forty-one faculty members, we found four who fell within the wider orbit of military scholarship: Barry Strauss is an MH1, as he teaches a course on military history and has written about wars; Chen Jian is MH2, having studied war in Korea and China; and two individuals are MH3: Isabel Hull, who published a book in 2004 entitled *Absolute Destruction: Military Culture and the Practices of War in Imperial Germany*; and Fredrik Logevall, who has written and taught a course about the Vietnam War.[65] We received two e-mails relating to Cornell, one from Hull at Cornell and the other from Penn's Peter Holquist, who once taught at Cornell. Hull wrote that, "Military history is regularly taught and has been since I've been here (31 years). Courses include: World War I, World War II, a new course on 'Battles,' and for years we had a very popular course on ancient Chinese military history." Hull also mentioned courses on terrorism. Holquist pointed out that Barry Strauss regularly teaches courses on military history, and, "thanks to an endowment from an alumnus, he recently introduced a team-taught course on military history with Edward Baptist." In addition, John Weiss (a veteran) teaches courses on World War II and other courses with a military theme.[66]

Of 164 courses taught during 2008–9, 8 came within the ambit of military history. There were three MH1 courses ("Introduction to Military History" by Strauss; "Strategy in World War II" and "The Vietnam War," by Logevall – the latter being perhaps a stretch), and one MH2 course ("The Cold War: Revolt and Revolution"). Four courses qualified in our estimation as MH3: "A Few Good Men: The American Soldier in the Popular Imagination"; "Seminar in History and Memory: The Asia-Pacific War"; "Subversions of Foreign Policy" (there were some military aspects in the course); and "Europe and Early Cold War."

62 University of Chicago, Department of Political Science, Faculty: http://political-science.uchicago.edu/faculty.shtml.

63 University of Chicago, Harris School of Public Policy, Program in International Security Policy: http://harrisschool.uchicago.edu/programs/beyond/workshops/pisp.asp.

64 Cornell University, Department of History, Faculty in the Department: http://www.arts.cornell.edu/history/faculty-department.php; Courses: http://www.arts.cornell.edu/history/courses.php.

65 Isabel Hull, *Absolute Destruction: Military Culture and the Practices of War in Imperial Germany* (Cornell University Press, 2005).

66 E-mail exchanges with Isabel Hull and Peter Holquist, Cornell University and University of Pennsylvania History departments, June–July 2009.

Cornell's Government Department's ample subfield of international relations is composed of nine scholars. Of these, six deal with national security issues: Matthew Evangelista, Jonathan Kirshner, Judith Reppy, Sarah Kreps, Christopher Way, and Jessica Weeks.[67] Cornell is also the home of the Einaudi Center for International Studies, a remarkably broad and sweeping program that deals with many angles of research, including peace studies, the causes of war and conflict, technology, and weapons proliferation.[68] Over the years, historians have participated in what is now known as the Judith Reppy Institute for Peace and Conflict Studies.[69]

Indiana University

(National Rank: tied for number nineteen with Texas and Virginia[70]) Indiana presents another example of a department that serves little classical military history, but a considerable menu of military history more broadly considered. It has no MH1 faculty members, and one in the category of MH2 (Nick Cullather, who teaches a variety of subjects, including courses on the CIA and OSS, American foreign policy, and military history). That said, we classified no fewer than eight faculty members as MH3, most of them dealing with memory and cultural issues. Accordingly, Indiana could be considered a relative hotbed of MH3 scholarship.

Our e-mail exchanges reflected this status. Referring to the History Department, Eric Wild Robinson said that "classical military history is taught not with great regularity at Indiana, but thanks to me and possibly one or two others, it is taught occasionally." James Madison wrote:

> Until recently, in my three decades at Indiana we have never had a historian who primarily specializes in military history. Rather, we have had scholars who treat military subjects as part of a related area. However, in recent years we have had more faculty drift into military history subject matter, particularly in teaching, so that each semester we have several courses with war in the title, some on a specific war (particularly Vietnam and Civil War) and some on broader thematic aspects of war.

Cullather has revived a military history course that he teaches in conjunction with the ROTC program. The head of ROTC asked him whether he wanted to teach it after the former ROTC instructor stopped teaching it, and it enjoys a large enrollment of ROTC and non-ROTC students. The course deals with

[67] Cornell University, Department of Government, Faculty by Subfield, International Relations: http://falcon.arts.cornell.edu/Govt/faculty/index.html.

[68] Einaudi Center and Associated Programs, Thematic Programs, Peace Studies Program: http://www.einaudi.cornell.edu/pdf/Programs2008.pdf.

[69] The annual reports provide information about faculty participating in the program: http://www.einaudi.cornell.edu/peaceprogram/publications/annual.asp..

[70] Indiana University, Department of History, People, Faculty and Research: http://www.indiana.edu/~histweb/faculty/; Graduate Program, Courses: http://www.indiana.edu/~histweb/grad/courses.shtml; Undergraduate Program, Courses: http://www.indiana.edu/~deanfac/class.shtml.

weapons, tactics, and strategy, as well as such "new military history" issues as gender and identity.[71]

Eight individuals teach international relations in political science at Indiana. Of these, three do research involving the military and war: Karen Rasler, William R. Thompson, and Abdulkader Sinno.[72] Meanwhile, the International Studies program at Indiana deals with issues other than war and the military: "Culture and the Arts," "Global Health and Environment," "Global Integration and Development," "Human Rights and Social Movements," "International Communication," and "Nations, States and Boundaries."[73]

Rutgers University

(National Rank: tied for number seventeen with Northwestern[74]) Rutgers' history department has sixty-seven regular faculty members, one of whom is an MH1 scholar in our view: John W. Chambers. Chambers has written extensively about war, peace, and the military, including editing the exhaustive *Oxford Companion to American Military History*.[75] Since 1982, he has been teaching a two-semester course at Rutgers University on "War, Peace, and the Military in the United States, 1607 to the Present." According to Chambers, other professors at Rutgers teach courses more specifically on particular wartime eras, including the American Revolution, the Civil War, World War I and World War II, and the Vietnam War. William O'Neil remarked:

> Military history is much neglected at Rutgers, especially since I retired three years ago. Before then I taught courses on WWI and WWII, both of which included a lot of military history, especially my WWII course. Since then only Professor John Chambers teaches any military history at all and his courses are more about politics, diplomacy, and the like than about the military as such.[76]

Chambers' and O'Neil's observations stand in contrast with those of Michael Adas. Adas responded, "A number of my colleagues and I teach courses on military history in a number of areas and time periods. I regularly teach courses on World War I as a global conflict, America's Rise to Global Power, and US Interventions Overseas. My courses on Imperialism, the Age of Global Empires

[71] E-mail exchanges with Eric Wild Robinson, James Madison, and John Bodnar, Indiana University Department of History, June–July 2009.

[72] Indiana University, Political Science Department, Faculty by Subfield: http://www.indiana.edu/~iupolsci/subfield.html.

[73] Indiana University, Center for the Study of Global Change, International Studies Program: http://www.indiana.edu/~intlweb/about.shtml.

[74] Rutgers, State University of New Jersey, Department of History, Faculty: http://history.rutgers.edu/index.php?option=com_content&task=category§ionid=24&id=56&Itemid=140.

[75] John Chambers, ed., *Oxford Guide to American Military History* (Oxford University Press, 1999).

[76] E-mail exchanges with John W. Chambers and William O'Neil, Rutgers University (New Brunswick) History Department, June–July 2009.

and the Twentieth Century also cover a good deal of military history."[77] Adas's definition of military history is considerably broader than the operative definitions of Chambers and O'Neil.

Rutgers' Political Science Department has a substantial national security cohort, including Jack Levy, Edward Rhodes, and others.[78] Rutgers also has a Center for Global Security and Democracy that is concerned with broad issues of democracy, the security of individuals, and human rights. The Center does address military-related issues, but these are downplayed on its web page.[79]

University of North Carolina and Duke

University of North Carolina (National Rank: tied for number thirteen with University of Pennsylvania) and Duke (Tied for number fifteen with Brown).[80] We treat the University of North Carolina (UNC) and Duke together, for they are closely linked in a programmatic sense, as we will explain.

The most prominent department in terms of military history representation is North Carolina, which has, according to our count, eight faculty members within the orbit of military history, including three who are MH1: Richard Kohn, Joe Glaathaar, and Wayne Lee, each of whom is a noted military historian. The other five are HM3, based on our judgment: Karen Hagemann (women's issues in the military); Roger Lotkin (impact of World War II on California, and so on); W. J. McCoy (Greek political, constitutional, military culture, and so on); Fred Naiden (new work on ancient warfare and the officer corps under Alexander the Great); and William L. Barney (Civil War). We only had access to Spring 2009 courses, but of these fifty-nine courses, up to eight were under the umbrella of military history, including six MH1 courses: "History of Sea Power"; "Global History of Warfare"; "War and American Society, 1903 to Present"; "The United States in World War II"; "Ancient Greek Warfare"; and "Intro Seminar in Military History." The other two courses were MH2 and MH3: a course on Alexander the Great and a course on the Civil War and Reconstruction.

In addition, the North Carolina History Department offers a special curriculum in "Peace, War and Defense" (renamed to mention "peace" after 1968), which "brings together faculty and courses from many disciplines to provide undergraduates with a wide range of approaches to the fundamental issues of

[77] E-mail exchange with Michael Adas, Rutgers University (New Brunswick) History Department, June–July 2009.

[78] Rutgers, State University of New Jersey, Department of Political Science, Faculty: http://polisci.rutgers.edu/.

[79] Rutgers' Center for Global Security and Democracy: http://cgsd.rutgers.edu/index.htm.

[80] University of North Carolina, Department of History, Faculty: http://history.unc.edu/faculty; Courses: http://history.unc.edu/courses; Duke University, Department of History, Faculty: http://fds.duke.edu/db/aas/history/faculty/alpha.html; Undergraduate Current Courses: http://fds.duke.edu/db/aas/history/courses_undergrad.html; Graduate Courses: http://fds.duke.edu/db/aas/history/courses_graduate.html.

human conflict and national and global security and defense."[81] (Such renaming of programs, centers, and institutes in reaction to the Vietnam War is common throughout higher education.)[82] North Carolina also offers a Program for Graduate Education in Military History, which is a collaborative undertaking with Duke University. The program has five core faculty members (Dirk Bonker, Joseph Glaathaar, Kohn, Lee, and Alex Roland) and fourteen "associated faculty." Its core courses include an "Introduction to Military History"; a "Research Seminar in Military History"; a "Colloquium in World Military History"; and a "Colloquium in American Military History."[83]

North Carolina is also part of the well-known Triangle Security Studies Seminar (along with Duke and North Carolina State), host to an ongoing seminar on "History of the Military, War, and Society," which began in 2006. The objectives of this seminar span the categories of MH1 to MH3:

> ...to provide a forum for historians working on issues relating to war, peace and society and in the field of a most broadly defined history of the military .... the seminar recognizes the rich and ever-growing diversity of approaches and methods that have come to characterize the study of the military, war and society. The seminar is open to approaches from political and diplomatic and institutional history as well as economic, social, cultural and gender history.[84]

The seminar is part of the Triangle Institute for Security Studies (TISS). Begun under a different name at UNC in 1958, it has resided at Duke's Sanford Institute of Public Policy since 1999. TISS has a broad membership of several hundred academic and nonacademic experts and interested citizens. Its operative definition of security is broad, and its membership includes professors of English, law, philosophy, anthropology, physics, religion, sociology, psychology, and communication studies, as well as political scientists, historians, graduate students, former diplomats, military officers, and other interested citizens.[85] TISS is the sponsor of *Soldiers and Civilians: The Civil–Military Gap and American National Security*, a leading volume on military–civilian relations.[86]

North Carolina is special in two senses. First, it gives prominence to all forms of military history. Second, members of the History Department are actively involved with centers or institutes outside of the department. This exceptional

81 University of North Carolina Curriculum in Peace, War, and Defense: http://www/unc.edu/depts/pwad/.

82 One interesting example is the Security Studies Program at MIT, which replaced the symbolic weaponry that adorned its institutional seal and stationery with less warlike symbols. Interview with Harvey Sapolsky, MIT Public Policy and Organization professor and former director of the MIT Security Studies Program, April 2008.

83 Program for Graduate Education in Military History: http://www.unc.edu/depts/pwad/military-history.html.

84 "History of the Military, War, and Society, A Research Triangle Seminar Series": http://www.unc.edu/mhss/about.html.

85 "About TISS," TISS home page: http://www.pubpol.duke.edu/centers/tiss/about/.

86 Peter D. Feaver and Richard A. Kohn, eds., *Soldiers and Civilians: The Civil–Military Gap and American National Security* (MIT Press, 2001).

status comes through in the e-mail correspondence. As Kohn informed us, "At NC, military history is integral to the history program at both the undergraduate and graduate level. It's looked at with some skepticism or ideological distaste by a tiny few, but my sense in my 17-years plus here is that the distaste has waned quite a bit." Kohn detects a similar trajectory for military/security studies nationwide. His colleague Naiden said military history at North Carolina is "integral," although he discerns a low status nationwide. Konrad Jarausch agreed: "At UNC military history has never gone out of fashion because we have a lively 'Peace, War and Defense' program (so named after 68) plus we are participating in the Triangle Security Studies Seminar." Significantly, an earlier generation of military historians was replaced by the contemporary crop – something that appears rare among the departments we have considered. Jarausch pointed to such older "distinguished" military historians as Gerhard Weinberg, Don Higginbotham, and Kohn, and such younger historians as Lee and Hagemann, the latter who "does also military along with gender from a European perspective."[87] (Since Jarausch's e-mail response, Higginbotham has passed away.)

Duke is strong in military history, but not as strong as North Carolina. Of sixty-nine faculty members, Dirk Bonker (who is also a core faculty member in the Program for Graduate Education in Military History, and whose main scholarly focus is military matters) and Alex Roland (military history and technology) are MH1. We ranked another faculty member, Anna Krylova, whose work deals with gender, women, and the military, as MH2, although her name did not come up among the three individuals who responded to our e-mail query. We selected three individuals for MH3, although one (Dominic Sachsenmaier) said he worked "in other fields": Bruce R. Kuniholm, whose numerous publications include such matters as foreign policy, security, the military, and the Cold War; Kristin Neuschel, who teaches the history of war; and Sachsenmaier, who treats the impact of World War I on China. Of 101 graduate and undergraduate courses (only Spring 2009 provided access to details), 4 fell under the umbrella of military history, all MH3: "Living Through the Great War"; "Love, War, Corsairs, Empire"; "History of World Wars"; and "Courts, Wars, Legacies" – taught by a nonregular faculty member.

Sachsenmaier and Bonker remarked that military history is taught with regularity, and that it is also a major within the department. Bonker also noted the Triangle Seminar in the History of the Military, War, and Society, as well as the Ph.D. program in military history. Roland concluded that military history as we defined it (dealing with war and security) was "offered regularly," but only by him. Otherwise, there is little interest in the security/defense aspect of military history. "The military receives more attention, but usually as a 'site' of social or cultural history." (Bonker is a primary example of this approach.)[88] Roland also

87 E-mail exchanges with Richard Kohn, Konrad Jarausch, Fred Naiden, and Wayne Lee, University of North Carolina History Department, June–July 2009.

88 E-mail exchanges with Dirk Bonker, Dominic Sachsenmaier, and Alex Roland, Duke University History Department, June–July 2009.

expressed pessimism about the future of military history at Duke, and commented in a later e-mail that no one has offered military history in the traditional sense since his retirement.

Beyond the History Department, in recent years Duke has sponsored extensive student and faculty engagement with the ROTC program and other military figures. Many non-military students take ROTC courses on leadership, physical fitness, and history; and the head of the Army ROTC unit has co-taught an undergraduate course designed for all undergraduate majors on civilian applications of military leadership. This course is taught through the aegis of the Hart Leadership Program, a long-standing undergraduate program that emphasizes the development of leaders in democratic society, and which has been absorbed recently by Duke's Sanford School of Public Policy.[89] Joseph LeBoeuf, a career military officer and former director of West Point's leadership curriculum, has taught this course several times. In addition, Duke hired General Anthony Zinni – a four-star general in the Marine Corps, former commander in chief of U.S. Central Command (CENTCOM), and an early critic of President George W. Bush's Iraq War strategy – to teach a course on "Leading in a New World." A teaching assistant for that course told us that "it was fascinating to see how students were mesmerized by his military examples. ... They couldn't get enough of them."[90] Zinni and a coauthor published a book that they developed in conjunction with this course.[91] The other teaching assistant in this course was an active-duty Army officer at Duke pursuing a master of public policy (MPP) degree in preparation for a teaching stint at West Point; he is working in a program partnered by the Sanford School and the U.S. Army. One of the principal instructors in this MPP program (Tom Taylor) formerly served as acting general counsel in the Pentagon. Needless to say, this is the type of productive friction we emphasize and recognition of the role that appropriate military presence has for liberal and civic education, as well as the practical importance of military knowledge in the teaching of leadership qualities and skills.

According to teaching assistant David Gastwirth, these programs associated with the Sanford School have gelled over the last several years. "You can't study public management and public affairs without thinking deeply about the military," he remarked. The military enterprise includes large amounts of funding and extensive bureaucratic operations, and it is a testing ground for many policies. "It is hard for undergrads or grads to go through the program without some understanding of the military as an institution and practice. We take the

[89] http://www.pubpol.duke.edu/centers/hlp/News%20Articles/military_leadership_course.html; http://www.pubpol.duke.edu/centers/hlp/portraits/teaching/leboeuf/leboeuf.html.

[90] Interview with David Gastwirth, Associate of the Hart Leadership Program, Duke University: http://news.duke.edu/2007/10/zinni.html.

[91] Tony Zinni and Tony Koltz, *Leading the Charge: Leadership Lessons from the Battlefield to the Boardroom* (Palgrave Macmillan, 2009).

'political' out of it. The military is there whether you like it or not, and has to be dealt with."[92]

University of Pennsylvania

(National Rank: tied for number thirteen with North Carolina[93]) Military history – at least broadly defined – has attained some status at Penn. Out of forty-eight standing members of the department, five fall within the realm of military history according to our interpretations: one MH1, Thomas Childers, who studies military issues as well as war and society; one MH2, Frederick Dickenson who studies World War II as well as memory of war in Japan (he possibly belongs in the MH3 category, but seemed closer to MH2 based on his work); and three MH3: Peter Holquist is a scholar of international law and war; Bruce Kuklick studies diplomatic history, but also teaches a course on war and diplomacy; and Arthur Waldron teaches and writes about the history of war. Waldron is an associate the Institute for Strategic Threat Assessment and Response (ISTAR) at Penn and has been associated with the Solomon Asch Institute for the Study of Ethnopolitical Conflict.

Most of our Penn e-mail correspondents considered military history to be in good standing in the department. The department has a concentration in diplomatic history, which provides some cover and support for military history. Waldron offers a two-semester sequence of lectures on "Strategy, Policy, Technology, and War" that is part of this concentration. Holquist has perhaps the most sanguine view, saying that military history is undergoing "a small boom" at Penn and his previous school, Cornell. Holquist alluded to Waldron's two-semester course, as well as work by Childers and Wally McDougal. Like others, Holquist stressed the resurgence of diplomatic history at Penn.

The most negative assessment was given by a source who asked to remain anonymous. This source viewed Waldron as the only one who teaches actual military history (although note that we placed Waldron as an MH3!). "As far as I know, there are no other faculty members or courses on campus dedicated to military history. This is a sad state of affairs." But this source acknowledged that Waldron has spawned greater interest in the field by historians who are not military historians proper. Because of this, "Penn has bucked the national trend regarding the study of military history. That is, we have actually gained courses in the last several years," while such departments as Virginia and Temple have "seen those programs fade away." In a later e-mail, this source also pointed out that two hires in political science had added to the security-related offerings at the university.

[92] Interview with David Gastwirth, Duke University History Department, June–July 2009.

[93] University of Pennsylvania, Department of History, Standing Faculty: http://www.history.upenn.edu/faculty/; Courses: http://www.history.upenn.edu/courses/undergrad/; http://www.history.upenn.edu/courses/grad/index.shtml.

Thus, military history at Penn is faring rather well because it is integrated with diplomatic and strategic approaches. Perhaps this is why Kuklick said that "Penn does itself proud in these areas without losing face in the profession." (In other words, military history has the cover of the other approaches.) In a somewhat similar vein, Kors opined that the positive status of military history at Penn is "quite strong" due to "several anomalies" and "what surely were wholly unintended consequences." Mainly, the university closely tracks undergraduate enrollments in allocating funds, and military-related courses attract a high number of students. These enrollments "are essential to all the race-gender-class-oppression graduate admissions," so the department is hospitable to military-related scholars. "So while the profession as a whole has generally abandoned diplomatic and military history, and the best work in these fields is now being done in International Relations in Politics departments ... Penn is very, very anomalous in this (undergraduate) regard, and the department hired [none of these individuals] thinking that it would turn out this way."[94]

As mentioned, Waldron is an associate of the Institute for Strategic Threat Assessment and Response. ISTAR is deeply integrated with other units at the university, and its focus is directly related to military and security concerns. Its interdisciplinary approach is centered on generating and evaluating "hypotheses, applications and policies for the detection, prevention and remediation" of strategic threats.[95]

ISTAR is linked to departments and programs across the university, including the Fels Center for Government and the Army War College's Strategic Studies Institute (SSI). The "Strategic Issues" listed on SSI's web page are: "Homeland Security and Defense," "Global War on Terrorism," "Military Leadership," "Military Change/Leadership," "Landpower Sustainment," "Strategy and Policy," and "Key Strategic Issues."[96] Meanwhile, the Political Science Department has seven members in the field of international relations, with five of them dealing with security and military-related issues: Avery Goldstein, Michael Horowitz, Edward Mansfield, Jessica Stanton, and Alex Weisinger.[97]

OTHER DEPARTMENTS

In brief, the situation at the other top-twenty departments mirrors what we have presented in the preceding sections. At Berkeley (tied for number two with Princeton), for example, Anthony Adamwaite reported, "Military history is not at all part of the Berkeley department" – a view supported by the other

94 E-mail exchanges with Peter Holquist, Bruce Kuklick, Alan Kors, and an anonymous source, University of Pennsylvania History Department, June–July 2009.

95 University of Pennsylvanian, Institute for Strategic Threat Assessment and Response, About ISTAR, Mission Statement: http://www.istar.upenn.edu/about/index.html.

96 United States Army War College, Strategic Studies Institute, Strategic Issues: http://www.strategicstudiesinstitute.army.mil/.

97 University of Pennsylvania, Department of Political Science, Faculty: http://www.polisci.upenn.edu/index.php?option=com_content&task=view&id=131&Itemid=73.

respondents, although some mentioned the subject's gravitation to other areas on campus. A correspondent at UCLA observed that there were no "purely military" courses being taught in the department, which is tied with Johns Hopkins at number nine. Similarly, Stanford's David Kennedy related that "we do not have a dedicated military historian on the faculty, and have not had in my 40 years here (possibly excepting Peter Paret, who departed for the Institute for Advanced Study some years ago)" – although Kennedy stressed that he and others incorporate some military history into their courses. (Stanford is tied with Chicago and Harvard at number four.) The situation is similar at Texas (tied for number nineteen with Indiana). Michael Stoff, who teaches in the Normandy Scholar Program, which instructs a select group of undergraduates about World War II at key battle sites in Europe, remarked, "We have taught [military history] in the past but our military historian (John Lamphear) retired a few years ago and we have not replaced him; unfortunately, the subject does not enjoy much prestige in our discipline." Lamphear himself lamented, "When I retired several years ago, no military historian was recruited to fill my position, and I believe military history has now completely vanished from the history offerings." David Bell has taught military history at Johns Hopkins, but he is now a dean and does not offer it. "There is no one else in the department who deals with these issues, or who has taught military history or security issues for the past 25 years." Michael Johnson, however, mentioned courses on the American Revolution and the Civil War as involving military history.[98] (We received no e-mail responses from Harvard faculty members.)

Northwestern (tied for number seventeen with Rutgers) is the one department in the "more major" category we did not examine, but its situation is similar to its partners. Yohanan Petrovsky-Shtern and Benjamin Frommer agreed with Michael Sherry (quoted previously along with Joshua Cole of Michigan) that classic military history is not dealt with much at Northwestern, but that social and cultural aspects of war are. In addition, Northwestern hired John Lynn to a part-time chair in military history in 2009.[99]

CONCLUSION

Several themes come to light based on our assessment of military history. First, military history, particularly conventional military history, has little or virtually no presence at several of the nation's leading history departments. This situation includes a lack of faculty who specialize in military history as well as the absence of a meaningful number of course offerings. For those committed to traditional military history, it appears that the glass is half empty at best – in some, it is

[98] E-mail exchanges with history professors Anthony Adamwaite (Berkeley), David Kennedy (Stanford), Michael Stoff and John Lamphear (University of Texas), and David Bell and Michael Johnson (Johns Hopkins), June–July 2009.

[99] E-mail exchanges with Yohanan Petrovsky-Shtern, Benjamin Frommer, and John Lynn, Northwestern University History Department, June–July 2009.

indeed empty. Second, there have been several notable instances in which military historians have not been replaced, even at some of the schools where military history had traditionally enjoyed regard. This is consistent with the findings of our survey in the previous chapter, which suggested that the decline of military history, in its more traditional version, may be through unwillingness to replace traditional military historians. Third, several universities hold military history in high regard, and in these universities, the glass appears half full or more. These programs also epitomize productive friction, with most programs with strength in military history actively building bridges with other academic units to enhance the quality and reach of the programs.

Although our analysis does not suggest that military history is in danger of extinction, we find some cause for concern. Perhaps most troubling is the fact that, at several of the nation's leading departments – most with well over fifty faculty members – there are *no* faculty who teach conventional military history and very few who even fall within the orbit of military history. Our normative framework in Chapter 2 provided several reasons that the study of war and the presence of the military contribute to a civic and liberal education – yet traditional military history is often left out of some of the nation's leading academic institutions. For example, why does a department such as that of the University of Michigan, with over one hundred faculty members, not have anyone who specializes in military history when there is such a diverse set of scholars in other areas? It seems more than a coincidence that, with all the different perspectives represented in these departments, there would be *nobody* who teaches conventional military history when there is, by the accounts that we have heard, substantial demand for these courses among undergraduates at institutions such as Michigan, Wisconsin, Northwestern, and Illinois. The existence of demand and the constraint on supply could be explained by the ideological conflicts that have been alluded to in previous chapters, yet we leave the causes of the dearth of military history to future research. With these findings in mind, we now examine the relationship among the military, realism, and security studies, the branch of the university most closely associated with policy governing matters of war.

12

Military Presence in Security Studies

Political Realism (Re)Considered

> I do the best I know how; the very best I can; and I mean to keep doing so until the end. If the end brings us out wrong ten thousand angels swearing I was right will not make any difference.
>
> – Abraham Lincoln, speaking of his leadership in the Civil War[1]

We have seen that there is reason to believe that military history – particularly traditional versions – is under threat. Although military historians have effectively raised the status of military history as a matter of public concern, there has been less attention to the role of the military in security studies programs. We now turn our attention to the status of military history and the military in security studies programs.

We examine the field of security studies in this chapter for several reasons. The debates among the models of security studies that we delineate in this chapter (in particular, the debate between political realism and its critics) raise profound empirical, normative, and philosophical questions that cut to the core civic and liberal education: What is the role of morality and ethics in international life, and what are the most effective means of promoting these goods? Is there such a thing as universal truth, or is truth contingent upon interest or social construction? Are ethical standards universal, or do they differ among different realms, such as private morality, economic relations, domestic politics, and relations among nations? How do power and the threat of force relate to citizenship, justice, and moral obligation? In what ways do the ethical and normative obligations of statecraft differ from those of everyday life and those of other endeavors? Finally, because security studies deal with the very existence of states and social order, they also impinge upon questions of life and death itself. (Hobbes, after all, rooted his argument for the state in self-preservation and the fear of violent death.)[2]

[1] Abraham Lincoln, quoted in Francis B. Carpenter, *The Inner Life of Abraham Lincoln: Six Months at the White House* (University of Nebraska Press, 1995), pp. 258–9.

[2] On how the themes in this paragraph constitute the core questions of liberal education, see Anthony Kronman, *Education's End: Why Our Colleges and Universities Have Given Up on the Meaning of Life* (Yale University Press, 2007). See also Thomas Hobbes, *Leviathan* (Cambridge University Press, 1991 [1651]).

In this and the next chapter, we look at the status of security studies and at a few specific programs for several more practical reasons as well. First, security studies departments comprise the arm of the university that is most likely to train individuals who will assume an active role in defining or implementing national security policy. As Gene M. Lyons and Louis Morton remark in their book on national security educational programs in the mid-1960s (*Schools for Strategy*), "The expert in national security ... is a professional in the deepest sense of the word. He must understand the role of force in society, be informed in international politics, and be capable of creative and analytical thought. These qualities can be developed only through rigorous and continuous training."[3] History departments primarily train academic historians, whereas security studies programs prepare not only academics but also practitioners. Accordingly, it is important to understand the degree of the integration of the military in these programs – indeed, from a policy perspective, integration of military presence within security studies programs may be even more important than the status of military history in history departments.

Second, security studies programs appear to be an area where integration of military history and those with military experience is essential to formulating good policy. Military solutions or threats can be called for in conflicts and disputes, even if we long for less violent options, especially if dangerous or violent leaders are not amenable to compromise or non-military solutions. Accordingly, students must be familiar with the protocols regarding the legitimate uses of military force.[4] In addition, military voices can provide a distinct perspective that is otherwise missing in scholarly or pedagogical debate. One example is the group of thirty military officers who took Jeremi Suri's online summer course on grand strategy in the summer of 2009 at Wisconsin. These student-soldiers debated the strategic implications surrounding the disputed election results in Iran that summer, including what course the Obama administration should take. The officers were united in a common concern: the fear that the president's statements could "lock in" certain military positions that the country and the military would regret – or that would make retreat from these positions difficult or embarrassing.[5] This perspective is intriguing not only for the policy analysis at stake but also because the response has a focal character in the sense that the officers appeared to be coordinated on it – in other words, it

[3] Gene M. Lyons and Louis Morton, *Schools for Strategy: Education and Research in National Security Affairs* (Frederick A. Praeger, 1965), p. 32.

[4] Numerous examples could include Slobodan Milosevic in the Baltics, Adolf Hitler, the Taliban in Afghanistan and tribal areas of Pakistan, and the Revolutionary Armed Forces of Colombia (FARC). In each of these cases, the aggressors utilized treaties or cease-fire agreements as opportunities to take advantage of the opposition and further their violent causes. On how European idealists who disdained the use of interventionist military power in international relations reconsidered their positions in light of Kosovo and similar cases, see Paul Berman's account in *Power and the Idealists, or, the Passion of Joschka Fischer and Its Aftermath* (Soft Skull Press, 2005).

[5] Discussion with Jeremi Suri, University of Wisconsin History Department; University of Wisconsin, Madison, "A History of Grand Strategy": http://iss.jasons.wisc.edu/.

appeared to be a *military* perspective. The point here is not to support any particular position in this debate, but rather to note how the military perspective added an important viewpoint to the class that would otherwise have been absent.

Third, as we will soon see, security studies (and the study of international relations, or IR) can be analyzed from a wide range of perspectives in terms of subject matter, methodology, and normative emphasis. We are interested in how much these programs are influenced by a distinctly military perspective as opposed to other approaches and emphases. One of the manifestations of military history in security is realism (which, as we defined the term in Chapter 2, includes both political and moral variants), which emphasizes historical conflict, the recurrence of war, and the importance of military power in understanding features of the international system.

Our pedagogical model suggests the importance of considering realism (as an approach that shares much in common with military history) along with the perspectives of those with military experience in order to encourage productive friction within security studies programs. Some may view a decline of Cold War–inspired security studies as an example of the broadening of intellectual horizons, but it is possible that nominally broader perspectives on security – including "constructivism" and "peace studies" – may have had the opposite effect by paradoxically excluding military history, political realism, and those with experience in military and security affairs. We are interested in finding out the extent to which security studies programs emphasize productive friction among the military, scholars, and students who will someday make policy.

Our findings should come as good news to military historians such as John Lynn, who, as we noted earlier, advocates a broader approach to security that emphasizes how war brings the problems of violence, illness, and economic threat together.[6] Although Lynn was speaking primarily to military historians and to the discipline of history, his insights are as relevant to the discipline of security studies. And while his perspective was somewhat pessimistic, our conclusions in Chapter 13 are more optimistic: *Many of the leading security studies programs are a source of productive friction in American universities because they bring military history, military personnel, and political realism to bear on real-world problems*. One of the reasons for our optimism is our finding that political realism continues to have a meaningful place in security studies programs, and that such programs honor realism by blending practical and theoretical forms of knowledge. Our findings thus suggest that security studies programs can be a model for integration of the military and military history within the university. We begin by reviewing our pedagogical model before describing the state of security studies historically and more recently in Chapter 13.

[6] See John A. Lynn II, "Breaching the Walls of Academe: The Purposes, Problems, and Prospects of Military History," *Academic Questions* (March 2008).

PEDAGOGY, MILITARY KNOWLEDGE, AND SECURITY STUDIES

Our pedagogical model stresses the importance of integrating diverse perspectives in order to formulate effective policy. In matters of national security, we view military history and military personnel as especially important for several reasons: (1) Their presence allows students to take advantage of the practical knowledge of those in the military, for military personnel are more likely to have experience in critical matters of national security, such as war; (2) their availability increases the number of contrasting viewpoints, thereby increasing the likelihood of reaching the "best" policy; (3) when all is said and done, military history and realism are the foundation of security studies rather than branches of it.

Our first rationale recognizes that soldiers have the most direct experience with the armed forces, which constitute perhaps the most important – or one of the most important – components of security. As such, military personnel offer a unique practical perspective to security studies, much in line with what education theorists call the "Third Way." The Third Way entails "practice-oriented education," in which students are exposed to the real-world aspects of their studies (for example, working in governmental or nongovernmental organizations, meeting with practitioners, participating in activities outside the classroom, and so on).[7] At the other extreme are scholars with primarily academic expertise. Academics may contribute substantial insight into international relations, but their knowledge is of a different sort from those with military experience. When combined with practical questions, such academic background can contribute to the "higher practicality" that we also discussed in Chapter 1, drawing from the thought of Hans Morgenthau.[8] Our pedagogical model does not suppose that one sort of knowledge is superior, but rather that those with military expertise offer a *distinctive* perspective on matters of war compared to those who approach the subject of war and security from a purely academic orientation. Similarly, traditional military historians, because they study the activities of soldiers, and political realists, because they study the role of power, power-seeking, and alliances in international politics, offer a perspective on war and the military that is critical to understanding not only war, but how to prevent it in the future.

Our second rationale for integration of the military perspective into security studies recognizes that increasing the number of contrasting viewpoints is desirable in education and in the formulation of policy. Diversity of viewpoints is one of the key elements of our pedagogical model. We do not suggest that military history or political realism typically supply the best answers, but rather that consideration of alternative perspectives increases the likelihood

[7] See Richard M. Freeland, "The Third Way," *Atlantic Monthly* (October 2004).

[8] Hans J. Morgenthau, "The Purpose of Political Science," in James C. Charlesworth, ed., *A Design for Political Science: Scope, Objectives, and Methods* (The American Academy of Political and Social Science, 1966), pp. 63–79.

of arriving at the best answer when it comes to key questions of national security.

This said, we stress that realism lies at the core of security studies, so it is essential to maintain realism as well as competing perspectives. Recall our definition of *realism* in Chapter 1, which included political and moral realism: a deeply held perspective that emphasizes the centrality of force or the threat of force in domestic and international politics, and recognition of the moral tensions that accompany a responsible acceptance of this fact. At its core, national security is fundamentally the study of force (or the threat of force) and its consequences, for a simple reason: The problem of dealing with and managing violence (internal and external) constitutes the core of social order;[9] and the practice of soft power and other more peaceful methods often lack credibility if they are not ultimately linked to power based on force. As such, we would view programs that lack these elements with suspicion, for any program that nominally seeks diverse perspectives while excluding military history and political realism would leave out the core of security studies.

There is little doubt that the Cold War led to the integration of security studies, the military, and the academy. We also know that with the decline of the Cold War University, various institutions – ROTC, the military, and traditional security studies – came under threat on various fronts. Our objectives in this chapter and the next are to articulate the tenets of realism, to consider the role of realism in security studies historically, and to determine the current status of military history, military personnel, and realism in security studies programs. What remains to be seen is how much of a role military history, military personnel, and political realism continue to enjoy in the discipline of security studies, and how to improve interactions between the military and security studies where this role is lacking.

TWO MODELS OF SECURITY AND INTERNATIONAL RELATIONS

Before we look more precisely at the field of security studies, it is useful to distinguish two basic approaches to the study of security and international relations: realism and liberalism. These models are "ideal types," so the reader should bear in mind that the actual field of study is very complex, and that the works of many scholars fall into areas between these poles. Indeed, the field of international relations constitutes a veritable growth industry, with many new approaches vying to explain international phenomena. Such approaches include constructivism, which argues that the dominant paradigms in international relations overemphasize power politics and fail to recognize that the international system itself is malleable, that is, socially

[9] See Douglass C. North, John Joseph Wallis, and Barry R. Weingast, *Violence and Social Orders: A Conceptual Framework for Interpreting Recorded Human History* (Cambridge University Press, 2009).

constructed.[10] Keeping these models in mind helps to place the significant changes that we will be discussing in perspective; furthermore, the models are especially relevant to the status of security studies in American universities, where the ideological and philosophical tensions that exist between the two models are most acute.

Like modern political realism itself, we begin our consideration by reflecting on the insights of Hans Morgenthau, one of the architects of realism in modern security studies. Morgenthau begins his classic work *Politics Among Nations* by anchoring his analysis in the tension between realism and idealistic liberalism:

> The history of modern political thought is the story of a contest between two schools of thought that differ fundamentally in their conceptions of the nature of man, society, and politics. One believes that a rational and moral political order, derived from universally valid abstract principles, can be achieved here and now. It assumes the essential goodness and infinite malleability of human nature, and blames the failure of the social order to measure up to rational standards on lack of knowledge and understanding. . . . It trusts in education, reform, and the sporadic use of force to remedy these defects.

The other school – Morgenthau's school of realism, which we will discuss more fully later in this chapter – believes that the imperfect world

> . . . is the result of forces inherent in human nature. Realism is a response to more optimistic theories of liberalism. According to realists, "to improve the world, one must work with those forces, not against them." This being inherently a world of opposing interests and of conflict among them, moral principles can never be fully realized, but must at best be approximated through the ever temporary balancing of interests and the ever precarious settlement of conflicts. This school, then, sees in a system of checks and balances a universal principle for all pluralist societies.[11]

Realism's fundamental policy implication follows from these sentiments – that force in relation to national and self-interest is a primary arbiter of disputes in the international realm, and failure to match a nation's ambition with countervailing force risks destruction of the international system. That said, the empiricism of Morgenthau and other realists compels them to take account of the actual ways in which international law and norms have indeed constrained behavior over time. In *Politics Among Nations*, for example, Morgenthau acknowledges how international law since Westphalia (1648) "has in most instances been scrupulously observed," although enforcement of violations has "not always

[10] Constructivists view realism and liberalism as emphasizing material interests, nation-states, and rational interests. Constructivists do not reject material interests, state centrism, or rationality as much as they suggest that preferences and interests are socially constructed, the state system is not "inevitable," and that intersubjective meaning and psychological considerations influence international politics. See Alexander Wendt, *Social Theory of International Politics* (Cambridge University Press, 1999); J. Samuel Barkin and Bruce Cronin, "The State and the Nation: Changing Norms and the Rules of Sovereignty in International Relations," *International Organization* 48, 1 (1994): 107–30.

[11] Hans J. Morgenthau, *Politics Among Nations: The Struggle for Power and Peace*, 3rd Edition, (Alfred A. Knopf, 1965), pp. 3–4.

been effective. Yet to deny that international law exists at all as a system of binding legal rules flies in the face of all the evidence."[12] The question of the binding scope and limits of such things as customary and formal international law is a central background issue in any honest inquiry regarding foreign relations and national security law.[13]

As we will see in this chapter, realism believes that the historical record teaches us that self-interest and striving for power constitute the primary form (or at least one of the primary forms) of state and human behavior; accordingly, force (or the plausible threat of force) is often necessary to protect a polity's existence or interests and the interests of justice. Peace and legitimate interest can be maintained only by a propitious balance of power to which relevant parties are committed. At the same time, a realist understanding emphasizes how such power can easily be abused. Although Morgenthau emphasized realism as a theory of international relations (a particularly appropriate realm for realism given the absence of an overarching authority in the international realm), a version of realism helped shape the thinking of America's Founding Fathers, and it lies at the heart of what Samuel Huntington conceived as the "military mind."[14] For the Framers, constitutional separation of powers tempered the threat of autocracy because each branch would defend its realm against encroachment by the other branches, resulting in a system of limited government. Properly understood, Morgenthau applied the Framers' political realism to interactions between or among nations. Although realism lies at the core of Morgenthau's thought, his school of realism also included a normative variant that we will discuss in a moment. For example, he developed a theory of national interest and political purpose that entailed commitment to national values. In *The Purpose of American Politics*, he wrote, "We know that a real nation worthy of our remembrances has contributed to the affairs of men more than the successful defense and promotion of its national interest. In order to be worthy of our lasting sympathy a nation must pursue its interests for the sake of a transcendent purpose that gives meaning to the day-by-day operations of its foreign policy." In America, these purposes are freedom and equality.[15] This understanding of national interest pushes us toward liberalism, which has often influenced American foreign policy. Throughout history, American foreign policy has embodied a tension between realism and liberal idealism, mixed

[12] Morgenthau, *Politics Among Nations*, p. 277.

[13] See Jack L. Goldsmith and Eric A. Posner, *The Limits of International Law* (Oxford University Press, 2005), ch. 1; Thomas M. Franck, Michael J. Glennon, and Sean D. Murphy, *Foreign Relations and National Security Law: Cases, Materials, and Simulations* (Thomson, West, 2008), chs. 2, 3.

[14] For an illuminating analysis of the Framers' understanding of constitutionalism and the propitious allocation of power, see Stephen Holmes, *Passions and Constraint: On the Theory of Liberal Democracy* (University of Chicago Press, 1995); Samuel P. Huntington, *The Soldier and the State: The Theory and Politics of Civil-Military Relations* (Harvard University Press, 1957).

[15] Hans J. Morgenthau, *The Purpose of American Politics* (Alfred A. Knopf, 1951), p. 8. See also Anthony F. Lang, Jr., "Introduction," in Lang, ed., *Political Theory and International Affairs: Hans J. Morgenthau on Aristotle's The Politics* (Praeger, 2004).

with its share of less supportable motives and actions. In our view, policy is best when liberal idealism is leavened by prudent realism; problems develop when either idealism or realism is completely forsaken.[16]

The other school draws its inspiration from the liberal internationalism of such figures as Immanuel Kant (who maintained in his essay "Perpetual Peace" that peace could prevail among nations if they adopted republican forms of government and concomitant respect for international law) and Woodrow Wilson, who led the fight for the League of Nations. Labeled (sometimes unfairly) "idealist," this school of thought has drawn inspiration from religious values, international law, and the belief in international institutions and human reason – phenomena that aspire to transcend the limitations of sovereign states. In Morgenthau's spirit, Robert Kagan has depicted the competing schools as Kantian (international law–oriented) and Hobbesian (power-oriented), or as the theories of "paradise" versus "power."[17]

The tension between realism and idealism has had a profound influence on security studies as a field. Paul D. Williams proposes a similar distinction among security study schools. One school asserts that security is a function of the accumulation of power: "In particular, power is thought to be the route to security: the more power (especially military power) actors can accumulate, the more secure they will be." The second philosophy "challenges the idea that security flows from power. Instead, it sees security as being based on emancipation; that is, a concern with justice and the provision of human rights. From this perspective, security is understood as a relationship between different actors rather than a commodity."[18] The latter orientation (broadly construed) has taken on several forms that we will discuss briefly later in this chapter, although the origins of the alternative approach can be traced to liberalism. Neoliberal institutionalism, with its emphasis on soft power and non-military sources of security, as well as the role of institutions in resolving the security dilemma, is a related response to realism and "neorealism."[19] Neorealism derives from axioms appropriate to the behavior of states, leading to the prediction that states are compelled to seek security, rather than power, because the structure of the international system is anarchic.[20]

[16] On the danger of forsaking realism, see Walter Lippmann, *U.S. Foreign Policy: Shield of the Republic* (Little, Brown, 1943). One reason that we were unprepared to deal with the rise of Hitler and Japan in the 1930s was that "a concern with the foundations of national security, with arms, with strategy, and with diplomacy, was beneath our dignity as idealists" (p. 49).

[17] Robert Kagan, *Of Paradise and Power: America and Europe in the New World Order* (Alfred A. Knopf, 2003); Immanuel Kant, *Perpetual Peace*, edited by Lewis White Beck (Bobbs-Merrill, 1957 [1795]).

[18] Paul D. Williams, *Security Studies: An Introduction* (Routledge, 2008), p. 6.

[19] See, e.g., David A. Baldwin, ed., *Neorealism and Neoliberalism: The Contemporary Debate* (Columbia University Press, 1993). Neoliberalism emphasizes that international institutions can constrain nation-states and that common economic interests can sustain cooperation even in hard economic times.

[20] See Kenneth Waltz, *Man, the State, and War* (Columbia University Press, 1959), and *Theory of International Politics* (McGraw-Hill, 1979).

The background empirical and normative (as well as methodological) disagreements of these schools can render any attempt at reconciliation futile. But there is no necessary conflict between those who believe injustice is a source of conflict and those who maintain that states act on the basis of power considerations.[21] Both are among the causes of conflict and war. The main disagreement lies in the degree of confidence one places in the malleability of human nature and the efficacy of such institutions as international law and organizations when they are disassociated from plausible threats of force as part of their package of attributes. Realism predicts that international institutions will reflect the balance of power and that they are likely to be ineffective in constraining states when the rules require behavior that harms the state's interests, while competing schools are more optimistic about the ability of individuals to design institutions that mitigate threats to international peace and prosperity.[22] We will encounter various aspects of this fundamental difference in the discussion of the vicissitudes of security studies throughout this chapter.

SECURITY STUDIES, THE COLD WAR UNIVERSITY, AND POLITICAL REALISM

The field of "security studies" is young, having emerged in the United States after World War II, primarily as a subfield of international relations (IR). Security studies' focus during its formative period (1955–6) was Cold War–related, concentrating on military issues relevant to the conflict between the United States and its adversaries. In an influential 1991 essay, Stephen M. Walt wrote that "security studies may be defined as *the study of the threat, use, and control of military force*. It explores the conditions that make the use of force more likely, the ways in which the use of force affects individuals, states, and societies, and the specific policies that states adopt in order to prepare for, prevent, or engage in war."[23] Research within the conventional security studies programs dealt with such issues as technological developments, deterrence and nuclear war, the arms race, coercion and escalation of conflict, the causes of war, and alternative strategies to win wars.[24]

[21] See, for example, the work of Donna Hicks (Harvard Weatherford Center for International Affairs), who stresses that the lack of respect and dignity is a major source of conflict. Donna Hicks, "Dignity for All," in Michael Henderson, ed., *No Enemy to Conquer – Forgiveness in World Affairs* (Baylor University Press, 2008). This theory resembles Hegel's tenet that the striving for recognition is the engine that drives human motivation.

[22] On how the major paradigms of international law in history reflect the strategic interests and values of the major powers, see Philip Bobbitt, *The Shield of Achilles: War, Peace, and the Course of History* (Random House, 2002).

[23] Stephen M. Walt, "The Renaissance of Security Studies," *International Studies Quarterly* 35, 2 (1991), p. 212. Emphasis in original.

[24] Examples include the works of such thinkers as Herbert Kaufman, Henry Kissinger, Thomas Schelling, Herman Kahn, and Albert Wohlstetter. See Walt, "The Renaissance of Security Studies," p. 214.

The early security studies programs privileged the nation-state and military power, viewing international politics as a history of war and preparation for war. But it was assumed that a thorough understanding of security and military capabilities is necessary to achieve peace. Relations among nations are analyzed not in terms of benevolence but rather in terms of how peace arises from the configuration of power in the international system. The moral of the story is that failure to understand the past can doom the future. To paraphrase Thucydides, history teaches that failure to appreciate military capabilities and power relations can contribute to war.[25]

The focus on military-related issues predominated during what Walt calls the "Golden Age" of security studies, which prevailed from the mid-1950s through the mid-1960s. (The late 1960s was a defining, turning point in the university's relationship with the military on several fronts, as we saw in Part II of this book.) Before World War II, intellectual work on strategy and military matters took place largely within military circles and institutions, with university personnel limiting their interest to the study of military and diplomatic history. But the advent of World War II transformed this arrangement, spawning unprecedented and extensive relationships among the military, the government, and higher education – a development chronicled by a large literature. World War II was the first war in which weapons technology (for example, jet aircraft, ballistic missiles, proximity fuses, and, of course, the atom bomb) changed dramatically during the actual span of combat, directly affecting the resolution of the conflict; and the development of this sophisticated technology called for the assistance of high-level research scientists, many of whom were affiliated with universities. Under these circumstances, as Alex Roland has observed, the laboratory became as important as the industrial base for weapons production and military strategy: "These developments convinced the services that the desideratum of modern war was shifting from the industrial production to technological development. The next war would be won in the research laboratory fully as much as the factory. Thus began the hothouse environment of military research and development."[26]

With the arrival of the Cold War, the government forged even stronger relationships with academia, broadening its outreach to include social scientists who conducted research on social and psychological issues bearing on democracy and Communism.[27] During this period, a strong commitment to national security blossomed, becoming what historians called the Cold War Consensus. Lyons and Morton depict the historical moment:

[25] Thucydides, *The Peloponnesian War*, translated by Rex Warner (Penguin Classics, 1954), esp. Book One, Chapter 1.

[26] Alex Roland, "Disciplinary Approaches of War: History of Science and Technology," in John Whitclay Chambers II, editor in chief, *Oxford Guide to American Military History* (Oxford University Press, 1999), pp. 222–3.

[27] See the essays in the symposium, "Universities and the Military," *Annals of the American Academy of Political and Social Science* 502 (March 1989).

The events from 1949 to 1952 marked an important turning point, both in American society's attitude to military problems and in the response of scholars and teachers to national security affairs. These events included the Soviet explosion of an atomic device, the United States' decision to develop a hydrogen bomb, the Communist victory in China, the Korean War, the establishment of NATO, and the presidential election of 1952 ... most important, there was no longer any doubt about the relationship between national security and foreign and domestic affairs. Scholars simply could no longer avoid the fundamental social and political problems in national security.[28]

As a result of these and other developments, major universities assumed the mantle of what observers have called the "Cold War University," an institution dedicated to assisting national defense efforts by conducting relevant research and teaching in the hard and social sciences.[29] The Vietnam War wrought discomfort to this cozy arrangement, however, as "the polarization that had occurred in the country and on campuses ... made even the attenuated presence of military-sponsored research intolerable at this juncture."[30]

The theoretical framework that governed much of the work conducted in security studies programs was supplied by political realism, which emphasizes the near inevitability of conflict:

If history is just "one damn thing after another," then for realists international politics is the same damn things over and over again: war, great power security and economic competitions, the rise and fall of great powers, and the formation and dissolution of alliances. International political behavior is characterized by continuity, regularity, and repetition because states are constrained by the international system's unchanging (and probably unchangeable) structure.[31]

Realism dominated not only security studies but also the field of international relations, in particular classical realism, represented by the works of such key thinkers as Morgenthau, Reinhold Niebuhr, George F. Kennan, E. H. Carr, Arnold Wolfers, and Raymond Aron. Realism and its more recent variants (including the neorealism of Kenneth Waltz, which stresses the causative influence of international political structures and systems more than Morgenthau did; defensive and offensive realism; "rise and fall" realism; and so-called

[28] Lyons and Morton, *Schools for Strategy*, p. 40.

[29] Jeremi Suri, *Henry Kissinger and the American Century* (Harvard University Press, 2007), pp. 3–99, 107–17, 122–39, 161, 191, 207. See Chapter 3.

[30] Roger L. Geiger, *Research and Relevant Knowledge: American Research Universities Since World War II* (Oxford University Press, 1993), pp. 194–5, and, generally, ch. 6. Seventy-six percent of federal funds during this period came from the Atomic Energy Commission (AEC) and the Pentagon. See also Arthur M. Cohen, *The Shaping of American Higher Education: Emergence and Growth of the Contemporary System* (Jossey-Bass, John Wiley and Sons, 1998), ch. 4, esp. pp. 262–3.

[31] Christopher Layne, "Kant or Cant: The Myth of Democratic Peace," *International Security* 19, 2 (1994): 10–11.

neoclassical realism) comprise a complex school of thought that defies simple definition or reduction.[32]

Realism also has powerful historical antecedents. Modern political realism is closely related to the writings of Thucydides, whose *Melian Dialogue* is the basis for the axiom that the strong do as they will, while the weak capitulate or risk annihilation (recall that the Melians chose slavery and death in the name of justice rather than capitulating to the Athenians, who pointed out that justice is for the stronger to decide). Realism also draws on Machiavelli, whose *Prince* accentuated effectiveness as a virtue rather than goodness; and Hobbes, who emphasized that absence of power is irreducibly anarchic and unstable. Each of these works was based on histories of relations among self-interested individuals and groups of people vying for control, each culminating in the view that power is the ultimate arbiter, not morality. Indeed, the proper arrangement of power is necessary *in order* for morality to prevail. We might also add to the discussion ancient military strategists Kautilya, who stated in *Arthashastra* that neighboring countries are natural enemies and that those countries' neighbors are natural allies, and Sun Tzu, who proclaimed in the *Art of War* that the pinnacle of excellence in battle is not winning one hundred battles in one hundred tries but rather subjugating the enemy without fighting. Military strategists in the ancient world emphasized power and strategy, rather than justice, as the primary concerns of a wise king.[33]

Because different realists share a common ancestry, the schools of realism embody certain core assumptions that continue to influence thinking about international relations. The major tenets include the belief that politics and statesmanship are fundamentally distinct realms (distinguished from such realms as economics, religion, and conventional morality) constituted by their own norms, interests, and obligations; the centrality of states as independent and self-interested power seekers in the international arena; the fundamental

[32] Several books articulate the various forms of realism, e.g., Jack Donnelly, *Realism and International Relations* (Cambridge University Press, 2000). Richard Ned Lebow recently articulated how classical realists demonstrated far more attention to historical contingency, domestic politics, and ethics than modern realists. See Richard Ned Lebow, *The Tragic Vision of Politics: Ethics, Interests and Orders* (Cambridge University Press, 2003), as well as Lebow's chapter on classical realism in Duncan S. Bell, ed., *Tragedy, Power, and Justice: Realism and Global Political Theory* (Oxford University Press, 2008). As noted earlier, Waltz, the leading neorealist, constructs a theory of international relations based on systemic, as opposed to historically contingent, factors. According to Waltz, states maximize security under the assumptions that the international system is anarchic and other states cannot be trusted. See Kenneth N. Waltz, *Theory of International Politics* (McGraw-Hill, 1979). Morgenthau's analysis is much more historically oriented.

[33] See Kautilya, *The Arthashastra* (Penguin Classics, 1992); and Sun Tzu, *The Art of War*, translated by John Minford (Penguin Classics, 2002). Modern theories of alliances also assume that states are instrumental in their behavior, with much of the debate centering on whether states pursue policies of balancing or bandwagoning. Stephen M. Walt emphasizes that perceptions of threat influence the decision to balance or bandwagon. See Walt, *The Origins of Alliances* (Cornell University Press, 1990).

structural or systemic fact of anarchy in international relations, a condition that resembles a Hobbesian state of nature lacking an overarching authority to enforce rules and impose order;[34] the assumption that individuals and states are committed to increasing their power and (predominantly material) resources;[35] the belief that human nature and state behavior have been essentially constant throughout history (empirical universality), thereby creating an historical and empirical basis for the generation of theory; and a belief that statesmen should deal with the world not as it "should be," but rather as "it is." The latter belief does not mean that statesman should be oblivious to higher moral standards, but rather that they cannot improve the world unless they take into account the self-interested and flawed nature of human beings. As Morgenthau wrote in *Politics Among Nations*, realism "believes that the world, imperfect as it is from the rational point of view, is the result of forces inherent in human nature. To improve the world one must work with those forces, not against them."[36]

Thus understood, realism is part of a long tradition that began its historical sojourn with Thucydides, picking up such important thinkers as Augustine, Machiavelli, the American Founding Fathers, Max Weber, and Reinhold Niebuhr along the way.[37] Unlike many contemporary IR scholars, Morgenthau and other traditional realists embedded their scholarship in political philosophy and classical learning as well as modern political science. In reading *Politics Among Nations*, the reader encounters numerous historical examples of states acting according to the tenets of realism; the reader also frequently comes across such figures or writers as the Framers, Weber, Tolstoy, the ancient Greeks and Romans, the Dead Sea Scrolls, *Hamlet*, and the prophets of the Old Testament.[38] Morgenthau does not use such thinkers

[34] As Morgenthau firmly acknowledges, international law and mores are important, as nations do strive, for the most part, to obey them for normative and strategic reasons. The problem is that powerful nations are largely at liberty to ignore (or to partially ignore) these strictures if they so choose. This result may not be typical, but a nation is expected to pursue its own interests when they are inconsistent with the demands prescribed by international institutions. Rule following, for a realist, reflects that fact that the institutions themselves are set up to facilitate the interests of the member nations that set up these institutions. This is the theme in Jack L. Goldsmith and Eric A. Posner, *The Limits of International Law* (Oxford University Press, 2005).

[35] Morgenthau looks to history and political thought to validate this point; Waltz considers these sources, but focuses more fully on the competitive pressures that are inherent in the anarchic system of international relations. Morgenthau uncovers principles of international politics from experience, whereas Waltz deduces them from particular conditions.

[36] Morgenthau, *Politics Among Nations*, p. 4.

[37] To wit, the *Federalist Papers* abound with discussions of how justice in democratic republics can be achieved only by taking human nature and self-interest into account. James Madison's famous analysis of checks and balances in *Federalist #51* is but one example, as are his comments in *Federalist #37* about the limits of human wisdom. See *The Federalist Papers*, edited by Clinton Rossiter (New American Library, 1961). Balance of power is also a remedy that Morgenthau stresses repeatedly in *Politics Among Nations*.

[38] Like Freud, Morgenthau considered the writings of the best minds to be data that provided knowledge and insight into human nature. On Freud's use of classic literature and thought as data, see Philip Rieff, *Freud: The Mind of the Moralist* (Doubleday, 1961).

merely as window dressing; on the contrary, his work is deeply interwoven with such thought. Indeed, one insightful commentator writes that Morgenthau's thought is profoundly normative, rooted in the traditions of practical morality represented by Christian Realism and other normative strands of Judeo-Christian thought. Cosmopolitan moral principles and recalcitrant morality exist in a dynamic, dialectical tension. From this perspective, Morgenthau's thought owes more to Augustine and Niebuhr than to Hobbes and Machiavelli. His thought emphasizes "the tragic presence of evil in all political action" – a fathoming that challenges the conventional norms of liberal democracy, as we elucidated in our discussion of the "moral dilemmas of liberal democracy" in Chapter 2.[39] In *Scientific Man vs Power Politics*, Morgenthau wrote:

> We have no choice between power and the common good. To act successfully, that is, according to the rules of the political art, is political wisdom. To know with despair that the political act is inevitably evil, and to act nevertheless, is moral courage. To choose among several expedient actions the least evil one is moral judgment. In the combination of political wisdom, moral courage, and moral judgment man reconciles his political nature with his moral destiny. That this conciliation is nothing more than a *modus vivendi*, uneasy, precarious, and even paradoxical, can disappoint only those who prefer to gloss over and distort the tragic contradictions of human existence with the soothing logic of a specious accord.[40]

There is some dispute about realism's assumptions concerning human nature. One school discerns realism as a precursor of the later "rational choice" approach to international relations, which stresses that states make decisions in the international arena based on rational determinations of their strategic interests in situations that can often be described by a strategic game. One of Morgenthau's comments in *Politics Among Nations* supports this connection:

> [W]e put ourselves in the position of a statesman under certain circumstances and we ask ourselves what the rational alternatives are from which a statesman may choose who must meet this problem under these circumstances (presuming always that he acts in a rational manner), and which of these rational alternatives this particular statesman is likely to choose. It is the testing of this rational hypothesis against the actual facts and their consequences that gives theoretical meaning to the facts of international politics.[41]

[39] A. J. H. Murray, "The Moral Politics of Hans Morgenthau," *Review of Politics* 58 (1996): 81–107.

[40] Hans Morgenthau, *Scientific Man vs Power Politics* (University of Chicago Press, 1946), pp. 195, 202–3. Quoted in Murray, "The Moral Politics of Hans Morgenthau," p. 106. See also Morgenthau's critique of political science as too divorced from the "higher practicality" in "The Purpose of Political Science." For a profound treatment of Morgenthau's moral anchor within the assumption of realism, see Christoph Frei, *Hans Morgenthau: An Intellectual Biography* (Louisiana State University Press, 2001).

[41] Morgenthau, *Politics Among Nations*, p. 5.

Morgenthau in effect proposed that the task of the analyst is to think of the underlying game confronting policy makers and to anticipate the equilibrium of the relevant game.[42]

Nevertheless, many of the classic realists hailed from Germany or other European countries and brought a more philosophical and pessimistic continental sensibility to the table. According to Ole Waever:

> Postwar "realism" often hides a tension between continental, historicist, and British liberal roots. To the former, states exist because they do ... they clash and struggle for numerous more or less rational reasons: ... Therefore, the rationalist, "six principles" reading of Morgenthau is misleading. In the classical realist world, conflicts are unavoidable because of the tragic nature of human interaction and the impossibility of fully rational decisions.[43]

The two positions can be reconciled to some extent by making a distinction between the inner motivation of the statesman – which is to do the most rational thing under the circumstances – and the external fact (which can also be part of the awareness of the actor) that the complexity of the world and human fallibility subject all decisions to potentially erroneous and even tragic consequences. However, irrationality is *in the actor* as well, complicating the internal/external distinction. We must strive to be rational in a world ridden with unknowns and human irrationality, including our own. Rational motivation constitutes a normative obligation for the statesman, regardless of the inevitable tragedy that follows from human action. In other words, rational choice can also be interpreted as a prescriptive theory suggesting how players should behave if they want to reap the best outcome in terms of their own self-interest.

Although classical realism drew on Germanic and European inspirations, many scholars have observed that IR has nonetheless been shaped from its inception by the needs of the American state, especially in the field's early years. Hence, IR and security studies have an inherent policy dimension that

[42] Not all situations are amenable to game theoretic analysis. Game theory becomes more appropriate when the stakes are high and individuals have incentives to think through their decisions. As long as the stakes in politics are sufficiently high, statesmen have incentives to think through their actions in the ways required by game theory. Morgenthau's sentiments suggest that the high stakes of politics increase the appropriateness of assuming rational calculation in the game theoretic sense, although we note later in this chapter that Morgenthau allowed for – indeed, his tragic sensibility *required* attention to – irrationality, mistakes, and human error in the political realm (features of human decision making that are, increasingly, the subject of economic analysis, including game theory).

[43] Ole Waever, "The Sociology of a Not So International Discipline: American and European Developments in International Relations," *International Organization* 52, 4 (1998), p. 720. Niebuhr's realism, for example, was steeped in tragic sensibility. The nature of organized life (domestically and internationally) compels states to act in ways that often contradict the moral principles of individuals, and the fallen state of mankind leads to unintended consequences that ineluctably bedevil us. See, e.g., Reinhold Neibuhr, *Moral Man and Immoral Society* (Charles Scribner and Sons, 1932). And Morgenthau constantly stresses the difficulty of knowing reality and the consequences of one's actions. See also Lebow, *The Tragic Vision of Politics*.

thrusts them into the most pressing issues of world politics.[44] But despite the importance of security studies to the Cold War University, the discipline of security studies has seldom enjoyed its own independent institutional base. Strategic and security studies either have been relegated to military domains or have been, in Richard K. Betts' words, "piggybacked on other disciplines – mainly history and political science – instead of securing an autonomous institutional home. There are no departments of strategy or war studies in U.S. universities in contrast to Britain."[45] According to Betts, this institutional dependency has inhibited the development of classical forms of security studies; it might also have exposed security studies to trends that were developing in history and other areas of the humanities and social sciences, some of which we examined in our earlier discussion of military history.[46]

Like other scholarly fields in the 1960s, security studies underwent ferment and challenge. Some of the leading challengers were indebted to the liberal Kantian school of thought that we juxtaposed to realism in our preceding discussion, whereas others drew inspiration from the Vietnam War–inspired mindsets that seriously questioned the military and its impact on American life. Walt discusses several forces that led to the relative decline of security studies defined as the study of military power and strategy: Traditional security studies work was not always empirically rigorous by contemporary standards, and assumed a narrow definition of politics that downplayed the influence of domestic influences on statesmen; the ascent of behavioral political science and other social sciences that opened the door to broader research agendas, as well as more sophisticated methodologies that generated doubts about some of realism's hypotheses; the fact that most of the graduate students of leading security study scholars went into government service rather than research at universities; and the effect of the Vietnam War, which discredited existing research, including the "techniques of 'systems analysis' and the application of bargaining theory to international conflict," and "also made the study of security affairs unfashionable in many universities."

Such external events as the rise of détente and growing interest in political economy also led to questioning of "the utility of military force. 'Transnational relations' and 'interdependence' became the new watchwords, as part of the explicit challenge to the realist paradigm."[47] Several developments challenged the realist paradigm, including the increasing prominence of countries that

[44] On the American character of IR, see Stanley Hoffmann's famous essay, "An American Social Science: International Relations," *Daedalus* 106 (1977): 41–59. On how American IR is distinctively American, although having different influences in other countries, see Waever, "The Sociology of a Not So International Discipline."

[45] Richard K. Betts, "Should Strategic Studies Survive?" *World Politics* 50, 1 (1997), p. 23.

[46] Of course, the military academies, such as the Army War College in Carlisle, Pennsylvania, are universities that go far beyond a department of war studies as far as integrating military history with a university education. There is a tradition in the United States of specialization in military affairs, but to see it, we have to look to the service academies and military universities.

[47] Walt, "The Renaissance of Security Studies," p. 216.

lacked military might (such as Japan) and the ability of international economic regimes to withstand economic crises in the 1970s. The traditional form of security studies would languish until the Vietnam War wound down in the mid-1970s. After this, it revived, but with a broader focus and with more competitors than before.

NEW MODELS OF SECURITY

As the military-strategy–oriented model of security studies licked its wounds, a host of alternative approaches rose to challenge its preeminence in both security studies and IR. Critics claimed that traditional forms of security studies were too beholden to "the four S's": states, strategy, scientific method, and the status quo.[48] Some of these reform movements consciously set themselves against traditional security studies' emphases, whereas other, more mainstream, movements more modestly aspired to expand the understanding of what comprises security. Both movements reflected the same expansion and breaking of scholarly boundaries that was taking place in other academic disciplines during this time (for example, history, as discussed in Chapters 10 and 11).[49]

Barry Buzan's book *People, States, and Fear*, published in 1983, is a leading example of the mainstream stretching of the meaning of security. Buzan argued that the concept of security should not be limited to the four S's; beyond military prowess, security involves such matters as political regime stability, economic security, societal security (the preservation of culture, religion, and identity), and the integrity of the environment.[50] A concern with *human* security – as opposed to the conventional preoccupation with the nation-state – can also be traced to this approach. The perspective seeks to open up the black box of the state and introduce broader security considerations to the field of international relations. According to Ken Booth, "Security is what we make of it. It is an epiphenomenon intersubjectively created. Different worldviews and discourses about politics deliver different views and discourses about security. ... It is possible – as Barry Buzan has shown above all – to expand 'international security studies' and still remain within an asserted neorealist framework and approach."[51] Of course, to say that security is what we make of it risks trivializing international security while we make academic distinctions. Does it help us understand matters of security when confronting the threat facing Jews in Nazi Germany, Kuwaitis in 1991, and Tutsi in Rwanda in 1994 (to use just a few examples) to say that security is "an epiphenomenon intersubjectively created"? Yet the

48 See Williams, "Security Studies: An Introduction," in Williams, *Security Studies*, p. 3.

49 Peter Novick, *That Noble Dream: The "Objectivity" Question and the American Historical Profession* (Cambridge University Press, 1988), esp. Part IV.

50 Barry Buzan, *People, States, and Fear: The National Security Problem in International Relations* (Wheatsheaf, 1983).

51 Ken Booth, "Security and Self: Reflections of a Fallen Realist," in Keith Krause and Michael C. Williams, eds., *Critical Security Studies: Concepts and Cases* (UCL Press, 1997), pp. 83–119. Quoted in Williams, "Security Studies: An Introduction," p. 98.

argument that security threats depend on our frames of reference appears undeniable.

This perspective suggests that Buzan's framework has simply expanded what constitutes security, including economic and environmental security, without necessarily leaving the neorealist framework. A practical consequence is a preoccupation with "securitization," which is the process by which issues come to bear on the security agenda of a particular nation. At the same time, the approach shows more concern with domestic politics and the process of defining the national interest. Neorealism, in contrast, had emphasized the structure of the international system without providing much of a role, if any, for domestic politics – although we have seen that classical realists were indeed concerned with domestic politics. In this respect, the securitization approach represents a return to the concerns of classical realism.

More critical approaches to security also entered the fray. "Peace studies" is perhaps the leading school in this camp. Pioneered by such scholars as John Galtung and Quincey Wright in the 1950s, it came into its own in the 1960s and 1970s.[52] A vast field of research, peace studies addresses the many factors that contribute to violence and war, including such matters as structural and cultural violence, psychological proclivities, and political factors that perpetuate (or fail to quell) conflict. It often employs systematic and scientific methods, although some versions of the field also tout an antipositivist edge similar to that of critical and postmodern approaches to security studies. A peace studies approach also brings a distinct normative and activist dimension to the table. Traditional security scholars "largely took war and other forms of violent conflict to be perennial, if tragic, features of an anarchical international system of sovereign states. In contrast, peace studies has always presented war as a problem in need of eradication."[53] According to David P. Barash and Charles P. Webel, editors of a compendium on peace studies, "The field itself differs from most other human sciences in that it is value-oriented – and unabashedly so. Accordingly, we wish to be 'up front' about our own values, which are frankly antiwar, antiviolence, antinuclear, antiauthoritarian, proenvironment, pro-human rights, pro–social justice, propeace, and politically progressive."[54] Today, peace studies programs populate many college campuses, often serving as a politically more palatable

[52] In essence, Galtung concludes that war is a product of wealthy countries exploiting poor countries. Waltz presents a serious critique of this position, arguing that it is reductionist and that it makes several simplistic assumptions about how wealth is created and about the implications of this process for international relations. Waltz, *Theory of International Politics*, pp. 31–5. Leninists and world-systems theorists had a similar perspective on war. For world-systems theorists, the capitalist core exploits periphery countries. See Immanuel Wallerstein, *The Capitalist World-Economy* (Cambridge University Press, 1979). Lenin believed that war was the final stage in capitalist development. See Vladimir Ilich Lenin, *Imperialism: The Highest Stage of Capitalism* (1917).

[53] Peter Lawler, "Peace Studies," in Williams, ed., *Security Studies*, p. 74.

[54] David P. Barash and Charles P. Webel, eds., *Peace and Conflict Studies*, 2nd Edition (Sage, 2009), p. xiii.

alternative to more traditional security studies programs. The International Peace Research Association's Directory Guide of Peace Research provides an expansive list of peace study programs in the United States and other countries.[55]

We should reemphasize here that Morgenthau and other realists have also held realism to be normative as well as empirical (Morgenthau's statement in *Scientific Man Vs Power Politics*, quoted previously, makes this quite clear), considering statesmanship based on realism to offer a more effective way to protect moral values. Beyond this consequentialist logic, we note that some moral realists also believe that it is ethically problematic *in itself* to ignore the harsher aspects of reality in favor of idealism. Sigmund Freud, for example, taught that accepting the tragic implications of human motivation and the reality principle is a moral imperative of ethical character, not simply a utilitarian requirement for successful living. In emphasizing the ethical character aspects of accepting the reality principle, Freud stood on the shoulders of Friedrich Nietzsche, who considered idealism a moral, not just a utilitarian, failing.[56] (Indeed, Freud's greatest ethical challenge to the Enlightenment was to show that the ethical impulse is not only in fierce competition with humanity's self-interested and aggressive instincts – but *rooted* in the aggressive instincts.)[57] We detect a somewhat similar moral posture in the authors of the *Federalist Papers* and in the works of Machiavelli and Max Weber. Accepting the limits of reality and the special demands of political leadership, while simultaneously acting to make the world a better place, is a sign of noble character. As Morgenthau observed in *Scientific Man vs Power Politics*, "To choose among several expedient actions the least evil one is moral judgment. In the combination of political wisdom, moral courage, and moral judgment man reconciles his political nature with his moral destiny."[58]

The field of critical security studies is less prominent than peace studies, but the field is also influential in some quarters of academe. It draws on several critical and radical philosophical schools, including the Frankfurt School's critical theory, and postliberal and postmodern thinking about the construction of reality through dominant discourses and power. The approach is postpositivist in that there is limited effort to make general statements about the incentives and behavior of nation-states. Proponents of critical security studies reject approaches that privilege the nation-state, focusing instead on marginalized

[55] See http://ipra.terracuranda.org/. For peace research centers in the United States (most on college campuses), see http://ipra.terracuranda.org/IPRA%20NORTH%20AMERICA%20regions.html#US.

[56] On this ethical aspect of Freud's thought, see Philip Rieff, *Freud: The Mind of the Moralist*, 3rd Edition (University of Chicago Press, 1979). On this aspect of Nietzsche's thought, see Peter Berkowitz, *Nietzsche: The Ethics of an Immoralist* (Harvard University Press, 1995).

[57] See Paul Ricour, *Freud and Philosophy: An Essay on Interpretation* (Yale University Press, 1970). Niebuhr makes much the same point in many of his writings, including *The Nature and Destiny of Man: A Christian Interpretation* (Charles Scribner's Sons, 1941).

[58] Morgenthau, *Scientific Man vs Power Politics*, p. 203.

groups within the nation-state. Critical scholars often share an activist bent with peace scholars. Proponents seek to deconstruct conceptions of the nation-state with the hopes of developing more progressive and inclusive international institutions that liberate oppressed segments of society. The approach, like peace studies, is defined in part by progressive, and sometimes pacifistic, ideology.[59]

There is no doubt that an increasing constituency steeped in peace and critical studies has arisen, but such work remains on the fringes of IR. Approaches building on liberalism and constructivism have had a more substantial influence on mainstream security study. Liberalism maintains that conflict and war can be ameliorated or eliminated by appropriate institutional, economic, and environmental change. Immanuel Kant theorized that international law and peace would prevail as more states adopted republican forms of government because republican government instills habits of cooperation and mutual respect that temper aggressive and martial impulses.[60] Meanwhile, economic liberals maintain that the internationalization of markets and trade (and growing economic interdependence) have fostered peace, as states and polities come to realize that peace and cooperation are necessary to the flourishing of markets and wealth. According to Albert O. Hirschman, liberalism's accommodation of self-interest and capitalism was a key factor in moving the West away from martial ideals in favor of commercial states, markets, comfort, and peace. Capitalism and liberalism do not deny passion, but sublimate it by turning it into the more peaceful pursuit of interest. The American Framers were part of this project, which places them at the edge of both realism and liberalism, as we have defined these schools here. Capitalism and democracy are related, but they are not synonymous, which suggests the possibility that common economic interests – as much as common political norms – govern peace between or among nations.[61]

Norms are not the only reason that democracies do not fight one another. Kenneth A. Schultz and Barry R. Weingast argue that democracies are less likely to fight wars because democratic political institutions increase credibility in international credit markets. Access to international credit influences how long a country can wage war. Democracies, because they are more likely to pay debts (this likelihood is being severely tested as we write in August 2011!), have better access to credit, and this reduces the temptation to go to war with a

59 See Ken Booth, Steve Smith, and Marysia Zalewski, eds., *International Theory: Positivism and Beyond* (Cambridge University Press, 1996); and Richard Wyn Jones, ed., *Critical Theory and World Politics* (Lynne Rienner, 2001), for an introduction to critical and postpositivist IR.

60 See Immanuel Kant, *Toward Perpetual Peace and Other Writings on Politics, Peace, and History (Rethinking the Western Tradition)*, edited by Pauline Kleingeld (Yale University Press, 2006).

61 Albert O. Hirschman, *The Passions and the Interests: Political Arguments for Capitalism Before Its Triumph* (Princeton University Press, 1977). For a more recent argument that capitalist countries tend not to fight each other, see Erik Gartzke, "The Capitalist Peace," *American Journal of Political Science* 51, 1 (2007): 166–91.

democracy.[62] The temptation for a democracy to attack another democracy is low because both countries expect a long, drawn-out conflict. This conclusion, of course, reflects both neoliberal and realist assumptions.

These forms of liberalism have contributed to the growing scholarship on "democratic peace": the theory that democracies and market states are much less likely to engage in violent conflict (at least with one another) than other types of polities.[63] Democratic peace theory has generated considerable empirical inquiry, provoking both supporters and critics. Most IR scholars believe that the theory is generally valid, although empirical work has refined the conditions under which it is most likely to prevail. Liberal institutions (republicanism, markets, international law, and international organizations) have indeed altered the incentive and security environment within which states operate and are correlated with peace among those countries that share in the community of liberal institutions. The democratic peace thesis, the Schultz-Weingast theory, and other economic theories of conflict are in many respects species of realism in liberal guise, as they are ultimately premised on the self-interest of political orders. Realism is not only about the influence of arms, but also the assumption that states' main motivation for action is self-interest.

A key historical development in the movement toward democratic peace has been Europe's reaction to World Wars I and II. Any meaningful vestiges of militarism remaining from the nationalistic triumphs of Napoleonic France, Prussia, and Germany were wiped away by the massive slaughter and carnage of these wars, leaving Europeans deeply reluctant to engage in military action – a posture that has engendered tensions with America in NATO and in the War on Terror. European soldiers consider the military essentially as a state job or occupation, whereas American soldiers are more prone to view themselves as warriors.[64] Europe has changed considerably since the days that Clausewitz celebrated a culture of war based, in John Keegan's words, on "the code of the warrior, of which physical courage, subordination to the heroic leader on 'might is right' are the ultimate values." Although "enlightened modernism" moved away from these values, they continued to coexist uneasily with nonmilitarist values during the Cold War period in the West, Communist states, and the Third World.

[62] Kenneth A. Schultz and Barry R. Weingast, "The Democratic Advantage: Institutional Foundation of Financial Power in International Competition," *International Organization* 57, 1 (2003): 3–42.

[63] For a good review of democratic peace literature, see Jack S. Levy, "War and Peace," in Walter Carlsnaes, Thomas Risse, and Beth A. Simmons, eds., *Handbook of International Relations* (Sage, 2006), pp. 358–61. This volume consists of sophisticated essays on the nature of the subfields by leading scholars.

[64] See James J. Sheehan, *Where Have All the Soldiers Gone? The Transformation of Modern Europe* (Houghton Mifflin, 2008). Background trends are related to Sheehan's thesis. For a thorough examination of the social, technological, and geostrategic factors that have made militaries more "service oriented," influencing military strategy, recruitment, retention, and the conception of military professionalism, see Curtis Gilroy and Cindy Williams, eds., *Service to Country: Personnel Policy and the Transformation of Western Militaries* (MIT Press, 2006).

But the calamitous events of the twentieth century in Europe and other regions of the world "are grounds for believing that at last, after five thousand years of recorded warmaking, cultural and material changes may be working to inhibit man's proclivity to take up arms."[65]

The last innovative theory we will discuss is constructivism, which has become realism's main challenger over the course of the last twenty years. Perhaps the leading architect of constructivism in IR is Alexander Wendt.[66] Constructivists accentuate norms, ideas, identities, and relationships, as well as perceptions in international relations. Cultures within the international sphere receive emphasis over material interests and individualism.

Constructivism is a very broad approach, leading to several important efforts to define more precisely what constructivism is. A coauthored work by Wendt and one of the leading rational choice scholars, James Fearon, attempted to clarify the key features of the approach. They maintain that constructivism has four central tenets: (1) It stresses the role of ideas in the construction of social life. As Fearon and Wendt put it, "Constructivism is not subjectivism or pure idealism. Instead, the emphasis on ideas is meant to oppose arguments about social life which emphasize the role of brute material conditions like biology, geography, and technology." (2) Agents or subjects are shaped by their social environment; they are not simply self-determining autonomous individuals. Consequently, (3) the most appropriate methodology for research should be predicated on holistic rather than individualistic criteria. And finally, (4) a belief exists that explanations of behavior should be "constitutive" rather than "causal." Causal explanations seek to find necessary or sufficient conditions for actions, whereas constitutive explanations deal more with "conditions of possibility."[67] Constructivism's commitment to constitutive explanations is one reason that some constructivists oppose the use of positive methodology in IR and social science, leading to philosophical and methodological disputes among some constructivists, realists, and rationalists about the nature of social inquiry.[68]

Social and state interests, therefore, embrace more than material and military resources; values, beliefs, and identities are also important phenomena. Empirically, we enhance our understanding of international behavior and relations by taking such entities into account; for example, the democratic peace phenomenon can be explained by the fact that countries are less likely to engage in violent conflict with each other if they share core political and moral values, not simply because they have superior abilities to finance war. Normatively speaking, the world can achieve this state by nourishing institutions and practices that enhance cooperation and mutual understanding; accordingly, many

[65] John Keegan, *A History of Warfare* (Vintage, Random House, 1993), pp. 49, 56.

[66] See Wendt, *Social Theory of International Politics*.

[67] These four tenets are presented in James Fearon and Alexander Wendt, "Rationalism v. Constructivism: A Skeptical View," in Carlsnaes et al., *Handbook of International Relations*, pp. 56–8.

[68] See, e.g., Theo Farrell, "Constructivist Security Studies: Portrait of a Research Program," *International Studies Review* 4, 1 (2002): 49–72.

constructivists – like liberals – are strongly committed to international organizations and law – or collective security, which is different from national security.[69] The authority of the latter is generated by the decisions of each state individually, whereas the authority of the former stems from supranational international organizations.[70]

On the one hand, constructivism shares the epistemology of critical theory, for it considers our perceptions of reality to be the products of social construction and interaction – not as the historically universal truths that realism discerns. The more critical side of constructivist studies points in this direction. On the other hand, more mainstream constructivist practitioners consider the theory to be a supplement to realism rather than an antagonist. One constructivist critique is that classical and neoclassical realism have not been able to account adequately for change, such as the demise of the Cold War and the rise of democratic peace, or even the rise of the modern nation-state system. Constructivists emphasize that the Westphalian state system created in 1648 is not an immutable feature of the world but rather one of several competing systems of order, including city-states and confederations of city-states.[71] Daniel W. Bromley, arguing from a similar perspective, suggests that we cannot understand *why* institutions change unless we understand the *reasons* offered for these changes. An implication is that understanding a phenomenon such as war requires an assessment of the particular reasons offered in justification for war rather than rationalizing war as a permanent feature of an anarchic international system.[72]

[69] See, e.g., Michael Barnett and Martha Finnemore, *Rules for the World: International Organizations and Global Politics* (Cornell University Press, 2004).

[70] International politics today is rife with disputes over the legitimacy and effectiveness of state sovereignty. See, e.g., Kagan, *Of Paradise and Power*; and Jeremy A. Rabkin, *Law Without Nations? Why Constitutional Government Requires Sovereign States* (Princeton University Press, 2005).

[71] See, e.g., J. Samuel Barkin and Bruce Cronin, "The State and the Nation: Changing Norms and the Rules of Sovereignty in International Relations," *International Organization* 48, 1 (1994): 107–30; and Bruce Cronin, *Community Under Anarchy: Transnational Identity and the Evolution of Cooperation* (Columbia University Press, 1999). See also Hendrik Spruyt, *The Sovereign State and Its Competitors: An Analysis of Systems Change* (Princeton University Press, 1996). Constructivist thought has also been influenced by the work of Benedict Anderson, who argues that the nation-state is an imagined construct. Nation-states arise because a collection of people invent a shared history and identity that unites them, a process that can be understood only with reference to the particular historical, economic, and political context that existed prior to the nationalist movement. See Anderson, *Imagined Communities: Reflections on the Origins and Spread of Nationalism* (Verso, 1983).

[72] See Daniel W. Bromley, *Volitional Pragmatism and the Meaning of Economics Institutions* (Princeton University Press, 2006). Bromley is critical of theories of institutional change that use history selectively to rationalize a particular theory, examples of which are Douglass C. North, *Institutions, Institutional Change, and Economic Performance* (Cambridge University Press, 1990); and North, *Structure and Change in Economic History* (Cambridge University Press, 1981). North assumes that societies will choose efficient economic institutions, such as private property rights, because these institutions maximize wealth, using particular examples from history to justify his argument. Bromley recognizes that such exercises do not actually explain *why* institutions change.

Some scholars argue that realism is more amenable to change than its stereotype suggests, and that constructivists and realists embody different, yet not necessarily exclusive, views of reality. For example, realists can describe change in the stability of international relations by referring to alterations in the balance of power; and they can explain conflict as a function of the lack of countervailing power, and peace as the emergence of a propitious balance of power. Similarly, although some realists may be less concerned with how the Westphalian system came into being, it is not hard to imagine realists articulating a historical account of the necessity of institutionalizing the state system in the aftermath of the Hundred Years' War as a manifestation of the state's interests, with the system itself reflecting the interests of the dominant powers. We do not believe anyone seriously questions that the Westphalian system was self-enforcing because it benefited the major powers of the time, or that the origins of peace did not to an extent reflect the fact that there was a relative balance of power among warring nations. Despite these apparent possibilities for a realist take on the development of international institutions and of systemic change, many constructivists remain convinced that realism and constructivism are fundamentally different research programs.[73] Accordingly, we read some of these distinctions to be more a product of disciplinary incentives to define constructivism as new and different than as the realization that political realism is incapable of analyzing change, reasons, or historical contingency.

In any event, several of the points of constructivist theorizing are uncontroversial and should inform any analysis, for it is clear that our understandings and perceptions of reality are often mediated by the assumptions and values that reside in our minds.[74] But this fact does not mean that there are not objective truths outside of our minds that have to be dealt with; one recalls Sam Johnson's alleged reply to Bishop Berkeley's claim that the physical world is an idea planted in our heads by God: He said Berkeley should kick a stone with his bare foot and see what happens. Likewise, threats posed by terrorists and state actors are often real, independent of the constructions in our heads. Nor does it mean that cultural variations are not ultimately the particularistic manifestations of underlying regularities or laws. The fact is that most of the important objects and processes that we deal with in the world are the products of social

[73] See the essays on constructivism in Carlsnaes et al., *Handbook of International Relations*.

[74] Economists, for example, have long looked to psychology to explain macroeconomic phenomena such as housing bubbles, depressions, and financial crises. See George A. Akerlof and Robert J. Shiller, *Animal Spirits: How Human Psychology Drives the Economy, and Why It Matters for Global Capitalism* (Princeton University Press, 2009). Behavioral economists certainly recognize that economies are socially constructed and that the beliefs of economic agents must be taken into account to understand why economies sometimes fall into hard times. Yet behavioral economists are not content to proclaim the tautologically true statement that markets are socially constructed (as markets are governed by rules that have human designers, they must be socially constructed), but rather seek to develop better economic models without rejecting model building as an endeavor. Constructivists in political science, in contrast, are more prone to reject model building once they reject rational choice – thus conflating rational choice with models and econometrics.

construction – including, among countless other examples, money systems, systems of government, and economic relations. But these systems themselves become part of the external reality that affects us. Take al Qaeda: While it is true that our reaction to it is constructed by many social and psychological factors, it is also true that it poses a definite threat to the United States.[75] In addition, realists such as Morgenthau have themselves stressed the important roles that ideology and cultural norms play in international behavior, as does Samuel P. Huntington in his famous work on the role of culture in international conflict.[76]

CONCLUSION

In this chapter, we have traced the main currents of security and international relations study. Our purpose has not been to stake a claim for one or two approaches to the exclusion of others, but rather to make a case for the importance of realism and its variants in the field. Far from constituting an amoral position and calculation, the best forms of realism are deeply normative in a manner that recognizes empirical historical realities and the tragic nature of existence and political life. Acknowledging the roles of power and force in the world is part of this reckoning, which is akin to the moral vision of the Framers of the American constitutional order. Needless to say, the military as an institution is intrinsic to this understanding. Thus, our emphasis upon realism is an important element of our position regarding the relevance of military presence on campus.

Having described the development of security studies and the philosophical debates that inform international relations, we now consider several traditional security studies programs to determine their perspective. We wish to determine whether they are "under threat," as Walt suggested, and how much they integrate the military into their programs.

75 For a discerning analysis of the relationship between what is socially constructed and what is not (and what to make of constructivism in general), see John R. Searle, *The Construction of Social Reality* (Free Press, 1995).

76 Samuel P. Huntington, *The Clash of Civilizations and the Remaking of World Order* (Simon and Schuster, 1996).

13

Security Studies in the Wake of the Cold War University

Paragons of Productive Friction, or Throwing the Baby out with the Bathwater?

> While military strength and political power are the preconditions for lasting national greatness, the substance of that greatness springs from the hidden sources of intellect and morale, from ideas and values.
>
> – Hans Morgenthau[1]

The theoretical discussion of the preceding chapter sets the stage for a consideration of military presence in security studies programs. In particular, we are interested in the degree to which security studies programs emphasize academic perspectives provided by military history and political realism, as well as the extent to which they integrate the military into their curriculum. To be clear, military history and realism are different academic approaches, yet they are intellectual cousins in their emphasis on the study of war and force in historical perspective, and for this reason, we underscore political realism as one of the critical components of military presence in the university.

Empirically, we present surveys of leading programs as well as several short case studies. We believe there are at least three reasons that our empirical focus is important. First, unlike existing surveys of international relations as a field, our emphasis is on security studies programs. The discipline of security studies requires special attention because it is the branch of international relations that is most likely to train individuals who participate in national security policy. Second, in contrast with existing studies of the discipline of security studies, which focus on the relatively narrow issue of funding and participation in some of the high-profile programs such as Human Terrain and the Minerva Initiative, we consider military presence within these programs – not simply physical presence, but the intellectual presence of military-related courses and content.[2] Third, because our emphasis is on the philosophical and normative significance of political realism in security

[1] Hans Morgenthau, *A New Foreign Policy for the United States* (Praeger, for Council on Foreign Relations, 1969).

[2] A recent Research Symposium in *Perspectives on Politics* considered the relationship between security studies and the military. The Minerva Initiative was the focal point of the discussion, with one side arguing that integration as epitomized by the Minerva Initiative is mutually beneficial, while the other side considered the costs of integration on scholars and the importance of figuring

studies, our empirical component continues the discussion that we initiated in Chapters 1, 2, and 12 regarding the importance of political realism in the discipline of security studies.

Of course, there are many more security studies programs than the ones we consider, and there are thousands of scholars who are experts in the subject. Accordingly, our analysis is necessarily incomplete. Yet we believe that our approach and information can help us to assess military presence in security studies and to think about the importance of military presence in such programs. If nothing else, we hope the discussion that follows encourages scholars interested in security and international relations to consider deeply the costs of excluding or drifting away from political realism, military history, and military presence on campus, and to think about the importance of seeking out diverse military perspectives in order to improve prospects for meaningful military participation in the formulation and implementation of security policy and education.

SECURITY STUDIES SURVEYS: BROADER PERSPECTIVES

To provide additional insight into the security studies programs, we surveyed several leading programs to determine their methodological and paradigmatic perspectives, and to assess how these programs assimilate the military into their agendas. Before presenting the results, it is important to comment on one of the leading surveys of scholars of international relations.

The extensive 2008 Teaching, Research, and International Policy Strategic Studies Institute (TRIP) survey on the state of international relations conducted by the Institute for the Theory and Practice of International Relations at the College of William and Mary provides interesting and important information.[3] TRIP researchers asked a variety of questions about research, teaching, and policy/political issues in the field of international relations in the United States and nine other countries, receiving 2,724 responses. They paid considerable attention to methodological, epistemological, and paradigmatic emphases. TRIP postulated three basic paradigms: realism, liberalism, and constructivism. In the United States, 21 percent of respondents identified themselves as realists (down from 25 percent in the 2004 and 2006 surveys), 20 percent as liberals, and 17 percent as constructivists. However, 26 percent reported that they were

out rules of engagement (there were also those who suggested that the gap between scholars and the military is overblown). Our perspective is that appropriate military presence includes policies such as Minerva, although we believe that the issue of military integration is much deeper than Minerva. Appropriate military presence includes not only participation of scholars in the security apparatus and in the field, but also the presence of military-related fields of inquiry and physical presence on campus. Our emphasis is on the benefits to the student and the scholar alike from broader military presence and its importance to civic and liberal education, not only encouraging the debates such as that arising over Minerva (largely a debate among professors), but also ensuring that we let the soldiers and students in the room. See "Reflections Symposium," *Perspectives on Politics* 8, 4 (2010): 1077–1124.

[3] The TRIP Survey report is available online: http://irtheoryandpractice.wm.edu/projects/trip/Final_Trip_Report_2009.pdf.

nonparadigmatic. In terms of "areas of study," 22 percent identified "international security" as their primary research interest. Although this figure was down 5 percent since 2004 (perhaps due to the decline of concerns about terrorism, a trend also reflected in TRIP's questions about pressing policy concerns), "at 22 percent it maintained its place as the most popular area of study or substantive focus of respondents."[4] International political economy was second on the list at 14 percent. Critical theory fared poorly in the TRIP analysis.

These findings suggest that constructivism is clearly gaining ground on more traditional approaches in IR, and also that security remains an important concern within the discipline. Yet the TRIP survey has at least two drawbacks. First, it does not consider explicitly the status of political realism in security studies programs, but rather more generally in the field of international relations. We have argued that political realism is important in two respects: It takes the military-related aspects of security seriously; and it is defined in part by a concern with practical, policy-relevant knowledge. Security studies programs are the arm of the university most likely to have an impact on policy. As such, it is important to consider explicitly the degree to which security programs feature political realism. Second, we have argued at length why inclusion of a distinctly military perspective is important for public policy, yet the TRIP survey does not consider the integration of international relations (or security studies programs) with the military. A consequence of these survey drawbacks is more knowledge of what is happening inside the Ivory Tower, but limited knowledge of programs' impacts outside of the Tower. For example, the survey asks about the status of critical theory, which is not the core of any of the main areas of international relations, but asks nothing regarding the relationship between security studies and the military, which is one of the more important dimensions of policy relevant to international relations.

Our purpose is not to engage in another large survey, but rather to point out that TRIP's survey questions do not emphasize security studies, the role of the military in security studies, or trends within the approaches to security studies – questions that we view as particularly important to the policy dimensions of international relations. We contacted individuals knowledgeable about security studies programs from fifteen leading security studies programs throughout the county. These programs included the leading security studies programs as determined by our impressionistic assessment, given the lack of *U.S. News & World Report* rankings of programs. To get an idea of our sample, we included three of the programs discussed in the case study section that follows (Yale, MIT, and Ohio State), as well as programs at Georgetown, Stanford, and Columbia, among others.[5] Our interest is in the development of security studies as a field, and for this reason we emphasized research orientations at the leading

[4] TRIP Survey Report, p. 6.

[5] Our list included Security Policy Studies, Elliot School of International Affairs, George Washington University; Georgetown University, Center for Peace and Security Studies; Triangle Institute for Security Studies, University of North Carolina, Chapel Hill; MIT Security Studies Program; Merrill

programs. For each program, we contacted directors or associate directors of the program with our survey. If they did not respond, we contacted associate directors or a randomly selected senior faculty member. This method of selection allowed us to contact individuals from each of the programs that we selected.

Our interest was to better understand the degree of emphasis in these programs of various perspectives. Unlike the TRIP survey, ours is directed at security studies programs rather than faculty who teach international relations. We also ask about political realism, military history, and military personnel in these programs. This sample provides us with some insight into the degree of interest in these programs and their integration with the military, as well as the influence of military history in some of the nation's leading security studies programs.[6]

We began by asking about the degree of interest in security studies on campus. The evidence (admittedly impressionistic) suggests that such programs generate a high degree of interest, with no one claiming that interest is "limited." Roughly two-thirds of the individuals from these programs viewed interest in their program as "great" and one-third as "good." This conclusion is consistent with those who note a high level of student interest in issues of national security and military history, which we have addressed often in this book.

To gauge trends in student interest in security studies, we asked whether interest and resources in these programs were on the decline. No one reported decreasing interest, and over three-fourths of our respondents indicated increasing interest. Respondents from nine of fifteen programs viewed resources for their program as increasing, while only two construed resources as decreasing. The issue of resources was somewhat less encouraging, but still strongly positive – not a bad situation in a period riveted by financial woes in higher education. The field of security studies does not appear to be "under threat," at least at the top programs.

As importantly, we were interested in the degrees to which the programs embrace different broad theories, in particular military history, strategic-military/national defense, neoliberalism or soft power, constructivism, and critical theory. We did not define these terms in the survey, assuming that directors and senior faculty of these programs understand differences between

Center for Strategic Studies, Johns Hopkins University; International Security Studies Program at the Fletcher School at Tufts University; Peace Studies Program, Cornell University; Kroc Institute for International Peace Studies, University of Notre Dame; International Security Studies, Yale University; Saltzman Institute for War and Peace Studies, School of International and Public Affairs, Columbia; Institute for Conflict Analysis and Resolution at George Mason University; Belfer Center International Security Program at Harvard; Program in Arms Control, Disarmament, and International Security at the University of Illinois; Center for International Security and Cooperation at Stanford; Five College Program in Peace and World Security Studies (Amherst College, Hampshire College, Mount Holyoke College, Smith College, and University of Massachusetts at Amherst).

6 As we were interested in the leading departments, our sample size was small. We leave to future research how much individual faculty members, rather than departments, emphasize military perspectives in their work.

the jargon such as "neoliberalism or soft power" and "constructivism," for example. Respondents were asked to describe the degree of emphasis in categories that included the following choices: "a great deal," "somewhat," "a limited amount," and "hardly any or not at all."

The results suggest that the greatest weight is on strategic and military security, with thirteen out of fifteen programs placing a "great deal" or "some" emphasis on strategic/military security. In terms of "a great deal" of emphasis, military history comes in second, but six programs weigh military history lightly or not at all. In contrast, only two programs emphasize strategic/military security, neoliberalism, or soft power a limited amount or not at all. Critical theory appears marginalized at the top security studies programs, and seven programs stress constructivism a limited amount or not at all. Only three programs accentuated critical theory a great deal or somewhat. The results are presented in Table 13.1.

Emphasis on military history is one aspect of productive friction, but it is also relevant whether military officers or personnel have some physical presence. As we found in our consideration of the experiences of ROTC cadets and non-military students, the physical presence of the military and military personnel often furnishes a source of diverse perspectives and discussions. Accordingly, we asked about how much such integration of the military itself exists in these programs, finding a reasonable amount. Respondents from nine programs stated that there is strong or some military presence in their respective programs, while six registered limited presence, almost none, or no presence in these programs.

Although nine of fifteen programs appear to provide substantial representation for military history, we have to remind ourselves that we are dealing with some of the top *security studies* programs in the county. Most of these programs view their mission as including training of a next generation of leaders in the areas of national security and national defense. For this reason, we must ask why

TABLE 13.1. *Orientation of Security Studies Departments*

	Military History	Strategic/ Military Security	Neoliberalism or Soft Power	Constructivism	Critical Theory
A great deal	6 programs (out of 15)	11 programs (out of 15)	5 programs (out of 15)	2 programs (out of 15)	2 programs (out of 15)
Somewhat	3/15	2/15	8/15	6/15	1/15
A limited amount	5/15	1/15	1/15	4/15	4/15
Hardly any or not at all	1/15	1/15	1/15	3/15	8/15

military history has little meaningful presence in *any*, let alone six, of the leading programs. Our pedagogical framework suggests that programs that fail to integrate military history into the curriculum are less effective on the dimension of productive friction, and that these programs would likely fall short of our pedagogical ideal, because they do not incorporate the military cluster.

As our interest in military affairs also includes the influence of ROTC in security studies, we asked individuals from these programs about ROTC. In all, eleven of fifteen programs felt that ROTC should have at least some role in security studies, while respondents from all but two programs believed that military history should have at least some presence in security studies. These results are propitious as far as military history is concerned, and it is also encouraging that more than two-thirds believe that ROTC should have a role in security studies.

One of the last survey questions asked about the degree of integration of the program with the military and whether or not it is increasing or decreasing. For the most part, respondents viewed it as remaining the same. A few believed it was increasing and a few believed it was decreasing. This suggests that there may be less to allegations of the decline of the Cold War University than Stephen M. Walt predicted. Several faculty members believed that even more integration would be desirable. Here are some responses:

R: We have a strong program of military fellows in our program and believe that the presence and involvement of military officers from all of the services makes an important contribution to the program and field of study.

R: The peace studies program can benefit from ROTC participation, but in our experience it is difficult to institutionalize because of the constant turnover in commanding officers, only a few of which are interested in encouraging contacts. Our most successful connections are usually the result of the junior officers doing graduate course work on the side.

R: It is vital for healthy civil–military relations in a democracy to have ROTC well represented, especially on elite campuses.

R: I'm a strong proponent of ROTC on campus – and of encouraging students to participate in the military. This is particularly true given the divide between business/political/economic elites, on the one hand, and military elites on the other.

R: Our university does not have any on-campus ROTC programs. Interested students take those courses at another campus. I believe it would be good to have an ROTC program, also to have more professors with some military experience. Many of our grad students do indeed have this kind of experience.

None of the open-ended responses suggested active opposition to the military in these programs. In fact, these responses suggest that there is a potential for a stronger role in these programs and not much in the way of hostility. One response in particular reflected our belief in productive friction:

R: 1. ROTC should definitely be on campus for two reasons. First, it is essential that military officers not live in a military culture-bubble, but rather live among the wider society and participate normally in its affairs. Second, it is essential that civilians understand the military perspective on policy and other matters (whether or not they agree with the military perspective). German militarism before World War I and Japanese militarism before World War II stemmed in part from the isolation of civilians and military officers into separate, mutually uncomprehending and sometimes mutually disrespectful social spheres. (See Martin Kitchen's work on Germany.) Welcoming ROTC onto college and university campuses is an excellent way to break down barriers between the civilian and military sphere so that both can deal more constructively with the other. Those who oppose war should be pro-ROTC, as it is a strong measure against militarism! 2. According to my experience, advanced security studies programs that train Masters and Ph.D. students will profit greatly from including military officers in the mix. The students learn a lot from the officers, and vice-versa.

Our brief survey of security studies programs has several implications. First, the field of security studies does not appear to be under threat, at least at the leading programs. Second, while there is widespread use of military history in the curriculum, and many programs do integrate military personnel, several of the leading programs do not incorporate the military and military history into their curriculum. While we do not believe that the military view should be privileged, we do believe that a military perspective is important to such programs for reasons we have reiterated throughout this book. Third, existing studies of the state of the discipline – such as the TRIP survey – would benefit from more specific consideration of security studies and the conflicts within these programs in order to better understand the policy significance of international relations. The large majority of international relations scholars and writings probably have a very limited impact on policy (as is the case with political science more generally), a lack that suggests the importance of considering more explicitly the branch of IR that has a more prominent influence in policy circles. While security studies departments appear to satisfy our conception of productive friction with respect to the discipline of military history, we suspect that in the broader context of international relations, there is considerably less effort by scholars of international relations to amalgamate military history or military personnel with their courses.

STABILITY AND CHANGE IN SECURITY STUDIES PROGRAMS: SOME REPRESENTATIVE CASE STUDIES

In this section, we take a look at a few of the nation's leading security studies programs. We make no pretense of providing a definitive overview of security studies programs, but rather hope to provide some insight into how a handful of representative programs operate and how they represent our pedagogical model. It is important also to bear a distinction in mind borne out by our foregoing discussion of security studies: between more pragmatic policy orientations and more academic-oriented study. (Of course, much research and the missions of many centers fall between these two poles, as we will see.) Regarding the pragmatic policy approach, Gene M. Lyons and Louis Morton raised a problem in 1965 that still applies today: the "perils of research," including the temptations of researchers to be "players" in the national scene in a manner that compromises their academic neutrality, as well as "the problems raised by classified information, and the restrictions on objectivity and academic freedom that may be involved. These are risks that scholars must recognize if they are to deal with contemporary issues of national security."[7] After the shocks of Vietnam visited the halls of academe, many programs and centers reformed their approaches to ensure greater independence from the government. At the same time, other programs continue to take traditional security claims more seriously, as some of our examples and the survey presented earlier in this chapter indicate. Perhaps this institutional trend supports what Walt foresaw as the "renaissance of security studies" in his 1991 article.[8]

We selected three programs with well-established reputations as leading academic institutions for the study of security: the Security Studies Program at MIT, the International Security Studies program at Yale, and the Mershon Center for Security Studies at Ohio State. We also examine the new, innovative Grand Strategy Program at Wisconsin. There are many other programs, but the first three are important historically given their prominence in studies of the field by Walt and their importance in the work of Lyons and Morton.

Security Studies at MIT

The Security Studies Program at the Massachusetts Institute of Technology is a model of the productive friction that we envision, although its clientele are graduate, not undergraduate, students. Federal dollars flowed into many defense programs at MIT, including the Radiation Laboratory (the most significant weaponry research project after the Manhattan Project), the Instrumentation Laboratory, and the Research Laboratory in Electronics, among others; and MIT's president, Karl Compton, served on the board of the National Defense Research Committee, established in the 1930s to deal with military matters. For a long time, MIT was also the leading recipient of funding by the Office of Strategic Research and Development, which opened shop during World War II.

[7] Gene M. Lyons and Louis Morton, *Schools for Strategy: Education and Research in National Security Affairs* (Frederick A. Praeger, 1965), pp. 182–3.

[8] Stephen M. Walt, "The Renaissance of Security Studies," *International Studies Quarterly* 35 (1991).

Many of the MIT programs were run as autonomous research centers that were less accountable to the university's normal rules and procedures, thereby arousing tensions with academic traditionalists.[9] MIT's relationship to the national security arms of the federal government has been special because of the school's scientific and engineering prowess, which has been highly valuable to the Department of Defense. In 1949, a faculty committee warned that "we must learn now how to incorporate research sponsored by a variety of external agencies into our plan in such a manner as to strengthen and sustain the educational program, without placing in jeopardy the freedom of thought and liberty of action that lend to academic life its very special flavor."[10]

Initially called the Defense and Arms Control Studies Program, the Strategic Studies Program was launched three decades ago. It is associated with the large Center for International Studies (CIS) at MIT, which promotes a wide range of international studies, focusing on how science and engineering relate to foreign affairs.[11] Founded in the 1950s, CIS dealt with a variety of topics relating to science and national security, and earned a reputation of nudging too close to the CIA. It concentrated on informing the citizenry about defense issues, communications, the processes of dynamic change within nations, and arms control. Concerns festered as the Center strengthened its relationship with the military during the 1960s, coming to a head at the end of the decade. "The strains in the Center's dual role became increasingly untenable as the political climate changed during the 1960s. Apologetics for American foreign policy, for which the Center became known, were received far differently during the Vietnam War from the way they had been during and after the Korean conflict."[12] As a result, the Center reorganized and decided to provide less direct assistance to government defense missions; it also broadened its base to embrace political science, which had not played a major role at the Center before this time. According to Roger Geiger, "*raison d'état* took precedence over academic inquiry in the CIS; and MIT was able to extricate itself from this uncomfortable situation with delay and difficulty."[13]

The Security Studies Program (SSP) is often considered one of the top programs in the United States along with security programs at Harvard and the University of Chicago. It has consistently brought the resources of the university to bear on the most pressing security problems of international relations. The 1985–6 Annual Report portrays the program's key priorities at that time, accentuating education, research, and public service, with the primary objective

[9] For instructive discussion of these and other MIT programs, see Roger L. Geiger, *Research and Relevant Knowledge: American Research Universities since World War II* (Oxford University Press, 1993), pp. 5, 22, 32–3, 63–73, and more generally.

[10] Lyons and Morton, *Schools for Strategy*, p. 155, quoting William T. Fox's report, "Civil Military Relations Research," p. 284.

[11] MIT Center for International Studies, "Who We Are": http://web.mit.edu/cis/wwa.html.

[12] Geiger, *Research and Relevant Knowledge*, p. 70.

[13] Geiger, *Research and Relevant Knowledge*, p. 70.

being the education of graduate students.[14] The program furnishes a locus for research and analysis of relevant technical, strategic, and political aspects of imperative national and international security concerns, drawing students from science, engineering, and the social sciences. Foci during this period included the technical feasibility and strategic implications of Strategic Defense Initiative (SDI), the ramifications of new antiballistic missile (ABM) technology for the ABM Treaty, nuclear winter and uncertainties pertaining to nuclear fallout and war, and decisions regarding the small single-warhead intercontinental ballistic missile (ICBM, or the "Midgetman" missile). The interdisciplinary program consists of ten MIT faculty members and senior researchers, fifteen affiliated fellows, three visiting officers from the U.S. military, and thirty graduate students. The faculty members are tenured in regular departments, and all five who do strategic security work reside in political science.

Stephen Van Evera, a core faculty member of SSP, spoke of the program's mission in language self-consciously indebted to Morgenthau's notion of the "higher practicality."[15] Although the program does sponsor and respect high-level abstract theoretical work, its primary emphasis is public policy and service. "We serve the world, not ourselves," Van Evera told us. He said that SSP faculty members are "less into the purely academic field debates" than other major security programs. "The focus is on policy and the world, but we are not headline chasers. We are broader. I am exasperated to have to distinguish policy from the theoretical analysis. These two approaches are tied at the hip. A good policy argument is theoretical. We have a social contract with society, so we consider it immoral to insulate ourselves." Military and strategic security issues constitute the centerpieces of the program, although it also makes room for such subjects as international political economy, environmental security issues, social justice, and human rights intervention. "The aperture is widening to include all things that cause and contribute to war. But violence remains the key focus." This focus echoes Samuel Huntington's definition of the military profession's central duty as the application of organized violence, as well as sociologist Eric Ouellet's advocacy in Chapter 2: The study of "organized violence" should be the "central construct" of military sociology.[16]

The Annual Report of 2006–7, written under the leadership of Barry Posen, professor of political science and director of the Security Studies Program, summarized the contribution of the MIT Security Studies Program and its objectives.[17]

[14] Defense and Arms Control Security Studies Program, MIT, Annual Report, Academic Year, 1985–6: http://18.48.0.31/ssp/Annual_Reports/AR-1985-1986.pdf

[15] See Stephen Van Evera, *A Guide to Methods for Students of Political Science* (Cornell University Press, 1997), esp. pp. 97–8.

[16] Interviews with Stephen Van Evera, July 2009 and November 2007; Eric Ouellet, "New Directions in Military Sociology," in Oullet, ed., *New Directions in Military Sociology* (de Sitter, 2005), pp. 22–3; Samuel P. Huntington, *The Soldier and the State: The Theory and Politics of Civil–Military Relations* (Harvard University Press, 1957).

[17] MIT Security Studies Program, 2006–7 Annual Report: http://web.mit.edu/ssp/program/MIT_SSP_AnnualReport2006-07.pdf.

The program strives to produce individuals with deeper knowledge about the political control of military force, avoidance of war where possible, and achievement of victory where necessary. The program is organized around several principles, most attributable to classic realism. Among them are that war is an extension of politics and policy and that war is increasingly destructive and complex. In Clausewitz's sense, policy must govern diplomacy, the preparation for war, and the conduct of war. A premise of the program relates to a central concern in this book and among those who are concerned about the relationship between the military and civil society: *Policy cannot govern war adequately unless politicians and their advisors understand how military forces work*. Such understanding includes the nature of military organizations and their members, the conduct of operations, the technology of weaponry, the nature of command and control, and the operations of intelligence. More generally, understanding how military forces work requires understanding military institutions and technology, both in the past and the present. But the MIT program also emphasizes the costliness of war and the desire to avoid conflict. As we have seen with the discussion of realism, one of the purposes of understanding war and military affairs is to reduce the need to use force and to understand when the use of force is appropriate. For realists, the main benefit of a strong military is to avoid war, not to fight wars.

As of 2009, the Security Studies Program had three priorities: increasing senior staff, contributing to debates about the nature of the grand strategy of the United States and the resources allocated to national security, and increasing the effectiveness of communication with leaders and the public. The program offers an increasingly broad range of perspectives on military-related matters. One of the distinguishing features of the MIT program is the weight it gives diplomatic and military history and the integration of these disciplines into courses and research. In 2009, the program had nineteen course offerings, many of which involve in-depth treatment of military matters. A sampling includes various foreign policy and international relations courses and such military and strategic studies as "Causes and Prevention of War," "Causes of War," "Innovation in Military Organizations," "Foundations of Security Studies," "Great Power Military Intervention," "US Military Power," "Comparative Grand Strategy and Military Doctrine," "Japan and East Asian Security," "Civil War," "Civil–Military Relations," "Understanding Modern Military Operations," and "US Military Budget and Force Planning."[18] The old Cold War emphasis on "hard science" appears to have waned, changing the disciplinary training of the permanent faculty, as nearly all members of SSP are now trained in political science or public policy. The director of SSP as of this writing (Posen) is a political scientist with research interests that include U.S. national security policy, the organization of military force (he is perhaps the

[18] MIT Security Studies Program, Classes: http://web.mit.edu/ssp/classes/index.html. Where course syllabi were available, we found that the courses offered substantial emphasis on military affairs and military history.

nation's leading expert regarding this issue), great power intervention into civil conflict, and innovation in military organizations. His course topics include innovation in military organizations, great power military interventions, comparative grand strategy and military doctrine, and issues in intelligence. Grand strategy is the set of political and military means and ends used to achieve national strategy. We were able to find substantial integration of military history – including what we have described as traditional military history – in many of these courses. Posen is also involved in training senior military officers.

Many of the scholars affiliated with the program have had substantial experiences in government. James Walsh has worked in nuclear proliferation and served as a visiting scholar at the Center for Global Security Research at Lawrence Livermore National Laboratory. Cindy Williams, a mathematician, was part of the National Security Division in the Congressional Budget Office and has worked in the Pentagon. Harvey Sapolsky is a well-known specialist on the military who concentrates on U.S. defense politics, including civil–military relations, the impact of casualties on the use of force, military innovation, and the performance of defense industries. Among other works, he has written *Science and the Navy*, which is a notable history of the Office of Naval Research and its relationship with universities.[19] Sapolsky has served as a consulting panel member of the Office of the Secretary of Defense, the Office of Naval Research, the Naval War College, the U.S. Army, the Department of Energy, and the John Hopkins' Applied Physics Laboratory. He has also headed MIT's ROTC committee and helped to lead movements dedicated to retaining ROTC on campus in the face of opposition in the late 1960s and later eras. In an interview, he provided a sketch of SSP:

> We don't really teach military people. Our focus is on the students. There are occasional military people that are students, but mostly we teach graduate students. [SSP] is a substitute for the War College; the Army allows a small percentage of people designated for war colleges – all the services do – to go to private institutions. They vary by service; the Army has the biggest number of people out, and the Navy has the least.

He also said of the program, "Well, we're the most focused, and probably the largest in the country, on training Ph.D.s. Some of them will go on to teach, and others will go on to work in government or other institutions. So there are a number of places Ph.D.s get trained, but not in the number that are here."[20]

Political scientist and international relations scholar Stephen Van Evera is an associate director of the Center for International Studies. His research interests include the causes and prevention of war, U.S. foreign policy, U.S. national security policy, and social science methods. His published work includes *Guide to Methods for Students of Political Science*, *Causes of War: Power and the Roots of Conflict*, and numerous articles on the causes of World War I,

[19] Harvey M. Sapolsky, *Science and the Navy: The History of the Office of Naval Research* (Princeton University Press, 1990).

[20] Interview with Harvey M. Sapolsky, MIT Strategic Studies Program, November 2007.

nationalism and the problem of war, American intervention in the Third World, American defense policy, and Europe's future international relations.[21] A proponent of the notion of "higher practicality," Van Evera is deeply concerned about making students aware of the issues of international relations, foreign policy, and war, and has striven to make students (undergraduates in political science as well as graduates) aware of research methods in order to enhance their understanding.[22]

Although military history is one component of productive friction, it is enhanced by the presence of those with military experience, for civilians and soldiers bring different perspectives and experiences to national security policies. Each cluster offers an important contribution to an integrated national security policy, and these clusters have traditionally been brought together in MIT programs for military fellows. In recent years, SSP fellows have included Colonel Harold C. Bass, who was deployed in Somalia and Kuwait; Lieutenant Colonel Louis Lartigue, who served as Tank Platoon leader in Desert Shield and Desert Storm; and Lieutenant Colonel Todd Piergrossi, an expert in cyber warfare who has commanded twice at the squadron level. Because of the small size of MIT's program, these student-soldiers will have significant interactions with faculty and their fellow graduate students.

This thumbnail sketch allows us to draw some very basic conclusions. In particular, we find substantial military influence in SSP, and a significant component of military history. Grand and lower levels of strategy are also stressed. SSP comes very close to embodying the normative pedagogical ideal that has formed the core of this book by integrating a broad understanding of security around a core focus on military and defense issues.

The core purpose of SSP is training graduate students who will be professors in research universities rather than training a large number of students who plan to work in the field of security. Nor does SSP train a large number of citizen-soldiers. Rather, the program offers superior academic training to a few military officers. It does not rely much on practitioners – those with fewer academic credentials who have practical skills involving the military or national security – to teach courses. SSP does not enlist an army of adjuncts with the same wealth of real-world experience that we find in, say, Georgetown's Security Studies Program.

Yale University's International Security Program

Yale's Institute for International Security Studies was a pioneer in the field of security studies, being established in 1935 by Nicholas J. Spykman. Spykman

[21] Stephen Van Evera, *Guide to Methods for Students of Political Science, Causes of War: Power and the Roots of Conflict* (Cornell University Press, 1997).

[22] See MIT Political Science Department, Faculty, S. Van Evera: http://web.mit.edu/afs/athena.mit.edu/org/p/polisci/faculty/S.VanEvera.html. Interviews with Stephen Van Evera, MIT Department of Political Science and Security Studies Program, November 2007, July 2009.

was one of a growing group of scholars concerned about foreign policy's response to the militarism advancing in fascist Europe at the time; indeed, many of these scholars were refugees from such states. Spykman and others published books in the 1930s incorporating realist theory as we depicted it in Chapter 12, stressing the need for power to counter power, while downplaying a reliance on international organizations and law, which had been the dominant intellectual preoccupation before the rise of fascism.[23] (In this sense, the realist belief that international institutions cannot be relied upon as the primary protectors of peace is based less on axioms than actual historical experience, in particular the failure of international institutions to prevent the rise of fascism and war in the 1930s.)[24] By 1950, the Institute had "achieved an enviable reputation," training professionals in strategy and in understanding "the relationship between military force and foreign policy." But the Institute moved to Princeton in 1951 because of policy disputes with the Yale administration, becoming part of the Woodrow Wilson School there.[25] Yale's new president, A. Whitney Griswold, was a leading national advocate of traditional liberal education who disdained applied research and research linked to external entities. Accordingly, he campaigned to ban institutes and centers fitting this description – undermining institutions that encouraged productive friction. "At the same time that organized research units were proliferating at other research universities, Griswold was purging Yale of them."[26]

Despite Griswold's hostility toward certain elements of the Cold War University, security studies ultimately mounted a comeback at Yale. One of the more recent institutional innovations was the creation of Yale's International Security Studies (ISS) program, which opened its doors in 1987. It has been directed by Paul Kennedy, the J. Richardson Dilworth Professor of History, since 1989. ISS strives to teach international history and grand strategy to future leaders, emphasizing international, diplomatic, and strategic history. It concentrates on the training of graduate students, but also provides access and fellowships to undergraduates and to postdoctoral students interested in military history and strategic studies. ISS also conducts an array of programs, publishing "Occasional Papers" that deal with a variety of issues pertaining to "International History and Security." A short list of the many past subjects includes "Apartheid on Trial: The International Court"; "South West Africa, and the Politics of Post-colonialism, 1960–66"; "Globalization and New

[23] See Lyons and Morton, *Schools for Strategy*, pp. 36–7, 61. Morgenthau was later among such scholars, having come to the United States in 1937.

[24] This was certainly the case for Morgenthau. See Christoph Frei, *Hans Morgenthau: An Intellectual Biography* (Louisiana State University Press, 2001). This is also a lesson that Henry Kissinger and a generation of Jewish foreign policy thinkers derived from Europe in the 1930s. See Jeremi Suri, *Henry Kissinger and the American Century* (Harvard University Press, 2007). For an interesting account of Jews' historical relationship with power as a means of survival, see Ruth Wisse, *Jews and Power* (Schocken, 2007).

[25] Lyons and Morton, *Schools for Strategy*, pp. 128–9.

[26] Geiger, *Research and Relevant Knowledge*, p. 88, and, generally, pp. 87–91.

Perspectives on Warfare, Security, and Strategy"; "The United States, France, and the NATO Dilemma, 1958–1969"; "The Army as the Forge of Political Loyalty: The Case of Chinese POWs in the Korean War"; "Strategies of Democracy Promotion in U.S. Foreign Policy"; "Early American Development of the Whitehead Torpedo: Industry, Technology, and Tactics"; and "The Ivy Scholars Program – Studies in Grand Strategy for High School Student Leaders."[27]

A centerpiece of ISS is the Brady-Johnson Program in Grand Strategy. The Brady-Johnson Program is affiliated with the MacMillan Center at Yale, which deals with such issues as identity; security; conflict; democracy past, present, and future; and distribution at local, national, regional, and global levels. Brady-Johnson is directed by Kennedy with the support of John Lewis Gaddis and Charles Hill. A Grand Strategy Program highlight is a year-long seminar, "Studies in Grand Strategy," which "teaches strategic thinking and the arts of leadership to a select group of undergraduate, graduate, and professional school students." The seminar is co-taught by Kennedy, Gaddis (the Robert A. Lovett Professor of Military and Naval History), and Hill (Distinguished Fellow and Diplomat-in-Residence at ISS).[28] Hill's recent book, *Grand Strategies: Literature, Statecraft, and World Order*, is a tour de force that probes how classic works of literature have illustrated the classic issues, themes, and dilemmas of statecraft, including the special obligations of statecraft that set it apart from other responsibilities and the need to organize power and violence in order to sustain and defend the polity. *Grand Strategies* fulfills the potential of combining strategic studies with the liberal arts.[29]

ISS launched the Project2000 for reasons that echo Morgenthau's notion of the higher practicality. On the one hand, fledgling future leaders needed to know more about strategic issues and thinking, including military-related matters. On the other hand, too many future leaders were being trained too narrowly and were not being exposed to the broader historical and cultural knowledge that is a necessary ingredient of education in strategic understanding. The project's brochure relates that the program was started to teach future leaders to think strategically, and to alleviate the growing problem of narrow specialization by striving to broaden the minds of students and by embedding the program in the liberal arts. The project spends about $750,000 annually for several activities: teaching, outside lectures, a summer program that includes high school students (the Ivy Scholars Program), the holding of conferences, interaction with government and the military war colleges, and other outreach activities.[30] Practicality is

[27] Yale University, International Security Studies, Schedule of Events: http://yale.edu/iss/schedule.html. See also the ISS home page: http://www.yale.edu/iss/.

[28] Yale University, International Security Studies Brochure, The Grand Strategy Project: http://alumninet.yale.edu/classes/yc1961/iss_brochure.htm.

[29] Charles Hill, *Grand Strategies: Literature, Statecraft, and World Order* (Yale University Press, 2010).

[30] Hill, *Grand Strategies.*

mixed with academic knowledge and theory. Hill underscored the program's indebtedness to integrating strategic thinking with the liberal arts

> The Grand Strategy Program at Yale was created in the late 1990s from a shared recognition by its originators – Paul Kennedy, John Lewis Gaddis, and Charles Hill – that higher education had largely divested itself of the ability to address the greatest issues of society, domestic and international, in a comprehensive manner. Disciplinary boundaries and methodologies, and fixation on quantifiable, empirical and manageable problems, however admirable and necessary, were not reaching the dimension of higher statecraft, the realm of presidents, prime ministers, commanders, and chief executive officers of major institutions. ... More expansively, the program recognizes that grand strategic thought is pre-disciplinary; that its most instructive examples are found in cases unbounded by the departmental fences of the modern university. Thus the humanities receive more attention in instruction than do the social sciences. ... Military history, case studies, and intellectual works provide the most obvious and well-developed educational material for the program and the foundation for our adding other layers to the program, such as grand strategy in the field of public health.

The program consists of graduate and undergraduate students drawn from a select group of applicants (graduate students are connected to other established programs), as well as several military personnel who have received Kenneth R. Miller, Jr., Fellowships, created in 2004 to honor Colonel Miller, a graduate of the program who was killed in Iraq in 2004. Hill described these fellowships as "the heart and soul of Grand Strategy's connection to the United States armed forces."[31]

The Grand Strategy Program offers a course on "Studies in Grand Strategy," taught by Gaddis, Hill, and Kennedy. Perusal of the syllabus indicates that the course integrates strategic theory and practicality with academic history and political theory – very much what Morgenthau meant by the higher practicality. The spring 2008 course dealt with major thinkers, statesmen, strategists, and/or topics, along with copious supplementary readings, including: Sun Tzu; Thucydides; the Romans; Machiavelli; Philip II and Elizabeth I; the Founding Fathers; Clausewitz; Kant versus Metternich; Bismarck and Lord Salisbury; Theodore Roosevelt, Woodrow Wilson, and Franklin Roosevelt; Imperial Geopolitics; Marx, Lenin, Stalin, and Mao; the Cold War; and the End of the Cold War.[32]

The course is open to undergraduate, graduate, and professional students. Faculty and visitors are primarily historians, and, as mentioned, the program is coordinated by historians. Hill enjoyed a career in the Foreign Service as a diplomat. A few affiliated faculty members are trained in political science or management. Paul Bracken, a professor in the School of Management and Political Science, sits on panels for the U.S. Navy and the Advisory Committee for Los Alamos National Laboratory. Kimberly Kagan, a former visiting fellow, was previously a professor at the U.S. Military Academy. She is a military

[31] E-mail exchange with Charles Hill, Yale University Grand Strategy Program, November 2010.

[32] The Brady-Johnson Program in Grand Strategy, Studies in Grand Strategy, Spring 2008: http://yale.edu/iss/gs/GS-syllabus-spring-2008.pdf.

historian with expertise on Roman military history and the surge in Iraq.[33] Kagan also founded the Institute for the Study of War, which was designed to provide civilian leaders and the electorate with awareness of military operations because of the perceived abandonment of military studies at American universities since the Vietnam War.[34] Scholars such as Kagan bring the belief in productive friction back to the university where it is often lacking. Both the Yale and MIT programs provide significant breadth of coverage, including a meaningful focus on military-related matters. But the programs are different in nature. MIT's Security Studies Program is a degree-granting program replete with nineteen courses, whereas Yale's program is not. Also, Yale's program is even more concerned with broader historical and international contexts and gives the study of the military less play than MIT's SSP, which is also more policy-oriented. And Yale provides more access to undergraduates. In many respects, the two programs represent apples and oranges: one more policy-oriented, the other more liberal arts–oriented. Yet both programs incorporate military-related knowledge and pedagogy in meaningful ways, at the same time that they reflect the trends that have arisen in security studies over the course of the last forty years. Traditional security study and military history remain the anchors of the MIT program, whereas they are less of an anchor at Yale, which is more oriented toward diplomacy and grand strategy. Yale's program would come closer to our model of pedagogy if it included more traditional military history and security study. For example, the Grand Strategy Program at the University of Wisconsin explicitly considers collaboration between the military and the university in its mission statement.[35] Yale's Grand Strategy Program represents a new collaboration between the military and academic worlds and a means of overcoming the divisiveness and political polarization that have characterized the relationship since the Vietnam conflict. It is a way for institutions and a new generation of academics to help policy makers think through contemporary problems and develop solutions with a historical perspective.

Wisconsin's New Grand Strategy Program

The influence of the military is even more apparent when we consider the leadership of the new Grand Strategy Program at Wisconsin, created by historian Jeremi Suri, who received his Ph.D. at Yale under the tutelage of Paul Kennedy. Scott Mobley, a captain in the Navy (Ret.), former commander of UW-Madison's Naval ROTC unit, and now a graduate student in the History Department at Madison, is the program coordinator and the military liaison; and William P. Tishler assists with the development of online courses and with

[33] See Kimberly Kagan, *The Surge: A Military History* (Encounter, 2008).

[34] Institution for the Study of War: http://understandingwar.org/.

[35] See http://grandstrategy.wisc.edu/.

media relations.[36] The program draws on the talents of several University of Wisconsin faculty members, including Jon Pevehouse (political science), John Hall (history), Kristopher Olds (geography), Paul Barford (computer science), Paul Wilson (nuclear engineering), Paul DeLuca (provost, nuclear engineering), Jonathan Patz (Nelson Institute and Med School), and coauthor Donald Downs (political science, law, and journalism). The program has contributed to productive friction at Wisconsin in meaningful ways (indeed, both authors were present at some of the early meetings of the program and learned much from them) and has engendered some discontent registered by a handful of Suri's colleagues who do not think that outreach to the military is appropriate. Unrelated to this dissent, in May 2011 Suri accepted an offer at the University of Texas and will be leaving Wisconsin. The fate of the program at Wisconsin is uncertain as we go to press.

One of the initial activities has been an online summer course for military leaders – taught by Suri with Mobley's assistance – on the history of the United States' wars, grand strategy, and diplomatic strategy. The course investigates how history informs current military policy.[37] An Associated Press story on the program in June 2009 placed the program in the historical context of Wisconsin:

> The University of Wisconsin–Madison, which saw some of the fiercest Vietnam War protests in the nation, is shedding its long-standing antimilitary image by hiring a military historian [see Chapter 11] and teaching a new course for military officers. The university also has improved services for veterans after hiring an assistant dean with a military background last year. "It really is a group effort to reach out to the military in a way we never have before, at least not in the last 20 to 30 years," UW-Madison history professor Jeremi Suri said. "... We're getting beyond this really silly notion people have that we're antimilitary." The image dates to the 1960s and '70s, when the university was a hotbed of Vietnam War protests. In 1970, four student radicals used a car bomb to destroy a building housing the Army Mathematics Research Center, killing a young scientist. ... Suri said he hopes to provide a new model for educating military employees if the class offered over the Internet is successful. "If we can be educating officers out there, I'm idealistic enough to believe we'll do a lot better job as a country," he said.

Joshua McAuliffe, a first lieutenant in the U.S. Army and an intelligence officer at a military prison in Iraq at the time he took the course in 2009, told the Associated Press he was taking the course "to better understand the historical backdrops that have led to the United States using military intervention," he wrote in an e-mail. "I hope through a better understanding ... I will come out as a better leader, one that is informed and able to speak intelligently on the subject."[38]

[36] See Grand Strategy Program, University of Wisconsin, Madison: http://grandstrategy.wisc.edu/.

[37] We attended one of the early meetings associated with the course, which was held at the Naval ROTC buildings on campus, observing firsthand productive interactions among ROTC cadets, officers, and other military personnel with academic historians and other members of the university community. Downs also audited this course.

[38] Ryan J. Foley, "UW-Madison Makes an Unlikely Ally: The Military," Associated Press, June 28, 2009: http://www.history.wisc.edu/home/announcements/associated_press_miltary.pdf.

Suri extended this approach in the undergraduate seminar that he conducted in the fall of 2009 and in the spring of 2011. The seminar consists of twenty students who study a full range of strategic subjects. A most noteworthy aspect of this course, in Suri's estimation, is a two-day grand strategy workshop in which several military officers from the summer online grand strategy course and a host of other guest mentors from government come to campus to join the undergraduate students. The mentoring base for the undergraduate students also includes military history professor John Hall, other faculty members from Wisconsin and other institutions, graduate students, and several local citizens. These individuals mentor students in dealing with crisis simulation exercises. The participants break into small groups, each assigned to hammer out policy prescriptions for the president in various crisis situations, such as how to respond to the 9/11 attacks or how to devise President-Elect Obama's national security plan a week after the 2008 election. Different teams were instructed to "think outside the box," to go to war if necessary, or to avoid war at all costs. "In each case," Suri related, "students had to hash out, in three hours, a brief for the president. ... You take all the politics out of it, and you challenge them as undergraduates have never been challenged before." The students informed Suri that, "It makes you realize how hard policy is, how actually hard it is. ... They all became friends, got to know the military officers, they stay in touch by e-mail. They are not 'children of light' anymore."[39] One interesting student reaction involved terrorism policy. According to Suri, the students entered the workshop very critical of President George W. Bush's antiterrorism policies. After the workshop session dealing with terrorism, they were less judgmental, acknowledging the fact that the actual pressures and responsibilities of the job create their own imperatives that can be independent of the values and assumptions that individuals bring to the office.[40] The Obama administration's ostensibly surprising adoption of some of the Bush administration's antiterror policies (not closing Guantanamo, restoring military tribunals, furthering special search authority under the Foreign Intelligence Surveillance Act [FISA], and so on) is the most recent example of this gravitational force.

As we saw earlier, Suri and his associates are active on many other fronts on and off campus to integrate military and strategic subjects with liberal and civic education. Suri related:

[39] Interview with UW-Madison history professor Suri, November 2009. As we mentioned in Chapter 1, the phrase "children of light" is an allusion to Reinhold Niebuhr's classic criticism of both unrealistic idealists and cynical realists in *The Children of Light and the Children of Darkness* (Charles Scribner's Sons, 1945). On the *sui generis* obligations of statecraft, see, e.g., Hill, *Grand Strategies*; Isaiah Berlin, "Special Supplement: The Question of Machiavelli," *New York Review of Books*, November 4, 1971.

[40] On how structural and environmental factors pressure presidents to engage in common policies regardless of the values and expectations that they bring to the office, see Jack L. Goldsmith, *The Terror Presidency: Law and Judgment Inside the Bush Administration* (W. W. Norton, 2007). This point is consistent with the theme of Hill, *Grand Strategies*.

I come at [the Grand Strategy Program] in two ways. One is what I would call the scholarly side. I'm really interested, and it is crucially important intellectually – the relationship between the military power and intellectual knowledge. I would argue that the United States did relatively well in the Cold War because we brought intellectual knowledge to bear on military power. We were lucky to have the Kennans, the Achesons, and the others. . . . I mean, military power by its very nature is a blunt instrument, and the United States has a lot of it. And one of the greatest problems when you have that power is figuring out how to use it effectively to serve political ends, to serve strategy . . . that to me is a crucial intellectual problem. . . . One thing is intellectual contribution to scholarship broadly defined. . . . In terms of citizenship, it is contributing to a dialogue about these issues. All sorts of things come together here, economic, social, political. If we don't put this together, we are a poorer society . . .

So without dumbing down the scholarly work at all, build forums so you can have serious scholarly discussion as well as public edification. . . . The Grand Strategy Program brings together military officers and undergraduates for serious scholarly activity, but also connectivity and a new kind of dialogue. . . ."[41]

Ralph D. Mershon Center at Ohio State

At its inception, Ohio State's Mershon Center for International Security Studies was rather unique. Its broad definition of national security included scientific and engineering knowledge (including, according to Lyons and Morton, such subjects as the biosynthetic potential of fungi and infrared astronomical photometry), and it benefited from substantial independent outside funding, rendering it relatively independent of foundations and the government.[42] The program was launched in the early 1950s with a major bequest from alumnus Ralph D. Mershon, a colonel in the Army reserve. A wearer of many hats, Mershon was a wealthy inventor and electrical engineer who earned many patents, as well as a man of public affairs. In the latter capacity, he was a leader in the institutionalization of ROTC as a national program. Mershon stipulated that at least half of the income from his bequest had to be used to "promote, encourage and carry on civilian–military education and training in the United States and its territories."[43] To guide its activities, the program formed a group called the Mershon Committee on Education in National Security. Under the auspices of this group, the program engaged in several security-defense–oriented activities in its first decade, including efforts to enhance the quality of ROTC education (now less prominent); sponsor courses in the departments of history, political science, and economics; hold lectures and conferences; and provide scholarship money.

A major project was a seminar in national security policy, modeled on the famous Defense Policy Seminar at Harvard, which was instituted as part of

41 Interview with Suri, November 2009.

42 Lyons and Morton, *Schools for Strategy*, pp. 171–2.

43 Lyons and Morton, *Schools for Strategy*, pp. 171–80. We draw heavily on this account in this early discussion of the Center. See also Mershon Center for International Security Studies, Mission and History: http://www.mershoncenter.osu.edu/about/mission%20and%20history/mission.htm.

Harvard's Defense Studies Program, administered by the Graduate School of Public Administration (renamed the John F. Kennedy School of Government in 1966).[44] Drawing on the expertise of many Harvard faculty members, including the rising stars Henry Kissinger and Samuel Huntington, the seminar was dedicated to the belief that "civilians should be trained in military matters if they were to participate constructively in policy making." Although it influenced many future security professionals, the seminar never became a regular part of an established department. "[T]he departments were little inclined to integrate the work in national security affairs into their traditional disciplines. This is characteristic of national security policy studies not only at Harvard but at other institutions as well."[45] The seminar soon fell under the umbrella of Harvard's Center for International Affairs, which was led by such formidable strategic thinkers as Kissinger, Thomas Schelling, and Huntington.[46] Other schools initiated similar programs, including Ohio State and Wisconsin – just as Yale's program in grand strategy influenced the later development of such a program at Wisconsin. But the original model and its progeny disappeared with the coming of the Vietnam War and its discontents.[47]

Today, the Mershon Center has foci that reflect the main currents in international relations: the subjects of military security/realism, constructivism, liberalism, and peace studies that we have discussed previously; the use of force and diplomacy; the ideas, identities, and decisional processes that affect security; and institutions that manage violent conflict. Mershon's overall mission is "to advance the understanding of national security in a global context."[48] Its oversight committee includes professors from several different departments and the commanders of Army ROTC, Navy ROTC, and Air Force ROTC. Thus, ROTC plays some role in steering the mission of the program.[49]

The Center does not offer courses in its own right, but it directly affects pedagogy and research in at least three ways: (1) by supporting the dissertations

[44] On this seminar, which we discuss in Chapter 4, , see Suri, *Henry Kissinger and the American Century*, pp. 132–4

[45] Lyons and Morton, *Schools for Strategy*, p. 149.

[46] Lyons and Morton, *Schools for Strategy*, pp. 149–51. Schelling, however, was an opponent of ROTC on Harvard's campus. Reflecting on the demise of ROTC at Harvard, Schelling stated, "Obviously Harvard lives in the real world but the idea is to minimize compromise with the real world, to preserve the idea of an ivory tower. Our service is to the culture, not to the national interest even when it's right." Charles D. Bloche, "ROTC: Making a Comeback," *Harvard Crimson*, April 8, 1981.

[47] Interview with University of Wisconsin political scientist David Tarr, June 2007; University of Wisconsin Oral History Interviews of David Tarr and Carlisle P. Runge: http://archives.library.wisc.edu/oral-history/guide/801-900/831-840.html#tarr http://www.archives.library.wisc.edu/oral-history/guide/201-300/241-250.html#runge.

[48] Mershon Center, Mission and History: http://mershoncenter.osu.edu/about/mission%20and%20history/mission.htm. See also Annual Report, 2006–7: http://mershoncenter.osu.edu/publications/2006–07%20Annual%20Report.pdf.

[49] Mershon Center, About Us, Oversight Committee: http://mershoncenter.osu.edu/about/oversight/oversight.htm.

and research of graduate students (in 2009, the thirteen students came from the departments of political science, history, sociology, geography, and the history of art);[50] (2) by including over sixty faculty members from a variety of fields on its roster of faculty;[51] and (3) by endowing three chairs, which consume 41 percent of its funds. The General Raymond E. Mason, Jr., Chair in Military History is currently held by Colonel Peter Mansoor, a Ph.D. in military history from Ohio State. Meanwhile, political scientist John Mueller holds the Wayne Woodrow Hayes Chair in National Security Studies. As of summer 2009, the Center was seeking a senior faculty member to fill its new Chair in Peace Studies.[52] The Chair in Peace Studies "will enable The Ohio State University to pursue in-depth studies of nonviolent resolutions to conflict as well as other peace-related issues." The Chair is funded by a $1.25 million gift from several sources under the aegis of the Ohio Council of Churches.[53]

Colonel Mansoor brings impressive military experience and expertise to the program. His command of the First Brigade, First Armored Division from 2003 to 2005 included thirteen months of combat in Operation Iraqi Freedom. After that, he was executive officer to General David Petraeus in Iraq. He published *Baghdad at Sunrise: A Brigade Commander's War in Iraq*, a work that followed *The GI Offensive in Europe: The Triumph of American Infantry Divisions, 1941–45*.[54] While working for Petraeus, Mansoor served on the "Council of Colonels," which assisted the Joint Chiefs of Staff in revising the counterinsurgency strategy for the Iraq War, leading to the surge. Mansoor is also the founding director of the U.S. Army–Marine Corps Counterinsurgency Center at Fort Leavenworth, Kansas. According to the Mershon Center website, "Under his leadership, the Counterinsurgency Center helped to revise the final version of the new *Counterinsurgency Field Manual 3–24*, which was published jointly by the Army and Marine Corps in December 2006. This document was the first revision of U.S. counterinsurgency operations in more than 20 years, incorporating lessons learned during conflicts throughout the 20th and 21st centuries."[55] Obviously, there are few faculty members in the country who command the level of practical and academic knowledge of military affairs and military experience of Colonel Mansoor. His appointment epitomizes

[50] Mershon Center, Graduate Student Research: http://polisci.osu.edu/faculty/jmueller/classes.htm.

[51] Mershon Center, Faculty: http://polisci.osu.edu/faculty/jmueller/classes.htm.

[52] Mershon Center, Endowed Chairs: http://mershoncenter.osu.edu/about/chairs/landing_fndowed.htm.

[53] Mershon Center, Chair in Peace Studies: http://mershoncenter.osu.edu/about/chairs/peace.htm.

[54] Colonel Peter Mansoor, *The GI Offensive in Europe: The Triumph of American Infantry Divisions, 1941–45* (University Press of Kansas, 1999); and *Baghdad at Sunrise: A Brigade Commander's War in Iraq* (Yale University Press, 2008).

[55] Mershon Center, Endowed Chairs, "Ohio State Selects Petraeus Aid as Military History Chair": http://mershoncenter.osu.edu/news/pressr/11.15.07.htm. See *The U.S. Army-Marine Corps Counterinsurgency Field Manual* (U.S. Army Field Manual No. 3–24, Marine Corps Warfighting Publication no. 3–33.5) (University of Chicago Press, 2007), with Forewords by General David H. Petraeus, Lt. General James F. Amos, and Lt. Colonel John A. Nagl.

bringing the military sphere to the university in a manner that embodies academic standards and values.

Mueller is an expert on international politics, foreign policy, defense policy, public opinion, democratization, economic history, post-Communism, terrorism, musical theater, and dance history. His recent books include *Atomic Obsession*; *Overblown: How Politicians and the Terrorism Industry Inflate National Security Threats and Why We Believe Them*; and *The Remnants of War*.[56] Mueller's courses since 2002 have included "War, Crime, and Violence"; "War, Violence, and Aggression"; "Ordering the New World"; "Security Policy During and After the Cold War"; "Terrorism; Threat Perception in International Relations"; and "Terrorism Policy: Threat and Response."[57]

Mueller is part of a large contingent of political science IR faculty (nine faculty members) at Ohio State who practice both constructivism and more traditional forms of security studies; many are associated with the Mershon Center.[58] The list of Mershon Center associates includes several individuals whose orientation to IR is identity-based, reflecting the development of constructivist approaches in IR, which we discussed in Chapter 12. Constructivist approaches emphasize formation of identity and the consequences of identity for how security is conceived and practiced. Constructivists in the program include Alexander Wendt, perhaps the nation's leading constructivist IR scholar, as well as Theodore Hopf, Richard Herrmann, and Pamela Paxton. The Center balances the constructivists with more traditional military historians and security study scholars, including the renowned Geoffrey Parker, Robert McMahon, Mansoor, and Mueller.[59]

The Mershon Center maintains close ties to Ohio State's History Department, which is one of the nation's leading military history departments. (We did not discuss it in our chapter on the top-twenty programs because its rank is number twenty-five overall.) The department offers military history as a field for graduate study, and has between twenty to thirty graduate students studying under no less than nine faculty members. (Ohio State has more military historians than North Carolina, according to our count.)[60] The History Department offers many military history and policy courses, including the following lecture courses: "World War I"; "The History of War"; "The History of European

[56] John Mueller, *Atomic Obsession* (Oxford University Press, 2009); Mueller, *Overblown: How Politicians and the Terrorism Industry Inflate National Security Threats and Why We Believe Them* (Free Press, 2006); Mueller, *The Remnants of War* (Cornell University Press, 2004).

[57] Ohio State University Department of Political Science, Faculty, Mueller, Classes: http://polisci.osu.edu/faculty/jmueller/classes.htm.

[58] Ohio State University, Department of Political Science, Faculty Webpages: http://polisci.osu.edu/faculty/index.htm.

[59] Mershon Center, Faculty Spotlight: http://mershoncenter.osu.edu/expertise/spotlight/landing_spotlight.htm.

[60] See Ohio State University Department of History, Courses, Military History: http://history.osu.edu//courses/curriculum/field_military.cfm.

Warfare (from the Renaissance to 1870; and 1870 to World War II)"; "American Military Policy (1607–1914)" and "American Military Policy (1914–1995)"; and "U.S. Diplomatic History and Modern Intelligence Theory." Seminars at the graduate level include "Studies in Military History"; "Studies in Military Thought and Strategy"; "Studies in the History of American Foreign Policy"; "Seminar in American Diplomatic History, I and II"; and "Seminar in U.S. Military History, I and II."[61]

Military historian John Guilmartin emphasized the substantial links between the military history program and other campus entities

> Military history is considered integral to the History program here at Ohio State. Indeed, one of the strongest aspects of our military history program lies in the fact that we military historians have good relations with colleagues in other fields who contribute materially to our effectiveness by offering minor fields to our graduate students, serving as second readers on dissertations, serving on general examination and dissertation defense committees and so on. The fields I'm thinking of include Business History, Japan, China, World History, Diplomatic, Women's, African and Ottoman. That having been said, there is a significant minority within our department that is adamantly opposed to military history and would love to see it excised from the program.

Guilmartin also pointed out that the Center used to have its own program in International Security and Military Affairs, but terminated the program in 1994:

> The closest thing we have to a security studies program now lies in our relationships with a number of military academic institutions who send us active duty officers for graduate training prior to service as instructors. We have had a steady stream of Army officers enroute to West Point, mostly captains and junior majors who are given two years to complete their MA. The Air Force Academy, Air Command and Staff College and Advanced School of Aerospace Studies also send us officers for two year MA programs and occasionally more senior officers for three year PhD programs. Finally, we occasionally get a newly-commissioned second lieutenant from the Air Force Academy who is given a year to complete the MA.[62]

In sum, although the Mershon Center does not have its own courses or house its own security center, it is a central station for an array of military history, military policy, and security studies at Ohio State. It funds significant graduate student research as well as panels and lectures; includes over sixty Ohio State faculty members on its roster of Center members; and supports three chairs whose publications and teaching address central aspects of military history and security studies. The Center's breadth reflects the broadening of security studies and military history that we have discussed elsewhere. By dropping the program in International Security and Military Affairs, it has moved somewhat away from

[61] Ohio State University Department of History, History Curriculum: http://history.osu.edu/courses/curriculum/curriculum.cfm. This site also includes sample course syllabi.

[62] E-mail exchange with Professor John Guilmartin, Ohio State University Department of History and member of the Mershon Center: June–July 2009.

the pedagogical model that we support in this book, but it has preserved a strong military dimension nonetheless.

The political science dimension of the program, however, appears less oriented toward providing skills for practitioners. The academic training offered to students with a military background occurs primarily through the discipline of history. In contrast, political scientists at Ohio State interested in security are increasingly of the constructivist persuasion. Wendt's approach, for example, appears primarily theoretical.

Ohio State, perhaps more than any other university that we consider in this book, brings the military cluster to the university – not simply because of the major program in military history or because of the Mershon Center, but because there is a large ROTC presence at Ohio State. The presence of the military cluster is promising, although we suspect that the trend in political science to emphasize theory over practical considerations has undermined opportunities to bring diverse perspectives together. The move toward theory is reminiscent of Morgenthau's critique of the scholastic tendencies of political science – a critique recently revived by Lawrence Mead.[63]

CONCLUDING THOUGHTS: THE STATUS OF SECURITY STUDIES

Our purpose in presenting this discussion of the various approaches to security studies was not to take a side in the debates that have proliferated in the expanding field. We had two different purposes. First, we wanted to provide a framework to cast light on the empirical findings that we presented earlier in this chapter. To make sense of these findings, one has to have a basic idea of the fundamental thinking and controversies in the field of inquiry. Our second purpose relates to the pedagogical theme of the book: to provide reasons for taking the study of military-related issues seriously. In the context of security studies, this means appreciating the classical approach to security studies, for that approach consciously includes military power as a central tenet. As stressed throughout this book, the point is certainly not to push a militaristic or pro-military agenda, but rather to demonstrate how the inclusion of military-related study can contribute to liberal and civic education. Indeed, as mentioned at the beginning of Chapter 12, the debate between realism and its critics raises profound empirical, normative, and philosophical questions that cut to the core of civic and liberal education: What is the meaning of citizenship? Is it rooted in universal principles, or is it socially constructed? What is the role of morality and ethics in international life, and what are the most effective means of promoting these goods? Is there such a thing as universal truth, or is truth contingent upon interest or social construction? Are ethical standards universal,

[63] Hans J. Morgenthau, "The Purpose of Political Science," in *A Design for Political Science: Scope, Objectives, and Methods*, edited by James C. Charlesworth (American Academy of Political and Social Science, 1966), pp. 63–79; Lawrence M. Mead, "Scholasticism in Political Science," *Perspectives on Politics* 8, 2 (2010).

or do they differ among different realms, such as private morality, economic relations, domestic politics, and relations among nations? How do power and the threat of force relate to citizenship and moral obligation? Classical security studies also pose questions regarding life and death.

In addition, it is evident that classical strategic studies and realism are still very relevant to political and international life. First, who can reasonably avow that self-interest and the will to power (at both the individual and the state levels) have disappeared as important aspects of human motivations and action? Even if wars are less prevalent than in the past, and if the theorists of democratic peace are on to something, the fact remains that organized violence remains part of our world; and it lies in the background of states and international orders within which the practice of democratic peace prevails.[64] (In other words, democratic peace must ultimately be backed by power, whether the power comes from international institutions – which have not had an unblemished record thus far in protecting peace and justice – or the commitment of powerful states or alliances such as NATO.)[65] Second, such rogue states and "revolutionary regimes" as Iran and North Korea are on the verge of possessing nuclear weapons as of this writing. If they attain these weapons, the nations within the realm of democratic peace will be obligated to deploy the doctrine of deterrence against them. Some strategic thinkers are now even reconsidering the previously rejected doctrine of the threat of limited nuclear war to deter such regimes.[66] Third, as many advocates of human rights acknowledge, sometimes military intervention is needed to secure those rights in the face of tyranny. And if such intervention does not come, the consequences are obvious, as the graves, hospitals, and rivers of blood in such places as Nazi Germany, Armenia, Darfur, Rwanda, Burma, Iran, and the Gulags of Communism have shown. Accordingly, sometimes peace is preserved not by pacifism or extreme reluctance to use arms, but rather by a plausible deterrent force.[67] If so, peace and war studies are not necessarily in opposition to one another, but can constitute two sides of the same coin. As MIT's Stephen Van Evera has remarked, most theories about the causes of war are also about theories of peace – and vice versa.[68]

[64] For an analysis of the relative waning of war, see John Mueller, *Retreat from Doomsday: The Obsolescence of Major War* (1989). Mueller's book was published during the unraveling of the Soviet Union and the thaw of the Cold War and before the eruption of violent jihadist Islam.

[65] On how the organization of violence is necessary to attain social order and peace, see Douglass C. North, John Joseph Wallis, and Barry R. Weingast, *Violence and Social Orders: A Conceptual Framework for Interpreting Recorded Human History* (Cambridge University Press, 2009).

[66] See Robert D. Kaplan, "Living with a Nuclear Iran," *Atlantic*, September 2010. Kaplan discusses the surprising renewed relevance of Kissinger's classic book, *Nuclear Weapons and Foreign Policy* (Council of Foreign Relations, 1957).

[67] See Donald Kagan, *On the Origins of War and the Preservation of Peace* (Doubleday, 1995). This is also a theme in the collection of essays edited by Robert J. Art and Kenneth N. Waltz, *The Use of Force: Military Power and International Politics*, 7th Edition (Rowman and Littlefield, 2009).

[68] Stephen Van Evera, *Causes of War: Power and the Roots of Conflict* (Cornell University Press, 1999).

Fourth, some scholars have empirically demonstrated that even liberal states with republican forms of government are considerably more likely to follow the strictures of international law when it serves their interests to do so than when it does not.[69] And fifth, what do we make of conflict that arises from the animosity of nonliberal states or groups that lie outside the realm of democratic peace? Sometimes this conflict is itself a product of the very practices that contribute to democratic peace – supporting classic realism's grasp of the tragic nature of life and international relations. As Philip Bobbitt has demonstrated in two magnum opuses, the rise of "market states" in the late-twentieth century – the products of economic interdependency – helped to fuel the jihadist terrorism that now threatens those very states. The economic relations and activities of market states extend beyond traditional physical borders, embedding market polities in international networks that sometimes defy the limits and perquisites of sovereignty. (Market states are prime examples of the decentering of the state.) This expansion of economic activity and power alienates fundamentalist Islamists, but also provides networks of communication and information that Islamic terrorists use to recruit members and obtain technological knowledge. In many ways, liberal democracy's conflict with terrorism epitomizes the tensions and dilemmas that beset international relations theory today: Dispute reigns over whether the conflict should be considered a war or a law enforcement matter, and the legal status of non-state terrorists who violate the rules of war is a matter of continuous dispute.[70] Is the threat posed by terrorism real, or is it also influenced by our constructions of the threat? The confrontation with international terrorism provides both vindication and refutation of all schools of security studies. But at the very least, realism and traditional security studies have something important to say about terrorism on a variety of levels.

Constructivism has usually been used to question realism's suspicion of international organizations and order. But a constructivist sensibility can also cut in the other direction. For example, some commentators have observed that some liberal internationalists and peace advocates project their own beliefs in goodwill and peace onto others whose purposes are much less benign. (Among a multitude of examples are Woodrow Wilson's faith in the League of Nations, Neville Chamberlain's views toward Hitler, Jimmy Carter's earlier views toward the Soviet Union, and George W. Bush's earlier assumptions regarding Vladimir Putin.) Accordingly, constructivism can be used to question the assumptions of all schools of IR, including its own when some of its practitioners unduly dismiss realism's claims.

[69] See Jack L. Goldsmith and Eric A. Posner, *The Limits of International Law* (Oxford University Press, 2005).

[70] See Philip Bobbitt, *Terror and Consent: The Wars for the Twenty-First Century* (Alfred A. Knopf, 2008); and Bobbitt, *The Shield of Achilles: War, Peace, and the Course of History* (Alfred A. Knopf, 2002). *Terror and Consent* is one of the most definitive and comprehensive works on terrorism as a phenomenon, and its legal, moral, strategic, and scientific implications.

Realism – including the "moral realism" as we have conceptualized of it in this book – and the traditional core of security studies remain highly relevant, even if responsible scholars and policy makers must account for alternative understandings. And since the project of this book deals with pedagogy, we are not obligated to pick a horse in this race. It is enough to acknowledge that the tenets of realism and traditional security studies are important regardless of one's policy or normative position, and that such tenets broaden and deepen the knowledge to which students are exposed in campus life today. Security studies programs remain hospitable to realism, and it is not isolated from the university or singular in its approach. In general, the security studies programs that we asked about are sources of productive friction to varying extents.

PART IV

CONCLUDING THOUGHTS

14

Conclusion

Placing the Military in the University

> The original sin stems from the pretension to be other than one's true self. It is our privilege to *try* to be whatever we wish; but it is vicious to pretend to be what we are not, and to delude ourselves by growing habituated to a radically false idea of what we are. . . .
>
> Not only does it [the university] need perpetual contact with science, on pain of atrophy, it needs contact, likewise, with public life, with historical reality, with the present, which is essentially a whole to be dealt with only in its totality, not after amputations *ad usum Delphini*. The university must be open to the whole reality of its time. It must be in the midst of life, and saturated with it . . .
>
> – Jose Ortega y Gasset[1]

One of the fundamental institutional conflicts in American society concerns the relationship between arms and the university. Several questions guided our inquiry into the nature and significance of the military and military-related fields of study in the academy. What is the status of the military and military-related fields of inquiry in American universities? Does an appropriate military presence contribute to civic and liberal education? Does appropriate military presence improve prospects for national security? Can appropriate military presence within a university enhance the relationship among civil, political, and military institutions in American society?

As we traveled the road of researching and writing this book, we became aware of the fact that this book is but a chapter in a larger story that was unfolding before our eyes: the embattled yet ineluctable reintegration of the military into the consciousness of the nation and the university. As we have elucidated throughout this book, American society has been attempting to bridge the gap that opened up between the military and society in the wake of several forces, including the fiasco of Vietnam; the advent of the All-Volunteer Force; the retreat of the socioeconomic elite and swaths of the middle class from service (the AWOL factor); the move of ROTC and military bases to more rural

[1] Jose Ortega y Gasset, *The Mission of the University: The Foundations of Higher Education* (Transaction, 1991). Emphasis in the original.

and conservative parts of the country; and the rise of a warrior ethos in echelons of the military that might have exacerbated the military's sense of isolation from the general society. As we embarked on this inquiry, pessimism was the order of the day regarding the breach. But as we wrote, trends that had already been percolating began to heat up, including the return of thousands of veterans to campus; intensification of awareness regarding the "gap" problem; national movements to "welcome" Vietnam vets back forty years late; the challenge to, and ultimate demise of, Don't Ask, Don't Tell; and the surprisingly quick response of some schools as soon as DADT's death knell sounded to seriously consider bringing ROTC back to campus, highlighted by the positive and historic decisions at Harvard, Yale, Stanford, and Columbia. Given the emergence of this new situation, it is evident that this book is part of a broader *zeitgeist*, or spirit of the historical time. And nowhere is this *zeitgeist* more surprising than at universities, especially those that had effectively barred ROTC and related programs during the heat of the campus wars over Vietnam.

As we have shown, the opening of the university's mind and arms is not without tension. Nor should it be. As we have taken pains to acknowledge, the university and the military are distinctively different organizations, and friction between the two is both natural and a sign that each is being true to its own nature. And such tension is good in order to resist any tendencies toward militarization that might arise in the future. But we have also presented evidence of the possibilities of "productive friction," which can come about by the nourishing of an appropriate dialectical relationship that can enhance each institution. Such a relationship will be fraught with both mutual respect and disharmony, as it can evoke creedal passions on both sides, as we have discussed in several chapters of this book. But such disharmony, as Samuel P. Huntington hoped, is both an expression of American democracy in action and a process by which we develop and grow as a people.[2]

We began our investigation by developing a theory relating appropriate military presence to one of the primary tasks of a university – namely, civic and liberal education. We conceptualized military presence to include physical presence of the military – such as ROTC – as well as intellectual consideration of the military and military institutions in such pedagogical endeavors as military history and military-oriented security studies. According to our theoretical framework, inclusion of a distinctly military perspective provides students with an opportunity to learn about the details and significance of war in society as well as to gain deeper understanding of the military itself. We recognized that

[2] In some respects, part of Huntington's work represents two bookends of this project. His seminal book on civil–military relations provided theoretical tools for understanding the differences between the military and the university, whereas his book on creedal passion and disharmony provided a model for discerning how a dynamic, dialectical relationship between the two can lead to productive friction and the enhancement of education. Samuel P. Huntington, *The Soldier and the State: The Theory and Politics of Civil–Military Relations* (Harvard University Press, 1957); Huntington, *American Politics: The Promise of Disharmony* (Harvard University Belknap Press, 1981).

the study of war and the presence of military institutions on campus are often a source of discomfort and discord; but it is precisely this sort of discomfort that enables students to broaden their perspective within a university. Indeed, in our theoretical framework, discomfort that arises as a consequence of academic and institutional diversity is one of the keys to fulfilling the university's special responsibility to educate students. Military presence, because it embodies a distinctive and important institutional and intellectual perspective, is of special utility to educators seeking to broaden students' horizons.

MILITARY PRESENCE AND A DIVERSITY OF LITERATURES

Our theoretical framework integrated several literatures. The first literature can be termed "diversity theory," which emphasizes the importance of diversity in learning. Scott E. Page, one of the nation's leading diversity theorists, provides a compelling argument why inclusion of diverse perspectives enhances the ability of people to solve problems.[3] A second literature considers civilian control of the military. One of the central problems of civil–military relations is establishing an effective means of control over the military and military institutions. There are several reasons that civilian control may erode. One is the fact that the military is increasingly professionalized. Huntington, in his seminal work on civilian control, accentuated the importance of civilian control amid increasing professionalization.[4] The defining feature of the military as a professional *institution* is the potential to inculcate its members with particular values and knowledge. Professionalization raises the specter of a civil–military rift that can destabilize political institutions because it ensures the military represents a distinct "cluster" in society.

A third literature considers the relationship among free speech, intellectual diversity, and education. Scholars interested in freedom of speech suggest that one of the tasks of the university is to encourage situations of discomfort, or what the Supreme Court has called the First Amendment principle of a "verbal cacophony."[5] Respect for freedom of speech on campus is important because it provides opportunities to challenge students in ways that may be uncomfortable but are nonetheless necessary for effective learning. In this sense, freedom of speech and the inclusion of diverse military perspectives on campus share an important purpose: Each contributes to intellectual and moral growth by exposing students to realities and perspectives that are beyond the ken of their normal experience. If discomfort results, this can be a good thing, for such discomfort is integral to the productive friction that augments knowledge.

[3] Scott E. Page, *The Difference: How the Power of Diversity Creates Better Groups, Firms, Schools, and Societies* (Princeton University Press, 2008).

[4] Huntington, *The Soldier and the State.*

[5] See, e.g., Donald Alexander Downs, *Restoring Free Speech on Campus* (Cambridge University Press and the Independence Institute, 2005); *Cohen v. California*, 403 U.S. 15 (1971), p. 25.

These diverse literatures often do not speak to each other, yet each has important insights regarding the status of the military on campus. Diversity theory has provided many insights into the sociology of learning, but the theory has not been utilized to better understand why military presence is important on campus. Studies of civil–military relations have not considered explicitly how military presence within the university can help to bridge the military–civilian divide – an issue relevant to citizenship as well as to civilian control of the military. Finally, most importantly to our project, studies of civic and liberal education have not considered explicitly military-related fields of inquiry.

In response to these limitations with existing literatures, we formulated a normative and theoretical framework that explicitly considered the relationship among military presence, education, and civil–military relations. There are several components to our theoretical approach. First, we explained why the military offers a diverse perspective. Appropriate presence of the military on campus promises to increase the ability of students as well as soldiers to think more broadly and to solve problems.

Second, we argued that the university is a laboratory of civil–military relations that enhances civilian understanding of the military as an institution. Studies of civilian control of the military usually emphasize formal channels of authority over the military – such as constitutional rules regarding the relationship between politicians and the military – or the breakdown of control, such as military uprisings against the state. Such perspectives are clearly important, but they furnish limited insight into how civil society comes to better understand the military as an institution – the understanding gap alluded to often in this work. And bridging the understanding gap is a two-way street: Military presence is important because it brings the military to the university, and in so doing increases the prospects for effective civilian control by creating better understanding of military institutions.

We then offered several specific reasons that military presence can enhance prospects for civic and liberal education. First, military presence increases opportunities to learn about the military as an institution, thereby improving the prospects for civic education. One cannot reasonably deny that knowledge of the military and military institutions is an important component of *civic* education. Second, military presence, because it concerns matters of conflict and war, provides a conduit for learning more about human conflict, the legitimate and illegitimate uses of violence, and human nature itself. Third, the presence of military personnel and military-related courses confronts students with moral difficulties inherent in liberal democracy. In particular, it compels students to grapple with such fundamental tensions as the desire for peace and well-being coexisting with the unfortunate necessity of employing force under certain circumstances, or the conflicts between benevolence and aggression. Finally, military presence is a source of intellectual diversity. Encountering the "military mind" and its emphasis on duty and command exposes students to a mentality or orientation that is different from the typical liberal norms and assumptions of civilian and campus life. The latter three points suggest the ways in which an appropriate military presence can deepen and expand *liberal* education.

Our normative and theoretical framework guided us in our sojourn into ROTC and military history. It bears repeating that this is a sojourn in the truest sense – we are not current or former members of the military, military historians, or experts in security studies. Yet we were able to speak to a large number of people who have experienced military life, who have dedicated their professional lives to the study of the military, as well as many who are deeply concerned about the military on campus – from the most ardent proponents to entrenched opponents. By acknowledging our own shortcomings, we were more than willing to ask questions from an increasingly diverse group of people – the diversity of which helped us provide more insight into the questions that we set out to answer.

ROTC AND THE UNIVERSITY

We began our empirical study by considering the explicitly physical military presence in the form of ROTC, finding that physical presence of the military is the historical norm rather than the exception within American universities. Under varying circumstances, universities have often figured out the appropriate presence of the military, one that did not require the removal of military institutions from campus. During times of total war, for example, military presence often increased substantially before returning to more "normal" levels at the conclusion of conflict. To be sure, this was less true for the Cold War University, but two points should be kept in mind regarding that unprecedented institution: First, government and military involvement after World War II were considerably less extensive than during World War II; second, the explosion of the "multiversity" and its remarkable range of government-oriented projects after World War II were the product of many factors, only one of which was military needs. And even when a military presence was overwhelming, the government and university leaders labored to maintain boundaries that preserved the university's basic integrity. Two obvious exceptions would be the failure of many World War I universities to protect basic principles of freedom of speech and academic freedom, as well as the abuses under McCarthyism in the early stages of the Cold War University.[6] In both cases – especially the former – First Amendment and academic freedom doctrines were not as developed as they are today, and the nation learned from these experiences in future years. Two points emerge from these two cases. First, they show that even if it makes national policy sense for the university to open its gates to the military, we must be vigilant in protecting the academic integrity of the university regardless how dire the emergency. This can be hard work, but it is a necessary undertaking. Second, responsibility for this problem was borne by the government,

[6] See, e.g., David Rabban, *Free Speech in Its Forgotten Years* (Cambridge University Press, 1993); Ellen W. Schrecker, *No Ivory Tower: McCarthyism and the Universities* (Oxford University Press, 1986).

not the military. McCarthyism was a political phenomenon, not a military phenomenon.

In Chapter 4, we introduced the idea of a sliding scale, in which the legitimate degree of military presence on campus varies proportionately with the extent of national necessity; the extensive – even overwhelming – presence of World Wars I and II was justified by the reality of total war. In other circumstances, universities must be more circumspect in granting access. Another issue of obvious importance is more prudential in nature: If the nation and its leadership believe it is necessary for the military to have a major presence on campus in wartime, there had better be sufficient consensus that the war is legitimate. Given the Vietnam War's lack of such consensus (and given the highly controversial draft that was used to supply it with troops), heated opposition to military presence could only be expected.[7] A nation asks much of its institutions and young in times of war, so the sacrifices that it requires of its campuses in such times must be legitimated by the support of the social contract. When this social contract is torn apart, we encounter what we saw in the late 1960s on campus.[8]

This book has not dealt at length with the question of military-sponsored research, focusing instead on pedagogical aspects of military presence; but our conclusions could have implications for research as well. We have argued that an appropriate military presence in the form of ROTC and military-oriented courses is not only justified, but even good for the reasons articulated throughout this book. In today's complex world marked by constant international dangers, it is legitimate and responsible for universities to sponsor such things as ROTC units and military/security-related courses. Research contributing to the national interest in security and defense raises different questions, but we believe it is appropriate if conducted in a manner that does not compromise academic principles.

The controversies over ROTC and research that marked the 1960s confirmed some important principles – mainly that courses and research must live up to academic standards and the principles of academic freedom. Accordingly, universities must apply consistent standards regarding staff and course content in ROTC and ensure that ROTC courses and courses dealing with the military embody standards of critical inquiry. For its part, research should follow the prescriptions of Harvard's James Conant, who banned secret research under the aegis of the university (see Chapter 4). If secret research meets standards of necessity, the standards for what constitutes necessity must be clearly articulated

[7] On the Vietnam War's deep strategic flaws, see Adrian R. Lewis, *The American Culture of War: The History of U.S. Military Force from World War II to Operation Iraqi Freedom* (Routledge, 2007), p. 220.

[8] One Cornell professor depicted the Cornell crisis of 1969 as "a Hobbesian state of nature," which entailed a dissolution of the social contract. See Donald Alexander Downs, *Cornell '69: Liberalism and the Crisis of the American University* (Cornell University Press, 1999). Our portrayal of the Columbia crisis in Chapter 5 depicts a similar state.

and set high, and appropriate bodies must determine that such necessity has been met. Meaningful review of such decisions is also needed.

After discussing the military and ROTC's status on campus before the 1960s (Chapter 4), our inquiry then shifted to the politics of ROTC, describing in detail the decline and resurgence of ROTC on campus (Chapters 5–7). In contrast with existing studies of war and the university (numerous books have been written from the vantage point of those who oppose the military), we emphasized the resurgence of ROTC more than the protest movement to remove the military from campus. Through interviews and historical evidence, we were able to articulate the reasons for the emergence of a promising – and ultimately successful – pro-ROTC movement at Columbia University. We found that the movement to restore ROTC reflected many of the rationales that we set forth in Chapter 2 – in particular, proponents of ROTC underscored the importance of diverse perspectives and also the significance of ROTC as a vehicle of civic education.

However, a reasoned defense of ROTC was not sufficient to win enough hearts and minds until the abolition of the Don't Ask, Don't Tell policy in December 2010. Protest movements benefit from events that coordinate individuals regarding the appropriateness of their actions.[9] The events of 9/11 enhanced support for the movement among students as the sliding scale began to shift in the direction of greater military presence; and the later abolition of Don't Ask, Don't Tell furthered this shift, encouraging pro-ROTC forces while weakening the case against ROTC in an era dominated by the civil rights paradigm discussed in Chapter 6. In Chapter 7, we chronicled the ultimate return of ROTC to two Ivy institutions that had "effectively barred" the program (Allan Silver's carefully chosen words) in 1969. These inclusions were the climax of a decades-long effort that could be construed as an uplifting sequel to *The Myth of Sisyphus*.

The final empirical dimension of our study of ROTC considered the perspectives of ROTC cadets and students at the University of Wisconsin as well as veterans at Wisconsin and Columbia. Our interviews with cadets suggest that they offer a distinctively military perspective, but also that they share common ground with students. The self-reported impact of cadets included giving the military a human face as well as "setting the record straight" on certain issues. In addition, many students reported being provoked to learn more because of the physical presence of ROTC. Our evidence suggested that the movement against ROTC and recruiters has real costs, in particular the costs of less diversity and

[9] Doug McAdam, Sidney Tarrow, and Charles Tilly provide a unified theory of political change that stresses the important role for symbolic events in the formation of protest movements. These symbolic events can be thought of as focal points that help individuals overcome a coordination problem that they need to resolve in order for collective action to be successful. The events of 9/11 were a focal point for movements seeking the return of the soldier to campus, as was the abolition of Don't Ask, Don't Tell (DADT). See McAdam, Tilly, and Tarrow, *Dynamics of Contention* (Cambridge University Press, 2001).

opportunities to learn. As such, we were able to conclude that by banning ROTC, universities lose out on important opportunities to encourage productive friction. In this section of the book, we also considered the impact on students of three University of Wisconsin humanities courses dealing with war. Although we had only a limited number of responses, they clearly revealed that the courses had an impact on those who responded. Students reported having to grapple with problems and aspects of politics, conflicts, and human nature that they had not confronted before. In some cases, students were explicit about the *sui generis* impact that the course had on them. These responses were in line with the theoretical model of civic and liberal education that we articulated in Chapter 2. This was especially the case with the course on "The Romance of War," which was intentionally designed to foster thought about the nature of humanity. The military history courses also had this type of impact, although in a less introspective manner.

MILITARY HISTORY AND UNIVERSITY EDUCATION

Our second empirical inquiry dealt with military history. The conflict over physical presence of the military in universities – from ROTC detachments to military recruiters to military funding of research – is well publicized, most notably the conflict over the military on campus that raged in the 1960s. A less-publicized conflict has involved the military as a field of inquiry, particularly what we refer to as traditional military history – the study of the military as an institution and the historical treatment of history's battles. This conflict has not involved protest movements, but it remains a critical and controversial part of military presence within universities. We concentrated on the status of traditional military history relative to newer forms of military history that emphasize the social, cultural, and psychological aspects of war.

For several reasons, we treated military history as a dimension of military presence. First and foremost, military history is the study of war in its purest form and war is one of the most important, yet also tragic, features of human existence. As such, understanding war can comprise an important element of liberal education. Second, failure to understand wars of the past may contribute to wars in the future. Thucydides is perhaps best known for his axiom that those who fail to understand history are bound to repeat it. He wrote, "It will be enough for me, however, if these words of mine are judged useful by those who want to understand clearly the events which happened in the past and which (human nature being what it is) will, at some or other and in much the same way, be repeated in the future."[10] These and related reasons suggested to us the significance of providing students with an opportunity to learn about war from those who are most knowledgeable about the facts of wars and battles, and how these phenomena relate to politics, society, and history.

[10] Thucydides, *The Peloponnesian War*, translated by Rex Warner (Penguin Classics, 1954), p. 24.

Armed with our belief in the importance of the study of the military and war for a civic and liberal education, we proceeded to inquire into the status of traditional military history on campus. There have been several inquiries into the status of military history, mostly by military historians.[11] So we must acknowledge that we are not the first to consider the status of military history. We are, however, the first to explicitly frame our inquiry based on traditional and new forms of military history, to consider its status through surveys of department leaders, and to examine the status of military history in security studies and political science departments. Hence, we provided a different perspective on a debate that has to this point transpired primarily within the halls of history departments, with the leading antagonists drawn from the ranks of military history.

Our study of military history produced several findings. First, we found substantial evidence that military history – especially traditional military history – is underrepresented at the top universities – both in terms of faculty with expertise in military history and in courses offered in military history. This gap at the nation's leading history departments is a disservice to civic and liberal education. This shortage in the nation's largest, best-funded research institutions suggests that there is something to the allegations of those who have sounded the alarm about the decline of military history. Perhaps more stunning is the lack of traditional military historians at the top history departments.

Second, in our broader surveys of the top one hundred history departments, we found that the threat to traditional military history appears to be in future hiring priorities. Our surveys of those in leadership positions in history departments – chairs, associate chairs, and the like – provide information regarding the status of military history today, but also insight into the future, because we asked about hiring priorities and replacement. Our findings reveal that the future does not bode well for traditionalists – most departments intend on replacing them with different approaches to military history, if they are to replace them at all.

Based on our evidence, we can offer some preliminary conclusions. On the one hand, scholars working in social or cultural versions of military history have cause for optimism. New military history is on the rise in history departments. The growing prominence of new military history bodes well for the future of military history, broadly defined. In addition, we found some evidence of courses that take traditional military history seriously while also incorporating meaningful aspects of the new military history. John Hall's new course on American Military History at the University of Wisconsin, Madison, is an encouraging example of this trend. A former Army major who takes traditional military history seriously, Hall is also expressly conscientious about integrating war

11 See, e.g., John A. Lynn, "The Embattled Future of Academic Military History," *Journal of Military History* 61 (1997): 777–89; Lynn, "Breaching the Walls of Academe: The Purposes, Problems, and Prospects of Military History," *Academic Questions* (March 2008); Edward M. Coffman, "The Course of Military History in the United States Since World War II, *Journal of Military History* 61 (1997), p. 761.

and society scholarship into his course, and student respondents to our questionnaires indicated the wide scope of the thinking that Hall encouraged.

On the other hand, the importance of war and the low representation of traditionalists in the top programs is cause for concern, one that leaves us feeling less than optimistic about the prospects for liberal and civic education at the nation's top history programs.

MILITARY PRESENCE AND SECURITY STUDIES

Our third empirical area considered security studies. Military presence in security studies was of particular concern to us because this is the branch of the university most likely to train individuals who will go on to have an active role in the formulation and conduct of national security. During the Cold War, an intimate relationship formed between security studies and the government.[12] The intimate relationship between the military and the university understandably and correctly raised serious questions, and many of the relationships forged during the Cold War University were challenged. While the Cold War University may have exceeded an appropriate military presence as far as security studies is concerned (as the distinction between research and national security objectives may have been blurred beyond recognition), it is important to remember that *appropriate* military presence remains an important source of diversity. The emergence of an inappropriate relationship in the past should not lead universities to forgo the challenge of striking an appropriate balance today. Yet the sliding scale may go too far in the wrong direction – which in the case of security studies would mean the excommunication of the military and political realism from security studies. For this reason, we found it necessary to examine the degree of military presence in security studies programs both now and in the past. We were particularly interested in the degree to which political realism and participation of military officers and those with military experience remains institutionalized, for these elements of security studies appear critical to formulating national security policy without risking the conflicts of interest that may have arisen during the heyday of the Cold War University.

We began our consideration of security studies with a theoretical inquiry into political realism, an excursion that produced several preliminary conclusions. First, political realism is best understood as the core of security studies as a discipline. The birth of security studies (a modern occurrence) was intimately bound up in realist political thought, which extends thousands of years back into history. More recently, alternative approaches – such as neoliberal institutionalism and constructivism – began to pose a serious challenge to political realism as the foundation of security studies. Based on our understanding of the

[12] See Stephen M. Walt, "The Renaissance of Security Studies," *International Studies Quarterly* 35 (1991); Eugene M. Lyons and John W. Masland, *Schools for Strategy: Education and Research in National Security Affairs* (Frederick A. Praeger, 1965).

development of security studies, we argued that political realism is integral to security studies as a discipline.

Second, political realism has conventionally emphasized historical knowledge and practical applications with a philosophical bent, or what Morgenthau referred to as "higher practicality." The practical and pragmatic dimensions of realism, as well as its tragic ethical dimension in the hands of such thinkers as Morgenthau and Niebuhr, distinguish it from the more modern schools of thought in international relations, such as neorealism, neoliberal institutionalism, and constructivism. Our theoretical inquiry suggested that political realism is a key component of security studies, and that without it, prospects for effective civic and liberal education – as well as for effective national security policy – decline.

Our theoretical inquiry allowed us to formulate an image of an ideal security studies program, one that recognizes the importance of political realism (without having to be dominated by it) and the integration of a distinctly military perspective – both through inclusion of individuals with military experience and through attention to military history – and a broader liberal arts orientation. Our limited evidence suggests cause for optimism. A substantive presence of military history and military personnel exists in some of the nation's leading security studies programs, such as MIT, Ohio State, and Yale, and they have integrated diverse perspectives in their curricula. The Grand Strategy Program at Wisconsin is also promising in this regard, although it is still a fledgling enterprise. Political realism remains a key approach in most programs. Yet several programs provide only a limited emphasis on realism, which suggests cause for concern because realism, in our reading of the discipline, appears to be the foundation of security studies rather than a branch of it.

Before offering some final words, let us consider some extensions of our study.

LEADERSHIP AND THE UNIVERSITY: STANLEY MCCHRYSTAL

Although it has not been our explicit focus, leadership is one of the central reasons that military presence is important to a university. How important is military presence for a university seeking to provide students with a deeper understanding of leadership? Our argument suggests that military presence can be very helpful in this regard.

An important example of military presence and leadership studies is afforded by the plight of General Stanley McChrystal, a top commander in Afghanistan and Iraq, who retired in the summer of 2010 after making comments in a now infamous *Rolling Stone* article that were interpreted as critical of the Obama administration.[13] His criticism of the administration raised important issues of civil–military relations and the chain of command. Was it appropriate for a

[13] Michael Hastings, "The Runaway General," *Rolling Stone* (June 22, 2010).

military leader to criticize the current administration? Should the words be forgiven in a time of war? Does the McChrystal incident reflect the deeper problem of a civil–military gap? Each of these issues is important, yet the reasons for (and the appropriateness of) his retirement are not our primary interest. We are mainly interested in where he landed – at Yale, teaching courses on leadership.

Shortly after McChrystal retired from active service, Yale's Jackson Institute for Global Affairs hired him as a senior lecturer. His responsibilities include teaching a graduate seminar on leadership.[14] There are several reasons that this appointment could epitomize productive friction. First, it recognizes that leadership is critical in the military. Second, students have opportunities to learn about the importance of leadership in the military, in particular leadership when the stakes are as high – perhaps as high as they can get. Third, they can learn about the appropriate role of the military in society more generally because they are taught by someone who was caught up in a conflict over appropriate civilian control over the military. In short, we believe that McChrystal's presence creates an exceptional opportunity to enhance students' liberal and civic educations.

To us, McChrystal's role represents *appropriate* military presence. Yet we can imagine many people believing that a general should not be teaching leadership, or that McChrystal should not have a place on campus. (McChrystal's alleged role in covering up Private Pat Tillman's death by friendly fire in 2004 has been raised by critics of his appointment by Yale. If the allegation is true – and we are in no position to assess its validity – then that would be a legitimate objection. But our praise of such an appointment is not based on McChrystal per se, but rather the idea of hiring a leading commander, even one with a controversial past.) Future studies of military presence in universities would do well to consider explicitly how much leadership studies promote productive friction by integrating the military into the design and plan of their curriculum and into the ranks of their faculty.

IN CONCLUSION: PLACING THE MILITARY IN THE UNIVERSITY

It is fitting to conclude by restating one of the fundamental themes of this book: The university benefits from military presence as much as university presence benefits the military. Many proponents of ROTC have defended its existence on campus because it places the university in the military. It seems undeniable that placing the university in the military is beneficial for society for reasons of civilian control and constructive civilian–military interaction and balance. To guard against any militarizing effects of ROTC, it is important that universities maintain the upper hand in terms of setting standards. As we have seen in Chapters 5 through 7, this concern was central to the politics of ROTC at Columbia University and other institutions. Columbia's University Senate

[14] See "Stanley McChrystal to Yale," *POLITICO* (August 16, 2010): http://www.politico.com/news/stories/0810/41101.html.

accepted ROTC's return on the condition that the program live up to the academic and antidiscrimination principles that the university appropriately held dear. It is upon such subjection to civil values that appropriate civil–military relations are built.

At the same time, we should think carefully about accepting uncritically the argument that ROTC is important simply because it places the university in the military, for such arguments capture only those benefits that accrue outside of the university. People may tolerate ROTC because they believe that the military is an institution that needs to be controlled by a more rational and educated civilian society. Yet civilians are unlikely to govern the military effectively unless they understand the military – a task that is made difficult when institutions of higher education do not encourage appropriate military presence. In particular, civilian control is expected to suffer unless civilians themselves understand the military. Civilian control can break down either because the military fails to understand society or because *society fails to understand the military*. If it is the former problem that society fears, then it is necessary to place the university in the military. Yet if it is the latter problem, then we should explicitly recognize the importance of placing the military in the university in order to facilitate civilian understanding of the military "other." One of our central themes is that the problem of civil–military relations is less the closed mind of the military than the society closing its mind to the nature and significance of the military as an institution. This problem is perhaps most clearly illustrated when the university, which is supposed to be the bulwark of defense against constraints on discourse and deliberation, closes its mind to the military because of disagreement with its policies and ends.

Thus, we should remember that the presence of ROTC is important because it also puts the military into the university. There are benefits for non-military students that only serve to buttress the argument for ROTC and military-related fields of inquiry. This sentiment may be disconcerting to some but, as we have stressed throughout this book, it is inconsistent with the concept of a liberal education to expect that the process of learning will be marked by comfort alone, or that students will be surrounded only by those who share their opinions, experiences, and aspirations. Learning requires encountering ideas that challenge or expand one's worldview. An appropriate physical and intellectual presence of the military should be encouraged because it can be a source of productive friction on campus that increases the ability of students to see the other side of an ongoing argument or discussion about the military in American society. It is for this reason that the university that takes seriously its mission to provide for civic and liberal education will do well to strive to figure out what constitutes an appropriate military presence on campus rather than excluding the military from campus as a matter of principle.

The trends delineated in this book provide reason for guarded optimism regarding the bridging of the gap that has opened between the military and the university and the society it serves. We hope this book and other projects will serve to further discussion relating to this end.

Index

ABM (Anti-Ballistic Missile) Treaty, 390
Abrams, Richard M., 105
Abu Ghraib, 191
Acheson, Dean, 400
Adamwaite, Anthony, 353
Adas, Michael, 347–8
Afghanistan, 8, 24, 173, 213, 250, 263, 357
  Human Terrain System (HTS), 24
al Qaeda, 3–4, 380
Alabama, 12
All-Volunteer Force (AVF), 6, 11, 15, 18, 78, 81–3, 85, 89, 94, 104, 213, 243, 250, 273, 411
Ambrose, Stephen, 338
American Anthropological Association (AAA), 24
American Civil Liberties Union, 138
American Creed. *See* liberal creed
American Federation of Teachers, 42–3
American Historical Association, 299–300, 303–4
American Historical Review (AHR), 19, 292, 304–5
American Political Science Association (APSA), 21, 44
American Psychiatric Association (APA), 170
American Sociological Association (ASA), 23
Americanism, 73–4
Anderson, Benedict, 378
Anderson, Martin, 85
Angell, Norman, 53
anthropology
  American Anthropological Association (AAA), 24
  involvement in Human Terrain System (HTS), 24
  military studies in, 24, 288
Appelbaum, Yoni, 175, 180–1, 199
Applegate, James, 186–7, 190, 192–3, 195–6, 200, 203, 208, 216–17, 219, 222, 260
Arendt, Hannah, 44, 57
Aristotle, 25, 45, 49, 67, 72, 77, 89, 331
Armed Forces & Society, 23
Armenia, 406
Armstrong, Charles, 336
Army War College, 292, 300, 353
  status of military history at, 371
Aron, Raymond, 366
Association of American Law Schools, 171
Association of NROTC Colleges and Universities, 153
Association of State Universities and Land-Grant Colleges, 78
Atomic Energy Commission (AEC), 122, 124
Augustine, Saint, 25, 49, 368–9
Avramenko, Richard, 275–6, 278, 280
Awn, Peter, 164, 202, 208, 217
Axelrod, Robert, 335–6
Axtel, James, 110

Bacevich, Andrew, 8, 10, 81, 104–5, 270, 276
Baltics, 357
Baptist, Edward, 345
Barash, David P., 373
Barford, Paul, 398
Barney, William L., 348
Barragan, Nico, 200, 218
Bartov, Omar, 333–4

Bass, Gary, 341
Bass, Harold C., 393
Beard, Charles, 110
Bell, David, 293, 322–3, 354
Bennett, Jake, 189
Bensel, Richard Franklin, 110
Benson, George S., 137, 165
Benson Committee, 137, 153
Benson Report, 137, 151
Berghahn, Volker R., 336
Bergovoy, Philip, 180, 182
Berkeley, Bishop George, 379
Berkowitz, Peter, 45–7, 55–6
Berlin, blockade of, 118
Berlin, Isaiah, 117
Berman, Paul, 52, 131, 357
Betts, Richard K., 17–18, 21–2, 210, 337, 371
Bhullar, Iman, 189
Bierce, Ambrose, 59, 271, 295
Big Ten universities, 137, 153
Bird, Austin, 177
Bishop, Morris, 108, 125
Bismarck, Otto von, 96, 128, 232
Bitner, Jack, 165
Black, Jeremi, 291, 297
Blight, David, 342–3
Bloom, Allan, 4, 77, 92–3
Bobbitt, Philip, 233, 251, 364, 407
Bok, Derek, 166, 171
Bollinger, Lee C., 88, 176, 185, 192, 195–6, 202, 207, 209, 217–18, 220, 222–3
Bonker, Dirk, 349–50
Booth, Ken, 372
Bosnia, 14, 194
Boston, 12
Boston University, 166
Bowdoin College, 106
Bracken, Paul, 396
Bradley, Bloch, 197
Brands, H. W., 289, 331
Breslow, Ronald, 220
Brewer, John, 293, 322
Brewster, Kingman, Jr., 142
Brick Murtazashvili, Jennifer, 24
Brinkley, Alan, 196
Britain, 21, 327, 371
Bromley, Daniel W., 378
Brown, Richard C., 299
Brown University, 112, 121, 165–6, 179
  attacks on ROTC at, 141
  in Revolutionary and Civil wars, 107–8
  status of military history at, 333–4
Browning, Reed, 292
Brozak, Steve, 194–5
Brzezinski, Zbigniew, 127
Buckley, William F., 166
Burdick, Charles, 300
Burk, James, 23, 82, 86
Burma, 406
Bush, George W., 351, 399, 407
Bush, Vannevar, 112, 124
Bush administration, 14, 399
Bushell, David, 107
Butler, William Francis, 3
Buzan, Barry, 372–3

Cabanes, Bruno, 342–3
Calhoun, John C., 25, 49
Calley, William, 191
Caltech (California Institute of Technology), 113, 115, 124
Cambodia, 135, 140
Campbell, William V., 217
Canada, 5, 327
Canadian Officer Training Corps (COTC), 5
Carnegie Foundation, 122
Carr, E. H., 366
Carter, Jimmy, 407
Chamberlain, Neville, 407
Chambers, John W., 298, 347–8
Chang, Chun-shu, 334
Chen, Eric, 181–2, 184, 199–200, 202, 223
Cheney, Dick, 10, 171
Chicago, 12
Chicago School, 85
Childers, Thomas, 352
China, 118, 331, 366
Christ, Jesus, 62
Christensen, Thomas J., 340–1
Churchill, Winston, 111, 163
Chwe, Michael, 83
CIA, 107, 113, 132, 146, 152, 389
CIA University, 301
Citadel, the, 78

Citino, Robert M., 292, 294–7, 305, 309, 312
citizenship, 6–7, 9, 18, 25, 28, 30–1, 41–2, 43, 45–7, 49–51, 62, 73, 81–2, 85, 88, 94, 122, 162, 168, 175–6, 200, 219, 233, 240, 251, 260, 269, 272–3, 279, 334, 400, 414
  liberal and republican visions of, 233–5
citizen-soldier ideal, 14, 77, 80–9, 185, 213, 233, 235, 237, 239, 241, 248, 264, 298
  clusterization of society and, 86
  idealist versus realist foundations of, 240
  in motivating military service, 233–5
  liberal versus republican foundations of, 85–6, 88
  non-military students' attitudes toward, 236, 263
  rationale for, 10–11
  realism and, 265
  republican basis of, 82
  warrior ethic and, 83, 89
City College of New York (CCNY), 192
civic and liberal education, 14
  and moral realism, 24–8
  and tensions between Americanism and internationalism, 73–4
  as engagement, 43–5
  as knowledge, 43
civic equality, 6–7
  contributions of ROTC to, 28–31
  defined, 41
  dialectically combined, 45–7
  philosophic education and, 45
civil rights, 7, 175, 184, 190, 193–4
civil rights paradigm, 172, 190, 196, 417
  and gay rights, 169–70
Civil War, American, 19, 59, 81, 84, 110, 233, 271
  Brown's role in, 107–8
  Columbia's role in, 108
  Harvard's role in, 106–7
  Ivy League's role in, 106–8
  Princeton's role in, 107
  Yale's role in, 107
civil–military relations, 8, 14, 34, 88–9, 98, 100, 228, 232–3, 237, 251, 270, 295, 412–14, 421–3
  gap in, 13–18, 92, 94, 179, 193, 199, 223, 231, 236, 249, 274, 414, 422
  ROTC's role in improving, 100–1, 181, 184, 224, 386
  university as microcosm of, 33, 414
Claremont Colleges, 137
Clausewitz, Carl von, 16, 37, 69, 284, 290, 295, 298, 307, 344, 376, 391
Clinton, Bill, 14, 29, 171–2, 192
Clinton administration, 15, 172
clusterization of society, 32, 86, 98, 104
  military as distinct cluster, 32–3, 413
  social clusters defined, 32
Coates, A. J., 97
Coates, Willson H., 283
Coffman, Edward M. (Mac), 268, 285, 287, 300–4, 308, 325–6, 337–8
Cohen, Eliot A., 82, 84
Cohen, William, 13, 15
Cold War, 11, 17–18, 21, 33, 49, 84, 105, 114, 118, 121, 132, 267, 289, 299, 301, 358, 360, 376, 378, 400, 403, 420
Cold War Consensus, 84, 120, 124, 129, 365
Cold War University, 115–16, 118–27, 134, 146, 154, 360, 386, 394, 415, 420
  and security studies, 364–72
  Columbia as a, 126–7
  Cornell as a, 125–6
  early controversies over, 127–30
  Harvard as a, 126
Cole, Joshua, 330–2, 335, 354
Cole, Lewis, 195
Coleman, James, 127
Colombo, Chris, 184
Colonna, Fabrizio, 50
Columbia University, 5, 18, 110, 164, 167, 206–7, 412, 417
  1968 crisis at, 145–6, 152, 154–5
  academic attacks on ROTC at, 149–53
  attacks on ROTC at, 134, 138, 144–60
  Barnard College, 188–9
  Columbia Spectator, 217
  Cox Commission Report, 144, 146, 148, 155–6
  Henkin Committee, 154–6

Columbia University *(cont.)*
  Henkin Report, 154–6
  Institute for Defense Analysis controversy at, 146–7, 152, 154–5
  Law School, 174
  Mansfield Committee, 155, 221
  Mansfield Report, 156–7
  NROTC Awards Ceremony demonstrations at, 148–9
  role as Cold War University, 126–7
  role in Revolutionary and Civil wars, 108
  role in World War I, 110
  role in World War II, 114–15
  ROTC movement at, 180–5
  ROTC's return to, 221–5
  ROTC's return to, incremental steps toward, 199–201
  ROTC's reversal of fortunes at, 208–12
  September 11 and drive to reinstate ROTC at, 175–9
  status of military history at, 336–7
  Students for a Democratic Society at, 144–8
  Task Force on Military Engagement at, 110, 208, 211–21
  Task Force on ROTC at, 175, 185–97
  Union Theological Seminary (UTS), 97, 186
Communism, 21, 84, 116, 118, 150, 366, 406
Compton, Karl, 388
Conant, James Bryant, 111–13, 119, 126, 416
Condorcet's jury theorem, 90
Congress, 7, 10, 17, 80, 82, 119, 129, 163, 168, 172, 174, 215
  House of Representatives, 15, 204
  Senate, 15, 204
Congressional Budget Office, 392
Connelley, Matthew, 336
Constitution, American, 43, 47, 56, 70, 80, 88, 117, 213
  Article II of, 117
  First Amendment to, 31, 43, 89, 172, 174, 176, 413, 415
  Fourteenth Amendment to, 204
  Second Amendment to, 80
constructivism, 272, 294, 358, 360, 375, 377–80, 401, 403, 407, 420–1
  and realism in security studies, 21–2
  at Ohio State, 403
  central tenets of, 377
  human nature and, 330–1, 361
  relationship with idealism, 377
  status in IR (TRIP survey), 382–3
  status in security studies, 385
  theories of change and, 378
Cooper, John, 285, 337–9
Cordier, Andrew W., 147, 156, 158
Cornell University, 106, 121, 133, 138, 165, 229, 352
  attacks on ROTC at, 139
  role as Cold War University, 125–6
  role in World War I, 108–9
Cosby, Bill, 286
Coumbe, Arthur T., 111
Craig, Gordon, 298
Crane, Stephen, 59, 271
creedal passion, battles of, 31–2, 43, 46, 91, 102, 412, *See also* liberal creed; Soldier's Creed
  at Columbia, 175–6
Cullather, Nick, 346
Cumings, Bruce, 344
Czechoslovakia, 118

Darfur, 406
Dartmouth College, 106, 121, 135
  attacks on ROTC at, 134–8
  role in World War II, 114
Dayton Accords, 29
Declaration of Independence, 107
Delbruck, Hans, 295, 298
DeLuca, Paul, 398
democratic peace, 51, 53, 376–8, 406–7
Department of Defense (DoD), 24, 122, 137, 140, 156, 158, 160, 166–7, 171, 173–4, 183, 205, 314, 389
Department of the Navy, 149, 151
Desch, Michael, 33, 86
Detroit, 12
Dewey, John, 110
Dickenson, Frederick, 352
Dickinson, Emily, 59, 271
Diman, D. L., 108, 112

diversity theory, 32–3, 413–14
Dobbs, Darrell, 45
Dodds, Harold W., 121
Dols, Monique, 190
Dominican Republic, 148
Don't Ask, Don't Tell (DADT), 34, 50, 91–2, 101, 163, 171, 178–9, 184, 186–8, 190, 192–4, 196–7, 199, 200, 202–9, 211, 214–16, 222–4, 229, 233, 250, 412, 417. *See also* gay rights movement and military; Solomon Amendment
  campus opposition to, 99
  law schools' opposition to, 171–5
  recruitment and, 171–5
Douglas, Mary, 61
Dow Chemical Company, 152
Dower, John, 293, 322, 344
Dowling, Brian M., 87
Downs, Donald, 95–6, 144, 183, 398
Doyle, Lyman, 189
Doyle, Michael, 337
draft, peacetime, 6
Dreyfus, Lee S., 78
Duby, Paul, 185, 193
Duke University, 286, 327, 349
  security studies at, 349
  status of military history at, 350–2
Duquesne University, 66
Dylan, Bob, 133, 208

Egypt, 213
Ehrenreich, Barbara, 276
Einstein, Alfred, 53
Eisenhower, Dwight D., 9, 16, 72, 98, 124, 129
Elish, Madeleine, 215
Elliot, William Yandell, 123
Emerson, Ralph Waldo, 81
Emerson, Thomas, 56
Engerman, David, 115, 124
England, 293
Eralp, Feride, 209
ethical realism. *See* moral realism
Evangelista, Matthew, 346

FARC (Revolutionary Armed Forces of Colombia), 357
fascism, 33, 111, 394
Faust, Drew G., 59, 203–7
Fearon, James, 377
Feingold, Russ, 9
Feldmeier, Elizabeth, 179
Ferguson, Adam, 81
Ferguson, Niall, 293, 322
First Amendment, 31, 43, 89, 172, 174, 176, 413, 415
Fitzgerald, F. Scott, 133
Fletcher, George, 67
Foner, Eric, 210
Foote, Learned, 200, 209, 223
Ford Foundation, 122, 127
Fordham University, 168, 177–8, 182, 192, 220
Forum for Academic and Institutional Rights (FAIR), 174
Foucault, Michel, 331
Founding Fathers. *See* Framers, American
Fourteenth Amendment, 204
Fox, William T. R., 158
Framers, American, 27, 48, 362, 368, 375, 380
France, 107
  Napoleonic, 376
Frankfurt School, 374
French, Shannon, 16, 66
French Revolution, 293
Freud, Sigmund, 53, 368, 374
Friedberg, Aaron, 341–2
Friedman, Milton, 85
Friedman, Robert, 144
Frommer, Benjamin, 354
Fukuyama, Francis, 53
Fussell, Paul, 250

G. I. Bill (Servicemen's Readjustment Act) (1944), 118
G. I. Bill (Veterans Educational Assistance Act) (2008), 164
Gaddis, John Lewis, 342–3, 395–6
Galanter, Eugene, 185
Galil, Zvi, 185
Galston, William A., 41, 45, 50, 81
Galtung, John, 373
Garrison State, 120, 129

Gastwirth, David, 351
Gat, Azar, 53, 330
Gates, Robert, 205
gay rights movement and military. *See also* civil rights paradigm: and gay rights; Don't Ask, Don't Tell (DADT); Solomon Amendment
Geiger, Roger, 389
Gelernter, David, 12, 61
Gelven, Michael, 29, 40, 62, 70–3, 276
Georgetown University, 393
German militarism, 387
Germany, 52, 370, 376, 406
  Nazi, 372
  Weimar Republic, 56
Geyer, Michael, 344
Gitlin, Todd, 210
Glaathaar, Joseph, 348–9
Glazer, Nathan, 127
Glendon, Mary Ann, 56
Glick, Edward Bernard, 23
Gluck, Carol, 336
Goehr, Lydia, 220
Goheen, Robert F., 140
Goldstein, Avery, 353
Gordon, Bette, 219
Graske, Ted, 65, 182–3, 203, 217
Grassey, Thomas B., 65, 67
Gray, J. Glenn, 57–9, 64, 66, 276
Gray Commission, 119
Greece, Ancient, 331
Greely, Reverend Andrew, 149
Greenwich Village, 169
Grimsley, Mark, 286, 297
Griswold, A. Whitney, 394
Gross, Jan, 340–1
Grossman, Dave, 191
group-think, 30, 34, 90, 92–3, 253
Guantanamo, 399
Guilmartin, John, 404
Gulags, 406
Gutman, Eric, 184

Haan, Phil, 267–8
Habeck, Mary, 343
Habermas, Jürgen, 20
Hackey, Shane, 184
Hadley, Arthur, 109
Hagemann, Karen, 348, 350
Haiti, 14, 191, 194
Hale, Nathan, 107
Hall, John, 268–9, 271–2, 274, 337–9, 398–9, 419–20
Hamilton, Alexander, 108
Hamilton, Lee, 9
Hamlet, 83, 223
Hanson, Victor Davis, 276
Harford, Lee S., 111
Hartwell, Sarah, 114
Hartz, Louis, 69
Harvard University, 5, 50–1, 71, 106, 115, 119–20, 122, 124, 126, 136, 171, 198, 202, 206, 219, 267–8, 389, 400–1, 412
  attacks on ROTC at, 138, 142–4
  Don't Ask, Don't Tell and ROTC at, 203–7
  Harvard College, 49–50
  Harvard Crimson, 206
  Harvard Regiment, 106
  Law School, 172–4
  return of ROTC through back door at, 166–7
  role as Cold War University, 126
  role in Revolutionary and Civil wars, 106–7
  role in World War II, 111–13
  ROTC and gay rights movement at, 166–7
  ROTC movement at, 183
Hawkins, Cameron, 344
Hedge, Chris, 276
Hegel, Georg Wilhelm Friedrich, 63, 300, 364
Helfand, David J., 210–11
Hemingway, Ernest, 59, 271
Henkin, Louis, 154
Herman, Richard, 403
Hibben, John Grier, 121
Higginbotham, Don, 350
Higham, Robin, 300
higher practicality, 25–6, 49, 68, 226, 359, 390, 393, 395–6, 421
Hill, Charles, 395–6
Hirsch, E. D., 41
Hirschman, Albert O., 375
Hitler, Adolf, 111, 357, 407

Hobbes, Thomas, 69, 122, 272–4, 356, 363, 367–9
Hodges, Albert G., 117
Holbrooke, Richard C., 29
Holmes, Oliver Wendell, 106
Holquist, Peter, 345, 352
Homer, 77
Hook, Sidney, 201
Hopf, Theodore, 403
Hormat, Robert D., 85
Horowitz, Michael, 353
Hovde, Carl V., 159
Howard, Michael, 343
Howell, William, 340
Hoy, Patrick C., 71, 98, 276
Hull, Isabel, 345
Human Terrain System (HTS), 24, 381
Hundred Years' War, 19, 379
Huntington, Samuel P., 14, 16, 18, 22, 30–1, 33, 46, 68–70, 77, 91, 98, 237, 239–40, 297, 362, 380, 390, 401, 412–13

idealism, 47, 52, 361, 374
  liberal internationalism and, 363
  relationship with citizen-soldier ideal, 240
  relationship with constructivism, 377
  tensions with realism, 27, 240, 363–4
Ienaga, Saburo, 344
Ikenberry, G. John, 341–2
India, 74, 220, 331
Institute for Defense Analysis (IDA), 126
  controversy at Columbia, 146–7, 152, 154–5
international relations (IR), theory and subdiscipline of, 21–2, 29, 55, 276, 319, 334, 336–7, 340, 346–7, 353, 356–80, 407. *See also* constructivism; liberal IR theory; realism; security dilemma; security studies
  rational choice approaches to, 369
  TRIP survey in, 382–4, 387
Inter-University Seminar (IUS) on Armed Forces and Society, 22–3
Iran, 357, 406
Iraq War, 8, 14, 24, 86, 184, 191, 194, 250, 263, 278, 402
Isaac, Jeffrey, 21, 49
Israel, 189, 191
Ivy League universities, 5, 82, 120, 129, 173, 175, 180, 202, 204, 206
  attacks on ROTC at, 138–59
  back door reinstatement of ROTC at, 165–8
  role in Cold War, 124–7
  role in Revolutionary and Civil wars, 106–8
  role in World War I, 108–11
  role in World War II, 111–15

Jackson, Kenneth T., 324, 336
Janis, Irving L., 93
Janowitz, Morris, 9, 14, 17–18, 22–3, 86, 237
Japan, 372
Japanese militarism, 387
Jarausch, Konrad, 350
Jefferson, Thomas, 67
Jervis, Robert, 337
Jian, Chen, 345
Jin, Ha, 344
Joas, Hans, 20
Johns Hopkins University, 323–4, 354
Johnson, Lyndon, 129, 148
Johnson, Michael, 354
Johnson, Samuel, 293, 379
Johnson administration, 133
Jones, Jeffrey Owen, 133
Journal of American History (JAH), 302–4, 321, 325–6. *See also Mississippi Valley Historical Review*
Journal of Military History, 19, 288
just war, 54, 95, 97–8, 186, 214, 251, 265

Kaba, Moez, 190
Kaegi, Walter, 344
Kagan, Donald, 294, 342–3
Kagan, Elena, 173
Kagan, Frederick, 285
Kagan, Kimberly, 396–7
Kagan, Robert, 363
Kalyvas, Stathis, 343
Kansas State University, 300
Kant, Immanuel, 62, 64, 122, 363, 371, 375

Kaplan, Robert, 298
Karsten, Peter, 165, 226
Kassamali, Sumayya, 214–15
Katznelson, Ira, 210
Kautilya, 367
Keegan, John, 67, 376
Kelley, Brooks Mather, 107
Kelley, Roger T., 157–8, 160
Kennan, George F., 366, 400
Kennedy, David, 354
Kennedy, Paul, 113, 302, 342–3, 394–7
Kent State University
  attacks on ROTC at, 134
  National Guard shooting at, 135, 166
Khademian, Anne M., 20
King, Martin Luther, Jr., 46
Kirk, Grayson, 126, 146–7, 149–51, 155–6
Kirshner, Jonathan, 346
Kissinger, Henry, 122–4, 126, 401
Kitchen, Martin, 387
Kohn, Richard, 286, 329, 348–50
Korean War, 84, 114, 116, 118–21, 366, 389
Kors, Alan, 332, 353
Kosovo, 14, 52, 357
Krebs, Ronald R., 83, 85, 89, 233–4, 240–1
Kreps, Sarah, 346
Kronman, Anthony, 58–60, 275
Krylova, Anna, 350
Kuklick, Bruce, 352–3
Kuniholm, Bruce R., 350
Kuran, Timur, 135, 144, 221
Kusch, Polykarp, 159
Kuwait, 372
Kwong, Jeff, 73–4
Kydd, Andy, 340

Laird, Melvin, 137, 140, 153, 155–6, 158
Lamphear, John, 354
Largigue, Louis, 393
Lasch, Christopher, 81
Lazarsfield, Paul E., 127
League of Nations, 407
LeBoeuf, Joseph, 351
Lee, Wayne E., 291–2, 294–8, 301, 303, 309, 321, 332, 348–50
Lefebrve, Georges, 283
Leitch, Alexander, 121
Lenin, Vladimir, 373
Leninism, 373
Levin, Matthew, 122
Levin, Richard C., 205
Levy, Jack, 348
Lewis, Adrian R., 84, 86, 105, 132, 273
Lewis, Harry R., 49–50, 66, 73–4
liberal creed, 46. *See also* creedal passion, battles of; Soldier's Creed
liberal democracy, moral difficulties in, 68
liberal IR theory, 360–4, 375–7, 382
  democratic peace and, 376
  idealist variant of, 361, 363
  neoliberal variant of, 363, 376, 385, 420–1
liberalism, 219
  role of discipline in preserving, 55–7
  tensions with military mind, 68–9
  tensions with republicanism, 85–6, 228, 233–5
Lincoln, Abraham, 3, 19, 117, 293, 356
Linn, Brian, 338–9
Linz, Juan, 127
Lipset, Seymour Martin, 127
Locke, John, 69
Log Cabin Republicans, 204
Logevall, Fredrik, 345
Los Angeles, 12
Lotkin, Roger, 348
Lovejoy, Doug, 165, 183
Lovett, Robert A., 342
Lovinsky, Joseph, 181
Lowe, Jim, 180, 182
Luhmann, Niklas, 20
Lyall, Jay, 341
Lynn, John A., 19–20, 287, 292–4, 296–9, 303–9, 321, 337, 354, 358
Lyons, Gene M., 357, 365, 388, 400

Mabus, Ray, 202
Macdonald, Dwight, 144

Machiavelli, Niccolò, 10, 50–2, 57, 117, 295, 367–9, 374
Machiavellianism, 27, 47
Madison, James, 28, 57, 330, 346
Mahan, Alfred Thayer, 112
Manhattan College, 168
Manhattan Project, 112, 115, 124, 388
Manning, Chandra, 341
Mansfield, Edward, 353
Mansfield, Harvey C., 142, 155–6
Mansoor, Peter, 402–3
Mao, Zedong, 118
Marrs, Theodore, 153
Marshall, George C., 16, 111, 126, 132
Marshall Plan, 126
Marx, Karl, 25, 49, 133
Mathewson, Tom, 185
Mawn, Paul, 183, 207
May, Ernest, 173
Mayer, Kenneth R., 20
Mazor, Ron, 208, 216
Mazur, Diane H., 101, 161, 163
McAuliffe, Joshua, 398
McCain, John, 201
McCarthyism, 124, 415–16
McCaughey, Robert A., 110, 127
McChrystal, Stanley, 104, 178, 421–2
McClelland, John, 178, 200–1, 213
McCoy, W. J., 348
McDonald, David, 338–9
McDougal, Wally, 352
McKnight, N. M., 149
McMahon, Robert, 403
McPherson, James M., 19, 107, 293, 324, 340–1
Mead, Lawrence, 49
Mearsheimer, John, 344–5
Meiklejohn, Alexander, 56, 59
Melville, Herman, 59, 271
Mershon, Ralph D., 400
Mettler, Suzanne, 118
Meyer, Ilan, 191
Michigan State University
  attacks on ROTC at, 134
Miles, Paul, 340–1
militarism, 8–10, 33, 48, 62, 69, 92–3, 148, 186, 210, 214, 262, 270, 288, 298, 376, 387, 394. *See also* German militarism; Japanese militarism
  new American variant of, 8
military, status in social sciences, 24
  anthropology, 24
  military sociology, 22–3
  political science, 20–2, 316–18
  psychology, 22
  sociology, 23
military and gay rights movement, 169–71
military and universities, basic differences between, 7–8
military and war, *sui generis* nature of, 60, 64, 242, 264, 271, 277–9
military history, 34, 48
  academic approaches to, 292–8
  alternative approaches to, 288–90
  anthropological approaches to, 288
  applied (or operational) approaches to, 291–2
  cultural approaches to, 288, 294–6
  definitional issues, 290–8
  diplomatic approaches to, 289
  economic approaches to, 289
  feminist and gender studies approaches to, 289
  history of science and technology approaches to, 289–90
  peace studies approaches to, 288
  political science approaches to, 290
  popular approaches to, 290–1
  psychological approaches to, 290
  recent skirmishes over, 285–8
  sociological approaches to, 290
  student responses to UW course in, 268–75
  traditional versus new approaches to, 294, 419–20
military history, status in security studies, 385–7
  at MIT, 391
  at Ohio State, 402–4
  at University of Wisconsin, 397–400
  at Yale, 397
military history, status of, 18–20, 283–319, 418–20
  at Brown University, 333–4
  at Columbia, 336–7
  at Cornell, 329

military history, status of *(cont.)*
at Duke, 350–2
at Indiana University, 346–7
at Northwestern, 354
at Princeton, 340–2
at Rutgers, 347–8
at Stanford, 354
at top history departments, 320–55
qualitative findings, 327–33
quantitative findings, 321–7
at University of California, Berkeley, 353
at University of California, Los Angeles, 354
at University of Chicago, 344–5
at University of Michigan, 334–6
at University of North Carolina, 348–50
at University of Pennsylvania, 353
at University of Wisconsin, 337–40
at Yale, 342–3
historical trends in, 298–302
in political science, 316–19
recent surveys of, 302–5
survey of historians' assessment of, 305–16
traditional versus new approaches to, 298, 309–13, 318–19, 324, 329, 331–2
military presence on campus, benefits of. *See also* ROTC presence on campus, benefits of
educating officers, 99–100
educating public about military, 100
enhancing civic education, 47–57
enhancing liberal education, 57–62
illuminating moral difficulties in liberal democracies, 62–8
improving civil–military relations, 100–1
promoting courage, 72
promoting intellectual and moral diversity, 68–74
promoting leadership, 100, 421–2
providing cheaper education for officers, 99
military presence on campus, objections to, 97–9
government and military control of ROTC, 99
opposition to Don't Ask, Don't Tell, 99
opposition to militarism, 97–8
tensions between liberal and military education, 98–9
military presence on campus, theoretical justification for, 89–96
military professionalism, 8, 16, 18, 33, 68, 77, 82, 87–8, 231, 413
military sociology, 22–3, 64, 296, 390
military's absence from campus, consequences of
constitutional and educational implications, 8–11
ignorance of military, 9–10
military's sense of moral superiority, 10
negative perceptions of military, 9
uncritical support of military, 8–9
military–civil relations. *See* civil–military relations
military-industrial complex, 9, 124, 128–9
military-industrial-academic complex, 20
military–university relations, gap in, 3–13
Mill, John Stuart, 40, 55, 89, 232, 266
Miller, Cheryl, 12
Miller, John J., 285–6, 297, 326, 338
Miller, Kenneth R., Jr., 396
Miller, Mary, 205
Miller, Richard F., 106
Millet, Allan, 300
Millis, Walter, 80
Mills, C. Wright, 129
Milosevic, Slobodan, 29, 357
Minerva Initiative, 381–2
Minutemen, 81
Mississippi Valley Historical Review, 303–4. *See also Journal of American History* (JAH)
MIT, 113, 115, 124, 166–7, 180, 206, 207, 267, 321, 421
security studies at, 388–93, 397
Security Studies Program at, 388–93
Mobley, Scott, 397–8
Mohr, Jay, 196–7
Montas, Roosevelt, 208, 216
Moody-Adams, Michele, 213–14
moral realism, 4, 374, 408
Morgenthau, Hans, 4, 25–6, 28, 49, 58, 68, 226, 240, 331, 359, 361,

362–70, 374, 380–1, 390, 394–6, 421, *See also* higher practicality
Morosani, Dan, 212
Morrill Act, 79, 100, 108–9
Morrow, James D., 336
Morton, Louis, 299–300, 302, 357, 365, 388, 400
Moskos, Charles, 23, 82, 233, 272
Mueller, John, 402–3
Muir, William Ker, 63–5
Mullen, Mike, 203
Murphy, Bill, Jr., 250
My Lai massacre, 13, 100, 191
Myrdal, Gunnar, 46

Naiden, Fred, 348, 350
NASA, 122
National Defense Act (NDA), 79, 100, 106, 108–9, 122
National Defense Education Act (NDEA), 157
National Defense Research Committee (NDRC), 112, 388
National Defense University, 21
National Guard, 84, 106, 135, 240, 254, 267
  shooting at Kent State, 135, 166
National Institutes of Health (NIH), 122, 126
National Science Foundation (NSF), 122
National Security Council, 123
NATO, 14, 29, 366, 376, 406
Naughton, Joe, 178
Naval War College, 334
Nazism, 116
Neiberg, Michael S., 79, 106, 120, 128, 134–6, 153, 160
neoliberal institutionalism, 363, 376, 385, 420–1. *See also* soft power
neorealism, 363, 366–7, 372–3, 421
Neuschel, Kristin, 350
New York, 12, 178–9, 218
New York University
  School of Law, 174
Niebuhr, Reinhold, 4, 26–7, 47, 52, 62, 111, 274, 366, 368–70, 399
Nietzsche, Friedrich, 62, 66, 70–1, 89, 231, 276, 298, 374
Nitze, Paul, 123
Nixon, Richard, 85, 134–5, 140
Nixon administration, 159
Nora, Pierre, 296
North, Douglass C., 378
North Carolina State University, 349
North Korea, 118, 406
Northwestern University, 23, 329, 337, 355
  status of military history at, 354
Norwich University, 78, 138
Novick, Peter, 326–7
Nuremberg trials, 210
Nussbaum, Martha, 30

Obama, Barack, 7, 15, 104, 201–2, 204, 208, 399
Obama administration, 357, 399, 421
Office of Chief of Military History, 301
Office of Naval Research, 122, 392
Office of Production Management, 301
Office of Scientific Research and Development (OSRD), 105, 114
Office of Strategic Research and Development, 388
Office of Strategic Services (OSS), 301
Officer Candidate School, 99, 111, 168, 191, 237–8
O'Gorman, Kate, 200
O'Halloran, Sharyn, 215, 219
Ohio State University, 286, 300, 321, 421
  Ralph D. Mershon Center at, 400–5
  security studies at, 400–5
Ohlin, David, 67
Olds, Kristopher, 398
O'Neill, William L., 144, 347–8
Oppenheimer, J. Robert, 113, 124
Organization of American Historians (OAH), 304, 326
Ortega y Gasset, José, 6–7, 25, 411
Ouellet, Eric, 23, 64, 296, 390

pacifism, 3–4, 7, 97–8, 105, 134, 406
Page, Scott E., 32–3, 90–2, 238, 251, 413
Pakistan, 357
Panama, 191
Pape, Robert, 344–5
Paret, Peter, 300, 354

Parker, Geoffrey, 293, 343, 403
Parker, Kevin "Kit", 206–7
Patz, Jonathan, 398
Paul, Saint, 67
Paxton, Pamela, 403
Peace and Conflict Journal of Peace Psychology, 290
Peace Corps, 207
peace studies, 68, 288, 358, 373–4, 386
Pearl Harbor, 111, 115
Pennsylvania State University, 300
Pentagon, 165, 173, 351, 392
Peters, Ralph, 83
Petraeus, David H., 16, 83, 178, 402
Pevehouse, Jon, 340, 398
Pew Research Center for People and the Press, 42
Philadelphia, 12
Piereson, James, 36, 230
Piergrossi, Todd, 393
Plato, 25, 49, 66, 72, 331
political realism, 361, 383
political science, 11, 20–2, 25, 49, 60, 181, 230, 251, 257, 277, 290, 295, 319, 334–5, 337, 342–4, 347–8, 352–3, 368, 371, 387, 389–91, 393, 400, 403, 405, 419. *See also* constructivism; international relations (IR), theory and subdiscipline of; liberal IR theory; realism
  American Political Science Association, 21, 44
  "Romance of War" course at University of Wisconsin, 275–8
  status of military history in, 284, 316–19
Posen, Barry, 390–2
positive feedback, 46
postmodernism, 21, 58, 373–4
poststructuralism, 20, 58
Powell, Colin, 69
Powell Doctrine, 69
Prague, 123
Princeton University, 106, 120–1, 138, 141, 160, 165, 217–18, 229, 300, 394
  attacks on ROTC at, 139–40
  Battle of Princeton, 107
  new ROTC movement at, 183
  role in Revolutionary and Civil wars, 107
  role in World War I, 110
productive friction, 14, 31, 33–4, 43, 71, 80, 89, 94, 96, 212, 219, 224, 226–8, 230, 232, 238, 242, 245, 252, 254, 257–60, 262, 266, 274, 278, 280, 309, 319, 333, 351, 355, 358, 385–8, 393–4, 397, 408, 412–13, 418, 422–3
Providence College, 141
Prussia, 52, 376
psychology, 290, 379
Purdue University, 19
Pusey, Nathan, 126, 143
Putin, Vladimir, 407

Quantico, 177
Quigley, Austin, 185

Raaflaub, Kurt, 333
Rashid, Fahmida Y., 198
Rasler, Karen, 347
rational choice, 370
Rauch, Jonathan, 94
Rawls, John, 54
  veil of ignorance, 54–5
Reagan, Ronald, 134, 259
realism, 21–2, 27, 97, 111, 123, 236–7, 239, 244, 272–3, 294, 299, 358–9, 366–8, 375–8, 380, 383, 391, 394, 401, 405–8, 420–1
  and constructivism in security studies, 21–2
  austere variant of, 240
  challenges to, during '60s, 371–2
  civic/liberal education and moral variant of, 24–8
  classical variant of, 366, 370, 373, 391, 407
  conservative variant of, 69, 239, 265
  core tenets of, 367–8
  human nature and, 330–1, 369–70
  importance of, in security studies, 360
  moral variant of, 226, 374, 408
  neorealist variant of, 367

political variant of, 358–9, 361–2
practical knowledge and, 22
relationship with citizen-soldier ideal, 240, 265
role in security studies during Cold War, 364–72
status in IR (TRIP survey), 382–3
status in security studies, 408
tensions with constructivism, 407
tensions with idealism, 27, 240, 363–4
theories of change and, 379
recognition, drive for, 94, 162, 170, 179, 184, 313, 364
recognition of military, ROTC role in fostering, 95, 238–9
Reed, Roy, 71
relativism, 67
Reppy, Judith, 346
republicanism, 17, 82, 238, 240
as basis for citizen-soldier ideal, 82
tensions with liberalism, 85–6, 233–5
return of the soldier on campus, 11, 34, 103, 138, 165
Revolutionary War, American, 19, 83, 130, 233, 270
Brown's role in, 107–8
Columbia's role in, 108
Harvard's role in, 106–7
Ivy League's role in, 106–8
Princeton's role in, 107
Yale's role in, 107
revolutionary wars, European, 19
Rhodes, Edward, 348
Ricks, Thomas, 15–16, 95, 104, 179, 274
Riga, 123
Robbins, Bruce W., 210
Robinson, Eric Wild, 346
Robledo, Jose, 71, 200, 202–3, 206, 216–18, 223, 225
Rockefeller Foundation, 122, 125, 127
Roland, Alex, 349–50, 365
Rome, 344
Roosevelt, Franklin, 105
Roosevelt, Theodore, 303
Rosen, Stephen, 198
Rosenblatt, Roger, 143–4
ROTC (Reserve Officer Training Corps)
Cadet Commands and, 136, 168
regional distribution of recruits, 11–12
status at elite and non-elite universities, 12–13
university attacks on, 134–8
ROTC presence on campus, benefits of. *See also* military presence on campus, benefits of
educating students about war and national security, 270–2
fostering citizenship, 272–3
fostering recognition of military, 95, 231, 238–9
illuminating aspects of human nature, 268–78
illuminating moral difficulties in liberal democracies, 239, 264, 274
promoting intellectual and moral diversity, 237–8, 241, 248–50, 262, 265
ROTC presence on campus, surveys on
civilian students' attitudes toward ROTC, 252–4
experience of ROTC students, 233–52
importance of ROTC presence, 241
motivations for joining ROTC, 254–5
perceptions of ROTC status, 254–5
positive effects of ROTC, 247–9
ROTC Vitalization Act, 128–9, 150
Roth-Douquet, Kathy, 12, 179
Rotsker, Bernard, 85
Roy, Rob, 5
Rudd, Mark, 131, 145–6, 198, 224
Rumsfeld, Donald, 14
Rusellai, Cosimo, 50
Russian military, civilian control of, 33
Rutgers College, 136
Rutgers University, 217
security studies at, 348
status of military history at, 347–8
Rwanda, 372, 406

Sachsenmaier, Dominic, 350
Sambanis, Nicholas, 343
Samet, Elizabeth D., 60–1
San Jose State University, 205
Sandholm, William H., 135
Santa Clara University, 205
Santayana, George, 29, 48
Sapolsky, Harvey, 94, 392

Sayre, Robert, 16
Schaeffer, Frank, 12, 179
Schelling, Thomas, 401
Schlesinger, Arthur, Jr., 120
Schmidt, Gary, 12
scholasticism, 25, 49
Schuck, Peter H., 174
Schultz, Kenneth A., 375
Seaton, Jennifer, 114
security dilemma, 55, 363
security studies, 21–2, 48, 301, 317, 319, 321, 333–4, 350, 356–80, 381–408, 419
  as source of productive friction, 358
  at Columbia, 337
  at Cornell, 346
  at Duke, 349–50
  at MIT, 388–93, 397
  at North Carolina State, 349
  at Ohio State, 400–5
  at Princeton, 341
  at Rutgers, 348
  at University of Chicago, 344
  at University of North Carolina, 349
  at University of Pennsylvania, 353
  at University of Wisconsin, 340, 397–400
  at Yale, 343, 393–7
  challenges to, during '60s, 371–2
  Cold War University, political realism and, 364–72
  constructivist approaches to, 21–2, 377–80, 385, 407
  critical approaches to, 374–5, 385
  importance of diverse viewpoints in, 359–60
  importance of political realism in, 360
  liberal approaches to, 375–7
  liberal versus realist approaches to, 85–6
  neoliberal approaches to, 385
  neorealist approaches to, 363, 373
  new models in, 372–80
  peace studies approaches to, 373–4
  pedagogy, military knowledge and, 359–60
  realist approaches to, 21–2, 408
  role of military in, 358–9, 385–7
  status of, 21–2, 34, 384, 387
  status of military history in, 317, 319, 359, 385–7, 391–2, 397, 402
  status of, in history departments, 307, 313–15, 319, 329, 333
Segal, David R., 15, 23
Segal, Mickey, 203, 217
Seidman, Gay, 167
Selective Service, 132
Selective Service Act (SSA), 119–20
September 11, 3, 5, 53, 82, 131, 138, 165–6, 175, 181, 197, 417
  impact of, on campus attitudes toward ROTC, 172–3
service academies, 238
Servicemen's Readjustment Act. *See* G. I. Bill (1944)
Seymour, Charles, 113
Shakespeare, William, 61
Shane, Peter M., 166
Shapiro, Jake, 341
Shaw, Martin, 290
Sherry, Michael, 335, 354
Shibusawa, Nakao, 334
Showalter, Dennis E., 292
Shy, John, 293, 297, 300, 312, 322, 334
Silver, Allan, 6, 93, 103, 129, 145, 147, 170, 175, 189, 195–6, 200, 203, 207, 210, 217, 222, 224, 273, 417
Silverstein, Samuel, 196
Singer, David, 336
Sinno, Abdulkader, 347
Skowronek, Stephen, 109
Slauenwhite, Timothy A., 72
Smith, Adam, 81
Smith, Gaddis, 109, 141
Smith, Richard Norton, 112
Snyder, Jack, 337
Society for Military History, 287, 327
sociology, 11, 22–3, 290, 296, 390
  American Sociological Association, 23
  Armed Forces & Society, 23
  Inter-University Seminar (IUS) on Armed Forces and Society, 23
  military sociology, 64
Socrates, 30, 45, 62, 331
soft power, 29, 52–3, 251, 317, 360, 363, 385
Soldier's Creed, 16, 73
  new and old versions of, 16, 244

warrior ethic and, 16
solipsism, 44
Solomon Amendment, 172–4, 193, 250
Somalia, 14, 393
South Korea, 118
South Vietnam, 129, 134
Southern Connecticut College, 142
Soviet Union, 11, 14, 21, 49, 116, 118, 122–3, 134, 366, 407
Sparrow, James, 344
Sputnik, 122
Spykman, Nicholas J., 393–4
Stam, Allan, 336
Stanford University, 5, 124, 165–6, 173, 180, 204–5, 300
status of military history at, 354
Stanton, Jessica, 353
Stark, John, 341
State Department, 113, 123
State University of New York, Buffalo
attacks on ROTC at, 134
Stephanson, Anders, 336
Stoff, Michael, 354
Strategic Defense Initiatives (SDI), 390
Strauss, Barry, 329, 345
Student Army Training Corps (SATC), 108–10
Students for a Democratic Society (SDS), 127, 131, 141–2, 144–8, 155, 210
Summers, Lawrence, 50, 166, 173
Sun Tzu, 298, 367
Supreme Court, 31, 43, 170, 173–4, 413
Suri, Jeremi, 122, 124, 337–9, 357, 397–9

Taliban, 357
Tan, Tao, 200, 216, 218–19
Tarcov, Nathan, 344
Tarr, David, 300–1
Tassel, Janet, 103
Taylor, Tom, 351
Temple University, 300, 352
terrorism, 18, 24, 29, 51, 53, 179, 251, 265, 345, 383, 399, 403, 407
Texas A&M University, 36, 229, 286, 300, 338
Third Amendment, 117
Thirty Years' War, 19
Thomas, Kendall, 190, 193–5, 197
Thomas Aquinas, Saint, 95
Thompson, William R., 347
Thorpe, Jennifer, 184
Thucydides, 21, 48, 57, 299, 365, 367–8, 418
Tillman, Pat, 422
Tishler, William P., 397
Tocqueville, Alexis de, 44, 56, 88, 170
Tolstoy, Leo, 201, 320
Tonkin Gulf Resolution, 129
totalitarianism, 112
Trilling, Lionel, 145
TRIP (Teaching, Research, and International Policy) survey, 382–4, 387
Trotsky, Leon, 330
Truman, David B., 133, 145–6, 149–52, 154
Truman, Harry, 87, 119
Trynosky, Stephen, 16, 105

United States Military Academy, 115
United States Naval Academy, 110
Universal Military Training (UMT), 119
University of California, Berkeley, 124, 127, 205, 314
attacks on ROTC at, 135
status of military history at, 353
University of California, Los Angeles
status of military history at, 354
University of Chicago, 23, 124, 126, 354, 389
status of military history at, 344–5
University of Illinois, 124, 153, 300, 304–5, 355
University of Kansas, 286
University of Maryland, 23
University of Michigan, 23, 124, 129, 153, 300, 302, 324, 326, 355
status of military history at, 334–6
University of New Hampshire, 178
University of New Haven, 142
University of North Carolina, 286, 327, 329, 337, 352, 403
status of military history at, 348–50

University of Pennsylvania, 165, 332
  attacks on ROTC at, 138–9
  Law School, 174
  role in World War I, 111
  status of military history at, 332
University of Pittsburgh, 66, 291
University of Texas, 354
University of Virginia, 352
University of Wisconsin, Madison, 4, 35–6, 49–50, 56, 59, 70, 87, 95, 124, 137, 153, 226, 228, 254–5, 285, 300–2, 326, 329, 332, 355, 397, 401, 417, 419
  Badger Herald, 265
  civilian student surveys at, 257–67
  Grand Strategy Program at, 397–400, 421
  reasons for conducting surveys at, 228–30
  ROTC surveys at, 233–55
  security studies at, 397–400
  status of military history at, 337–40
  student responses to military history course at, 268–75
  student responses to "Romance of War" course at, 268–78
Updike, John, 103

Van Evera, Stephen, 25, 390, 392–3, 406
Veterans Educational Assistance Act. *See* G. I. Bill (2008)
Vietnam War, 5, 10, 15, 19–20, 22, 78, 81–2, 84–5, 94, 100–1, 104–5, 116, 120, 128–9, 131, 146, 148–9, 154, 157, 159–60, 164, 168, 173, 175, 198, 213–14, 219, 228–30, 243, 257, 270, 272, 288–9, 298, 300, 349, 366, 371–2, 388–9, 397–8, 401, 411–12, 416
  effect of, on attitudes toward military, 132–4
  My Lai massacre, 13, 100, 191
  Tet offensive, 133–4, 141
Vietnam War University, 132
Virginia, 12
Virginia Military College, 78
Vorenberg, Michael, 334

Waever, Ole, 370
Waldron, Arthur, 352–3
Walker, Nate, 187, 193–4, 196
Wallace, Schuyler, 115
Walsh, James, 392
Walt, Stephen M., 364–5, 367, 371, 380, 386, 388
Waltz, Kenneth, 366–8, 373
Walzer, Michael, 344
war and military, *sui generis* nature of, 60, 64, 242, 264, 271, 277–9
War Department, 108, 122
War on Terror, 105, 205, 251, 298, 376
warrior ethic, 16, 52, 66, 83, 89, 177, 198, 243, 276, 298, 376, 412
Warsaw, 123
Watson, James, 143
Way, Christopher, 346
Webel, Charles P., 373
Weber, Max, 26, 64–5, 175, 368, 374
Weeks, Jessica, 346
Weigley, Russell F., 84, 295, 300
Weinberg, Gerhard, 350
Weingast, Barry R., 41, 375
Weisinger, Alex, 353
Weiss, John, 345
Weiss, Michael, 32
Wells, Tom, 135
Wendt, Alexander, 377, 403, 405
West Point, 60, 71, 109, 250, 404
Westin, Alan, 145
Westphalian state system, 361, 378–9
White, Dixon, 108
Wilentz, Sean, 341
Wilkes, Sean, 176, 182–4, 186–7, 189, 200, 202, 209
Williams, Cindy, 392
Williams, Paul D., 363
Williams, William Appleman, 116
Williams College, 106
Wilson, David A., 124
Wilson, Paul, 398
Wilson, Woodrow, 363, 407
Winks, Robin R., 113–14
Winter, Jay, 342
Wisconsin State University, Stevens Point, 78
Wisse, Ruth, 51, 57, 203, 241, 261
Witherspoon, John, 107

Wolfers, Arnold, 366
World War I, 7, 53, 84, 376, 387, 415
  Columbia's role in, 110
  Cornell's role in, 108–9
  Pennsylvania's role in, 111
  Princeton's role in, 110
  Yale's role in, 109
World War I and II University, 115–17
World War II, 7, 14, 19, 22, 53, 57, 62, 72, 82, 84, 86, 105, 118, 125–6, 149, 170–1, 250, 257, 261, 288–9, 299–301, 303, 322, 340–1, 364–5, 376, 387–8, 415
  Columbia's role in, 114–15
  Dartmouth's role in, 114
  Harvard's role in, 111–13
  Yale's role in, 113–14
Wright, Quincey, 373
Wriston, Henry Merritt, 121

Xue, Mark, 189

Yale University, 13, 15, 61, 106, 113, 120, 174, 205, 300, 302, 397, 401, 421–2
  attacks on ROTC at, 138, 141–2
  International Security Program at, 393–7
  Law School, 174
  role in OSS, 113
  role in Revolutionary and Civil wars, 107
  role in World War I, 109
  role in World War II, 113–14
  security studies at, 343, 393–7
  status of military history at, 342–3
Yellow Ribbon Program, 164, 202, 215
Yerxa, Donald A., 286–7
Yohanan, Petrovsky-Shtern, 354
Yu, Liya, 219–20

Zaidi, Riaz, 177
Zaragoza, Alfred, 181
Zenk, Christopher, 291–2
Zinni, Anthony, 351

12/04/2012 $34.99